A Distant Calling

One Young Man's Journey into Alaska.
And *more…*

Wishing you all good things. Safe travels
George

GEORGE W. BENSON III

For information, write to
adistantcalling@comcast.net

Library of Congress Cataloging-in-Publication Data
has been applied for.

Cover design by Karen O. Benson

This is a work of fiction.
Names, characters, places, and incidents
either are the product of the author's imagination,
or are used fictitiously.

Prologue

They say that you can never really start to think. You can't start, you don't stop. That it's all connected, like some crazy, mixed-up jangle of memories and dreams. Facts and bullshit. But I guess with a story it's different. Like at some point, you have to say GO. And then, if it's good enough, people get to the place where you quit and they stop. I don't know.

I remember standing on the banks of the Yukon one spring afternoon as the river was breaking up, and the roar was unbelievable. I saw a special about it once, on National Geographic, and I thought I understood. But you never do unless you're there. It moans and groans and then explodes with the muffled sounds that only the frozen Yukon River can make when it starts to come unglued. Millions and millions of churning and bubbling tons of ice.

And then, just when you think it can't possibly get any louder, the ground begins to shake and all hell breaks loose as giant chunks of ice, the size of houses, go squirting up into the air. Creaks, cracks, moans, groans, and then this giant B-O-O-M! And above it all, you hear the voice of Pinto yelling – "Jump! Jump!"

And so you do.

And for the next seven or eight hours, and one or two miles, the two of you hang on to what seems to be an incredibly small chip of ice, surrounded by a tray of ice cubes, drifting out to sea. Like two pathetic caribou that have wandered out onto an ice flow in the middle of the Yukon River, waiting to be shot from shore. Seven or eight hours and a couple of miles of bobbing and freezing. Giant chunks of ice, exploding all around.

"And for what?" I asked him later.

"Memories," he said. "Something to remember."

And so, it seemed we lived our lives for that. "Shitcans full of memories" he called 'em. Shitcans full of thumbing north, thumbing east and thumbing north again. Union Halls. Card games. And washing dishes in between. There was gold, money, frozen ravioli and a place called Prudhoe Bay. A state so big, we called it The Country. And people. All the crazy, crazy people. Kolis. Meat Man.

3

Over the Bridge Eddie. And the girl who smelled like an inner tube on a hot September day.

And all the while we would harass and cajole each other to "Take notes." "Take notes" or "Write it down." But of course we never did. It was more than that. Like the man who summits Everest with a camera strapped around his neck. He knows the best thing is to walk away.

And so, in time, you come to stand alone in the freezing cold on a clear December night, and you begin to watch the lights as they dance above your head. Whites, reds, blues, and purple. Neon greens and on into red again. You shiver and shake in the forty-below, until the cold you felt is gone, replaced with a strange, almost welcome numbness. Like someone has taken your entire life and encased it in a solid block of ice.

You stand and watch, but now you listen, because you think you hear what very, very few have heard before. The crackling of the lights. Like a sizzling steak gone out of control, they fry above your head. Swirling, splitting, patterns of light, that eventually crackle and burn themselves out of the midnight sky and into the cells inside your brain.

They say that you can never really start to think. And yet, from beneath the lights you begin the search. You begin to remember back to another time. Another place. And then somehow, from beneath the lights, between the memories and dreams, you reach down deep inside and begin to pull something out of the original can.

Chapter 1

There was a lady on the other end of the phone, asking me questions about Mandarin oranges. They were on sale, she said, down at Kroeger's Bi-Rite, and she wanted to know if I thought they would be OK for Arthur to take on his trip. It was the spring of '75. The year of the Watergate Scandal, the year the Vietnam War ended, and the year the Mandarin oranges went on sale down at Kroeger's Bi-Rite.

I had met Arthur Kingpen sometime before that. A small, wispy guy in a paisley shirt. Our paths first crossed at a card game late one night. He was a strange looking character, who would have reminded you more of a caricature than a person. Like a picture an artist would have drawn of you at a carnival, with short spindly knees and nervous eyes. Like someone would have looked in their second grade class picture. Except Kingpen was older. Maybe 19 or so.

It had been during the card game when I first told some friends I was driving north. To Alaska. The Last Frontier. Over the next couple of weeks, Kingpen must have called me a dozen times.

It was his dream, he said, to see the state. It had been his dream since he was a kid. He had read about it, watched movies and collected maps and brochures. I felt sorry for him in a way, and began to think that at the very least he could help with expenses. So with a couple of months to go before I left, I told Arthur Kingpen to keep in touch. And until the day we left, he did.

There was another guy I asked to go. An acquaintance I had known from high school. Six-foot-one and over two hundred pounds of solid muscle. Robert Beamish. Been to Canada twice, loved to camp, and knew a hell of a lot besides. An all-around guy you'd have wanted in your corner. That's what you would have thought if you had known Beamish.

They say anticipation is more rewarding than the journey. I'm not so sure, but God did we anticipate. The three of us started getting together at my house on weekends and nights to plan the trip. Pouring over Kingpen's books and magazines, it just kept getting better.

I bought a '64 silver Buick Special from a lady down the street and then Kingpen, Bob and I began to fix the clunker up. New tires, brakes and shocks. We even got some chicken wire and wrapped it around the headlights and radiator, the way one of Kingpen's books showed, to keep the gravel out.

In a way, it was all kind of crazy. Like a part of you knew it could never get any better than the dream. But then another part of you held on to something Arthur had said.

"We can never know beforehand the adventures that we'll have," he told us.

And though Beamish was right when he said that it sounded like something you'd find in a goddamned fortune cookie, I knew what Arthur meant. So the day finally came when, without knowing what adventures lay ahead, I lifted a forty pound bag of dog food onto my shoulder and hooked a leash to my collie. I grabbed my backpack, left my parents' house, and started off to pick up Bob and Kingpen.

We were heading to Alaska. It was April 1, 1975.

Looking back, I remember driving down a side road to the bottom of the hill, and then stopping there and watching all the cars go by. Chevys, Fords and Plymouths. Then a transit bus. A couple of trucks. And the whole time I was watching, all that I kept hoping, all that I kept thinking, was that somebody that I knew, or even somebody that I *didn't* know, would stop and ask it.

"Where ya' headed?" they would ask me. And then I'd turn real slow and tell 'em what I wanted to shout out. "ALASKA," I would say. "The Last Frontier. Diamond Tooth Gertie's. The Red Dog Saloon. No Named Mountains. *Grizzlies, caribou and wolves.*" And so I sat there for a minute, but they kept on going by. Then I made a left, passed a convenience store and headed west.

I followed Bob's directions to his house for six or seven miles. I drove down a couple back roads and eventually I found it. He was standing in his front yard, in a pair of Redwing boots he had just bought. He was surrounded by a sleeping bag and Coleman stove, a backpack and a rifle that he had for bear. He had a six-man tent and a camera. Everything you could have had, Beamish had it.

"I even got a bottle," Beamish told me. "To celebrate the trip. You like rum?" he asked. Then he pointed to this bulge inside his North Face backpack.

Together we began to pack his gear into the trunk. I really didn't have that much myself. A couple cans of food, an old Boy Scout

6

sleeping bag, and then this forty-pound bag of small-nugget dog food. I didn't even have a coat back then, although I did plan on buying one. In Chicago. At the Eddie Bauer Store. But anyway, we finally packed the gear in the trunk, got inside the car, I took the wheel, and we started to roll.

We had never been to Arthur's. Either of us. And as we followed his directions, we came to one of the fancier parts of town. Landscaped yards, expensive cars. "Glitter Gulch," Bob called it. Then he pointed up ahead.

There was a large stone colonial, with a statue of a little black man holding a lantern standing out in front. And when we drove up the driveway we could see Kingpen, looking out a window.

I pulled up to the curb just as Kingpen opened the door. He was carrying two big grocery bags, one under each arm. "My mother thought we might want some of this on the trip," he said. He came over to the car and handed me the bags. I put them in the trunk, and then he walked back to the house.

He took a little while, but then when he did finally come out, he seemed to have everything. A sleeping bag, a suitcase, the travel books, and an inexpensive camera that was hung around his neck. He stood with his mother for a while, but all I heard him say was, "I've really gotta go." Then he came on over to the car, handed me his suitcase, and climbed into the back.

Beamish decided to drive. We got in the car, he started the engine, Arthur waved, Beamish honked, and then he drove it out. Drove it out the way we had come in. Past the little black man, the lawn sprinklers, and all the fine trimmed lawns.

We passed the mailman that day. He was walking down the street like I guess he always did, giving out the mail. We passed the mailman, the sidewalks, the parked cars, and all the people in their homes, doing what they did. But somehow we were different. We were finally on our way. And it was just like Beamish said. We were passing all the bullshit and leaving it behind. *We* were heading north. North to Alaska. North to the future.

Chapter 2

Beamish took the Buick to the Beltway, then ran it up I-70, and we headed west. All these cars around us, and the thing that I remember thinking was, we had to be the only people driving to Alaska that day. At least the only people driving there from Baltimore.

I was looking at my Eddie Bauer Catalogue and according to the magazine, this Eddie Bauer place was *huge*. The catalogue itself was huge, with page after page of these glossy photographs of backpacks, hiking boots and tents. There were sleeping bags, life rafts, dehydrated foods. Every piece of outdoor gear you ever could imagine. Even special bags to carry down your trash from a mountaintop. And then on page twenty-six, there it was. The jacket that I wanted. One hundred percent goose down, rip-stop nylon, and Velcro fasteners. "Built for Alaska." That was what the ad said.

"And I just *know* Eddie Bauer wouldn't bullshit you on *that*," Beamish told me. And then he started laughing this loud, crazy laugh he had.

In the months before we left, we had decided we would each put $300 into a common pot that would go for gas or breakdowns or anything the three of us would need. Then if one of us wanted to get something extra, we could buy it with whatever other money each of us had brought along. Which in my case wasn't much. I had about $300. And part of that was going for my jacket. And then I had expenses for my dog. But anyway, Beamish was in charge of all the money, so when we pulled up to the toll booth for the Pennsylvania Turnpike, he took $4 from the $900 pot, gave it to the lady, and we kept on going west.

God, we were excited. Just looking at it all, but always driving on. Driving on to places we had never seen, but tried to picture in our minds.

I remember there were things to make you *think* back then, as we drove along the Turnpike. Stupid, crazy things - to make you think these thoughts you'd never really thought before. Like a shoe or something lying on the side of the road. And you'd wonder for the longest time how it ever got there. *Shoes, boots, pieces of rope.*

We saw the Appalachian Mountains later that same day. Saw and then drove through them. Thousands of fluorescent lights, then coming out the other side, we heard an auction. The first and last I've ever heard on a radio.

"Table! Table!" the announcer would call out. And then he would describe it and the listeners would phone in to bid. "Ten dollars!" "Fifteen dollars!" On and on, until someone would win. Ping-Pong tables. Ironing boards. It really didn't matter. He even auctioned off a birdcage.

We were just outside of Middletown, Pennsylvania, heading to Mechanicsburg. None of us were hungry. But it was just like Beamish said, it was the *idea* of the trip, so he pulled the Buick over to a little picnic place on the side of the Turnpike. We got a can of beef stew from the trunk and put it on the Coleman stove to heat it up. And I remember that I didn't have a spoon back then, so I borrowed one from Kingpen, who was going off to take some pictures.

"Think he'll make it to Chicago?" Beamish asked me.

But before I could answer, Bob went back to the trunk, got the bottle he had brought, unscrewed the cap, took a long hard pull, put the cap back on, and tossed the bottle to me.

"C'mon Kingpin," he yelled. "Let's go to Alaska." With that, we put the stuff back in the trunk and got in the car. Beamish merged us into traffic.

And we kept on heading west.

We drove a couple hours. Beamish did. Then we stopped along the road at a fast food place for Kingpen. We both went in. Me and Kingpen. We walked up to the counter to this generic looking girl and Kingpen told her, "Plain burger with extra salt, please."

"Gimmee a plain!" she yelled to the back. And then she told us it would be a couple minutes.

We went up by the front window and sat there at a table, with a plant hanging up above our heads. You could tell it was just watered from all the water on our table top.

"Still getting that jacket in Chicago?" Kingpen asked me.

"Yeah," I told him.

"Well you won't need it after May," he said. "It's gonna be too warm."

He started playing with these drops of water on the table, while I looked around the room. Nobody was there. Just this girl at the counter and some workers in the back. No customers to eat the food. Just dozens of these hamburgers sitting underneath the little metal steamer, trying to stay warm. Hamburgers with everything. Mustard, ketchup, mayonnaise, and pickles.

"Ever seen a Minnesota license plate?" Kingpen asked me.

"What?"

"A license plate from Minnesota. Ever seen one?"

"Yeah," I told him, even though I wasn't sure I had.

"Remember what they say?" he asked.

"What?"

"The license plates."

"From Minnesota?"

"Yeah, the license plates from Minnesota. Remember? 'Land of 10,000 Lakes.' That's the Minnesota motto," he told me. "They have 10,000 lakes of five square acres or more."

"No kidding," I said.

"And you know how many lakes are in *Alaska*?

"No," I told him. "But I'll take a guess. *Nine* thousand?"

Kingpen shook his head. "Not even close. There's a million of 'em.," he told me. "Can you *imagine* that? Over *one million* lakes at least five square acres each."

As if to make his point, he tapped his fingers on the water that had dripped down from the plant. It splattered apart and spread all around the table. Then the girl called his order and he went up to the front, while I sat there staring. *Staring, staring, staring,* at all these drops of water on the laminated tabletop.

———————

According to Arthur, we were right on time. He loved figuring stuff like that out. But it was Beamish who said we'd be *gaining* on the time if we kept on driving. Because of the time zones. So we kept on driving.

"Did you visit *THIS* or take in *THAT*?" people asked me later. And I'd nod my head and tell 'em that we had, even though we hadn't. They'd have never understood. It was just like Beamish said. We were balls to the wall. From Glitter Gulch to North Dakota. On to Watson Lake. Driving. Always driving. And if, by chance, the road that we were on had passed within a half a mile of the Grand Canyon, or even just a quarter mile, I can tell you one thing for sure – we *never* would have stopped. There wasn't any way. We would have blown right past that hole, without even looking back.

Alaska. It drove us on.

We were crossing into Ohio on our way to Eddie Bauer. A silver bullet on a winding golden thread. Road signs for Windham, Drakesburg and Shalersville. Olmstead Falls and Birmingham. Yet for all of our driving, not that much had changed. Oh, the license plates were different, the signs and stuff like that, but the scenery was the same. Four lanes heading west. And four lanes heading east. You never even saw the towns. It did start getting cooler though.

"The wind's from Lake Erie." That's what Arthur said. And when you looked at Kingpen's maps, it all made sense. You never actually *saw* the lake, but thanks to Rand McNally we could tell that it was there.

We drove past Elmore and Perrysburg, and then just east of Toledo, we stopped so I could feed my dog. Small nuggets that you mixed with water, stirred, and watched, as it all turned to gravy. At least it was *supposed* to. But of course we didn't have any water, so he ate the nuggets dry. He didn't seem to mind. He ate most of them. Beamish pried off a hubcap and I poured the nuggets in. Then a couple minutes later, we took the nuggets that were left, along with the hubcap, put it all on the back seat floor, got in the car, and started off again.

We were driving in the far left lane back then, still heading to Chicago. And even though it was getting dark, if you looked real closely, you could start to see the snow. It wasn't coming down where *we* were yet, but you could see it on the cars and trucks that were coming our way. Tractor trailers especially. We saw the snow and then we started driving into rain. A sprinkling drizzle first, and then these tiny little flakes of snow, that would slide on down the windshield and melt before they hit the hood.

"Starting to get cold," Beamish said. He flipped the button up for the heater and for two or three minutes the heat came pouring out. Hotter than normal. Then a loud *click, click, click* - and nothing but cold air. Then hot air. Then cold air again.

"Fuckin' *heater's* gone up!" Beamish yelled. "Son of a *bitch!*" But the worst part was, we couldn't get the fan off, so the windshield starting icing up.

11

"Here," Kingpen said. He handed me a handkerchief and I started wiping off the glass. I got it cleared off a little, so we kept on driving.

We drove another ten or twenty miles, then the small flakes turned to larger ones. They starting laying on the windshield, the road signs, the hood, and finally on the road. Another thirty, forty miles and it was really coming down. Coming down and piling up. Even in the dark you could see where it was deep, especially alongside the government fencing that ran along the Interstate.

"Maybe we should stop and call the weather number," Kingpen said. "Check it out ahead."

But Beamish just ignored him, took a slug of rum, the tires of the Buick started slipping in the snow, but we kept on going.

It was eight or nine o'clock by then. It might have been the time of night, but it seemed to me the more we looked, the fewer cars we saw. There were hardly any heading east. And most of those with us, the ones heading *west*, were pulling to the side or going off the exit ramps.

We kept on driving though. Beamish did. Thirty, sometimes forty miles an hour. He would sit behind the wheel, sip his rum, give the car a little gas, pump the brakes, and then step down on the gas again. God that guy could drive.

We went around a lot of cars that night. Cars, salt trucks, and at least a dozen graders. Snow was tugging at the Buick, underneath the car. And then just when I was sure there was no way we could make it, Beamish stomped down on the pedal and ploughed the Buick through another drift.

We were about a hundred miles from Gary, Indiana. That's what Kingpen said, but I don't think he really knew. You couldn't read the signs with all the snow. But anyway, we hadn't gotten to Gary when we started up this exit ramp, Exit 31 on the Indiana Toll Road.

"Gotta get some gas," Beamish said. He stepped down on the pedal and we started up this long, winding ramp. And I'll tell you, if it had been any steeper, we never would have made it. We did though. Went up the ramp, passed by the stop sign, and drove onto a short, narrow road that led us to a dull orange glow.

"HoJo's," Kingpen said. And that was where we were. The Howard Johnson's with the gas station out front, at Exit 31 on the Indiana Toll Road.

I got out of the car and went into the building, while Bob and Kingpen got the gas. The restaurant wasn't all that crowded. I guess a lot of people couldn't make it up the ramp for one thing. There were only six or seven people sitting there, drinking HoJo sodas or eating all the clams that they could eat.

"What'll it be?" I turned to see a girl about my age, in an aqua and orange uniform, standing back behind the counter.

"I'll take two large root beers and one large water. No ice please," I said. She got it all together, I paid her, and then I started out the door.

"Road's closed west of Gary, if you're headin' that way," a man behind me said. "First time ever."

And even though I didn't tell him, I remember that I *thought* it. *Headin'* that way? Headin' *that way*? We're driving to *Alaska*. That's what I remember thinking. *Grizzlies, caribou and wolves*. Then I nodded my head and kept on heading out the door.

I couldn't see the Buick, but I did see some headlights flash off and on. Then Beamish drove the headlights to the entrance of the restaurant. Kingpen let my dog out and I put the cup of water on the ground. You could tell that he was thirsty, but he couldn't really drink it very well.

"Here," I said to Kingpen. I handed him a root beer and he reached into his pocket for some change. "Keep it," I told him.

I stood there for a minute, until my dog knocked the cup over. Then he jumped back in the car. I got in and we all sat there for a minute.

It was snowing like a bitch. More snow than *I* had ever seen, at least back then.

"A guy in the restaurant told me that the road was closed, west of Gary," I said. "It's the first time ever," I told Beamish. Then he started driving.

We went maybe sixty yards down the entrance ramp to where a grader had been working, before we hit some ice. I knew we were in trouble. We only started sliding first, but then we went into a spin.

"*HOLD ON!*" Kingpen screamed. I reached back for my dog, but then Beamish started yelling.

"WIPE *dammit*, WIPE!" Beamish yelled. So I handed Kingpen my root beer, picked up the handkerchief he had given me before, and started wiping the windshield. *Wiped and wiped and wiped*. But even then, I knew that we were going to crash.

13

"WIPE!" Beamish screamed. Then he pulled down on the left side of the wheel and floored the Buick. I swear to God, it was just like in the movies. With only fifteen yards to go, we did a full 360, straightened out, and kept on sliding down the entrance ramp. *Front-end* first. Kingpen never said a word.

We barreled down the ramp, from one side to the other. "Tacked it," Beamish told us later. "Just like a fuckin' *sailboat*." We ploughed right through this drift that another plough had left behind, and made it to the Interstate.

The car rolled to a stop and Beamish told us, "*Bagged.* I'm in the fuckin' bag."

And then he passed out after that.

I put the car in park and turned around to Kingpen. "HoJo's spilled," he said. There was root beer everywhere you looked, except you couldn't really see it because it was so dark. You could *feel* it though. On the seat, on the floor, but mostly on my dog.

"Give me another napkin," I said. But Kingpen wasn't listening.

"Look," Kingpen told me, and pointed out the window.

He opened his door, stepped out of the car and then I got out and followed him. I'll never forget it. We were out there on the interstate and no one was around us. Nobody. No thing. Absolutely *nothing*. No cars, trucks, or noise. Absolutely nothing, except for us and millions of snowflakes coming down. "Do you believe this?" Kingpen asked me. "Do you *believe* this?" And I've gotta tell you, it was pretty unbelievable standing out there on the interstate without any cars.

We got my dog out of the Buick and then trudged on over to the median strip four lanes away and stood there in the snow. Stood there in the snow and off behind us we could just barely hear the electric wires buzzin' back at Howard Johnsons. That's how quiet it all was.

"We can never know beforehand the adventures that we'll have," Kingpen said. And then we stood there for another couple minutes before we trudged back to the car.

We got Beamish in the back seat and started off again, keeping track of our progress by the light poles that we passed. We peaked out at twenty-seven one hour. It was a whole different world and it seemed like we were the only ones out there trying to see it. Me and Kingpen and my dog. *Unbelievable,* we kept saying, and the snow kept coming down and piling up.

"Maybe we should find a place to pull off," Kingpen said. But it wasn't all that easy. You couldn't really see that well for one thing, between the iced-up windows of the car and the snow that was coming down. And then there were all the snowdrifts. But anyway, I kept on driving until Kingpen just happened to turn around and look out the back window where my dog had licked a place clear.

"STOP!" Kingpen yelled. "We passed it!"

I put the car in reverse and backed it up until we could see the little turn-off. "Look," Kingpen said. It was almost like a driveway that ran off from the interstate and went back into an empty lot that was all cleared out. I pulled the Buick in, put it in park, shut the engine off, and within a half a minute, the windshield was completely covered with snow. "Kinda like we're in an igloo," Kingpen said.

I could hear Beamish stirring in the back. Then he began to mumble.

"Gimmee the keys," he said. "Gimmee the keys."

I thought he wanted to drive, but that wasn't it.

"I'll get the bags," he said.

I turned around and he didn't look so good, but I didn't want to argue. He took the keys from my hand and got out of the car.

"You think he's OK?" Kingpen asked.

I shrugged my shoulders and we started to wait. "Maybe the snow will insulate us," I said. "And we won't be all that cold." Maybe *this.* Maybe *THAT.* Then just as I started my next sentence, we heard this loud, piercing scream from behind the car.

I pulled back on the door handle, pushed open the door and stepped down into the snow. It was up to my knees. "Beamish!"

"Come back here," he called. "Wait until you see this. Come here!"

I followed his voice to the back of the car. He was sitting in the snow, holding his side. "I can hardly talk, I've been laughing so hard," Beamish said. "Look in the bags."

"What bags?" I asked.

"Kingpin's," he said. "Wait until you see 'em. He's a goddamn Chinaman."

15

I wanted Beamish to show me but he was laughing so hard he couldn't even walk, so I went to the trunk myself.

"Forty-four cans in both bags. I counted 'em," Beamish said.

But it turned out he was wrong. There were really forty-seven, when you counted the ones that had fallen out. Forty-seven cans of Mr. Ming's mandarin oranges. And the funny thing was, Kingpen told us later, he didn't even like 'em.

───────────

I was down deep in the bag, the way I used to sleep on Boy Scout trips. Crunched way down, trying to stay warm. Then I felt Kingpen's hand on my leg, groping around.

"Gimmee the keys!" he said. "We gotta go."

I stuck my head out of the bag, and remember thinking we were in an icebox. That's what I remember thinking. We were locked inside a solid box of ice.

"Gimmee the keys!" he said again. There was something frantic in his voice.

I handed him the keys. He jammed one in the ignition, gave it a turn and the Buick started up with this low, muffled sound that came from the tailpipe being down in the snow.

"We gah, gah gotta go," Kingpen stammered. He was shaking from the cold. "We gotta go."

But we couldn't start to go because we couldn't even see. That's what I remember. "Wipers are frozen," Kingpen tried to say, but his teeth were chattering so badly I could barely understand him.

He rolled his window down, got a face full of snow, stuck out his arm, and tried to wipe the windshield off. But because it was still dark out, you couldn't see a thing, until he flipped on the lights.

"*Now* we're gonna go," Kingpen said. He put it in drive and gave it the gas. You could hear the engine. It revved all up, except we didn't move an inch until we heard this real loud *CCRACK!*. Then we started off.

"Ice," he said." "We were frozen in."

There was another loud noise, but not from the Buick. A loud *CLACK, CLACK, CLACK,* a bright oversized light, and then we heard this heavy, rolling noise coming at us from the left. I reached in front of Kingpen, threw the lever into Park, and we watched as a snow plough went right past us a couple feet away.

That was close, I thought. But I never said a word. Neither did Kingpen. We just sat there for a minute, then Kingpen put it back in Drive, but we didn't move.

At first I thought it was Kingpen's feet. He was still in his sleeping bag and I didn't think that he could keep his foot down on the pedal. But that wasn't it. And it wasn't the ice. It was something else. "Transmission," Kingpen said. So I told him to put it into Park.

Kingpen began to move the lever back and the Buick lurched ahead.

"Neutral," he said. "Now Drive is Neutral."

Beamish would say later that it had something to do with the linkage, and maybe it did. I don't know. We never had it looked at. But anyway, we rolled down our windows to help us see, and then for a while we kept driving in circles, trying to get out of the pull-off.

You could hear the *BEEP, BEEP, BEEP's* of the salt trucks backing up, and see the graders rolling by. I really thought for sure that one of them would hit us. We made it though.

We finally found the driveway out, and took it to the Indiana Toll Road. We pulled off to the side and then stopped for a while to brush the snow off of the car with our arms. That took a long time.

And then just as we got finished, we saw that the sun was coming up. The snow had stopped and it wasn't easy going, but I knew by then that we would make it. The sun was up behind us, the sky was clear, and everywhere you looked, just miles and miles of snow. Bright, glaring white. And all around us, there were cars. Only thing was, most of them weren't moving.

"Look," Kingpen said. And you could see them on the road. Hundreds of them sitting there, abandoned from the night before. When we listened to the radio, we heard these advertisements. Mostly from the cab companies that were giving out rewards of $50 to anyone who could bring one in. From the way they explained it, "the keys are under the seats and all you have to do is start 'em up and bring 'em in." And I guess we could have made a lot of money that day, but like I said, we were heading to Alaska. Kingpen did get some pictures, though.

We were driving into Gary, the first real town we'd seen close up. Off in the distance, you could see the smokestacks of the steel plants, like sea anemones, reaching for the sky.

"Ex-Steel Town Capital of the World," Kingpen said. And we kept on driving.

We were still on I-80/90, but it was different now. All around, you could see the towns. Gary, Hammond and Calumet. Low-cost housing, people shoveling out. More low-cost housing. Then we drove on into Chicago, before we even got to Illinois. East Chicago. That's what Kingpen said. And it was right there on the map.

"Now where's this Eddie Bauer's?" Kingpen asked me. "I think we're getting pretty close."

I took this crumpled up piece of paper from my pocket and straightened it out. There were two addresses. One was the home of my mother's friend's son in Fairbanks, Alaska. And the other was the address of the Eddie Bauer store.

"123 North Wabash," I said, and I held out the map. I was never very good at directions and figured Kingpen could find it faster than I could.

"We'll take Shore Drive," he said. "Down by the lake."

We went another couple miles, drove into Illinois, made a right on Wacker and got on South Shore Drive. We could see the lake. There was water on the right for as far as we looked.

"Lake Michigan," Kingpen said.

And I thought it would have frozen, but it hadn't. There was just a lot of wind, whipping up the waves.

We drove a little farther. More and more into neighborhoods, getting closer to the store all the time.

"This should do it," Kingpen said. "It's not that far from here."

We found a place to park against a giant pile of snow on my side, so I couldn't open my door.

"Now what about Beamish?" Kingpen asked.

I looked in the back and there was Bob, stretched out over the seat, with my dog on the floor.

"They'll be all right." I said. "Come on."

We got out on Kingpen's side, walked down the street to Wabash and then kept on going, on top of these piles of snow. Never walking on the sidewalk, because the people were shoveling there. So we ran and jumped and slid and fell on all these giant piles of snow, until finally we made it. "123 North Wabash," Kingpen said. It was the Eddie Bauer's store in Chicago.

If you've ever been there, I don't have to tell you what it's like. A long glass showcase, about a half a block long, with the words *Eddie Bauer* written up high on the outside wall.

18

There was a skiing scene in the window. A couple of dummies were skiing down a slope, with other ones pretending to camp or walk around. And they all had their Eddie Bauer gear on. Every one of them. Down jackets, mittens and boots. There were a couple of mannequins standing by an electric fire. You knew they weren't real, but if you looked closely enough, you could almost see them smile. And then you'd think you'd hear them say, "Look at that poor son of a bitch out there freezing his ass off, while we're standing here next to our Eddie Bauer's fire, staying nice and warm."

And then you saw your reflection in the glass, Standing there without a jacket, the wind would start to blow and your ass would freeze some more. God, I remember thinking I was cold back then.

But anyway, the display was pretty good. But the best part was, my *jacket* was there. Two inches away, on a guy in the window. He was one of the mannequins off to the side. Rip-stop nylon. Velcro fasteners.

"There it is, Kingpen," I said. "Made for Alaska." It was just the one I wanted. In royal blue.

"Closed," Kingpen said.

We turned to look at each other.

"It's supposed to be open," he said. "But I guess because of the storm…"

I walked over to the door and gave it a pull, but of course it didn't budge.

"Damn it!" I said.

There was a little sign on the glass door and it gave the times they were supposed to be open or closed. Kingpen was right. They were supposed to be open.

I didn't want to walk by the window again, so instead we walked around back, and found this other place that was open.

It would have reminded you of a Woolworth's or Ben Franklin's. A place like that. All kinds of parakeets and plenty of goldfish. But anyway, off in the back, I found this jacket for sale. Just my size and the label said royal blue, but it looked more black. Eighteen dollars and seventy-five cents. There wasn't much to it. Real lightweight and stuffed with some kind of filler.

"It might not be made for Alaska," Kingpen said, "but it's a nice looking coat."

19

And I tried to remember that later, when the stuffing came out and I nearly froze. I guess it was a good-looking jacket when I bought it. But the truth of it was, Beamish had it right.

"That fuckin' jacket," he told me later, "wasn't made for Alaska. It wasn't made for shit."

Both of us were hungry and I knew that Kingpen didn't want something from the trunk, so I started looking around for a place where we could buy something to eat.

We finally got the name and directions to a restaurant, from a lady we had helped with her car that had been stuck in the snow.

"Jimmy's," she said. "Up ahead."

We walked about a block before we saw the sign. Kingpen saw it first. A long, narrow sign hanging from the second floor. You read the letters down. *Jimmy Franklin's* it said. That was all.

We went up a stairway to the restaurant, pushed open a big, red wooden door and went inside. The place was kind of dark, but looked pretty classy from what I could see. Deep plush carpeting, crystal chandeliers, and mirrors on the walls.

"Just look at this place," Kingpen said. "And we're the only people here, not counting the employees."

We walked to the back and then sat in big leather chairs, at a large, round table with a dark green tablecloth. A waiter came, left us some menus, and walked back to the kitchen.

"I wish I was going to Ketchikan with you," Kingpen said. "You want to take my camera?"

"I don't think so," I said. "But thanks."

It was a long drawn-out story. I had written to these people, Mr. and Mrs. Kraxin, who lived in a place called Ketchikan on the Alaskan panhandle. It was one of a half-dozen towns, like Juneau, Sitka and Haines. All strung out along the Alaskan southeast coast, none connected by roads.

Anyway, I had gotten these people's names out of an old tourist magazine. I wrote for some information before I knew that Kingpen and Beamish were going on the trip. The Kraxins had run a small tourist business in the town. It took a while before I got anything back, but Mrs. Kraxin eventually wrote and said they had retired.

Even then, she was nice enough to send some brochures and other information. And a few weeks later, I got an invitation to visit.

"Would be pleased to have you come visit and spend some time with us, if you make it this far," her letter said. And I had accepted.

So, that was the plan. Kingpen and Beamish and I would drive to Prince Rupert, a small, scenic fishing town on the northwest coast of Canada. From there, I'd take the Alaskan Ferry up the southeast coast to Ketchikan, spend a day with the Kraxins, and then come back to Prince Rupert. Then the three of us would head north on this shortcut road that Kingpen had found in one of his books. We'd take that to Watson Lake, and drive the Alcan to Alaska. That was the plan. You can see it better than I explained it, if you look at a map.

"Rain Capital of the World," Kingpen said. "Ketchikan got 302 inches of rain last year alone. I hope you brought a poncho."

The waiter came back and I told him I would take a Reuben sandwich. He wrote it down and turned to Kingpen, who was glancing through the menu.

"I'll take the chopped sirloin," he told the guy. "With extra salt."

The waiter left and so did Kingpen. Out to make a phone call. By the time he got back, the food had come, on dishes as hot as the food.

"Called home," Kingpen said. And I nodded my head.

We sat there for a while after that, eating our meal and talking about the trip.

"Been pretty adventuresome so far," Kingpen said. The waiter came back with a bag for the leftover hamburger that Kingpen couldn't eat, and handed us the bill on a silver tray. Twenty-four dollars and nineteen cents.

"Whew," Kingpen said.

But I have to tell you it was worth every penny. That's what I was thinking. Because that was one ritzy place. Even the silverware was stamped with the initials of the restaurant. I looked at the bill, told Kingpen I would pay it, and then I put down two twenties. Enough for the meal and a tip - and the rest for the spoon that I took.

It was the soup spoon really. About six inches long with all of these etchings. And on the back of the handle, right there at the top, like I told you, I could see the initials.

J.F. Just like mine, for Jesse Fitch.

Chapter 3

"Red line," Kingpen said, pointing to his map. "No toll."

We were driving out of Illinois and crossing into Wisconsin, home of the Packers. "America's Dairyland." That's what the license plates said. Except we never saw any cows.

We were leaving behind places named Pittsburgh, Cleveland and Gary -and driving into Token Creek and Waunakee. We could tell there were even Indians around, from the little brown tepees on one of Kingpen's maps that showed the reservations.

The Buick was on Highway I-90/94, heading north. And Beamish was driving.

"I still can't believe you guys stopped," Beamish said. And then he punched down on the pedal, as if that would make up the time. "Can't believe it," Beamish said again. And he shook his head.

We were moving along pretty well. At least for a while. The snow was dry, for one thing, and the wind would blow it off the road. Just little wisps of snow, and we'd follow 'em on up the interstate.

It was starting to get dark, and it was right about that time that Beamish got us lost. He stuck with I-90 where the interstate split up, where he should have gone with I-94. Twenty miles back.

"She *IT*!" Beamish said to himself. But he didn't turn around. I didn't think he would. We went another couple miles, made a right at Sparta and headed north on 27.

"Gray line," Kingpen said.

It was a gray line on the map, but the road was mostly white. A lot more snow, with lots of little drifts we kept on driving through. A long, winding country road. But it wasn't so bad. It was like Beamish said. It gave us more of a chance to see the state. Only problem was, we didn't see that much, because, like I told you, it was getting dark.

We went a little bit farther and Kingpen asked if he could stop to get something to eat.

"You've got two hundred fuckin' cans of Mr. Ming's Mandarin oranges in the trunk," Beamish said. But Kingpen just ignored him.

"How about this place?" Kingpen asked.

We had come to a small general store in a very small town called Cataract, so Beamish pulled up to the front. When we looked inside, we could see they were about to close.

"I'll hurry," Kingpen said.

He got out of the car and went into the store.

"Where's the map?" Beamish asked.

I looked around and found it on the back seat, underneath my dog.

"Here," I said, and I handed it to Beamish.

Beamish pulled the car up closer to the light of the store and took the map. Then we sat there in the Buick, looking at Wisconsin.

"Hey Fitch. Whaddya say we camp?" he said at last. "Set the tent up on the Chippewa River?" He pointed on the map, to a small green triangle about 70 miles away, near a place called Altoona.

"Sounds good to me," I said.

Kingpen came out of the store with a couple of sandwiches and a box of cookies. He got in the back, unwrapped a sandwich and gave it to my dog.

"He doesn't seem to like those nuggets anymore," Kingpen said. And then he pointed down to where there were dozens of 'em lying on the floor.

"Anybody want a cookie?" Kingpen asked. He started to pass them around, then the light from the store went out and we sat there in the Buick, in the dark, eating vanilla wafers, trying to stay warm.

"Better go," Beamish said. "We don't have a reservation."

We started north on 27 again, passed a small town called Shamrock, and then it wasn't that much longer till we joined up with I-94 again, at Black River Falls.

"Another hour," Beamish said, "and we'll be camping on the river." But it wasn't like that. Not exactly.

We stayed on 94 awhile. A long red line, stretched across the Dairyland. Miles and miles of dark, snowy fields. But the interstate was clear, so at least that was nice. Then we started passing signs for Northfield and Osseo, Foster and Cleghorn.

"There's *Brackett*," Kingpen said. "We're getting close."

We drove a little farther to the exit for Altoona, but we still weren't there.

"Next one," Kingpen said. "The next one." So Beamish kept on driving.

We drove around the town of Altoona, staying on 94, until we came to Exit 17 and a sign for Caryville.

"This is it," Kingpen said.

Beamish made a left, went down the exit ramp, and crossed over to a narrow, tree-lined, winding road that was packed with snow.

"Should be down here a couple of miles," Kingpen said. "On the right." So we started to look, but we couldn't see that much, because there weren't any lights. Just this narrow back road that went to a little town called Caryville, with the Chippewa Campground somewhere along the way.

"There's the town," Kingpen said. "We've gone too far. We've gotta go back."

Beamish drove a little farther, pulled the car into somebody's driveway, and then started to back the Buick out. You could hear the tires, spinning in the snow.

"We're off the asphalt!" Kingpen yelled. Then Beamish put it in Neutral, stepped on the gas and started to tack it, the way he had done back at Howard Johnson's.

The porch light came on as we went across the lawn. You could see a lady and man looking out their window. Beamish gave it more gas, then we fishtailed across the snow, dropped into a gully, and bounced onto the road.

"Sonova*bitch*," Beamish said. Then he waved to the people, and we started looking again.

"It'll be on the left this time," Kingpen said.

"No shit," Beamish answered. But we missed it again, and went back to the exit. Then we missed it again, and again.

We were on our way to Caryville for the sixth or seventh time, when I noticed there was something different up ahead on the right side of the road. The trees were more thinned out for one thing.

"Stop the car," I said.

Beamish swung the car around until the front faced toward the woods, and then he put it into Park. We were at a ninety-degree angle to the road, but it really didn't matter. We were the only ones there.

I got out of the Buick and started to walk back into the woods. The snow was deeper than I thought it would be, and it came up to my knees as I trudged the fifteen or twenty yards to a small mound of snow. "Look underneath it," one of the guys yelled. So I did and I saw there was a stubby, wooden post with a sign nailed on.

"Flip on the brights!" I yelled.

Beamish punched the lights and I stepped back a couple feet to read the sign.

Chippewa Campground
Open April 15-Sept. 15

I could hear Beamish yelling, but I couldn't make out the words. I turned my back to the car and looked back to the woods. There was probably a road, down under the snow. A road that meandered back through the trees and back to the tent spaces. A road that kept on going back to the Chippewa River.

"Ain't no way," I yelled. "The snow's too deep."

I floundered past the sign and back to the car. My feet were numb. That's what I remember. Big hunks of snow, up inside my pants legs and down inside my tennis shoes. God it was cold. I brushed off the snow and climbed into the car, then I got into my sleeping bag and we headed back to Caryville.

We didn't go far. There was a ploughed-out space on the side of the road. It was back in the shadows and a dumpster was there. The trash bin for the campground, that's what I think it was.

Anyway, Beamish pointed to the spot, swung the car around, drove it in, and then backed it up to a pile of snow. It wasn't much, but it was like Kingpen said, "Just be thankful that we're off the road."

We spent at least a couple hours after that, trying to get the tent up - getting it out of the box and fooling with the poles. But the hard part was, we couldn't find the pegs, at least not for a long time. Then when we did, we couldn't get them in. The ground was frozen solid.

"Here," Kingpen finally said. "Found 'em."

They were in a little leather bag, deep down in the trunk. Sixteen brand new aluminum stakes you were supposed to put through these loops that were connected to the tent, and then pound them all into the ground. Except we didn't have a hammer.

"So use your fuckin' head, and figure it out," Beamish told us. Then he climbed into the dumpster and pulled out a ragged piece of concrete. One of those things like a shoe or a boot, or a piece of rope. And it made you wonder how it ever got there.

"Here," he said. "Try *this*."

We took it back to the tent that was all spread out, to the sixteen little loops waiting to be staked. Then we started on a corner. I held the stake, while Kingpen tried to get it into the ground.

"*Hit* the sonovabitch!" Beamish yelled. So Kingpen let loose and brought the concrete down and bent the stake in half.

That was how it went that night. We'd bend the stakes, straighten them out, and then bend 'em all again. It never got any better.

"*Permafrost,*" Beamish said. "Fuckin' *permafrost.*"

There was frozen gravel all around. Broken bottles. A couple of old tires. And the wind was picking up. I remember that. The wind and the trash. It would lift up out of the dumpster and then blow across the road.

"Here," Beamish said.

He was back in the trash bin, calling out to Kingpen. You couldn't really see him, but you could hear his echo.

"Take these." "*Take these,*" he said. He handed out some metal things. "Put 'em on the corners to hold them down." "*Put 'em on the corners . . .*"

He climbed out of the dumpster, took off his belt and tied it to one of the tent's window flaps.

"Let's get this sonovabitch *up,*" he said. And believe me, we tried.

Kingpen went inside the tent to hold it up, but he wasn't tall enough to support it, so I went in. We finally got it. Beamish tied one end of the tent to the Buick, and the other to the trash bin. We never did get any of the pegs in, though.

I left my dog in the car that night. We got the sleeping bags into the tent, crawled inside and tried to go to sleep. But of course we never did. Not for a long time. You'd lie and listen to *EEE EEE EEE*. And then, *CLANG CLANG CLANG*. And the metal of the dumpster would whine and cry out, and the top of the bin would slam against the side and you'd think to yourself that two days before, *just two days before*, you were sleeping in a warm bed.

The tent collapsed sometime that night. All of us knew it, but none of us cared enough to fix it. It didn't seem to matter. I closed my eyes and pushed down deeper in my bag. I think I fell asleep, but I didn't know it for a while.

"C'mon," Kingpen said. "We gotta go."

I opened my eyes and stuck out my head. I could hear Kingpen breathing, but I couldn't really see him because the tent was all around us like a giant canvas blanket.

"C'mon," he said. "We gotta find the door."

We pushed and crawled our way around. You couldn't stand.

"Here," Kingpen said. But it was only the window.

He went back to looking for the door, while I looked out the screen. The sun was coming up. It was just getting light, dull shades of black turning to gray.

There was a car on the road. A rust-colored Olds that was heading our way. A couple of adults and a little girl. The car came to a crawl and then the lady rolled down her window. I thought they had some trash at first. A litter bag or something.

"Take a picture mommy," the little kid said. "Take a picture."

"You take it honey," her mother told her. And then she passed the camera to the girl.

I pulled away from the window and tried to get up, but I couldn't. We were trapped. Trying to fight our way out of a giant canvas bag, we had become a part of the scenery.

"Made it," Kingpen said. "I'm out."

I heard the car drive off. Then I followed Kingpen's voice to an opening in the tent.

"Where's Beamish?" I asked.

Kingpen pointed to the Buick and I could see Beamish in the front, finishing off his bottle from the night before.

"I'm going to walk your dog," Kingpen said.

I went back to the tent and started to fold it up, but there were pockets of air that I could never flatten out. So I gathered it together and jammed it in the trunk, along with the bent metal pegs that I figured we would need again before too long. *Just get it all in.* That's what I remember thinking. And then I told Kingpen that I'd sit in the back.

We got in the car, Beamish started it up, and we pulled away from the dumpster and the permafrost. We hadn't gone far when Beamish pointed to his left and slowed the Buick down.

"There it is," he said. "The Chippewa River."

But as much as he wanted to see it, I know he never did. The Chippewa River, near a place called Altoona.

Chapter 4

We got to the bridge around eight that morning.

"Mississippi River," Beamish said. But the sign said St. Croix, and it divided the states. At least it did where we came in.

We stopped on either side for Kingpen to take pictures, and then we drove on into the Twin Cities. First St. Paul, then Minneapolis. I think that was it. We weren't there very long.

We stayed on I-94. Passed a park, crossed over a river, and drove through a business district. It got a little tricky once, where 94 runs into 12. We made it though. Up Nicollet Avenue, on to 7th Street, Highway 52, and back to I-94 again.

"Making good time," Beamish said. And Kingpen nodded his head.

We drove a lot that day. Beamish especially. Kingpen and I would try, but the glare of the sun on the fields of snow would put us to sleep. We'd squint and we'd stare and blink our eyes. Glaring bright and white. That's what I remember. Then we'd pull it over to the side and let Beamish drive some more.

We were wiping off the frost from the inside of the windshield and the windows, so we could watch it all go by. Farmland, lakes and patches of trees.

"Look," Kingpen said. He pointed to his map. "Wyoming."

There was a small gray circle on his map of Minnesota. A town so small, the map didn't show a population.

"Probably a place called Minnesota out in Wyoming too," Beamish said. "There's a Pennsylvania in Maine."

"There's even a place called Unalaska in Alaska," Kingpen added. We looked out the windshield and began to pass Albany, Freeport and Alexandria. Always following the red line across these giant fields of snow, up into the corner of the state. *Squinting and staring and blinking our eyes.*

It must have been about one that afternoon when we crossed the Red River of the North and went into North Dakota.

"Some of the very few," according to Kingpen. And when I asked him what he meant, he told me, "More people leaving this state than coming in or staying," he said. And when you took a look around, you could understand why. There was nothing there. Not after Fargo. Just lots of windswept land, with all these tumbleweeds blowing across the snow.

We branched off of I-94, near a place called Jamestown, then we swung a right, got on 52, and headed north toward Canada. The yellow color on the map. "We'll look for Bigfoot," Beamish said. And he started howling.

We were a little higher than the first O in North Dakota on one of Kingpen's maps, about 40 miles south of Kenmare. It was exciting, in a way, to be driving into Canada. At least for me. I had never been there before.

"You're gonna love it," Beamish said.

We were about ninety miles from the border, with the insurance papers in the glove box and the money in Bob's pocket. That was all you needed, according to the pamphlets we had read. No passports or visas. No red tape. Just insurance for the car and a reasonable amount of money to get us to Alaska. And of course our driver's licenses, which we had.

"Twenty miles," Kingpen said. You could tell he was excited.

We were just outside of Bowbells, USA. Eight o'clock at night. There was a long narrow road, Highway 5, that ran parallel to the border, so we got on that and headed west.

According to the map, there were five roads we could take. All of them branched off, and then went north, through a Customs Station. We took the first one. Highway 52. Then we drove for about six miles, until the highway widened and we saw a small brick building on the left hand side of the road.

"U.S. Customs," Beamish said.

He explained how we wouldn't go through that one, because it was just for people coming in.

"They don't give a damn what you take out," he told us.

So we drove another half a mile, until we came across this guy sitting in a car by the road. He needed fifty bucks, and it all made sense. He was driving to Alaska, and they told him up ahead, at the Customs Station, that he needed $700 dollars to go through. And he only had $650.

"I'll pay you back on the other side," he said.

So we talked it over, and Beamish gave him fifty bucks.

"We'll follow you through Customs," Beamish told him. "You can give us back the money about a mile down the road." And I really think he would have, if we had gotten there.

We followed him down the road to another building, like the one we'd seen before, made of brick and all lit up. There was maple leaf that said, "Welcome to Canada." And then beneath it was a long list telling you what you could and couldn't do.

"Better declare your gun," Kingpen said. But Beamish just ignored him and rolled his window down.

There were two guys to a car. One went through our gear, while the other one asked questions. Beamish did the talking. We were heading to Alaska. We didn't have any drugs. Then Beamish showed them the gun.

The guy in the Chevy, with our fifty, pulled ahead, then the inspector for our car checked our insurance. Beamish showed him the money, and we got ready to roll.

"Papers," the man said. "For the dog."

Beamish pointed to me and the guy came around to my side of the car.

"Rabies," he said. "I need papers for rabies."

But of course I didn't have them, so we had to turn around and head back south. Back to North Dakota and Highway 5. "Screw it," Beamish said.

We headed west again right after that, deciding what to do. Then we made a right on Highway 40 and headed north again.

"A whole new ballgame," Beamish said. "Port of Estevan."

But it was the exact same thing. Without the papers, we couldn't cross. So we drove on back to Noonan, a little town about ten miles from the Canadian border, found a rest stop and went inside.

"Forge it," Beamish said. "Just *forge* it. We'll type a letter at the library. Then we'll sign it from a vet."

But Kingpen said it wouldn't work.

"Then we'll *really* be in trouble," Kingpen told us. "That's criminal," he said.

So I figured I would drive the Buick back to Estevan and see exactly what we needed. Then find a vet in Noonan.

"I'll go with you," Kingpen said.

It didn't take us long. We left Beamish at the rest station, then we drove back to Estevan, to the Canadian Customs Station. When we stopped the car, this older guy, an agent we had never seen, came out.

"Heading to Alaska?" he asked. And Kingpen told him that we were.

"Lotta people heading that way," he said. "*Lotta* people."

His face broke into a grin and he told us to go ahead. So I turned the key, put it in Neutral, and we started to move.

"Want to see the insurance?" Kingpen asked. But the man just waved us on.

We were a good two miles into Saskatchewan. We came to a Shell Gas Station with a sign that said, *Last stop for gas, before the U.S.* But you couldn't really get any. The station was closed.

"Why don't you stay here?" I told Kingpen. "Take care of my dog. I'll go back for Bob."

They got out of the car, I gave Kingpen his sleeping bag and the gun, and I started back to Noonan. When I got there, Bob was outside, shaking like a leaf.

"They came and closed the fuckin' rest stop," Beamish yelled. "Right after you left. Where have you been?"

He got in the car, scraped the inside of the windshield and started driving, as I told him what had happened.

"Changed shifts at midnight," Beamish said. "I didn't think of that."

We pulled up to the maple leaf again and I could tell that Beamish had been right. It was the same older man, working all alone, only this time he didn't smile. He looked at me and said, "Aren't you the one who was going to Alaska? With *another* guy?"

He started searching after that. From the brake lights to the headlights, he tore the car apart, looking through our gear. He checked our licenses, the insurance. All you could imagine. He even made us count the money. $731.47. Just barely enough, he told us, to let us through. But anyway, after an hour and a half, he finally let us go.

By the time we got to Kingpen and my dog, it was after 3:00 that morning. The two of them crawled into the Buick, and that's where the four of us spent the night. Three miles from the Port of Estevan, on the Canadian side. *Last stop for gas before the United States.* The Shell Gas Station.

We were there.

Chapter 5

The Gas Station opened at six. We drove out right after that, when they woke us and told us to leave. We drove less than a mile to a small campground and pulled the Buick into a cleared-out area next to a frozen stream.

"This is nice," Kingpen said. And it was in a way, with a table and a couple of benches.

Kingpen got out the bread and some eggs we had bought. He started to cook breakfast on our little Coleman stove, while Beamish and I walked around. We let my dog out of the car, and the three of us started down the stream. *Walking, walking, walking.*

"Frozen solid," Beamish said. Except for that, we didn't talk much. Just walked a quarter mile or so, and when we got back to the car, Kingpen wasn't there. He was a good ways off. Beamish saw him first.

"Must have had to take a crap," Beamish said. *But Kingpen was too far off for that.* That's what I remember thinking.

Beamish started cooking the eggs while I went to go see Kingpen. And it wasn't all that easy. Walking back in the woods, without any boots, it seemed the snow was always deeper than it looked. Every ten or fifteen steps, I'd pull a leg up, and my shoe would still be down there in the hole I'd left behind. I finally got there, though.

"Look," Kingpen whispered. He pointed up ahead. "A fox."

I couldn't really tell, but something was up there.

"I'll get these enlarged," Kingpen said. He took another picture, the animal walked off, and we trudged back to the car.

I ate a couple of the eggs, Kingpen gave my dog the toast, and the four of us got ready to leave.

"I'm gonna throw the dog food out," I said. "We don't need the extra weight."

It had started with this beef stew I had given him. Then the chopped sirloin, left from Jimmy Franklin's. Then sandwiches. And toast. He had gotten to the point where he wouldn't eat the dog food.

"I'm going to dump these nuggets here," I said. I pointed to the ground, next to the table.

"Yeah, something will come and eat them," Beamish told me.

Beamish started the engine and we started to drive away, real slowly at first, because the three of us were looking at the spot where Kingpen had seen the fox.

"Could have shot it with my thirty-ought-six," Beamish said. And then he scraped a hole in the ice on the inside of the windshield, stepped on the gas, and we were on our way.

It wasn't long before we passed the towns of Yellow Grass and Drinkwater. A few hours later, we connected up to Highway 1, right there at Moose Jaw.

"I'll drive," I told Beamish. And I did for a while. I drove two or three hours and got us to Swift Current, but I could barely stay awake. The same thing happened when Kingpen tried to drive. So Beamish drove some more.

We were pretty far north of Gull Lake when I opened my eyes. The Buick was stopped, and the two of them were out of the car, looking over a valley. Bob was shaking his head.

"Ever seen anything like that?" Beamish asked.

I got out of the car and I couldn't believe my eyes. There were thousands of spruce trees. Hundreds of thousands burned to a crisp, all through the valley. Like a Christmas tree farm, painted over in black. And for the longest time, we thought that it would never end. It did though, after forty-one miles. Kingpen kept track.

Forty-one miles of burned down, burned up, crispy trees, for as far as you could see. Even the ground was black, covered in charcoal and ash. Kingpen said it would eventually be good, to bring the moose back in, but it looked obscene at the time. Like we were driving through a three dimensional, surrealistic painting. It was pretty weird. It did give you a sense of perspective, though.

It was like Beamish said. "How many places could you go where they didn't even have a fire hydrant for forty-one miles?" And he was right. There weren't any fire hydrants, there weren't any buildings, and we'd only seen a couple of other cars.

"Wilderness," Kingpen said. "Even though it's all burned up. We're getting into *wilderness*." And he pointed to his map.

Beamish pushed the Buick on. Six, six-thirty that night, we drove into the city of Calgary. We got Kingpen something to eat, fed my dog, and checked the oil. Except for the transmission, the Buick was running great.

"Time change," Kingpen said.

We were gaining another hour, and according to the brochures that Kingpen brought along, we were heading for some pretty spectacular scenery.

"Wait until you see it," Kingpen said. He was talking about Banff National Park, on Highway 1. The Trans Canadian Highway. It ran up the foothills of the Rockies and into the Park for at least seventy miles. And then for another hundred twenty miles or so, we could see on the map where we would be riding along the mountain crests on Highway 93, the Icefield Parkway. After that, we would drive through another Park called Jasper.

"We'll look down from the mountain tops," Kingpen told us. And he couldn't keep from smiling.

We came to an entrance station east of Banff. There was a welcome sign next to a little building. We pulled to a stop, paid $2, and the ranger put a little sticker on the car. It's probably still there.

"Now, that's good for two days," he said. "Good for Jasper, too."

We picked up a couple of extra brochures and then started driving into the Park and I wish you could have seen it. We never saw it *all*, but the entrance was spectacular.

"Majestic," Kingpen said. We got about halfway up Highway 1 and it started getting dark.

There was a big resort about fifty miles ahead. They had skiing, camping, and a gas station. There was even a lodge where you could spend the night if you wanted. Lake Louise – that's what it said next to the dot on the map.

"You want me to drive?" Kingpen asked.

Beamish was beat. You could see it on his face. Total exhaustion.

"Yeah. That would be good," Beamish said. He pulled the car over, went to the trunk, and came back with a can of Spam.

"Want some?" he asked. But nobody did. Not even Beamish. I think it was frozen.

Kingpen started to drive, and I pushed myself down deeper in my sleeping bag. God it was cold.

We were always in the bags. That's what I remember. Kingpen especially. Not Beamish so much, but Kingpen was - even when he drove.

"Gonna get us killed!" Beamish used to scream. But Kingpen was too cold to care.

We passed the lodge later on that night. Chateau Lake Louise. Then we passed the ski gondolas.

"Like something you would see in Switzerland," Kingpen said. It really was impressive.

We were going up into the mountains. Gradually at first, but even then there were times we could have seen for miles, if it hadn't been so dark.

"This is something, isn't it?" Kingpen said. And I told him that it was.

There were dozens of hiking trails and ski trails, picnic areas and pull-offs with fantastic views. We stopped at a couple of them. Like Mosquito Creek, where we looked for animal tracks for a while with Kingpen's flashlight.

We drove on up to Bow Summit after that, on the Icefield Parkway. Nearly 7,000 feet high. And according to the brochure, there was a short trail near the top that went down to this lake called Lake Peyote.

"A glacial, meltwater lake." That's what the article said. But anyway, it sure was pretty. We saw pictures of it in the pamphlet, this real pretty turquoise. So we thought it would be worth seeing and figured we would hike on down, even though it was dark.

We parked the car on Bow Summit, found Kingpen's flashlight, and made sure we took the brochure.

"We better cover Bob up," Kingpen said. So we took Kingpen's sleeping bag and put it around Beamish the best we could. We started down the trail and I've gotta tell you, with all of that snow, it wasn't easy, but we made it.

"Ever seen a turquoise lake?" Kingpen asked.

I shook my head and he started to laugh.

"I can't believe that it's turquoise," he said.

But for as much as we wanted to think that it was, it turned out that it wasn't. Like everything else that night, except maybe the snow, it was gray or black. But at least it wasn't frozen when we finally got there. Not completely.

"Here," Kingpen said. "On the pamphlet."

I aimed the flashlight onto the brochure, so we could see exactly what it would have looked like in the light. Then Kingpen turned the picture until he thought he'd lined it up with the *real* lake sitting out there.

"See that mountain?" he asked, pointing across the lake. "That's *here*." And he pointed to the picture while I flashed the light of the flashlight back and forth to get the overall effect.

"Hold this," Kingpen said. His hand was shaking from the cold as he gave me the brochure. Then he reached into his pocket, bent down, and filled a little glass container with some water from the lake where it hadn't frozen over. "I can't wait to see the turquoise-colored water," Kingpen told me. And I told him that I couldn't either.

But when we looked at it the next day as we headed to Prince Rupert, it was just like Beamish said. It only looked turquoise when you held it to the sky.

We drove the Buick to the clouds that night. To Sunwapta Pass. We were seventy-five miles from Lake Louise and we started to climb. You could feel the engine strain. Higher and higher we went up, until we could hardly see.

"Fog," Kingpen said. But really it was the clouds. With the Columbia Icefield on our left and Mount Stewart on our right, we were driving in the clouds.

Up and up we drove and drove, and then Kingpen stopped the Buick. He got his camera and he stepped out into the middle of Icefield Parkway at Sunwapta Pass. He stood there in the dark, in the middle of the cloud, and then he took a picture. I watched him.

And then I remember I said, "It'll never turn out." That was what I told him.

He got behind the wheel, put his camera on the seat, and I swear to God, he said, "I know. But when I see it, I'll remember."

The road got crazy coming down the other side. Hairpin turns, avalanche signs. So at three or four o'clock that morning we decided to pull into this little picnic place and wait until we had some light. "Tangle Creek," the park map said, "with a view of Tangle Falls."

36

And while we never really saw it, with a good imagination we could hear it.

"Listen," Kingpen said. And I told him that I thought I could hear the water.

We were the only people in the park. At least that was what it felt like. All alone. We sat there in the car and listened to the wind blowing down the creek and through the trees, and then they started swaying around us. All around the car. Big, giant spruce trees. And every now and then, they'd drop a bunch of snow and you'd hear it on the roof of the Buick. Little pats at first, and then – THUMP!

I saw the windshield icing up where the opening had been. I dug down in my bag and closed my eyes, but even then I felt it. It was Kingpen, shaking like a leaf behind the steering wheel. God, it was cold.

And there was no way to escape it, unless maybe we just died there freezing to death.

We were rolling down a hill. That's what I remember. A long, steep, gravel road. Faster and faster, into the black. We were out of control and couldn't stop.

"GET IT!" Kingpen yelled. "GET THE BRAKE!"

I remember diving down and hitting my head on the steering wheel. I could feel Kingpen's hand, down by the floor.

"I've got it," he said. "Put it in Park!"

I tried to push the gearshift up, but it was already in Park.

"Hold it down," I said. "I'm going out."

I pulled up on the handle, opened the door and stepped outside. I could hear the wind blowing down the creek and through the trees.

"We haven't moved," I said. "We're right here where we were. Right here where we parked."

But Kingpen didn't believe me. Not for a while.

"Come here," he said. "And hold the brake."

So I climbed in the front and held the brake down with my hand while Kingpen went outside.

"See?" I said. "We didn't move."

Kingpen didn't answer. Sweat was running down his face. He didn't look so good.

"We must have been dreaming," I said. "The exact same dream." And the more that we talked, and the more that we thought, I think Kingpen finally agreed.

We left right after that. It was really spooky. Kingpen got in the Buick, I started it up, and we started driving away. Driving away from a picnic stop called Tangle Creek, with a view of Tangle Falls that we thought we heard, but never really saw.

We drove thirty or forty miles and it started getting light. Not all at once, because of the mountains, but more like uneven shades. Subtle reflections.

"Look," Kingpen said, and he pointed up ahead.

You could just barely see them. Little dots of tan, high up on a mountain.

"Sheep," Kingpen said. "Dall sheep."

And we watched them for a while, but we never saw them move. I think they were asleep.

We stopped to take a picture, then we kept on driving another twenty-five or thirty miles. We drove out of the park, heading northwest on the Yellowhead Highway.

"Look," Kingpen said. Then he pointed up ahead. "British Columbia. We're headin' into British Columbia."

I stopped the car and he handed me the camera. I know he wanted me to look ahead and take a picture. But instead I looked behind, turned around and took one. Geez, it was pretty. Ragged, jagged peaks on all kinds of mountains, covered with snow. The sun was coming up and it was really something with the sun rays and the shadows. We saw the glare of white on white that morning, and little bursts of green and brown. Kingpen took another picture.

Then I started the engine, put it in neutral, stepped on the gas, and we left Saskatchewan behind.

We were on Highway 16, coming into a place called Tete Juane Cache, a community named after a blond-haired Iroquois trapper and guide. It was an intersection, really. You could take Highway 5 south to a place called Kamloops or stay on 16, the Yellowhead Highway, like we did.

But anyway, I got us to the intersection and we stopped to get some gas. Kingpen got out of the car. He walked across the road to read a sign, and I picked up his camera, followed him out and took his picture. I still have it tacked up on my wall. Arthur Kingpen in his brown corduroy pants and paisley shirt, wearing this big smile. He had on his navy blue jacket and his Totes rubber boots, and his hair was blowing in the wind.

The picture shows him standing by the sign. You can see it in the picture, just as big as Kingpen. "Prince Rupert," it says. "697 Miles."

Chapter 6

We got the gas, then Beamish started driving. We stayed on 16, the Yellowhead Highway, driving alongside the Cariboo Mountains on our left, with the Rockies on our right. Then we crossed the Frazer River. We started winding through these miles and miles of trees. Lots of spruce, more rivers and mountains. That's what Beamish said. I don't know. I was asleep.

We were north of McBride, near the Goat River. Kingpen was asleep in the back and I was barely awake.

"So you never saw the Falls?" Bob asked. And then he started laughing his crazy laugh.

"Never saw it," I said. Then I started drifting off again. I couldn't stay awake. *Fucking glare,* I thought.

Then I thought that I was dreaming I was in a zoo. Not because of anything I saw, but I sure could smell it. Then I started thinking that I'd never smelled a dream before, so I thought I was awake. And it turned out that I was. I'd only had my eyes shut and thought I was asleep.

But the smell was still there. Old rotten egg shells, empty Spam cans, and dog nuggets lying on the floor. Moldy bread and little broken bags of mayonnaise and ketchup that Kingpen had picked up in different places, even though he knew he'd never use them. God, that Buick stunk.

And then there was my dog. Wet, mangy fur. I thought that I was gonna puke, so I started looking out the windshield at the glare. Then I know I fell asleep, because his screaming woke me up.

"HOLY *SHIT*!" Beamish yelled. I opened up my eyes just in time to see us swerve into a gully. "Get the hell on *out*!" Beamish screamed. "Get *out*! Get *out*!"

I pulled up on the handle and watched as Beamish opened his door, went in back and dragged Kingpen onto the ground, sleeping bag and all.

Then Beamish came around to my side and started pointing to his face. "Look!" he screamed. "Look here at my face. Am I *bleeding*? I was driving down the road and felt his jaw against my face. Do you see any blood?"

I looked and told him *no*, but he wanted me to look some more. So I looked some more and told him *no* again. "Only foam," I said. And that was when he really lost it.

"*BULLSHIT*!" Beamish screamed. "It isn't foam. It's goddamned rabies. And there's no excuse! No excuse at all. You knew he needed rabies shots!"

My dog was lying on the back seat, staring straight ahead.

"It's even on the *windows*!" Beamish yelled. "And look there on the seat."

And when I looked, I could see that he was right. The foam was everywhere. But mostly it was coming from my dog's mouth. Like Beamish said, "A fuckin' foam machine."

Kingpen started toward the car. "I don't think it's all that bad," he said. He reached inside the back with his hand and started scraping off some foam that was frozen on the inside of the window. Then he held it out to Beamish.

"You fuckin' *nutcase*!" Beamish yelled. But Kingpen just ignored him and squished it in his hands.

"Toothpaste," Kingpen said. "I put some on the windows for his breath. It really stunk and he was always licking off the ice from the inside of the windows. We never give him any water, because it's too cold to go outside. So I thought that if he licked toothpaste…"

It was the one time on the trip that I thought that Bob was really gonna hit him. I really did. Especially when Kingpen told him next, "Look, at least you don't have rabies."

But in a way, I think Bob really was relieved. His whole entire body kind of sighed, and then he got behind the wheel and wiped the toothpaste off his face.

"You just clean that shit up," Beamish shouted, "all of it." And he threw the handkerchief at Arthur, the one that we'd been using since Chicago. "Clean it up!" he yelled again.

Then Kingpen and I got back inside the car. Beamish put it in Drive and revved the engine. Then he must have remembered, because he dropped it down to Neutral and muscled us out of the gully. He got it on the road, and we headed toward Prince Rupert. "Sonova *BITCH!*" Beamish yelled.

It was after noon, but we didn't stop. Beamish and I got a couple of cans of something out of the back to eat while we were driving and Kingpen said he thought that he could manage until we got to Prince Rupert. Another three hundred fifty miles.

There were hardly any towns along the way. Oh, there were a couple, but mostly there were rest stops. Little roadside places where you could stop to eat or sleep. "Roadhouses," Kingpen called them. But *we* never stopped.

"Gonna keep on driving," Bob said, "until we get to Prince Rupert." So we kept on driving.

We crossed the Bulkley River and went through Telkwa, Smithers and Moricetown. By the time we got to Kitwanga it was dark.

"Don't forget the shortcut," Kingpen said, and he handed me the map.

Kingpen had twelve maps of the road. At least. But of the dozen or so he had of the Yellowhead Highway, there was only one that had the shortcut. We called it *The Map*.

He had gotten it out of an old National Geographic, and it had faded colors and names that were hard to read. But about fifty miles this side of Prince Rupert, there, on *The Map*, was a thin, black, dashed line that broke off from the Yellowhead Highway and went north to the road we would eventually need to meet up with. The Alaskan Canadian Highway. The Alcan for short.

Of course we were still going to Prince Rupert, so that I could take the ferry. But after all that, when I returned from Ketchikan, we'd backtrack fifty miles and head on up. It was that or drive back to Prince George and head north from there. You should really look at a map yourself to understand it.

But anyway, Kingpen had it all figured out. We would save one thousand, two hundred fourteen miles by using the shortcut. If we could find it.

But of course we never did. At least not on the way into Prince Rupert. We started looking about sixty miles west of the town. We'd slow down and look, and then drive along some more. Bob finally said that he thought it was stupid and that we should look for it coming out. So he kept on driving.

We drove along the Skeena River on our way to Prince Rupert, and even in the dark you could see them. All these islands - big ones, small ones. hundreds of them, all shapes and sizes. If you've ever seen the Thousand Islands, it would remind you of them. That's what Beamish said.

We smelled Prince Rupert before we really saw it. It was kind of like Ketchikan was later on. Except instead of the sweet smell of a pulp mill, it was more like rotten fish. That's what I thought. But Kingpen said it was a processing plant, to turn fish into fertilizer. But whatever it was, that place really stunk - even from inside the car. It was like Beamish would say later, "Welcome to Prince Rupert, Armpit of the World."

We drove into the town and the very first thing we saw was a large, modern building with an old totem pole out front. It was a little before nine that night and the place was all lit up. The sign said *Recreation Complex*, so we parked the car and went inside to check it out.

There was a basketball court with ten or eleven guys standing around or shooting hoops, and a small gym off to the side. And lockers and showers. The whole thing was free. It wasn't a club.

"The facility will close in ten minutes," the announcer said.

"Must close at nine o'clock," Kingpen said, looking at his watch. So we waited in the building to stay warm ten more minutes, then left and got back in the car.

"Maybe you guys can shower before I get back from the Kraxins," I said. "You're really starting to smell."

"Screw you," Beamish said, and he started to laugh. "Let's go see the town."

It wasn't very big and not that much was going on. We ended up in a laundromat on McBride Street. We were there maybe an hour, smelling the fish fertilizer and watching some other people's clothes going around. It was the only place that was open. The only place we could stay warm.

"We can do some laundry tomorrow," Kingpen said.

We left at eleven that night. We had to. It was really depressing. The place closed. Then we got in the car and we weren't really sure where to go at first. So we looked at one of Kingpen's maps, made a left, and went down Park Avenue for about a mile and a half, until we were outside the town.

There was a small, flat-topped hill. A plateau, I guess you'd call it. But anyway, we drove up this frozen, gravel road to the plateau and crossed over a broken metal chain. There was an old white van farther back on the hill, with some people standing around. But aside from them, we were the only ones there. *Prince Rupert Campground* - that's what the map said.

We had a campfire that night. "A beacon," Kingpen called it. We couldn't get it going at first, because the wood was all wet and hard to find under the snow. We finally got it going though. We never set the tent up and had to sleep in the car. But we did have a fire.

It was later that night when Kingpen and Beamish went into the Buick. I stayed outside looking at one of Kingpen's maps. It was a map of the continent and for a while, I thought I was there. On page 34. A small, red dot on the left hand side of North America. But then I closed the atlas and looked down the hill. There was a small Esso gas station that had closed for the night, but the lights had been left on. Beyond that, there was the ocean, about a half a mile away. This never ending blackness that you felt more than saw. And then the wind began to blow. God it was cold. But I remember I still stood there. Stood there on the hill, smelling the ground up fish. Then I watched as the lights of the town began to go out, one by one.

Remember, I thought. **This** *is Prince Rupert. The next time you look at the dot on the map,* **THIS** *is what it is.*

Then I set the last piece of wet wood on the fire, went into the Buick, got down deep in the bag, and tried to go to sleep.

Chapter 7

Arthur cooked me a great send-off breakfast the next morning - scrambled eggs, toast and Spam.

"I'll bet Mrs. Kraxin can't cook like this," he said.

"I hope to hell not," I said and we started to laugh. It was six-fifteen. The sun was comin' up. The ocean was out there.

"It's gonna be a good one," I said, and I took a bite of toast.

"I wish I was going," Arthur told me.

The ferry left at seven. The dock was two miles down the road. We drove over the broken campground chain and went down the hill. You could still smell the fish or the fertilizer or whatever it was.

When we got down to the dock, we could see it was packed. This one huge parking lot, jammed with all these cars leading to the ferry. Cars, trucks, and a couple dozen campers.

"You don't need to get in *that* line," Kingpen said. "You can walk right on."

We parked the car and sat around awhile, watching the people and studying the brochures. It was like Kingpen said. If you didn't have a vehicle, you didn't need a reservation. You just bought yourself a ticket and walked on board. It was pretty cheap, really. Eighteen dollars for a six-and-a-half-hour ride.

"We'll clean out the Buick while you're gone," Kingpen said. "Take a shower and wash some clothes."

I got my gear together, said goodbye, and began to walk on down the line of cars. There were license plates from everywhere: Mississippi, Oklahoma, Texas. There was even one from Florida.

I bought a ticket at the little building and then I had to go through Customs. U.S. Customs. To get into Alaska. I got through there and headed to the ferry. There was one ramp for cars that went down below - and then the other one, for people like me, who were walking on. I got to the top, turned around, and saw Kingpen take my picture.

"Say hello to Alaska!" Kingpen yelled. Then I saw Beamish get inside the car.

You've probably seen the ferry on a TV ad, in the movies, or maybe in a brochure. But let me tell you, it was really something. A lot bigger than I had pictured. It was blue and white, with a gold-colored line that ran along the sides. There was a big viewing room in front, and lifeboats were hanging up over the deck. An American flag and an Alaskan flag were both hanging off the back of the ship. *The Taku.* That was its name.

But anyway, they got all the vehicles on, the engines started up, there were two long blasts from the whistle, and then we pulled away from the dock.

"See ya," somebody yelled.

For about a half an hour I stood on the deck as we headed up the coast. Miles and miles of coastline with no buildings or roads. That's what I remember. Just this never-ending forest. And ravens. Plenty of ravens.

We headed into open water after that, so I decided to look around the ferry. Almost all the people were inside, where it was warm, sitting on lounge chairs, looking out the glass. There were even private rooms where you could spend the night. Or, if you wanted to, you could sleep outside, in the solarium. And then there was a gift shop.

I found a shower on the second floor. It was for anyone who needed it. Walk-ons mostly, I figured, because the private rooms had their own. I must have been in there for an hour. I didn't have any soap, so I just stood under the water staying warm. Then I dried myself with some paper towels, the brown kind that come in the dispenser. I must have used at least thirty of them. Then I put my clothes back on and went outside.

We were along the coast again. No cities, cars or towns. Just giant spruce trees. Spruce trees and ravens.

We crossed into Alaska soon after that. "The Alaskan border," the captain announced. And I don't know how he knew it, but anyway, we went on in. We stayed by the coast after that.

Sometime later, one of the passengers on deck with me pointed up ahead. "Ketchikan," he told me. It was somebody with binoculars. And when I looked where he had pointed, I could just barely see the littlest town, hugging the coast.

"Ketchikan," the Captain announced. "Gateway to Alaska."

It was starting to rain, drizzle mostly. And it was getting foggy. But even then, I could see where the hills had been cut bare. "A logging town." That's what the Kraxins had said. And as we got a little closer, I began to smell it. Like the fresh, sweet smell of a lumber yard.

The town itself was a couple of miles long, all strung out along the bottom of a big hill called Deer Mountain. It was a neat looking place, kind of disorganized. Buildings on pilings over the water. Floatplanes landing and taking off. But the thing I remember most was the steps. Wooden stairways, leading up the hill. I saw them as we passed the town, and then we docked just to the north.

It didn't take long to get off the boat. I thought that with all of the cars it would take a while, but it wasn't like that. I went down the ramp with some other walk-ons. A few of the cars followed and the rest stayed on the ferry to continue on to Juneau, Wrangell or Haines.

"Jesse Fitch!" someone called. I looked into a crowd and out walked Mrs. Kraxin. She looked just like the picture she had sent me that I left back in Prince Rupert. She was a nice looking lady, a little bit tall with a real pretty smile. She was about 55 or 60. She had on a dark green poncho with a fur-trimmed hood. "Jesse Fitch," she said again. "I'm Ellen Kraxin."

We got into her camper, a Volkswagen bus. We drove up the hill and on to Third Avenue. Hers was the fourth or fifth house after we turned. She parked the bus in a little space behind the house, opened a gate, and we went in from the back. The front of the house hung over the hill.

"Charlie's under the weather," Mrs. Kraxin said, "or he would have picked you up."

She opened the door, and we went through the kitchen and into the living room.

"Welcome to Ketch," Mr. Kraxin said. He was sitting on the sofa with a banged up leg. "Fix the boy a drink," he said. "Whaddya want? A beer?"

"Yeah. That would be great," I said.

"How about a shower first?" Mrs. Kraxin asked. "Let him take a shower first, to freshen up, and then we'll have some lunch."

There was a little apartment downstairs that the Kraxins rented out. It was vacant at the time, so I went down there. I took a shower with soap, dried off with a regular towel, put my clothes back on and went upstairs.

We ate in the living room after that, in front of a big picture window. We watched the float planes come in and the ferry leave. I had a beer, some smoked salmon, halibut, and herring with sauce on top. And they were just the hors d'oeuvres. Mrs. Kraxin had fixed us pasta and a homemade apple pie for dessert. "Want some ice cream on that?" Mrs. Kraxin asked. But before I could answer, she piled some on. They couldn't have been nicer.

"Now tell us about this trip," Mr. Kraxin said. So I told them about Kingpen and Beamish. About the storm in Chicago.

"A pretty rough trip," Mr. Kraxin said. "Are you planning on working up north?"

"Working?"

"Plenty of work," Mrs. Kraxin said.

I shook my head and told them no. "Just want to see the state," I said. Then we looked out the window and watched another floatplane take off.

It was like a Sunday afternoon when you sit around the house, read the paper and watch TV. They didn't have a television set, but that's what it was like. Real relaxing. I remember thinking that it must have been like that for Kingpen and Beamish too, with nowhere to go.

We sat around and talked most of that day. Talked, listened to music, drank more beer, and watched the floatplanes come in and take off. For supper, we served ourselves from a three-foot carousel that was built into the dining room table that Mr. Kraxin had made. Halibut, scallops and these big giant shrimp. "Prawns," Mrs. Kraxin called them. And we turned the wheel, took off more food and kept eating, while we looked at some slides Mr. Kraxin had taken.

"Old sleeping cars," he said, as he showed us a slide of McKinley Park. There was a small hotel with some trains out front. Four or five coaches on a hundred-foot piece of track. "For the overflow," Mr. Kraxin said. And then he went on to the next slide.

There was a dirty, yellow school bus on the side of a hill. "Park tour bus," he said. "Goes back into the park."

There were pictures of mountains and rivers. Some moose. He had one of a bear. "Didn't get one of McKinley," he said. "It was socked in that day." And then, he had slides of Southeast. Sitka and Haines.

"Go and see it yourself," he said. "You and your friends. You'll see it." He turned the projector off and I helped him with the slides. "You get some sleep. There's a bed downstairs."

I thanked them for everything and went down the steps. It was a few minutes after eleven that night. I remember lying on the bed and looking at the clock on the wall. It's funny, when you travel. You're one place one day, another the next. And still, you think of people that you know, and the patterns that they keep. I thought of Kingpen and Beamish, miles and miles away.

Five after eleven, I thought. And I could picture it clear as day. The two of them were just stepping outside. Leaving the laundromat.

We went to a whorehouse that next morning, Dolly's on Creek Street. It was an ex-whore house really. From twenty years before.

The creek started on the hill and ran down Deer Mountain. By the time it reached the bottom, it was twenty feet wide, and shallow or deep, depending on the tide. There was a whole group of buildings built over the creek. Built on wooden poles. There were at least twenty-two. There was a little wooden walkway that ran around them all. Ketchikan named it Creek Street, but the people who lived there said, "*Crick* Street."

It had been a red-light district years before. "Where men and salmon came to spawn," Mr. Kraxin said. But anyway, the town and some people had taken over the buildings and fixed them up. Dolly's was a museum. There were some gift shops and art stores. One place was a law office.

I saw a lot that day. Mr. Kraxin's leg was doing better, so the two of them took me around until twelve-thirty or one, and then we all went back for lunch. More prawns, chicken salad, and these abalone Mrs. Kraxin had gotten from the beach. And you should have seen those shells. Like alabaster with all these pink and white translucent colors. I stuck one in my pocket to show to Kingpen later.

"How about you take the VW, go on out, and drive around?" Mr. Kraxin said. "You can stop back for dinner, or later, if you want. Whatever."

"We'll be here," Mrs. Kraxin said, and she started to laugh.

He tossed me the keys. I thanked them and started out the door. "Now don't worry about getting lost," Mr. Kraxin said. There are only thirty-five miles of road.

49

One part of it went south, into town, the part we had taken before. So I got in the van and headed north and drove out a ways. Six or seven miles, and I started to see the smoke. Smoke or steam, I wasn't sure. There were a couple of huge brown buildings that were interconnected, with a big sign out front that told you what the place was, in case you didn't know. *Ketchikan Pulp and Mill.* You should have seen it. Seen it, smelled it. Steam pouring out from all these pipes, with tens of thousands of these huge logs lying all around, waiting to be turned into pulp. That place was really something.

I must have sat there thirty, forty minutes, just watching. Guys using forklifts and loaders in the snow. Giant cranes to move the logs around. Lots of *beep, beep, beep*'s. Kinda like the pull-off, where we parked the car that night outside Chicago. Except here it wasn't dark, so you could see it all. *Beep beep!* Lookout, I thought. And then I started laughing to myself.

I drove out to another place right after that. Totem Bight. It was really pretty neat. Totem Poles. More Totem Poles. There were some that were old. *Really* old. Then other ones were newer. And one was being carved. I think the place was supposed to be a tourist spot, but nobody was there. No people, just giant ravens flying all around, like the ones down in Prince Rupert – *Caw. Caw. Caw!*

I got back to the Kraxins' and they were playing dominoes, sitting by the window, watching everything go by.

"I thought you might be back for dinner," Mrs. Kraxin said.

Those people were the best.

"You like king crab?" Mrs. Kraxin asked. So I told her I had only tried the kind we had back east. From the Chesapeake.

"Well if you like *them*, I know you'll like *these*," she said.

She went back to the kitchen and brought out a platter full of giant legs. "Just crack 'em open, get the meat out, and dip it in the butter," Mr. Kraxin told me.

So that was what I did. And I have to tell you, they were great, which is what I told the Kraxins. But the Maryland blues are really better. Even with the butter, it wasn't near the same. No way they compared.

And that was when I *knew* that someday I would do it. Send some blues up to the Kraxins. A couple dozen, real hot and spicy, and a couple soft crabs to go with them. *Just wait*, I kept on thinking. And then Mr. Kraxin handed me another beer, and I opened up a leg, dipped it in the butter, and stuck it in my mouth.

Mrs. Kraxin drove me down to the terminal that night. I had to leave at eleven. I had come in on the Taku, but I was going back on the Malaspina. I waved to Mrs. Kraxin from the deck and shouted one more time to give my thanks to Mr. Kraxin.

"Now make sure and have a safe trip," she called out. "Say hello to Kingpen and Beamish for us."

"I will," I shouted back. Then the whistle blew a couple times and the ferry pulled away from the dock.

Because it was night, you couldn't really tell when we were going along the coast. You couldn't see a lot of things, but you knew that *they* were out there. *Grizzlies, caribou and wolves.* You *could* see all the stars that night, though. Millions of 'em, shining from the black.

I went upstairs and slept out on the deck that night. I had a cushioned chair and I tried to sleep there in my sleeping bag. But I don't think I ever fell asleep. I got down in the bag and at first I thought that it was the cold. But it wasn't. My head was keeping me awake.

We can never know beforehand the adventures that we'll have. That's what I remember thinking. And my mind went to the next thing. In a crazy kind of way I started missing 'em. Kingpen and Beamish, my dog and the Buick. Thinking. *Always thinking.*

And not long after that, I started smelling rotten fish. *Getting there*, I thought. I stuck my head out of the bag, and off in the distance I could see the fuzzy lights of Prince Rupert.

And just for a second, I thought of the dot on the map, but then I remembered the chain that was broken. The campfire, the ocean, and the Esso gas station that were all there. *Armpit of the World*, I thought. And I started to smile.

51

Chapter 8

We pulled up to the dock. I was the first one down the ramp, except for a deckhand. I got off and started looking around, then I finally saw the Buick in a far-off corner of the parking lot. It was covered with mud and snow and looked more gray than silver. I gave a wave and waited for the lights, but they never came on.

Probably still asleep, I remember thinking, as I walked over to the car. And in a way, I was right. Even the guy who fell out of the driver's side when I opened the door - he wasn't awake.

He slumped out of the car onto a frozen puddle of water down by my feet. I thought that he was dead at first. He looked about twenty-three or twenty-four years old, wearing cowboy boots, a pair of jeans and a red plaid shirt.

"Don't worry," he blubbered. "I *know* the man."

His head began to wobble like one of those little bobble heads that you see, where the head is connected to the shoulders by a spring. And when you moved him - *WOBBLE, WOBBLE, WOBBLE.*

"I *know* the man," he told me again. "The one who owns the car." And then he curled all up, right there on the frozen puddle and tried to go to sleep.

I stuck my head in the car and started to gag. They had to be dead. They had to be. Nobody could be alive and live in that smell, I thought. It was like somebody had thrown up, which I'm sure they had, all inside the car. And then shook up some beers and sprayed them around to top it off.

There were empty Spam cans, dog nuggets, and more toothpaste on the windows. But it was the beer smell mostly, from all these cans that were there in the car. Dozens of 'em. Crushed and smashed, or ripped in half.

"KINGPEN!" I yelled. But he didn't move a muscle. He was over on the passenger side, all crunched up in his sleeping bag, with his head on the armrest and his feet on the dashboard. Beamish was stretched out in the back.

I reached down to the ice and picked the guy up; the one who said that he knew me. Then I put him on the seat.

"Just who the hell are *you*?" I asked. But the spring from his shoulders to his head had broken and he couldn't talk, so I pushed him over toward Kingpen and I got in the car. Somebody had left the key in the ignition and as soon as I turned it, the engine started up.

I checked the fuel gauge. We had plenty of gas. I put the Buick in Neutral and we started across the parking lot, up a little embankment and out onto Park Avenue. I stopped it once at a little curve in the road where you could look back to the dock. I got out of the car and started to wipe off the windshield with a sock I'd found on the floor. Wiped and wiped and wiped.

Then I got back in the car and thought that I was gonna puke, so I rolled the windows down. But it didn't help that much, because when you didn't smell the vomit and the beer and the toothpaste, you smelled the rotten fish being ground up into fertilizer.

I went down Park Avenue, made a right on McBride Street and stopped at the Recreation Center. I pulled the guy with the cowboy boots out of the car and hauled him up to the entrance of the building. "Here," I said. "Five more hours and you can go inside."

It took a couple of tries but I finally got him set, all propped up with his back to the wall and his legs stretched out. I took out a five and put it in the pocket of his shirt. "Get some coffee later," I told him. But I know he never heard me.

I went back to the Buick, climbed in, and sat there for a minute watching him wobble. *WOBBLE, WOBBLE, WOBBLE.* And then he started swaying, back and forth. *Timber*, I thought. And then I watched him topple over, sinking to the frozen ground.

I was going to set him up again. I really was. I started to get out, but I never did. *Sometimes*, I remember thinking, *you just have to go.*

And that was when I drove the Buick out.

I drove us out at five or six o'clock that morning, with the windows down. God it was cold. The wind would whip on in and you'd catch it in your mouth; but you couldn't breathe through your nose, because then you'd smell the fish and the vomit and the beer and the Spam.

"WAKE *UP* you sons*abitches*! WAKE *UP*!" I yelled. But neither of them did. Even my dog looked dead, lying underneath the dashboard.

The sun was coming up as I drove along the Skeena River. I headed east, into the early morning rays, looking for the logging road that we'd never found a couple nights before.

I drove a long time after that. Nearly two hours - a long time for me. Then I started looking, right before we got to Terrace.

There was a roadside store about a quarter mile ahead. A general store. They had groceries, hardware and gas. *It must have started as a house*, that's what I remember thinking. At least that was how it looked. And then, they'd added on a room and then another and another. It didn't really look like a roadside store as most people would imagine it. But anyway, the place was open, so I stopped to get some gas. An older guy came out and started the pump, and I asked him about the logging road.

"Only two roads here. The one you're on and the one that runs back behind the store. I've never been on that one," he said, as he turned his body toward it and waved his arm.

"Does it get much traffic?" I asked. He shook his head and looked around. "Not that I can see."

I paid him and pulled the Buick to the side of the store. I could see the little road that went back into the trees. If you hadn't known, you would have thought it was part of the parking lot.

We can never know beforehand..., I thought, and then I started up the road, the one that started by the store and went back into the trees.

It was a pretty well-built road for the first part. Good solid gravel, a lot like the Yellowhead Highway for twelve or fifteen miles. I got us to a large plywood sign that was nailed to a pole. Off to the side of the road. It was what was left of a sign, really - blasted away by people who had shot it.

W RN NG
BEFOR START G ON TH S ROA
Y U NE D THE FOL O ING:

And then there was a list – except I couldn't read it. It was all blown apart.

I shut the car off, sat there and thought for a minute. I even got the maps out, and the mileage charts, and that's what kept me going. It would have been over three hundred miles just to get back to St. George, then all the way up Highway 97 to Fort St. John and on to the Alcan. About a thousand miles of extra driving. It would have been at least another day.

"The adventures that we'll have," I said real quietly to myself.

And then I started the Buick and kept on driving. Kept on driving where the gravel meets the dirt, and around the first week of April it all turns to mud. You can see it if you ever go there.

It was still pretty early, about eight-thirty or nine, but it started warming up and the snow began to melt. Not all of it, of course, but the snow that did melt ran into the road and made it all sloppy. Sloppy and black. Muck. That was what it was. Thick, muddy *muck*. Except Beamish didn't think so. "Fuck the muck," Beamish told me later. "This stuff's more like unadulterated elephant shit." That's what Beamish told us. But that was sometime later.

It was pretty interesting, driving. When you looked in the rearview mirror you could see the tire marks, at least a couple inches deep. And then the mud would suck it all together and they'd all disappear. It really made you wonder if you'd ever even been there.

Kingpen finally woke up. We were an hour from the store, when he finally opened up his eyes.

"Just what the hell went on back there?" I asked. But Kingpen said he didn't know.

"Met the people in the van," he said. "Asked us over for a drink."

I handed him *The Map*, the one with the long hyphenated line that ran up the page.

"I'm pretty sure we're on the logging road," I said. "Whadda *you* think?"

It was a pretty stupid question. Nobody could tell. Not from where we were. For one thing, there was nothing there. No signs, stores or pull-offs. There weren't even any cars. Just this long, strung-out, muddy rut that ran between the trees. And it wasn't getting any better.

"Let's stay on it," Kingpen said. Then he rolled up his window and crawled down deeper in his bag.

We kept on moving, but in another couple hours, you could tell that we were *really* slowin' down.

"Breakup!" Kingpen said. "That's what this is. It's *breakup*." And he started looking through his books.

"Listen," Kingpen told me. "Here it is… '*Breakup is the time of year usually occurring in late spring or early summer, when the snow begins to melt in an unusually violent manner, and causes the*

55

surrounding land to become water soaked.' It's *breakup*," Kingpen said again. And I kept on driving.

We were fifty-five to eighty miles north of the warning sign, sloshing through the soup. We'd drive along and you could hear the sounds. *MWAP, MWAP, MWAP.* Little implosions as the tires sucked at the mud.

Kingpen looked at *The Map*.

"Noticed any curves?" he asked.

I shook my head.

"Looks pretty straight here, too," he said, pointing to the hyphenated line. And the more we drove, the more we knew. This was it. The long lost logging road we had found in the magazine. The one that started near the store, went into the trees and ended near Watson Lake, on the Alcan.

"Four hundred fifty miles to go!" Kingpen yelled. The two of us started cheering, and the Buick pushed ahead, through little valleys and hills, but always going in a straight line. Always forging on – *MWAP, MWAP, MWAP.*

We stopped for some lunch late that afternoon, right on the muddy road. We gave my dog a can of corned beef out of the back, and Kingpen scrambled some eggs and made toast for us.

Then he took some pictures. One was great. We had just come down a hill and the car was sitting at the bottom where the water had collected. It was almost to the doors, and the way he shot the picture, you'd have thought that we were sitting in a lake - this '64 silver Buick Special, all covered in mud, floating in the water.

I drove a lot that day. Not so many miles, because we couldn't go that fast, but I drove a lot of time. From about five-thirty or six that morning until nine or ten that night.

It started getting dark and it was really getting hard to drive. Just staying on the road was tough. No curbs or yellow lines, and you'd slide off to the side and maybe hit a stump.

"Halfway there!" Kingpen said. I drove a little farther, and then I remember we came to a tree in the middle of the road. We saw it in the headlights. It divided the mud into left and right roads.

I put the car in park and we sat there a minute, while Kingpen found his flashlight and he looked at *The Map*. "Nothing like this on *The Map*," he said. "Is there a *sign* on the tree?"

I punched on the brights and both of us saw that nothing was there. "Whaddya think?"

He didn't say a word, but I knew what he was thinking. *Suppose this wasn't it? Suppose we weren't supposed to be here?*

"I'm going left," I said, and I started around. God, I was tired. I remember it all started looking the same. Black on black. The mud, the sky, the trees.

"Ever heard of a whiteout?" Kingpen asked me. "Well, this is a *blackout*," he said. And then he gave a nervous laugh.

I drove a little farther, until I couldn't see a thing. *Nothing.* "Blackout," Kingpen said again. "Just shut the engine off and we'll start again tomorrow."

I turned the key, turned around, and got my sleeping bag from the back. Then I crawled down, deep inside.

"I'll see you tomorrow Kingpen," I muttered.

But I know he didn't hear me. He had his flashlight out - and I just knew that he was staring at *The Map*.

Chapter 9

We were sitting on a cliff. I swear to God. Right there at the edge.

Kingpen and Beamish were already out of the car, so I got out of the bag and opened the door.

The road went another six or seven feet, stopped and disappeared. There was a riverbed below, and when you looked across you could see the other side. But I don't think the road had ever been there.

"Now *that* would have been some ride," Beamish said. And he picked up a rock from the ground and tossed it over the edge. We watched it tumble down about two hundred feet, over the boulders and grass and snow. There were three cars down there.

"Maybe there still are some people in 'em," Kingpen said.

But Beamish shook his head. "Look at the rust on those old clunkers. They've been there for years."

We stood there for a couple of minutes after that, shaking our heads and talking about what might have been.

"Life's a funny thing," Kingpen told us. "Another couple feet . . ."

"Fuck it. Let's go," Beamish said, so we walked back to the car. I got in the back seat, underneath the bags, and Beamish started driving. We went back to the tree and made a right this time. Made a right, and somehow we followed the mud that we called the road, and went over a little wooden bridge.

"Not quite two hundred fifty miles to go," Kingpen said.

It wasn't long before the sun began to shine and the snow began to melt, and pretty soon you could hear the familiar *WAMP, WAMP, WAMP!* More little implosions, as the tires started sucking at the mud.

Beamish drove all morning, but the road was getting pretty bad, especially the dips. Two or even three feet deep. They were filled up with water and we'd slosh our way on through .Then we'd test the brakes and keep on driving – *WAMP, WAMP, WAMP!*

"*LOOK!*" Kingpen said. *WAMP, WAMP, WAMP!* He pointed up ahead. There was a good-sized log sitting there in front of us.

"Must be from a logger's truck," Beamish said, even though we'd never seen one.

I remember thinking we were going to move the log at first. That's what I remember thinking. Hook it to the car and pull it to the side. But Beamish didn't think so.

"We'll just drive on over top it," Beamish told us. He stomped down on the pedal, gave the car some gas, and we lifted up and then came down hard. Right there on the log. And then we didn't move.

"Son of a *BITCH*!" Beamish yelled. "I think we're *stuck*." So we got out of the car to take a look.

"I think we're balancing more than we're stuck," Kingpen said. And when you looked at the car, you could see he was right.

"Son of a *BITCH*!" Beamish said again. "Well, maybe we can *rock* it."

He went around to the front and leaned down on the hood, while Kingpen and I began to lift up the trunk.

"Up-Down! Up-Down!" Beamish yelled.

You could see and feel the car, like a see-saw, going up and down and back and forth. And the funny thing was, it started to work. But not like you would think. The car didn't move but the log started to sink.

"Up-Down! Up-Down!" Beamish kept yelling. And in another half an hour the car was sitting on the mud.

"That'll teach those loggers to screw with us," Beamish said. Kingpen looked at me and we both shook our heads.

We got in the car, and we could feel the tires in the back as they ran over the log.

We kept on heading north to Watson Lake. It was late that afternoon, after we had eaten, when it started clouding up.

"How many more miles?" Beamish asked. "We're running out of gas."

Kingpen looked at *The Map*. "Maybe a hundred."

"We'll never make it," Beamish told us. "We might have to hike on in."

We drove another hour after that, another twenty miles or so.

"Look!" Kingpen said, pointing to the windshield. There was a drop of water, and then another, and another, and then it started coming down. Never really a storm, just a long, steady drizzle that made it really hard to drive.

"Hold on," Beamish said. We were headed toward a puddle that wasn't very deep, but the mud was pretty thick because of the rain.

"I don't think we're gonna make it," Kingpen said. And you could feel the Buick going down.

Beamish gave it some gas, the tires began to spin, and the *WAMP, WAMP, WAMP* changed into this real high pitched *ZEE-EEE-EEE!*

"Shee-*IT!*" Beamish yelled. And then he gave it more gas.

I remember sitting in the back and feeling the trunk when it hit the mud and bottomed out.

"Stuck!" Beamish yelled. And then the car shut off. "Fuckin' tailpipe must be down in the mud!"

We were sitting at an angle, ass-end down. And when you looked through the windshield, you could see the sky, with the clouds and the rain all coming at us.

"Maybe we can rock it," Kingpen said. "Like we did before." But Beamish never said a word. None of us did after that, at least not for a while.

We just sat there, watching it get dark. Then we climbed out the windows, because we couldn't open the doors, and we started doing what we didn't want to do.

The mud was up to our shins, and when you looked at the tires on the back of the Buick you could just barely see them. Beamish climbed back through the window, got behind the wheel, and Kingpen started digging out the tailpipe. He just about had it, when he let out a scream and held up his hand.

"Oh *God*, it hurts!" Kingpen whined. He had burned it on the tail pipe.

"Just stick it in the mud!" Beamish yelled. He turned the key and the Buick started sputtering to life.

We were still in the mud - that hadn't changed - but the rain was *really* coming down. When Beamish flipped the lights on, we could see the road getting washed away. All around us, everywhere we looked.

"Try to lift it!" Beamish yelled.

So that was what we did. Tried and tried to lift it, but the car still wouldn't budge.

"Won't budge!" I yelled.

"We need a fulcrum," Beamish called back. He climbed out of the window. "Maybe we should cut down a tree."

But we didn't have a saw, so we just stood around the car, deciding what to do.

It was pretty bad. It really was. And the worst part was, it was just like Kingpen said - even if we got out of this mess, how far could we go?

"Let's work for half an hour. We'll give it our best shot," I said.

But after a couple of minutes, we were covered with mud, and as fast as we dug, the mud came oozing back. So finally we just stopped and stood there in the dark.

"Let's get in the car," Beamish said. So we climbed back in and rolled the windows up behind us. The seats were soaking wet but the worst part was, we'd brought all this muck inside the car. Everywhere we sat or put our legs, hands, or feet.

"Sonova *BITCH!*" Beamish said, as a big glob of mud fell out of his hair. And then he turned on the lights so we could see the road, but they only pointed at the sky.

"Maybe a plane will see us," he half joked, flipping them off and on.

"Well at least we're not washing away yet," Kingpen told him.

Beamish turned off the lights and rolled down his window. The rain was starting to let up a little, so he climbed out of the car.

"I'm going to the trunk. Anybody want something to eat?" he asked.

"Get me a drink," I said. "If there's anything back there." Which was kind of funny, now that I think back, with all of the water coming down.

I moved behind the wheel and stared out through the windshield toward the dark. *Suppose a logging truck came down the road tonight and crushed us all?* I thought. *A logging truck with big chained tires that could stay on the road. A logging truck with huge, giant logs like the ones that I saw, back at the pulp mill.*

Beamish came back with a can of Spam and a big brown bag.

"Here," he said. "It was all I could find." He handed me the bag, and I reached inside and felt dozens of cans.

"I thought you could drink the syrup," Beamish said.

I took one out and looked over at Kingpen.

"Go ahead," he told me. "I've never even tried them. I don't want any. Help yourself."

Beamish passed me a can opener and we settled into the bags. God it was cold.

And that's when I remember thinking that it really didn't matter. *We'd never even know what hit us. Just WHAM! We'd never even know it.* That's what I remember thinking.

I hooked the opener we kept up on the dashboard to the lip of the first can and turned it about a third of the way around. That way, I figured it would keep the little oranges inside when I turned the can up to my mouth. It was sickening at first, this sweet, orange syrup. But I was really thirsty. And it seemed the more I drank, the thirstier I got. I finally must have drunk at least nineteen of the cans.

The temperature started going down, and none of us could sleep.

"Hey FITCH. You awake?" somebody would call out. And then, "Hey BEAMISH . . . Hey KINGPEN. You *dead* yet?" All through the night.

It was four or five o'clock in the morning. Freezing cold. And you could feel the mud getting solid all around you. In your shoes. In your socks. Your hair. Even in your ears. This cold, black, muck. God, it was cold. I was down deep in the bag and started to shake. And then I guess I hit the horn.

"LOOK *OUT*! GET *DOWN*!" I screamed. I thought it was the logging truck. And then I started sweating.

But for all of the reasons that I couldn't get to sleep, the one that stood out was that sweet orange syrup. I really had to *go*.

I put it off for as long as I could. Finally, I crawled out of the bag, rolled the window down, and climbed outside. I almost fell at first, right outside the car. I slipped on some ice but I caught myself, then I stood there peeing for a minute by the front left tire. And all at once, it hit me. I was standing *on* the mud. Not *in* the mud, but on it. And that was when I knew. I *knew* that we were gonna make it.

I went back to the door, climbed in through the window, pushed the sleeping bag over, and got behind the wheel.

I turned the key in the ignition. *Come on*, I thought. *Come on.* The Buick started up, I turned on the lights and stepped down on the gas.

You could hear it, but you *felt* it more than heard it. The Buick lifted up, broke free, and began to pull out of the hole. I heard this loud popping sound coming from the two back tires.

We were right there on the edge, pulling out. I gave it more gas and the Buick lurched ahead. You could hear the ice. Like a thousand panes of glass, shattering beneath us.

"I'll get the windshield," Kingpen yelled, as he worked his way out of his sleeping bag. Then he pulled his hand up inside his sleeve and started to wipe.

"Look," Beamish said. And he told me what I already knew. "Frozen." He pointed up ahead.

There were ripples mostly. You could see 'em in the headlights. Frozen ridges and gullies, where the water from the snow and the rain had cut through the mud. It made it easier to drive, for one thing. You could just steer the car until the tires got into a groove. Then you could step down on the gas or the brakes as you were moving, so you didn't slide too much.

The sun was coming up. We could see it on our right.

"GO!" Beamish yelled. "Before it starts to melt."

I stepped on the gas, and we began to pick up speed. Twenty, sometimes thirty miles an hour. We were flying over the gullies and riding on the ridges.

"GO!" Beamish yelled again. And even as we drove, we could feel the mud getting softer underneath the tires.

"Fifteen miles to the Alcan," Kingpen said. "Twenty at the most."

And in another five or so, the mud turned to gravel, and I knew that we were getting close.

There was a Jeep up ahead. Stopped on the road, it was facing our direction.

"Better warn them," Kingpen said.

So I pulled up alongside and rolled my window down. There were two of them in there. A couple of guys in matching red jackets, and they didn't look too happy.

"Road's a bitch," Beamish said. "But maybe in your Jeep . . ."

"You know it's *closed*," the driver said. "It opens in May, but that's only to loggers."

He took out a pen and asked his buddy for the ticket book. "Unauthorized use of a logging road." That's what the ticket said. Three hundred fifty Canadian dollars, but of course we never paid it.

"Gimmee the ticket," Beamish said. Then he set up the Coleman stove on the back seat of the Buick as we drove away. As he held the ticket to the flame, I kept on driving. And in another ten or fifteen miles, we met up with the Alcan.

I made a right and we headed east to Watson Lake, about twenty miles away. Named after Frank or Bob, the books didn't seem to know, the town wasn't very big, and we couldn't see the lake. They did have a gas station though. We drifted in, as we ran out of gas.

"Perfect timing," Kingpen said. But we were a little early. It opened at seven and it was still closer to six.

There was a laundromat open across the road. It was open twenty-four hours a day, seven days a week. *Far North Laundry*. That's what the sign said.

So we walked across the Alcan and went inside. Nobody was there. Not even an attendant. Just this laundromat that was a lot more modern than the one in Prince Rupert, with much bigger dryers and more washing machines.

"Feels good just to be warm," Kingpen said, as he took off his coat that was covered in mud.

"Might as well do our laundry, now that we're here," Beamish said. He peeled off his jacket and shirt, and threw them in a washer. "How about those sleeping bags, Kingpin? They need to be washed."

Kingpen put his jacket back on, went out the door, and headed toward the gas station, while Beamish started walking toward the back of the laundromat, to a little closet-like room.

Ten minutes later, Kingpen came back in. You could hardly see him. He was carrying the bags, all three of them. And for the next few minutes, the two of us stuffed them into washers. The big industrial kind you've probably seen, but never had to use.

"Here," Beamish said. "Get my pants." When I looked to the back, I could see them, hanging on to what turned out to be the restroom door. "I'll just buy new underwear," he said. "This pair's shot."

I threw his clothes in the washer and put a dollar in the machine. That's what they took. Just dollar bills. Two bucks for each of the bags.

"Don't let anyone back here, in the closet!" Beamish yelled.

"Why not?" Kingpen asked. And then Beamish shouted something that I didn't understand.

"Maybe we should take his clothes, and drive away," Kingpen whispered. And he started laughing.

We spent the morning there, in the Far North Laundry at Watson Lake. We washed our clothes in the regular machines, and then washed ourselves in this little basin, back in the closet that had the bathroom. We scraped off the mud, mostly. We got back in our clothes, and it was like Kingpen said... Even though we had washed our clothes, we could still see the dust fly up when we sat on a chair.

That was because we'd hadn't used any soap. But the clothes were dry and it wasn't that bad. The worst part was the bags. We should have read the labels, Kingpen said later. But of course nobody had.

"*Feel* 'em," Kingpen said, as we were taking the sleeping bags from the washing machines. I could feel the globs. Big, lumpy bunches of feathers, all stuck together. Mine wasn't so bad - it was only made of cotton. But the other two were wrecked, along with their jackets.

"Maybe when we dry 'em, they'll fluff back up," Kingpen said, "in the industrial dryers."

But they never did. You could tell it when you held them. All airy and loose up top, and then sagging with big lumpy bunches of goose feathers down at the bottom.

"C'mon," Beamish said. "We gotta go."

We packed up the bags and walked back over to the car, across the road. The gas station had been closed when we first drifted in, but I remember it being open when we went back. It was about eleven o'clock by then. We pushed the Buick to the pump, filled it with gas, and then went inside the store. Kingpen got some cookies and a couple of little pies, then we left and started driving with Beamish behind the wheel.

It was six hundred miles to Alaska. That's what Kingpen told us. "It won't be long," he said. And then he got this far-off look.

We were finally driving on the Alcan and for maybe an hour we looked at a long, winding river off to our left.

"Rancheria," Kingpen said. And God, it was pretty. We couldn't see the water because it was still frozen, but for forty miles or more we drove alongside the ice and snow, that was covered with animal tracks. We thought we saw a moose once, going back into the woods. And that's what it was like, all along the way. Frozen scenery like you wouldn't believe. Miles and miles of forests and dozens of picnic stops. We crossed frozen streams and little bridges. We could see the Cassiar Mountains on either side of the road, and then we crossed over Screw Creek and passed Swan Lake.

"Four hundred and fifty miles," Kingpen said. And the more we drove, the more wound up we got.

"Tonight," Kingpen said. "Sometime tonight."

And he pounded on the dashboard, and we all began to cheer.
Sometime tonight.

Chapter 10

It was different driving on the gravel, different than the mud. The car seemed to bounce more, and rattle and jiggle. Kind of like a boat, when it rocks in the water.

It was three or four o'clock and we stopped to have some Spam and a can of beef stew. Kingpen cooked some eggs.

"Look," Beamish said. And when he pushed down on the trunk, you could see the back of the car bouncing up and down.

He crawled under the Buick, and then he crawled out and told us what he'd found. "Shocks," he said. "Look at this."

I got down on my knees and looked underneath.

"Here," he said. And he pointed to these holes that were in the metal pieces the shocks were bolted to. I don't know what they were called, but anyway, they weren't supposed to be there. The holes. And it was all just gonna keep getting worse. The holes would keep getting bigger and bigger, until the shocks fell through and the car collapsed. That's what Beamish said.

"Must have been that logging road," Kingpen said. "All the ups and downs."

But I knew it wasn't that. It was the way we'd put them on.

"We'll have to get 'em welded," Beamish said. We threw the cans in the back of the car and started driving again, bouncing down the Alcan.

We couldn't go as fast as we'd been going. Maybe only thirty miles an hour. And then every once in a while, we would stop and check underneath the car.

We got some gas near a town called Teslin, just as it was getting dark. There wasn't much there. Some trailer homes and a little museum. It was an Indian village, really. That was what it said in Kingpen's book.

We drove another thirty miles to the Teslin River Bridge. Then Beamish punched on the brights so we could read the point-of-interest sign. "1,770 feet long." That's how long it said the bridge was. Then it went on to explain that the bridge had been built as high as it was, so the steamers could pass underneath, on their way to Teslin from Whitehorse.

"Prior to the construction of the Alaskan Canadian Highway, all freight and supplies for Teslin traveled this water route from Whitehorse," Kingpen read.

And then we started across. We made it halfway and then Beamish stopped the car. He shut off the lights and we sat there awhile, in the middle of the bridge. Nobody was there except for my dog and us and the Buick.

"Imagine those steamships," Kingpen said. "Comin' up the river. Just picture them." But it was kind of hard to do with all of the ice that was there.

Beamish flipped on the lights and he started to drive, eight hundred eighty-five feet to the other side.

"We're in the Yukon," Kingpen said. "But it isn't the first time." He turned on his flashlight and I looked at his map.

"See how the road runs?" he asked. "Back and forth, and back and forth?" He pointed to the map. "*Here*, we were in British Columbia. And *here*, we're in the Yukon." We were in one or the other depending on the road.

"How much farther?" Beamish asked.

"About three hundred fifty," Kingpen said. But Beamish didn't pound the dashboard. He was getting tired. You could hear it in his voice.

"I'll drive," I said. "I like to drive at night."

Beamish pulled the Buick over. We let my dog out, and then Kingpen went underneath the car with his flashlight and laid there on the frozen gravel, to check on the shocks.

"The holes are a little bigger," he said. "But I think we'll be all right."

Beamish climbed in back and got into his bag. "Gimmee a wakeup call when we hit the border," he said. And then he tried to laugh.

Kingpen and I stayed outside for another minute, before we switched seats.

"He doesn't look too good," Kingpen told me. "Maybe he's sick."

"He's been driving an awful lot," I said. "I think he's just beat."

But it wasn't Beamish Kingpen was talking about. "Not Beamish. Your *dog*," Kingpen said. "I think he's really sick."

He was over by some trees, and Kingpen was right. He didn't look that energetic.

"Maybe he's hungry," I said. I went to the trunk and got out a can, turned the key around the edge, dumped the meat out, and offered him some.

"C'mon boy, it's Spam," I said. But he only hung his head.

"Try something else," Kingpen said. So then I got a can of corned beef, but he didn't want that either.

"Put it on the floor. Down in the back," Kingpen told me. "Maybe he'll eat it later."

So I put it down on the back floor, underneath where Beamish was sleeping. Then the three of us got in the car, and I started driving.

It was about six-thirty at night by then, maybe seven o'clock, and I know we hadn't seen more than a dozen cars on the road. Not since the laundromat. Or even Terrace, for that matter. Hundreds of miles, and you never saw a soul.

Suppose we broke down? Then what would we do? But of course I never said it. Just kept on driving. *Driving, driving, driving.* Bouncing along and thinking of the next thing.

Then it started getting dark, and after a while, we noticed this strange, almost eerie glow, off in the distance.

"*Look*," Kingpen said. And he pointed up ahead. "It's Whitehorse. Capital of the Yukon. We oughta get some gas."

It was another forty or fifty miles until we finally saw the town. Larger than I had expected. Fifteen thousand people lived there. That's what Kingpen told me. It had hotels and restaurants. We saw a couple of churches.

It was all pretty flat. That's what I remember. We drove into Whitehorse from the south, on a little access road, passed the airport on our left, went over some railroad tracks and then drove along a river to our right.

"The Yukon River!" Kingpen said. And he rolled down his window.

I stopped the car and we looked out into the black, away from the lights of the town.

"The mighty Yukon," Kingpen said.

And I looked and I imagined, till he rolled up the window, and I started driving again.

We were on a road called 2nd Avenue, and like a lot of towns we drove through, they had 1st and 2nd Avenue, and then came 3rd and

4th. I found out later that sometimes the places we'd go through might go up to 12th, depending on how big the town was.

"Look," Kingpen said. He pointed to a gas station, so I drove on over. We filled the Buick up and put in a quart of oil.

"Driving to Alaska?" the attendant asked. I told him we were, and he nodded his head.

"Lotta work up there," he said. But I told him we didn't know anything about that. "Just going to see the state," I said.

"Wish I were going," he told me. "I used to be a welder."

So that was when I asked him all about the shocks and the holes in the metal. He looked underneath the car.

"Needs to be welded, all right,' he said. "But there's nothing open now. Not around here. Can you wait until morning?"

I looked over at Kingpen, and then back at Beamish, asleep on the seat.

"I don't think so," I said. "I think we're gonna go."

I gave him the money, he figured out the exchange rate, handed me the change, and waved us off.

"Have a good trip," he said. I honked the horn and we pulled away.

"Stay on 2nd all the way out," Kingpen told me. So I did.

We drove past city hall and a fire station, out through the town and up a long winding hill.

"Not that much ahead," Kingpen said. "Not for a couple hundred miles, at least."

We got back on the Alcan and started driving west. Kingpen got in his sleeping bag and I put mine across my lap.

Kingpen was right, in a way. There wasn't much ahead. But in another way, there was. Snow covered hills. Frozen rivers and streams. And miles and miles of trees.

We stopped at a place called Cracker Creek, about eighty miles from Whitehorse. We got out of the car and looked underneath. The holes were getting bigger all the time.

"Maybe half an inch," Kingpen said. And what he meant was that there was that much metal left until the bolts fell through.

"I think we'll make it," I said. But I wasn't really sure.

Kingpen turned off his flashlight and we got back in the car. I started it up, put it in Neutral and pressed down on the pedal.

"Getting a little seasick?" Kingpen asked me.

"Just a little," I said. And the Buick floundered on, like an old wooden rowboat, bobbing in the waves.

We went another nine or ten miles. It wasn't far. Looming out in front of us we could see the mountains, but we didn't know what they were called. Kingpen flipped on his flashlight and looked at his map.

"The Kluane Icefields," he said. "The St. Elias Mountains." You could see they were covered in ice and snow, even in the dark.

"There's Mt. Hubbard," he said, pointing up ahead. "Mt. Vancouver and Logan - over 19,000 feet."

"Reminds me of Banff," I said. "Except they're all to one side." They weren't all around us, like they had been farther south.

I drove another ten or fifteen miles to where the road split... South to Haines, or you could branch off, go north and stay on the Alcan, like we did. And even with it being so damn cold, we rolled the windows down to see the mountains on our left, the forests on our right, and about thirty feet of gravel road lit up ahead.

"Wilderness," Kingpen said. "We're surrounded by it. See?"

And I told him that I did.

But like a lot of things back then, I felt it more than saw it. That's what I remember. The soft green glow of the dashboard lights. The hard, crunchy sound of the gravel underneath the tires. Millions of stars and no one there to see them. Just us. Driving all alone in the middle of the night. Moving. Always moving. To places we had never seen and could only imagine. Bouncing along, like a rocking, silver bullet. And the further we went, the more incredibly small I felt, until, even with my eyes closed, I knew what Kingpen meant.

We started seeing signs, before too long, about a mile apart. Off to the sides, in the fields of snow. We could just barely see them in the shadows of the headlights, so I stopped the car and we walked across the Alcan. Kingpen turned on his flashlight and we looked toward the mountains.

"There," I said. He aimed his flashlight toward the sign, and we could just barely see it, because his light was getting dim.

"CAUTION – BEARS IN AREA," he read. But then he told me, "Don't worry. I'm almost sure they're hibernating now."

Kingpen shook his flashlight and tried to make it brighter as we walked across the road.

"How much gas do we have?" he asked.

We got in the car and I turned the key. "Three quarters of a tank." I pulled the lever down, stepped on the pedal, and we started to go.

"A lot of people carry bells when they go back in the woods," Kingpen told me. "For the bears. To scare 'em away."

"I'd rather carry a rifle with me," I said. "Beamish has one in the trunk, if you want to get it out."

But Kingpen didn't answer. He got inside his sleeping bag, turned his flashlight on and looked at one of his maps.

"Nothin' much ahead . . . Except for a lake, about fifty miles away. Why don't you wake me when we get there," he said. "You OK to drive?"

I nodded my head. "I'll try not to go over any cliffs."

Kingpen laughed, and just then the flashlight finally died and Kingpen put it on the floor.

"I'll see you later," he said, settling back in the seat.

Bells? I thought... And I kept on driving.

I drove for a while, maybe an hour. Just rockin' along, kind of in a daze. And then I started to notice this star up ahead. One, out of millions. But this one was different.

Look at that, I thought. And as I drove and I watched, and I watched and I drove, it turned into the moon. And then back to the star. And then it stayed like that for a while. I shook my head, rubbed my eyes, listened to the gravel underneath the tires, and kept on driving.

I drove another mile, maybe two. Then the same, one star, changed into the moon again. Only this time it *shattered* into *thousands* of stars. Another mile or two, and the star came back. Then changed into the moon, and exploded again. Over and over. From one to the other. Then these massive explosions that I never really heard.

"STOP!" Kingpen shouted.

I jammed on the brakes, we slid on the gravel, then stopped and I rubbed my eyes.

"*LOOK!*" Kingpen said.

It was building to the moon.

"Two seconds," he said. And by the time he had counted, you could see 'em coming down. Millions and millions of pieces of light.

"Must be a flare," Kingpen said. "Somebody's in trouble."

So I stepped on the gas and we started driving again.

I asked Kingpen how long he had been awake.

"Maybe ten minutes," he told me.

We looked through the windshield again, but nothing was there. All kinds of stars, but none were getting any bigger.

"Maybe they ran out of flares," I said.

The trees were thinning out, off to our right. We could see spaces of black, and then miles and miles of ice.

"Kluane," Kingpen said. "I think it's Kluane Lake."

It was forty miles long, according to Kingpen. We followed it for a long ways, until we both saw the glow.

We came to a clearing, but it was off in the woods. We couldn't really park there. So we sat in the Buick, in the middle of the road, and we looked across the lake.

"See it?" Kingpen asked. And he pointed past the window, to the area that was shining. "*See* it?"

It was kind of like Whitehorse, this strange eerie glow.

"Another town," I said.

But Kingpen shook his head. "You just don't understand." He reached for his flashlight, then threw it back on the floor. "Come on."

We got out of the car, went around to the front, up near the headlights, and Kingpen held out his map.

"Look," he said. "There's nothing that way for at least a thousand miles."

We looked across the lake, and the glow was getting bigger.

"There's *something*," I said.

I reached through the window and shut off the lights.

"Kill the engine," Kingpen yelled. So I turned the key.

Quiet. That's what I remember. Just this absolute silence, like back in Chicago. No crickets or little sounds of the night. No other cars. Just me and Kingpen standing by the Buick in the freezing cold, watching the glow spread into the dark.

It's changing, I thought. But I didn't want to say it. And then all of a sudden, all at once, the colors came. Reds, blues and violets. Awesome shades of green. Over the lake and out into the night. Winds of color that would blow across the sky, and sway and vibrate and blend into patterns of neon lights, that would disappear and then start up again.

73

"Come on," Kingpen said. We left the Buick and started through the clearing, down to the lake, watching the lights as we trudged through the snow.

There was a tower on the shore, right by the ice. What was left of a cache. That's what Kingpen said. Four wooden poles with a platform on top. It was at least a dozen feet high.

"We'll watch the lights from up there," he said, "but I'm gonna get the bags." Then he turned and started back toward the car, while I looked around.

And I have to tell you – it was pretty neat. It really was. Like something the Indians had made and left, from a thousand years ago. Hand-cut poles, with a homemade ladder. It would have made a great picture, especially at night, with just the silhouette.

I got up on the platform and stood there awhile. Maybe five or ten minutes, until Kingpen came back. He got halfway up the ladder.

"Here," he said. And he handed up the bags. "I tried to wake Beamish, but he wouldn't get up."

Kingpen pulled himself onto the platform. We stepped into the sleeping bags and then sat on the snow. There was just enough room for the two of us.

"How high do you think those lights are?" Kingpen asked. But I couldn't really tell.

"Probably higher than they look," I said.

We sat there for hours after that, freezing our asses off and watching the lights. Unbelievable colors that would run across the sky, like electric currents in the night, filling the black, and then blowing away. And then one of us would shout out, "Over there to your left," or "There back behind us. *Look! Look!*" And they'd all start up again.

They finally died out. Not all at once. It took a while. Then we climbed down the ladder and walked back to the car.

"Wildest thing I ever saw," I said.

And that's when Kingpen told me, "You'll see 'em again."

And it turned out he was right. But for all of the times I've seen them since, it was never like that. Not like the first time.

The Northern Lights. The night they started as a star, grew into the moon, and then shattered into millions of neon colors that blew across the blackest sky.

By the time we scraped the windows and started the car, it was a little after four that morning. We got back in our sleeping bags and started to drive.

"A hundred and fifty to go," Kingpen said.

We drove through Destruction Bay, and about ten miles later we saw a little sign. *Burwash Landing*. That was what it said. But all we saw were trees. Silhouettes, really, because it was still dark. But anyway, it really didn't matter. We never stopped.

We were moving along for at least another hour until the road fell apart. I thought it was the car at first. I thought the shocks had gone through. We went into a hole and then we heard it coming from the back. There was no way we couldn't.

EJONG! EJONG! EJONG!

"Holy *Shit*!" Beamish yelled. And he jumped up in the back.

I stepped on the brakes and waited for the car to collapse. Just totally collapse.

"Look," Kingpen said. And when he pointed through the windshield, you could see the giant potholes.

"Gravel's busted up," he said. "We better take it slow."

So I started off again, going five miles an hour, sometimes ten, with Kingpen looking out for holes.

The road got better once. But in a way, I wish it hadn't. The road was looking pretty good, so I stepped down on the gas and must have had the Buick up to nearly forty miles an hour.

"Lookin' good," I said. And then Kingpen pointed up ahead, held on to the dashboard and let out a scream.

"Look-*OUT*!" he yelled. "More potholes!"

I swerved to the left, right, then left again, all while pumping the brakes and sliding into the holes. Another four or five miles, and we were back to good gravel. Then bad gravel. Then good gravel again. Anyway, that's what it was like. You were never really sure how long it would last.

The sun was coming up. Right there behind us. And it was just like Kingpen said. It made it easier to drive because you could see further out. Fewer surprises.

"Another eighty miles," he told us. A little while from there, we stopped to get some gas at the Pine Valley Motel. They had a gas pump, some cabin rentals and a little café. I thought they'd be closed, but they weren't. We got a bag of cookies, filled the Buick with gas, and started driving again.

"Fifty!" Kingpen said. Then forty. And before too long, we got to Beaver Creek, a town of about a hundred. There was Ida's Motel and Café and a little information building. Then when we saw the Alas/Kon Border Lodge, we knew that we were getting close.

We passed Canadian Customs, and I was kind of surprised, because I thought it would have been on the border. But it wasn't.

"Twenty," Kingpen said.

The road got narrower and harder to drive. Real winding and torn up, but at least you could see it. We crossed Snag Creek on an old plank bridge and passed a lake to our right. We were almost there.

"Look," Kingpen said. And he pointed to the hills. "The *border!*"

I wiped the ice from the windshield with a sock, and looked up ahead. I remember looking for a fence.

"*There,*" Kingpen said again. "See it?"

And when I squinted my eyes, I *could.* About twenty feet wide, a clearing that ran through the trees for as far as I could see. Like the one I had seen from the ferry.

"That's *it,*" Kingpen said. And sure enough, in another mile or so, we came to a pull-off with a plaque and some other markers that told us about the border.

"*Note the narrow clearing marking the border,*" one of the signs read. "*This is part of the twenty-foot/ six-meter-wide swath, cut by surveyors, from 1904 to 1920 along the 141st meridian (from Demarcation Point on the Arctic Ocean south 600 miles/966km to Mt. St. Elias in the Wrangell Mountains) to mark the Alaska-Canada border. This swath continues south to mark the boundary between southeastern Alaska and Canada. Portions of the swath are cleared periodically by the International Boundary Commission.*"

We stayed there awhile, right between the countries. Kingpen got out his camera and started taking pictures of me and Beamish and all of the plaques.

"If you want to ask me, it all looks the same," Beamish said. "Both sides of the border."

But when we got in the car, and I drove into Alaska, I knew that it wasn't. It was like Kingpen said. You could *feel* the difference.

We didn't go far, maybe a half mile to the U.S. Customs Station. Two men came out, and one checked the car.

"Going up to work?" the other one asked.

"Just sightseeing," Kingpen answered.

Beamish flashed him the money and I showed him my license.

"What's in the trunk," the first guy asked. So I went around back and showed him the cans.

He was supposed to check out the car, in case we were smuggling anything in from Canada. That's what Beamish had said. "He'll go through the trunk, check under the seats, even behind the dashboard. But don't let it rattle you," Beamish had told us. "It's all pretty standard. He'll check the car out pretty good."

But it turned out he didn't. He started to at first, but then I think he was so disgusted with the corned beef and nuggets, the Spam, and the smell of the vomit and toothpaste and beer, that I think he changed his mind.

"Go ahead," the other guy said. And then he shook his head and waved us on.

It must have been 8:30 by then. Except for the snow on the ground, it was a lot like the morning we'd left back east. Sunny and bright. It was a lot, lot colder though.

We stopped at a place called Border City Lodge and got a bag of powdered donuts and a dozen eggs. Beamish checked the shocks.

"They don't look too good," he said. "Whaddya wanna do?"

"Well I guess we'll just have to get them fixed as soon as we can," I said. But I wasn't sure where.

"Didn't we get them at Sears?" Kingpen asked. "Maybe there's some kind of warranty." But I told him I thought that was only if *they* had installed 'em. "Yeah, maybe," he said.

We got in the car and Beamish started to drive, while Kingpen looked for the warranty in the glove box.

"Let me know if you find it," Beamish said. "I think there's a Sears right over this hill." Then he started to howl, and we kept on going.

The road had improved ever since the border. Most of it was paved, but then we hit a bad stretch for about twenty-five miles and had to take it kind of slow. All torn up, the road started getting kind of narrow again, and curved all around.

"Suppose this is the *good* part?" Beamish said. But it turned out that it wasn't. The road started getting wider and the paved part started again.

We were bouncing along, eating our donuts and watching it all go by. For another thirty-five or forty miles, and nineteen little powdered donuts, we kept on pushing the Buick, until we started seeing roadhouses and rest stops, a trading post and a general store.

We went a little further, into a town called Tok - another intersection, really. It made me think of *shoes and boots and pieces of rope,* and I wondered how it got there. Just suddenly this strung-out little town, with nothing else around it.

"Why don't we call Information," Kingpen said. "See if they have a Sears."

So we found a phone booth, got a Canadian quarter we had picked up from some place, put it in the slot, and gave it a try. But the operator only laughed. That's what Kingpen said.

"She told me there's a Sears in Anchorage and another one in Fairbanks, Kingpen said. "You want to drive that far?"

We got out his map and took a look. A triangle. That's the best way to describe the roads. We were at the right hand bottom corner, and if we kept on toward the top, we would go to Fairbanks. If we went down toward the left, we would end up in Anchorage. Then there was a completely different road, the Parks Highway, that connected those two places.

"Two-o-five to Fairbanks. Three twenty-eight to Anchorage," Kingpen said. "What do you think? It's your car."

"Might as well go to Fairbanks," I said, "If they've both got a Sears."

We let my dog out for a minute, he jumped back in the car, and then Beamish drove us out of Tok. We passed a half-dozen hitchhikers and another couple roadhouses. Then we got back on the Alcan and headed to Fairbanks.

"Not a bad road," Beamish said. And it wasn't for a while. But about ten miles later we started hitting hills. Not like the ones out in San Francisco that you hear about, just these giant rolling lumps.

"Frost heaves," Kingpen called them. And then we started bouncing up and down like you can't even imagine. Up and down. Up and down. And all the time, you could hear it in the back – *EJONG! EJONG! EJONG!*

"Son of a *BITCH*!" Beamish yelled. And then he started slowing down, which helped a lot. Except it made you kind of sleepy. We'd lumber down the road on these long, gently rolling lumps and it would really put you out.

At least that's what I think happened to me. Between the lumps and the *EJONGS*, I think I fell asleep.

78

Chapter 11

I woke up at the Santa Claus House in the town of North Pole. I swear I did. You can see it on a map. Fourteen miles south of Fairbanks.

"Just look at that son of a bitch," Beamish said. And when I looked out the window, I could see Santa Claus. Fifty feet high and twenty feet wide.

Welcome to the Santa Claus House, the sign on his stomach said. And when we looked right behind him, we could see this long, stretched-out, castle-like building that was really a store. It was covered with paintings of reindeer and candy canes, little elves and a sleigh. We were gonna go in, but like a lot of things back then, it was closed.

"Let's drive around the town," Kingpen said. So after we saw Santa Claus, we drove around awhile. It didn't take that long. We stopped and got some gas, just as we were heading out.

"You ought to stop over at the post office," the attendant said. "Get yourselves some envelopes, with the *postmark.*"

So we drove on over to 5th Street and got there just as it was closing. We bought maybe a dozen envelopes, along with the stamps, and sent them to our friends back east. Not any letters, because we didn't have the time, but we did send the envelopes.

"Wait till they get a look at these," Kingpen said. And we stood there and watched while the lady stamped them by hand. "North Pole, Alaska," they said. Every one of them – we checked. Then we dropped them in the box, thanked the lady, walked outside, got in the Buick, and Beamish started driving.

It was a little after five and we were moving right along.

"I think Sears closes at six," Beamish said. But I thought it was nine.

"Probably won't be able to fix it until tomorrow anyway," he said.

We were on a modern two-lane highway, driving into Fairbanks. As we started getting closer, we could tell it was a pretty big town.

"Turn up here," Kingpen said. "And we'll look for a phone."

Then we made a left on Gaffney, turned right on Cushman, and there it was. We saw it right in front of us, while we were looking for a phone.

"Look," Beamish said. "The Sears sign."

And it looked just like the ones I had seen back east.

There were two little buildings connected together. One was the catalog store and the other was for cars... *Sears Automotive*. That's what the sign said. So we parked the car there, right at the door.

"Come on," Beamish said. So we followed him to the door and tried to go in. But it was just like the Santa Claus place. Locked. So we went in the catalog store.

"That automotive shop closed down a month ago," a lady told us. The manager went up north to work and took all three mechanics with him."

"Where up north?" Kingpen asked. "Bethel? Kotzebue?" He was flipping through the pages of his atlas that he had. "Barrow? Rampart?"

"Something Valley," another lady said. "*Happy* Valley, I think. But I don't know for sure."

"There's another Sears in Anchorage," the first lady said. "If you want to drive down there."

We kind of nodded our heads like the guy from Prince Rupert. *WOBBLE. WOBBLE. WOBBLE.* Then we started walking out, past the washing machines.

"Demonstrators," Beamish said.

Kingpen picked up a catalog as we walked out the door.

"Maybe we can use this to start a fire sometime," he said. Then we got in the car and he threw it on the back floor, with the nuggets and corned beef and everything else that was there.

It was getting dark, but even then I just assumed we would be heading down to Anchorage. We didn't though. "What's the rush? We can drive down in the morning," Beamish told us. "Why don't we look around the town?"

We drove out to the University after that, out on College Road. Big modern buildings, not like I expected. One was pretty neat.

"The Student Center," Kingpen said. And it turned out he was right. Like a modern day museum. That's what Kingpen said it reminded him of, with a huge slanting roof and lots of glass.

We went inside and it was mostly empty space. There was a counter on the left, where they sold some things, like candy bars and magazines.

"Listen," Kingpen said. And you could hear the bowling alley, way in the back, by the Ping-Pong tables. There were T.V. areas with people sitting around, informational bulletin boards, and people shooting pool.

The second floor was a balcony, with a stretched-out snack room and plenty of tables where you could eat your food.

"This is really something," Kingpen said.

And it was. You should have seen it. But the best part was, when we walked inside we saw these stairs that started up – and just kept on going. Up into the air. I'm not kidding. Right there in the center, in the middle of the building. Up and up and up, into the air.

"Come on," Beamish said. And so we started up these stairs, nearly two hundred steps and four people wide.

There was a platform on top, with a table and chairs, so we sat there awhile. Sat there, right under the slanted ceiling, and kept looking all around.

"Why don't you go out to the car and get some maps?" Beamish said. "Maybe there's some place we can visit on our way down to Anchorage."

Kingpen nodded his head and started down the steps. We watched him pass the candy counter and then go out the door. We could see everybody from up there. Everybody and every *thing. And no one could see us* – that's what I remember thinking – even though *we* knew we were there.

I started telling Beamish about McKinley while we were waiting for Kingpen. All of the stuff the Kraxins had told me about the park, with the bears and the mountains and even the train cars out front.

"You'll love it," I said. "We can really explore."

We saw Kingpen come back with an armload of pamphlets and maps. Then he climbed up the steps and set them on the table.

"How far's McKinley, and which way would we go?" Beamish asked.

I picked up one of the atlases and started looking through it.

"About a hundred and ten miles to the entrance of the park," Kingpen said. "It's right off the Parks Highway. The one we're taking to Anchorage."

We found it on the map. A big patch of green, near the center of the state.

"Look," Kingpen said. And he pointed to the scale. He sized his finger to the line and put it on the Park.

"Over a hundred and thirty miles long," Kingpen said. "It's gonna be huge."

We sat there awhile after that, maybe an hour, looking over Kingpen's maps and brochures.

"Wait till you see it," I said, and I started describing the slides. "Dozens of mountains without any names."

Beamish reached in his pocket and pulled out the money.

"Whaddya say we count it?" he asked.

We pushed the papers to the side and split up the bills. I got mostly tens, with a couple of ones.

"Five hundred and twelve dollars and thirty-two cents." That's what it turned out to be, when we added it all together. "I thought we would have had more than that," I said.

But Beamish shook his head.

"We spent some down at Prince Rupert," he mumbled. "I didn't think you'd mind. Kingpen looked at the floor.

"C'mon," Beamish said. "Let's celebrate. Let's hustle up some food."

We picked up the books and brochures, Beamish took the money, and we headed down the stairs.

"This way," Kingpen said, and he led us to the snack room. It was a cafeteria really, but not all that big. A counter with sandwiches and a guy cooking on a grill. Anyway, we each got a tray and started pushing it along the metal bars.

"Let's celebrate and take it out of the pile," Beamish said, pulling out a couple of twenties.

We ate real well that night, for the first time in a while. Lasagna and salad, French fries and chocolate pie. It was kind of nice for another fifteen minutes or so. Until the announcer came on. "Ten minutes," he said, "and the Center will close."

I remember it was like Kingpen said. We'd be in these places that were getting ready to close, and you could feel your body tensing up, already starting to get cold. We picked up the books and walked around, soaking in the heat, until they finally kicked us out and we went to the Buick.

I let my dog out for a while. I tied his leash to the handle of the car, put out a bowl of water, and then I got inside and shut the door. God, it was cold. Kingpen and Beamish were already down in their bags.

"McKinley tomorrow," Kingpen's muffled voice said. I waited about fifteen minutes before opening the door, and my dog jumped in. I got down deep in the bag and then I tried as hard as I could to go to sleep.

When we woke up the next morning, I thought I'd feel funny waking up in the car, out in the parking lot with people around. But the windows were iced up and nobody could see us.

"I'll scrape the windshield," Beamish said. And he picked up an empty can and got out of the car.

I started the Buick and we sat there a minute, looking at the map.

"This is gonna be *great*," Kingpen said. And I nodded my head.

Beamish got in, with the can he had used for scraping and the bowl I had forgotten from the night before.

"Look," Beamish said. And he turned over the bowl of water. "Frozen fuckin' solid," he said, tossing it all onto the back seat floor.

Kingpen was looking at one of his maps.

"Go down here," he said. "And make a left."

We got on Airport Road and went maybe a mile, before we saw the police cars and a crowd by the road.

"Something's happened," Beamish said. "Slow down."

I stepped on the brakes and brought it to a crawl. There were hundreds of people there and dozens of cars.

"Probably a shooting," Beamish told me. "There's a lotta guns up here. *King Pin*, go up there and see what it is," Beamish told him. So that's what Kingpen did.

We sat there for a minute, on the side of the road. Watching the people and waiting for Kingpen.

"Look," I said. I could see him through the windshield, waving his arms. "He's trying to scream something." But I couldn't understand what it was, until I rolled the window down.

"Hamburgers," I said. "He's shouting something about hamburgers."

Kingpen came back to the car and pointed behind him. You could see the arches.

"McDonalds," he said. "The hamburgers. It's their anniversary or something, and the hamburgers are all on sale for ten cents apiece, with a limit of twenty. Maybe we should get some to take to McKinley."

Beamish looked at me and shook his head. But we got out of the car and the three of us went into the crowd, which eventually formed into lines. There were security guards and people with badges.

"Come on," one worker said. "Keep it moving. Keep it moving."

And as crowded as it was, that's what we did. Kept moving, because of the waitresses mostly, who were running up and down the lines, taking our orders. We were still outside in the parking lot, and all around we heard, "Gimmee *twenty*. Gimmee *twenty*."

"People filling their freezers." That's what Beamish said.

We were there at least a half an hour, shuffling along, and then the waitress came up to our part of the line to take our order.

"Tell me you're not gonna ask for 'em plain," Beamish said. "You can just wipe off the fuckin' pickles and mustard yourself."

Kingpen nodded, and then each of us told her the same two words she must have been hearing all morning. "Gimmee *twenty*."

It was another hour before we got to the counter. Beamish gave them six dollars and they handed us the bags. Three of them - medium sized, brown grocery bags, with sixty hamburgers inside.

We walked back to the car, let my dog out, and took him for a walk. Beamish and I did, up the road a ways by some telephone poles. Then we headed back to the Buick.

Kingpen was there. He was taking a picture and I swear to God, he had every single hamburger, all sixty of 'em, out on the hood. All stacked up like a pyramid, and he was standing there with his camera, taking a picture.

"What the hell are you doing *now*?" Beamish asked him. "I'll be a sonova*bitch*!"

He grabbed the one on top, took off the paper, and threw the wrapper in the car.

"Here," Kingpen said, handing me a couple. "Here are a few for your dog."

We put the rest of them in the bags and got in the car. Beamish started driving. We turned left, turned right, I don't know, but somehow we got on the George Parks Highway and headed toward McKinley, scraping, or eating our hamburgers, depending on who we were.

It was ten or eleven o'clock by then. The sky was blue, and the scenery was just unbelievable. It really was. And I know it would never enter your mind, but *Africa.* That's what I remember thinking, at least from the pictures I had seen. Just miles and miles of open land for as far as we could see, and no other roads except the one we were on. *Frozen veldt.* That's what it was like.

We were crossing a bridge on the Tanana River, and driving into a little town.

"Nenana on the Tanana," Kingpen said. But there wasn't all that much there. We did stop at a gift store though.

"Want to buy some tickets?" the lady asked. She could tell from our look that we didn't know what she meant.

"For the Ice Classic," she said.

It was a contest they had every year. Whoever came closest to guessing the time and the date that the ice on the Nenana River broke up would win a lot of money. They placed a tripod out on the ice, and then a little farther down, there was a rope stretched across the river, hooked to this giant clock. At some point, the ice would break, the tripod would drift down the river, hit the rope, and stop the clock. "You could win a lot of money," she said.

"Last year somebody won a hundred and thirty thousand dollars."

There was a chart up on the wall with the winning dates and times from the last ten years, to help you figure out your guess.

"Let's get some," Beamish said. He pulled out a ten. "We'll buy 'em from the pile."

We bought ten tickets and wrote down our guesses for the dates and times.

"I bet you're going to win," the lady said.

"I hope so," Kingpen told her. The lady smiled.

And the way it turned out, maybe we did win, but we never found out, because we lost the ticket stubs before the river broke up.

She couldn't have been nicer. She let Kingpen fill up his canteen from a basin in the back, and we kept on thanking her as we walked on out.

"Can you just imagine winning all that money?" one of us asked out loud. And then the three of us promised to split it, no matter who won.

"Over forty-three thousand dollars each," Beamish said. Then we got in the Buick, threw the stubs down on the back floor and started driving.

We hit some frost heaves after that and took it slow for a while, all the way to Healy, where they mine the coal.

"Another ten miles to the entrance to the Park," Kingpen said. But in another mile or so, we felt like we were there.

We were driving through canyons, over frozen rivers and streams, and most of the names were pretty neat. There was Bison Gulch and Moody Bridge. Dragonfly Creek and the Nenana Canyon. *"Watch out for rock slides,"* the signs read. And then we'd look up at mountains, covered with snow.

It seemed it started getting cloudy all at once, and then the wind whipped up, and it got pretty cold. Even colder than it *had* been. It never really rained or snowed that day, but the weather sure changed fast when we drove into the park.

"There," Kingpen said. We looked to our right and saw a narrow gravel road somebody had plowed out.

"That's *it,*" Kingpen said. And even though we never saw a sign, we knew it was the road that would take us to the Park, so we started back between the piles of snow.

"Wait until you see these train cars," I said.

We drove about a mile to where the plow had stopped plowing - and then of course we had to stop.

"Shee-*IT*!" Beamish said. "The road isn't even open." But it wasn't really closed. You just couldn't drive anymore because of all the snow. Like an ocean full of white. That's what it looked like, with hundreds of these giant drifts that reminded you of waves.

"SON OF A *BITCH*!" Beamish yelled. And you could hear it echo in the hills: "SON OF A *BITCH*! . . . Son of a *bitch!*. . . Son of a *bitch*. . ."

But the good thing was, we were right at the train cars. I couldn't believe it. Right near the hotel, so we walked around awhile. Nobody was there. We climbed on the sleeper cars, but couldn't get inside. They were locked.

Then we trudged up through the snow, to the porch of the hotel, and looked into the window of the lobby. It was all we could do.

We went back to the car to let my dog out to run – but he wouldn't get out.

"Offer him a burger," Beamish said. "Throw one in the snow." But that didn't help.

Then Beamish climbed on the hood of the car. "Which way is McKinley?"

Kingpen got out a map.

"That way," he said. "About eighty miles." And he pointed toward a tree.

"Give me my camera," Beamish said.

Kingpen handed him his camera. Beamish took it, then he climbed up further, onto the roof, and held the camera way above his head. You could hear the button click.

"There," Beamish said.

He climbed down to the ground and we all stood there for a minute just looking around, trying to think.

"How about climbing a mountain?" Beamish asked. "There are lots of 'em around."

We got in the car, went back to the highway, and started driving up and down the road, looking for a mountain. There were plenty of 'em there, just like Beamish said. All along the road and off in the distance. Giant hills, I'd call them now, but back then I didn't know.

"There's one," Kingpen said. But it was too far off the road, and we would never have been able to walk back through the snow. That's what Beamish said. So we kept on looking.

It started getting gray, with the clouds coming in. Dismal and dreary. It looked almost prehistoric, with the mountains all around.

"*There!*" Beamish said.

He pointed up ahead, and we knew it right away. That was the one, the mountain we would climb.

It was back off the road, but not that far back, covered with snow, except for some rocks. We could see the ridges we could take to the top.

Beamish pulled the Buick to the side of the road and then Kingpen left a note underneath the windshield wiper.

"Just a precaution," he said. "In case we don't come back."

"We'll come back," Beamish said. He opened the trunk.

God, it was exciting. It really was, just looking at that mountain and picturing yourself up there.

"I'll bet *nobody's* climbed it," Kingpen said. And I knew he was right. Not because of its size, but because there were so many other mountains, everywhere we looked.

"FITCH!" Beamish yelled. He threw me these rubber galoshes. "Put 'em on," he said. "You can't go up there like that. Not in tennis shoes."

We spent maybe twenty minutes getting ready to climb, looking at the mountain and stuffing our pockets. *Twenty-seven hamburgers -* that's what I figured we took. I took eleven.

"C'mon," Beamish said. And then we started off across this wide, snow- covered gully on the side of the road.

"This will be the worst part," he told us. And even when the snow was up to our hips and we were freezing cold, we kept on pushing.

"C'mon," Beamish said. We helped each other to the other side, and then we started off across this little field. Before we knew it, we were heading up, real gradually at first, so we hardly even noticed. But then we started toward the first ridge, and we could tell. We were climbing. We were really climbing, except when we would stop to eat.

It was two-thirty, maybe three o'clock by then, and the higher we got, the harder it was to tell exactly where we were. Not like on the road, where we'd stood and looked up at the peaks and ridges and valleys of snow.

"Just remember to keep going *up*," Beamish said. So that was what we did. Kept on climbing, moving up along this path between the mountainsides. Always heading higher, up toward the clouds. We were trudging and climbing and starting to sweat.

"Look," Kingpen said.

We could see the mountaintop, about a quarter mile away. Kind of craggy, with patches of ice. It wasn't that much higher, just farther along the ridge.

We kept moving on for another couple hours, with Beamish in the lead. Then we came up to this really narrow ridge and stopped, deciding what to do.

"Maybe we should tie our belts together," Kingpen said. "Like in the movies."

It really didn't look good, especially when we looked over the sides. It was a *long* way down.

"Maybe we can hump it," I said. "Put a leg over each side."

But then nobody said anything. Not for a while. We just stood there on this ridge, balancing ourselves.

"It's only about twenty feet farther, for the narrow part," I said. "That's not very far." After that, the ridge widened out, and I knew that we could get to the top.

"Maybe we'd just better go back," Beamish said. Then Kingpen turned around.

"C'mon," I said. "It's only twenty feet." But they didn't want to try it, so I started off alone.

I just sat there at first. I got down and sat there, on the ridge that was two feet wide. Then I dangled a leg over each side.

"Just pretend you're on a horse," Beamish said.

So I tightened my thighs and started across. *Scared shitless.* That's what I remember. *God, I was scared.*

"Don't look down," Kingpen called. So I started staring at a spot on the other side, dug in my heels, and began to slide my ass ahead, one inch at a time.

Then it started getting even narrower. Really, really narrow. Really, really fast. Narrower, and icier, and hard to hold on.

"Fall to the right, if you feel yourself go," Beamish yelled. "It's not as far down. Maybe only two hundred feet."

I wanted to look, but was too damned scared.

"Halfway there," Kingpen called out. "You're at the narrowest part."

I couldn't really see it, because I was staring at the spot up ahead. My legs could feel it though. Six inches wide, maybe seven at the most.

"GO!" Beamish yelled.

And then my legs started shaking, but I kept on moving. Kept on moving, just a little at a time. Then it started getting wider, and I knew that I was gonna make it.

Five more feet, I thought. And it must have been another ten or fifteen minutes, but I got there.

"You made it!" Kingpen screamed, and he started to cheer.

I stood up, and then started to the top. It wasn't very far away.

And when I got there, I wish you could have seen it. The mountaintop that I'd thought was all alone was actually connected to the other mountain tops by dozens of wider ridges.

"You ought to see it up here!" I yelled. "Snowcapped peaks, all tied together. With ridges you can walk on, just underneath the clouds."

"C'mon," Beamish called. "It's gonna get dark. We gotta go."

But I told the two of them to go ahead.

"I'm gonna walk the ridges," I yelled back. "They're not really narrow at all." And I wish they could have seen them.

"Well how long you gonna be?" one of them screamed.

"I'll start down in an hour," I yelled back.

"Well, we'll start on down, but in case you get lost, I'll shoot off the rifle," Beamish yelled. "So you'll know where we are."

"All right," I called. We waved to each other, and I watched as they started back, walking down the mountainside.

I stood there a minute. If you've never really been there, on top of a mountain, it's hard to explain the feeling you can get. All quiet, and white, and up in the clouds. Just mesmerized. That's the feeling I felt mostly, like I was standing up there in a different world. And I guess I really was.

I started walking back, away from the road, along the crests and the ridgelines, to the different mountaintops. The sun was dipping down and every mountain seemed different, with all the reflections from the ice and the snow. God, it was pretty. I even saw some sheep, down in this rocky part, off to my right. But the thing that really surprised me was this building that I saw.

It was a bright orange spot against a background of white, about a hundred feet away. I couldn't really miss it. All modern aluminum, with an antenna on top. It wasn't much bigger than somebody's bathroom. I hiked over to it, kicked some snow aside and opened the door. It didn't have a lock. I guess it didn't really need one, sitting where it was.

The place was filled with equipment, lots of gauges and maps. *Maybe it's a weather station*, I thought. *Some kind of an outpost.* There was a stool and a desk, some papers and pens. They even had a short-wave radio, but I couldn't figure it out, so I just sat there a while, trying to stay warm.

I'll bet that sonovabitch fell off the ridge and froze to death, I pictured Beamish saying, as they waded through the snow down by the road. Then, I picked up a magazine that was lying there, started looking through it, and stayed warm some more.

I found a pen and a piece of paper, and tried to write, but the ink didn't come out.

"*Frozen*," I thought. And then I tried another pen and another, until I got one that worked.

"To whom it may concern," I wrote. And then I pulled out a hamburger and left it right there on the desk, underneath the note.

I opened the door, stepped outside, and took a look around. The wind was starting up. And even though it was getting dark, I could see these swirls of snow, blowing across the ice.

I closed the door behind me, and started walking back the way that I had come. Back across the mountaintops, until I finally made it to the ridge that I had crawled across.

And to tell you the truth, I didn't even try it. The wind was whipping down and all I could picture was this tall, skinny guy, going over the wrong side of the ridge, and I wondered if his scream would really make a sound, with no one there to hear it. But of course there was me, so I figured that *I* would... at least for a while.

No way, I thought. So I just stood there for a while, watching it get dark. And then I started down. Down and down and down. Down the mountain I had crossed the ridge to reach. Down a couple feet, and then down a little more. *Down and down and down*. That's all that I kept thinking. *Just keep on going down. And somehow*, I figured, *I would make it*. But then it started getting deep.

I spent five or six hours coming down that night. And the worst part was, when I got to the bottom, the road wasn't there. Just a snow-covered field and then another couple mountains.

The clouds were gone by then and the stars were out. I could see them twinkling in the sky. God, it was cold. The wind was blowing and my feet were almost numb when I started off across the field, pushing through the snow. It was up to my knees. I'd plough through it awhile, then try to step over it, then plough on some more.

And my hands would start shaking . . . *SHAKIN'. SHAKIN'. SHAKIN'*. I couldn't get them to stop. So I stuck them in my pockets, and remember feeling ketchup and mustard and frozen pieces of meat.

I got halfway across the field and threw out the food. And as dark as it was, these ravens started coming out. Flew by and landed in the field. Four or five of 'em, like vultures, waiting for me to die.

"CAW. CAW. CAW!"

I was getting kind of scared by then. I went another twenty-five feet, stopped, and listened for the rifle. But of course I never heard it. Just the ravens fighting for the bread or the meat, or sometimes a pickle.

So I started off again. And then, at some point, I thought I saw a light, off to my right, around the side of a mountain. Just for a second, and then it was gone. But it was enough of a reason to change the direction I was going. *Just maybe*, I thought. And after another hour or so of pushing through the snow, I saw it again. *Headlights*. That was what they were, about a quarter mile away. The road was closer than I thought.

I got across the field to some low-lying bushes and then I sunk down in the snow. I was stuck down in a gully and couldn't get out. Not for a while. It was up to my waist. I tried jumping up and down and waving my arms, yelling for the Buick. I finally stretched and grabbed hold of this prickly little branch and pulled myself out. And that's the way I made it to the road, pulling on these sticker bushes, from one to the next.

I could see something coming down the highway with its headlights on. Then the lights began to flash. It slowed down, and I could see it was the Buick.

"Where the hell have you *been*?" Beamish screamed. "We thought you were dead.

"I got lost," I said. "I came out the back." I pointed behind me, but they all looked the same. Three or four mountains, all covered with snow.

"Look at my boots!" Beamish said. He pointed to my feet, and all that was left were these loose bands of rubber, up around my ankles. Each connected by a set of buckles. That's all that was left. The bottom half was gone.

"Sorry," I said. "I guess it was the rocks."

We got in the car. Beamish started the stove, Kingpen started to drive, and I started to shake. That's what I remember. I started to shake and I couldn't stop. Not for a while. I had snow in my jacket, down in my shoes, and up inside my pants. *SHAKING. SHAKING. SHAKING.*

"We'll drive up here to Ice Worm Gulch," Kingpen said. And then we headed north.

We passed the entrance to the Park, and in another couple miles we came to a bridge with a pull-off on the side. Ice Worm Gulch, which is where we stayed that night – in the pull-off next to the bridge that went across the canyon. Kingpen stopped the car and turned the engine off, but we kept the Coleman stove going. At least for a while, until the fuel ran out.

You could hear the wind echoing through the canyon, blowing under the bridge, and then rattling the car.

"Must be ten degrees," Beamish said. "Twenty below, with the wind."

And every time we talked, it got colder than the last time.

"Thirty below!" Then, "Forty!"

"Watch this," Kingpen said. He took a napkin out of one of the hamburger bags and dipped it in his canteen.

"Watch this," he said again. Then he rolled his window down, left half an inch of napkin inside the car, and rolled the window up.

"One, two, three . . ."

He got to thirteen, rolled the window down a little, and then pulled the napkin back inside the car. "Frozen solid," Kingpen said, and he tapped it on the window's glass. "Now *smell* it." It was just like rotten eggs.

"Must be a factory around here," Beamish said. We thought it was the wind at first, but it turned out that it wasn't. It was in the canteen.

"Sulfur water," Kingpen said.

And that was what it was. We couldn't even drink it. You couldn't get it past your tongue.

The sun came up a little after that. I don't think we ever got to sleep. We drove back to Healy to get some gas for the Buick and some propane for the stove. Then we turned the car around and headed south again, over the bridge, and past the Park entrance.

"To Mount Fitch," Kingpen said. And then he raised his canteen and pretended to drink. But it was like I said before – you just couldn't do it.

Chapter 12

Beamish drove after that. Drove and drove. Kingpen and I fell asleep just south of the Park entrance, but for five or six hours, Beamish kept going. He took us through Cantwell, Trapper Creek and Talkeetna, down past Houston and Wasilla. By the time I woke up, we were just about there. We were where the George Parks Highway turns into Highway 1, about thirty miles from Anchorage. We could tell that we were getting close.

"Fewer and fewer bullet holes in the signs along the road." That's what Beamish said. And if you've ever driven in that way, you know what he meant.

"We're getting there," he said. And it was none too soon, because even as flat as the road was, we were bouncing like a boat.

It must have been two o'clock by then. We pulled into an empty weigh station on the side of the road and stopped the car. Then Beamish went back to the trunk to get us some cans of ravioli to eat.

"I don't think I've ever seen a weigh station that was open," Kingpen said. I told him that I couldn't remember if I had or not.

I tried to get my dog up, and out of the car, but he wouldn't move.

"I think he's sick," Kingpen said.

"Me, too," Beamish told me.

He didn't look too good, real depressed and hardly moving.

"Maybe you should ship him out," Beamish said. "Send him back east where it's warm."

We got in the car and headed south again. We passed a big mobile home park, a little private airport, and then came in on 5th Street, the way everybody does, past buildings and restaurants and stores.

There's an old Alaskan joke about this tourist who flies up to see the state, stays in Anchorage awhile, and then flies back home to the Lower 48. As he's flying back, the pilot says to the guy, "It's a real damn shame," he says, "you got so close, but never saw Alaska." Of course the tourist never gets the joke, but that's what Anchorage was like. The Lower 48.

We stopped at a phone booth and got the address of Sears... 700 E. Northern Lights Boulevard.

"That's easy," Kingpen said. "Go down here."

We went two or three blocks, Beamish swung a left on Gambell, and we kept on going to where it turned into Seward Highway.

"*There*," Kingpen said. We could see it right on the corner.

It wasn't like the Fairbanks store. This place was huge. Twenty or thirty stores, all put together. *The Sears Mall* - that's what the signs all said. We parked down at the end, where the car place was, then the three of us got out of the car, and Beamish got on the ground.

"One-sixteenth of an inch," Beamish said. "That's all we've got left." Then he crawled out from under the car.

We went into the shop and explained the situation. I thought we'd have to wait, but we didn't.

"Bring it in," the manager said. "We'll see what we can do."

Beamish drove it in, parked it on the lift, and got out of the car.

"Take it on up," the manager said, and somebody punched a button.

There was a real low hum, then the car started upward. Higher and higher, up toward the ceiling.

"Look," Kingpen said. He pointed up above us. "Forgot to take your dog out." And I could see him looking down through the window.

We went into the waiting room after that and sat there awhile, reading the magazines and talking with some of the customers.

"Holy cow!" one of them said. "All the way from Maryland?"

He was listening to Beamish, who was telling him stories of Chicago, Prince Rupert, and the logging road.

"You can see the fucking mud," Beamish told him, pointing toward the car. "And look at these goddamn clothes." He slapped his pants leg and the dust flew up. "That's *after* washing them."

A mechanic came out with an estimate in his hand. He gave it to the manager and went back to the garage.

"Has to be welded, all right," the manager said. "It'll cost around a hundred and fifty bucks."

Beamish reached in his pocket, but then pulled out his hand, without any money.

"Isn't this *guaranteed*?" he asked. "For a full six months? It hasn't even been six weeks."

We went out to the car and stood underneath. The way the guy explained it, the problem wasn't the shocks.

"It's the bolts," he said. "They're wearing holes in the chassis of the car."

"Then they weren't put on right," Beamish said.

Kingpen opened his mouth, but before he could talk, Beamish cut him off.

"Were they?" he asked. *"Were they?"*

"If you don't want to pay, we can't do the work," the manager said. "It's as simple as that. Take her down."

Somebody hit the button. You could hear the hum, and then the car started down, with my dog inside.

"Just *explain* it," Beamish said. "It doesn't make sense. Don't you guarantee your work?"

We went back to the waiting room and they argued awhile, going back and forth.

"Maybe I can be of some help," a customer said. He was the one who had been listening spellbound to the stories Beamish had been telling.

He stood up from his chair and took off his coat.

"Christ!" Beamish said. And when you looked at the man's collar, you could see he was a priest, or a minister, or something.

"What seems to be the trouble?" he asked.

We went back to the garage, the manager hit the button, and we watched the car go up again. I could see that he was right. It wasn't the shocks. It was the way we'd put them on.

"See what I mean?" he said. "Take it down." The Buick started toward the floor.

"Now look at that ad," Beamish said. And he pointed to a poster, stuck on a wall. It was an ad for their shocks, with a picture of a desert, some lizards and a cactus. And then right beneath the picture, in big letters, it said, *BUILT FOR THE MOJAVE.*

"But not for the *Alcan?*" Beamish asked. And then he added, *"Huh?"*

There was a little pause, and when the minister cut in, I knew the manager was going to change his mind.

"Maybe you could just help them out," the minister said. "They're all the way from Maryland and probably low on money. Would it be *that* hard to fix?"

The manager walked away, over to his office. He stood there by the door, and yelled over to a mechanic.

"Take it up," he shouted. "Take it up and fuckin' weld it. I'm sick of it all."

He went into his office and slammed the door. The mechanic punched the button, and the Buick started toward the ceiling again.

"It'll be about an hour," he said.

If you've ever gotten a phone call from someplace in Alaska, you know what it's like. Lots of little echoes, and you have to learn to wait, so you both don't talk at once. *Satellites*. They're the problem. You learn to stop and wait an extra second, till the other person's voice bounces off.

"Hello? Hello?" I said. "Is that you . . . that you?"

I could hear my mother on the other end.

"You sound so far away . . . far away," she said.

And I guess I was. About five thousand miles.

I told her about my dog and how he didn't look that good.

"I might have to ship him home . . . ship him home," I said.

We talked for a while and she asked where we were. I told her I was at the Sears Store in Anchorage.

"What's it like?"

"Just like the a mall back east," I said. "Lots of shoe stores and people walking around . . . .around . . . Anyway, we're having a great time . . . great time," I said. "I'll call you later . . ."

"Well take. . ."

" . . . you later," I said.

" . . . care . . . take care." And I hung up the phone.

"You should have heard that," I said to Kingpen. "Everything was double."

He nodded his head, but I knew I hadn't explained it very well. *Very well*, I thought.

We walked back to the car place and we could see the Buick sitting in the lot. We went inside the office and signed a piece of paper, then walked out the door and got in the car. Beamish started it up, and we sat there for a minute, not knowing where to go. It was pretty funny in a way.

"Now what?" Beamish asked. "Now that we're here." And where he meant was Alaska. It was really pretty funny, now that I look back.

"How far's the airport?" I asked.

Kingpen looked at his map.

"Not all that far," he said. "You gonna send your dog back?"

"Maybe I should check it out," I said. "Why don't we go down and see?"

Kingpen gave directions. We waved to the minister as we drove off the lot, and then went down Northern Lights Boulevard to a narrow road called Aircraft Drive.

"Turn left," Kingpen said.

And for all of the times that I've driven down it since, I still don't understand exactly what it is. There were fences on the sides, fifteen feet high. And every hundred feet the fences opened up and a landing strip was there - right across our road. They even had these little lights and signs - *WATCH OUT FOR LOW-FLYING AIRCRAFT*, they said. And we would laugh, and joke, and pretend to look, but it really wasn't all that funny, not knowing where we were.

We went maybe a mile, passed a pond on our left and could see the airport up ahead. It was a lot more modern than I would have thought. But even then, we didn't have to pay to park. Nobody did. No tickets or machines or lifting gates.

We parked at the curb, right at the terminal. Then we got out of the car and walked into the building, through some electronic doors.

"Let's check the schedules first," Beamish said. So we looked at the flights that were up on the boards. Dallas, Tulsa, L.A. and Miami.

"There," Kingpen said. "He'll fly on Northwest Orient."

And when I looked at the board, I could see the connections… Fairbanks to Anchorage to Seattle to Chicago.

"On to Baltimore, see?" Kingpen said.

We went down to Northwest Orient, at the end of the building, and talked to an attendant behind the desk.

"You want shipping," she said. "That's out on Frontage Road."

She wrote down the directions. It wasn't that far, maybe five minutes away.

There were six or seven buildings, with the names of the Airlines - United, Lufthansa and a bunch of others.

"There it is," Beamish said. And he pulled the Buick in, right beneath the big sign, *Northwest Orient.*

The door was in the back. We went around the building, kicked the snow off of our shoes, and walked inside.

"Arctic entrance." That's what Kingpen said. But it was almost like a closet till we opened the next door.

"Cuts down on the wind and weather," Kingpen added. Then we went on in.

It wasn't a big place, but then maybe it was. Just so filled with junk, it *looked* kind of small. Crates, packages, and lots of cardboard boxes.

"Help ya?" a voice boomed. And there, in the corner of it all, was this big, husky guy. Bigger than Beamish. A football player. That's what he looked like. A linebacker, with his arm in a sling.

"I want to ship my dog back east," I said. "You have some kind of rates?"

"Depends on the size," he said. "And where you want to send him."

He gave me a form and I filled it out, and then he looked it over.

"Have a container?" he asked. I shook my head. Then he wrote something down on the form and totaled it up.

"A hundred and twenty-seven fifty," he said, "and that includes the box. There's a flight out at one o'clock this morning, if you want to put him on it."

"Now what if he dies?" I asked. "Is there much of a chance of *that*?"

"He'll die if he stays here," Beamish said. "Then what'll you do?"

I reached in my pocket, pulled out the money and handed it over.

"Only had one go in seven years," the guy said. "Heat system failed and he froze." He looked at his watch and gave me a receipt. "It's four o'clock now. I'll need him here by seven."

We walked out the doors and got in the car. In a way I felt relieved. The decision was made. Beamish was right. *What if. . .?*

"How about Earthquake Park?" Kingpen asked. You could tell he was excited. "It's right down Aircraft Drive. *It shows us the results of the Great Alaskan Earthquake of 1964.*" Kingpen read from one of his brochures.

"How about it?" he asked. "It's not that far away."

We got on Aircraft Drive, and drove between the fences, around the blue colored lights and past the little signs.

"Keep your head down," somebody said. I gave a nervous laugh, and we pretended to duck.

Kingpen was right. It wasn't that far. A couple of miles, it was at the end of Aircraft Drive. That's what the map said. But as hard as we looked, we couldn't find it. At least, not for a while.

There was only a pull-off where the park should have been. So we parked the Buick there, on top of a cliff, overlooking some water.

"Knik Arm," Kingpen said. And when you looked across the water, you could see downtown.

"Anchorage," Kingpen said.

And even for a city, it looked pretty good, with these gigantic, snow covered mountains behind it.

"Give me your camera," I said.

I took Kingpen's camera, stood there and took a picture. I didn't see it for a while, but it turned out great. I only wish that you could see it. If you're ever in the airport, there's one something like it in a big gold frame that's hanging on the wall. It's not nearly as good as mine, but you'll get the idea. Big pieces of ice floating in the water and hundreds of shades of gold and magenta. The sun was just starting to go down. You can see these reflections of buildings and trees and lights from the town.

"Look at those mountains," Kingpen said.

And I got those too. Towering, snow covered peaks. Bigger than life. It's the very best picture I ever took - and it should be in a magazine.

"How about something to eat?" Beamish said. "We can drive into the city."

"You two go ahead," I said. "I'm going to walk my dog around."

I pulled him out of the car and shut the door. Then Kingpen rolled down his window and Beamish started to drive away.

"We'll get you a burger," Kingpen said. "A burger with everything," he yelled. Then the two of them were gone.

My dog and I stood there on the cliff for a little while, watching the reflections muddle together. *Sure doesn't last long*, I remember thinking.

"C'mon boy," I said.

I gave a yank on the leash but he didn't move.

"Come on now," I said. "Come on."

He started to move, but not all that fast. Just this real slow walk, toward one end of the pull-off where the ground sloped down and went into some bushes and trees and hilly land. We went maybe twenty feet down. And then I saw it. This little plaque that was welded to a pipe.

EARTHQUAKE PARK
Left as a Reminder of the Great Alaskan Earthquake of 1964.

The land before us was supposed to show *the results of unbridled nature in all its fury.* That's what the sign said. But the land before us wasn't that big a deal. Not the part I saw. Covered with trees and shrubs, it was a little bit hilly, but except for the sign, you really never would have known.

"Come on," I said.

It was getting dark and I remember thinking that maybe they'd get lost, but they didn't. It wasn't long before they came back to the park. But before they did, I counted up my money. All twenty-seven dollars and thirty-seven cents. That's what I had left.

Beamish flashed the lights and the Buick pulled in.

"Here," Kingpen said. And he handed me a bag with a couple of hamburgers.

"Took it out of the pile," Beamish said.

I told them about the plaque, and then Kingpen loaded some batteries into the flashlight and went down in the bushes.

"Doesn't look like much," he said. You could tell that he was disappointed.

Beamish got out of the car with a shopping bag and set it on the snow.

"I thought I'd change the oil," he said. "I got some 10-40 weight at the store. And a filter and a pan."

He took the flashlight from Kingpen and crawled under the car.

"Go take a break," he said, as he unscrewed the plug.

You could hear the oil draining into the pan.

"We could be here all winter," he said. "And we'd never get it all. That's the thing about oil. Just *drip, drip, drip.*"

He worked for a long time after that, trying to fix little maintenance things on the car. He couldn't do everything, though. For some of it, he needed a special wrench. That was what he said. And of course, we didn't have it.

I remember he crawled out for a napkin once, and then he went back underneath.

"What the *hell*? *Look at this!*" he said.

101

I got down on my knees and looked under the car. I could see the oil dripping into the pan.

"Down *here*," Beamish said. "Where the snow is mashed flat." He scanned the ground with the light. "*Look* at that."

And like little balloons, stuck in the snow, there they were. Dozens of these condoms, probably hundreds of 'em, frozen in the ice.

"Frozen, fuckin' rubbers," Beamish said. "Will you look at that?" And so for two or three minutes, that's what we did.

Beamish screwed the plug in, filled the car with oil, then threw the empty cans into a trash barrel by the cliff.

"How about the pan?" Kingpen asked.

"We'll just take it with us," Beamish told him. "Come on. We gotta go."

We got in the car and pulled away, with the pan full of oil on Kingpen's lap. I thought for sure that he was gonna spill it, like the Ho-Jo Root Beer, but he didn't. The drive back wasn't that long. A couple of minutes and we were there, at the Northwest Orient building.

"Here," Beamish said. He took the pan from Kingpen and set it in the snow, on the sidewalk, next to the building. "Somebody will get it."

We had to practically carry my dog inside, through the arctic entrance and into the room. The same guy was there, nailing some crates and taping some boxes.

"Ready to go?" He scratched my dog on the head. "Here's the crate." It was almost like a doghouse, made of pieces of plywood with lots of reinforcements.

"Looks pretty sturdy," I said. He nodded his head.

"Whaddya want for thirty-two dollars?" he asked, and started to laugh.

"It even has a little door," Beamish said. He swung it open.

"Here," Kingpen said.

He had this thin cotton blanket from his sleeping bag that he folded over and put it into the crate.

"It'll be getting warmer soon," he said. "I won't really need it."

"Why don't you go ahead and put him in there for now," the guy said. "I'll walk him a little later."

I thought we would have to coax him in, but we didn't.

"Look at that," Kingpen said, as my dog walked into the crate.

102

"He'll be all right," the guy said. "Was he up here long?"

"Just a couple of days," Kingpen said. "But the trip was pretty rough."

"Especially the logging road," Beamish added. And then he started with the stories.

"It sounds like you guys could use some fun," the football player said. "Ever been out on the town?"

"To a restaurant or something?" Kingpen asked.

"Yeah. Or something," the guy told him. "Get out and see it all. There's Christie's, there's Ernie's, the Aurora Review."

"Maybe you're right," Beamish said. "We deserve some fun."

So he took down the names of the places and Kingpen got the directions.

"Just don't go to the Embers," the guy told us. And he pointed to his arm.

"Pretty rough, huh?" Beamish asked.

The guy nodded his head, and started to laugh. "Got the shit kicked out of *me* last time I was there."

I reached in the crate, patted my dog on the head, and told him I'd see him back east. Then we started toward the doors, but Kingpen stopped.

"Hold it," he said. "I almost forgot."

He reached in his pocket and pulled out a rolled up, narrow piece of paper.

"Here," he said. "I got it for the crate."

He unrolled the sticker and peeled off the back.

"I got it at the airport," Kingpen said. "At the gift shop, when you were talking to the attendant."

He walked back and stuck it on the crate. Right on top…

I DROVE THE ALASKA HIGHWAY

Then we turned around and walked out through the arctic entrance, the way we had come in.

Chapter 13

We got to the Igloo about eight-thirty or nine o'clock that night, mostly because we got lost. It was the first on the list that Beamish had written down, and was out in the middle of nowhere. I don't think we ever saw a street sign.

"There it is," Kingpen finally said. But the way that he said it, you couldn't really tell if he wanted to go in, or stay in the car.

"What do you think?" he asked.

"Here's what I think," Beamish said. "I think we should have a drink." He pulled out this bottle he had picked up along the way. "It's cheaper than the drinks inside. He unscrewed the cap.

"Want some?" he asked Kingpen.

Kingpen shook his head. "I'll have a beer inside."

We must have split at least half of the fifth, me and Beamish, and then the three of us went inside. As soon as we walked in, I thought of Jimmy Franklin's. I've gotta tell you. That Igloo was really classy. Red velvet carpet all over the walls and mirrors on the ceilings. They had six or seven strippers spread around the room, up on little stands, dancing to the music. And it was just like Beamish said, any place you sat, you could see every one.

"There's some empty seats," Beamish said. "Over at the bar." So we walked past some tables and climbed up on the stools.

"Gimmee a shot of rum," Beamish told the guy behind the bar. "And give my buddies whatever they want." He put a twenty on the bar, the guy got the drinks, and put down three dollar bills right in front of Beamish.

"Keep it," Beamish told him.

And the thing I remember thinking was that I could only afford to buy one round. Three drinks, I thought, maybe four. And then . . . *busted.*

By the time Kingpen bought the next round, Beamish and I were sliding off the bar stools and chewing on these little straws.

"Man, they're pretty," Kingpen said. But they were more than that. They were beautiful. They really were. All seven of them, dancing on the platforms and taking off their clothes.

"*Look*," Kingpen said.

And we watched them in the mirror, the one behind the bar. Wall to wall, and five feet high. We could see it all.

I was sitting in the middle, with Kingpen on one side and Beamish on the other. I remember Kingpen was saying something, but I couldn't really hear him with all of the music.

"Igloos," he shouted. "They were never in Alaska."

"We're *in* one," I said.

But Kingpen shook his head. "Not a *real* one," he told me. "They're in Canada. Or they *used* to be." But I didn't give a shit.

Kingpen wasn't making sense, but Beamish was the one who really needed help. His eyes were all glassy and he was staring at the mirror in front of us, mouthing something to me that I couldn't understand. He'd form his mouth like an M and then blow out through his lips.

I gave Kingpen a nudge. "Loogatim," I mumbled. "Whatizit he's sayin'?"

"Why don't you ask him yourself?" Kingpen said. So I told him I had never thought of that, turned to Beamish and tapped him on the shoulder.

"Whaddya tryin' to tell me?" I asked.

He turned to face me, but I still couldn't hear him because he kept mouthing the words.

"UMPIRE?" I shouted. "You wanna be an *UMPIRE*?"

"I wanna *GO* there," he said. "TuhtheEmbrrs."

He slid off the stool and started toward the exit. I took one last look in the mirror and saw Kingpen mouth two words. "Oh God."

We got out to the car and Beamish got behind the wheel.

"Move over," Kingpen said. "You don't like to drive at night."

"Why don't we go to Kristie's?" I said. "That sounded pretty good."

"Yeah," Kingpen said. "That's OK by me."

Beamish reached over, turned the key, and the Buick started up.

"Let's find a phone booth," he said. "I'll get the address."

And in a little while he had it and we were heading toward the Embers. It was in the middle of the city, near a bunch of other bars, and before we went in, we could see what it was like.

"Sleazy," Kingpen said. And as fancy as the other place had been, this was just the opposite, with people going in who looked a lot like us. All disheveled and I was sure they all smelled. *Yeah*. A *lot* like us.

"Let's go," Beamish said. We went around the block, came back, and a parking space was empty, right in front.

"C'mon," Beamish said, and he staggered out of the car.

We followed him in and Kingpen was right. It was pretty sleazy. There was a stripper in the corner, dancing on a table. A bar was in the middle of the room, and further back, in another room, there was a pool table.

"You watch the girl," Beamish said to Kingpen. "We're gonna shoot some pool."

Beamish and I walked toward the back. The table took two quarters, so I put 'em in the slots and pushed the lever in. *SLAM!* The balls dropped down and started rolling toward me.

"Here," I said. I handed Beamish my twenty-dollar bill. "Get what you want, and get something for Kingpen."

I put the balls on the table, found the wooden triangle hanging on the wall, and racked them up.

"You go ahead," I said, when Beamish got back. "Go ahead and break."

The game didn't last that long. Normally I'm not very good. I shoot too hard and choke on the tough shots. Except when I drink – then I'm hard to beat.

"Rack 'em!" I said.

I beat Beamish again. And then again and again. I just couldn't lose.

"Let's take a break," he finally said. We went up to the front, got another drink and sat there with Kingpen.

"Your dog ought to be leaving now. It's a little after one," Kingpen said.

"So how about a toast?" Beamish said. He lifted up his glass and took a gulp, but there was no way I could do it, I'd had too much to drink. So I just raised my glass, and then I put it down on the table.

"I'll be back in a minute," I said. "I need to get some air."

I went out the front and looked up at the sky. It was cloudy and gray and the snow was coming down. Tiny flakes that fell on snow that had been there for weeks.

You made it up the Alcan, I thought. *You can fly back east.*

I went back in the bar after that and we started shooting pool, until Beamish finally won one. At least we *thought* he had, but we weren't really sure who had the different numbered balls. One-thirty, two in the morning, and we could hardly stand up.

"I'll get this one out of the pile," Beamish said. And I asked how much we had spent.

"Less than a hotel," he told me. "And we're staying just as warm."

Then he peeled off a twenty and bought another round.

I thought they'd close at two, but instead it started picking up. More people came in, and then another girl went on.

"Look!" Beamish said. Six or seven guys in motorcycle jackets came in the door. Some stopped at the bar, but a few came back and stood there by the table.

"Got winners," one of them grunted. Then he put two quarters down.

The game was almost over. It wasn't even close. I banked the eight ball off the side and sunk it in the corner.

"Rack 'em!" I said.

The guy was pretty lousy. He reminded me of me when I hadn't had a drink. He shot too hard and couldn't put 'em in. At least not when it counted.

"Watch this," I said. It was a pretty easy shot. I put it the stick behind my back and dropped the eight ball in the pocket.

"Rack 'em!" I said again. *Man I was hot.* I couldn't be beat.

"How about playing for some money?" he asked.

He pulled out a roll of twenties, as big as my fist.

"Two hundred dollars?" he asked. "Three hundred? More?"

I thought I had three dollars, maybe four with some change.

"Here,'" Beamish said. And he handed me the pile.

"How about fifty?" I asked.

So we started off with that. Then seventy-five, then a hundred and a quarter, and I still hadn't lost.

"Double or nothing," the guy said. Two hundred fifty bucks. And then he started getting lucky and the game got pretty close.

"Shee-*IT!*" Beamish said, right after a shot that nobody should have made. The guy had careened it off two balls and put it in the side.

"*Damn*," Beamish said. And I knew what he was thinking, that the guy was getting lucky. But I *knew* I could beat him.

The place was getting crowded. That's what I remember. Especially where we were. Motorcycle guys mostly, but even Kingpen was there.

It got down to the eight ball and *I* had the shot. But I knew it would be tricky without the cue ball going in.

"Five hundred says you scratch," he grunted. "Plus the two-fifty we already bet."

"Make it a thousand," I said. "And you're on."

I looked over to Beamish, but he was saying something to Kingpen. Then he walked back to the table and looked at the ball.

"Doesn't look like a hard shot to me," Beamish said. "But it's an awful lot of money."

"Well you'd better fuckin' *have* it," the motorcycle man said. So Beamish told him we would check.

"We'll go into the bathroom and count it," Beamish said.

It was a shitty little bathroom, with lots of graffiti. And the place smelled like mildew and vomit and beer.

"Smells a lot like the inside of the Buick," I said. But Beamish just ignored me.

"Gimmee a hand," he said. He bolted the door and reached up to a window. "Here. Give me a lift."

"I'll dust it," I said. "If I spin it just right . . ."

Beamish grabbed me by the coat and pushed me to the wall.

"*Then* what?" he asked. "Do you think they're gonna fuckin' *pay* us? *Do* you? Like *Hell!* They're gonna kick our *ass.*"

He was starting to sweat and was getting all shaky.

"And if you *miss* it," he said. "*Then* what'll we do? We're five hundred short. Maybe *more.*"

I couldn't lift him up, so I got on his back and knelt on his shoulders.

"Tap it," he whispered.

But the window was frozen, from the ice outside.

"*Here,*" he said. He handed me the tank top from the toilet that was there.

"Bang it!" I remember him saying. "*Bang it!*"

So I gave the window frame a whack with the top from the tank and heard the frame break loose.

"Got it!" I said.

I pushed the window open and tried crawling out.

"Still snowin'," I said.

"Look," Beamish said. "Try *this.*"

There was a radiator there, right up on the wall. Steaming hot, with the paint peeling off.

"Gimmee your foot," Beamish said. So I did. And then he put it on the valve, I put my weight against it and I started to push.

"Go," Beamish whispered. And then a little louder, "Go, go, GO!"

I went out through the opening and must have fallen two or three feet, down into the snow. I was on the outside of the building, in what looked like an alley.

"Hey," Beamish called up. "Grab hold of my belt." He had taken it off and then tried to toss it to me three or four times.

"Grab it," he said.

I caught hold of the buckle and tried to pull him up, but he almost pulled me back inside the bathroom. Then he stood there a minute, shaking his head.

"I didn't want to do it," he said. "But there's no other way."

He sat on the toilet and took off his boots. Then he pulled off his socks, and put his Redwings back on.

"There's just no other way," he said.

Once he got started, he didn't even falter. I've gotta give him that. He just dove toward the radiator and started clawin' his way up.

"*Help* me!" he yelled.

But I couldn't really reach him, so I kept on saying things like, "Two more feet." Or, "Come on. You can do it." And finally he did it, but it wasn't very pretty.

If you've ever seen plastic when it burns in a fire, you've seen how it bubbles and melts and sticks to everything. That's what it was like. Big hunks of nylon melting off his jacket, with hundreds of feathers floating to the floor. He had his socks on his hands, but even then, I know his fingers must have gotten burned when he pulled himself up. I never could have done it.

"Just one more foot," I told him.

He got up to the window and I tried to pull him out.

"Try and put your foot on the valve," I said.

So he did. It took him a minute, but he finally found it.

"Got it," he said.

He made a final push up, but then the valve broke off. I know because I heard it hit the floor, and then the steam came pouring out. *PSCHTTT* . . .

That really got him moving up and out. He fell into the snow and then he started up the alley and back to the car.

"Come *on!*" he yelled. "We gotta *go!*"

But you know, it was funny in a way – I almost went back. I looked through the window, past the steam pouring out, and all the melted nylon and the feathers on the floor, to unbolt the door and walk back to the table. I *know* I could have made it.

I'll dust it, I thought. *If I spin it just right . . .*

"Come *on*! Beamish screamed. "You're gonna get us fuckin' *killed*."

So I backed away from the window and started up the alley, following the feathers back to the car.

Kingpen was in the car, already driving. They'd had it all planned. I dove into the back of the car and he gave it the gas. I could hear the tires, spinning on the ice.

"*Stomp* it!!" Beamish yelled. Then he put his foot on top of Kingpen's shoe and pushed the pedal to the floor. The tires wore through the ice and grabbed the asphalt - and the Buick took off.

"GO!" Beamish screamed. "GO, GO, *GO!*"

We went sliding down the road, but it was really hard to see. There was something on the windshield.

"A ticket," Kingpen said.

But he didn't stop to get it. He rolled down his window and when the wiper came over, he pulled the paper off.

"Read it," he said.

But I'd had too much to drink, and so had Beamish, so Kingpen read it to himself.

"Gabriel's," he read. That's all I remember. Then it started getting kind of fuzzy, and I think I fell asleep.

I could feel him tugging on my jacket and the words were coming in, but they didn't make much sense.

"Wake up," he said. "We've gotta get some sleep."

I opened my eyes and the car was stopped in front of a small ranch-type house, the kind you'd see back east, with a little picket fence.

"What time is it?" I asked. It was darker than hell.

"Come on," Kingpen said. "You've gotta get up."

We left the car and Kingpen helped me to the house. Beamish was at the door, pushing on the doorbell. *Brrnngg. Brrnngg. Brrnngg.*

The porch light came on.

"Where are we?" I asked.

The front door opened and I'll never forget this tall, willowy guy in a full-length nightgown.

"This is Gabriel's," he said. "I am Brother John. How may I help you?"

Beamish handed him the paper, still wet from the snow.

"Could we stay here?" he blubbered. "We've gotta get some rest."

Brother John didn't say much. He nodded his head and we followed him in.

"This way," he said.

We went up the stairs to the second floor. He turned on the hall light and we looked in the rooms.

"Why don't you two stay here?" he said.

There were three or four bunk beds with two empty places. Beamish and I went in.

"You can stay across the hall," he said to Kingpen. Then Brother John turned off the light and went downstairs.

I remember thinking later, it was a lot like Kingpen said, "You never really know *where* you'll end up or even how you'll get there. You can think the strangest thing, and it always ends up more."

That was what he said. Not *different,* or some other word, but "*more.*" That's what Alaska was like.

I thought I heard from God later on that night. The room began to spin and I knew I heard His voice. Real husky and deep. I could hear it right above me.

"Do not go down to breakfast," He said. "Unless you like to sing."

And then the room began to spin, I held on to the bed, and it all turned black.

I hadn't slept two hours when Beamish woke me up.

"Come on," he said. "We've gotta go."

The sun was coming out and it was starting to get light. We went across the hall to look for Kingpen, but no one was there. Just a lot of rumpled blankets.

"What if he's the guy from Sears?" Beamish asked.

"Kingpen?"

"No. Brother John."

I tried to remember, but they all mixed together. The mechanic, the manager and the guy in the nightgown.

"Come on," Beamish said.

We got halfway down the steps, and you could smell the food. Then we heard the piano and they started to sing.

"Don't even look," Beamish said. "Just go out the door."

So that was what we did. But I couldn't close my ears.

It was Kingpen's voice, real nervous and shaky, with five or six others, singing this real high-pitched gospel. And none of them could sing. Not even Brother John. "Red and yellow, black and white. They are precious in his sight…"

"Come on," Beamish said. So I closed the door behind us and we started toward the Buick. We waited ten or fifteen minutes for Kingpen to come out. Beamish started the car, while I counted the money.

"Three hundred forty-two dollars," I told him. And we were just about out of gas.

Kingpen came out and got in the back. Then we drove to a gas station and Kingpen filled it up, while I called back east. That was pretty crazy. I had three dollars and sixty cents to spend on one minute.

"Hello, hello," I said.

Because of the echoes you couldn't talk too fast. But then you only had a minute, so you couldn't talk too slowly. My mother got the point.

"Dog will arrive at five . . . Dog will arrive at five . . . But I only have a minute . . . minute."

"Your time is up," the operator said. Just like they said she would at the beginning of the call. And then the phone went dead. She never even asked if I wanted more time.

I walked back to the car and an attendant was there, talking to Beamish and looking at the tags.

"You've really come a ways," he said. "You going up to work?"

"Just seeing the state," Beamish said. "Driving around."

We talked another minute and then another car came in, so we pulled the Buick out.

"See ya," Kingpen yelled.

"Where to?" Beamish asked. But of course nobody knew, so we drove around some more.

We finally headed toward the city. We were going to wash our clothes.

"Look," Kingpen said.

There was a giant St. Bernard, standing all alone at the corner of Cordova and 15th. All fluffed up, he was really looking good.

"A show dog," Beamish said. "I wonder where his owner is." We looked all around, but we never saw a person with a leash.

We went another half a mile, turned left on 9th, made a right on A Street, and passed the Anchorage Museum.

"Look *OUT*!" Kingpen yelled. But there was nothing we could do. The guy was backing out a driveway and rammed us in the side.

"Shee-*it*!" Beamish yelled, as he jammed on the brakes. Kingpen grabbed his camera and started taking pictures.

It wasn't that bad. Nobody got hurt. The other guy's car wasn't even dented and the only thing wrong with my car was that the left back door was crunched a little bit. And except for the fact that you couldn't keep it closed, like I said, it wasn't all that bad.

But anyway, we spent the rest of the morning at the insurance adjuster's office, filling out forms and showing him the dent.

"I'm telling you, I wouldn't take less than eighty dollars," Beamish whispered.

But I knew I'd only paid a hundred for the car, not counting tires and the shocks we hadn't put on right.

"Let me see what I can do," the insurance man said. He started making phone calls. And after maybe half an hour, he told us, "There's not a one in the state. I've been calling all the body shops, and junkyards. Not a one." What he meant was a left back door for a '64 Buick Special.

"I can't get it fixed," he told us. "I'll have to give you a check."

Then he got out a pamphlet and started looking through it.

"Sixty-four. Sixty-four," he mumbled. Then he must have found what he was looking for, because he wrote something down.

"Three hundred dollars. That's the best I can do," he said.

"Three hundred dollars?!" Beamish shouted.

"Well, I'll give you five hundred. But that's it," he told us. "That's *it*."

He wrote me a check. I put it in my pocket with my dime and two nickels, and then we all shook hands.

"Come on," Beamish said.

We went out to the car. Beamish took his belt, closed the door and buckled it shut.

"That oughta hold it," he said. "Where you wanna go?"

But of course we still didn't know, so we drove around some more.

It was Kingpen who said we could get a reward for the St. Bernard, if we could find him again and turn him in.

"Maybe a hundred," Beamish added.

So Kingpen got out a map and we went back toward Cordova.

"Eleventh," Kingpen said. And we were getting pretty close, but none of us saw him. Not for a while.

"Probably gone," Beamish said.

But then we saw that he wasn't. He was there in a gutter, all covered with blood. Beamish slowed the car and we could see the dog was dead. And it was like Kingpen said - it really made you sick.

"Makes you wanna vomit," he told us.

Shoes, boots, pieces of rope.

"What do you think will happen to him? I asked.

"Somebody will get him," Beamish said. And then we kept on driving.

We went to Earthquake Park after that - not for anything special, but because we knew that it was there. We stood on the cliff and looked across Knik Arm, to the city.

"Doesn't look as good as it did last time," Kingpen said.

And I knew what he meant. Somehow it was different.

"Listen," Beamish said. "This might sound pretty crazy. But remember up in Fairbanks? Remember that center with the stairs?"

"At the University?" Kingpen asked.

"Yeah. That's it," Beamish told him. "They had these bulletin boards in there and I remember seeing signs about a dance. They're having it tonight. Whaddya say?"

We grabbed something to eat and drove out on 6th Street, the one everybody takes, to the highway we'd come down on the day before. Highway 1. "Three hundred fifty-seven miles back to Fairbanks," Kingpen said.

It was one or two o'clock and I was sitting in the back, getting pretty sleepy. I made it as far as the weigh station, though.

"Closed," Kingpen said. "What did I tell you?" I heard him ask me.

Then, I shut my eyes and drifted off to sleep.

I slept through Wasilla and Willow, Montana Creek, and the Park. Ice Worm Gulch and the town of Nenana.

"Ester," I heard Kingpen say. I opened my eyes. "Right on up the hill, if you follow that road."

Ester was a little town near Fairbanks with a hundred people or so. Then we crossed the railroad tracks and passed another weigh station that was closed.

"You should have seen those mountains," Kingpen said. "When we went through the Park. So icy and white."

We crossed Sheep Creek Road and went another mile. We made a left and we could see the University.

"There's the gym," Kingpen said. It was the first building that we saw, so we pulled into the lot and sat there a minute.

"We can walk up to the Center," Beamish said. "But we don't need to go now. It's only nine o'clock. How about a drink? We can run into town and pick up a bottle."

His eyes lit up and he started the car.

"I'm still hung over from the night before," I said. "I'm going to go into the gym and try to find the showers."

I reached toward the door, felt the belt and went out the other side.

"You go ahead," I said. "I'm gonna clean up."

"How about if we meet you in an hour?" Kingpen asked. And then the Buick pulled away.

If you're ever in a gym and need to find the showers, just smell for the chlorine. It'll lead you to the pool. Once you get there, it's not any trouble. The showers are always close by.

I must have spent an hour standing under the water. Probably not that long, but it sure felt like it. I'd turn it hotter and hotter the longer I was there. Boy, it felt good. I finally turned the shower off, and then just like on the ferry, I dried myself with some brown towels that I got from the dispenser.

115

Then I put my clothes back on and sat there on a bench. Nobody was there. *Probably at the dance*, I thought. And then, just as I was thinking that, Kingpen came in with a pack of razors.

"Thought you might want to shave," he said. "You know . . . for the dance. I got these at the store." There were five or six razors, the kind you throw away.

"You all about ready?" I asked. But Kingpen shook his head.

"I think we're going back," he said. "To get another bottle. He finished the first one – a bottle of wine."

"I'd better go," he finally said. "I have to drive. I'll see you in a while."

I went into the bathroom next to the showers and opened the package. But I never really shaved. I started to. I took the little cover off the blade and pulled the razor down my face, till it hurt so bad I couldn't stand it anymore. Then I started with another razor. And another. Scraping across these whiskers that were a little too long to shave and a little too short to cut with scissors. I guess I could have done it, if I really wanted to. But I kept on looking in the mirror, and then after a while, it didn't seem to matter. I got all caught up, staring at a face.

I guess you think you're one thing when really you're not. You could be something else. That's what I remember thinking. You picture that you look a certain way from glances in the mirror, snapshots from a camera and thoughts inside your head. But you never really look like that. I mean, not exactly. Like potato chips you eat and hear fifty times louder than the people around you. It's not really that loud, but then maybe it is. I guess you never really know.

Beamish told me later, it was just the trip. "You haven't had the time to look the same," he said. "And on top of that, you haven't *seen* yourself for at least a week."

But for two or three minutes, I can tell you one thing. The face that I was looking at was the face of somebody else. I think it started out as me, but the more I tried to focus, the more it wasn't. Or maybe it was. Try it for yourself and see who *you* see. I could never really tell.

"Hey, Fitch!"

The face turned away and I saw Kingpen coming through the door.

"Hey, Jess," he said. "Come on. We're gonna go."

I stuffed the razors in my pocket, put on my coat, and we started out. Out past the lockers and the weight room, up out of the basement and past the basketball court.

"I don't know about Beamish," he said. "He's had a lot to drink."

We got to the car and he was sitting in the back.

"One of you drive," he said. "It's getting kind of dark."

"It's been dark," I said. "It's after eleven. And besides, we're not driving any more. We're going to a dance."

Beamish handed me his bottle, put his head back on the seat, and raised his thumb into the air.

"Drink up," he said.

It was a pint of rum, but a third of it was gone. There was a wine bottle on the floor. The cap was gone, but it really didn't matter.

"Are you mixing this?" I asked.

It was getting pretty cold sitting there in the car. The windows were icing up and the seats were getting hard.

"Go ahead," Beamish said. "It'll warm you up."

We must have spent an hour, or an hour and a half, finishing the bottle and making big plans.

"I *know* him," Beamish said. "He can get you in the school."

He was telling me about this guy back east who could get me into Law School.

"You should try it," Beamish said. "What else you gonna do?" I shrugged my shoulders in the dark and told him that I didn't really know.

Kingpen drove us to the Center. It was a couple hundred yards from where we were. We got out of the car and walked inside, past the candy on the counter and all the magazines.

"*Listen*," Kingpen said.

And when we listened, we could hear the band upstairs. So we went on up. And when we got there, we found it back behind the snack bar, in this giant closed-off room we hadn't seen the first time we were there.

"*Look*," Kingpen said.

And when he pointed to a little sign, I thought that we were screwed.

"*Must show student I.D.*"

But the way it all turned out, we didn't have to.

"Just flash 'em your license," Beamish said.

117

So that was what we did. They couldn't tell the difference, it was so dark.

There were hundreds of students there and the band was pretty good. Then the drummer hit the cymbals and the lights came on.

"Thank you for coming. Thank you *all*," somebody said.

"Play one more," another person yelled.

But of course they never did. That was it. "The dance is *over*," Kingpen said.

The people came pouring out of the room and we lost Beamish in the crowd. Then Kingpen went off to the bathroom, so I walked around alone.

I remember wondering if I was drunk from drinking in the car, or maybe just still drunk from the night before. Maybe I had *almost* been sober, but when I *started* drinking in the Buick . . .

I was pretty well shot, whichever it was. I talked to this girl for a while, but we didn't hit it off.

"What happened to your face?" she asked.

I figured out later, she'd meant, "Why is it so patchy?" But I didn't know it at the time.

"It's the trip," I said. And then I told her all about how I hadn't seen myself, for at least a week.

Then she nodded her head and walked away. She couldn't understand.

I climbed to the ceiling right after that, and sat at the table and looked around. I could see it all. The Ping-Pong tables, the bulletin boards, and a guy counting money in three separate piles.

"Hey, *BEAMISH*!" I yelled down.

But I don't think he heard me. He was too far away. Too far away and too far gone.

"HEY, *BEAMISH*!"

He was three floors down, if you included the stairs to the ceiling. By the time I got there, he was walking away.

They say you can tell a lot about a person by the way that they walk. That's what I was thinking, following him along. Something had changed. Something was different. I could see it in his footsteps.

He walked over to a post, put his back against it, turned his head, and then saw me standing there.

"TEN MINUTES TO CLOSING," the intercom announced.

"Is it me, or is it getting colder?" I asked.

Beamish slouched against the post, slid to the floor and sat there.

"I called back east," he said. "I think I'm flying home."

I didn't get it at first. "For Law School?" I asked.

He shook his head.

Neither of us said anything for a minute. And I really couldn't blame him for feeling like he did. It hadn't worked out the way we had thought.

"I called the airlines," he said. "And I know this might sound kinda crazy, but…."

"But what?" I asked.

"It's eighty-five dollars more if I fly out of Fairbanks."

He reached into a pocket and pulled out some money. Then another pocket and some other money.

"It's the pile," he said. "I split it into thirds. With my share, and my own money, I've got just enough, if you don't mind going back… To Anchorage, I mean. I'll buy you a drink at the Embers," he said and tried to laugh.

We took a big breath of our last warm air, went out the door and then walked to the Buick. Kingpen was there, huddled in the back at the bottom of his sleeping bag.

"You take the passenger side, I'll sleep behind the wheel," Beamish said. Then we got into the bags and tried to go to sleep.

We spent the next morning lounging around in the Student Center, watching TV and staying warm.

"I saw this same show back east," Beamish said.

But there was no way that he could have. The guy on the show kept saying it was live.

"But I've *seen* it," Beamish said. "Watch *this*."

He pointed to the TV. Then he told us ahead of time what the guy would do, what he would say, and how he would act.

"*Watch*," Beamish said again. And it was exactly like he told us it would be. The guy picked up his coffee, touched his ear, and scratched his forehead.

"And now he's going to go to a commercial," Beamish said. And that was what he did. It was all pretty strange.

We finished watching the show and then we went up to the snack room and got some lunch. I bought Beamish a sandwich because he didn't have any money, except his money for the ticket.

"Get a drink," I said. But he only got water.

I had a hundred and fourteen dollars, my share of the pile, plus the check for five hundred. Altogether, not that much less than I'd started with.

"You think you guys will get a job?" Beamish asked. "I mean if the money gets tight? Maybe you could be a mountain guide, Fitch," he said. And he forced out a smile.

We went down to the first floor after that and picked up some candy bars for the trip. Then we went out to the parking lot and got in the Buick.

"It's too bad you're flying at night," Kingpen said. "It would be nice to see the state. When are you leaving? Eleven?"

Beamish nodded his head and started the car.

We went down past the gym, got on the highway and took it out toward Ester.

"That would be a neat place to live," Kingpen said, as we drove past the little town. But you couldn't really tell. It was back up on the hill.

"Now you two make sure and send me a postcard," Beamish said. "And tell me what happens."

"I'll send you a letter," I promised.

Nobody said much after that. At least I don't think they did. I made it to the bridge just north of Nenana, and then I fell asleep.

"Still frozen solid," was the last thing I heard.

I guess Beamish kept on driving after that, south through McKinley and Trapper Creek. On past Talkeetna, Houston and Wasilla.

"Closed," I heard Kingpen say. "What did I tell you?"

And when I opened my eyes, we were passing the weigh station.

Beamish got us to the airport. We were two hours early.

"Plenty of time," Beamish said.

We walked down to Northwest and paid for his ticket. Then he put it in his pocket.

"Come on," I said. "I'll buy you a drink."

We walked down the lobby, past the picture like mine and another one that I hadn't seen before.

"Wonder Lake," the title said. It was one of those pictures of a lake with reflecting mountains. You could have turned it upside down, and it would have still looked the same.

Anyway, we rounded a corner and went into the lounge.

"Must be a group of tourists from Texas," Kingpen said.

And when we looked, we could see all these guys with cowboy hats and leather boots.

"A junket!" Beamish told us.

We sat in there a long time. And the place wasn't cheap - five dollars a drink. But nobody cared.

"SET 'EM UP!" somebody yelled. And that somebody bought all of us a drink. Every person there. Over a hundred of us. Kingpen counted.

"Nearly five hundred bucks," Beamish said.

We left the lounge a little after ten and went out to the Buick. We opened the trunk to take the stuff out, and I thought I was gonna puke.

"Snow must have melted and leaked inside the trunk," Kingpen said. And when we looked with the flashlight, we could see all the water in the bottom of the trunk. But it wasn't only water. Everywhere we looked, there was slimy, green mold. Sometimes, it was brown and even shades of black.

"Shee-*it*," Beamish said.

We started pulling all his stuff out and put it on the parking lot. I wish you could have seen it. Everything was moldy. I almost dropped the rifle once. Even in the case, it started slipping from my hands.

"Watch it!" Beamish yelled.

But everything was like that. The rifle case, the backpack, his clothes... all covered with this slippery, slimy mold. The tent was the worst.

"Maybe you can kill it with some bleach," Kingpen said. "After you get home."

"I think I'm just going to toss these clothes," Beamish said. Then he took them all out and put them by the side of the car. "Somebody'll get 'em."

I handed Beamish the gun case, but he put it back inside the trunk. Up out of the water.

"You'll probably need it," he said. "You can give it to me later."

Kingpen shut the trunk and we started toward the terminal, dragging the gear. We couldn't really carry it. The mold kept getting on our clothes.

"What if they won't ship it?" Kingpen asked. "What if it's too moldy?"

Beamish stopped just short of the door and tried untying his pack. He couldn't get it for a while, 'cause like everything else, it was really pretty slimy. He finally got it though.

"Here," he said. "I've got something for you."

He reached in his pack, felt around and pulled out a can.

"Cross and Blackwell crab soup," he told us.

The label was wet and was peeling off, but still, you could read it. And that's what it was. Twenty full ounces of Maryland crab soup.

"I was saving it, Beamish said. "For a special occasion. But I want you to have it. You can eat it when you want."

He handed me the can and we started through the door and walked down the lobby to the Northwest counter. He didn't have much time. The attendant looked at the gear and I know I saw him shake his head. But he never said a word. Just tossed it on the conveyer. Then we waited and watched as it all moved along. *Moving. Always moving.* And then all of the stuff disappeared behind the flap, and Kingpen told us, "Only hope it's not contagious."

Beamish handed in the ticket. "Come on," he said. And we followed him to the gate.

"You give me a call when you get back east," he told me. He slapped me on the shoulder and looked over to Kingpen. "And I want to see those pictures, Kingpen."

The two of them shook hands and then Beamish started down the aisle. He never looked back. That's what I remember. The feathers coming out of his jacket, and his pants slipping down. He never turned around.

"What about your belt," Kingpen shouted. "Do you want me to get it?" But Beamish didn't answer. I don't think he could.

The plane pulled away, out into the dark. You know what it's like. You squint and you stare, but you're never really sure.

"*There*," Kingpen said. And when he pointed to the sky, we convinced ourselves we saw it.

We got back in the car. Then I started the engine and we pulled away.

"Watch out for planes," I said. Kingpen started looking as we went out the back, on Aircraft Drive and down to Earthquake Park.

We stayed on the cliff that night. Eleven years after the earthquake, we were there. I turned the can opener around and we sat there, eating Maryland crab soup and looking over Knik Arm.

"Kind of pretty," I said. And it was, from a distance. The lights of the city, all sparkling and bright.

"We can stay here in Anchorage," I said. "There's no real reason to drive back up. To Fairbanks, I mean."

Kingpen nodded his head. "I guess we should decide," he said. "And then stay put for a while."

He found a nickel on the floor and held it in his hand.

"Heads we stay, tails we go," he said.

He flipped it in the air, but then lost it in the dark.

"Let's just sleep on it," I said. "We can decide in the morning."

Then Kingpen climbed into the back, and we got in our bags.

"First time I've had room to stretch," Kingpen said, "since we left on the trip."

"Except for Brother John's," I told him.

And then just for a minute, we sat there in our sleeping bags and started to laugh this wild and crazy laugh that reminded me of Beamish.

Chapter 14

It was kind of like that time I woke up in the car, right outside Chicago. I opened my eyes, but couldn't see out. The windshield was covered with snow.

"We're driving to Fairbanks," I said.

I got out of the Buick and brushed off the snow. Then I started the engine and waited a minute.

"Did you hear me?" I asked. But Kingpen was asleep or faking it, trying to stay warm.

I took us to a gas station and was filling it up, getting ready for the trip.

"Still driving around?" the attendant asked. "Didn't I see you guys last week?"

"We lost two," I said.

It was snowin' like a bitch, so I asked him about it.

"When's spring coming?"

"Just winter and summer," he answered. "Maybe two more weeks. Do you have any tickets?"

"No. Cash," I said. And he started to laugh.

"I mean for break-up," he told me. "The Ice Classic. You can really win some money."

"Yeah. We got some," I said. "But we don't know where they are."

I gave him the money and took us out on 6th Street, past the private airport and all the mobile homes. It was really coming down by then. Big fluffy flakes everywhere you looked. That didn't stop us, though.

Kingpen woke up right before the weigh station.

"Look," he said. And he thought it was open. Both of us did, with six or seven tractor trailers sitting by the building. But it wasn't.

"I guess they're just waiting out the storm," Kingpen said. Then we headed toward Wasilla.

We were driving over train tracks and train tracks and more train tracks.

"Sure must be a lot of trains up here," I said. Even though the only one I'd ever seen was in the Park, and it didn't run.

I pulled the car to a stop and looked both ways.

"There's only one. From Fairbanks to Anchorage and back again." That's what Kingpen said. "It's all the same. It winds around the mountains and keeps crossing the road, but it's still the same track."

We were someplace north of Houston and the snow was letting up.

"First time I've seen all this," I said.

I kept on driving where Beamish must have driven. Past Willow, Wasilla, and finally Talkeetna.

"Town's a base camp for McKinley," Kingpen said. "That's where the glacier pilots live."

But anyway, I drove it *all* that day. From Earthquake Park to where I parked the car in Fairbanks.

"Come on," I said. And we walked into the bank.

I had my check in my hand, but they told me I could only cash it if I opened an account.

"Then I can give you the money tomorrow," the lady said.

So that was what I did. Opened an account, and then we left.

We drove back to the University right after that. Picked up some sandwiches at the Student Center and took 'em up to the ceiling.

"How about some Ping-Pong?" I asked.

We looked down at the tables and a couple of them were free, so we finished the sandwiches and went on down.

We played five or six games, and I know I could have won them all. But I got so far ahead each time, I stopped trying, so he beat me.

"Give up?" Kingpen asked.

I told him no, so we played one more and he squeaked by again.

We went up to the snack room and got some hot chocolate after that. Then the intercom came on and I started feeling cold.

"TEN MINUTES TO CLOSING," the intercom announced.

We were walking past the candy and all the magazines, and I remember I was telling Kingpen, "We could get up early."

"We'll take a shower at the gym," I said. "And wash our clothes. Maybe sometime later, tomorrow night, we can go out on the town. Maybe meet some girls."

"Well, yeah," Kingpen said. "I guess we could. I mean I guess we can if you want to. But . . ."

"But what?" I asked. He was acting really funny. Nervous and edgy. And he kept staring at the floor.

"Listen," Kingpen said. "I feel kinda awkward telling you this, but I think, I mean if you don't mind, I think I'm gonna go on down to Haines."

We each took a deep breath and walked into the arctic entrance, then out the other door.

"You mean that place past Tok?" I asked. "The last stop for the Ferry?"

"That's it," he said. He took another deep breath, but forgot about the cold. He started to cough, so I pounded on his back.

"I met this girl. Remember at the campground, those people with the van? She was one of them."

"Yeah," I said.

"Well anyway, we really hit it off. She lives in Haines, and I'd like to go and see her. I mean, if you really wouldn't mind."

"I don't mind," I said. "Do you have her address?"

"Well, she owned the van," he told me. "And it's not that big a place. A couple thousand people at the most. I think I can find her." He paused. "Marie. That's her name."

Marie *what*, I was going to ask him, but I didn't think he knew.

"Sounds good," I said.

Then he told me all about how much it meant to him that I hadn't gotten upset.

"I think she's really something special," Kingpen told me. "If it doesn't work out, I'll be right back."

"No problem," I said. "She sounds like a great girl."

We got inside the Buick and then we sat there for a minute.

"Would you mind," I asked, "if we drove down to the gym?"

I always felt funny, sleeping by the Center.

"Of course not," he said. "Would you mind," he went on, "if I left tomorrow morning?"

"No problem," I told him. "Are you going to take the bus?"

"No. There's no bus that goes down there. I guess I'll hitchhike," he said.

I drove to the gym and we slept there that night, in the parking lot, up by the building. We must have been there a long time. I was down deep in my bag, and then I heard this *Rat tat tat… Rat tat tat.* I could hear it in my sleep.

"No camping in the lot," somebody said.

I stuck my head out of the bag, opened my eyes and looked at a face, staring through the glass.

126

"No camping in the lot," he said again. *Rat tat tat. Rat tat tat.* He wouldn't stop tapping on the window.

"We're on our way to Anchorage," I said. But I don't think he heard me, because he wouldn't let up.

"Get moving. You're not allowed to *sleep* here," the guard said.

So I told him again. "We're *driving*," I said. "We're on our way to Anchorage. Nobody's sleeping."

Kingpen climbed over the seat and started the car. "We're going," Kingpen said. "He's just confused. We've been driving back and forth, and back and forth. He thought he was awake. And I thought that I was. We're moving," Kingpen told him one more time. Then he put it in Neutral and stepped on the gas.

We went downtown and had breakfast. Twenty-four dollars. That's what it cost... twelve apiece.

"How you doing for money?" I asked.

Kingpen got out his wallet and counted the bills.

"Sixty-seven," he said. Which was a little more than I had.

It was sometime after ten, so we went to the bank and I emptied the account.

"I guess you want large ones," she said. "Like everybody else?"

"Whatever," I said.

She opened a drawer and reached inside.

"One. Two. Three. Four. Five." *Hundred-dollar bills.* The first I'd ever seen.

I stuck them in my pocket, and then the two of us walked out.

"What about food?" I said. "Do you want to take some cans? There are still plenty in the trunk."

"I think I'll pick up a burger or something later," he said. "I don't want to take that much. Just my tent and my sleeping bag and my suitcase. And I can't forget the camera."

We got in the car and when I looked over, he seemed more relaxed. That's what I remember thinking. And it didn't seem quite right, when I thought of all he had ahead of him.

"Eight hundred miles?" I asked. "Where you gonna sleep?"

But he only shrugged his shoulders and shook his head.

I drove toward Delta Junction for about twenty miles. "This oughta help," I said. "At least it will get you started."

I pulled the Buick over and we both got out. Then I handed him his gear.

127

"I really hope you find her," I told him. "I mean it. I wish you the best." And then I thought of something.

"Let me see your money," I said.

He reached into his pocket and gave it all to me. Then I handed him three of the hundred-dollar bills. He didn't want to take them at first, so we called it a loan.

"I'll pay you back next time I see you," he said.

He hung his camera around his neck and we stood there a minute, not knowing what else to say.

"Well, I'll see you," Kingpen said.

He picked up his gear, but there wasn't any traffic.

"I guess I'll walk awhile," he said.

So that was what he did. *Walked and walked and walked.* I watched him get started. He took off down the road toward these hills, miles and miles away. Carrying his suitcase, his tent, his sleeping bag and camera, and three hundred-dollar bills. He turned around a couple times, stopped and waved. I swear to God, I stood there for at least a half an hour, looking, always looking, until I couldn't see him anymore.

I remember thinking later, it was all pretty funny. Everybody gone - and me sitting in the car.

"Where you headed?" they would ask me.

But I was already there. No-named mountains.

Grizzlies, caribou and wolves.

———————

If you've ever played "In Between," you know that you can lose pretty quickly. I lost everything I had in less than fifteen minutes. I had gone back to the Center and was eating a sandwich and watching TV, when I got into a card game with these guys at the University.

"Five-Jack," the little guy said.

So I bet twenty-five dollars against what was in the pot.

"SEVEN! Take it," he said. So I took out what I won.

"Three-Nine." And the next guy bet.

"Fifteen bucks," he said. But the next card was a ten, so he threw his fifteen dollars into the pile.

We went around the circle one time and then it got back to me.

"Three-Queen. Can you get in between?"

"I'll make it a hundred," I said. Then he flipped over a King.

"Pay it," he said. So I threw in a hundred-dollar bill.

You couldn't really lose if you had enough money. You just doubled your bets and kept on going. You even had the odds, if you waited long enough.

"Four-Seven"... "Nine-Queen"...

"Deuce-Bullet. It's to *you*," he said. And they all looked to me.

You know it doesn't get any better, if you've ever played the game. I counted my money and put it near the pile.

"Two hundred forty-one dollars," I said.

And then he flipped up a two.

"Busted," he said.

I pushed the money in the pile and could hardly stand up.

"Seven-King." And the game kept going.

I went back to the Buick and sat there in the lot, looking out the windshield and picturing the cards. Deuce-Bullet. Deuce-Bullet. *Busted*, I thought. Son of a *bitch*.

I went down to the gym after that. I took a hot shower and then used the paper towels. *If I could just get a job*, I thought, *I could win it all back.*

I found a new place to sleep that night. I was still in the car, but the parking spot was different. About a quarter mile away, in a pull-off by the road. I had a half a tank of gas and found some quarters on the floor. And I still had the cans in the trunk. I crawled in my sleeping bag and put my head on the arm rest, then I tilted my neck and looked for the lights. Neon greens, reds and different shades of purple.

But the clouds were there and I never got to see them. Then it started to snow.

I tried to buy a paper that next morning, but they didn't come out until four in the afternoon. *The Fairbanks Daily News Miner* – that's what it was called. Like something from the Gold Rush.

But anyway, I left the car and hitchhiked into town, so I wouldn't use the gas. Then I started looking for a job.

I could have shoveled snow. That's what I remember thinking. But I didn't have a shovel and I couldn't even buy one. So then I thought that I could be a salesman, but I didn't have the clothes. And then my thoughts went to the next thing and I thought I didn't even have a phone. And if they asked for my address, just what exactly would I say? That I was living in a pull-off on the side of the road?

I finally got a paper and cut out an ad for "general help" for Far North Music Machines. That was what it said, followed by a phone number.

I couldn't find a phone booth, not for a while. There were a couple on the street, but the cords had been cut. They take the phones each fall and replace 'em in the summer, somebody told me later. But I didn't know it at the time. Anyway, I finally found a phone inside someplace. I made the call, but they had just gone out of business. That's what the tape said. So I tried it again.

"Far North Music Machines. We are unable to answer your call. We are currently out of business."

And as I listened to it the second time, the thing that I kept thinking was, *that's what it was like*. Even when I finally found a place where I could work, I couldn't.

I started walking back to the University and then I hitchhiked a little, but I never got a ride. My heart just wasn't in it and nobody picked me up. *Busted*, I thought.

It was a little after six when I got back to the car. I opened the trunk and took out a can, turned the opener around, took off the lid and stuck my Jimmy Franklin's spoon inside. Ravioli in meat sauce. That's what it was. But anything I'd had would have tasted just as good. I got a can of peaches, and sat there off the road, slurpin' 'em down and drinking the syrup. Natural, heavy syrup. That's what the can said. Geez, it was good.

And then I thought, *screw it*. So I turned the key and the Buick started up. *How much could it use, to go a quarter mile?*

It was sometime after seven that night when I parked it in the lot. Then I went inside the Center and stood there getting warm. And I kept on thinking, *What would be the worst thing that could happen? Would I die there in some gutter? Or maybe in the Buick with a thousand empty cans?*

"Excuse me," I said. "Could you help me a minute? I'm looking for a job."

There was a girl at the counter with long brown hair, arranging the candy and stocking the shelves.

"Do you know of anything? Maybe here at the school?"

"You can check upstairs," she said. "Try up in the snack room."

But they didn't have a thing. That's what these two guys told me.

"Try down at the Commons," one said. "They always need some help."

"The *cafeteria*," the other guy said. "Halfway to the gym."

I had seen the building and knew just where it was. But I couldn't get in, because I didn't have a card.

"I'm looking for a job," I said. But the girl just shook her head.

"You need a student card."

There were people behind me, waiting to get in. So I turned around and started out the door.

"Check around back," somebody called out.

So I went behind the building to the loading platform. There was a dumpster there and a guy was crawling out.

"Can I go in *this* door?" I asked.

He gave me a wave and lifted himself up. "Come on," he said. "I'll take you in."

We went up the steps and through the door. *EMPLOYEES ONLY.* That's what it said. When we walked inside, we were in a kind of storeroom. There were big jars of mayonnaise and applesauce, with people running all around.

"There," he said. "You looking for a job? That's the man to see."

He pointed to an office that was over in the corner, and when I looked through the glass, I saw him, about 40 years old, kind of squatty and fat.

"Excuse me," I said. "Could you help me a minute? I'm looking for a job."

"What list are you on," he asked me. "A, B, C, or D?"

I shrugged my shoulders and told him that as far as I knew, I wasn't on any of them.

"But I guess I could get on one, if it would help me get a job," I said.

He pulled his desk drawer out and got a piece of paper.

"Fill this out," he said. He handed it to me. "There's a pencil on the table."

It was an application for employment. And there were a dozen or so questions. Like "Where were you born?" "Where do you live?" *On and on and on.* Questions I couldn't answer the way I knew he wanted, so I filled in the blanks with imaginary names.

"I've gotta have the name and the phone number of the last place you worked," he said. "Too many damn people coming through this town. I need a local name."

"No problem, I said.

But then I couldn't remember if it was "Boxes" or "Machines," so I got out the paper and copied it down. "Far North Music Machines." And then I wrote the phone number.

"Just give 'em a call and ask for James Larew," I told him. "The work was slowing down so they had to let me go. But he can tell you more about it."

"I'll give you a call tomorrow," I said. "I don't know that I'll be home, if I'm out looking for a job."

I handed him the application and started toward the door.

"When can you start?" he asked. "Could you start tomorrow morning?"

We went back into the office and talked about the job.

"If you don't mind washing dishes," he said, "I can pay you six dollars an hour." Which I thought was pretty good.

"Seven o'clock tomorrow?" he asked.

"Sounds good," I told him. "I'll see you in the morning."

"Great," he said. And then we shook hands, and he told me, "You can call me Mr. Milt."

I didn't get much sleep that night. I was afraid that I'd be late, because I didn't have a clock, so I rolled the windows down. God, it was cold, and the wind would blow. I kept checking the radio, but none of the stations were on all night, so that didn't really help.

But it didn't matter, because it turned out that I made it. Right on time. I parked at the gym and walked on up to the back of the building where the loading platform was.

Employees only, I thought, and I went on in. Nobody was there. Not in the storeroom, except for Mr. Milt, who was sitting in his office.

"Morning," I said. And I gave him a wave.

He came out with an apron and a little white hat, then he handed them to me and I put them on.

"Out *this* way," he said. He pushed open a pair of swinging doors and we walked on through, out into the cafeteria. There were two huge rooms, one full of tables and the other full of food. Hotcakes, sausage, eggs and fruit.

"You'll be working over here," he said. He took me to a room that was off to the side.

"This is Kolis," Mr. Milt said. "He'll tell you what to do. They'll be coming in soon," he said. Then he turned around and walked back to his office.

I guess I expected a sink and a bottle of detergent. Maybe some towels. I don't know. But it really wasn't like that at all.

The first thing I noticed was a machine that was sitting there, right in the middle of the room. It was like a miniature car wash, but kind of narrow and long, with a conveyer inside. And all of it was automatic, so the dishes went in dirty, but came out clean.

Almost everything was different than I would have pictured. I mean, I *knew* there would be dishes, but not like they were *there*. Hundreds of them. I mean *hundreds*. There were six or seven columns, stacked as high as I could reach. Even higher. All clean and white. And you should have seen them swaying back and forth.

"STACK!" Kolis said. Then he pointed to some plates that I figured had been washed the night before. All clean and empty, shiny and white.

"Worked here long?" I asked. But Kolis didn't answer.

"STACK!" Kolis said. "*Chinese* style."

He was hard to understand, because he talked so damn fast, in this real shrill voice. And he never said a sentence. Just short, choppy words, like a high-pitched, female machine gun. That's what Kingpen told me later. *Berp! Ber, ber, ber, ber, berp!*

The people started coming in, like Mr. Milt had said. Students mostly, but some teachers were there, too. They'd push their trays along the metal bars and pick out anything they wanted. Then they'd go into the other room, to sit and eat their food.

Two dollars, I thought. Because that was what I'd already made and I hadn't done a thing. But to tell you the truth, I really couldn't wait until I got a dish.

Come on... Come on, I thought.

Then this girl finally came up and handed me her tray through the window. Two hotcakes and a sausage. That's what was left.

"Just throw it in the trash?" I asked. But Kolis didn't answer, so I took the plate and banged it in the rubber trash can. That's all I had to do. Then I put the empty plate and the tray onto the rack on the conveyer. I pushed the button in, and it all started moving along.

"Here you are," somebody said. He handed me his plate of eggs. Next was coffee and French toast. There were lots of bowls of oatmeal. It really wasn't bad. Honest to God, I think I almost liked it.

Sensuous. That's what I remember thinking. I had these big black rubber gloves to wipe off the plates, but they were so damn bulky, I pulled them off, put 'em to the side, and started using my bare hands. Sticky, smooth, greasy, and soft. It was pretty amazing what the food felt like. And the funny thing was, if you did it long enough, you could almost do it with your eyes closed and still tell what you had. Scrambled, fried, ham and cheese omelets, or even over easy. *Oatmeal*, I thought. But instead it was grits.

"You stack. I wipe," Kolis told me.

And when I looked back behind me, I couldn't believe it. There were nine or ten columns, five or six feet high, some higher, swaying back and forth.

"*Chinese* style," Kolis said. "You stack *Chinese* style."

And when I asked him what that meant, he pointed to the ceiling.

"High as you can. Then *higher*," he said.

I guess it helped the dishes dry. That's what I remember thinking. But they had all seemed pretty dry to me, when I had taken them off the conveyer.

"*HIGHER!*" Kolis said again.

And then I really stacked 'em up. Not as high as his, but they were up there pretty far.

"What if they fall?" I asked. "Won't we both get *fired?*" But Kolis didn't care, or at least he didn't seem to.

It started slowing down by eleven o'clock, which was a good thing, because we really needed the time. The trays had been piling up in front. But it wasn't that big a deal. Mr. Milt never came out to bug us, and as long as you paced yourself, it all got done.

"Lunch time," Kolis said. And it was for him. But I didn't have the money.

"You go ahead," I said. "I'll meet you in a while."

Kolis reached up and took a plate from the column. He grabbed a tray, hot off the conveyer, and went over to the food.

I washed another load of dishes and went out to the table. Some kind of soup, a ham and cheese sandwich, and lemon meringue pie. That's what Kolis had. There was a lot more to choose from, but that's what he got.

"Chicken noodle?" I asked. But he shook his head.

"Chinese."

And then I figured it was egg drop.

He was a pretty interesting guy, about thirty-six years old. He had traveled the world and seen it all.

"On motorcycle," he said. And he showed me a picture.

"What'll it do?" I asked. "Can you go very fast?"

"*FASTER!*" he told me. And he put the picture back in his wallet.

The place was gearing up for lunch and we got pretty busy scraping the plates and running the conveyer. There were lots of little dishes we hadn't seen at breakfast.

Kolis climbed on a stool and lifted up some plates from one of the stacks that was swaying back and forth.

"Need them in kitchen," he said. *Berp. Ber, ber, berp.* And he went out the dish room door.

I really wish you could have seen it. But even if you had, it was more than that. More than what you saw. Like the smells for instance. Hot, humid smells from the washing machine, when it steamed the breakfast and lunch food off of the plates. Syrup and ketchup and sometimes mayonnaise. Anything that was left, after I wiped the food off of the plates.

Psshtt, and the water would spray.

And even the gloves. You could smell the hot rubber, when Kolis reached into the steam near the back of the machine.

Psshtt... and the water would spray. And everywhere you looked, these high stacks of dishes were swaying back and forth.

The day went pretty fast. Kolis left at three and there wasn't much to do, except for wiping off the tables. But boy, I was hungry. Just watching all that food that I'd have to throw in the can.

"Here," somebody said. And she passed me a tray with a soda and part of a sandwich, and a half a bowl of soup.

I got off at four, and then another guy came on. Jeffrey Margolis, from downtown New York.

"Started last night," he said. "But I'll be leaving pretty soon. The work is picking up."

He looked in the dish room, and I could tell by his face that nobody had shown him how to do the dishes.

"What's *that*?" he asked, pointing to the stacks swaying back and forth.

"Chinese style," I said.

And I told him how to do it. "High as you can. Then higher."

"Did Kolis tell you that?" he asked.

I nodded my head then I hung up my apron and took off my hat. There was a long, long pause and then Margolis looked away.

"You know he's retarded…" he said.

I left after that, but stopped in the office to say goodbye to Mr. Milt.

"Get something to eat?" he asked. But I told him I had forgotten my money.

"I'll make sure and remember tomorrow," I said, with a laugh.

And that's when he told me.

"Employees eat free," he said. "As long as it's your shift. For example, you couldn't eat dinner tonight, but breakfast and lunch would have been all right."

Of course it had all been put away by then. The ham and cheese sandwiches. Pizza and soup. Olives and French fries.

"How did it go?" he asked. "Was everything OK?"

"Went great," I said. "I'll see you tomorrow."

I went out the back, climbed down from the loading platform and walked past the dumpster.

Employees eat free, I thought. And that's when I first thought I might be coming back! I had been down, but not out. Down to mandarin oranges, ravioli in meat sauce and a half a tank of gas, but I was still in the game. *Deal 'em,* I thought. Yeah, that's what I remember thinking.

I was down by the gym and I was going to go in. Maybe take a shower, or shoot some hoops.

"Hey, Jess," somebody yelled. "Can you come over here and help me?"

He was sitting on the trunk of the Buick, with his sleeping bag, tent, and suitcase. And his shoes were off. I remember that.

"Jesse," he called out. "I can't stand up. I need some help."

He had taken off his socks by the time I got there, and everyplace I looked, I saw blisters. Big, silver-dollar sized ones.

"I can't stand up," he said again.

"What happened?" I asked.

"I couldn't get a ride. I walked twenty-five miles. Maybe more."

I helped him into the Buick and looked at his feet.

"Maybe we can pop them," I said. "The blisters." But we couldn't find a pin.

"I found a new place to sleep, though," I said. "I'll show it to you later, but first let's get some food."

Kingpen got out his wallet and handed me two hundreds. "Let's go up to the snack room," I said. And I drove us to the Center. But Kingpen couldn't walk.

"I'll get you a burger," I said.

But I couldn't. They didn't have the change.

We didn't do much after that. We went to the pull-off and I told him about the job. Then we ate a couple of the cans of ravioli and split a can of corn.

"Maybe you can work there," I said, "if Margolis doesn't stay. The pay is pretty good and it's all the burgers you can eat."

Kingpen found his alarm clock at the bottom of his suitcase. A magnetic one that you could stick to metal, so we stuck it on the dashboard right under the mirror.

"Eleven-o-three. Back East time," Kingpen said. And he turned the hands back five hours.

It was six-fifteen when we settled in the bags. We talked another couple hours, until it started getting dark. I wasn't even tired. Kingpen was, but I wasn't. I was more excited.

"Wait until you see it," I said. "All the food." But I know he never heard me, because he was already asleep.

And then I leaned my head back on the armrest and started staring at the sky. I started seeing 'em real faintly at first. Little glows and distant reflections. I wish you could have seen them. Brilliant flashes and splashes of color, all across the sky. God, it was something. And that's when I knew.

Fitch, my man, you are coming BACK!

Chapter 15

The alarm went off at six. I pushed the button in and turned the key.

"Gotta go," I said. And the Buick started up.

I drove us to the gym, climbed out of the sleeping bag, and opened the door.

"I'm going to take a shower," I said. "I'll leave you the keys. Do you think you can drive?"

"Maybe with my shoes off," Kingpen said. "I'll wear two pairs of socks."

The gym doors were open. But I never took a shower. I heard this sharp metallic sound in the basketball court, on my way to the pool, then I looked in to see what it was.

"FOIL!" somebody yelled. And then, *CLANG! CLANG! CLANG!*

There were a couple of fencers really going at it. They had the helmets with cages and foam covered pads, and the long skinny swords with the little plastic tips. Six in the morning, and *CLANG! CLANG! CLANG!*

I left before seven and walked to the Commons. Kolis was there doing pushups in the dish room.

"For the Olympics," he said. "I do them *Chinese* style." And then he did one more.

I put on the apron, stuck on the hat and put on the gloves.

"I'll take these to the kitchen," I said. And then I lifted down some clean plates from a column that was swaying back and forth.

It was really pretty sad. And you couldn't tell him any different.

"How would you ever get there," I asked him. "To the Olympics? And what about your job?"

But Kolis didn't care.

We didn't get very busy until lunchtime that day. It was always like that on Sundays. That's what Kolis said. But lunchtime was a bitch. Lasagna and salad and all kinds of Jello in little glass cups.

"FASTEST!" Kolis yelled. And he punched the third button at the front of the conveyer, the one that really made it move.

Berp. Ber, ber, ber, ber, berp!

"*Chinese* style!" he yelled. And after he hit that third button, we really busted ass. *Worked and worked and worked.* But let me tell you, by the time I walked away that day, I was so damn full, I could hardly move my feet. Hotcakes and French toast, sausage and biscuits, big plates of lasagna.

"You eat this way at home?" Kolis asked. But I couldn't remember. It was so long ago.

"Gotta eat *right* to go to Olympics," Kolis said. And he went into the dish room and started doing jumping jacks.

I stopped in the office on the way out the door and got an application for Kingpen.

"Worked with me on the Music Boxes," I said. And Mr. Milt nodded his head.

"Do you think he could start tomorrow?"

"I'll ask him," I said.

Kingpen was waiting outside. I got in the Buick and gave him the application.

"You can start tomorrow," I said. "If you think that you can walk. But you have to stand a lot. Whaddya think?"

"Gimmee a pencil," Kingpen said. So I reached back and found one in all the junk on the floor.

We drove to McDonald's that night. I went in and got Kingpen a burger, but I couldn't eat I was so darn full. Waffles and fruit and three kinds of soup, ham and cheese sandwiches.

"Wait until you see it," I said.

Kingpen reached in his pocket, pulled out his wallet and got a piece of paper, a small, little scrap he had written something on.

"Want to go to a party?" he asked. And then he told me about this guy he had met at the Center.

"He cashed one of the hundreds for me," Kingpen said. "This is where he lives." He handed me the piece of paper.

It wasn't a house. Not even an apartment. Just a room in Stevens Hall.

"It's a dorm," Kingpen said. "It's right near where you work."

And after he described it, I knew just where he meant.

"It's a party for one of his friends who's coming back to town," Kingpen said. "He told me you could come. It's this Friday night."

And that's when I told him, "Maybe it would do us good to meet some people. Sounds good to me."

Kingpen finished his burger and it was only five o'clock, so we drove around. Down past the Sears place and to a military base at the end of Airport Road.

"Fort Wainwright," Kingpen said. We pulled up to the guardhouse, but nobody was there, so we drove on to the grounds and took a look around. Acres and acres of military housing. An airfield with planes.

"Let's go," Kingpen said. "Maybe we'd better leave." So I turned the car around. We went back past the guardhouse and started off down Airport Road. That's when I remembered and reached into my pocket.

"Look," I said. It was the paper I had brought with the address of the son of a friend of my mother. "I thought it sounded familiar. Airport Road. He must live near here."

But when we finally found it, we figured he didn't. Even though I think he must have, now that I look back. *The Christ Church Homeless Shelter.* That's what the little homemade wooden sign said. So we kept on driving.

We stayed on Airport Road and because of the name, you had to know it went out to the airport. Six or seven more miles and we could see the planes. Big cargo carriers sitting on the runway.

We parked the car and then we started walking toward the building.

"Feet are feeling better," Kingpen said. We walked a little farther and when we went inside the airport, the very first thing we saw was a bear. You couldn't really miss it. Five or six feet high, he was standing in a box made of Plexiglas, or plastic, and his lips were pulled back so that you could see his teeth.

"Look," Kingpen said. And all throughout the lobby there were wolves and moose and lots of kinds of birds.

"Five Mile, Dietrich, Prospect Creek," a girl announced on the intercom. "Meet at the Alyeska counter."

It was a pretty busy place, for as small as it was. And a lot was going on. People moving back and forth with duffel bags and steamer trunks.

"Look at those guys," Kingpen said.

And when I looked, I could see these guys getting off a plane. Glassy-eyed and all spaced out. "Like zombies," that's what Kingpen said.

We drove back past the gym and parked near the Commons.

"That's him," I said. "The guy who works at night." He was reaching in the dumpster and taking out a bag.

I told Kingpen about Kolis and the dishes and how to wipe the tables, how to stack the trays and fill out the time cards.

"We can really make some money," Kingpen said. "If we only work a month, together we can put away twelve hundred bucks. Maybe more, if we keep living in the car. Then we could really start to travel. Maybe take a floatplane to a lake out in the Bush, or see the Arctic Ocean on one of those tours."

"It's a beginning," I said. "At least we won't go hungry."

And with that, I started the Buick, drove it off the lot, and took us back to the pull-off where we lived.

The alarm went off at six, as usual, and we went right up to the school.

"You can show him what to do," Mr. Milt told me. He took Kingpen's application and handed him an apron.

"Is it everything I said, or what?" I asked.

"Better," Kingpen answered. And we sat there eating bacon, eggs and sausage, and drinking orange juice.

"I only wish Beamish could have seen all this," I said. "Things have really turned around. No more just getting by and always feeling hungry."

"And I think it's getting warmer, too," Kingpen said.

We were the only ones who worked that day. Kolis didn't show up and Margolis had quit.

"And the other guy's not coming in tonight." That's what Mr. Milt said. "Do you think you two can work until nine tonight?"

"Sure," we said. "No problem."

So that was what we did. For fourteen hours we worked and worked and worked. Especially at dinner, when we really got backed up. We made it, though. And it was just like Kingpen said. You couldn't quite believe it. Eight hours at six dollars. And six hours at nine.

"We're really pulling it in," Kingpen told me.

By the end of the night, we had made over a hundred bucks apiece. Not to mention all that we could eat. And just for washing dishes.

141

We thought that we had lost the paper, but we found it in the glove box, along with some bullets Beamish left behind.

"Room Two-o-seven," Kingpen said. We walked into the dorm and started up the stairs.

It was a typical room for people to live in while they were going to college. There was a bed on each side of the room and a couple of desks, a couple of closets and a little TV. Six or seven people were there, sitting on the floor or up on the beds.

"Here," Kingpen said. And he handed the guy who invited us a bottle we had picked up downtown.

"Thanks," he told us. "Help yourself." And he gave us back the bottle with some red plastic cups.

"Who's the party for?" I asked.

"Brian Rockett," somebody said. "He's flying in at ten."

"Well here's to Brian," I said. I filled up my cup, raised it to the ceiling and tossed it down. "Here's to *him*," I said again and then I poured myself another drink. And the thing that I kept thinking was I was sitting there feeling warm, with a stomach full of all kinds of food, and money in my pocket. *And I'm even off tomorrow.* That's what I remember thinking.

"Here's to *you*, Fitch," I said. Except not all that loud. Then I poured myself another drink and drank it down.

It was getting near eleven and things weren't making sense. There was a ball game on TV, and I knew that I had seen it.

"Watch *this*," I said. And right after I'd said it, the pitcher threw the ball and knocked the batter to the ground. "Knocked out!" I said. And sure enough, within another minute, they brought a stretcher out and hauled him outta there.

"I'll bet five hundred bucks, I know who wins this game," I said. "I'll even give the score."

"Boston over Philly, eight to two," somebody said. And they started to laugh. "It's all shipped in. Everything we see. It's all on tapes. About a three-week delay. Even the news."

It was sometime after midnight when Rockett finally came. But nobody noticed at first, they were all too drunk.

"Oh, bullshit!" this guy kept saying, that I was talking to. "Bull *shit*! Bull *shit*!"

But I knew that I was right. "Just *watch* it," I said again. "Keep watching."

There was a picture on the wall that was swinging back and forth. Not all the time, but when it did, you couldn't miss it. "Just watch," I said. And then all at once, it jumped off the nail and crashed to the floor.

"Now was *that* bull *shit*?" I asked. "Did you see *that*? Whaddya think *NOW*?" But nobody heard me. They were looking at a piece of paper being passed around the room.

"Rockett's paycheck." That's what Kingpen said. So I gave it a glance and passed it on.

"I can't believe you *quit*," somebody said. "Making that kind of money and you left after a week? You've gotta be nuts!"

"Well why don't *you* try washing walls for thirteen, fourteen hours a day, seven days a week - and see how long you last?" Rockett asked him. "Especially up *there*."

"Where's that?" Kingpen asked. And Rockett told him.

"Prudhoe Bay. Where have *you* been?"

"Well maybe you could get a job with us, washing dishes," I said. "We could sure use the help, and the money's great."

"Did you see how much he was making?" somebody asked.

And I told them about four hundred and fifty a week. Which was a little more than I was making with the overtime.

"That's *TAXES*," the guy said. And he passed the check around so I could take another look.

"Twelve hundred and thirty five take-home," somebody said. "Plus all you can eat. And we're talking the good stuff... steak, lobster, prime rib and king crab. Isn't that right, Rockett?"

"*Screw* it. I don't need it *that* bad," Rockett said. And then he grabbed the check out of my hand and left his party.

We didn't stay long after that. But we did stay long enough to hear about this Pipeline they were building through the state. The Trans-Alaska Pipeline. Six hundred miles long, from a place called Prudhoe Bay to an ice- free port, that was spelled Valdez, but pronounced "Valdeez."

"Five or six unions working on the project," the guy who had invited us to the party said. "And all of them are full, except maybe the Laborers. That's what Rockett's in. But even then, you have to sign up on the list and by the time they let you in, the project will be over. No use even trying." I nodded my head.

Anyway, we left right after that. And the funny thing was, when we went outside, there were all these flashing lights from the fire

143

trucks and police cars that were there. Flashing lights and hundreds of students standing around.

"What happened?" I asked a girl standing near me.

"Earthquake," she said. "Didn't you *feel* it?"

We stood around for a little while and then we went back to the Buick. We took it to the pull-off and tried to go to sleep, but my mind wouldn't stop and I couldn't turn it off.

"Hey Kingpen," I said. "You still awake?"

"You thinking what I'm thinking?" he asked.

And as tired or screwed up as we were that night, the two of us both knew. First thing Monday morning, we were gonna sign up on that list.

Chapter 16

Kingpen found it in the telephone book. Alaska Laborers Union Local 942. It was next to this little grocery store we had been to downtown. It was closed on Sunday, but we went down there anyway, just to see what it was like.

There was a big plate glass window and we could see inside to a large, open room with a counter and a metal screen.

"We'll come down here tomorrow," I said. "Instead of eating lunch. We can see what's going on."

"This Pipeline we're hearing about must be the project the Sears guy went up to work on," Kingpen said. "The one who took his mechanics."

And when you thought about it all, a lot of things made sense that we hadn't understood before. Especially the bumper stickers. Like, *Let the Bastards Freeze in the Dark*, and, *Alaska For Alaskans – Yankees Go Home*.

"Come on," I said. "We'll drive back down tomorrow."

We didn't do a lot that day. Went back to the snack room and got something to eat, sat around and watched TV. But I had seen the shows, and even if I hadn't, I couldn't concentrate - not on that.

"Twelve hundred dollars a week," Kingpen said. "Just for washing walls."

"And that's *take-home*," I said. "Plus all we can eat."

We got up the next morning and drove to the Commons. Kolis was there in a red and white sweat suit and brand new tennis shoes. Stacks of dishes were swaying all around.

"What do you know about this Pipeline?" I asked him.

"Have one in China," he told me. "Long as this one. Then longer," he added.

We were going to leave at one-thirty, then changed it to ten, but we left at eight-thirty instead.

"We'll be back in an hour," I said. "We'll work through lunch." But Kolis didn't care.

"Come on, Kingpen," I said. "We gotta go."

Kingpen and I got in the Buick and headed down the road.

"Do you think it's open yet?" I asked. And it turned out that it was. It opened at eight and there were close to a hundred people milling around, filling out papers, and talking to each other.

According to the paperwork they gave us, there were five different lists you could join for the Union, and they were called A through E. To get on the A list, you had to have worked at least eight hundred hours out of the Laborer's Union, which I didn't really understand, but Kingpen thought he did.

"In other words, you can't *start* there," he told me. "Or the B list for that matter," he said. And when I looked at what we needed to get on the B list, I saw what he meant.

"Two hundred hours working out of the Union. That leaves us out, too."

So we looked for the C list qualifications and they didn't look all that great either.

"Must have proof of having worked in the construction trade for two full years," Kingpen read.

So we went on to read about the D list.

"Alaskan resident," it said. And we weren't really sure what we needed for that, but from all that we read, we *knew* we could get on the E list. Because that was what it said: *Everybody else.*

"That's us," Kingpen said. "Everybody else."

We walked around the room. On one of the walls, there was a map of the state, with a long, thin line that ran down through it, with the names of all of the construction camps.

"Look," Kingpen said. And he pointed to some of these little dots on the line that said Happy Valley, Dietrich, and Prospect Creek. "Look," he said again. And up there at the top was Prudhoe Bay.

The Union called out the jobs at nine-thirty each morning for the people on the A and then the B list. And depending on your number and what list you were on, you had a choice of the jobs that were called out. And then any jobs that were left over were called out at one-thirty that afternoon, for the C and then D, and then E list. Then after you took a job, your name came off the list, until you got laid off or quit. And then it was put at the bottom of whatever list they figured it should be on then. The point being, you had to work your way up to the A list.

"Over twenty thousand names on the E list," somebody said. "And I've never seen anybody get off of it yet."

"The D list either," somebody else said. That's how bad it was.

"Hopeless." That's what Kingpen called it.

"We'd better get going, or we won't even have the jobs we have now," he told me. So that was when we left.

We got in the Buick, took Cushman past 2nd and 1st Avenues, and then I punched down on the pedal and we flew up College Road.

"Let's go in the front way," I said, "so we don't have to pass Mr. Milt."

But the girl wouldn't let us through.

"You don't have a student ID," she said.

So we went around the back, past the dumpster and then up and over the loading platform.

"Hey, Jess!" Mr. Milt roared. He was back in his office behind some gallons of fruit. "You two gonna work till nine tonight? I really need the help."

"Yeah, sure," I said. We pushed through the swinging doors, into the dish room, and started unstacking the plates.

We had to work our asses off that day. Kolis left early and the guy who worked at night didn't do a damn thing, except bag up people's half eaten steaks. *Meat Man.* That's what we called him. He'd bag 'em up, hide it all in the dumpster, then climb in later and get it all out.

"Maybe he has dogs," I said. But we didn't think he did.

"Makes you want to vomit," Kingpen said.

And then for some reason, all at once it hit me.

"Didn't you work for a construction company back east?" I asked. "Isn't that what you told me?"

Kingpen dropped a plate and it shattered on the floor.

"Isn't it?" I asked.

Kingpen nodded and reached for a broom.

"Suppose we got a letterhead," I asked. "On a blank piece of paper. You've gotta know *somebody*. How long were you there?"

Kingpen stared down at the floor, at the pieces of dish and looked to be thinking a minute.

"Six months," he said.

"Well?"

"Well what?"

147

"We could write our own letters," I said. "To get on the C list. Whaddya think?"

Kingpen squinched his eyes and nodded his head. "We could try it," he said. "But what if we get caught?"

"So what if we do?" I asked. "We'll just drive away. Whaddya think?"

"Well, maybe," he told me. "I could call this guy named Barry Moran. He works in the office. Maybe he would do it."

"Well, go call him," I said. And I took the broom.

Kingpen was gone awhile. He went to the gym and used a phone down there. Fifteen or twenty minutes, and then I let him back inside.

"He didn't sound too happy," Kingpen said. "I forgot about the time. It was one in the morning back there. I think I woke him up."

"Well, what did he say?" I asked. "Is he gonna do it?"

"He told me he'd try," Kingpen said. "I asked him to send anything he could to the post office downtown, General Delivery. We can check down there in a few days."

I hung up my apron and we started out of the dish room, past all the tables, through the swinging doors, on into the storage room.

"Shouldn't forget the lights," Kingpen said. He reached back behind me and turned off the switch. "I guess we're in charge now." And it sounded so simple, but it still felt pretty neat to be the only ones there in the whole damn building.

"Don't forget to lock it," I said.

We walked out the door and Kingpen pulled it shut. Then he checked it and checked it again.

We were both pretty beat.

"Come on," I said. "Let's go home."

We got in the Buick and went down College Road, drove in to the pull-off, and I turned the engine off.

"Wanna sleep in the back?" I asked.

"No. You go ahead," he told me.

So I climbed over the seat and got down in the bag.

"Must be warming up," I said, because the smell of the beer and the dog food in the carpet on the floor was stronger than before.

"Won't be long," Kingpen told me. "Breakup will be here soon."

And then I remember looking out the window. Ice and snow, everywhere I looked, except on College Road. And the only reason that I ever thought it would all turn green was from the pictures that Kingpen had shown me, in his books and magazines.

Chapter 17

It was the last week in April or the first week in May when both of us got paid. I got two hundred and sixty-three dollars and seventy-four cents, and I would have gotten more, but I had only worked four days. I had started on a Tuesday.

"First check," Kingpen said. And he held it in the air before he stuffed it in his pocket and went back to the dishes.

"Maybe you can cash them," I said. "When you go to check the mail. Think it'll come today?"

"Maybe," Kingpen said.

It had been nine days and every single day, Kingpen had taken the car and gone downtown.

"Nothin'," he'd say, when he got back to the dish room. "*Nothin', nothin', nothin'.*" Nine days in a row. And it was the same thing that day, when he got back after lunch.

"Nothin'," Kingpen said.

We were working longer hours, starting at six and working till seven, eight, or even nine o'clock at night.

"Working this weekend?" Mr. Milt asked. "I could really use the help."

And I knew he really could. Because nobody was left, except for me and Kingpen and sometimes Kolis, who let us know he wouldn't always be there. 'Cause he was exercising.

"*Chinese* style," he said. "Then more."

"The Olympics aren't even until next year," Kingpen told him once. But Kolis didn't care.

We worked all through the weekend. Twenty-seven hours total, Saturday and Sunday. Twenty-seven hours, scraping the plates and steaming off the trays.

"How many plates you think are in this room?" Kingpen asked one night. And there must have been two thousand, maybe more. "Wanna count 'em?" he asked. But I was too damn tired, so instead we decided to take a picture.

Kingpen got his camera from the Buick and then we started stacking up the plates, as high as they would go.

"*Chinese style*," Kingpen said. And then we started laughing and stacked 'em even higher, on up near the ceiling till we were sure that they would fall. Six or seven stacks, swaying back and forth. And then we laid out all the trays in different kinds of patterns.

"Let's put on the gloves," one of us said. Then we got on the aprons and put on the hats.

It was ten or ten-thirty by then. Sunday night and nobody was there.

"It'll take about five seconds," Kingpen said. And he punched the little button and the timer went on.

Bzzzz. . . Cuh-LICK!

"That's it," Kingpen said.

And it turned out great. Even better than we would have thought, because the lights in the dish room gave off a strange, eerie glow. We couldn't see it at the time, but it turned up later in the picture.

We were going to leave, but it was like Kingpen said, "Suppose we have another earthquake and the dishes come down? Better unstack 'em," he said.

So we must have spent at least another half an hour there, taking down the plates. God, I was tired.

We finally shut the lights off, went through the building, and locked the doors. Then we got in the Buick and headed to the hundred square feet of asphalt we called home.

"You'd think somebody else's car or truck would be here one of these times," Kingpen said. But nobody's ever was.

Kingpen set the clock and I thought that we had hardly shut our eyes when we heard, *BRNNG! BRNGG! BRNGG!*

"Come on," Kingpen said. "We've gotta go."

He started the Buick and we drove to the Commons. We went in the *Employees Only* entrance, walked through the building, and went back to the dish room.

"Feels like I never left," I said. And in a way, I never had.

"Look," Kingpen said. And he pointed to the apron I still had on, from the night before.

"How about tonight?" Mr. Milt asked. "Think you guys can work? I could really use the help."

"Well, what about some students?" I asked. "Don't *they* want a job?"

"Not during exams," he said. He threw up his arms and walked out of the room, back to his office near the gallon cans of food.

"How about something to eat?" I said. So I got us some fruit cocktail and we sat there a minute. Then the people started coming in. Not many at first, but they always ate a lot. The early people did. Ate a lot and used a lot of dishes. Little cups and saucers and cereal bowls.

Kolis never showed up. Then the breakfast turned to lunch and we never had a break. Bacon and eggs and then suddenly soup bowls, hot dogs and half-eaten sandwiches.

There was a counter in the front, where the people put their trays, then we'd pull 'em into the dish room. But they kept on piling up.

"Here," somebody said. And he tried to lift his tray up over the pile.

"Just put it on the floor," I told him.

Then everybody did. Trays, dishes, salad bowls and glasses, all piling up on the floor in front of the counter. I mean, we really got swamped. I was sure that Mr. Milt would come in to complain, but he never did.

"Too embarrassed to see how hard we have to work." That's what Kingpen said. And I think it got to one point where every dish we had was there on the counter or out on the floor.

"Hit the third button," Kingpen said. But even then, we couldn't do it.

"We'll never catch up," one of us said. So we gave up trying and decided to eat.

We got a couple of plates and washed them off, and then went in and got some food. But we couldn't relax, because all of the time the trays were piling up. Trays and dishes and forks and spoons - nobody cared.

"Suppose somebody touches that pile on the counter?" I asked. "And it all comes crashing down. Then what'll we do?"

"We could always drive away," Kingpen said.

We looked at each other and started to howl. Laughed so hard, I thought we would get sick.

"Screw it," I said. "I'm gonna get a sandwich. You wanna piece of pie?"

"Lemon meringue," Kingpen told me. "*Chinese style*." So then, I knew he wanted two.

We finally got the dishes cleared. It was some time after four and we were wiping off the tables, waiting for the supper crowd.

"I'm going to check the mail," Kingpen said. He picked up an apple to eat on the way. "I'll see you in a while," he said. And I nodded my head.

Boy, I was tired. And it would only get worse. I could tell from the menu. Veal parmegian. Mashed potatoes and gravy. Macaroni and cheese. All this sticky stuff. You'd wipe and you'd scrape and you'd finally give up and put the plate on the conveyer, and only hope the steam would melt off whatever was still there.

Mr. Milt had gone home, but another guy was there. Leonard Pratt, *Night Manager*. That's what Mr. Milt said he was. But he never did a thing. I think he was a student, majoring in business. Sometimes he would stop back in the dish room, maybe once or twice a night, and check things out. But he always left by seven.

"How's it going?" he asked. And after he asked, I'm sure he wished he hadn't.

"Up to our asses in dishes," I told him. But by that time, they were clean. All stacked up and ready for supper.

"We were here till nine last night," I said. "Wiping the tables and cleaning the plates. What are the chances of us getting a raise?"

He thought for a minute and started scratching his head. "I can't give you more money," he said. "We're only allowed by the company to give a certain dollar per hour amount per employee. But how about more hours?"

"More hours?"

"Yeah," he said. "Anything after seven, just double your hours. If you work until eight, just put down nine."

"And if we work until nine, we put down eleven?"

"That's it," he said. "Is that all right with you?" And I told him it was.

Leonard went back to the office. I punched the first button and the conveyer started up. The three or four dishes that were left on the rack went through the machine and came out through the steam. Dry and white and squeaky clean.

"Got it," somebody said. And when I looked at the doorway, Kingpen was there with a large manila envelope. "Came in the mail," Kingpen said, holding it up.

He got a steak knife from the counter, slit the envelope open, and pulled out some papers. There was a note from his friend and a couple of pieces of stationery, with the company's name on top.

"Let me see the note," I said. And before he could stop me, I took it from his hand.

"Dear Nanuk," it said. "How is it up there? Shoot any bears yet? We've had two timekeepers since you left and the second one just quit. Here are some papers. I didn't understand exactly what you wanted, but I hope these are OK. Stay warm, Barry . . . P.S. What is the fishing like? I hear it's pretty good. Barry."

There were two tan-colored pieces of paper. Completely blank, except for some words at the top of each page: *Zimmerelli Contractors, since 1941.* And then there was a little symbol of an eagle with a shovel.

"What do you think?" Kingpen asked. "Do you think these are OK?"

"They're great," I said. "But we can't mess them up. We've gotta do it right. Every single word."

"I'll put them in the Buick, on the dashboard," Kingpen said, "till we know what to do."

"We can type them tonight," I said. "If the library's open."

Kingpen walked away and I tried to do some dishes, but all I kept thinking about was typing those letters. *We could get a manual,* I thought. *One that shows you how to type business letters, references and resumes. An instruction booklet. That was what we needed.*

We worked till eight that night.

"Put down nine," I said. And I told Kingpen about the raise.

"Double time and a half," he said. And then we went out through the store room, turned out the lights, locked the doors behind us, and started looking for the library.

Kingpen saw it first. Or at least he knew what it was. Big, plate-glass windows and slabs of marble. "That's it," Kingpen said. And then we started up some steps and went through a set of doors. "Another arctic entrance," Kingpen said, then we went through another set of doors. Kingpen had been right. *The Rasmussen Library.* That's what the sign said.

Kingpen had forgotten the papers, so he went back to the car, while I looked around. There were plenty of books, but nothing you would read. Research stuff mostly.

"May I help you?" somebody asked. I looked back behind me and a girl was standing there. Eighteen or nineteen, with a real pretty face, big brown eyes and long brown hair.

"I need to write a reference letter," I said. "But I'm not sure what to write. I need to know the *style*."

She wrote down a number on a little piece of paper, handed it to me and pointed toward the stairs. "Try downstairs," she said. "I think it's in the basement."

Kingpen came back and we started down the steps.

"Look at that," he said. There were dozens of paintings, hanging on the wall next to the stairs. "Bush pilots," Kingpen said. There was Joe Crosson, Harold Gillam, and of course Noel Wien. A painting of Russel Merrill, Eielson, and a guy named Ellis.

We went down to the basement and sure enough, we found a book. *The Art of Writing a Resume.*

"Just what we need," I said.

Kingpen had a pencil. Then we got some paper towels from a bathroom dispenser and wrote down the style. Just like in the book. It even gave examples.

"To whom it may concern," one said. And they followed that with a paragraph about a guy who had been a clerk and was looking for a job. "Mature, efficient and works well with others."

"We can use that sentence in our letters," I said. And Kingpen nodded his head.

We found a typing room after that. All the way in the back on the fourth floor. *Thursday night and we were there.* I wrote the letters out by hand at first. On the brown paper towels we had gotten from the bathroom.

"Just make me a general helper," Kingpen said. So I wrote that he had worked at Zimmerelli Contractors for two and a half years. *General work*, I wrote. *Hard worker. Always on time.*

"I'll make myself a laborer," I said, and wrote something down that I thought would be OK. Then came the hard part.

"Ever typed?" I asked. But Kingpen shook his head.

"Neither have I," I said. "Not very much."

I turned the paper in the roller until the eagle was on top. Then I sat there awhile, looking at the book.

"Well, here goes," I said. And I pushed down on a button.

We were there a long time after that. Looking at the paper towels and staring at the book and punching at the buttons, one by one. But we did it. Kingpen looked at his and then read mine.

To whom it may concern. This is to acknowledge that Jesse Fitch has worked as a laborer for our company, Zimmerelli Contractors, for the past three years. He is mature, efficient and works well with others. John Zimmerelli

Kingpen held the letters up and you could see them shaking in his hands.

"These really look good," Kingpen told me. But I told him he was wrong. They were better than that.

"They're *DAMN* good," I said. That's what I remember saying.

The alarm went off at five, but we had been awake for a while looking at the letters and planning what to do.

"If Kolis comes in, we can go down at eight," I said. "We can turn in the letters and get on the list."

"Twelve hundred a week," Kingpen went on. And he started the car.

We drove around, then went up to the dish room, got some breakfast and started the conveyer.

"Go to Olympics in two weeks," Kolis said. And I nodded my head.

We left the dish room at eight-fifteen and by the time that we got to the Union Hall, a crowd was in the room. Most mixed-up group of people I think I'd ever seen. Seventy-five or a hundred of them, mostly in a line, but a few were sitting in metal, folding chairs that were set around the room. Old people, young people and people in between. In all kinds of clothes, from tattered rags to business suits. Men and women. Even kids were there, standing with their parents. Whole families.

"Get on this sonovabitch, and we'll be rich," somebody said.

"Just like the Gold Rush," another guy said. "We'll have so much money..."

And that's how they kept talking. Everywhere you listened.

"We'll be eating lobster and burning hundred-dollar bills," this one guy told his buddy. "We'll have so much money..."

"You go first," Kingpen said. So I got in the line, Kingpen got behind me, and we stood there for about forty-five minutes, moving along, up toward the window.

"They're gonna close down," somebody said. "It's almost nine-thirty. Time for the A list call."

But they didn't close down. At least not until they finished with us.

"NEXT!" the guy yelled. He was the guy at the window, looking at the letters, and talking to the people.

"Come on," he said. "Let's *go*. Let's *GO!*"

There was one person left between me and the window. About forty years old, he looked like a teacher.

"I've gotta have a *letterhead*," the union man said. "You could have written this yourself."

"But they went out of business," the man told him. "I *can't* get one. I've tried," he said. "I sold everything to get here. Now what?" he asked.

"I can put you on the E list," the Union guy said. "That's the best I can do. Number twenty-two thousand, one hundred and six."

The man who looked like a teacher signed a piece of paper, handed out ten dollars, and started to cry. That's what I remember. Walked to a chair and just sat down and cried.

"Sold everything I owned," he said out loud. "Everything…"

"NEXT!"

I handed him my letter and just for a minute, I really felt sick. Suppose he asked me for a number? Suppose he said, "I'm gonna call back east and check this out." Suppose he said *THIS*? Suppose he said *THAT*? And then I started thinking about perjury and forgery. Ten to twenty years.

"C list. Forty-nine eighteen," he said. "How much you wanna pay? It's ten dollars a month."

I gave him twenty dollars. I signed a piece of paper and he gave me a receipt. *Paid through June*. That's what it said. That, and then it had my number, *C List 4918*. There was a lot of little typing that told about the Union, but the main thing was, you weren't really in it until you got a job. You were on the waiting list until then. That's what the money was for. Ten dollars a month to hold your spot.

Kingpen went next. Forty-nine nineteen.

"You two work together?" the man asked. But he didn't want an answer.

"That's it!" he announced. "No more for today."

Kingpen signed the paper and gave him twenty dollars. We started to leave, but decided to stay. The line broke up and the people drifted out, then some other ones came in to listen for the jobs.

"People on the A list and B list." That's what Kingpen said. And when you looked at them, somehow they were different. Like the ones at the airport we had seen the week before. Weathered. Spacey. Set apart.

"Listen," Kingpen said. And we stood there with the crowd and you would have thought they made it up, the stories that we heard. *Grizzlies, caribou and wolves.* Eighteen-hour work days and hundred-dollar bills.

The metal screen went up and the people settled down. Then a guy with a microphone came to the window and started reading off the jobs.

"Prudhoe Bay – nineteen general laborers . . . Happy Valley – seventeen." Franklin Bluffs. Chandalar. And on and on it went.

"Anybody under a hundred on the A list?" the guy called out. And three men went up. Eighty-three and forty-seven, the first two said. But the third guy got first choice.

"Twenty-seven," he said. And what that meant was his number. The first twenty-six people weren't there, or they didn't want the job. The main thing was, this guy got his pick.

"Prudhoe," he said. And the way that he said it, you could tell that he had been up there before. He signed a piece of paper, got his dispatch slip and walked out of the Hall.

"We'd better go," I said. I pictured the dishes stacked up Chinese style, swaying in the dish room. As high as they could sway and then higher. "Come on," I said again. We got out to the Buick, shot up College Road, parked in the back and went in past the dumpster.

We really had to push it in the dish room after that. Kolis had gone and we were trying to catch up.

"We'll get it," Kingpen said. And we almost did. But then at quarter after one, we went back again. Back to the Hall for the C list call.

"Come on," Kingpen said. "We've gotta go." And then he pushed in the button that shut off the conveyer, we snuck out the front way, went around to the back, got in the Buick, and shot back down College Road.

It was a lot more crowded than the last time we were there. Hundreds of people. We barely got in. We did though. We stood in the back by the soda machines, along with some people who were sitting on the floor.

"Burnouts." That's what Kingpen said later. They were sharing a doughnut and drinking from a canteen.

"The calls are picking up," somebody said. "They're gearing up for summer."

And then the screen went up and the dispatch man who had been there that morning spoke into the mike. "No calls today," he said. And almost as a group, the crowd let out a moan.

"Damn," somebody muttered.

But then, "Tomorrow," someone else said. "I know we'll go tomorrow."

And then the screen came down and we all walked out together. C-listers, D-listers and people on the E list. The most mixed-up group of people I think I'd ever seen. Young people, old people and people in between. All walking out, holding onto the dream.

Get on this sonovabitch, and we'll be rich. You could see it in their eyes.

And all we had to do was be there.

Chapter 18

They say Alaska has two seasons. Winter and summer. And it's supposed to be a joke, but in a way, it's true. It was the first week of June and spring came all at once. The snow melted, the birds came flying in, the rivers broke, and even the tripod went out with the ice, tripped the clock and somebody won a little over $130,000. But it wasn't us.

But the thing I remember most was the trash. All along the roads. In the ditches and the gullies. Everywhere the snow had been. All this trash, lying there, until hundreds of people went out and picked it all up. "Spring cleaning." That was what they called it. And everyone pitched in. Boy Scouts, students, people from the churches and regular people.

And by the end of the week, summer had come. Longer days with lots of sunshine.

"I wish Beamish could have seen this," I said. "He would never believe it."

Rolling hills covered with green for as far as you could see. People wearing shorts. But the funny thing was, if I hadn't been there a couple of weeks before, I couldn't have imagined the winter with the ice and all the snow.

It was like Kingpen said. "When the rain is pouring down, you can never picture sunshine, and when the sun is out, you have trouble picturing the rain."

But geez, it was nice. Flowers. That's what I remember. Especially the ones up at the University. One day there weren't any and then the next day, there were hundreds. Even thousands. All in bloom, all over the place. And you'd swear they hadn't been there just the day before.

"It's the daylight." That's what Kingpen said. "Longer hours." And then he showed me in his book about the Matanuska Valley. Ninety-pound cabbages and giant zucchini. Watermelons so big you couldn't lift them up.

"We'll see 'em," he said. And the way that he said it, I knew that we would.

We got a new place to live right after that. The Chena Campground, on the Chena River. About a half a mile from the school, it was really pretty nice. About eighty-five tent spaces, and it didn't cost a thing. Kingpen got us in. He ran into a family when he was down at the Hall. The father was on the E list and had given up hope.

"We're moving out tonight," he told Kingpen. "Driving back to Selma."

So we took their space that night. We set up Kingpen's tent, on a ten-by-twenty piece of dirt, with a picnic table and a barbecue grill, and called it home.

"Pretty darn lucky." That's what Kingpen said. And we were, in a way. Because it was damn near impossible to get a space. It seemed like every single person who had signed up on a list, and most of their families, were living at the campground. All these desperate people.

We would sit around our campfire, on into the twilight, 'cause it never got really dark, and listen to these people talk about the money they were going to make.

"It's my patriotic duty," one guy said. "It'll make us less dependent."

And then they talked about the Arabs till you thought that you were gonna vomit.

It must have been a Friday, because that's when we got paid. Every Friday morning, Mr. Milt would come into the dish room and hand us our checks.

"What's *this*?" he asked. And you could tell that he was hot. All steamed up about something on the time sheet. "How could you have worked twenty- *seven* hours this day?" he asked, "when there are only twenty-*four*? How could you have *done* that?"

It took me a minute, but then I remembered.

"It was Wednesday," I said. "The machine broke down and then a pipe burst after that. You should have seen it. Water spraying everywhere. So we worked until three. Until we got it fixed. We could have used a plumber that night," I said, and I started to laugh.

"That's still not twenty- *SEVEN*," he yelled. He was getting all upset.

"Sure it is," I said. And I explained the double hours and then he really hit the roof.

"I'll be a *son* of a *bitch*," he screamed. "You can't make more than *me*. And then he handed me my check for over eight hundred dollars, with the taxes taken out. *Take-home*. That's what I remember thinking.

"No more double hours," he shouted. "Things will change tomorrow." And then he stomped past the fruit cans to his office in the back.

The day didn't get any better after that. There weren't any calls down at the Hall and when we got back to the campground, everything was gone. The tent. The bags. Everything we owned, except what was in the Buick.

It was ten o'clock that night and when we got to our space, there was a couple there from Denver.

"Hitched up here so we could work up on *the Line*," she said. They didn't even have a car.

"The space was empty when we got here," the girl said. And you had to believe her.

So, we started walking. *Walking, walking, walking*. All around that night. Looking for our sleeping bags, the tent, the rifle, and our jackets.

"Boy is Beamish gonna be upset," Kingpen said. And he meant about the gun.

And then just about when we had given up hope, Kingpen noticed something, right there at the entrance.

"Look," Kingpen said. And there, inside a little Ranger Station where you came into the Campground, was our stuff. Piled into a corner.

"Help you with something?" the Ranger asked. And we told him about our gear that was sitting in his little building.

"Day man must have taken it," he said. "He's a tight-ass son of a gun. He likes to go by the rules. There's a fifty-dollar confiscation fee," he told us, "but I won't charge you anything. You just need to keep on moving. Every five days. You aren't allowed to stay in one space any longer, so find someone to switch with, like everybody else." He pointed to the rules on the side of the building. "And as for the gun," he said, "You've gotta keep it in your car." I nodded my head, then we got our gear together and carried it out.

"Thanks," Kingpen said.

We walked to the car and threw everything in. Piled it in the back. Then we got in the front and drove around awhile on the skinny dirt roads of the Chena River Campground, passing different colored tents, beat up campers and a couple mobile homes. *Looking.* Always looking for a place to park the Buick.

"Nothing," Kingpen said. And I knew he was right, so we went back to see the people from Denver. And like everyone else in Fairbanks in the summer, I knew they'd be awake. One-thirty, two in the morning - nobody slept, because of the light. They'd be out cutting the grass, or playing ball. Even little kids. You'd see them riding around on their bikes.

"Mind if we park the car here tonight?" I asked. And then I explained what had happened.

"No problem," they told us. And then Kingpen and I got all of the gear out, except for the rifle, and went down to the river. It was the only place you could camp that wasn't a tent space and where you wouldn't get caught. It was down in the weeds, on the side of the bank where the bushes were filled with brambles and the mosquitoes were hatching their eggs. And the funny thing was, other people were there, too. In *their* sleeping bags and homemade tents.

"Here," Kingpen said. "Gimmee a hand with the tent." But because of the bushes, we never set it up. So we just lay there in the bags, but never got to sleep. It was like Kingpen said - we were on too much of a slant.

The alarm went off at six and you would have thought that it was noon, as light as it was.

"Gonna be a hot one," Kingpen said. We packed up the gear, zipped it in the tent, carried it to the car, and dumped it all in.

"Maybe we can get a tent space tonight," I said. And then I started the Buick and we headed toward the school.

———————

It was pretty typical for a Saturday morning. There weren't that many dishes, with the students sleeping in. Kind of like a Sunday… and then my mind went to the next thing.

"How about Monday?" I asked. "Do you think they'll have some jobs?"

"At the Hall?" Kingpen asked. "It's picking up. They had thirteen last week. Thirteen jobs for the afternoon calls and the last one went to 3792 on the C list."

But none of it made sense.

"The twelfth job went to 3712. Now what about those other eighty people? Where were *they*?" I asked.

"Who knows?" Kingpen said. "Who knows? We just need to be sure *we're* there. That's all."

I parked behind the dumpster, we went up on the loading platform, and through the door. And there was Mr. Milt, going through some paperwork.

"How ya doin'?" I asked. And then I waved. But he never really answered. Not exactly.

"I'll be in later," he said. "To see you two work." And we were the only ones he could have seen, because no one else was working. At least not in the dish room. Even Kolis had left, to go to the Olympics.

Like I said before, it always started kind of slowly, but then it started picking up for lunch. By twelve-thirty or one, we started getting jammed.

"Push the second button," I said. And then we really had to hustle, as the cups and the dishes came out faster through the steam.

"What's the hold-up?" someone asked. And when I turned around and looked, I could see Mr. Milt taking off his sport coat and loosening his tie.

"Go get the plates," he said. "And scrape off the food."

He put on an apron that was over by the door, and then he came back where I was, at the end of the conveyer.

"Go scrape the plates," he said again, "And give 'em to Arthur. He can put them on the rack." Which was really just some rubber holders, attached to the conveyer.

Anyway, I got over to the window, and if you've ever washed dishes in a dish room, you know the first thing you do is set up your trash cans. Two big rubber trash cans, if you have them, one on each side. Then you pick up the plates, bring 'em down inside the cans, turn your wrists just right, and hit the plates on the rubber. *BOO-BOOM*! Knocks the food off of 'em almost every time.

Almost there, I thought.

"Come on. Come on," he said. "Get those plates and hand them back to Arthur."

So I picked two up, one with burned toast and the other one with pancakes and brought 'em down inside on the rubber. *BOO-BOOM!* A little to the left, I thought.

"*FASTER!*" he yelled. And by then I had the trashcans set just right. Everything was perfect. "*FASTER!*" he kept yelling. And I looked back to Arthur and motioned toward the button, the one on the end that we hardly ever used.

The trays were too easy, so I left them on the sink and began to pass back all the cups and little white saucers. Knives, forks, all the utensils. The stuff that got hot and was hard to lift out.

"There are some gloves back behind you, Mr. Milt," I said. And just as he turned, Kingpen pushed the button in.

BOO-BOOM! BOO-BOOM! I was really knockin' 'em down. Coffee cups, glasses, plates and utensils. *BOO-BOOM! BOO-BOOM!*

If you've ever seen a racehorse right after a race, that's how Mr. Milt was starting to look, dripping with sweat, or maybe it was steam from the washing machine. Covered with lather.

"Not too busy today," I called back.

And Kingpen yelled out, "Not yet. But just wait until supper," he said. "It'll really pick up."

And then even as we spoke, we kept filling the conveyer. We'd watch as it carried the bowls and the dishes and all the little saucers through the little rubber flaps and into the steam, and finally back to Mr. Milt, who looked like he had drowned.

BOO-BOOM! BOO-BOOM!

He was going to explode, that's what I remember thinking. He was as red as the ketchup that we steamed off the plates. His veins were sticking out and his moustache was dripping with sweat. *BOO-BOOM! BOO-BOOM!*

It was a fork that finally got him. A prong went through his left rubber glove, and he stopped to take a look, then dove for the cup, but by then it was too late. It crashed to the floor - and then a saucer and plate. *SA-MASH! SMASH! SMASH!*

"SON OF A *BITCH!*" he yelled.

And then two little glasses, steamed clean as could be, rolled off the conveyer and crashed to the floor.

"What's the hold-up?" I called back. But by then, he had lost it. Bowls. Plates. Little fancy dishes. Then a couple more glasses. *SMASH! SMASH! SMASH!*

165

"Turn this fuckin' thing *off*!" he screamed. "Turn it fuckin' *off*!"

Kingpen punched the button and the whole thing stopped.

"Damn it all to *hell*!" Mr. Milt shouted. "Look at this mess. Clean it up!" he roared. "Clean it *up*!"

He stomped out of the room, still wearing his apron, telling us he'd come back, but of course he never did. It was like Kingpen said... He belonged in his office.

Kingpen swept the floor, while I finished up the dishes. Then we started saying how we both deserved another raise for all the work we were doing.

"Ought to be at least five people back here washing dishes," Kingpen said. And that's the way we talked until the supper crowd came in and we started getting busy.

We worked until ten that night. Then we walked to the car, got out the tent with all of the gear, and walked down to the campground, a half a mile away. Dragging the tent with all the stuff inside it.

"I'm starting to feel like a snail," Kingpen said. And then he hoisted his share of the tent a little higher on his shoulders and we kept on going.

We got ourselves set up in the weeds again that night, except it was a little better place about four feet from the river. Flatter. And the mosquitoes weren't as bad. But the weeds were still there, so that even if somebody had passed us from the river, I don't think they ever would have seen us.

"We'll keep trying for a tent space," Kingpen said. Then, we drifted off to sleep.

Chapter 19

It was the first part of June, eleven at night and we were finishing with the dishes, when the water pipe broke. It was a small leak at first and then the more we tried to fix it, the worse it got.

"Watch out!" Kingpen yelled. It started to spray scalding hot water, out of control. There was a valve near the leak, but you couldn't really reach it without getting burned. Kingpen grabbed his gloves and a mop and I gave him a top from a big rubber trashcan. Then he went at the water like an ancient Roman Gladiator.

"Get it!" I yelled. And I was laughing so hard I was nearly doubling up. But Kingpen wasn't laughing. That was the funny part.

"Lower!" I yelled. "And more to your left." Because he couldn't really see it with his shield.

"I can't do it," Kingpen yelled. But of course he finally got it, with the help of my directions. He stuck the handle of the mop in this hole in the valve and turned it to the right, till the water stopped.

"Now suppose that valve hadn't been there?" he asked. But I was laughing so hard, I couldn't talk.

"Sure, it's funny," he said. "But suppose it hadn't been there? What could we have done?"

"We'd have gotten it," I said. But Kingpen didn't think so.

"I've *had* it," he told me. "And on top of all this, now I guess we've gotta clean it up? Look at this mess!"

And when I took the time to look around, I knew that he was right. It was pretty depressing. Nothing was dirty, but everything was wet. All the plates and utensils and little fancy cups.

"Let's try the fan," I said. So we got out a giant floor fan and tried to dry things out. But it never really worked. All it did was push the water around to different places on the plates.

Kingpen never said a word. He just hit the second button and put the plates on the conveyer. Plates, utensils and little fancy cups. Hundreds of 'em, clean and bright and sparkling white. And the only thing that changed as they went through the machine was how less wet they were when they came out at the end.

"We oughta get a raise," Kingpen said.

"Or else we'll quit," I told him.

167

And from midnight till we finished the dishes, that was how we talked. Like a couple of people with pockets full of money, until by five in the morning, we'd convinced ourselves to talk to Mr. Milt.

We turned out the lights, went out the back, locked the door, and headed toward the car.

"Let's sleep in the Buick," I said, and Kingpen nodded his head.

They say that every day brings with it a new philosophy. That's what I was thinking as we planned what we'd say when we talked to Mr. Milt. For all of our talk earlier that night and into the morning, something had changed.

Maybe our outlook or sense of perspective, but it had to have a name. A total contradiction that could well up inside you and ask for the moon, but not give a damn if you got it or not. To care so much that you really didn't care. To know you knew. That's what it was. To be in a position where you could screw or be screwed - and it really didn't matter. And after I thought it through, I knew the word that described it all. The philosophy I would often come to fall back on in the years ahead.

"But suppose we ask him for more money and he fires us instead?" Kingpen asked. "Suppose it all falls through?"

Fuggit, I thought.

I saw a car go by and park up by the dumpster. Mr. Milt got out, then he went inside the building.

"We gotta stick together on this one," Kingpen said. I told him we would. We got out of the Buick, then we followed Mr. Milt in, through the *Employees Only* door, past the cans of fruit and back to his office.

Seven twenty-five an hour. That's what Kingpen and I agreed on. But when we got in the office, it seemed like a lot. That's what Kingpen said later. So he asked Mr. Milt for six-fifty.

"We've been working really hard," Kingpen said. And he told him what had happened with the pipe that had broken.

"I'll have to get a plumber," Mr. Milt said. "That'll *really* cost me some money." Then he started to tell us how the company we

168

worked for was a part of another one, back in Philadelphia. "Things are tight," he said. But then I started to think about Kolis and Jeffrey Margolis and people who had quit but were never replaced. There had to be a budget for the dishwashing crew.

"Six twenty-five?" Kingpen asked. "Would that be too much?"

He was really getting nervous and kept glancing over to me.

"How about eight dollars?" I asked. "For all that we do, I think that would be fair."

Mr. Milt started to laugh and then he shook his head.

"Then I guess we'd better go," I said. And I got up from the chair.

Kingpen looked down, but was right there with me. I had to give him that. He reached in his pocket and pulled something out, but his hand was shaking so bad, he dropped it to the floor.

"Here's the key," he said. He picked it up off the floor and put it on the desk, then looked over again at me. "I guess we'd better go."

We got to the jelly, right outside the office. Big five-pound jars that were packed in cardboard boxes.

"Now hold on! Hold on," Mr. Milt shouted. "I didn't say I couldn't pay it."

I turned back to look and he was starting to sweat. Little beads of water, right above his eyes.

"Maybe I could do it," he said, "if I could cut back on your hours. Would that be all right?"

"It's OK with us," Kingpen said. And he looked back to me. "It's OK with us. Isn't it?"

I nodded my head, but I didn't understand how he could cut back on our hours and still get the work done.

You can think the strangest things, I thought.

And so of course I started thinking. "But it always ends up more."

That's what Kingpen used to say. "You can think and imagine, but it always ends up different. More." That was what he'd said. "It always ends up *more*." And it turned out he was right.

"We'll work it out," I said.

Kingpen got the key and we went back to the dish room. "Hit the first button," I said. And then Kingpen pushed it in and we started on the dishes. The ones from the early people who had already eaten.

"You think he's on a list? Kingpen asked. I scraped some hotcakes from one of the plates and put it on the conveyer.

"Mr. Milt?" I asked. "What list would he be on?"

"Culinary," Kingpen said. "There's a Culinary Union."

And it sounded pretty silly when I first thought about it. Mr. Milt on a list to get into a Union. All I could picture was him back behind the jelly, pushing his papers.

"I don't think so," I said. But I wasn't really sure. Kingpen had a point. People were leaving damn good jobs from all over the state. "Top notch jobs." That's what Kingpen said. You could read it in the papers. Accountants and teachers and bankers and lawyers. Even a mayor walked away from his town to take a job up north.

"Just imagine," Kingpen said, "how far we could go if we had a normal job. With everybody gone, we could really move up fast." But that was just it. Except for washing dishes, we were just like the mayor. Holding to the dream. Just waiting to get out.

"We could really go somewhere," Kingpen said. And then I turned off the machine, we snuck out the front, got in the Buick, and shot down College Road.

It was twenty after nine when we got down to the Hall. I remember it was crowded with lots of people from the C, D and E lists.

"Just like us," Kingpen said. "They're all waiting to get out." And then ten minutes later, the screen went up and they started the call.

"Fifteen general laborers needed at Pump Station One... Seven twelves," the man called out. And what that meant was you were guaranteed twelve hours a day, seven days a week. "Fourteen laborers at Happy Valley. . . Seven tens." They wanted twenty-two people at Atigun Pass, twenty more at Dietrich, eighteen at Coldfoot, and forty-one at Prudhoe Bay.

"All right! All *right!*" somebody yelled. You could feel the excitement from the people in the crowd. Not from the ones on the A or B lists who were there to get a job, but from people like us who had shown up to watch.

"Whaddya think?" Kingpen asked. "You think they'll trickle down?"

And of course what he meant was, would there be any jobs at the end of the call? Jobs that weren't taken and would go down to *our* list later that day.

"It's picking up," somebody said. "The work is picking up."

And somehow, I knew, in a matter of hours, we would be just like the people who were heading up front to the dispatch screen.

"Four seventeen," somebody said. And when you looked to the people who were standing by the dispatcher, people on the A list, you saw them glance around. And when no one was lower, "You got it," the dispatcher said. "Where you wanna go?"

And without a moment's hesitation, the guy said, "Prudhoe. Prudhoe Bay." And that was that. He got this far off look, a dispatch slip, and a job that would pay him $1,500 a week.

"Six thirty-two," somebody said. And then seven twenty-four. And the more we stood and watched, the more we knew the guy was right. The guy we heard when we first came in the Hall. The work was picking up, and the time was getting close.

"Come on," Kingpen said. We walked past the people sitting at the soda machine and went out the door. Then we got in the Buick and shot back up College Road.

"Whaddya think?" Kingpen asked. I told him I thought there would still be some jobs that would go down to us.

"It could be a good call," I said, and Kingpen nodded. And even though he never said a word, I knew what he was thinking. The time was getting close. And all we had to do was *be there*.

We got back to the dish room and the plates were piling up. Leftover sausage, eggs, and French toast.

"Push the second button," I said. And then we humped it for a while, pounded the plates and sent 'em through the washer. But we couldn't stop talking. That's what I remember. Pounding the plates and wiping the syrup... and the whole time we were talking and making big plans.

"Maybe we should tell him," Kingpen said. "Tell Mr. Milt that we're not coming back."

But how could we tell him after getting a raise? That's what I remember saying. So we figured we would wait.

The eggs and French toast turned to tuna and salad and pie, and you knew it was lunchtime. "We're falling behind," Kingpen said. It wouldn't have mattered, except we were leaving to go to the Hall.

"It'll look pretty messy if it keeps piling up," Kingpen told me. "Mr. Milt might realize we're gone."

"So just bring it all in," I said. And for ten or fifteen minutes, that's what we did. Brought it all in. We handed the trays to each other. The ones on the floor and up on the counter, trays full of plates and utensils and little salad bowls, with leftover lettuce and dressing. But the worst part was the drinks - leftover milk and all kinds of juice.

"Watch it!" we'd say, but as careful as we were, as hard as we tried, a lot of it spilled, and then it got to the point where we didn't really care.

"Just get it in here," I said. "We've gotta go." So we got kind of frantic and started piling it all up, right there in the dish room, as fast as we could. Hundreds of plates with leftover noodles and half eaten hotdogs and all these bowls of sauerkraut, that I guess nobody liked.

"Come *on*," Kingpen said again. "We've gotta *go*."

Then we headed out the back with some big plastic trash bags, so it looked like we were working. We tossed them in the dumpster and jumped in the Buick.

"C'mon," Kingpen said. Then I turned the key and the engine roared to life and we raced down College Road, past the little pull-off where we used to live.

Talking. Always *talking*. And even as we drove, the excitement kept building, until there was no more we could say. You just had to be there. Not just at the Hall, but there on College Road. Driving to a $1,500 job on the Trans-Alaska Pipeline. That's what we were doing. It was the middle of June in Fairbanks, Alaska - in 1975 - on College Road. And we were *there*.

We turned right on Cushman, went over the Chena River Bridge and then about a half a mile later, turned right on 3rd.

"Look at that," Kingpen said. We could see the people standing on the sidewalk. "Hall must be jammed."

And then we thought we knew what everybody else must have known. That day there were gonna be a lot of calls. A *lot* of calls.

"Look," Kingpen said." He pointed to a place to park and I edged the Buick in. Then we got out and started off across the street to mix in with the crowd.

"There were thirteen jobs left over from the morning call," somebody said. "Thirteen jobs. Now where the hell did *they* go?" And when we looked at the door of the Hall, there was a yellow cardboard sign, hanging on the handle.

"NO C LIST CALLS TODAY," it said. And to top it off, the door was locked and you couldn't get in.

"Thirteen jobs left over from this morning," another guy said. "They should have gone to us."

"We oughta sue. This just ain't right," somebody moaned.

And from what little I knew, I didn't understand it either.

Then a guy who said he *did* know, started to explain. "They have twenty-four hours," he said. "To fill all the jobs. They'll put 'em through again tomorrow on the A list and B list. And then, if they aren't taken, they'll come down to us."

"That's *crap*," somebody yelled. "We oughta get the jobs."

But the door stayed locked and after a while the people drifted off.

"Maybe tomorrow," I heard one of them say.

"Yeah, *tomorrow*."

We fired up the Buick, but the transmission got stuck, so I popped the hood and we looked around. "We need Beamish," Kingpen said, and he started to laugh.

It took us a long time, but we finally found the problem. A little metal rod had come unhooked from another metal rod. "We need a piece of wire," Kingpen said. "Or something that'll hold it."

So we walked around awhile and ended up at a place called Sampson's Hardware, where we got a cotter pin. That's what finally fixed it, at least for a while. A little brass one, about a half an inch long. I should have bought a couple of 'em, but I didn't.

Anyway, we got the Buick going and headed back toward the University. It was kind of depressing just thinking about the Union. But when we got back to the dish room and saw all that mess, we really got depressed. And the worst part was that we had the supper people coming in two more hours.

"Hit the third button," I said. Kingpen pushed it in and we worked that day like we'd never worked before. Steaming the plates and racing around, tossing out the hot dogs and sauerkraut. Boy, we were busy.

We did it though. Kicked some kinda ass. And then right after supper, Mr. Milt came into the dish room and handed each of us a piece of paper.

"Here's your new schedule," he said.

When we looked at the hours, they were all chopped up. Seven to ten, eleven to one, and four to seven.

"No more overtime," he told us.

I started asking how we'd ever get the work done, but Mr. Milt didn't answer. He just walked out and went back to his office.

"It doesn't really matter," Kingpen said. "We'll just have to work as hard as we can. But if we don't get it finished…"

"*Fuggit*," I said.

We worked until nine or nine-thirty, then went to the Buick, took out the stuff and hauled it to the Chena River Campground.

I wish you could have seen us. Walking down University Avenue, ten o'clock at night. The sun was shining, and the two of us were dragging this two-man tent with everything we owned, zipped up inside it.

And nobody even gave us a glance. That was the thing. The cars went by and nobody honked, gave us a weird look, or even pointed.

"I like this place," Kingpen said. And the thing about Fairbanks was, you fit right in. No matter what you were like or what you were doing.

"It's a pretty crazy place," I said.

And I guess looking back, it was people like us who made it that way.

Chapter 20

We got halfway to the University, before we remembered we didn't have to be there until seven o'clock. "Let's go to the dorm," I said.

So we went into Stevens Hall and sat in the rec room. We watched TV with a couple of other people who were already there. Nothing was on, just some old news shipped up from the states. But anyway, we stayed there awhile, then we walked to the Commons and went in the back.

"All set?" Mr. Milt asked. He came out of his office and the three of us walked past the boxes and cans and back to the dishes, where the food line started. But the dishes weren't there. Not exactly.

"Paper plates," Mr. Milt said. "And plastic spoons and forks and plastic knives. Styrofoam cups. Let's see how *this* works."

Kingpen and I went to the dish room and waited for the people to bring up the trays.

"Know what today is?" Kingpen asked. And I think I told him Thursday and he nodded and said yeah. "But it's something else. It's summer solstice," he said. "June twenty-first. Longest day of the year."

Somebody came and handed me their tray, then I held it over the trashcan and called out to Kingpen. "Watch this," I said, and I tilted the tray and everything slid off. First a fork and a knife, then a paper plate with syrup, a napkin, and then a Styrofoam cup.

"Here," I said. I gave the tray to Kingpen, he put it on the conveyer and we waited for the next person. That's all we did from seven to ten. Slid the stuff off the trays and stacked the trays on the conveyer. Then every half an hour or so, we'd hit the first button and send 'em through the steam.

"I can handle *this*," Kingpen said. And we thought we had it made.

At ten o'clock, Kingpen left to call his mother, and I went out to a table and sat there for a while. There were hardly any people. There hadn't been many all morning, but I didn't think much about it at the time. I got some pancakes and cereal and sat there some more, and then Kingpen came back.

"I told her we'd be leaving in another week or so," Kingpen said. "Going up north and working at Prudhoe or one of the camps."

I stuck my fork into a pancake and a prong broke off. Then all I could think of was how things had changed. I tried to tell Kingpen, but he didn't understand.

"You mean how two months ago," he asked, "we were living in a house back east and now we're Alaskans, going up to work on the Trans-Alaska Pipeline?"

But that wasn't it.

"Have you ever seen a college catalog?" I asked. "With hundreds of pages that tell about the school? We've changed it." I held up the fork. "We've changed it," I said.

And looking back, I can picture it now. Sitting at the table and picturing thousands of students and how they used to eat on regular plates with metal knives and forks and the way it all had changed. And you'd have seen it, too, if you had been there that summer. You would have *used* the stuff. Red paper plates, plastic utensils and Styrofoam cups.

And like I told Kingpen, it was all because of us.

———————

At five till eleven, we went back into the dish room and waited for the people to bring us their trays.

"Whaddya think?" Kingpen asked. And of course what he meant was, what did I think about the jobs? So I told him I thought they were building up. Like the ice on the Nenana, I thought.

"It's gonna break soon," I told him. And he nodded his head.

The time dragged on and then at five-after-one, we got into the Buick and went down to the Hall.

"I'm feeling pretty good," Kingpen said. And when we got to the door and it didn't have a sign, we both felt that way.

"C'mon," Kingpen said. We walked past the soda machine and the burnouts and then up to the window to be with the crowd.

"It's one-thirty!" somebody yelled. And in another couple minutes, the screen went up and you could feel the excitement building.

"Mornin'," the dispatcher said. "Or should I say good afternoon?" But nobody cared.

"Whaddya have?" somebody called out. And the guy let out a smile and that's when we knew.

"*Today*," Kingpen told me. "We're going out *today*."

"Now listen up," the dispatcher announced. "I'm gonna say this once. Four general laborers at Pump Station One. Seven twelves," he said. And then he waited just a minute. "Two general laborers at Five Mile. Seven tens. Two for Coldfoot. Seven tens. And three for Prudhoe Bay. Seven fourteens. Is there anyone with a number lower than a thousand?" he asked. And when nobody said a word, you could feel it in the crowd.

It was time to pack your bags, the gravy train was headin' out.

"I bet we go today," Kingpen said. "Stuff happens on the solstice."

And now that I look back, I think that he was right.

"Anyone lower than fifteen hundred?" the dispatcher asked.

And still nobody answered. They were either already out working, had been called off the list, or had gone down south to the Lower Forty-Eight.

Bottom line was, for whatever reason, they weren't *there*. That's what Kingpen said.

"Two thousand? Anyone . . .?" But he was cut-off before he could finish.

"I'm twenty-three seventeen," somebody said.

But then some other guy had twenty-two eleven, so that's where we started. Twenty-two eleven. He got first pick and then twenty-three seventeen went next. And the strange thing was, the last job left went to thirty-one eleven.

"That's lower than the last time we were here," I said. And I remembered a job had gone to thirty-four fifteen.

"They're all coming back," somebody said. "People from Outside who signed up last year."

"From the Lower Forty-Eight," Kingpen said.

We watched thirty-one eleven pick up his dispatch slip and walk out of the Hall.

"We're seven steps closer," Kingpen said.

But when I thought about my number, forty-nine eighteen, it was pretty depressing.

"Two thousand people?" I asked. "Between us and a job?"

But it was like Kingpen said. It could have been worse. "Over twenty-seven thousand on the E list," he told me. "And the list is getting longer every single day."

We went out the door and walked around awhile. Went to the bakery and got a couple of doughnuts and then stopped in the public library, about two blocks from the Hall.

It was a pretty neat place. It's not there anymore. The building is, but the library's not. Anyway, it was this old three-room house with a porch outside, and you could get a book and read it on the steps.

We stayed there about an hour and I found this beat-up old book about early Alaska. And in one of the chapters, they told about some towns up north that had started as gold rush towns, but now they were deserted.

"There are lots of those places," Kingpen said. "They had plenty of people, but now nobody's there. Ghost towns. Full of broken-down cabins and stuff like that."

"How about if we go back to the Hall?" he asked. "And talk to someone there. Someone who *works* there. We'll ask them to give us an idea when we'll get out."

So we put away the books and started toward the Union Hall again.

"We can ask 'em in the office," I said. So that's what we did. Talked to a lady who was a secretary there.

"Whaddya think?" Kingpen asked. And he told her our numbers.

"Well now don't hold me to this," she said, "but I would guess about a year."

"A *year*?" Kingpen asked.

And all at once I felt my body sag and wondered why I'd ever thought it would be any different than a lot of things back then.

If you lived in a house and you needed a phone, you had to wait a year. A safe deposit box was a year. And even when we applied for our post office box, we were told to wait a year.

"At least," the lady said. And then she told us what the guy had said that morning in the Hall.

"The guys are comin' back up," she said. "The ones who signed in last year. The work will pick up, but more people will be coming. And then the layoffs should start around the middle of October.. Maybe by next summer," she told us. "But I can't say for sure."

My body sagged some more and then Kingpen thanked her. We walked out of the building and got in the Buick. There wasn't much to say.

We drove back to the University and by the time that we got there, it was almost four o'clock.

"Spaghetti," Kingpen said. But it didn't really matter, because it all went into the trash can. I mean it wasn't like before, when we scraped it off the plates. It was a pretty easy night, with not that many people, and only trays to send through the machine.

"Seventeen more trays," Kingpen said. And then Mr. Milt came into the dish room.

"You two have a minute?" he asked. And he started looking nervous.

"I want you two to know how hard you've worked for me," he told us. "You've really busted ass and I want you to know."

"We know it," Kingpen said. And he started to laugh. "But I think these plates will help." He picked up a paper bowl from one of the trash cans.

"Well I'm glad that you know it," Mr. Milt said, "because I have to let you go. The school year is over and there's nothing I can do. If you're looking for a job the first part of September, I can put you back to work." He paused. "Anyway, here's your pay," he said.

And he gave us each a check. "Thanks again," he said. "Make sure and get yourselves something to eat before you leave."

Kingpen had been right. *Stuff happened on the solstice.* There were parties and cookouts and lots of celebrations. There was even a ballgame played under the midnight sun.

But *we* didn't go. It was getting close to twelve and we were sitting in the weeds on the banks of the Chena, throwing gravel in the water and watching it all go by.

"Whaddya think?" Kingpen asked. Then he looked at his alarm clock and told me that in another couple minutes the days would start to get shorter.

"We'll be losing seven minutes a day," Kingpen said, "until the middle of winter, when there's hardly any light. It's kind of like our job. And down at the Hall. Except I think we peaked out early."

"But I don't think we did." That was what I told him.

For now, I thought, *for another couple of minutes at least, we were still rising stars. And regardless of whether we had jobs or not,*

179

or when we got out, we were a part of it all, the means heading to the end.

And like I told Kingpen that night, what I thought, what I believed, was that we were right there on the edge.

"Kingpen," I told him, "We're right on the cusp."

The alarm went off at six, I opened my eyes, stuck out my arm and hit the button with my fist.

"I've been waiting to do that for a month," I said. And then I tried to go back to sleep, but I couldn't. The sun was too bright.

"Come on," I said. I unzipped the front screen of the tent, pulled myself out of the bag and crawled into the weeds. *Sons of bitches are already out*, I thought. I could see the mosquitoes buzzing around.

"Whaddya wanna do?" Kingpen asked me.

And it reminded me of the time we got gas when we weren't really sure where we were going, that time down in Anchorage.

"I don't know," I said. "We could clean out the Buick." But of course we never did. We walked up University Avenue, got in the car, and then sat there a minute.

"Let's go get something to eat," Kingpen said.

So I started the car and we drove downtown, past the Union Hall to the Arctic Pancake House. That's what it was called. Like a lot of things back then, and probably today, if it wasn't called the Aurora or Far North something or other, then it was the Arctic.

But anyway, the food was pretty good. But expensive as hell. It really brought back how easy we'd had it with all the free food.

"Maybe we should get a job," Kingpen said. "Or at least have a plan until we get out on the Line. Do you think we should stay up here all year, or do you wanna go back east?"

"Well, we know we won't get off the list for the next eight months," I said. "So if we go back now, it really won't matter."

"Exactly," Kingpen said. "But maybe we should wait another week or so, just to be sure. In case there's a big call. Whaddya think?"

"What time do you have?" I asked. He took out the alarm clock that he carried in his pocket and turned it to face me.

"Forty-five minutes," I said.

We paid for the breakfast and went down to the library to kill some time. Then fifteen minutes later, we went out the door, down the porch steps, and raced over to the Hall.

We were a couple of minutes early, so we looked at the map that was up on the wall. The one with the line that ran through the state, from Prudhoe Bay to the Port of Valdez. It showed all of the camps and all of the pump stations.

"Now this is the Slope," Kingpen said. And he pointed just above a squiggly line that was supposed to represent some mountains. "That's the Brooks Range," Kingpen told me. "And just to the north, where it slopes to the Arctic Ocean is where *we'll* probably go. *The North Slope.*"

And the way that he said it, I couldn't imagine that I'd ever go to work there. Take a tour maybe, and see the oil workers, but that was about it.

"We'll get there," Kingpen said. "Don't you worry about it."

And just as he tapped the Arctic Ocean with his finger, the screen went up and the people on the A and B lists settled down to listen to the call.

"Mornin'," the dispatcher said.

Then the people as a group mumbled something and the man read off the jobs. "Two general laborers for Dietrich... seven tens. Four for Coldfoot... seven twelves. Thirteen for Prudhoe Bay... seven fourteens. And eight for Atigun Pass... six tens," he called out.

And you could hear the people *boo*, because it was only sixty hours.

"Now *those* jobs might go to us," Kingpen said.

And for a while, I thought they might. "I mean who would want to sit there in a Pipeline camp, in the middle of nowhere, and just work six days a week?" he asked. But eight people did. We watched them take the jobs.

"Nothin' left for us," somebody in the back said. And the way that he said it, I knew he was a C, D, or E-lister. It was really depressing.

"I guess the lady knew her stuff," I said. And then Kingpen and I went out of the Hall and drove to the bank, where I had opened my account.

I had twenty-six hundred dollars, when I included my last check. And Kingpen had two thousand.

"Not bad for washing dishes," I said. "Beamish won't believe it."

181

"All hundreds?" she asked. I nodded my head and then remembered what had happened up at the snack room.

"Better make one twenties," I said. Then she peeled off five and put 'em on the stack.

"Two thousand, six hundred fifteen dollars and twenty-one cents," she said. She handed me the bills, two dimes and a penny, and then Kingpen got his money.

"We'll be back in the spring," he said.

We walked out of the bank, got in the Buick, and went up College Road to the post office where we used to go. The College Branch, about a half a mile from the University.

"Any mail?" Kingpen asked. And the lady checked General Delivery, but nothing was there. "How about the box?" Kingpen asked. "Does it look any better?"

"Not until the spring," the lady told us. "Maybe even summer. There's still a waiting list."

"Well, give us a call," Kingpen said, "if anything comes up. We're going back east." He got a piece of paper and wrote his phone number down.

"I'll have to call collect," the lady said.

And Kingpen told her, "Sure. Call us anytime."

We went outside, and for over an hour we cleaned out the Buick.

Shoes, boots, pieces of rope. Everything you could imagine. And *more*.

We gathered it together and tossed it all into this big green dumpster, back behind the post office.

"Remember this?" Kingpen asked. And he held up the big piece of concrete we had gotten from the other green dumpster back in Wisconsin. The concrete we had used to bend all the stakes.

"Toss it in," I said. And Kingpen let go, but it made so much noise, I thought we'd better leave.

"Come on," I said. Then Kingpen shut the trunk and we got in the front. We took the Buick out on College Road and up toward the school.

"What would you think about leaving the car here?" Kingpen asked. "We could fly back east and then when we come back, it would already be here."

But I wanted to drive. That's what I remember saying. And then Kingpen got a little nervous and said he thought that he would fly, if it was OK with me.

"I'll drive back with you, if you really want me to," he said. But he knew I wasn't like that.

"You go ahead and fly," I said. "I'll take the Buick back. When do you want to leave?"

"How about tomorrow night?" he asked.

It was sometime after lunch, and for the rest of the day we took care of things that had to be done. We went down to the Hall and paid up through the following May. Then we went back to the tent and figured out the gear.

"Why don't you go ahead and take the tent?" Kingpen asked.

There wasn't much left that had to be done.

"How about your ticket?" I asked. "Don't you need a reservation?"

But Kingpen didn't know. So we drove down to the airport.

We walked in past the bear and it was just like before. Dozens of these guys, most with southern accents, all milling around. "Welders," Kingpen said. And the way he could tell, he told me, was from the type of hat they had on. "They always wear it backwards. It's their trademark," Kingpen told me.

Then he pointed to the far left corner of the building, and there was Northwest Orient, the airline Beamish had taken back east. "That's it," Kingpen said.

There wasn't a line and the lady told us he didn't even need a reservation. In fact, he could have gone that night, but decided to wait.

"I think I'll stay another day," he told me. "And have a look around."

But he did buy a ticket. "Round trip," he told her. And the lady explained how he had a year to use it.

"I'll be coming back next spring," Kingpen said.

As we got ready to go, I noticed the Bush plane company's counter, next to the Northwest one.

"Look at that," I said.

There was a lady behind the counter, and on a board behind her, there was a list of places all around the state. Up and down the Yukon River mostly, with a few farther north. Places in the Bush that most people didn't know existed, like the places that I'd seen in the book at the library.

But anyway, we asked her, and she told us that they chartered too.

"That's good to know about," Kingpen said. "We're coming back next spring."

"Well I'm not so sure *we'll* be here," she said. "The owners had this idea to fly tourists out to little ghost towns up north. But it's not working out. Not enough interest for one thing. And the landing strips up there are all breaking up. Need to be replaced. Takes a lot of money. Anyway, with the regulations as they are, we have to keep it going for another year and a half. So probably after that, they'll shut it down and try something else. I don't know."

We went out past the bear, got in the car, drove it to the school, parked near the Commons, and then walked down to the tent. We had left it in the weeds, so we wouldn't have to haul it up and down the road.

"When do you think you'll leave?" Kingpen asked.

I told him I thought it would be another week or so.

"Well give me a call if you think we can get out," Kingpen said. "I'll fly back up."

We found our way to the tent, but nothing had changed. The weeds were still there and so were the mosquitoes, buzzing all around.

"How about if I take you out tomorrow night?" Kingpen asked me. "Someplace really fancy."

And then we got in the bags and looked out the screen, past the mosquitoes and out to the river that was moving along.

"Where do you think that goes?" I asked.

But Kingpen wasn't sure. "Probably runs into the Tanana," he said.

———————

It was the first of July, and the only way we knew it, was because of the date on Kingpen's ticket.

"You'll be home for the Fourth," I said. Kingpen nodded his head, but I don't think he cared.

"We better go," he told me. Then we got out of the tent, walked up to the University and got in the car.

It was around eight-thirty, so we knew we had an hour. We drove around awhile, stopped in the College branch, and checked for the mail.

"Nothin'," the lady said.

Then we told her we were leaving and wouldn't be back. "Not until the spring, anyway," Kingpen said.

"Well, you have a good trip," the lady said. "And like I told you, I'll give you a call if a box becomes available."

"We'd appreciate it," Kingpen told her. We all said good-bye and Kingpen and I walked out to the Buick.

By the time we got downtown, it was quarter after nine. It was a lot like the C list call we had gone to before, with the people on the sidewalk, standing around.

"Probably no call," Kingpen said. But that's not what the sign hanging on the door said.

"Only people on the A and B lists are allowed in the Hall for morning calls from now on," it said. And when we listened to the people who were standing on the sidewalk, they gave you the impression it was more of the same.

"They don't want us to know how many jobs there are," somebody said. "So this is what they do."

Somebody else said we'd need proof, before long, of how long we'd lived here. "Whaddya mean?" somebody asked.

"Driver's licenses. Credit cards. A Post Office box. You think they're gonna keep letting people come here from outside the state?" the first man asked. "To take all their jobs? *Hell no!*"

We stood around outside for a while, until eleven o'clock when the people on the inside came out of the Hall. "Nothin' left," one of them said. "The jobs are all gone." And then eight or nine people gave out a sigh.

"Come on," I said. "We'd better wash your clothes if you're going back east."

We got in the Buick and went up College Road. "How about the dorm?" Kingpen asked. And I thought it would be closed, but it wasn't. There were still some people there.

"You go ahead," I said. Kingpen got out of the car and I told him I'd be back. "I'll go down to the tent and get your stuff together."

Kingpen went into the dorm and then I went down to the campground. I loaded up the car with his suitcase and camera and sleeping bag, with the lumps still at one end. I was going to take the tent down and stay in the car, but I decided to leave it up and sleep there that night. I got his stuff into the car, zipped up the screen in the front of the tent, swatted some mosquitoes, and started the Buick.

I made it back to the dorm and Kingpen was there, standing on the steps, with his hair soaking wet.

"I forgot, I didn't have a thing to wear," Kingpen said. "I mean, if I put my clothes in the washer..." And he pointed to his pants. "So I just took a shower."

He got in the car and I remember it was twenty after one, so we really had to move to get to the Hall.

"You better gun it," Kingpen told me. So I pushed the pedal to the floor and the Buick lifted up.

"Suppose that guy was lying?" Kingpen said. "About no more jobs? Suppose there really are some?"

And the more we talked, the faster I drove. Over College Road, over the bridge and then I swung a right on 3rd and skidded to a stop at the building with the sign on the door. "No C list call today," it said. And then somebody honked and we pulled away.

We drove around some more. We picked up some burgers and then headed out of town on a road we'd never been on, the Steese Highway. That's what it was called, but it wasn't a highway like *you* would imagine. It was just a couple of lanes and as we drove along, we began to pass this cleared out area about an eighth of a mile square, with hundreds of pieces of pipe.

"This is it," Kingpen said. "The *Pipe Yard*. This is where it starts."

And for the very first time, it all seemed *real*. Dozens of trucks waiting to be loaded. Heavy equipment.

"This is *it*," Kingpen said. And there it was. Forty-foot-long sections of pipe, four feet in diameter. They were loaded onto a truck and we followed it out, down the Steese Highway to a town called Fox, that was only a couple of buildings. And then we made a left.

"The Haul Road," Kingpen said. "It goes to Prudhoe Bay."

I pulled off to the side and we sat there a minute. "Four hundred and sixteen miles," Kingpen said.

It was hard to believe we were really that close.

"There's a checkpoint at the Yukon. Ordinary people can only drive that far. Another fifty-six miles. Only workers go beyond that," Kingpen told me.

We watched the dust from the truck as it headed up the road. You could hear the driver, running through the gears.

"We'll get up there one day," Kingpen said. And then we sat there in the car and watched until the truck disappeared over a hill.

"Come on," I said. I turned the car around and we headed back to town.

It was quarter after five so we went to a phone booth and looked in the yellow pages for a restaurant.

"How about this one?" Kingpen asked, and he pointed to an ad on one of the pages. Ivory Jacks, out on Goldstream Road.

"Sounds good to me," I said. So that's where we went. Kingpen got us there. It was a huge log house that was made into a restaurant and according to the ad, there were lots of things to choose from.

"Suppose we need a tie to get in?" Kingpen asked when we pulled up front. And I hadn't thought of that. But we went on in anyway and the funny thing was, nobody had one on. Not one person there, even though the place was pretty crowded.

"I like this place," Kingpen said. And then we went upstairs and sat inside the logs. Big eighteen-inch diameter ones, not like the ones you've probably seen. Not like from a kit.

"Look how tight they fit," I said.

And Kingpen told me how they were all hand-scribed to make them fit like that. "Then they cope 'em at the ends," he said.

I got a bottle of wine for each of us and then we got half-crocked and ordered up some salmon. "Fresh from the Yukon." That's what it said on the menu. And the fish couldn't have been better.

But the best part was when this guy flew in and landed his plane, right behind the restaurant. "Look at that," Kingpen said. We watched him bring it down on a short gravel airstrip right behind the building, and then he came inside and bought a round of drinks for everybody there.

"Here's to *you*," I said, and I tapped my glass to Kingpen's. And after we finished, the waiter brought the check. A hundred and forty-seven bucks and change. That's what it was and worth every penny.

"Do you split the tips with people in the dish room?" Kingpen asked. And I knew what he was thinking. So when the waiter said he did, I took a hundred and a fifty out and Kingpen did the same, and we left it all on the table.

"Come on," Kingpen said.

We floated down the steps and went outside right after that.

"Ten-thirty," Kingpen told me, putting his alarm clock back inside his jacket. "I guess we'd better go."

We got to the airport fifteen minutes before his plane took off. He turned in his suitcase and bag, and then we raced upstairs to sit for a minute.

"You ever notice how you leave from the building for a flight that goes outside the state?" Kingpen asked me. "For any flight that takes you someplace in Alaska, you walk out on the tarmac and get onto the plane. Not like this." There was a walkway from the building to the airplane, and the people went through that. "Ever notice?" Kingpen asked again. And I told him that I hadn't.

He got ready to go, I slapped him on the shoulder and then he went through the detector. But the buzzer went off and they made him come back.

"You must have an awful lot of change," the lady said. But he only had a nickel, so that wasn't it.

"It's the alarm clock," he said. He handed it to me and went through again. "You might as well keep it. You'll need it more than I will." He gave me a wave and went into the walkway.

And then right after that, I heard it all again...

"Five Mile, Dietrich, Prospect Camp and Prudhoe Bay," the speaker blared.

And it was just like Kingpen said. You could stand there at the window, eleven at night, but the sun was out, so you could see it for yourself. Ten or twelve people crossing the tarmac to get into a plane that would fly them somewhere else, but always in Alaska.

"Last call," the voice announced. "Five Mile, Dietrich, Prospect Camp..."

But before he could finish, the plane had taken off, circled right and headed north.

Chapter 21

I stayed in the tent a long time the next morning, looking out the screen and watching the rain fall into the river. I thought it would let up, but it never did. I finally walked up to the University in the middle of the storm and went into the library.

The Rasmussen Library that I told you about, but except for the Bush Pilots, no one was there. At least not any students. Just librarians, who were keeping it all going. I stayed three or four hours reading some papers and looking at magazines.

Then I left and walked to the Buick and drove down to the Hall. Two general laborers for Livengood. That was all they had. And both of the people who got out that day had numbers under three thousand on the C list.

"We wanna go to work!" somebody shouted, but the guy at the screen didn't give a damn. He didn't want to hear it, so he pulled the screen down, and then the rest of us drifted out the door.

I remember I was partly depressed, but at the same time excited, about going back east. Looking forward to watching it all go by. But then I started picturing I'd get lost, so I went back to the school and Xeroxed an atlas that was in Rasmussen. It wasn't that expensive. A hundred twenty pages at ten cents a page. It was under fifteen dollars.

There was a mountain on the front cover and when I looked inside the page, the credit said it was McKinley. Mount McKinley, Alaska. And that's when I decided.

Suppose I don't get back next spring, I thought. *I never will have seen it.* So I decided I would go. Drive down to McKinley Park and drive and drive and drive some more, until I saw it.

I picked up the atlas, put it on the counter, then I stapled my copy together. At least I tried to, but there were so many papers the staple wouldn't go through, so I just gathered all the papers together and took them to the Student Center.

Lots of people were there, but not many students. I found that out later. But just as I went in, I got to talking to this guy named Artemus Tischman, that I had met down at the Hall. *Artemus*

Tischman. He had a big, bushy beard with a handlebar moustache and his briefcase that he always carried – every time I saw him.

"Whaddya have in there?" I asked. He opened it and hundreds of papers were there. *Hundreds* of 'em. All shapes and sizes, with all kinds of writings and drawings and pencil notations.

"It's my *book*," he said. *"The Life and Times of Artemus Tischman."* And it turned out he really was a pretty interesting guy, who had been to a lot of places and seen a lot of things.

"That's why I want to go on up to work," he said. And he meant up on the Line. "So I can put it in *here*." He held up his briefcase. "You gonna go somewhere?" he asked. He pointed to my copy of the atlas, with McKinley on the front.

"I think I'm gonna drive back east," I said.

Artemus shook his head. "You oughta *hitchhike*," he said. "That's how I got up here. All the way from Cape Horn. And I wrote it all down."

We spent another couple minutes talking, then I went up to the ceiling and sat there awhile. It was like a lot of things, I guess. The briefcase would get lost, or his work would never be accepted. Something would screw up. But I can tell you one thing. If it doesn't, and you're ever in a bookstore and you *do* come across it, don't pass it by. *The Life and Times of Artemus Tischman*, by Artemus Tischman. I can tell you now, it'll be one helluva book.

There was a newspaper that somebody had left on the table at the top of the stairs. The *Anchorage Times*, from a couple days before. I started to read it and then I stopped and started looking down awhile at people playing Ping-Pong and watching TV.

And then I thought, *You really oughta count your money Fitch.* That's what I remember thinking. So I reached inside my pocket, and I know you think the money wasn't there. But it was. I don't think I've ever lost anything I kept inside my pockets. Twenty-four hundreds, three twenties, two tens and a one. I stacked 'em all in little separate piles, right there on the paper. And the funny thing was, *that* was how I saw the picture. When I picked up the money to put back in my pocket.

There was a picture on the front of the *Anchorage Times* of Kolis in his sweat suit, with his finger pointed to the sky. And underneath the picture was the caption. *Another special winner.* Of course the article was all about the Special Olympics, and the reporter went on to tell about the race. They even had an interview.

Chinese style, I thought. And that's exactly what he said when they asked him how he'd won. "Ran as fast as I could. Then *faster*," Kolis told them. *"Chinese style."*

I tore the picture out to put in my pocket and take back to Kingpen. Then all at once it started. "ATTENTION! ATTENTION!" a man announced. He was in the back of the building with five or six guards. University Security people. He had a big red megaphone and was waving his arms. You couldn't miss him. "Only those people with a student ID will be allowed to stay," he said. "The rest of you must leave. Too many transients."

Then the guards fanned out and began to walk to the front side of the building, chasing everybody out. I could look below and see it all. Maybe three hundred people dwindled to a hundred, then seventy and finally twenty-five. Twenty-five students, where there had been hundreds of us. People on the lists. Just hanging around, waiting to get out.

I put the picture in my pocket, went down the steps, snuck out the back, went around front, got in the Buick and headed toward the campground. The rain had stopped by then, but still, the tent was soaking wet. I took out the stakes and pulled out the poles, then I bundled it together with all the stuff inside and threw it in the back of the car.

McKinley, I thought. And then I looked around to see if I had left anything behind.

I got in the Buick and began to drive away from a bunch of weeds down by the water. Just outside of the Chena River Campground, where we used to live.

Chapter 22

"One hundred twenty miles." That's what I remember Kingpen had said. And I was already someplace out near Ester, so I figured it was less.

But *I* didn't care. I couldn't have cared less how far it was. There were dozens of pull-offs all along the way. Scenic overlooks. That's what the signs said. The ones we'd never even seen the last time we drove down, because of all the snow.

God, it was pretty. Just as far as you could see, for hundreds of miles, nothing but rivers and forests and sky. And never a road, except the one that I was on. Train tracks, then train tracks. Another set of train tracks. I went over the Nenana, passed Fish Creek, saw Ice Worm Gulch, and knew that I was getting close.

Then I went another couple miles and could see it on the sign. *Mount McKinley National Park.* And on the second of July, I made a right and drove into the Park.

I drove out of McKinley Park on the Fourth of July, turned the Buick south and headed to Anchorage. It was about two hundred forty miles to the city, according to my copy of the map. Between two hundred twenty and two hundred sixty. That's what I had figured.

I had seen this sign at McKinley, on a bulletin board, about a fireworks display down in Anchorage, so I thought that I would go. They were having it that night, with a lot of other stuff like food booths and games. It was supposed to be held in a small park, just inside the city.

I was a hundred miles out, or a hundred and twenty, from my finger tip to knuckle. I was heading south and things were going great. And the more I drove, the more I thought. *Thinking. Always thinking.* About Kingpen and Kolis, and working in the dish room. About Artemus Tischman and how he had hitchhiked up to Fairbanks. *Just imagine*, I thought, *standing by the road and waiting for a ride. All these crazy people, passing you by.*

It was quarter after eight when I looked at the alarm clock. I had it right on the dashboard, held down by the magnet. *Closed*, I thought. And when I drove by the weigh station, I saw that it was.

I stopped to get some gas and then I went in on Highway One, like we always had, and followed the traffic down to the park. It was right there in the city, not far from the YMCA, maybe just two or three blocks. But it was kind of like Chicago, in a way, because I couldn't find a place to leave the car. At least not at first.

I went around and around on 7th and 8th, then cut back along C Street and finally found a spot. It was back in an alley, behind somebody's house. Nine-thirty, ten o'clock at night. I started to the park and passed by a bakery. That's what I remember. And the funny thing was, it was open.

"I'll take one of those," I said. And I pointed to some doughnuts, but I didn't know their names. Crullers, pastries, pop-overs. I didn't know the difference. Not back then. But anyway, I paid him, he handed me the ones I had pointed to, and then I started out the door.

"Going to the show?" he asked. And I told him, "Yeah."

I *was* going to the show, but just for a minute I stood there on the sidewalk eating a doughnut, looking around and thinking some more.

There was a little room, right next to the bakery, with a window that I think the people who ran it wanted you to look in. It was supposed to be a Reading Room. That's what the sign said. But nobody was there. There was a book opened up that was sitting on the shelf there in the window. It was part of a display. But I couldn't really read it because of the reflection that was coming off the glass. Ten-thirty at night and the sun was still out, so I kept squinting and staring, but the only thing I could see was the book or my face depending on the glare. *Health is not a condition of matter*, I finally started to read, but then my face came back, all covered with blood from the mosquito bites I'd gotten back at McKinley. It was kind of like the time I looked in the mirror, back at the gym, in a way. I finally gave up.

I finished one of the doughnuts and then followed the crowd to Delaney Park. It was a long, narrow strip of land back behind 4th Street, and food booths were there. Food booths and people throwing Frisbees and flying kites, with dozens of kids all around. Everyone was waiting for the fireworks display to start.

"This is gonna be great," somebody said. "The biggest one in years." And then before too long, people started getting out their blankets and chairs and started sitting together.

"You want to sit with *me*?" somebody asked. I turned to see a sixteen-year-old girl, maybe seventeen, with short curly hair and big-rimmed glasses. "You look a little lost," she said. "You wanna sit with me? I'm Zoey."

Neither of us had a blanket or a chair, so we sat on the grass. Then for maybe an hour, we talked. About traveling mostly. "I'm gonna get a car," Zoey told me. "Just as soon as I get some money. And then I'm gonna see it all. Seattle and L.A, and even New York. I'm gonna get myself a car and drive and drive and drive."

I asked her where she was from and she told me, "Right here. Anchorage. But I'm leaving pretty soon."

"Just as soon as you get money to buy that car," I said.

And she laughed and told me, "Right!"

We heard a muffled pop and then a series of explosions, and then the crowd let out a moan and kids pointed to the sky. POP! POP! POP! – Ka-*BOOM*!

But it was a lot like that waterfall someplace in Banff. You heard it, more than saw it, because it wasn't all that dark. Twelve o'clock at night and it was darker than in Fairbanks, but not pitch black. It wasn't that bad though. The display lasted an hour, and then hundreds of people all headed home with their blankets and chairs and picnic baskets.

"You want a ride home?" I asked. And then just for a minute, I thought I'd take her with me. To Seattle and L.A. and even New York.

"If you don't mind," she said, so we started to the Buick.

It was just six or seven blocks, and at one point I got lost, but then I saw the bakery and remembered where I'd parked. "Over this way," I said. And we began to follow these three guys back into the alley.

"Watch *this*," one said. And he started throwing fire crackers everywhere he went. All along the sidewalk, in the street, up on people's porches. And then he threw one on the Buick.

The car was all banged up and completely beat to shit, mostly from the logging road. There was no way he ever could have hurt it, but that's not what I was thinking.

194

So I grabbed him by the neck and threw him up against the car. "What's the big idea?" I said. And I thought that would have scared him, but he didn't even get upset. He just put one hand inside his coat, I heard the hammer of a gun click back, and I thought that I was dead. That's what I remember thinking.

"How about I blow your fuckin' head off?" he said. "Is there any other big idea you think you oughta know?"

And that's when I got scared. *Really* scared.

"I just don't like you messin' with my car," I blubbered. "No big deal."

I let go of his neck, then he straightened his coat and walked over to his buddies.

"No big deal," I said again. I unlocked the Buick's door and Zoey got inside. God, I was scared. I got into the car and sat there a minute, deciding what to do.

"You really need to watch it here," Zoey said. "There's an awful lot of guns around."

And within a half a minute, right after she had said that, a car came up behind us, flipped on its brights, and tried to block us in.

"It's *them!*" Zoey said. And that was when I turned the key and the Buick came to life.

"*HOLD ON!*" I hollered. God, I was scared. I had to back it out. That's what I remember thinking. *Back it up and get the hell out!* So I got it in Reverse and stepped down on the pedal.

If you've ever seen these demolition derbies, that's what it was like. We rammed the other car, and began to push it back. A little more, a little more, I thought, and then, "*HOLD ON!*" I yelled again. I flipped the stick to Neutral, stepped down again, and the Buick lifted up and took off, racing down the alley with the other car behind us, right there on our tail.

We made it to the road, but just barely got out. Everything was jammed. Cars and people, everywhere you looked.

"Maybe if you honk your horn," Zoey said. But nobody cared.

We were on a one-way street, two lanes, and we were in the left hand side, not moving very fast. Then all at once I saw them, pulling up beside us on our right. I saw the gun come up and then the guy took aim –

"*GET DOWN!*" I screamed.

I took Zoey's head and pushed it toward the floor, pulled a hard left on the steering wheel, and punched down on the pedal.

EEEEEEE! The Buick lifted up again, swung left, and I held it to the floor. EEEEEEE! You could smell the rubber burning everywhere.

And for as scared as I was, I've gotta tell you, that car was hauling ass. We were *really* movin'. Driving up this one-way street we should have been driving down and even then, the road was closed. That's what the sign said. Barrels in our way, with flashing lights, but they didn't even slow us down.

I looked in the mirror and another car had pulled up right into our spot. Right where we had been. And the guys who were chasing us never had a chance. They were still in the traffic, back where we had left them. But I knew *that* wouldn't last.

The best thing was, I had plenty of gas. But the worst part was, I didn't have a plan. *I've gotta think*, I thought. And then, all at once, it hit me. *In the mold and in the slime... Somewhere, it was back there.*

I swung down 7th, made a right on 9th, and headed to the airport, out past the Sears place. I got on Crossfield Road and then drove out the back way, down Aircraft Drive, where you had to look for planes, and then I drove the Buick back to Earthquake Park. But even then, we didn't stop. Too many cars. *People getting laid.* That's what I remember thinking.

"Come *on*," I said. I swung the car around and we started toward the airport, back up Aircraft Drive, and then I pulled the Buick over and went back to the trunk.

"Look out for planes!" I yelled.

It was getting lighter than it had been. The sun was coming back, pushing over the horizon. Another seven minutes lost, I thought. But it really didn't matter. It wasn't hard to find. Slippery, slimy, gooey and wet. I could hardly lift it out, it kept sliding in my hands. I got it though. *The rifle case*, I thought. And I began to pull the zipper down.

I didn't know that much about rifles at the time. But I did remember Beamish telling me that the one that he had brought would put down a bear. "Maybe not a Kodiak," he'd said. But a black bear, at least.

But then I couldn't find the bullets. Beer cans and dog food and even used toothpaste, but I couldn't find a fuckin' bullet. Until I remembered. "The glove box," I said.

There were three of them there. Brass-coated, shiny, about an inch and a half long, they were mixed in with some junk we had stuffed in the box.

"Stay in the car," I said. I took the bullets out and tried to put them in the gun, but it took me a while. I didn't even know if I had them in right until I'd shot off the first round.

"Hold on," I said. "I wanna make sure this is right." I shouldered the rifle, pulled back on the trigger, and a bullet blasted to the sky. Ka-*BOOOOM*!

"*Holy shit!*" Zoey yelled. "We're right next to the *airport*."

And that's right where we were. A quarter mile away, if you came in from the back, by the sign on the fence that told you to look out for low flying aircraft. And the funny thing was, I might have shot one down that night, if it had been flying up above us. Maybe not a 747, but a little piper cub, at least.

"Here," I said. I handed Zoey the gun and she put it in the back seat. I got behind the wheel and turned the car toward Earthquake Park.

"I've really gotta go," Zoey said. And I thought she meant home, so I told her I would get her there.

"But we've gotta be *careful*," I said.

We'd gone a half a mile or less, and gotten back to Earthquake Park, when I heard the sirens coming toward us.

"Police cars," I said.

And all at once, everybody at the Park must have pulled their clothes back on and started up their cars.

"Come on," I said. And then we got behind the other cars and started driving out, back toward the city. There were twelve or thirteen cars, and I was sure that the police were gonna stop us, but they never did. We all just pulled a little to the right and watched them fly on by.

"I've *really* gotta *go*," Zoey said again. And from the way that she looked, I think it finally hit me. But there wasn't any place to take her. At least not near there.

"How about the park?" Zoey asked. "Where they had the fireworks display? I think there was an outhouse there."

"Delaney?" I asked. "You've gotta be nuts."

But that was where we went.

We drove back to the park and Zoey was right. There was a little Spot-a-pot that the city had set up for the people at the fireworks display.

"Now suppose those guys come back?" I said. "Then what are we gonna do?" But Zoey didn't care.

"I've *really* gotta *go*," she said.

There had been hundreds of people there three hours earlier. Picnic baskets, lawn chairs and blankets. A fireworks display. But none of it was left. Nobody was there. Nobody but us. Just this long, strung out strip of land, with an outhouse in the middle and a sixteen-year-old girl, maybe seventeen, with short curly hair and glasses, sitting inside. And then there was me. Sitting in the Buick with a rifle in my hands. Looking. *Always looking*. For things I never saw.

We've really gotta go, I thought. But the longer she took, the less I really cared. *A Kodiak*, I thought. *I bet I could put one down if I hit it just right -*

Zoey came back and climbed into the car. She looked like she'd been crying. I kept my finger on the trigger and looked out through the windshield.

"You wanna sit here a minute?" I asked.

But Zoey wiped away a tear and told me. "No. I think you'd better take me home."

I followed her directions to her house. "Go left on A Street," she said. "Turn right on 6th." And then we went out to Highway One, the way I'd come in, and went a couple miles. "Turn here," she said. I made a left and she pointed up ahead. "That's it."

It was a small, shingled house that needed some paint, but the thing that I remember was the porch light. It was the only one on in the neighborhood.

"Oh, no," Zoey said. And before I stopped the car, a man had come out, followed by a woman who I figured was his wife. "I really better go," Zoey said. "Have a nice trip."

I started to wave as she walked to the house. "I hope you get your car," I said.

The three of them went in and turned off the light. I sat there for a minute, and then I tried to go, but the car wouldn't move. Son of a *bitch*, I thought. I popped up the hood and just as I had figured, the cotter pin was gone. I couldn't find it anywhere.

Shoes, boots, pieces of rope.

198

But the only thing I found was a little piece of string that was lying in the gutter. And that didn't work.

I guess I could have hitchhiked back to town to buy a cotter pin or asked Zoey for some wire. I could have called a tow truck and had the Buick fixed. I guess I could have done a lot of things I never did.

Instead I figured *fuggit*, and then I started taking it all out. Everything I needed for the trip. My backpack, Kingpen's tent, the alarm clock, my sleeping bag, the copy of the atlas and the thirty-ought-six, in the moldy rifle case. I had my jacket on, with my spoon in the pocket, and that was it.

I found a pencil on the floor and a piece of paper in the back and I began to draw a map of the place in the engine where the cotter pin went. "Right here," I wrote. And then I drew a little arrow.

I wrote it all down. How to put it in Neutral if you wanted to go. Watch out for water that'll get in the trunk. And to change the oil filter, just as soon as she could. It oughta get you to New York, I wrote. Which was really pretty funny, because except for Zoey, I never met a person who wanted to *leave* Alaska. At least no one who'd been born there.

I took a few steps back and then stood there for a minute. I started to walk, but I kept on glancing back. Because that's the way I am. I've always been like that.

And the way I had it figured, Pinto had it right when he told me sometime later...

"Just *know* it's going by," he used to say. "Make yourself remember. You're only living for the past."

Chapter 23

You hitchhike out on One if you want to go to Tok, about three hundred fifty miles away. From there, you can try to get to get a ride to Haines, which is another four hundred fifty miles. And then you take the ferry to Seattle.

That's what I was gonna do. And then catch a ride back east, about five thousand miles altogether. That's what the copy of my atlas said. But I guess like Kingpen, I felt like walking for a start. So that was what I did. At least for a while.

It was five or six o'clock that morning and the sky was kind of patchy. Misty, cloudy, with splotches of sun. I walked in it all for maybe an hour, and then I stuck out my thumb and hoped for a ride. It didn't take long.

"You can throw it all in the back," the man said. He had a pickup truck with out-of-state tags. Vermont, I think they said. But he was only going down to Palmer, about forty-five miles away.

I was in the Matanuska Valley and I wished Kingpen could have seen it. Farms and fields of green and gold, everywhere I looked.

"Settled by the Scandinavians," my driver said. "In 1935. It was part of Roosevelt's New Deal." I nodded my head.

We drove about an hour, then he pulled the pickup over, helped me get my stuff out, and then got back in the cab.

"Been working up North?" he asked.

And I told him I had. "Been washing dishes," I said.

But that's not what he meant. "What Camp?" he asked.

So I made one up. "Aurora," I told him.

"Never heard of that one," he said. "I'm on the waiting list myself. Heavy equipment, Operator's Union. Six months to a year till I get out. That's what they told me."

"Well, good luck," I said.

"And good luck to you," he said back. And then he asked how far I was going.

"Baltimore." I said. Except I probably pronounced it like everybody else back there does, because then he asked me, "Bawlmer? Where's that?"

"Back east," I told him.

"Well good luck," he said again. And as he started driving off, I thought of what I'd said, and it sounded pretty stupid. Like Hong Kong. Or Australia. On the far side of the world. *Nobody would have said that*, I thought. So I thought for the next time I would tell the person Tok. Or Haines. Any place but *Baltimore*.

I was still on Highway One, and if you've ever walked past Palmer on your way to Glennallen, you know what it looks like. A town of a couple thousand people and not that many buildings, off to your right. Beautiful scenery. Like a picture on a calendar from a farm equipment company. That's what it was like. I could have stayed there for a while.

I walked a couple miles, put down my gear and stuck out my thumb. There were plenty of cars. Cars, campers, and pickups hauling boats. It was ten or fifteen minutes and then a semi came by. I heard the *Psschtt* of the air brakes and then I knew that he was gonna stop.

"Hop on up," he hollered down. So that was what I did. Hopped up on this piece of grate, opened up the door and climbed into the cab. "You can put your gear back there," he said, and pointed to the sleeper back behind the seat. "Been waiting long?" he asked. And I told him I hadn't.

We began to pull away. You could feel the trailer catch and then he started through the gears. I watched him. He pushed the gear knob forward, then pulled it back, then pushed it up again. *Vibrating power.* That's what I remember thinking. You could hear it in the engine but even more, you felt it all around you. This *veh-veh-veh...*

And in ten or fifteen seconds, we had picked up speed, and there I was - eighteen wheels beneath me, sitting up there, bouncing like hell and looking all around. *Artemus Tischman*, I thought. I'll never forget that. My first tractor trailer ride, right outside of Palmer.

We went ten or fifteen miles and passed a small town. "Sutton," he said. But nothing much was there. A post office, a restaurant and a couple of gas stations. There was a river to our right, that we drove along for a while. The Matanuska. It started at the Glacier, about forty miles ahead, but I never saw it. At least not that day. I think I fell asleep.

I was tired from all that had happened on the Fourth of July. And the way that the truck rocked, it was kind of like the Buick, riding on the frost heaves. It just put me to sleep, for a hundred twenty miles, until we got to Glennallen. I felt him tap me on the shoulder, then I opened my eyes.

"You never told me how far you were headed," he said. "Do you wanna get out here? This is Glennallen."

But I was headed to Tok. That's what I remembered I was gonna say. So I told him, "I'm heading to Tok, if you're going that far." And he told me he was.

We went another couple miles, to a truck stop on the outskirts of the town. I thought we would stop, but we didn't.

"I'll fuel up when we get to Tok," he said. And then we kept on driving, past thousands of spruce trees and hundreds of foothills without any names, until we got to the Gulkana River.

Some Natives were there and they were selling permits to fish from the shore. That's what the trucker said. "They own the land, so they sell out passes. Forty bucks a day to fish as much as you want. The kings are running now," he said. "It's a pretty good deal." I remember looking down into the river as we went over the bridge.

I was starting to wake up and felt kind of bad that I'd been sleeping so long. I mean, I don't think I'd like it, if I'd picked somebody up and they slept the whole time. So then I started asking questions.

"How ya like driving?" I asked. "You been doing it long?"

"Thirteen years," he said. "Seven years up here," and he started to laugh. "I came up here when this asphalt wasn't down," he told me, and he pointed through his windshield. "None of it. Just a two-bit half-ass road when I came up here in my camper. And the one thing I remember is my cereal."

He pointed to his right and began to wave his arm. "Know what that is?" he asked. And then he told me. "The Wrangell Saint Elias National Park and Preserve. Two times larger than New Jersey. That's where I'm from… New Jersey. And I'm never going back."

We drove another couple miles to Tulsona Creek and suddenly he remembered what he'd been telling me before. "My cereal," he said, "was inside my camper when I first came up here. A brand new box I had packed back east. I was gonna pour myself a bowl when I was staying at this campground somewhere on the Highway. And do you know what? I poured a bowl of dust."

He started to laugh and pounded on the dashboard. "A new unopened box of cereal and I poured a bowl of fuckin' dust. But that's what it was like," he said. "That time when I came up here. So much dirt and dust that they had to oil the roads. And not just once a week, like they do it now. They had to oil 'em every day. And the gravel - you don't know about the gravel. It would fly up in the air and break apart your windshield. And I *never* had *both* headlights. One was always out. But that's what it was like. I was chokin' on the dust and ducking from the gravel, but I wasn't going back. And I didn't either. Been here seven years, which is thirty years too late, as far as I'm concerned." And then he started staring through the windshield and I *know* I saw him duck once.

We drove along the Copper River, but couldn't always see it. It depended on the road. But you knew it was there. Sometimes you could hear it and then other times, you could tell from the empty space back behind the trees.

"How about some lunch?" he asked. He reached back behind his seat and pulled out a paper bag. "Grilled moose steaks," he said. And I've gotta tell you, they were great. "Because I marinated them." That was what he said. "Ever fix a moose?" And I shook my head, so he told me how to do it. And I guess he knew what he was doing, because like I said, they were really good.

We kept on driving. Boy, it was pretty. Mountains, rivers, forests and creeks. It reminded me of April when we had driven up before, except now there wasn't any snow. And the funny thing was, this was the road we would have driven on, if we had taken the car to Anchorage instead of Fairbanks, when the bolts were wearing through.

Athel Creek, Porcupine and Carlson. Then we drove up over two thousand feet to Mentasta Summit and down the other side. Nobody was there. Mountains to our left, mountains to our right and rivers in between. Rivers, lakes, and millions of trees - and we never saw another car or truck.

"Was it like this in New Jersey?" I asked. And he pounded the dashboard and we started to howl.

We crossed the Little Tok River and in another five miles, we crossed the regular Tok River. And the funny thing was, I thought the second one looked *smaller* than the first one. And maybe it was. I don't know. *I'll have to ask Kingpen*, I thought. And then we kept on driving.

We drove another half an hour and went into the town. It was just an intersection, really. Like I told you before. You can see it on a map.

"I'm going to Haines," the driver said. "So I'll let you out up here."

And now, looking back, I know I should have told the guy, "Aw, what the hell. I'll go on down to Haines. What I had to do in Tok wasn't *that* important."

But of course I didn't. I just sat there too embarrassed to say anything. And the worst part was, there were nine or ten people standing by the road with backpacks and tents, and all kind of gear.

"This is a bottleneck," he said. "For people going south, people without cars. The border's just ahead and it's hard to get a ride." But I didn't understand.

"Drugs," he said. "If you pick somebody up and it turns out they've got dope, you can lose your car. They'll confiscate your vehicle at the border up ahead. You know you've gotta go through Canada to get to Haines. They could be here for a month." He pointed to the people. "But I guess it could be worse. It could be New Jersey." He started to laugh, ran down the gears, and I could hear the semi coming to a stop – *Psschtt.*

"You know somebody here?" he asked. And I told him I did. "Well, you have a good visit," he said. And then he helped me get my stuff out and I gave him a wave.

I walked behind a building after that. I watched him fuel his rig and then take off down the road to the place where I was going. And then I walked on over to the crowd.

"You can go right to the back," somebody said. And when I asked him what he meant, he said there was a line. They weren't all there together. The newest ones were last. "I been waiting for two weeks," a guy up near the front said. And the people in the back had only been there *three* days. That was what they told me. So that's where *I* went. All the way in back, behind the guy who had a sign that said *HAINES.*

"You'll *never* get *that* through Customs," he said. And he pointed to the rifle case I was holding in my hand. "You oughta ship it out."

So that's what I did. Walked two or three blocks to the post office and mailed it to Beamish. The case had dried out from the sun, so I didn't have to special-wrap it, but I did have to take the bullets out - the ones I had put in the rifle back near the airport. I wasn't quite sure how to do it, so the lady helped with that.

"It should arrive back there next week," she told me.

It was sometime after five and I was getting kind of hungry, so I went across the street to a grocery store and made myself a deal. I would get something that I wanted. Something that I *really* wanted, and then I'd hitchhike until nine-thirty that night. If I didn't get a ride, I'd go ahead and eat it. That way, I figured, I couldn't lose.

They had doughnuts, little pies, and bags of colored candy, but the thing I knew that I was gonna get was the can of pie filling. For blueberry pie.

There was a picture on the front, showing lots of syrup. All gooey and blue. And the berries were there. I even had my spoon from Jimmy Franklin's in Chicago. But I didn't have an opener because I'd left it in the Buick, so I bought one of those when I got up to the counter. The kind you squeeze and turn, except they hardly ever work.

Only four more hours. That's what I was thinking. Because in a way, I was hoping that I *didn't* get a ride. *Only four more hours.* And then I went back to the crowd and stood there at the end of the line.

Things were pretty much the same. One person had left, but his stuff was still there. You could save your place by leaving your gear. That's what the other guys said. But it really didn't matter. Hardly anybody came. I stood there for hours. Thirteen cars, one van, and a pickup drove by. And not one of 'em stopped. Sixteen minutes, I thought. And then sixteen minutes later, I picked up my stuff and started down the road to a clearing that I'd found.

It was back in a valley and a tent was there. It was so quiet and peaceful at the bottom of this mountain that I decided to leave them alone and find another spot.

"Hold on. Who's that?" somebody called. Then he crawled out of his tent to see who I was. He was a photographer, he said, for a geographic magazine. He would be leaving the next morning to go up in the mountains.

"I specialize in *sheep,*" he said. Then he showed me his equipment. Thousands of dollars' worth of cameras and lenses. It was pretty impressive.

"How about some blueberries?" I asked.

I think at first, he thought that they were fresh because he held out his hands. But when I showed him the can, he went to get a bowl.

"I can put them on my pancakes in the morning," he said. And the way that he looked, I could tell that he liked them, so I poured out most of what was in the can.

"If you want to get up early, I'll fix you some pancakes tomorrow," he said.

I scraped the bottom of the inside of the can and ate what was left, then we sat there awhile talking about sheep. Bighorn mostly.

"I better get some sleep," he finally said. And then I told him I'd see him the next morning to try out those pancakes.

I walked back to my gear, opened Kingpen's tent and began to set it up. There were still some mosquitoes left inside from back at the Park. From McKinley. Big splotches of blood all inside the tent. It would have made you sick.

But anyway, I remember the clouds started rolling in that night. They came in from the north and then I watched as they crossed over the mountains. Then they kept on going south, heading down to Haines.

And then there was me. *How long would I be there?* That's what I remember thinking. And then I checked my pocket for the money and drifted off to sleep.

I could smell the hotcakes cooking before I woke up. A kind of bready, fluffy smell, but most of all warm. It really made you hungry. I unzipped the zipper, opened the flap, and crawled out of the bag.

"Mornin'," I said. And I gave him a wave. I put on my shoes and then I started to his tent.

"Mornin'," he said. And he took another bite.

He was running kind of late. That's what he said. And so he didn't think he'd have the time to make another batch. "Sorry," he said. And I stood there and watched till the blueberry syrup ran down his chin and then I went back to my tent.

Fuckin' prick, I thought. And then I got my stuff together and walked out to the road.

There were sixteen people standing there, including three new ones since just the night before. A ragtag bunch of people, all staring up ahead. I got at the end of the line at seven, stood there until nine-thirty, then ten, and by ten-twenty-five, we were all still there. Plus two more guys who had shown up later.

Eighteen people waiting for a ride by the side of the road. Waiting. *Always waiting.* Kicking at rocks and looking up ahead.

And there was hardly any traffic. A couple of cars but that was about it. So I stayed another half an hour and then, *Screw it*, I thought. *I think I'm gonna walk.*

It was ninety-two miles to the Canadian Border. But I didn't know it at the time. The guy who took my place told me when I stepped out of the line.

"You'll never walk that far," he said. And he probably was right. But I could hitch along the way. It made as much sense to me as standing in the crowd. But first, before I started, I was going to get an ice cream at the Far North Ice Cream Parlour, about a quarter mile away.

The sign said, "Old Fashioned Goodness at a Reasonable Price." They opened at eleven, which was just when I got there with another guy named Phil. We sat there and ate ice cream and talked about sheep. I swear we did.

And everything I said, I'd learned from the guy who'd eaten my pie filling. "*Ovis aries*," I said. And Phil nodded his head.

He was making a movie and somebody had told him the best place to go to take pictures of sheep was down at Kluane. "Sheep Mountain," he said.

"And how about bears?" I asked. Because I remembered those signs; the ones Kingpen and I had seen, down by the lake.

"You think there would be *bears*?" he asked. You could tell he was excited because his ice cream kept melting and he didn't even care.

"You think *you'd* wanna go?" he asked. "You could really help me out. You could kind of be the guide, since you've been there before."

We got out the maps from the atlas that I'd copied and looked through the states. Alabama, Arizona, Arkansas. "Here," I said. I had found it in the back, where it is a lot of times. "Alaska."

And we looked at the road that ran out of Tok, went southeast and into the Yukon. *The Alcan*, I thought. And I remembered the Buick, the frost heaves and the bolts coming through. *Ejong! Ejong! Ejong!*

"I could help you for a couple of days," I said. "But then I'm heading down to Haines." And I told him all about how I was taking the ferry and then hitchhiking back east. "To *BALL*-TUH-MORE," I told him.

"Well this will put you on your way," Phil said. He got out a map with all kinds of details and we figured it out. "About two hundred miles to the mountain," he said. "Maybe a little more. And another two hundred to Haines. Whaddya say?"

"I say we'd better get some cans," I told him. "Because there aren't that many places to pick up any food. Let's *hit* it," I said.

We finished our ice cream, went out the front and got in Phil's truck. "Rented it in Anchorage," Phil said. It was one of those trucks that you rent from a place where the cars are all wrecks. *Rent a Bomb*, or something like that. Nothing really fancy, which was OK with me.

I pointed up ahead and we went across the road and down a little ways, to the store I'd just been to the night before. "We can get some stuff in here," I said.

Then we went in the door and looked around. Nothing had changed. Same old boxes and cans on the shelves. Spaghetti and puddings, big jars of pickles. And next to the Jell-O there was one can left. Pictures of berries and syrup all over the label, twenty-one ounces of blueberry pie filling. I took out three dollars, gave it to the lady and we walked out to the truck.

It was sometime after noon when we finally got going.

"*That* way," I said, and we started to roll and creak down the road.

"Now who the heck are *they*?" Phil asked. He pointed to the people kicking the rocks and staring off into space. Seventeen people, all in a line.

"Travelers," I said. And I think he thought it was a bus stop, but he wasn't really sure, because one guy had a sign.

But the thing that I was thinking was, it's funny how you care what other people think. Even when you think you don't. People that you know, or even people that you don't. Or people who you think you thought you knew.

I wonder what they'll think , I thought, *as they see me driving by*? And then I started slouching down in the seat as we got closer to the group. I was getting kind of nervous and covering my face, glancing away, but still trying to see. Slouching. Always slouching. Curled up like a dog.

Then my mind went to the next thing , which was what I'd heard somebody say once. *Every dog has it's day*, I thought. And that's when I began to sit up straight.

"Know 'em?" Phil asked. And I told him that I didn't. "But I'll give 'em a wave."

Then I rolled down the window and wished them all good luck. Seventeen travelers, all in a line. People kicking rocks and staring off in space. One guy with a sign.

"Wonder where the bus will take them?" Phil asked me.

And I remember telling him that I didn't know.

We were driving where Kingpen and Beamish, my dog and I had been before. Except now we were going the other way on the road they made the bumper sticker for.

"The Alcan," Phil said. And we began to drive through rolling hills of aspen, birch, and cottonwood.

"Been here long?" Phil asked.

And I told him a while. "Two or three months," I said. And then just for a minute I was gonna tell him all about the trip. But I stopped, thinking that sometimes you just get tired of telling everybody.

Phil had flown up. That's what he said. And like most people in Alaska, he was from someplace else. "Kentucky," he told me. But he didn't have an accent. He told me how he'd just gotten in a couple days before. "Rented this truck and just started driving," he said.

We passed a little gravel turnoff to our right, that went seven or eight miles back into Northway. An Athabaskan village. That's what Kingpen had told me, so I passed it on to Phil, who nodded his head.

Then a little farther along, we came to a river that ran beside the road. The Chisana, with hundreds of ponds as far as we could see. Ponds that I had never seen when we were coming up. Probably thousands of 'em. Pockets of water all sparkling and bright.

"Look at that," one of us said. And I remember Phil stopping the truck, and we sat there a for a long time looking at it all. "Ever seen a Minnesota license plate?" I asked.

We got to Beaver Creek at two-thirty or three that afternoon.

"Customs," Phil said. And we stood there and watched while they looked through the truck.

Go ahead, someone motioned. They never seemed to talk.

So we got back in and Phil started it up. We crossed the old plank bridge, and in another mile or so we saw the Wrangell Mountains off to the west, their ragged, jagged peaks covered with white.

"Never lose their snow," I said. And it might have been pure bullshit, I don't know. But it was near the middle of July, so that's what I figured.

We were creaking and rocking and rolling along. But looking. *Always looking.* For things we never saw. Bighorn, Dall and Stone.

"Look, " Phil yelled. But it wasn't anything. And then a little while later, some gravel flew up and spider-webbed the windshield.

"Son of a *gun!*" Phil hollered.

And now that I look back, that's when I think that *he* started to think about turning around. "Now am *I* gonna have to *pay* for this cracked windshield?" Phil asked.

And I remember telling him, "No friggin' way."

We were racing into the rain. That's what I remember thinking. Like at the start of our trip, when we caught up with the snow storm just outside of Gary.

"Look at *that*," Phil said, pointing to the sky. And when I looked up, I saw 'em. Giant black clouds that began to fill the sky - and then it all came crashing down.

"Buckets." That's what Phil kept saying. Buckets of rain and torrents of water, until it got so bad we couldn't even see.

"I've gotta stop the truck," Phil said. And then he looked over at me. I nodded my head, he stepped on the brakes, and we slid to a stop.

"We'll never see them now," Phil said. And when I asked him what he meant, he told me the sheep. "We'll never see 'em now with these torrents of water. I'm gonna have to turn around," he said. "When these buckets of rain let up."

We sat there awhile, maybe twenty-five minutes, watching the water drip into the car, where the windshield was cracked.

"Do you see anything? Any cars or trucks?" Phil asked. And I told him I didn't because of the rain. "Then I'm turning around and we're going back." he said. He fishtailed the truck and we started back to the border.

The rain was letting up in the direction we were heading. It was more like a shower and in another mile or so, it turned into a drizzle.

"Look," Phil said. There was the lodge we had passed awhile before. The lodge - and then we went another half a mile and crossed over the bridge that spanned the White River. There was the lake to our west, then we re-crossed a creek. It was all coming back. Every little thing we had passed on the way.

And that's when it hit me. I remembered the people kicking the rocks and staring ahead. "You can let me out up here," I said. "I think I'm getting out."

Phil hit the brakes. We slid for a few seconds and then came to a stop at a creek. It even had a number. *Dry Creek Number Two.* That's what the sign said, but the creek was all *wet.*

"You can let me out right here."

"But you'll get soaked." That's what Phil told me. So I pointed to the place where the creek ran through, down underneath the road.

"I can stay down there," I said. "In the pipe for the water."

Phil nodded his head. I opened the door and got my stuff. The sleeping bag, Kingpen's tent, and my jacket.

"Here," Phil said. And he handed me the can of blueberry pie filling.

"I hope you get to Haines," he said. And I told him I would.

"I hope your movie works out. I bet I'll see it on TV," I said.

I pushed against the door, the tires began to spin, some gravel flew up, and Phil was on his way.

It wasn't raining buckets and the torrents had let up, but I guess what you'd call drizzle was still coming down. Drizzle and showers - and everything was wet.

There was a little embankment that went to the creek, ten or fifteen feet to the bottom of the hill. Mostly rocks, so I didn't get that muddy. But anyway, I stood there for a minute and looked up above me. Water was crashing down from up in the hills, for as far as I could see. Over the rocks and down through the trees, and it all came together as Dry Creek Number Two. The water ran into a round metal pipe that went underneath the road, which is where I went. Into this pipe about twenty feet long and six feet wide.

There was a log in there that I managed to turn and set just right, so that I could sit with my gear and not get wet. *It was all so cozy.* That's what I remember thinking, with the rain coming down and the creek going by right under my feet. Rain all around me, but I wasn't getting wet. It was almost perfect.

Then I got out the can, hooked in the opener and began to turn the handle. It would slip and catch, slip and catch, and it took me a while, but I got it. The top came off and I took out my spoon from Jimmy Franklin's and sat for a long time eating my pie filling. God, it was good. All of these berries, twenty-one ounces, all gooey and blue. And I ate every one.

The rain let up after a while. I buried the can, picked up my gear, and began to walk away from Dry Creek Number Two.

And the funny thing was, it all looked so different, which is what I think happens once you start walking. You see things in a different way, once you slow down. There were thousands of flowers all along the road, with dozens of colors, all growing wild. Flowers and tundra and muskeg. And then a raven flew by... *CAW! CAW! CAW!*

The sun was coming out. The clouds were breaking apart and floating off, and the sun began to shine. Fields and forests all sparkly and wet - and then the gravel started to steam. That's what I remember.

Walking down the Alcan, all by myself, looking up ahead to where I had been and back to where I thought I'd been going. Walking through the steam, as it came off the gravel, and somehow it reminded me a little of the dish room.

Hit the third button, I thought, and then I laughed and started walking just a little faster.

I walked a long time after that. Miles and miles of kicking at the gravel and looking up ahead. But moving. *Always moving*. Passing things I had already passed by twice before that day.

And then as I walked, I thought back to Kingpen and something he had said. "You really gotta write this down," he had told me.

And it was that day on the Alcan, that day I was walking, that I remember thinking to myself that maybe he was right.

I was right by the bridge, maybe fourteen, fifteen miles from where I had started, when a pickup truck came by. I could hear it back behind me, rolling on the gravel, with a trailer pull-along.

All RIGHT! I thought. And I knew I had a ride. Because the way I had it figured, *nobody* would pass me by, standing out there in the middle of nowhere like I was.

They did though. At least for a while. Drove right by - and the worst part was, they were driving all the way to Maryland. That's what their license plate said. I saw it when they passed.

They got up to the bridge, about a quarter mile away, and then they stopped.

"Come on," a lady yelled. And she leaned out her door and began to wave her arm. "Come on. Come on."

They started to back up and I ran ahead, until we finally came together, not too far from the Whitewater Bridge.

"Need a ride?" the lady asked. And I thought of the time I had hitchhiked to Tok when I meant to go to Haines.

"Sure do," I said. "All the way to Maryland."

They were people who'd retired, the lady and her husband. Really nice people who had saved all their lives to go across the country.

"We were gonna see it all," the husband said. "And we did. The Arch in St. Louis, the Golden Gate Bridge, the Tetons, the Canyon, the Pacific, and now this."

He pointed up ahead and off to our right to the mountains that were there. Mountains like you'd never see back east. "Aren't they *something?*" he asked. And I told him they were.

"The Saint Elias Mountains," I told him. And the reason I knew was because Kingpen had told me, when we were driving up.

We passed the White River Lodge that Phil and I had passed earlier that day. Nothing had changed. The Lodge was still there with some cabins on the side, a little café, and a grocery store with "Beer to Go!"

He pointed to the sign. "But it won't be going with *us*," my driver said, and started to laugh.

We kept on moving. Geez, it was pretty.

And then it started getting dusky, so it must have been near ten when we pulled in to get some gas, at the Pine Valley Motel. "Fill her up," my driver said. Then he and his wife went into the office, while I walked around outside.

I noticed a bulletin board, covered with small cards. Hundreds of 'em. It was really a collection of business cards, from people who had stopped and put them there. *Ed Logan's Towing* and *Carl's Machine Parts. Easy Kote Painting* from Brooklyn, New York.

213

Salesmen and junkyards. Chemical labs. And dozens of cards for electricians and plumbers.

There was even a card for business cards. *"Use Our Cards"* was printed at the top. So that was what I did. I took it off the bulletin board, walked back to the truck, found a marker on the dashboard, and turned the card over. Then I walked back to the board.

The couple came out. "We've got a problem," the man said. And he told me how he had figured on driving all night.

"We had hoped to catch the ferry," he said. "But I'm really kind of beat. Do you think you could drive? If not, we could spend the night right here." He pointed back behind him to the motel. "Or we could sleep here in the trailer."

"You two go to sleep," I said. "I can drive to Haines." And I told him how I loved to drive at night, and I even knew the road.

"There's a lake up ahead," I said. And I told him of the time the star had grown into the moon. "Kluane Lake," I said. I pointed up ahead to where the lights had rolled across the sky. "About another fifty miles."

"Well, if you really wouldn't mind," the lady said. I told her that I didn't. Then they climbed into the back, in the trailer pull-along.

I started the truck. I put it in gear and stepped on the gas. Real slow at first, until the trailer caught hold. Then I pulled around the pumps and stopped at the bulletin board with the hundreds of cards.

And I know you think I never found it but I did. Even in the dark. Tacked up in the left hand corner of the board, next to another card that advertised a Rental Hitch. You can see it for yourself if you ever drive by.

It's not that fancy though. It just says, *Fitch.*

––––––––––

I was back in the saddle and it was all pretty good, until we got to Quill Creek. That was where I started getting sick. Boy, was I sick. Thirty-some miles past the Pine Valley Motel, I finally had to pull the truck over. I was hanging on this sign by the side of the road, which is how I knew the name of the creek that was there. *Quill Creek.* And the more the Creek gurgled and bubbled along, the more my stomach churned - and the sicker I felt.

The trailer door opened and the lady from Maryland looked out. "You gonna be all right?" she asked. She aimed her high-beamed flashlight down at the blue gooey mess, down by my feet.

"Why don't you come in here," she said, "and lie down for a while?" Then her husband came out and said that *he'd* drive. That was the worst part.

"We'll go up front," he said. "You get yourself some sleep." But of course, I never did. Almost all the way to Haines, I was back there in the trailer. Riding down the Alcan, sitting on a toilet.

We drove past Burwash Landing, Destruction Bay, Lake Kluane, and the Star Dust Motel, but *I* never saw them. At least not that time.

I would start to feel better and then after a while, when I thought I could drive, I'd think of the label and start to get sick again. Thousands of berries in sticky, blue syrup, all gooey and sweet.

Ten minutes to one, I saw on the alarm clock. We turned off on Exit Three, Haines Highway, and went past Haines Junction. I saw it out the back window - a couple of lights. We started to head south, past Kathleen Lake, Dezadeash, Klukshu and then we drove along the Tatshenshini River into British Columbia. "Logging capital of the world." That's what Beamish used to say.

We were driving on a road that went up through the mountains, up to a place called Chilkat Pass, where the Gold Rush people went. Up and up, until at last we were there. *Chilkat Pass*. The wind began to blow and I could feel the trailer swaying back and forth. Then I guess I fell asleep.

It wasn't that much later, I heard a tapping on the trailer door. "Can we come in?" somebody asked. I pulled up my pants and told them they could.

"Customs," one guy said. And then I knew we were there. At the border of Alaska.

It's hard to explain, but if you look at a map, you can see how the road goes. Alaska, then Canada, then Alaska again. They didn't stop us very long.

"Go ahead," he said. And my driver told him we were heading down to Haines, to catch the ferry.

"One's leaving there at nine," the Customs officer said. It was only three in the morning, so we knew we had it made.

I sat up front after that. I offered to drive, but it wasn't that much farther. That's what the man said. So he drove us in. We went another forty miles, and it reminded me of Banff, with mountains and hills and different shades of gray.

"We'll see it all soon," I remember the lady saying.

And before long, we did.

If you've ever been to Haines, you know that you can only come in on the Highway, unless you want to fly or go in on the ferry. You come in on the Highway and then you turn right after that. We went down 2nd, crossed over Main, went out on Lutak, and started toward a campground that was four miles past the ferry terminal. Which was three miles from where *we* were.

"At least, we'll get a couple hours' sleep," my driver said.

There was a forest on our left that rose up a hill. Water on our right, Portage Cove. And even in the dark we could tell we were someplace special. Someplace *spectacular*, but in a serene kind of way.

"Now I've *really* seen it all," the lady said. And after she said that, nobody said a thing. We just drove along the narrow gravel road, looking out across the water to the mountains that were there. Like the pictures that you see of fjords in Norway, except that it was dusk.

We went another couple miles and up on our right we saw some cars. Cars, pickups, and a couple of trailers. "I guess they're waiting for the ferry," somebody said. And I thought back to Prince Rupert and what it had been like there.

"Maybe we should stop," the lady said. "And check about the tickets."

But her husband said he was tired, so we kept on going for another four miles, until we made it to the campground. Or at least we *thought* we made it to the campground. But the funny thing was, we never saw a trailer or a car. Not even a tent. Nothing, except for an old wooden picnic table sitting on the grass - and we only saw *that* because of our headlights.

"No place but Alaska," the lady said. And she told me how the campgrounds had been so crowded down in California. "Such a thing to see. And now - look at *this*." It really was pretty neat, this little park-like setting with nobody there.

We got out of the truck, and then the man must have reconsidered and decided to go back. "Maybe we should," he said. "At least find out what's what. You can come down with us," he told me, "or stay here if you want. We shouldn't be long."

So I told him I'd stay. "I'll catch you in the morning," I said. And they got in their truck.

I pulled Kingpen's two-man orange tent from the nylon bag and began to stake it out. The earth was soft, so I pushed the pegs in with the bottom of my shoe. Five or ten minutes and I had the whole thing set up.

But I didn't go inside. Not for a while. I heard this *SPLASH! SPLASH! SPLASH!* a little further up the road, so that's where I went. Around and up the hill, to the lake with a small wooden sign. *Lake Chilkat.* Like the name of the pass you might have seen in the famous picture from the Gold Rush.

SPLASH! SPLASH! SPLASH! I stood there a long while looking for a boat, but there weren't any around. No boats or motors. Not even any people for me to see, or for them to see me. Nobody there. Just the lake and the mountains and me. All alone, except for the fish.

I could see them in the moonlight. *SPLASH! SPLASH! SPLASH!* And I know I saw 'em by the dozens. Hundreds maybe. Two and three-foot salmon, jumping in the night.

I stood there and watched until the water smoothed out. Then I walked back to the tent and set the alarm for a couple hours' sleep. I pulled the button out and put the clock down like I always did, at the bottom of the tent, so I wouldn't turn it off if I rolled around at night. And then I got inside the bag.

And the thing I remember most before I drifted off to sleep was that it all seemed so perfect. It all seemed so *right*.

———

They began to filter in from someplace far away. Little human voices that broke into my dreams and slowly convinced me that I wasn't asleep.

"Over here!" one of them shouted. And they started to get closer. Whining, broken voices. Dozens of them, screaming all around.

"I'll race you to the lake," one of them yelled.

And then, "*NO!* Let's play *ball.*"

"Let's go *fishing.*"

"Let's go *swimming!*"

And all the time you heard their feet, tromping right outside the tent.

There were a couple of them on the picnic table then, almost right beside me.

"You think somebody's *in* there?" one of them asked.

And the other kid said, "No."

But then the first one said, "Yeah. There *has* to be. *Watch*." And then he must have thrown a piece of gravel or a stick, because something hit the tent.

"Let's look inside," one of them said. They started toward the back, to look through the air flap. But just as they got there – *BRRRRNNGGGG!*

"SHIT!" one of them yelled. And then they took off running, scared to death.

I pushed the button in and sat there for a minute, deciding what to do. *Maybe I could wait*, I thought. They would all go away. All disappear. Then I could pack up my bag and the tent, my spoon from Jimmy Franklin's, and the other stuff I had, and walk down to the ferry.

"How about the food?" a little squeaky voice asked. "You wanna put it on the table?"

"You might as well," somebody shouted. And that's when I knew. It would only get worse. More gravel. Then rocks. They'd look in the tent and then after a while, well - the only thing you could count on was that it would turn out *more*.

"Come help me with the food!" somebody yelled.

And that's when I decided I had to get out. Pack up the gear, fold up the tent, and then I'd walk on down the road, looking straight ahead.

I threw the clock in my backpack, rolled the sleeping bag up tight and sat there for a second. It wasn't very long. Then I unzipped the tent flap, turned myself around, and started backing out, so it looked like I was going in.

"Did you sleep in there?" this one kid asked. I pretended not to hear him, but another kid was there.

"Do you live in there?" he asked. And I told him that I didn't. "Well not *exactly*," I said.

I gave the tent a yank and it lifted off the ground. The stakes flew everywhere, and then I threw them all inside my pack and put the whole thing on my back. *University Avenue*, I thought. And I started toward the gravel road, looking straight ahead.

"Where you gonna go?" another little kid asked. "Back up in the woods?"

And for the first time, I noticed that they all looked the same. Each one was blue. *Cub Scouts*, I thought. And that's who they were.

"You guys on a trip?"

"Cookout," one said. And they told me they'd been fishing and playing some ball.

"Well, I hope you all have fun," I said.

A truck was coming down from up above the lake. It was coming down the hill and stopped where I was walking.

"How about a lift?" the stranger asked. "Going into town?"

"Headed that way," I said. "Going to the ferry." Then he nodded his head and told me one was leaving pretty soon.

I tossed my stuff in the back and as I turned to get in, I saw a sign I hadn't seen before. Back near the place where I'd slept in Kingpen's tent. *NO CAMPING – PICNIC AREA*, it said. And when I asked the guy where the campground was, he pointed up the hill.

"Up there past the lake," he said. "You've gotta go on up the road."

We started down the gravel, with the forest on our right and the water on our left. Boy, it was pretty.

"Something, isn't it?" he said. And it really was. Beautiful mountains reflecting on the Cove.

"Where else but Alaska?" he said. Then we drove four miles, came to the ferry, and he let me out.

"They're really packed today," he said. "I bet they'll wait a week." I thanked him for the ride and got out. Then he gave a wave and started off.

The ferry terminal was right next to the water, for people to buy tickets. And from that point on back, there were over two hundred vehicles waiting in line. Campers and cars, trucks and travel pull-alongs. Anything on wheels.

"I been here two days," somebody said. And you could tell there were more cars than they had places to put them on the boat.

The ferry was the M.V. Malaspina, which looked a lot like the one I had been on before. Blue and white and gold, except I think that it was bigger.

But anyway, I went into the building, stood there awhile, and heard the ticket sellers telling people it would be at least another day. Maybe two. They were all booked up, and the way they had explained it, you had to have a reservation. "Unless you're walking on," they said. "Then you don't need one."

I remember it was one hundred fifty-eight dollars from Haines to Seattle. So I handed him two hundreds, and he handed me a schedule that I put in my pocket, along with the change.

The boat was leaving in an hour. They never blew a one-hour warning whistle like you see in the movies, but I could tell from the alarm clock. There was just enough time to see the people from Maryland, so I started walking down the line. Pickups and Broncos, little two-seaters. And back toward the end, about three-fourths of the way down the line, sat a pickup truck and a pull-along, with Maryland license plates.

"We were going to come back to get you," the lady said. "But we thought we'd lose our place in line. I just don't know what to think. They said we might get on. But then again, we might not."

The line began to move as they loaded up the ship. "Let's hope," the lady said. And they got real close, but they didn't get on.

"Tonight," somebody told them. "There's another ferry coming."

"Well, I guess we'll go on *that* one then," the lady said. "If we don't get out of line."

"You want to stay and wait with us?" her husband asked me. "If you do, we can drive you all the way."

But I told them I was gonna go. "I might stop off in Ketchikan," I said. Because according to the schedule, I thought I could get off there and stay awhile, and then catch another ferry after that.

"Well, whatever you think," the lady said. "We just wanted you to know."

"Well I *do*," I said. "I really do." And I told them how much I had appreciated the ride, all the way from Whitewater Bridge. "You two are the best," I said.

"Well, good luck," the man told me, and we both shook hands. The lady put her arms around me and gave me a hug.

"Now you give us a call when you get back east," she said. I told her I would, but of course I never did. I mean, I wanted to, but I didn't have their phone number. And now that I look back, I never even knew their names.

I walked up a little wooden gangplank to get onto the ferry. Then I kept on going higher, up the stairs, to get a better view.

It was a little bit different, but kind of the same as the ads that you see of people leaving the dock. People on a cruise.

"Isn't this *exciting*?" someone asked. And I guess from *our* side it was. Lifeboats and portals and people with cameras. I mean *that* part was the same.

But the one thing in the ads that you almost always see, is the crowd on the dock. The people waving goodbye. Some with balloons, others tossing confetti, holding onto flowers, or maybe throwing a kiss. The people are happy.

But I remember that when I looked at the dock down below me that morning, these people were different. These people weren't like that. These people were *pissed*.

———

The engines started up with a deep, low rumble that I could feel in the railing I was leaning on. "We're underway!" someone shouted. And in five or ten minutes, we had left the terminal behind, started past the town, and headed south.

I was standing on the top deck and we were moving down the Lynn Canal. That's what one guy said. And it was even better than the last time, because for most of the trip I could see the land on either side. At least for a while. Boy, it was something. Snowcapped mountains, forests - we even passed a waterfall. And there were never any people or buildings to see.

"Look!" somebody shouted. The rest of us looked and there on the shore, we thought we saw a bear, running down the beach.

"A Kodiak," somebody said. And we kept on moving.

It was getting close to noon. The snack room had opened, but before I went in, I walked down to the lockers and put my stuff away. Then I took a quick shower, put my clothes back on, and went to get some food. Two ham and cheese sandwiches and a pickle.

I went up to the lounge deck and lounged there in a chair. All stretched out, one sandwich on my lap, the other in my hand, with the pickle in my mouth. And the thing I remember thinking was, *it had all changed so fast.* That's what I remember thinking. *If Phil could see me now*, I thought. And then I bit another bite.

It started clouding up a little after that. The mist came in and it started to rain.

"This is typical," somebody said, reading from his tourist guide. He looked over to me and I nodded my head.

"Know how many inches of rain Ketchikan gets in a year?" I asked. I could tell he didn't know, so I told him. "A hundred and eighteen. *Rain Capital of the World.*" And we both looked out the window.

It began to rain a little harder after that, never pouring down, but more of a long, steady drizzle. Misty, foggy, kind of hard to see.

"Auke Bay!" the Captain announced. You could hear him on the speaker. "Auke Bay." And I remember, that was when I started getting nervous.

Auke Bay? I thought.

You read about people who end up in Zimbabwe when they meant to go to London, or Belgium, or maybe Australia. And then even when they get there, where they thought they meant to go, they're not really sure. Like Hilo, when you fly to Honolulu. But anyway, that's what it was like. I looked at my schedule, and according to the chart we were supposed to stop at Juneau. But we never really did.

"For those planning to depart, you can go down to your vehicles," the captain announced. And it wasn't very long after that, we pulled up to the dock, and there we were. *Auke Bay*. About fourteen miles from Juneau, capital of Alaska.

The rain was coming down, so I looked out through the window at the cars driving off. There weren't that many, maybe seven or eight. Then some other cars drove *on*. "I wonder how they manage that?" somebody asked. "How do they know to load them just the way they do?" But I didn't know.

We weren't there that long. The engines started up and we began to pull away. It was kind of like Haines, because in five or ten minutes, we began to pass the town. *Juneau*, I thought. But it wasn't. It was Douglas, on the island in front, and there back behind it, on the side of the mountain was Juneau. You can see it on a map.

We went another couple hours and the Inside Passage opened up. Water, water everywhere, and by five or six o'clock that night, you couldn't see the land. Just water. Gray and dreary and rolling with mist, it began to blend with the sky. And after a while, you couldn't tell the difference, because it all looked the same.

I got another sandwich after that. I went down to my locker to check on my stuff. Then I walked back to the lounge chair, settled down, and then I guess I fell asleep. Fell asleep and slept through

Stephens Passage, while the ferry passed forests and fjords, Kupreonof and Kake.

"PETERSBURG!" the speaker blared. And I looked at the alarm clock. It was ten minutes to midnight and there we were. *Petersburg.* "The most picturesque town in all Alaska," the Captain announced. And even though I never saw the town because it was so dark, the lights looked pretty good.

A few cars got off, none got on, and the engines started up again. The night was clear by then, so I went out on the deck and stood there as we pulled away.

The thing that I remember most is that it all looked so alone. Petersburg did. A lonely blotch of lights with pitch black all around. Not even any roads you could drive on, to leave the town. And the thing I remember wondering was how it even got to be there. Thinking about *this*. Wondering about *that*. *Thinking about wondering.*

And as I sat there thinking, an older lady walked to the back of the ferry, when no one else was there. Twelve o'clock at night. She had a small wooden box that she was holding in her hands. And when she took the lid off, all these ashes scattered into the dark. She dropped her head and stood there for a minute, and then she walked away.

After that, I stood by the railing and watched the silhouettes of the mountains as we moved on down the coast. Miles and miles and miles - and I never saw a light. I remember Kingpen or Beamish, one of them saying on the way up the road, "We're getting there." And what they meant was, to wilderness.

But there, on the ferry, I thought I really saw it. I watched it awhile and then I looked back behind me, to all the people sleeping on the boat, huddled in their staterooms or bundled in their lounge chairs. Then I looked back to the coast.

Wilderness, I thought. And back then, I really thought I knew just what it was.

We got into Wrangell a little after four that morning. The sun was coming up, and as we left, we passed by the harbor where the fishing boats were going out. Gill and seine netters mostly, dozens of them, starting toward the ocean.

We went around Zarembo Island, started down Clarence Strait, and headed toward Ketchikan, about six hours away.

I could get them some lunch. That's what I remember thinking. We'd get there at ten or maybe eleven, then I'd pick up some lunch and take it to the Kraxins.

"Now you shouldn't have," she'd say. He'd offer a smile and we'd sit there with our rum and cokes and watch the float planes come in.

The boat was waking up by then. People were moving around and collecting their things. Blankets and sleeping bags. Parents telling their kids, "Get up! Get up!"

It was all so different from when you went to sleep. I mean it was natural at night. We were almost like a family. People were sleeping on the floor or curled up in their chairs. But the thing about the morning was, you couldn't get caught in the half of the crowd that woke up last, because then it wouldn't *look* right. It was embarrassing, I guess. Because of the light.

"Come on," I heard a lady say. "Before the other people see you."

We were out in open water and off to our right we began to see land. "Prince of Wales," somebody said. And I thought it was a town at first, but it wasn't. They said it was an island. And the way that the sun was coming up, you could see it all glisten. All the trees and the hills and the beaches and the coves.

I took a shower after that. By the time I was finished, the cafeteria was open, so I went on in and sat there eating pancakes, while I looked out the window. I thought I saw a humpback once. You can almost always see a whale, if you travel on the ferry and look hard enough.

I finished a small glass of juice I had bought for a dollar, then I went down to my locker to get my gear. I could see it was ten minutes to ten on my clock. I checked to make sure the button was in, then I took everything out and went up on the deck.

A lot of people were there. Maybe forty to fifty of them, leaning on the rails or walking around. There wasn't much to do. It wasn't like a cruise ship.

"Ever seen an Eskimo?" I heard somebody ask.

And the other guy said, "Yeah. The time I went to Barrow."

"McKinley wasn't bad," I heard somebody else say. And that's how they were talking, all about their tour stops.

The sky was clouding up, so I knew that we were getting close. Ten or fifteen minutes and then I heard it on the speaker.

"Ketchikan!" the Captain said. "Over to our left." But you couldn't really see it, because of all the rain. And the thing that got me was, we didn't even stop. *Auke Bay*, I thought. I figured we would dock just north or south of town. But we didn't. We didn't stop at all. And when I looked at my schedule, there was a little star next to Ketchikan that was supposed to let us know that.

I went down to the lounge deck to get out of the rain and looked through the window, back to where we'd passed. But the only thing I think I saw was some steam from the pulp mill. And even then, from all the mist, I'm not so sure I really saw it.

We were moving down the channel. Revillagigedo. About a hundred miles long. *Raining Raining. Raining.* I remember that. For five or six hours, we were moving through the mist.

An island here. An island there. Misty fiords off to our left.

Then we went across the border, right there in the water. That was what the Captain said. "CANADA!" he announced. And even though we didn't know what to look for, everybody looked.

I left the lounge deck right after that and went back outside. Then I stood there in the rain, looking back to Alaska. And as sure as I could have been about anything right then, I knew that I'd go back. *I know I will*, I thought. Then I started smiling.

The clouds began to lift. We went by Dundas Island into Chatham Sound. And just like the last time, I smelled the place before I ever saw it. *Prince Rupert*, I thought. *Armpit of the World.*

And in another half an hour we had docked, where I had first gotten on the ferry months before. Nothing much had changed. The parking lot was full, with dozens of campers and cars, and all kinds of trucks. And Customs was open, with people filing through.

"Gonna be here awhile," I heard somebody say. And when I looked at my schedule, I knew what he meant. Arriving at four, departing at six-thirty. So I decided to leave the boat and take a look around.

And I know just what you're thinking. But if there's one thing you don't want if you go to Prince Rupert, you don't want to get *stuck* there. Which was all I kept thinking. So I double-checked with the purser and even asked if the time zones had changed. Then I went down to the lockers, jammed in my gear, walked off the boat, and started through Customs.

"Visiting," I said, when they asked me why I was there. And then I handed them the clock, and they let me put it in my pocket.

"Go ahead," he motioned.

I knew just where I was. At the point of the road where the Yellowhead Highway dead ends at the water. I could only go back toward the town. I went across the lot and on up the hill.

By then, the cars had started off the ferry. One guy drove by and honked to give me a lift, but I waved him on. I really felt like walking, after being on the boat.

I looked at the clock. It was four thirty-five. I set the alarm for six, pulled out the button, and kept on walking. It was two or three miles to the center of town, which was where I was going. But then I started getting nervous. I wasn't sure I could make it back to the ferry in time, so I decided I would just walk to the campground where we'd stayed.

It wasn't that far. Another half a mile, then I went off on the side road, around and up the hill, where the broken chain had been. Except it wasn't like the last time this time. This time it was *packed*. Campers and trailers and hundreds of tents, everywhere you looked. People cooking dinners on little Coleman Stoves. Kids playing ball.

The campground's building was there. The one that was locked the last time, but this time it wasn't. It was partly an office and partly a store. Cupcakes and milk, some apples and pears, and over on one side, a desk was set up.

"Only spaces left are on the side of the hill," I heard the campground lady say. "The top parts are all taken, at least until tonight, when the Ferry comes in. Then they'll start to leave. You think you want to wait? Egh?" she asked.

And the customer said, "Yeah," he thought he would.

I looked around awhile and then I finally bought one thing. Two things really, if you figured in the stamp. It was a postcard with a picture of the campground on the front. I flipped it over, picked up a pencil on the table and started to write…

"Hey Beamish," I wrote. "Wish you were here."

Then I filled in the address, put on the stamp, and dropped it into the mailbox. It was the kind you see at campgrounds and hotels. Just a little cardboard box.

"Thanks," I said. I turned and walked away.

And even now, now that I look back, I see that campground one of two ways. Packed and jammed with millions of people, campers and tents. Then sometimes I see it empty, like the first time we were there. Jammed full or empty, but never in between. Never partly full.

Come on, I thought. *I've gotta go.*

I started walking faster, so I wouldn't miss the boat. And I didn't miss it either. As a matter of fact, I even got there early. Five fifty-seven, I was standing there at Customs, but American this time, because we were going to Seattle.

Five fifty-eight. Five fifty-nine. "Anything to -

BBBRRNNGGG!

"Oh, my *GOD!*" the Customs lady screamed.

I took out the clock and pushed the button in.

"Oh my Lord! You really had me scared," the lady said. And then she looked at me a minute and told me to go through.

I walked up the gangplank, showed someone my ticket and went onboard. My stuff was still there, packed inside the locker.

One more thing, I thought. I put the clock on top the tent, shut the locker door, and except for what I had on and the money in my pocket, everything I owned was in there. Even the spoon that I had bought from Jimmy Franklin's.

The engines came to life, we began to pull away, and I went up to the deck to watch it all go by. The fertilizer plant and washing machines. The Recreation Building with the ravens outside. The campground on the hill and the Prince Rupert Hotel. "I *know* the man," he'd said. *Yeah*, I thought. Him, too - The Wobble Wobble Wobble Man.

And the thing that was so strange was that now I was right where I'd been *looking* months before. Out there in the water that I never really saw back then, because it all had been so black. Looking for *this*, looking for *that*.

And it took me a long time to realize it, but I think do now - I was starting to look back.

I just didn't know it at the time.

Chapter 24

It takes almost as long to go from Prince Rupert to Seattle as it does from Haines to Prince Rupert. Another thirty hours. That's what it said on my schedule. With nothing in between except mountains and forests, and hundreds of islands.

I got a sandwich in the snack bar and went to sit in the lounge chair that I had been sitting in, but someone was there. You couldn't reserve them, not unless you left a coat or a jacket or something to hold it, which *I* never did. But a lot of other people did it, so I never got a chair. Not for a while. I just walked around and ate, and then went up on the deck and stood at the front of the boat, looking straight ahead.

I went into the dark like that. I saw the sky turn inky black and the water lose its depth. The stars began to shine and it started getting cold. Not like back in Banff. Just chilly, I guess. Then I went to my locker and got out my sleeping bag.

There were twelve to fifteen people sleeping on the deck that night, right on the floor. I put my bag down with them and crawled inside.

"Where ya headed to?" I heard somebody ask.

"Seattle," I said. "And then I'm going east."

"Signed up on a list?" the guy behind me asked.

"Laborers," I told him. And he let out a laugh.

"Signed up with them last fall," he told me. "It's almost been ten months. Screw 'em. I'm finally wising up. Going home to Pittsburgh. I never should have left."

We laid there after that and he drifted off to sleep. But I never did. Not for a while. The engines kept me up as they rumbled through the deck.

I found myself just staring at the sky. Billions of stars, all sprinkled on black. And then, all at once, the lights came out. Nothing like Kluane, but I could tell that they were there. And for forty minutes to an hour, I sat and watched them. Faint traces of colors that would roll and sweep across the night.

Back beyond Prince Rupert, the Armpit of the World.

"Look," a lady said. "There up ahead." And when she pointed, I could see the killer whales. White on black, and black on white. We followed them south into Queen Charlotte Strait, back behind Vancouver Island.

I had put my things away and was standing on the deck with some other people. Tourists mostly. The kind who slept down in the cabins.

"Now *that's* the way to go," I heard one of them say. He pointed up ahead and you could see a cruise ship, coming up the strait. It started getting closer and everybody waved as the boats began to pass. *Sun Princess*. That was its name. And just the way it looked, you could tell it was a nice one.

"Top of the line." That's what one guy said.

I went down to get some breakfast after that. Pancakes and sausage and a dollar glass of juice. Then I went to take a shower and stood there with the water beating down. I didn't even use the soap. I just stood there with the water beating down. And the neat thing was, I remember thinking, it really doesn't matter if I'm eating pancakes or I'm sleeping or I'm standing in the shower. It really doesn't matter, because we're moving all the time.

We saw another couple cruise ships after that. For fifty, sixty miles, maybe more, we rode along with the shorelines to our left and to our right. British Columbia and Vancouver Island. Long gravel beaches, where we saw a couple of bears, some black tail deer, and then eagles. Dozens of them, flying all around or up on tops of trees.

"*There*," somebody said. We saw another whale and the cameras all began to click.

We passed an island on our left, a town called Cambell River on our right, and then the water opened up. And that's the way it stayed until we got down to Seattle. Except for some islands, I don't think we ever saw the shores again that day. At least not close up.

"About another two hundred eighty miles," I heard somebody say. It sounded pretty close, but it wasn't. It was kind of like the railroad that ran from Fairbanks down to Anchorage. You could get there faster with a car.

I got a hot dog and bun and some potato chips for lunch, four bucks, and then I got lucky because I found an empty chair, so I sat there and ate. I think I drifted in and out of sleep right after that. I'd open my eyes and watch it all go by and then I'd close them for a while. Mountains and forests off in the distance. Islands going by. And then I'd be there in the Buick, with Beamish driving and me sleeping in my dream, or working in the dish room. "Anybody under thirty-seven twelve?" somebody'd shout out. And then I'd open my eyes and see islands again.

It was the most relaxing day, that's what I remember. Over three hundred miles and I never saw a cloud. Lounging kind of weather, where the whitecaps roll and glisten and the spray flies up. You couldn't beat it.

Maybe I should check my stuff in the locker, I thought. And then I figured, *fuggit*, and drifted back to sleep.

We went down past Powell River, Saltery Bay and Courtenay. And then kept on, passing Langdale, Horseshoe Bay and Nanaimo.

"Look at that," somebody near me said. And all along the way we saw these islands. Dozens of them, all different sizes and shapes. Private Shangri-La's, where you could go and they'd never ever find you. That's what one guy said.

The sparkle wore off. It began to get dusky and then before it got dark, I thought that I would see it one last time. I went up on the deck like I had the night before, but the thing that was so different this time was seeing the lights of all the towns. Up and down the coasts and even on some islands, they were there, pushing out the dark.

"Vancouver," someone said. "A city of a million."

And off to our left, there it was. A distant hazy glow that reminded me of Whitehorse the time we saw it in the distance. Except this time, it was bigger.

We crossed the imaginary line and the Captain called out, "We are entering the United States." And I guess he would have told us all about the swath if there had been one, so I figured that there wasn't.

We passed Saltspring Island, Swartz Bay and Sidney.

"Victoria!" somebody called out. And you couldn't miss it. Sparkling lights all sitting on the water, it almost looked kind of pretty, and then we started passing even more islands, larger than before.

"San Juan," the Captain announced. And you could tell from the tourists who were still on deck that we were starting to get close.

But then it all got so different. Between someplace and Bellingham, somehow it changed.

The lights along the shore began to bunch up. They clustered together and started to branch out. Forests became towns and I started to see planes. Single-colored lights, moving across the sky.

And then sometime after that, *think the strangest thing,* "Bellingham!" the Captain called out. "We're at the end of our journey." And just like with Auke Bay or Hilo, we came in close, but not exactly where I thought we would, in Seattle.

"You can go down to your cars," I heard the Captain say. So I went down to the locker and got out my stuff.

It didn't take long to dock. Another couple minutes and we had stopped for the first time since Prince Rupert. We all began to leave, and the thing that I remember was I never had to show my ticket stub. There was no one there to see it.

And now that I look back, I guess I could have bought a ticket just to Auke Bay for fifty-seven bucks and never gotten off. From there, I could have just kept on going down to Bellingham. It seemed that way to me. And I guess you still could do it. I don't know.

When you walk off of the Ferry in Bellingham, you go on to this road that's called Alaskan Way. I swear to God. Pinto told me later, "They name a lot of stuff like that, because in a way, they really want to be there - in Alaska. But in another way they don't. So they name their streets and other stuff like that. You can really see it at the airport in Seattle."

Anyway, I started walking down the road to a street lamp. I took out the maps I had Xeroxed up in Fairbanks... Vermont, Virginia, *Washington.* But even though I had a map, it didn't help that much. It wasn't that specific. So I figured I would just start walking south, the way the ferry would have gone if it hadn't stopped to dock, but gone on to Seattle like I thought it would. And then I thought I'd make a left the first chance that I had and head back east.

Cars were coming down the road. Cars and pickups, and a of couple travel trailers. Almost all of them were coming off the ferry. And the way you could tell was from all the dust and the mud and the windshields that were cracked.

Well if I'm ever going to get a ride, this is it, I thought. So I turned around and stood there, on the sidewalk, and stuck out my thumb. One-thirty, two o'clock in the morning. Sometime in July.

And there I was, hitchhiking south to Seattle on Alaskan Way. I had Kingpen's tent sitting on the ground beside me with my sleeping bag. The alarm clock was in the pocket with my spoon, and then I had my other pocket full of money. And I must have looked like a pig that had rolled in shit, even though I'd had three showers in the last two days.

A couple cars slowed down, but none of them stopped. Campers, trailers, pickups and cars that were covered in mud. I saw 'em all go by and remember wondering how many of the drivers I had talked with just the day before. Then the regulars began to drive by, people who had never made the trip. People who had normal-looking cars, with windshields in one piece.

It was two o'clock. It might have been two-thirty when one car finally stopped. "Toss it in the back," he said. Then he pulled the front seat forward and helped me with my gear.

I was going to tell him I was only heading south to get to the highway that would take me east. But I never did, because he never even asked me where I was going. In fact, he hardly even talked, and I never offered much. I was too damn tired. So we kept on driving.

Like a barber with a customer who's not really sure how much they want to say, so he sticks to what he's doing. "Trim?" "Yeah." "Taper?" "Yeah." "Leave it dry?" That's the way it was. I even laid it on at one point and told him that his car, which was just a pile of junk, was really something special.

"Thanks," he said. And kept on driving.

He drove a long time after that. Nothing like Beamish, but at least a couple hours. I fell asleep. But the thing that I remember, just before I did, was that I started feeling nervous, not knowing where I was or where I was going. Being driven all around, this way and that.

But then, I started thinking, it didn't really matter. I had a pocket full of money and in another couple hours, the sun would be up and I could see where I was. I'd be *someplace*. Just like I was then. *You always are*. That's what I remember thinking. And now, looking back, it was a highlight of the trip. The night I figured out, you're always *someplace* with yourself.

We must have gone over a bump. I woke up and then he told me, "Just about there. I can let you off up here, just over the hill, or in another couple miles, there's a little town. Whaddya think?"

"Maybe I should get out here," I said. And by that time, things were dead. A little after four in the morning and nothing was around. No cars. No people. "Well, I appreciate the ride," I said.

"Yeah," he told me. He handed me my stuff, and I watched him drive off toward the little town. Then I stood there for a minute.

I went into a field after that. I think it was part of a farm. I climbed through long strands of wire and tore my jacket apart on the sharp metal barbs. Fluffs of polyester began falling to the ground. And the thing that I remember thinking was that you might have thought a pigeon died there, if you saw it in the morning.

Twenty after four. Almost four thirty. I set up Kingpen's tent, put my gear inside, and then crawled down deep in the bag. But even then, as deep as I was, I started to hear birds. *Chirp! Chirp! Chirp!* Then I drifted off, but I know I only slept for a couple hours. Then I packed it all up and started off again.

I walked toward the buildings, and even though the cars were passing by, I didn't try to get a ride. It wasn't very far. A mile and a half, maybe even less. I walked into the town, but not much was there. A Methodist church, some restaurants, a laundromat, and little drugstore. So I went in there.

"Morning," the clerk said. And at first I didn't see him back behind the counter. "Help you?" he asked.

I looked down at the candy counter. "Any Sky Bars?" I asked.

The man just shook his head. "Don't think I've ever seen one," he said. So I told him what they looked like. Four or five different flavors, each with its own section.

"You oughta get some," I told him. "I think they'd really sell." And then I bought a chocolate bar for breakfast.

I went out to the parking lot and took a look around. There were license plates from California and Oregon and one from Arizona, but mostly from Washington, like you would figure.

"You looking for a ride?" I heard somebody ask. I turned around and when I looked, a man was walking down the sidewalk to his car. A Jeep, really. A bright red CJ5. "I'm driving down to Portland, if you want to come along. You going to California?"

"Not exactly," I said. "I'm trying to go east."

"Well you can get on I-84," he said. "It's right outside of Portland, if you wanna come along." So I climbed up in front, put my stuff in the back, and we started driving out.

"Had it long?" I asked. And he knew I meant the Jeep. His eyes lit up and he shifted through the gears.

"A couple months," he said. And then he asked me if I'd ever had one.

"Not really," I said. And then I told him all about the Buick.

"Well now *this* is what you need," he said. "Especially up there. Four- wheel drive." He pointed to the gearshift.

We were driving on a highway and it was starting to get crowded with more trucks, cars and signs. "Spend much time in Oregon?" I asked. And then, I remember, he put his finger to his head and I thought that he was going to shoot himself.

"Or-eh-*GUN*! Or-eh-*GUN*! *GUN*! *GUN*! *GUN*! You're not from *these* parts, are you?" he asked.

And I told him I wasn't.

"Well anyway, you really oughta see it down the coast. Do it while you're young."

The Interstate split up, we headed right and began to cross a river.

"Tell you what I'm gonna do," he said. "I'll drive you up to Highway 18 if you want to see the coast. It's right outside of Portland. Then you go a hundred miles, on into Otis, and then down along the ocean, 101 to California. How about it? You'll love it." So I told him I'd do it.

We went across the city, passing Killingsworth, Banfield, and Freeway, then we crossed another river and went down Highway 5 to Tigard.

"You oughta get a ride here," my driver said. He pulled off to the side and helped unload my stuff. "Just take it to the end, then turn south after that. I hope you have a camera." And I didn't, but I told him that I did.

He turned around and started heading back to Portland. "Don't forget. Get yourself a Jeep," he shouted. I waved and then I reached inside my pocket, took out the alarm clock, and started winding. It was ten twenty-five.

I got myself something to eat, went out to the road, and stuck out my thumb. It got to be a game of trying to predict who would pick me up and who would pass me by.

No… No… *Here's one*, I thought. A blue Chevrolet began to go by, about five or six years old, with one guy inside. *Here we go*. And I thought he would stop, but he didn't. Just kept on going.

So I stood there and waited and began to watch the people. And some of them watched me. But others didn't. That's what I remember. They stared ahead like I wasn't even there. And the thing that I kept thinking was, *they're the ones who* really *want to look*. That's what I remember thinking.

I walked and stood and walked and stood, and a couple miles from Tigard I finally caught a ride. But I didn't know it for a minute. The car went by and then I heard a horn and they started backing up - two kids and a couple from New Hampshire.

"Want a ride?" the lady asked. And they all got to laughing. Even the man. "Need a ride?" the lady asked again. "We're driving to the ocean." So I climbed into the back, held my stuff on my lap and off we went..

There wasn't that much room when you considered the car. It was a big Ford station wagon, brown on white. The kind you used to see, but don't see now, at least not that often. And the reason it was cramped was from all of the crap they had jammed inside. Stuff for a vacation. Boxes and bags and golf clubs and water skis. A bucket with sand toys. And up on the roof, there were bicycles mounted to the car.

Everything was there except the kitchen sink. And if you would ever need to wash your hands, well, she'd brought these moist towelettes. That's what Barbara said. And then, there was her daughter, Isabella Rose, who was nine, her son Charlie, who was seven, and her husband Johnson, who didn't talk much, but smiled a lot.

"Have you ever seen the ocean?" Isabella asked. And I told her I had, but that was back east. "The Atlantic," she said. "I saw *that* one, too!"

Barbara told me how Isabella and her brother had gone to their grandparents' house in New Jersey. "We went out in the waves," Charlie said. He told me all about a fishing boat they had been on, except they didn't catch a single fish. And then I told them of the ferry and McKinley and the time we'd driven up the road.

"Ever see a bear?" they asked.

"The only time I did, I was up there on a hunt," I said. "Wilderness. No houses. No stores. Not even any roads. They had to fly us in with all of our supplies. Three of us. The pilot flew us to a place where no one else had ever been. It wasn't even named. Soaring mountains all around, forests and valleys, and rivers that were frozen. And the morning of the hunt, we decided to split up. 'I'll walk along the ridge tops,' one guy said. And the other guy went between the mountain peaks and valleys.''

"And where did *you* go?" Isabella Rose asked. So I told her. "In the brush. Down by the river. Back in the brush."

"And *that's* where you saw him?"

"No. Not for a while. But I *heard* him," I said. "You ever hear a pig?" And they nodded their heads. "Well this was louder. Like five or six *HOGS*. Branches were breaking and I knew he was close, so I lifted up my gun."

"And you *shot* him?"

"He *said* he couldn't even *see* him," Charlie said. "Only that branches were breaking."

"That's right. And sometimes when you're out there, the sounds get all confused. You think it's coming from the left and it's really coming from the right. Well, the next thing I knew, he charged from the front."

"And you *shot* him?"

"Ka-*BOOM*! Right between the eyes. But it still didn't stop him. Not for a second. And I thought I was dead, because I only had that one bullet in the rifle. But then he started falling. Took two steps and started coming down."

"Tim-*BER*," Charlie said.

"Yeah. Tim-*BER*," I said. "Right on top of me. And then I took a long time crawlin' out. Maybe an hour. And by that time it was dark."

"So what did you do?"

"Well, I'll tell you," I said. "But it wasn't very pretty."

"What? What?" Isabella Rose asked.

"Well, it started getting cold. Kind of nippy. And then it started getting *really* cold."

"Like down around zero?"

"Oh, a lot colder than that," I told them. "So the only way I *knew* that I could stay alive for sure, was to gut him. Cut out his innards and then crawl inside."

"*JESUS*!" Johnson cried.

"Well, what else could he do, Hon?" Barbara asked him. "He had to stay warm."

"So that's what I did. And of course that took a while. Three or four hours, and by that time, it was midnight, maybe one in the morning. But at least I was warm."

"And you fell asleep that way?"

"Yeah," I said. "Except the next morning, I couldn't get out."

"*WHAT*?!"

"The bear was frozen solid. All around me."

"The bear was frozen *solid*?"

"Yeah. The bear was frozen solid. I could just barely move."

"Oh my *GOD*!" Johnson looked in his rear view mirror and then back at the road. "Then what did you do?"

"Well, I tried to get up, and I'd get up and fall, and get up and fall, but then after a while, I had it. I was walking in the bear."

"WALKING?!"

"Yeah. Then I went down by the river."

"But how did you ever see?"

"Through the hole," I said. "The one that I'd shot between his eyes. But anyway, I guess I walked a mile. Maybe more. And then, looking up, I saw them. Up there on the ridge."

"More bears?"

"No. My buddies. So I started calling out, but I guess they couldn't hear me so I began to wave my paws. Then one guy raised his gun. Ka-*BOOM*!"

"You're kidding?!"

"No."

"Did he hit you?"

"Yeah he hit me. Knocked me on my tail and I guess it knocked me out, because the next thing I knew, when I opened up my eyes, I was lying on the ground and they were standing over top of me, pointing their guns."

"Then what did you do?"

"I told 'em my name. I called out, 'HEY! It's me. It's Jesse Fitch!'

And one guy understood so he told the other one, 'It's Fitch! Don't shoot! It's *him!*' And then they got me out."

"And after that, you flew back home?"

"No. We had to walk," I said. "Had to hike it out. The plane never showed."

"SONUVA *BITCH!*" Johnson yelled. "You're lucky you're alive."

And the way that he said it, he convinced me that I was.

———————

I always think it's funny when I'm driving to the ocean, because if the ocean weren't there, I probably wouldn't drive that way. And if I didn't drive that way, I'd never see the ocean. I mean, it doesn't really matter now, because everybody knows it's there, but a thousand years ago, I wonder if they did. Twenty miles away, just like we were then. Right in their back yard, and you wonder if they knew it.

"Maybe they heard rumors," Barbara said. "Of something that was there."

"But you think they ever saw it? I mean fifteen miles away and maybe they would go, but you think they would at fifty? Sixty?" I asked.

"Well, think about Mohammed," Johnson said. "Suppose that you died right *before* he was born. Just one or two days. Or Jesus? Or Buddha? It's almost the same."

But it wasn't. "With *them*, you never could have *known*," I said. "With the *ocean*, you *could*. If you *looked*."

"But what about *God*?" Charlie asked. "Can't you look for *Him*?"

And Barbara told him, "Sure. Sure you can."

And then Isabella asked her mother, "Really Mom? Even if you're *dead*?"

We were driving west, on down Highway 18, and I bet we'd must have passed a dozen wineries by then. It started getting cooler, and off in the distance, it started looking different. More sky. More blue. And then we drove into Otis, like the guy with the Jeep had said I would.

"Now don't blink," Barbara said, "or else we might miss it." And then we all started laughing, made a left on Highway 101, and in less than a mile we came to a pull-off.

It was right at the ocean. Next to a river. But you wouldn't have known, except for the sign. *Shortest River in the World, the D River.* That's what it said. And it came from a lake back behind the road.

"How about a picture?" Barbara asked. So like a lot of people there, the four of them smiled while I pushed the button in. *Ca-Lick!* Then we walked down to the ocean.

It was just like the Atlantic in a lot of ways, I guess. The water, the waves and the beach. But somehow it was different. Some things *weren't* there, like chairs and umbrellas. But other stuff was, like driftwood. Hundreds of pieces of driftwood, all gnarled and worn, and you wondered where they came from.

"Did you know the Eskimos used to think that wood came from the water?" I asked the kids. It was something Kingpen told me once. "They didn't know about trees, because they'd never seen them. Not up in the Arctic."

"No kidding?" Johnson said. And then he started staring out at the ocean.

"Look at *this!*" Charlie yelled.

Barbara and I went to where he was and saw a horseshoe crab swimming in the surf. First live one I'd ever seen. "Looks a million years old," Charlie said. And it did, with its long spiny tail and gray plated shell. Like something from the Stone Age.

We walked along the beach for forty-five minutes after that, maybe an hour. Watching the seagulls and the people flying kites of all different colors. Reds and yellows, oranges and blues. Then we walked back to the table at the pull-off and I helped them fix lunch. Braunschweiger sandwiches, pickles and soda.

"How about some mustard?" Johnson asked. But I told him I had eaten and thought that I would go.

"You all deserve to be alone," I said. "I'm gonna hike on down the road."

"But we're leaving in a minute," he told me.

"We're going to California just as soon as we clean up. Why don't you come along?" Barbara asked.

And that's the way they were. Nicest darn people you would ever want to meet. Which is why I finally left. "I think I really have to go," I said.

"Well at least give us your address."

So I wrote it on a napkin and handed it to Isabella Rose. "Jesse Fitch. General Delivery. College, Alaska," she read. And then I told her that was it, and to drop me a line.

"Well, I think I'm gonna go," I said. Then we all said good-bye and I thanked them for the ride. I figured I would walk on down the beach, so they wouldn't have to pass me after they cleaned up.

"You want to take an orange?" Barbara asked. She handed me an orange. I put it in my pocket, got my things from the car, and got ready to go.

"Well, have a good trip," Johnson said. The two of us shook hands and I started off.

The sun was out that day. I remember from the glitter, all across the water. The waves lifted up and then billions of diamonds shimmered and rolled and washed up on the beach. They soaked into the sand and I walked on the foam.

And I'll tell you, it was really something. *Really* pretty. Not like Alaska, but as pretty as any postcard that you've seen of any other place. Not that many people, the sky as blue as it could be. And off in the distance, there were boulders in the water, out in the Pacific. Giant rocky shapes. I know, because I saw them as I walked along this long stretch of beach. And then I came to Lincoln City.

If you ever want to go there, you can come in from the north, down 101. Or drive in from the east, on Highway 22. You can even come up from Toledo on 229. But I came in an even different way, from the west, up the wide wooden steps that connect it to the beach. The *back* way, I guess.

But however you get there, it all looks the same. Dozens of hotels and motels and restaurants, but tourist shops mostly, with seagulls for sale. Every shop I looked in had ceramic or sometimes plastic seagulls, standing all by themselves or together on little driftwood piers. The shops even had these hats, with bird crap, I guess, all over the front. "DAMN SEAGULLS," the hats said. And they looked pretty good, if that's what you wanted. Pretty realistic.

I spent a long time there, in the middle of the city. Five towns really. That's what one of the brochures said. In 1965, five small coastal towns consolidated into one. And there I was. Lincoln City, Or-eh-*GUN*. *Kite Capital of the World.* I was walking on its sidewalks and looking at its seagulls. Walking and looking, and looking and walking.

And I kept *on* walking after that. I walked and walked toward the outskirts of the town and then I came to a small seaside shop that sold burls. Giant redwood burls, which are kind of like the knots you've seen on trees, except that these were *huge.*

"From redwoods to the south," the saleslady said. Benches and beds. They even had clocks and lamps that were bent and gnarled. But the thing I remember best is a table that was there. Maybe eighteen feet long, it was five feet wide, or six, or nine, depending on where you measured. It was never the same. All around the edge, it twisted and curved, like a shoreline, I guess. With inlets and bays.

But anyway, it was thirteen thousand dollars. That's what the price tag said. "Don't know if I'll ever sell it," the lady said. "I've had it for three years." But I told her she would.

I left and started up a side street after that. It must have been nearly five o'clock when I got to 101. I put my jacket on the ground, along with Kingpen's tent, held out my arm, stuck out my thumb, and watched it all go by. *ZOOM! ZOOM! ZOOM!*

Then after twenty minutes one guy passed, pulled to the side and hollered back. "Need a lift?" he yelled.

"Yeah," I said.

"Well get yourself a jack and hook it to your ass!"

He began to pull away, but just for a minute, I imagined he couldn't. His tires caught in the gravel and they started to spin. I would walk to his car and open the door. "Whaddja say?" I'd ask. But by then he wouldn't be able to talk. Six-foot-four, over two hundred pounds and he would be shaking like a leaf. "Get myself a jack?" I'd say. "Is that what you just told me? Get myself a jack and hook it to my *what*? Maybe I should jack *your* ass around a little bit!" I'd say. And then I'd reach down in the car and pull him out and lift him over top my head and drop him to the ground. Ka-*BOOM!* "Don't fuck with *me*," I'd tell him, I thought. Then I picked up my jacket with the stuffing coming out, my sleeping bag, my backpack and Kingpen's tent, and started walking.

I walked a quarter mile, maybe less, then another guy pulled his car over to the side and hollered back, "Need a lift?" But by then, I wasn't sure. "I'm going down to Florence, if you wanna ride that far. You wanna ride or not?"

"Yeah," I said. I climbed into the car and the thing that I remember thinking was, *just where the heck was Florence?*

He got the car on the road and shifted through the gears. "From around here?" he asked. "Bellingham," I said. "I'm heading back east, but I thought I'd see the coast."

"Well, it's something," he said. "There's no way you can beat it. Just like on a postcard." Then he told me how the beaches were all

241

parks. Almost all of 'em, he said. All along the coast. "They belong to the state." He lifted his thumb. "You won't see no construction *here*."

"You mean in Or-eh-*GUN*?" I asked.

"Yeah. It's not like California. Ever been down there?" I told him I hadn't.

As if to make his point, we began to pass pull-offs and parks like Depoe Bay and Rocky Creek. "Otter Creek," he said. And then came Devil's Punchbowl State Park and Beverly Beach. We drove along the cliffs and even saw a lighthouse once.

"Agates are down in there," he said. And he pointed to our right and asked me if I'd like to stop but we never did, because the tide was too high. "You can find some good ones, when the water's right," he said. "Especially in the winter."

We kept on driving. Down through Newport, right there on the Bay. Fishing boats and sea gulls and restaurants with a view. "Like crab?" my driver asked. "And shrimp? Any kind of seafood? You'll never get it better," he told me. But it turned out he was wrong.

He reminded me of people I had seen from in the dish room. People handing me their trays and sitting at the tables. "Going to school?" I asked.

He told me he was, but was off for the summer. "College. Up in Portland."

"You go to school back east?" he asked.

"Yeah," I said. "At least I used to." And then I told him how I might go into law, and I thought it sounded kind of funny just as soon as I had said it. But I think *he* thought it sounded good. "You can make some bucks with that," he said, and gave a thumbs up.

We were driving out of Newport on a bridge that went across the Bay. Then we went into the hills, but always on the coast. Always on the Highway. Highway 101. And the thing that I remember thinking was, *I wonder how they do it? How do they build it over the rivers and right along the cliffs?*

"It's *something*, isn't it?" my driver asked. I pointed my thumb up and told him it was.

We drove another ten or fifteen minutes and went by Driftwood Beach. We crossed another bridge, went through a tiny town, and kept on going south, past Beachside Park. A lot of names were Beach. And then we started through the forest, riding down the

Highway in between the trees. *The Siuslaw National Forest.* That's what the sign said.

"You could walk that way for miles," my driver said. And he pointed to our left. "Twenty, thirty miles and it's forest all the way. Hemlock, cedar, Douglas fir. Twenty, thirty miles and you'd never see a road."

But we did see logging trucks, which had driven out from someplace. They were coming up the Highway from someplace farther south.

"Mapleton," my driver said. And unless you were there, you couldn't really picture the loads they were carrying. Fifteen, maybe even twenty giant logs, three to four feet wide, maybe forty feet long. All stacked together, so they hung off the sides of the trucks. And the only things that held them there were these chains. Heavy duty logging chains that were strapped over top, then down through the rungs, and held there with clamps.

"You'd think that they would snap," I said. But they didn't. And then even as they passed us on a level stretch of Highway, you began to hear the strain of the engines in the trucks. *Bbrruugghh* – the engines winding out and the drivers shifting through the gears. I can hear 'em even now.

"I'm going to see my folks," my driver said. "If you want a place to spend the night, they've got an extra room."

"Thanks, but I think I'll keep on going," I said. "Maybe camp out down the coast."

"Whatever. I can take you to the other side of Florence. We should be there pretty soon. Maybe half an hour." And we kept on driving through the trees.

We'd been seeing signs since Newport, all along the coast. "Sea Lion Caves" every couple miles. "You take an elevator down," my driver said. "Twelve miles north of Florence. You ride it down into a cave and the sea lions are right there." But it turned out that it was sunny, so we saw 'em from a pull-off, just before a tunnel.

"Look!" I said. And you could see 'em in the ocean, down there off the coast, swimming in the surf and lounging on the rocks.

"It's something, isn't it?" my driver asked. It really was, so we sat and watched them for a while.

We drove down 101 into Florence after that, and because we had stopped, it was nearly dark when we got there. "I'll drive you to the other side," he told me.

"You'll find some campgrounds further south," he said.

I thanked him for the ride. I picked up my stuff and stepped out of the car. "Thanks again," I said. I pushed against the door to close it.

"Have a good trip back east," he said. He waved and I watched as he turned the car around and started back to Florence.

There wasn't that much traffic like up near Lincoln City. I remember even with the town nearby, it was still pretty quiet. *I'll walk awhile*, I thought. And then I took the orange Barbara had given me, broke the skin with my front teeth and started walking down the road.

I was walking into the sunset that night. The sun was going down and there I was, right outside of Florence, walking and thinking and eating my orange.

And then after a while, it was maybe a mile, I was burping it back up. Pieces of orange I thought that I had eaten, but really I hadn't. I chewed 'em up again and swallowed 'em back down. And I never really used to think about it much, until Pinto told me once, "Different foods are like that. Oranges, tomatoes, sometimes even ice cream." *Burp-up foods* he called 'em. "You can never keep 'em down until you chew 'em up again."

And the *best* thing about 'em, the burp-up foods was, they helped you out, so you wouldn't be that bored when you were out there on the road. That's what Pinto used to say.

And now that I look back to walking on *that* road, right outside of Florence, I think that he was right.

———————

There's a town outside of Florence. I know from little lights I saw back off the road. Fifty, sixty lights. Then after you walk by, it all turns dark and you wander down the Highway, waiting for a ride. *Waiting. Waiting. Waiting.* Then you start to picture things.

I was picturing the tent, down there on the beach, with the waves and the sand. So even when a car came, and I thought I had a ride because it started slowing down, I turned my head away and started walking west. Started walking west, through the trees and a field, around a little pond, and then I felt it underneath me. *Sand.* And I thought that I was getting close.

It wasn't hard to tell just where I was at first. The trees were right behind me, and even in the dark, I knew enough to keep on walking, toward the lighter shades of black and gray, and the purple streaks the sun had left behind.

Go west, young man. Go west.

I walked until I couldn't see the trees behind me, and the purple blended into night. Then I sat there on the sand and listened for the waves. And the funny thing was, I really thought I heard them, crashing to the beach, not too far away.

I remember listening and walking. Then I started thinking. I thought back to the time when I had walked along the drifts on the way to Eddie Bauer's, because that's what it was like. At least when I first started. Shifting grains of sand that piled up into dunes, five and ten feet high, but then I pushed on through the ridges up to higher piles of sand. Forty, fifty feet. Then a hundred feet and higher. I swear to God.

You should have seen 'em. Giant mounds of sand that lifted to the sky. And the thing you'd never guess is that they stretched out there for miles. Massive, rolling shapes of gray, as far as you could see. And the reason that I know, is because I climbed them.

I never made it to the water. I tried to pitch the tent somewhere on a dune, but of course I couldn't get the stakes to hold and everything collapsed sometime in the night. Just like at the dumpster. But it really didn't matter. At least I was warm. *Fuggit*, I thought. And I kept on sleeping.

The sun came up at five-fifteen, according to my clock. I got out of the tent, packed it all together and started walking back into the sun. Up and down the dunes. Trudging up and sliding down. It must have been three hours before I made it to the Highway.

And it was right there where I came out to the road. I saw the sign. *Dunes Park*. It even had a little carving of the dunes next to the words.

I started walking after that, but I didn't go too far, because my legs were cramping up. Little knots that made it hard to walk, so I sat there on my sleeping bag and waited for a car. I didn't wait that long.

There was a Plymouth coming down the Highway. The place that I had picked to sit was where the Highway curved around, so he started slowing down. *C'mon*, I thought. I got up from the bag and stood there with my thumb, moving back and forth, and then he pulled the Plymouth to the side.

"Only going to Westlake, but at least it's a ride," he said. "You wanna come along, or you wanna wait?"

"Well to tell you the truth, I'd really appreciate the lift," I said. We put my gear and a couple pounds of sand into his car, then we started down the road.

"Had anything to eat?" he asked. I told him that I hadn't. "Well you can eat with me," he said. "When we get down to the restaurant. I'm on my way to work. Bill's Café and Grill. I'm Bill Sneer."

I told him I was Fitch. "Jesse Fitch."

"You ever see that *sand*?" I asked. "Out there on the beach? It looks like the Sahara."

Bill Sneer nodded his head. "It might not be as *big*," he said. "But it's *higher* there in some spots. A couple of those dunes are over three hundred feet high. *I* wouldn't try to walk it. It's close to three miles from the Highway to the ocean. Nothing but dunes." And I told him that I knew.

We drove another minute or two. "Well, I said I wasn't going far. We're almost there," he said. We pulled off to our left on a narrow road, went a half a mile, and there we were. *Bill's Café and Grill.* "Been here two months," Bill said.

The place was kind of small and reminded me more of a country grocery store than a café and grill.

"You oughta try the French toast," Bill said. "We make it with fresh eggs and cinnamon. You really oughta try it." So I told him that I would.

We went up on the porch, through a screen door, and I saw maybe half a dozen people sitting at tables.

"Where the *hell* you been?" the man behind the counter shouted. "You're a half an hour late. Now get back to the dishes." And the way that Bill ran off, you never would have known he knew me.

I sat down with my stuff at a table over by the wall, and I looked out through a window to something like a lawn that went into some scrub. "We hold our barbecues out there," the man who brought the menu said. "But only on the weekends."

And the way it all turned out, the French toast wasn't all that great.

But the syrup sure was thick. I remember that I sat there wondering if Bill squished it through his fingers and smeared it on his hands before he steamed it off the plates. Two months, I thought. And then I figured that he did.

Chapter 25

When you drive on down from Westlake, south on 101, the scenery starts to change. Not so many cliffs, so you're closer to the beach. Sometimes right there *on* it when the wind begins to blow. Little drifts of sand come across the road, where the dunes come to the highway. You can see it for yourself if you ever get there. Swirling, grainy flakes of tan. It reminded me of North Dakota and Wisconsin, when we had driven up in the Buick.

"Something? Isn't it?" I asked. And the ladies I was with agreed. "Beautiful," one said. And the other one said, "Grand." I pushed down on the pedal and we kept on heading south.

If you've never really hitchhiked, you probably imagine there's a certain kind of person who would never pick you up. Like older single women and people with new cars. But sometimes people like that will. You take a rock and throw it to the ground, and where it breaks, you'll find there was a crack or an air hole, something you can analyze. But *people* aren't like that. There's no way to predict. The only thing you're left with is what they chose to do. At least that's what I can tell you from the people who would stop to pick *me* up. Or wouldn't.

"Where you ladies from?" I asked. And the one who told me "Grand," said someplace up in Canada. Chilliwack, I think. And then she told me they were driving south to visit California. "We're going to see the Bay and ride the cable cars," the other lady said.

We were someplace south of Reedsport. And now that I look back, it sounds just like a movie or a title to a book where something special happens. *"Someplace south of Reedsport."* But nothing ever did – not while I was there.

I'd been driving since they picked me up. "Do you think that you could drive?" they asked. So I told them that I could. And I really didn't mind. "I *like* to drive," I said. And I took us down past Winchester Bay, Saunders Lake and Hauser. All along the dunes until we got down to the bridge that goes across Coos Bay.

"North Bend," I said, because I'd seen the sign. Then we started toward the town with the pulp mills. You could smell 'em in the air. "They cut a lot of wood down here," I said. And I know that I was right, because in another couple miles, we started passing logs. Thousands of 'em, out there in the water, right off to our left. "Waiting for the ships," I said. And then we crossed another bridge.

It started getting cloudy after that. A storm was coming in and I remember that we stopped at a restaurant, there by the water. *Brandon by the Sea.* That was what it said at the bottom of the menu. For an hour and a half, we looked out through the windows and watched it coming in. Sweeping sheets of rain and lightning on the ocean. We sat there eating lunch and listened to the thunder rolling all around. *BOOM! BOO! BOOM!*

"Storm Watching Capital of the World," the waiter said. He gave us some brochures that told about the town, and the lectures and programs on the weather that they offered. "This is a pretty interesting place," he said. And you can see it for yourself if you're ever out that way. Right there at the mouth of the Coquille River. It's called *Brandon by the Sea.*

We started driving into forests after that. Twenty, thirty miles, then we crossed a fishing town and started seeing beaches. Long, sandy beaches, the kind you see in travel magazines with giant rocky boulders, out there in the water. It was really pretty. Flower-covered fields that ran down to the sand and we hardly ever saw a soul. "Most of these are parks," I said. "You won't see much construction."

"Have you ever been a tour guide?" the lady back behind me asked. "You sure know a lot of things." And I told her that I hadn't. "Well you *should* have been," she said. "But he *is* one," the other lady told her. And I guess back then, I was.

We didn't talk a whole lot after that. I kept on driving south and the one thing I can tell you, if you don't get to Alaska, at least go see the coast. You can start right there at Ophir and head down to the beach. *Gold Beach.* You cross a giant bridge where the river hits the ocean and as far as you can see, looking up the Rogue, there are forests, hills and streams.

But then you keep on heading south, down along the coast. Winding, twisting curves through places like Sebastion. And you wonder how they got there. Giant granite boulders, sitting in the water.

Shoes, boots, pieces of rope.

Then you drive up into cliffs and for ten or fifteen miles, you look down from above, until you come down into Brookings. Right there on the ocean. Only thirty, forty miles, it isn't very long. And I can tell you – it's really something.

We got to California sometime after five and the thing that I remember is, we had to stop the car, right there at the border, while a Customs agent checked for vegetables.

"Bringing any in? Peppers, or tomatoes? Any kinds of fruit?"

"Only had an orange. But I ate it twice a couple miles ago," I said.

"Any kinds of grapes? We're checking cars for fruit flies. Peaches?" we all began to shake our heads. "Well go ahead," the man told us.

And he waved us into California.

In case you've never been there, it's kind of like New York, from what I've heard 'em say. People that I've talked with tell me there are two parts to the state.

"Beautiful," the ladies said. And the first part was. We went around the Bay, and passed by Crescent City. Then we started through the redwoods, and they're everything you'd ever think they would be. Giant stands of trees that stretch up to the skies. All you can imagine. "They're majestic!" one of my riders said. And then we kept on driving on the road that curved and wound around the trees. A couple times, I swear to God, we drove right through their trunks.

"Maybe we could stop and fix some dinner. Have a little cookout," one of the ladies said. There were campgrounds all along there, except we had to keep on driving until we found a little store and bought some hot dogs. Hot dogs and rolls and coleslaw and Jell-O. Everything for supper. I know, because I bought it. I changed one of the hundreds that I had. "My treat," I said. And the man who checked me out put everything we bought into a brown paper bag.

"There's a campground up ahead," he said. "Another couple miles." So we thanked him for the food, put it in the trunk and started back down 101, to a turn-off that had a picture of a tent. "I think it's further back," one of us said. So I drove a little while and we found it, set back in the trees. Fifty, sixty spaces, each with a barbecue grill and table and a place to put your tent. And your car, if you had one. But first, you had to pass a little gatehouse and pay a couple dollars, if you didn't have a sticker.

"Park system," the gatekeeper said. "Three bucks." So I took out three one dollar bills, handed him the money and we started down a narrow, gravel road, looking for a place to cook our hotdogs. But there weren't that many places. Nearly every one was taken.

How about the weeds? I thought. But of course I didn't say it. We just kept looking and looking, until we finally found a spot. Just like all the others, it was underneath the redwoods.

"A canopy from heaven." That's what Mae said. Mae and Mary Ellen. Those were their names.

"How about we start a fire? I'll go and get some wood," I said. I went to go and get some, except there wasn't any there. Standing in the forest and I'm telling you, I couldn't find a stick.

"I might be a while." I called back. Then I started looking everywhere, back behind the campsites and underneath the bushes. But I never found a single piece of wood. Pristine. That's what it was like.

It was starting to get dark and I remember I was thinking that the sun was going down. But it turned out that it wasn't. The leaves were blocking out the sun. And when I looked up there to see them, I saw the thing I couldn't find. *Branches*. But not along the *sides* of the trees. Not where you'd expect them. No. Go and see 'em for yourself. They're only at the top. All up there at least a couple hundred feet. Sonuva *bitch*, I thought. And then I went back to the ladies.

"Well, don't you worry. I think I saw some wood, back there at the gatehouse," Mary Ellen said. "All tied up in bundles."

They even had two kinds. "Solid and kindlin'. Five dollars each." That's what the man said. And he thought I needed both. "You're never gonna get it started with just *solid* sticks," he told me.

But I did. *I'll use the bag that's holding all the food*, I thought. And in maybe half an hour, Mary Ellen, Mae and I were standing by the fire, and mostly it was quiet. Except for once in a while. You'd hear, *Pschttt, Pschttt, Pschttt*, when the hot dog grease began to drip into the flames. "And you never even used a match," Ellen said. "You knew enough to use the lighter from the car."

We stayed another hour after that. Then we packed it all together and I told them both, "I guess we'd better go."

"Now what about the wood we didn't use?" Mae asked.

"Just leave it. Somebody will get it," I said.

We drove out past the gatehouse, got on 101 and started south across the Klamath River. "You wanna drive all night?" I asked. By that time, it was seven, maybe eight o'clock. "We could get down there by two," I said. "Or if the two of you want, you can stop along the way and stay in a hotel. Whatever you want. But if you stop, just to let you know, I think I'll keep on going."

"Well, would it help you if we didn't stop?" they asked. "You might not get a ride." But I told them that I thought I would. "But the two of you decide," I said. "I'll be glad to drive, if you want to keep on going. But if you want to stop, well that's fine too." And like a lot of things, I guess, nothing was decided. No decision made. So I kept on driving, until we got down near Eureka, where the ladies fell asleep.

It was starting to get dark. I kept on passing signs for little towns like Rohnerville and Alton, Pepperwood and Meyers Flat. And then I got somewhere near Leggett and the road divided up, so I pulled off to the side and found my Xerox copy of the map of California.

There were two ways I could go. I could stay on 101, or go on down the Coast Road. Highway One. Which is what I finally did, because I thought I'd see some scenery. But of course it turned out that I didn't. For thirty, forty miles, I drove on in the dark, and then it started getting misty. Almost foggy. And all that I kept picturing was driving on the cliffs, and then going over, just like on the mountain. *AAAAHH!* And then I saw the lights.

I couldn't really tell if he'd been waiting on the shoulder or had pulled out from a side road, but suddenly a pair of lights was there. Back lights from a semi. For twenty, thirty miles, they helped keep me on the road. Then all at once he started slowin' down and I passed him and he followed *me* for a while. On the edges of the cliffs, curving all around, back and forth, back and forth, until we got down near the Bay and he flashed his lights good-bye. And we'd never said a word.

I woke the ladies after that. I thought they'd want to see the bridge. "Golden Gate," I said. But it wasn't like we'd pictured. Construction crews were working on it that night and everything was orange from the lights that they were using.

"Come *ON!* Come *ON!*" somebody yelled. And a man waved a little flag. And even then, late at night, the cars were backing up, because the far left lane was closed. "Come *ON!* Come *ON!*"

That night, we inched our way through air hoses and machinery and workers everywhere. Misty, hazy orange. And cement dust in the air. "Come *ON*! Come *ON*!" And the generators rattled and the jackhammers banged. *Rah tah tah tah TAT*.

"Do you know where you're gonna stay?" I asked. But they didn't, so we looked around awhile. And if there's one thing that I learned that night, it's that you've got to have a reservation, at least in San Francisco in the middle of July.

"Try Berkley," a motel clerk told me. So we went over there, five miles away. And the funny thing was, you should have seen the signs. *VACANCY! VACANCY!* Everywhere we looked. "What about *that* one?" Mary Ellen asked. She pointed to a motel where the rooms were on the ground floor and built around a courtyard that was all lit up.

"We'd like to treat you to a room," Mae said. But it turned out that they couldn't, even if I'd let them. There was only one room left. So I told them I was gonna go on down the road. "There's another place down there," I said. They tried to give me money, but of course I wouldn't take it.

"I'll get your things," I said. After I brought all their stuff inside, I got my gear together and told them both good-bye. "I don't think I'll see you in the morning," I said. "I'm gonna try and get an early start."

"But you never even told us where you're going."

So I told em. "Ball-tuh-more," I said. "It's a place back east."

"Well, we wish you all the best," Mae said. And the way that she said it, I knew they really did.

I started walking after that, walking down the sidewalk to the place that I'd seen. *The Breezeway Motel*. But by the time that I got there, it was three forty-five. I checked on the alarm clock. And the one thing that I thought was, I couldn't see paying forty, fifty dollars for a couple hours sleep. So I walked a little farther, waiting for the sunrise. Then I sat down on the curb and started leaning up against an eight-foot-high, wire mesh fence that ran around a warehouse. *Vacancy*, I thought.

I'd only closed my eyes for just a minute when I heard 'em coming at me. Crazy sounds you can't imagine. Snarling, vicious dogs.

Sweat came pouring off me. My legs went numb and I started shaking. *SHAKING, SHAKING, SHAKING!* There, an inch or so away, were a couple German shepherds and a Doberman. Attack dogs, snapping at my face.

Gonna die! I thought. *Right here in the gutter.*

Then I turned and rolled, and that's when I first noticed they were behind the fence. *GUARDED BY ATTACK DOGS.* That's what the sign said. I saw it as I crawled away.

Hit the third button, I thought. And I couldn't even stand up, but I kept on moving. Moving and crawling, sweating and shaking, dragging myself along, until I made it to a beam, up underneath a bridge, where I finally fell asleep. And I guess you'll never do it, but it's better than you think.

You lie there all alone and you watch it all go by. Then you close your eyes and listen till you hear it in the dark. Whoosh. Whoosh. *Thump!* Whoosh. Whoosh. *Thump!* People going by. You can see 'em down there on the road, and feel 'em right above your head. Moving. *Always moving.* They never even know you're there, but *you* know that you are.

That's why I think you'd like it. Your mind begins to wander, and before you fall asleep, you think about what might have been. Like dying in the gutter.

You can spend your life with others, but you always die alone. That's what I remember thinking.

Shoes, boots, pieces of rope.

And then I heard a raven. *CAW! CAW! CAW!*

––––––––––

The sun was coming up, but I couldn't really see it with the buildings in the way. I started walking backwards, down from underneath the bridge, like the time I backed out of the tent in Haines. Then I slowly turned around. Restaurants, banks, hotels and stores. I came across a gas station that was closed, but the bathroom wasn't.

So I went inside, and while I was sitting there, I saw a poster stapled to the wall. Summer school at the University of California at Berkley. There was a list of courses and a map to show you how to get there. Telegraph and Bancroft. Just a couple miles away. The way I had it figured, I could go and take a shower, maybe buy some clothes, and then go out on the town. Go and see the cable cars, Chinatown and Alcatraz.

I took a last look at the map, started out the door, and headed down the street, going with the traffic. Then against it for a while. But walking. Always walking. Kicking stones along the way and looking for the University.

And the one thing I can tell you, if you ever want to walk there yourself, is you'll never know exactly when you get there. You sort of wade on in, from about a half a mile away, with people selling tee shirts, handicrafts and jewelry. Coffee bars. Bookshops and people passing leaflets. And at some point, I guess, you begin to pass a line, from the neighborhood to campus, and then suddenly, you're there. In the middle of it all. With your Jimmy Franklin spoon, your sleeping bag and Kingpen's tent. And you wonder when it was that you really got there.

I walked into a shop and bought a shirt and pair of pants and socks, and then I walked a little further to a building where I took a shower. They even had a swimming pool with bathing suits, lounge chairs and towels. And I never saw a soul.

Now keep your chin tucked in, I thought. I dove and swam and I took a couple showers and I lounged around awhile, then I threw away my old clothes, put my new ones on, and walked out through the door, underneath the sign: *University of California at Berkley. Alumni House.*

Well I'll be a son of a bitch, I thought. And it really made me feel like I had gone to school there.

I caught a bus. I looked down on the Bay as we went across the Oakland Bridge and into San Francisco. "*Look*," somebody said, pointing to a building that looked like a pyramid.

And I was going to see it all. That's what I remember thinking. And in a way, I guess I did.

I had dozens of maps and brochures I had picked up back in Berkley, so I started looking for a place to stash my stuff. *The airport*, I thought. I could take my stuff out there and put it in a locker while I walked around the town. Or, I could put it on a chair in a library, walk out, and come back to get it later.

But then I saw exactly what I needed on the map. *Golden Gate Park.* Three miles long and a half a mile wide. With all the bushes and the trees, I just knew I'd find a perfect place to stash my stuff.

"Transfer up at Third," the driver told me. "Take another bus to Geary, and then go up Van Ness."

Sometime after noon, there I was at Stanyon Street, looking at the Park. It was just like I had pictured, with bushes, flowers, and trees. Except lots of people were there, riding horses and bikes. Kids were playing ball. The more I walked, the more I saw. Japanese gardens with bridges and ponds. Buffalo. Roving herds of buffalo. And if you don't believe it, call the Park. They'll tell you.

I finally found a place to hide my stuff. It was underneath some bushes, down along a hill. I scooped a little hole, got my gear in there, and then I covered it with branches I'd found back in the woods. *Now nobody'll find it,* I thought. Then I checked to feel the money in my pocket and started down the hill, until I made it to the road.

A pocketful of money and everywhere to go, I thought. But I wasn't sure just how to get *anywhere*, so I went into a store, and listened while they told me. "Go another couple blocks and the bus stop will be there. The bus will take you right downtown," they said. And it did.

Fifteen, twenty minutes and there I was. Broadway and Columbus. And like I said, I thought that I would see it all, so I started up the pyramid you always see in pictures. The Trans America Pyramid. Except you can't get to the top. That's what I found out. "Those rooms are offices," the lady in the lobby said. "They're not for observation."

I left and walked around some more. Up and down the hills. I would have gotten on a cable car, except that they weren't running that week. "Maintenance," another lady said. "It's done every other year. They shut 'em down a week." So I kept on walking.

I went to Chinatown. And it's not at all like Berkley, when you're walking toward the school. There's an archway with a dragon, so you know just when you get there. And once you go inside, it looks just like you picture. Lots of bright red paint and little golden Buddhas. Carved ivory pieces in the windows. There were grocery stores with dried fish, roast duck and spices. Lots of spices. "Hoisin sauce," somebody shouted.

And everywhere around me, I could feel it. People filling up their lives, looking in the windows, talking to each other, buying some of *this*, selling some of *that*. And people watching people. That's what I remember thinking. People even watching *me*, I thought. And then I got myself an egg roll and kept on walking.

I spent a couple of hours there in Chinatown. Then I walked down to the wharf, and I think that you would like it, except that it was pretty crowded. Fisherman's Wharf, where the boats come in around three or four o'clock and they sell you crabs a couple minutes old. Crabs and shrimp and even abalone. I know because I saw 'em. Baskets of them coming off the boat.

But it's not just fishing boats and crabs. Other things are there, too, like restaurants and fish markets, people playing music, and people in lines – for tour boats mostly.

But the longest line you'll see will be the line to see the island. Alcatraz. Where I was gonna go. But the wait would be three hours. That was what they told me when I went to buy a ticket. So I never got in line, but I still thought I could see it. I put a quarter in the slot and started looking through a telescope that was right there at the water. Twenty-five cents for a minute, but it started getting foggy.

The mist came rolling in, so I left, and it must have been nearly six o'clock when I went to catch the bus. I walked up and down the hills and depending where I was, the mist was thick or thin, gray or white. And I know just what you're thinking – that I never saw the sights. That it started getting cloudy, then it started getting dark, and I never saw the prison or the cable cars or the pyramid or *any* of it. But I did. I walked up Hyde Street to Washington, to Laguna, up near Geary. And right there by the Church, next to the Cathedral, I saw everything I missed.

I walked out of the Gallery, made a left and kept on walking six or seven miles until I got back to the Park. By the time I got there, it was dark. Silhouettes on silhouettes. Bushes, trees and gravel paths. *A little over there*, I thought. *There's* gotta *be a hill*. And there was, but it didn't have the bushes. And then I found a clump of bushes, but they weren't up on a hill.

So I kept on walking. Walking all around and stumbling in the dark. Then I thought I'd plot it out. I'd plot it like a graph. I crisscrossed back and forth. Looking. Always looking.

Think the strangest thing, I thought, and then I figured I would end up sleeping underneath a bridge again. Except I didn't. It was *more*.

I finally gave up looking and knelt down by a bush, one like all the rest. It was short and squatty, and I had to keep my head down to keep from getting scratched. That was where I slept. I curled up in a ball, down there by the roots, and the fog came rolling in. Thin, then thicker, then *really thick*. That's what it was like. Really, really *THICK*. Like sleeping in a cloud. Whitish gray with softness all around. *I'm sleeping in a cloud*, I thought. And then I drifted off to sleep.

A breeze was blowing off the Bay, the air got cool, and the fog began to lift. When I opened my eyes, the stars were shining overhead. But the thing that woke me up was the ringing, out there in the dark. *Think the strangest thing,* I thought. And for all of my looking, it turned out that I *heard* my stuff, before I ever saw it. *BBRRIINNGG! BBRRIINNG! BBRRIINNGG!*

I got there in a minute. I crawled out from underneath the bush and started walking toward the sound. *Push the button in*, I thought. And then I did and looked down at the clock. *Five-fifteen - I've gotta go*.

I picked up Kingpen's tent, my sleeping bag, and a couple other things, and started walking. Moving in the night. I walked in circles for a while, and then noticed it was getting lighter in one part of the sky, so that's the way I went. Back on through the park, heading toward the light. And the way it all turned out, I got a bus to Berkley, went back across the bridge, and ended up in Oakland somehow. Right next to a factory. Then I stood on a corner and stuck out my thumb. And the thing that I remember was that it started getting hazy. I could barely breathe.

My eyes began to water, as the cars began to come. I never really saw the people who were driving, but I knew that they saw me. Tears were running down my face and I must have spent a half an hour there. Then I heard it. "How about a ride?" somebody called. So I stumbled to the car and threw my gear inside.

I learned a lot that day. To go out to the truck stops was the main thing. I must have gotten thirteen, fourteen rides, and I wasn't even all that far from where I started. Two miles here, another couple there. A lot of them were like that. "I'm going all the way to Sunol," one guy told me. And it turned out that was only thirteen miles.

So I thought and I figured that the way that it was going, it would take me thirty-seven days to hitchhike back to Maryland. I counted all my money and divided it by forty. Forty-two bucks a day, and change. That's how much I finally figured I could spend each day.

But anyway, I was someplace east of Oakland. Southeast, I guess. It was starting to get dark, when a station wagon pulled off to the side. "Need a ride?" the driver shouted. "Where ya headed?" So I told him back to Maryland. "Well you oughta take the Interstates," he said. "You'll piss away your time on *these* roads. Get on in. I'll take you out to Ninety-nine, and you can catch a ride to Forty."

I threw my stuff in back, then we sat there for a minute, looking at my maps. "Used to hitch a lot myself," he said. "Twenty, thirty years ago. All across the country. Colorado, Utah. Ever seen Montana? Beautiful... You oughta try and see it. I'd go back there myself, except my wife don't like to travel."

He pointed to a black line that would have been a red line in the atlas that I copied. "I'll take you down to here," he said. "Modesto. You can catch a ride to Bakersfield and head back east from there. Ever seen the canyons?" I told him that I hadn't. "Well, wait until you do," he said. "I wish that *I* could go."

We drove about an hour after that, then began to see the signs. Modesto - eighteen, fourteen, then seven more miles. "There's a truck stop up ahead," my driver said. "I *know* you'll get a ride." And in a little while we saw 'em. Forty, fifty trucks, with a diner in the middle and a sign that reached up to the sky. CROSSROADS TRUCK STOP.

"Gonna get some food?" my driver asked. "How ya fixed for money?"

"Still have thirty-six bucks for today," I told him.

"Well, you can always buy some paint," he said. "Get yourself a little paintbrush and go around to neighborhoods. Ten cents for a number. "You can paint all the addresses. That's what got *me* through. Use this for the paint." He reached into his pocket and handed me a ten. "Even if you never buy the paint, I'd like for you to have it." He jammed it in my hand, looked out through the windshield and began to nod his head. "Please don't give it back. This way *I* can go."

I put it in my pocket, opened up the door and took out all my stuff. "Stand here by the ramp," he said. "This is how they'll leave." He offered me his hand, I shook it, then he turned his car around. "Don't forget. I'm with you." Then he blinked his lights and gave a little wave.

I waited six or seven minutes after that. A truck came rolling off the lot and started down the ramp. And right there where it should have picked up speed, I heard it slowing down. PSSCHTT!

"Driving down to Bakersfield," he yelled. "If you wanna come along, it's a couple hundred miles."

A couple hundred miles? All RIGHT!! I thought. I climbed up in the cab and thanked him for the lift. But the one thing I was thinking, the thing I was regretting, was that he didn't stay to see. The guy back in the car. He didn't stay to see me climb into the cab and then head out to the canyons.

"Where you coming from?" my driver asked. "San Francisco?"

And I told him someplace east of Oakland. "Southeast."

He shifted through the gears. "Good place to be *from*," he told me.

We went down the ramp and merged into the center lane. Then for a couple hundred miles, we drove along, with the mountains off to our left.

"Sierras," my driver said. And even in the night, I think you would have liked them. Nothing like the mountains in Alaska, but they still were pretty good. All strung along together - and reaching for the stars.

"Where ya' goin' *to*?" my driver asked. "L.A.?"

"East," I said. "Going back to Maryland."

"Out to see the country?" And I told him that I was. "Well see it while you can. There's a lotta shit out there. *Lotta* shit," he said. "That's why I like *this* job." And he patted the dashboard.

I fell asleep sometime after that. Some place south of Fresno, where the road loops off and you start to see signs that tell about a giant forest. I fell asleep, and by the time I woke up, there we were in Bakersfield, in the parking lot of Mrs. Kibby's Frozen Foods.

"Whaddya wanna do?" my driver asked. "I don't unload till six. You can sleep here," he said. So that was where I slept some more.

The guy pulled across a curtain, back behind the seats, and climbed up in the cab, to a little bunk that he had fixed up. Then he pulled the curtain shut and left me sitting all alone, looking out the windshield, to a little neon sign: *MRS. KIBBY'S FOODS.*

They really do *go someplace*, I thought. All the trucks you see, out there on the roads. They really *go someplace*, like raindrops that come down or waves out on an ocean. Snowflakes, leaves or people passing by. We always end up *somewhere*.

Then I stretched my legs across the driver's side, pushed the button down, put my head against the door, and drifted off to sleep.

If you've never been to Mrs. Kibby's Frozen Foods, I'm sure you think it's cold. But it's colder than you think. People walk around in refrigerator suits and every time they talk, you see their breath come out of their mouths.

"Ready to load up?" I heard somebody ask. My driver said we were, so we backed up to the dock, workers brought in a forklift, and they started loading up the truck. Pot pies mostly, but a lot of other stuff, too. Little frozen cakes, pizza pies, and all kinds of desserts. Even frozen egg rolls.

"Ever eaten any of this shit?" my driver asked. And I told him that I had, but I wasn't really sure. "Lemon pies aren't all that bad," he told me, and he walked back to a freezer, came out, and handed me a box. "Here," he said. You can save it for the road."

I spent four more days driving after that. Not me, but the people I was with. Truckers mostly. I went across the Mojave Desert and my pie began to thaw, and there I was. "Want some lemon pie?" I asked, and my driver told me no. "Just ate," he said, and he kept on driving. Past Kingman, Flagstaff, and Gallup.

One guy picked me up, and for eighty-seven miles he thought that we were going west, when we were really going east. I would have told him sooner, but I think I was asleep.

"I hear the ocean's great," he told me, going into Albuquerque.

"Yeah," I said. And I thought he meant the Atlantic, because that's where we were headed.

"Ever been to California?"

I told him I'd just been there.

"When?" he asked.

I told him earlier that day.

"Holy *SHIT!*" he yelled. Then he stopped the car, turned it around, and told me he was sorry. "Headin' the wrong way," he said.

When I got out of his car, I remember that I told him I had done that, too. "Lots of times," I said. Then I watched him drive away.

From there, I think I stayed on Forty. *Riding, riding, riding*, except this one time.

I was really beat. Standing on the side of this road, in the middle of the night. Someplace down in Texas. *Should I try to get a ride, or should I go to sleep? Anchorage or Fairbanks?*

Then this little Volkswagen came by and the guy asked if I could drive. "I'm really *high*," he said. "I just can't do it anymore." So I got behind the wheel and it really started pouring down. *RAINING, RAINING, RAINING.* This guy was all screwed up, I was driving in the rain, and it kept on getting worse. *Pop! POP! POP!*

"What?" he asked.

"What?" I asked him back. *POP!* God I was tired. And then I'd start to fall asleep and - *POP!*

It was really coming down. "Look at that," he said. "The rocks are moving all around."

And when you looked at the road, even in the night you could see that he was right. All these little rocks were moving *this* way and *that*.

"Rain must have sent them down the mountainsides," he said. But that wasn't it, because everything was flat for as far as you could see.

I was falling asleep. My head would drop down, hit the horn, then I'd think about the logging truck. I'd wake up and see these rocks moving in the night.

"I can't do it anymore," I said. "I *can't*. I've gotta get some air."

I pulled the car to the side, and even though the rain was pouring down, I opened the door, and got out. That was when I really saw 'em. Hundreds of turtles all across the road.

Pop. *POP! POP! POP!* And I thought that I was gonna puke.

Chapter 26

I finally made it home. Walked up the same sidewalk that I'd walked down months and months before. I stood on the porch and knocked on the door.

"Well look who it is," my mother said.

I stayed home for a while and it was really kind of nice. I even got a landscaping job, so I could think.

After another month or so, they told me they were going to have to lay me off, because the work was slowing down. But the phone rang that night. And *think the strangest thing...*

"You're never gonna guess," Kingpen said. "I called the Hall this morning and they went above our numbers. Fifty-three twenty-seven."

And right away, it started. *Grizzlies, caribou and wolves.*

"I think we oughta go back," Kingpen said. I told him that I knew.

"All we've gotta do is *be* there," I told him.

And I could picture Kingpen nodding his head.

———————

Kingpen had called in to reserve the tickets, and for all of our connecting flights, you'd think they would have screwed them up. But they didn't.

The tickets were perfect. Baltimore to Chicago, then we'd fly to Seattle, on up to Juneau, wait four hours, and then catch a flight back down to Ketchikan.

"We'll get a hotel up there," I said. "In Ketchikan. We'll get a hotel, go see the Kraxins and then come the next morning, we'll fly on to Fairbanks."

"Arrival one-o-five p.m.," Kingpen read from his ticket. "We should get there just in time. We'll shoot down to the Hall and pick up our dispatch slips. Then we'll head on up to Prudhoe."

"We'll take the train," I said. And we both knew what I meant. The Gravy Train. Hundred-dollar bills. A thousand bucks a week.

"We'll sleep up on the Slope tomorrow night," Kingpen told us.

We paid for our tickets and walked down to the gate. And when we looked at the people, it really made us wonder who would make it to Alaska and who would get off somewhere else along on the way.

"We'll find out when we get there," Kingpen said. And I figured that we would, except a lot of them had coats and ties, and we just knew *they'd* never make it.

"Chicago," Kingpen said. "I bet we lose 'em in Chicago." And it turned out that we did.

The pilot pulled the plane up to the walkway, the one that was connected to the building. In another couple minutes we had gotten on the plane, fastened our seatbelts, and were headed down the runway.

"Here goes," Kingpen said. And I felt it all around me. The rumble of the engines. Then my stomach pushed back against the seat, we lifted to the sky, and we headed toward Chicago.

I guess you'd never know it's all laid out the way it is, unless you see it from the sky. Perfect lines rise up and run across the land and intersect with other roads, then other roads crisscross across the ground. Always perfect lines, until you start to get out west.

Then it turns to squares. Giant squares of grass and grain, green and gold and different shades of brown. That's what I remember seeing from the plane when the clouds broke apart. Perfect order. "Symmetrical." That's what Kingpen said. And you wondered how they did it.

We flew into Seattle late that afternoon and Kingpen told me not that much had changed. "Still raining. Just like the last time I was here," he said.

I'd forgotten he had been there a couple months ago. "Must rain a lot," I said. And Kingpen nodded his head.

We went into a subway after we landed. Right there at the airport. We took a little train that went around the airport, out to all the gates. And even now, I can hear the deep voice on the tape: "HOLD ONTO THE RAIL. *PUH-LEEZ.* HOLD ONTO THE RAIL."

"This is it," Kingpen said. The subway stopped and we walked off of the train. We started toward the gate that wasn't near the others. Alaska Airlines.

"That's us," Kingpen said, and we started up the steps to the second floor. When we got up by the window that looked out on the airfield, I wish you could have seen 'em. Maybe half a dozen planes with pictures of Eskimos, salmon, or old-time sourdoughs on the tails. Red and blue and white.

"Alaska Airlines," Kingpen said. I could feel my heart begin to pound.

We had about a thousand miles to go to Juneau, and three thousand miles to Prudhoe, but you could feel it at the gate.

Alaska. *Land of grizzlies, caribou and wolves.*

"Look at this," Kingpen said, pointing to a photograph display.

"Alaska: Land of Enchantment," with photographs of glaciers, moose and the Northern Lights.

We stood there, looking at the pictures, then we went back down the steps to a small open lounge, and you could feel it even more.

You felt it when you saw the clothes they had on mostly. Thermal tops they wore instead of shirts. Goose down vests and scraggly beards. And every one of them, every single one, had this far off look.

"Alaskans !" Kingpen said. And there they were. Fifteen, twenty of 'em, maybe more, sitting in the lounge, waiting for the plane.

That was when I realized... *this was it*. Where you really start to feel it. Where it really all begins.

Grizzlies, caribou and wolves.

Where you get off of the subway and walk out to the gate.

"Alaska Airlines!" the man announced. "You are free to board. Welcome to our state."

I don't think you ever fly down into Juneau and think you're gonna make it. You almost always come down flying through the clouds. And then for six or seven feet, before you see the runway, you swear to God you're gonna crash. All you see is water, whitecaps, foam and waves.

Then your plane begins to drop. Lower, lower . . .

"Holy *SHIT*!" you think. Sweat pours from your skin, and right there, where you know you're gonna take a dive, the runway comes up and the pilot takes her in. Right there at the water.

"Son of a *BITCH*!" I said. And the guy in front turned halfway around.

"Crazy place to put a runway. Isn't it?" he asked.

And Kingpen told him, "Yeah."

We got off of the plane, walked across the tarmac, and went into the airport. And if you've never seen it, I can tell you that it's smaller than you'd think. Just one huge room with a cafeteria built on, except we never got to go in because the sign said, *CLOSED*.

"Reminds me of the Union Hall," I said. Kingpen laughed.

There wasn't all that much to do, so we sat for a while in these molded, plastic orange chairs. Sitting and looking. *Looking, looking, looking.*

"Look at those boots that guy has on," Kingpen said. They were twice as big as any that *I'd* ever seen. "*Look* at that!" Kingpen told me. There were valves on the sides. Big white boots, with air valves, so he could blow 'em up.

We sat there four hours that day - from late afternoon, on into the night. It must have been about the third hour, when we got this great idea from all the boxes that were there. Boxes, steamers, duffel bags and suitcases that were over by the wall.

I think of the two of us, *I* was the one who noticed first. "There's no storage room," I said.

But Kingpen thought there *had* to be. "*Every* airport has one," Kingpen told me. But Juneau didn't. There weren't even any lockers. So then we started thinking.

"We could make a *FORTUNE*! Just fifty cents apiece, or a dollar," Kingpen said. "Even two." And then we started counting. Two hundred thirteen . . . fourteen . . . fifteen boxes, bags and duffel bags, along with fishing rods and hunting rifles.

"And this isn't even *tourist* time," I said. "You know *they'll* want a place to store their stuff. We could get a storage van and store their stuff in there. Give the people tickets.

"Four hundred thirty bucks a day," Kingpen said. "And that's *off-season!*"

The intercom came on and a man announced that we could go out to the plane. "Alaska Airlines. The flight to Ketchikan is ready. You can walk out on the tarmac and begin to board."

"I guess we'd better go," Kingpen said.

265

We walked across the room and over to the door. We passed them one last time, and I can see 'em even now. A couple hundred boxes, trunks and duffel bags.

"We should *DO* it!" Kingpen said. "I mean, come back here one day and really *DO IT!*"

And at the time, I think we both thought that we would.

When we flew *out* of Juneau, it wasn't quite as scary. It was dark for one thing. And for another, we were going *up*. But the crazy thing was, we started heading south, because those were our connections. North to Juneau, south to Ketchikan. And the following morning we'd fly up north to Fairbanks.

"We should get to Ketchikan by seven," I said. "We'll get ourselves a room and then go and see the Kraxins. You're really gonna like them."

We weren't up there flying all that long. It might have been an hour, then the pilot cut back on the engines, and we started to descend. But not down through the clouds. Not like back in Juneau. Right then we were gliding through the black. Miles and miles of clear, black sky - and we never saw a light. At least not for a long time.

"Water," Kingpen said. "We're flying over water." But we weren't.

The moon was out that night. A full moon. And as we started going lower, I could see the forests down below. Silver white, from snowfall on the ground. I was right next to the window, and I wish you could have seen it. Miles and miles of frozen mountain lakes and hilltops full of giant trees.

"*LOOK!*" I said. And just then when I said it, Kingpen saw it, too, because the plane began to bank. Everywhere we looked, there was wilderness, frozen in the moonlight.

We went another couple miles, saw a light, then another and another. Then groups of lights and finally we saw it, like the ancient armies that you see in movies, camped out for the night.

"Ketchikan," I said. And there it was. A burst of lights, surrounded by the black.

We landed on the runway, got out of the plane, and started off across the tarmac to the airport. "Windy, isn't it?" I said.

And in another couple minutes, we thought we knew why. We were walking on an island. This tiny, little island. "Whoever would have thought they'd land the planes out *here?*" I asked. But it really didn't matter, because that was how they did it.

"So now what?" Kingpen asked. I shrugged my shoulders, shook my head, and we kept walking to the airport.

There was a sign inside the building that told about a ferry you could take. Over to the mainland, which was really just a larger island. *EVERY TWENTY MINUTES, $2 PER PERSON.* And underneath *that* sign, there were another couple signs for hotels, rooms and laundromats.

"Whaddya say we sleep *here?*" I asked. I pointed to a little handmade cardboard sign, tacked up to the wall. *Rooms, twenty bucks a night.* "I know just where it is," I said. "Not that far from Creek Street."

"Well go ahead and call 'em," Kingpen told me. And I did, except it took a little while. You weren't supposed to put the money in, until you heard the person on the other end. That's the way the phones worked, and probably still do. You never got a dial tone.

I dropped a quarter in the slot and punched the numbers, but I never got an answer. I never even heard it ring.

"I think it's broken," I said. We tried to find another phone, except that was it. The one and only phone. So Kingpen looked at the directions.

"Do not deposit coin until the other party *answers*," Kingpen read. So we tried it all again. I punched the buttons and heard somebody's voice.

"Hello?"

"Hello," I said.

"Hello?"

"Hello?"

"Drop the quarter," Kingpen said. "Drop the quarter in the slot." So I dropped the quarter in and heard him ask again. "Hello?"

"Hello," I said.

"Hello."

"We're looking for a room," I said. "A couple of us. Flying up to Fairbanks. We're looking for a place to stay."

"Well, I've got one here, for thirty bucks a night," he yelled into the phone.

"Thirty bucks?"

"Thirty bucks!" he shouted. But not because he was upset, but because of all the music blaring in the background.

"All right," I said. "We'll take it." I told him we'd be there in an hour.

We left the airport, walked out into the wind, and started down a set of wooden stairs that was built on top of boulders.

"Look," Kingpen said. And at the bottom of the steps, I could see it in the moonlight. The ferry. But it wasn't like the one that I had been on earlier that year. This one only held a couple cars. Maybe three. It was mostly used for people.

"People who fly into the airport and then need to get to Ketchikan." That's what Kingpen said. We gave the man our money and stepped onto the boat. He waited till another six or seven customers got on, then he started up the engine, and we headed off across the water.

God, it was cold. "Trip won't take that long," the Captain said. "But you can stand around the inboard if you want. It'll help to keep you warm."

So that's what everybody did. Everybody there, except for me and Kingpen. We went up front so we could see and feel it all. The lights across the water, the salt spray in our faces, and the moonlight coming down.

"Don't forget this," Kingpen said. And I told him that I wouldn't.

Then I pictured what it must have looked like to the people looking down, because a plane was taking off just then. It lifted up behind us, circled twice and I can tell you what they saw.

Miles and miles of water, and then down there in the waves, I know that they could see us in the moonlight. Me and Kingpen, in a little wooden boat, pushing toward the lights. Like thieves out in the darkness, stealing toward the town. With the salt spray on our faces, we were crashing through the waves and heading to the lights.

October 31, 1975. Halloween night. We were there.

From where the ferry dropped us off to where we had to go, it must have been eight miles. Maybe seven. So we walked awhile and then we caught a ride.

"Going down to dockside," our driver said. I told him that was fine. And the way it all turned out, he dropped us off a block away from where we were going to stay.

"Appreciate the ride," I said. Then we got out of the car and Kingpen saw him first. "*Look*," Kingpen said. And when I looked, I saw this big, sleazy guy behind us.

"I think we're being followed," Kingpen whispered. So we went across the street and started up the block, but so did he, so we walked around another building, but he still stayed with us.

"I bet he'll try to rob us," Kingpen said. We decided to split up and see what he'd do, but then that was when we saw it.

"Look," Kingpen said again. And there it was. *Coho's.*

"That's it," I said. But in a way, it wasn't.

The first floor was a bar, and you could hear it from the outside, before you started in. "A band," Kingpen said. We could hear it, blaring on the street.

"I don't really know about this," Kingpen said. But when we looked across the street, the sleazy guy was standing there, so we figured we'd go inside and ask about the room.

"Thirty bucks," the guy behind the bar said. So we handed him the money and he pointed toward a narrow set of stairs that went up to the second floor.

Like Kingpen said back then, it really wasn't much. There was a single bed against the wall, a little table and a bathroom. No phone.

"I was gonna call the Kraxins," I told him. "But I guess we'll just go."

"Well, would you mind if I just stayed here?" Kingpen asked.

Kingpen started to get nervous. I never knew exactly why he didn't go, but he didn't.

"No problem," I said. "I'll see you in a while."

Then I started out the door, but thought about the sleazy guy and the money that I had. "I'm gonna keep five bucks," I said. "In case he tries to rob me. Take this," I said.

I handed Kingpen the rest, about a hundred forty bucks, and told him maybe he should put it in with *his* money. "Then put it all together in a hiding place," I said. "A good one." Kingpen promised me he would.

I left the room and started down the narrow steps. Then I went out through the bar, past some lumberjacks.

"A lot of people have a gun." That was what she'd said. The girl back at the park.

A lot of people have a gun, and if *he* did, I figured I would turn my pockets inside out and give him all my money. "That's it. Five bucks," I'd say. But the way it all turned out, I never even saw him.

I started walking after that. Walking and looking and looking and walking. *That's him*, I thought. But then I looked again and it wasn't. So I started walking, until I caught a ride to First Street, then started up the hill.

There was a light on in the window and everything was just the way it had been. The Lazy Susan on the table, the dominoes and giant pillows. But nobody was there. *Son of a gun*, I thought. I thought they would be back before too long, so I waited and I waited. It must have been three hours. Sitting on the steps, and thinking while I sat, until I thought I'd better go. And what I remember thinking, when I finally walked away, was that they'd never even know that I had been there.

I walked back down the hill. After ten or fifteen cars, I got a ride. "Going down to dockside," my driver said. I told him that was fine. And in another couple minutes, that's where I was.

"Well, I appreciate the ride," I said.

"No problem. Going to a bar?" he asked. And I told him, "Not exactly. I'm staying in a room down here. I'm flying up to Fairbanks in the morning."

"Going up to work?" And I told him that I was.

I thanked the guy again and started walking toward the bar, about a block away. *A lot of people have a gun*, I heard her say. And then I kept on walking.

I walked into the bar sometime after twelve and it was getting kind of wild. Like the TV shows that you see of how it was Out West. Rough looking guys, some pretty drunk, and a piano playing in the background.

"Ring the fucking bell!" one guy yelled. Then I heard a bell ring and I started up the steps.

The door was locked when I got to the room, so I took the little key that they'd given us, pushed it into the hole, and turned until it clicked. Then I pushed against the door.

EEEEEEE – I could hear the hinges.

Then I saw him on the floor.

He looked the way you'd think that anybody would have looked after they'd been shot or stabbed or had the shit kicked out of 'em. He was all scrunched up, with his knees against his chest.

Dead, I thought. *He's fuckin' dead.* Except it turned out that he wasn't. Kingpen was asleep.

He was lying on the rug, by the foot of the bed, and the way that he was lying there, he reminded me of a painting that I'd seen. *Man's Best Friend.* It was a painting of a lap dog and a fireplace, except you never saw the man.

But anyway, I got a blanket off the bed, threw it over Kingpen and then I laid down on the mattress and tried to go to sleep. *Go to sleep. Go to sleep.* Except I couldn't. There was too much noise. Music blaring down below and the walls began to shake. And then I heard a fight break out, and then another, which was why he'd left the light on. That's what I remember thinking.

The bathroom light was on and I was gonna turn it off, except I never did. I kept on lying there. And I know I must have laid there for a couple hours, before I finally got to sleep.

And the only reason I *did* get to sleep was because the bar closed down. CLOSING TIME. *Think the strangest thing*, I thought. And then all at once it stopped. The music, the fights, the shaking walls. And then I started to drift off, and, *BBRRNNGGG!*

Damn, I thought. I banged down on my pocket and kept on banging till it stopped.

"Got it?" Kingpen mumbled.

And I told him, "Yeah."

I explained to Kingpen what had happened. How nobody had been home.

Then I went into the bathroom of our room. "Ever see that guy again?" Kingpen asked. "That sleazy guy?" And when I told him that I hadn't, he gave a little smile.

"Try and find it," Kingpen said.

"What?"

"The money," Kingpen told me. "Try and find it. I hid it really good."

But before I could look, he asked if I had given up. "You give up?" he asked.

And when I didn't answer right away, he pointed to the bathroom. "I put it in the light," he said. "Turn the screws. The globe comes off."

There were a couple little screws that held the globe in place. I gave a little twist, and then the cover came off in my hand.

"Careful," Kingpen said.

And then he told me something else, but I was staring at the money. The bills were wrapped around the light bulb and all of them were brown and brittle, and depending on their order in the stack, they had holes the size of quarters, dimes, or silver dollars.

"*LOOK* AT THIS!" I yelled.

Kingpen took the bills, I heard them crinkle in his hand, and then he looked down at the floor. "A hundred ninety bucks," he said. "Everything we had. I'll make it good somehow."

But when I realized that all he'd had was forty bucks, I let it drop.

"Come on," I said. "I guess we better go."

We walked out through the bar and out onto the street. When we looked up at the clouds. it looked like it was gonna rain, even though we knew it couldn't. "Too cold," Kingpen said. But still, it looked that way.

We kept on walking. We passed a couple bars, a Ben Franklin's and a grocery store. Then we started walking down the main road that ran along the water.

"Salmon," Kingpen said. And he pointed to a building. "That's where they freeze the salmon, halibut and crab." And by that time, we were down by Phillip's Frozen Storage.

We caught a ride a little after that. We got back on the ferry, but we almost didn't make it.

"Four bucks," the Captain said. "Two bucks each." So I handed him the five I'd had in case the sleazy guy had robbed me, and the Captain gave me back a one. "Now don't go spending all of it in one place," he said. Then he started laughing.

It took us ten or fifteen minutes till we got back to the steps that were built on top of boulders. Then we walked up to the airport, but hardly anyone was there.

"We've got about an hour," Kingpen said. So we sat around awhile and watched the people, then we heard it in the air.

"Wien Airlines. Flight 922 to Fairbanks is ready to board."

"That's us," Kingpen said. "I guess we better go."

We walked out through the door, out onto the tarmac, to the smallest plane I'd ever been on up to then. "Twelve-seater." But not that many people boarded. Maybe only half a dozen.

"We'll feel it when we drop down in the currents," Kingpen said. And then the engine started up.

We didn't see a whole lot after that. We flew into the clouds and then we flew above them. Just miles and miles of dirty piles of cotton. That was what it looked like. And maybe once or twice we'd see a patch of frozen mountains, trees or lakes. But almost always, it was cotton. And as fluffy as it looked, you would have thought you could have walked right on it, but you knew you couldn't.

We crossed into another time zone, someplace west of Ketchikan, and then we started going down. You could feel it in your ears.

"Too soon to be Alaska," Kingpen said. It turned he was right. Because the pilot took us down inside of Canada. And the only way we found that out was because they wouldn't let us off the plane.

"Doesn't make a lot of sense for you guys to go in and out of Customs just to see the airport," the pilot said. So we sat and watched the other people get off, then we saw a pickup drive out across the snowy field and pull up to our plane.

"*Look*," Kingpen said. He pointed to his ticket and a silver colored star at the bottom of his schedule. "Stopover," Kingpen said. "I guess that's what this is."

Some workers took a large, covered crate from the pickup and put it into the plane. Right there in the aisle, up behind the pilot, where the first class section would have been, except of course they didn't have one.

"Now how is anybody gonna walk past *that*?" Kingpen asked.

The pilot fired up the engine and then I knew it didn't matter. No one else was coming. "Two hundred people flying out of Baltimore and now we're all that's left."

"Yeah. And a lot of 'em never even made it past Chicago," Kingpen told me.

Then we started down the runway and right before we lifted off, it started. You could hear it coming from the crate. *"AHOOOOO. AHOOOOO."* It really wasn't all that bad at first.

"Malamute," Kingpen said. And he went up to the crate and lifted off the cover and sure enough, that's exactly what it was. "Pressure's getting to his ears," Kingpen told me. "It shouldn't last that long."

But of course it turned out that it did. All the way to Fairbanks. A couple thousand miles of *"AHOOOOO. AHOOOOO."* And then we'd drop down in these air pockets and he'd really let it rip. *"AR AR AR AHOOOOO!"*

Sonuva BITCH, I thought. And then a couple hours later, right before we landed, right before he took her down, the pilot's door swung open and he yelled back to the crate, "SHUT the FUCK *UP!*"

And it was pretty quiet after that.

We started seeing hills as we were coming down. Hills and little trees and a winding, frozen river that went on for miles and miles. *Almost there*, I thought. And then, sure enough, we kept on going lower, and we saw it spread out in the snow.

"Dodge," Kingpen said. And of course it wasn't. It was Fairbanks, but we called it that sometimes.

The intercom came on. "Prepare to land," the pilot said. "You both might check your seatbelts. Approximate landing time 1:03 p.m. Current temperature is twenty-five degrees." And then he paused for just a second. "Below zero. Thank you for flying Wien."

The dog began to whine and the words kept rolling in my head. "Twenty-five below. Twenty-five below. Do you know just how *cold* that is?" I asked. But Kingpen didn't know.

"Maybe it's like Ice Worm Gulch," he said.

Our plane landed on the runway and the dog let out a howl. We started down these steps they had pushed up to the plane and *then* we knew how cold it was. *So cold we couldn't breathe.* That's what I remember thinking. Every time we'd try, the air would freeze our throats and then we'd start to cough and cough, until I finally figured what to do.

"Try *little* breaths," I said. "Breathe in through your nose."

So we did that for a while, and breathed out through our mouths. Little bursts of air. In our nose and out our mouths. In and out.

And the thing that was so crazy was I thought back to McKinley. *Wonder Lake*, I thought. *But then it was mosquitoes.*

"I think that helps a lah…" Kingpen said. And then he breathed in through his nose. "Lot," he finished saying.

We walked across the runway to the airport and the bags were coming out. Nothing yet from *our* plane, but other stuff was there. Bags and boxes. Duffel bags with duct tape.

"Happy Valley. Coldfoot. Prudhoe Bay." a man announced.

And then we heard on the intercom, "Kingpen… Mr. Arthur Kingpen and Mr. Jesse Fitch, go up to the counter, please. Wien Airlines. Go up to the counter."

Kingpen thought we were supposed to check back in through Customs. But that's not what it was. Our luggage hadn't made it.

"Still down in the States," the guy said. "It might get here tonight." But you could tell, the way he said it, he knew it never would.

"We'll send it out, just as soon as it gets up here. Just give us your address," But of course we didn't have one.

"At least we didn't tell him we were gonna camp." That's what Kingpen told me later.

"Just send it up to Stevens…Stevens Hall. At the University." I said.

He wrote it on a card and then Kingpen and I started out the door.

"Maybe we can catch a ride," I said. We kept on walking.

It was just like Kingpen said. You felt it in your nostrils first. Little tiny nose hairs that would freeze and then your eyes would stick together.

"Look," Kingpen said. He only closed his eyes for six or seven seconds and his lashes stuck together. "FROZEN!" Kingpen said, then rubbed them with his fingers. We started blinking after that.

We kept on walking down the road, breathing in through our noses and out through our mouths - and blinking all the time. In and out. In and out. *Blink. Blink. Blink.*

The cars kept going by and I know the people saw us. "Imagine what we look like," Kingpen said. And we kept on walking.

We finally got a ride. "I'm going down to 2nd Avenue," the driver said. We got inside the car, he took us down to 2nd, and then we walked a couple blocks. We made a right, went back to the Hall, and saw it on the door.

The sign.

But neither of us read it. Not out loud. We read it to ourselves, but even then it made you wanna puke. *No C list calls today.* But we went in anyway.

Not that much had changed. The room was still the same, the map was on the wall, and over by the screen, the one they lifted up, the lady we had talked to was talking on the phone.

"All right," she said. "All *right*. But I'm telling you, they're starting to lay off. You won't get out till spring, but *you* do what you want. She put down the receiver and turned to me and Kingpen.

"Remember us? We told you we'd be back," Kingpen said.

The lady looked at me, then turned to look at Kingpen. I could tell that she didn't, but even if she had, I knew she wouldn't care.

"I called a couple days ago. The jobs went past our numbers," Kingpen said. "A couple hundred past."

"Well it might have been a special job," the lady said. A powder man or a driller. A *specialty*," she said. "But anyway, they're laying off for winter. Are you both on the C list?"

We told her that we were and all she did was shake her head. The phone began to ring and she put it to her ear. "Well *you* do what you want," she said. "But I'm telling you, they're laying off."

We walked over to the Coke machine and stood there for a while, planning what to do.

"We'll come back tomorrow," Kingpen said. "I think that we'll get out."

We walked to Cushman and made a left. Then we both stuck out our thumbs, but we couldn't get a ride. Not for a while. A couple cars slowed down, but they couldn't find a place to stop, so they kept on going.

We kept on walking to the Chapel of the Chimes, about a half a mile away. "How's *this*?" Kingpen asked. It was a funeral home. *Northern Lights Chapel of the Chimes*, with a place where cars could pull off from the road.

"Looks great," I said. Then we both stuck out our thumbs.

We got a ride up to the post office. But the way it all turned out that day, we didn't get the mailbox. The lady we had given all the information to wasn't even there.

"Got a job up North," The new lady told us. And she didn't even have us on the waiting list. "You'll have to fill *this* out," she said. Then she handed us an application - exactly like the one we'd filled out before. "You might get a box in March," she said.

Kingpen filled out the form again, then we started through the door. We walked down the road to the long, wooden, snow-covered steps that took us up the hill. And there it was...

"Home," Kingpen said.

The campus reminded me of April in a way, when we saw it first with Beamish. With the snow and the buildings spread all around. Everything was there. Exactly like we'd left it. Not a thing had changed, except for us.

"How about we go up to the ceiling and figure what to do?" I asked.

So that was what we did. We went into the Student Union, through the arctic entrance, and started past the counter.

"How about a candy bar?" I asked. "They're not more than a dollar."

"You go ahead and get one," Kingpen answered. But of course I never did. "I'll get your money for you somehow. Don't you worry," Kingpen said. Then we started up the stairs.

It was just like every other time we'd been there. No one else was there. We sat up by the ceiling, just the two of us, and took a look around. Then we started counting all this burned up, crispy money. A hundred eighty, ninety bucks we couldn't spend. And then we had one dollar that we could.

"How about we *split* one candy bar?" I asked. But we never did.

We went to Stevens Hall a little after that. It must have been five or six o'clock, because the students I'd thought were gonna be there weren't.

"Dinner," Kingpen said. And I wondered if they still were using paper plates.

"Maybe we should go see Mr. Milt," Kingpen said. "Go see him, and then we oughta find a place to stay."

"Maybe we can get the keys and sleep back in the dish room," I told him. So that was what we figured we would do.

We walked across the snow, over to the dumpster, climbed up on the loading platform, and pushed against the door.

"Locked!" Kingpen said. So we went around to the front, but of course the girl at the entrance wouldn't let us in. "You've gotta have a *student card*," she said.

So we walked on back to Stevens and watched TV. "We can try again tomorrow," Kingpen said. "If we don't fly up to Prudhoe, we can go back to the dish room."

I went up to the TV and flipped through the channels. We finally settled on a show I had seen a month before. *How to Tie a Fly, with Your Fishing Host Bill Bertram.*

"Know who'd really like this?" Kingpen asked.

"Beamish."

"Yeah. Beamish," Kingpen said.

We sat there for a while watching Mr. Bertram tying all these flies. Then all at once we heard it.

"Listen," Kingpen said. And I can hear it even now. *Ping. Pong. Ping. Pong.*

We went down to the basement, to a room right near the washers. "Rec room," Kingpen said.

A guy was standing there with a paddle in his hand. He had the table up against a wall and was playing by himself. "Haven't lost a game yet," he joked. "You two wanna play?"

"You go ahead," I said. "You play a game with Kingpen. I'll play winner."

They warmed up for a while and they both said how they hadn't played for years. Then Kingpen won the serve.

"Net ball," the other player said.

So Kingpen tried again and for ten or fifteen minutes….. back and forth, back and forth.

And the thing that was so crazy was when they got down to the end. They didn't know the rules. Twenty-one to twenty. But you had to win by two. That's what Kingpen said. But then the other guy said no, you didn't. But neither of them knew. Not for sure. So they played another game.

Ping. Pong. Ping. Pong.

It was seventeen to fifteen, and Kingpen was ahead. Then the other guy came back, twenty-seventeen, and tossed the ball to Kingpen.

"Your serve," he said.

And then Kingpen hit the net, and all at once the game was over. Just like that.

"You play," Kingpen said. He handed me the paddle and stood against the wall. "*You* go ahead and beat him."

I guess I felt it on my fingers first. Then I rubbed it on my palm and I *knew* I couldn't lose. *A sandpaper paddle.* Just the kind I liked. With the tiny bits of sand worn almost to the wood. And the other guy had sponge.

I'll keep the ball down low, I thought. *He'll lose all his control and every time he lifts it up – SLAM! SLAM! SLAM!*

"Need a couple minutes warm-up?" he asked.

But that's the other thing. I *never* warm up. *Ever.* I start right there with the game.

"You go ahead and serve," I said. But he handed me the ball.

"You first."

It dropped down from my fingertips and right before it hit the tabletop, it must have been an inch, I hit it with my paddle.

BOOM. BOO BOOM!

The ball bounced up from *my* side, flew across the net, and barely hit the other end, right there to his left.

"One zip," I said. *BOOM, BOO BOOM! BOOM, BOO BOOM!*
Bang 'em in the cans, I thought.
PING. PONG. PING. PONG.
"Five-zip," I said. "Your serve." And I tossed the ball across.
"Two more for a shut-out," Kingpen said.

His name was Rodney Cornfield. That's what he told us later. But for now, he got this real determined look and said I'd never do it.

"I'm really not that good, but I know you'll never shut me out. You wanna bet a buck on *that*?" Cornfield asked.

And I told him that I did.

If there's one thing you can't fake, it's the way you're gonna serve, by the way you hold your paddle. *High and easy.* That's what I remember thinking. To the middle of my right-hand square. And when the ball came over just like that, I brought my paddle down. *SLAM!* Right into the net. I swear to God. The ball went right into the net, but with the topspin that it had, it started climbing up, until it almost started over. Then suddenly it stopped and dropped back down to my side of the table.

"Sonuva *BITCH*," I said. And then Cornfield took my dollar.

The score was one to five, but by then it didn't matter, so we started up another game.

"I'll give you fourteen points," I said. "I'll even let you serve. You wanna bet me back my buck?"

And Cornfield said he did.

Ping. Pong. *SLAM!* Ping. Pong. *SLAM!*

His serve was getting better, but I had him twenty-seventeen. And then I pulled my paddle back to fake a slam, tapped it just a little and Cornfield never had a chance.

"*GAME!*" I said. And then he gave me back my dollar.

We kept on playing after that, doubling the money. First he owed me one, then a couple, then four, eight, and finally sixteen.

"Sixteen bucks," I said. "You wanna play one more?" But Cornfield wanted nineteen points.

"Well you've gotta win by two," I said. And then I let the ball drop down from my fingertips.

Boo Boom *BOOM!* Ping. *PONG.* Ping. *PONG.*

His game was getting stronger, but it hurt him in a way, because then I changed my tactics and I wasn't still the same.

Tap. Tap. *BOOM!*

"Overshot again," Cornfield said. And by then the score was twenty-seventeen, but I knew that I could win it if I didn't choke.

"Your serve," Cornfield said. "I only need one point."

But the thing that I was thinking was *karate*.

If you've ever seen 'em break a board, you've seen just how they do it. They tighten up their hand and bring it down – *Ka-BOOM!* But that's not how they do it in their head. They picture that the board is really down another extra foot, convince themselves it's there, and then *Ka-BOOM!* They never feel the real one.

Just push the limit out and there's no way that you'll choke, I thought. *Just figure you need thirty.* So that was what I did.

It was twenty-one to twenty, then twenty-two to twenty-one. And that's the way it went. Back and forth and back and forth. Twenty-seven twenty-six and then I looked off to my left and slammed it to my right.

"*GAME!*" Kingpen yelled. And I thought I'd won it. Over thirty bucks. But Cornfield didn't have the money.

"You wanna play some cards?" he asked.

We went up to his room and it must have been nearly nine or ten o'clock by then. *Twelve o'clock in Ketchikan*, I thought. And I was really feeling kind of beat. Not to mention hungry.

"I'll let you have these poker chips," he said. And then he gave me thirty-two and I handed Kingpen ten of them.

"Five card stud?" Cornfield asked. And I told him that was fine.

It was like the game we'd played before, it all just went around. Back and forth and back and forth. I'd lose a couple chips and then I'd get 'em back.

"No peek?" Kingpen asked.

We told him, "Yeah." Then he started with the deal.

The place was waking up. I could hear it in the hall. Eleven, twelve o'clock at night and all throughout the dorm, things were going on. People coming in and stereos began to blare.

"Listen," Kingpen said. And I could hear it. Rock and roll. But that's not what he meant.

"Someone's honking," Kingpen said. And when I listened, I could hear it, out there in the cold.

"Just somebody here to pick somebody up," Cornfield said. And we could see it from the window, underneath a light.

"Arctic Cab," Cornfield said. And we heard *HONK. HONK. HONK.*

Then we went back to our game.

They say the chances are a couple hundred thousand to just one that you'll ever pull the card you need to fill an inside straight. But I don't think they are. I've pulled the cards I've needed, maybe six or seven times, and I don't think I've played a million games.

"One card," I said.

HONK! HONK! HONK!

But the card that Kingpen gave me wasn't even close.

Busted, I thought. But I never said a word. Instead, I raised the pot, the two of them dropped out, and I won back all the money I had lost the hand before. Round and round and round. Back and forth and back and forth.

HONK! HONK! HONK!

A couple minutes later, a guy came to the door and asked me if I knew me.

"Know a guy named Mr. Jesse Fitch?" he asked. And I told him that was me.

"Well your cab`s outside," he said. "Can't you hear it *honkin'*?"

I went out to the parking lot. He had come out from the airport.

"I've got your stuff," he said. "It got here from Seattle." And when I looked behind his seat, I saw everything was there. The tent, my backpack, and Kingpen's suitcase.

"Here," he said. "You've gotta sign this form." He handed me a pen, but I only got as far as Jesse Fit before the ink froze. But anyway, I got our stuff out of the back and I reached into my pocket for a tip. But I couldn't find the money for a long time, because of all the chips.

"Here," I finally said. I handed him the dollar that I had, but he never said a word.

I got back to the room. It must have been a little after one by then, and Kingpen couldn't stay awake.

"How about Monopoly?" Cornfield asked. "We'll give him time to sleep and then we'll go back to the cards."

"Sounds good to me," I said, because I knew that we would die if we camped out in the cold.

So Cornfield got the board, and round and round we went, from one street to the next. Cornfield had the racecar and my piece was the dog.

And the way that Cornfield played, you couldn't just *deal* the cards. *No.* "You have to *land* there," Cornfield said. "And *then* you get to buy it."

We must have played an hour after that. And I *think* I stayed awake. I was never quite asleep, never quite awake, but either way, I always knew that I was warm.

"*SIX!*" Cornfield yelled. I trotted down to Boardwalk, to Cornfield's big hotel. "Two thousand bucks," he said.

I thought I didn't have it, but Cornfield said I did.

"*MORTGAGE!*" Cornfield told me.

He started taking houses from my properties and turned over half my cards. He handed me some money from the bank and then he took it *from* me.

"*My* turn," he said. Then he shot the dice across the board and bought another railroad.

He was really pretty good. And like a lot of people that you see, who can never slow down, that's what he was like. "Driven." That's what Kingpen told me later.

"Your turn," Cornfield said. He handed me the dice, I dropped them on the board, and landed on Vermont.

"Three houses. That's it," Cornfield said. "There's no way you can pay it. Even passing *GO,* you're a couple hundred short. You wanna play again?"

But I told him that I didn't.

"Well how about Parcheesi?"

God, I was tired. "How about we rent your room?" I said. "I've got twenty seven chips and Kingpen's got thirteen. We'll leave tomorrow morning."

"You going up to work?" Cornfield asked.

And I said I thought we were.

I got Kingpen off the bed and we put our sleeping bags down on the floor. The only thing that kept the light out of our eyes was the table top above our head.

"You'd think he'd fold it up and put the card table off somewhere," Kingpen whispered. "Or at least turn out the light."

But it turned out that he needed it to play solitaire over by his desk. "Black king. Red four. Ace of diamonds. Red eight." On and on, throughout the night.

But the thing that really got me was the dust balls.

"Look," Kingpen said. And right there at eye level, giant balls of dust would blow across the floor. Bigger dust balls than I'd ever seen before. They were bigger than my fist. Like something from the dustbowl, you would see out West.

"You'd think that he could sweep the floor," Kingpen whispered.

Then we put our hands across our mouths before we fell asleep, so we wouldn't breathe 'em in.

Kingpen woke me up. "Come on," he whispered. "We've gotta go. Come on," he said again. "We'll go downtown and see what's at the Hall, then go see Mr. Milt."

We got out from underneath the table and began to roll up the bags. And there was Cornfield, sound asleep over at his desk, with his head down on his cards.

"Come on," Kingpen whispered. We got our stuff together and started out the door.

I couldn't really picture lugging our stuff downtown, so we went back to the TV room. Just off to the side there was a little closet, so we put our gear in there.

"I don't think that anybody's gonna take it," Kingpen said. I told him that they wouldn't.

We walked across the snow, breathing through our noses, blinking all the time. Then we started down the long wooden stairs to the bottom of the hill.

"You think a bank would swap the money?" Kingpen asked. "I mean, you think they would *exchange* it?"

"We can try," I said. But it turned out that we didn't. It wasn't open yet, because it was so early.

But the temperature was there. On their giant sign. Temperature and time: Thirty-two below and 8:21.

"*Geez,*" Kingpen said.

It didn't take that long to get a ride. We stood there on the corner shivering for six or seven minutes. Then a car came by, we got in, and off we went.

"Going to the Hall?" the driver asked.

And Kingpen told him, "Yeah. Laborers.'"

"Just got riffed myself," the driver said.

"Got what?" I asked.

"Laid off. Pink slipped. Reduction in Force."

"Oh. Yeah," I said.

"I'm going to the Hall to get back on the list," he said. "But I don't think I'll get out till the spring. The jobs aren't even going to the bottom of the A list anymore."

"How about the C list?" Kingpen asked.

But all the driver did was laugh.

We stood around outside awhile and then we managed to get in. The metal screen went up and the speaker told the crowd, "Just one job today."

"Happy Valley - seven tens." And the way that we were feeling, we didn't even stay around to see what number got it.

"I guess we oughta go see Mr. Milt," I said. Then we went out past the Coke machine and started walking to the Chapel of the Chimes.

Kingpen said it best. All we had to do was hold the course, and someday we'd get on. Maybe not today, and maybe not tomorrow, but someday.

"All we've gotta do is *be* there," Kingpen said. And we *would* be there. At least that's what we kept saying.

We made it to the dumpster, went up on the loading platform and this time it wasn't locked.

"After you," Kingpen said. And when I went in through the door, everything came back. The food, the smells and all the crazy people.

"Well *there* you are," he said. Mr. Milt was standing in his office, grinning ear to ear. "Where the hell you *been*?" he asked. "You two want a job?"

We walked into his office and a couple things had changed.

"I've gotta split you up," he said. "I'll need one of you up at the Student Center, working with the food. The other one can work back here. Stay back in the dish room, eight o'clock to four, seven-fifty five an hour."

"We'll *take* it!" Kingpen said. Both of us were hungry, so we asked him when the soonest was that we could start.

"How about an hour? Go get yourselves some food and figure which of you will want to work back in the dish room."

We walked out past the cans of plums and over to the trays. "Why don't you go ahead and work up with the food?" I said. "I don't mind the dish room." So that's what we decided. Then we planned on meeting back at Stevens Hall at quarter after four.

The lunch was coming out and we were first in line. Not a dollar in our pockets, at least not one that we could spend, and there we were with everything we ever could have wanted. Soups and salads, sandwiches and pies.

"Isn't this great?" Kingpen asked. And I told him that it was.

Mr. Milt came up a little after that, then he and Kingpen walked out past the girl who didn't know we worked there.

"Quarter after four," Kingpen called back. And he kept on walking.

I went back to the dish room and a couple guys were in the room. One of them was Meat Man, but the other guy, the skinny one, I didn't know. He must have been near seven feet and skinny as a rail, but he had the kind of muscles that would ripple when he moved. "Sinew," Kingpen told me later.

But anyway, he strutted more than walked. Everywhere he went. He had these long pink rubber gloves for washing dishes and these sunglasses he wore. *Keep on Truckin' Tom.* That's what people called him, because every time you saw him he was Truckin' like the decal that you see. Everywhere he went, strutting like a turkey. But the thing that I remember was this look he used to get.

I was in the dish room ten or fifteen minutes before I saw it for the first time. He strutted over from a stack of dishes to the conveyor belt, and all at once he stopped and started staring off in space. And then he got this crazy little smile that kept on getting bigger.

"We're gonna pop Lon," he said. And then his eyes got kind of glassy and you knew that he could see something in his head that no one else could see. "We're gonna *pop* Lon," he said again. And then he came out of his trance, strutted out the door and went to wash some tables.

"Now *that* son of a bitch is *crazy*," Meat Man said. He took a chicken leg off of a plate, put it in his plastic bag and started to the dumpster.

They say you never get to know exactly who you are unless you go off by yourself. You only see the way you are through other people's eyes. But I don't think that's right. I think you always know exactly who or what you are. *You always know yourself.* And then

285

through other people's eyes, you get to see exactly what or *who* you're not.

But still I had to wonder. Meat Man, Kolis, Keep on Truckin' Tom. And then there was *me*.

"*Here*," somebody said. She handed me her tray with a plate of mashed potatoes, then I turned my wrist just right and knocked 'em in the can. *BOO- BOOM!*

Push the button in, I thought, and then I pushed the button in, and another couple plates came in through the window. Onion rings and gravy. Sauerkraut and pickles.

And I knew that it was coming back.

BOO BOOM! BOO BOOM! I saw the food drop from the plates but by then I *felt* it more than saw it. *Felt* it. *Smelled* it. *Breathed it in.*

PSSHHTTT! Just send it through the steam, I thought. Then I sent it through the steam.

I worked till four that afternoon. I grabbed a sandwich as I left, said goodbye to Mr. Milt, and went outside to look for Kingpen.

"Hey Fitch," I heard. I thought I saw him in the dark. "Hey Fitch."

"How'd it go?" I asked.

"Just fine," Kingpen said.

"It isn't like the dish room," he told me. "I'm working more with food. Cutting up tomatoes, slicing cheese and grating lettuce. A little bit of *this*. A little bit of *that*. Filling in for people when they need to take a break. I even worked the grill. I cooked a couple hot dogs and then I did the register. I think I'm really gonna like it," Kingpen said. And I told him I was glad.

We went up to the dorm and checked inside the closet to make sure all our stuff was there. Then we watched TV awhile.

"Where you wanna stay tonight?" I asked. But Kingpen didn't know.

So we stayed right where we were. I curled up on the sofa and Kingpen took a chair that was stuffed with lots of foam.

"This isn't all that bad," I said. And it wasn't for a while.

I felt her tapping on my arm at first, then screaming in my ear. This fifty-year-old lady.

"*YOU'VE GOTTA GO!*" she shrieked. "You two can't *SLEEP* here! Get *up*! Get *UP*! You've gotta *GO!*"

Kingpen jolted from his chair and nearly crashed into a wall. "I've gotta have I.D.," she said. "You two guys aren't *students*. You think that you can *SLEEP* here?"

"Well, we were thinking . . .," Kingpen started, but he never got to finish.

"Come *ON!*" she hollered. "I'll show you out the door."

We packed up all our stuff and walked out of the TV room. But once we got outside, we knew we wouldn't last.

"Watch this," Kingpen said. He spit a blob of spit, and I guess he thought that it would freeze before it hit the ground. Except it didn't. It *did* freeze once it hit the sidewalk though.

"C'mon," I said.

We went around behind the dorm and started counting windows after that. "Three, four... *There* it is," I said. Kingpen packed some snow and tossed it toward the glass.

We saw him start to look outside, but then he walked away.

"That's him," I said.

So Kingpen made another snowball and tossed it up again. *SPLAT!* Cornfield came back to the window and raised it up this time.

"How about a game of monna... monna... mon-pleh," I asked. But I couldn't say the word, because I couldn't keep my teeth from clicking. "Monna... monna... mon-pleh," I said.

Then Kingpen finally shouted "CARDS! How about a game of cards?" he yelled up to the window.

Cornfield yelled down, "Sure. Just come on up."

But we told him to come *down*. "We'll meet you at the door," Kingpen told him. So that was what we did.

We never saw the lady again after that. Not *that* night. But her name was Mrs. Grobbus.

"Grab Ass," Cornfield said. "She goes through all the dorms every night at twelve, tossing people out who aren't supposed to be here."

"Like you two," Cornfield told us. "But there's not much she can do, unless she finds you in the TV room or down there playing Ping-Pong. Just stay in here," he said.

Kingpen closed the door and Cornfield went to get the cards.

"Guess what?" Kingpen whispered. He reached inside his pocket and pulled out a little wad. "I was waiting to surprise you. Here."

And then he showed me all this money. "A hundred ninety bucks. Take your hundred forty-five."

"But… "

"Shhh," Kingpen said. And he put his finger to his mouth.

Cornfield came back and began to deal the cards. "Five card stud?" he asked. And we told him that was fine. "One dollar limit?" And we nodded our heads.

"Gimmee twenty dollars' worth of chips," I said.

It was a little like the last time we had played. The money went around and around. The only way it was determined who had won or lost was by the time we had agreed to stop the game. "We'll play another twenty minutes," Kingpen said. "It's quarter after three."

"And then we'll play Parcheesi," Cornfield told us.

Kingpen set our clock and at twenty-five till four we heard it.

BRRNNGG!

"Push the button in," I said. And Kingpen shut it off.

"How'd you do?" he asked. And I told him I was up eleven dollars.

"Anybody wanna cut the cards?" I asked.

"I'll cut you once for ten," Cornfield said. He shuffled the deck. "You go ahead and draw."

I pulled a five and Cornfield drew an eight. "Gottchya," Cornfield told me.

And the thing that I remember thinking was that after three and a half hours, I was up a buck.

"How about we draw again?" I asked. "This time make it *twenty*?" But Cornfield didn't want to.

"I'd rather play Parcheesi."

"Don't you ever have to go to school?" Kingpen asked. "Don't you have some classes?"

"Not till ten o'clock this morning," Cornfield told him. And he went to get the game.

Kingpen took red. He put his pieces on the board. Cornfield took blue. And I got green.

"What kind of courses are you taking?" Kingpen asked.

"Mass communications."

"Like subways, planes and buses?"

"No. Like radio and TV. You're thinking of mass *transportation*," Cornfield said. "They don't need that up here. But there's gonna be a lotta jobs for radio and TV. *ANNOUNCERS!*"

Cornfield boomed in an announcer kind of voice. "You wanna hear my tapes?"

In a way we really didn't, but in a way we kind of did. Anything not to play Parcheesi. "We'd love to," Kingpen said. So Cornfield got them from his desk and put one in the tape machine.

"Part One, Side One. *Choosing the Right Job.*" We sat there for an hour after that, listening to Cornfield's voice recite a list. Bartenders, bakers, painters and shoemakers. On and on and on - until I thought that it would drive me nuts.

"I never knew there were so many jobs," I said. But Cornfield told me that was just the start. "I've got two thousand on the list," he said. And Kingpen told him that was great.

"You learn about the different jobs, but my tapes are all progressive," Cornfield said. "You learn how to apply and interview, and then you finally take the job. But you've gotta *learn* about the jobs before you can apply."

God, I was tired - *and only for a dollar.*

"Sailor, repairman, surgeon and watchmaker."

"Do you think that we could lie down on the floor, while we listen to the tapes?" Kingpen asked. When Cornfield said we could, we went and got the bags, and got inside them, underneath the table.

"Cowboy, cartoonist, plumber and model."

And everywhere I looked, giant dust balls would roll across the room. Even as I watched 'em, I could tell that I was driftin' off to sleep.

"Car salesman, ventriloquist."

Then just about the time the tape ran out, I heard it...

BBRRNNGGG!

Fireman, I thought.

Kingpen hit the button. The two of us got up, packed our gear, left Cornfield's room, and started toward to the closet.

"Let's try and find another place to stay tonight," I said.

When we got outside, I branched off toward the dumpster and Kingpen started to the Student Center. "Save a bone for Meat Man," Kingpen shouted.

I went into the cafeteria from the back, walked past all the plums and started to the dish room. *Heat*, I thought. *Gimmee lots of heat.* And when I walked in through the doors, I stopped breathing through my nose and started breathing through my mouth.

289

It was a pretty easy morning, once I started waking up. I had some help for one thing. Meat Man and Keep on Truckin' Tom were there.

Piece a cake, I thought. And then I took somebody's tray.

Mr. Milt came in at ten. "Gonna have a meeting. Right outside," he said. "Out there in the lunch room. Two-fifteen. Everybody's coming. Be there!" he told us. And then he stomped back toward the plums.

I was thinking I was gonna sneak out after lunch and go down to the Hall, but after Mr. Milt came in, I thought that maybe I should stay.

"He didn't look too happy, did he?" I asked. But the only person I was talking to was Keep on Truckin' Tom. So of course he didn't answer. Not exactly.

"We're gonna *POP* Lon," he said.

And then I nodded, he smiled, got that real far-off glassy look and strutted out the swinging doors.

We worked our way through lunch. It must have been near two o'clock, when things started slowing down and the people started filing in. Everyone who worked there. Even on the late shift. People who took tickets, ordered all the food or cooked it. People who washed floors and people who washed dishes. And it wasn't just us, the people who worked in the cafeteria.

"What's up?" Kingpen asked. And I told him that I didn't know. But a lot of people thought they did.

There were close to twenty of us there, sitting at a couple tables.

And all at once it started…

"I bet we're gonna get a raise," somebody said.

But then another one said, "Turkey. Thanksgiving's coming up," she said. "I bet he gives each of us a turkey."

But another person thought that it would be a ham. "I just *know* that each of us is gonna get a ham," she said.

But that's not what it was.

Mr. Milt finally came out and stood there at the front of the table. "Look at *this*," he said. And then he reached down in his pocket. He pulled some papers out, and every one of us could hear them crinkle in his hand.

"Just what the hell *is* this?" he roared. "Every day, we tabulate the money. Put it all together from the cafeteria and the Center. This here money's *burned!*" he shouted. He was really pissed.

290

"Why would anybody want to burn their money?" Meat Man asked. But Meat Man missed the point.

That's what Mr. Milt said back to him. "How the hell do *I* know? You miss the whole damn point. We don't *take* this kind of money! And if I ever catch anybody working here who's taking burned up, crispy bills, they're fired. Understand? *FIRED!* Now get back to your *JOBS!*" he roared.

I was gonna look at Kingpen, but then I thought I'd better not, so I started toward the dish room and passed Mr. Milt along the way.

"Maybe you could take the money to a bank," I said. "You think *they* would exchange it?" But he never really answered.

"I'll take care of it," he said.

———

It was just like Kingpen used to say…

We had a job, we had a goal, and we had a place to stay out of the cold.

"The only thing we don't have is someplace we can *sleep*," Kingpen told me. "We oughta look around. There are probably a lot of places we could sleep from four to twelve. At least we've got a place to spend the night."

"Yeah. As long as we play games and listen to those stupid tapes," I said.

We were on our way to Cornfield's and it must have been a Friday night, because I knew if I could stay up nine more hours I could go to sleep.

"We'll go up to Rasmussen or the Student Center," Kingpen said. "We'll find *someplace*."

"Part Two, Side One. *How to Prepare for the Job You Choose*." He started with the shoes you were supposed to wear, and then your socks, and how to comb your hair and on and on and on.

"You really know your stuff," I said. But that was just the icing.

"The icing on the cake." That's what Cornfield said.

"How about my *tone* and *resonance*?" he asked. Kingpen said they sounded great.

"You wanna play gin rummy? How about Careers?"

"Yeah. Careers," Kingpen said. "Let's all play Careers while we listen to the tapes.

Cornfield got the game, then each of us came up with a formula to win. Fame, happiness and money. You figured out percentages, but you couldn't tell the others. Then you tried to fill the little hearts or stars or dollar bills by going around the board.

"*Seven*," Kingpen said. "I rolled a seven." So he went on into College and I think he won a scholarship.

We played a couple hours after that. *Moving. Always moving.* Little plastic cars that would drive each of us around the board, so we could try out every kind of job.

"Don't forget to shine your shoes," the tape would say. And then you'd roll the dice and find out that your plastic piece was gonna fall in love or win the Derby.

"Don't forget to use your antiperspirant, wear a matching tie... " and on and on and on. And I never even found a job. Not one that I liked.

"*ELEVEN!*" Cornfield shouted. "*PAYDAY!*"

And after it was over, we traded our papers, and looked at what the other two had written down.

And now that I look back, it all seems kind of funny. I ended the game with piles and piles of money, Kingpen won the hearts, and Cornfield had the fame.

"Now don't forget to check your zipper," Cornfield's voice announced.

And then I looked down at my pants, put my head on the board, and I guess I fell asleep.

Chapter 27

"Seven minutes," Kingpen said. We were walking to the bank and he was pointing to the clock. "Seven minutes every day." And I knew he meant the light. "We're losing it," he said.

It was the first part of November and a lot of times back then, we never really felt we had a feel for what was coming next. But *that* day we could feel it.

"Winter," Kingpen said. And we could feel it getting colder every time we walked out of a building. Colder. Darker. Things were locking up. Thirty-six below that day. You could see it on the bank's clock, and it really made you wonder.

"Just how much colder do you think that it could get?" I asked. But Kingpen didn't know.

It was like you picture being on an iceberg, but you don't have any clothes. Then someone comes along and wraps you up in cellophane. *Wet* cellophane. And then it starts to freeze and you keep on getting colder. Colder than you ever could imagine. That's what it was like.

Freezing. Always freezing.

Walking in our tennis shoes and wearing gloves we'd found along the way. Gloves that didn't match.

Shoes, boots, pieces of rope. Just trying to stay warm.

Except for no jobs at the Hall, things were going pretty well. We'd figured out a schedule and depending on the time and day, I'd either be down working in the dish room, sleeping at Rasmussen, or up in Cornfield's dorm room, listening to tapes and playing all those crazy games.

"What kind of tape you think we'll listen to tonight?" I asked. But Kingpen didn't know, so I told him what I thought.

"Part Three, Side One," I said. *"How to Write a Resume."* And that's exactly what it was.

According to the tape, the hardest resume you'd ever have to write would be the resume you'd write to get the *first* job. After that you'd have some references. Some background.

"A *PORTFOLIO!*" Cornfield's voice boomed. But until then, you had to be *creative*. "*Stretch* yourself a little. Don't exactly lie, but *embellish* anything you've ever done."

"Two pair," Kingpen said. And when he saw I didn't have a thing and Cornfield missed his straight, he gathered all the chips.

"Your deal," Kingpen said.

They say you're really most at ease when you're on some kind of schedule. Some kind of routine. And now that I look back, I think they might be right.

We were sticking to our schedule, living our routine. Washing dishes, fixing food, playing cards and sleeping. And we never got out of the Hall that month, but we'd gotten to the point where I think it really didn't matter.

"Ever think you'd like to live your life like this?" Kingpen asked. "It's really not that bad." And I guess we had it pretty good.

But then things began to change.

It was sometime near Thanksgiving and the Health Department closed the Student Center down for one thing. Closed it down or *said* that they were gonna close it down.

"How about you two work from four to twelve tonight and really get that place in shape?" Mr. Milt said. We told him that we would. So after I had finished working in the dish room, I went up to the Center.

"Mostly it's the floors," Kingpen said. "We've gotta mop the floors, and back there in the storage room, it's really pretty bad. But the dish room was the worst.

It was a quarter of the size of the one down at the Commons and it only had a little sink. It didn't even have a washer.

"Wasn't meant for volume," Kingpen said. "Just for snacks and stuff. But anyway, I think the guy who works here quit. He wasn't here last night and I don't see him now." And everywhere we looked, all we saw was grease and grime.

"How about we go out to the front and grab a bite to eat before we start?" Kingpen asked. "My treat." And of course he didn't pay, because he worked there.

And when we went to our some food, I saw that everything was different. Like the lemons for example.

I was going to get some tea, and the lemons that were there were cut in little, fancy shapes. Plus, the napkins on the tables were folded like the ones you'd see in restaurants.

"What the hell is *this*?" I asked. Even on the menu, up above the counter, lots of stuff was added. Pigs in a blanket, different kinds of omelets.

"Whose idea was this?" I asked. And Kingpen told me it was his.

"You know, I really like this kind of work," he said. I told him that was great. "No, I mean I *really* like it," Kingpen said again. "I think that I could do this for a living, if we weren't going up to Prudhoe."

We straightened up the storeroom, then we started on the dishes, but we didn't wash 'em there. We packed them in some boxes that we found, hauled 'em down to the Commons and then sent them through the steam… *Psschtt.*

"Just like old times," Kingpen said.

Then we took 'em, bright and shiny, back up to the Student Center.

"I guess we oughta mop the floors," I said. And it couldn't have worked out better with the timing.

"Two minutes until we close," the guy announced. So everybody left, we put the chairs up on the tables, and by twelve o'clock exactly, we were done.

"Just wait till Mr. Milt sees *this*," I said.

We went to Cornfield's after that. He had Monopoly all set up, but before we even got around the board, I knew I couldn't do it.

"How about we give you thirty bucks?" I said. "Just to let us sleep."

"Well, can you listen to the tapes?" Cornfield asked.

And Kingpen told him, "Sure."

So Cornfield took our money and pushed the button in. "Part Four, Side One. *The Interview*."

It was different than the last tape.

This one had two parts - The Interview-*er* and The Interview-*ee*. "I understand you're looking for a job?" Cornfield asked. And Cornfield said he was.

I put the bags down on the floor after that, underneath the table, then we got down on our knees and crawled inside.

"You don't mind if *I* play? Do you?" Cornfield asked. He sat down in his chair, his feet inches from my face, and then I heard him roll the dice above my head. "*ELEVEN!*" he shouted. "Kentucky Avenue. I'll *take* it!"

"Questions you'll be asked," his taped voice announced. And then the interviewer started, but I never got to hear exactly what he asked.

"Dusba...," Kingpen croaked. "Dusba... " He pointed to his throat, his eyes began to water, and his face was turning blue. He started coughing, until I thought that he was gonna die. But just before he did, he opened up his mouth, stuck his fingers in, reached way down and pulled it out...

"Dust ball," Kingpen said.

And I thought that I was gonna puke.

———————

Things started getting crazy in our lives soon after that.

People mostly. Kingpen said it had to do with cabin fever, but our schedule started getting crazy, too.

"I'm gonna need the two of you to jump around," Mr. Milt said. "Any problem there? I need some flexibility," he told us. "Sometimes you'll be *here* and sometimes you'll be *there*."

We were sitting in his office, so all he really meant was that sometimes we would be *here* at the cafeteria and other times we'd be *there* at the Center.

"Might mean some overtime," he said. "Think you guys can do it?" And Kingpen said we could.

"Well, start down here for now," he said. "And later on tonight, Arthur, you can work up at the Center. And Fitch," he turned toward me. "You can stay here in the dish room, if that's OK with you. I really appreciate it guys. You know, you two are my best."

But when we walked back to the dish room, I realized that it wasn't saying much.

"Who's *that*?" Kingpen asked. He pointed through the open window of the dish room to a table in the lunch room.

"That's Keep on Truckin' Tom," I said. He was sitting by himself with his elbows on the table, staring at his cereal.

"Does he always wear those long pink rubber gloves?" Kingpen asked. "Even when he eats?"

"Even when he eats," I said.

"And how about those sunglasses?"

"He wears them, too," I said. "Almost every time I've seen him."

He got up from the table and started truckin' toward us. Struttin'. Always struttin'.

"How ya doin'?" I asked.

Kingpen said hello.

"We're gonna *Pop* Lon," Keep on Truckin' Tom said. And I guess his eyes got glassy, but I couldn't really tell. "We're gonna *POP* Lon," he said again. Then he started with his smile.

Kingpen told me later, "Just be glad you're name's not Lon. Did you see all that sinew? That guy could tear you limb from limb."

"But that's not what I think he's gonna do," I said. "I think he's gonna *SHOOT* him."

"Shoot who?"

"Lon," I said. "He's gonna fuckin' *POP* him. Don't you get it?!"

The people started coming in, we started getting busy, then sometime near ten-thirty Kingpen left and went to call the Hall.

"A couple jobs, but nothing going to the C list," Kingpen said, when he got back.

Since we didn't have the Buick, one of us had come up with the idea to phone down to the Hall and check things with the lady.

But nothing. Always *nothing*. Every single day.

"Maybe she's just saying that," Kingpen said one time. So for a few days we'd gone down to the Hall, but it turned out she'd been telling us the truth.

"*Nothing!*" Kingpen said. And we'd stood there for a minute, staring at the sign.

Later that day, sometime near five-thirty, maybe six o'clock, we were at the cafeteria. Things were pretty quiet for a steak night.

"It reminds me of May, when people start leaving," Kingpen said. "It's a little bit like that. But now they're leaving for Thanksgiving." And I think that he was right.

"Why don't we go up to the Student Center?" Kingpen asked. "And get that place in shape."

"You go ahead," I told him. "I'll be up in a minute."

Kingpen took off, I pushed the button in, and that's the night it started. People lost control.

I was over by the sink and four of us were there. Me and Meat Man, Keep on Truckin' Tom, and a new guy Mr. Milt had hired a couple days before. A new guy from L.A.

"Now just what the hell is *this*?" the guy from L.A. asked. And he picked up Meat Man's plastic bag of bones. "Anybody know what *this is*?" he asked again.

"You just leave that bag alone," Meat Man said.

297

But of course the new guy didn't.

"You couldn't have a dog," he said. "These are chicken bones."

And everything was there. T-bones, chicken bones, even bones from fish. Three days' worth of savings.

"Look at this," he said. And he held one in the air. "You like to nibble on these bones?" he asked. But Meat Man didn't answer. Not exactly.

"FUCK YOU!" Meat Man shouted.

And then he grabbed a dish, threw it, and *SA-MASH!* It barely missed the guy from L.A.'s head and broke against the wall.

"We're gonna Pop Lon!" Keep on Truckin' Tom said.

And after that, everything broke loose.

There was a space back in the corner, underneath a counter, and I got there just in time. *SA-MASH! MASH! MASH!*

"Gimmee back that bag!" Meat Man yelled.

But the only thing the guy from L.A. said that he was gonna do was give Meat Man a bone.

"Here," he said. And he lifted up a T-bone, raised his hand behind his head and let it fly. *THUMP!* "Now how about a chicken leg? A *ham* bone? A fillet of *fish*?" THUMP! THUMP! *SPLAT!*

Things really started flying after that. All across the room. Little bowls and cups. Then a dish would shatter as it hit against the ceiling. Every kind of bone you ever could imagine was sailing through the air.

"We're gonna *pop* Lon," Keep on Truckin' Tom kept saying. And even though I never *saw* him, I pictured he was smiling.

But as crazy as it was, the thing that I remember was that one thing was consistent. *Thump, splat, crash, smash*, but there above it all, you always heard it in the background. The ever-constant *PSSCHTT!*

Push the button in, I thought. And then I crawled out of my hole.

I made a dash across the floor, up onto the counter, over top the trays, and out into the big room where everyone was eating.

"Just what the hell's going on back there?" I heard somebody ask.

But I never said a word. Just kept on moving. *Moving, moving, moving*, until I made it to the door about forty feet away. And even then, as I left to go outside, I heard it all behind me...

"Cluck! Cluck! Cluck! Wanna nibble on a chicken bone?"

"FUCK YOU!" Meat Man yelled.

SA-MASH! SMASH! SMASH!

I went up to the Student Center, walked into the kitchen, then I started telling Kingpen. "Shoulda seen it. Dishes flying everywhere."

"Well I bet I know who's gonna clean it up," Kingpen said.

And I knew that he was right. But the one thing that we didn't know, or at least we couldn't quite remember, was if the guy who'd started just the day before had ever said his name.

"You think that he was *Lon*?" I asked. But Kingpen didn't know.

"It's kind of like the Foreign Legion down there in the dish room," Kingpen said. And I knew exactly what he meant.

We worked till after one, then headed off to Cornfield's.

"Here's forty bucks," I told him when we got there. "We're really kinda beat and are gonna have to bust our asses first thing in the morning."

"Dish fight," Kingpen said. But Cornfield didn't care.

"I got an interview for a job," he said. "Tomorrow. One-fifteen. Radio announcer."

They had a little station at the school and sometimes we would hear it.

"It'll only be part-time if I get it," Cornfield said. Kingpen told him that he thought that sounded great.

I opened up the bags and the dust balls blew across the room. We got down on the floor, and Cornfield pushed the button in...

"Part Seven, Side Two. *How to Know When to Apply for the Job You Choose.*"

"Holy Shit," I thought. But it was better than you'd think. And different than you ever would imagine.

If you didn't know his voice, you would have sworn he was a doctor.

"Biorhythms," Cornfield's taped voice said. "Everybody's got one." Then he told how every person had a cycle. "You need to *know* yourself," he said. And even as he talked, he handed me these graphs and different kinds of charts.

"Timing," Cornfield's real voice said. "It all comes down to timing things to meet your peak. That's why I asked to interview at one-fifteen," he said. And he pointed to a graph of his biorhythms.

I didn't sleep very well that night, and neither did Kingpen.

299

"How many plates you think got smashed?" he asked. And I said a couple dozen.

"That was when I left," I said. "So it's gotta be way more."

"Well, I guess we'd better go," he said. "It's almost six o'clock. Maybe Mr. Milt will be there and he can let us into the building."

We walked outside from Stevens and as usual, everything was dark.

But you should have felt the snow. That's what I remember. Walking through this snow, except it didn't *feel* like snow. It felt more like powdered sugar.

"Ever been around any other snow that felt like this?" I asked. But Kingpen didn't hear me.

"Look," he said. He pointed up ahead and we both could see it. A light was on, over in the Commons.

"Maybe Mr. Milt's in there," I said. But it turned out he wasn't.

We got up on the loading platform and Kingpen pushed the door in.

"Listen," Kingpen whispered. And I could hear it in the distance, like some ancient tribal chant. *Thump, thump, thump, thump. Thump, thump, thump, thump.* "We're gonna *pop* Lon. We're gonna *pop* Lon."

"Listen," Kingpen said. "It's Keep on Truckin' Tom." And I told him that I knew.

We walked on past the office. Everything was dark except a light back in the dish room. We snuck around the plums, until we got up to the door that went into the main room where everybody ate. Then we looked back around the corner.

Kingpen told me later, it reminded him a little of the way a jazz musician looks when he's really into playing what he's playing.

"*Focused,*" Kingpen said. And that's exactly what he looked like.

Keep on Truckin' Tom was sitting on the floor with a T-bone in each glove, banging on these pots that were resting on his knees. And staring. Always staring at the light that was up above him on the ceiling. But I guess it didn't matter, with his glasses.

Thump, thump, thump, thump. And everything was spotless. Not a cup or plate or saucer anywhere in sight. Everything we'd had was completely smashed to hell, but you never would have known it.

"*Clean and empty.*" That's what I remember thinking.

"I bet he's been in here all night," I said. "Cleaning up the room."

And when you listened to his voice, you could tell that he was getting tired.

"Listen," Kingpen said. "Listen to the words."

And they all began to blend and jumble with each other. "Werg on pop Lahn." *Thump, thump, thump, thump.* "Werg on pop lahn."

And then it hit me all at once. "Holy shit," I thought. He was just like one of us, holding to the dream.

Catch the gravy train and you'll be rich, I thought.

And when I turned to look at Kingpen, he began to shake his head. "Come on," he said. "I think we'd better go."

We snuck back past the cans of plums and went down to the gym to take a shower.

It was just like Kingpen said. You didn't know if you should laugh or cry. "I *know* he isn't on the A or B list," I said.

"He isn't even in the union," Kingpen answered. "At least not the one that *we're* in. I mean, *I've* never seen him."

Kingpen turned the crank and handed me some paper towels.

"You ever seen him down there?" And I told him that I hadn't.

"Even if he's signed up at another Hall, which I don't think he is, he won't get out till spring," Kingpen said. "I feel sorry for the guy. He's living on delusions."

We walked around the gym awhile, then back up to the Commons. We walked in past the office and there was Mr. Milt, pacing back and forth.

"You two are all that's left," he screamed. "Everybody else has left. Sons a bitches ran off with the dishes, cups and saucers, so we'll go to paper plates again!" he roared.

It was a pretty easy day except we worked a lot of hours. Two a.m. and we were up at the Student Center, mopping the floor.

"Only need six more hours and we'll have put in twenty-four," I said.

But Kingpen wasn't laughing.

"And now we've gotta go and listen to that stupid tape," he said.

———————————

Cornfield said he got the job. "I start tomorrow. One to three o'clock, then five to six. How about some cards?"

"Well, we can play a couple games," I said. "But we're really kind of beat."

"Five card stud," he told us.

I guess we finally stopped for good at six o'clock, but all through the night, we'd start and stop and start, depending on the time, the moon - anything that had to do with Cornfield's chart.

"I'm *timing* all the games to meet my peaks," Cornfield said. And he ended up that night with close to twenty bucks.

"I'll flip you for it all," I said.

But Cornfield didn't want to, and Kingpen said we had to get some sleep.

"We can play again tomorrow night," Cornfield told us. "Just make sure and wake me up before you leave this morning. I wanna practice for my job before I start."

The alarm went off at seven forty-five, we shook Cornfield awake, and then we walked down to the Commons.

"Fitch, I want you to work right here in the dish room, but Arthur, you can go up to the Center," Mr. Milt said. "Fix it up real nice."

And what he meant was for Thanksgiving. "Put some fancy decorations out. Any kinda shit." And Kingpen told him that he would.

We only worked till ten that night and right before we left, Mr. Milt stopped in to see us.

"I'm gonna get some dishes, then I'm gonna get you both some help," he said. "I know I've told you both before, I know you're not machines. I'm working on some schedules, too. And another thing... Here."

He handed us a bottle. "For Thanksgiving. You know tomorrow's Turkey Day. Thanks for everything."

We went up to Rasmussen after that. We grabbed a couple hours sleep, then *BRNNGG!* Right there in the library.

"Come on," Kingpen said. "We'd better go."

So we went out through the arctic entrance, just as they were closing, then we started off across the snow to Cornfield's.

"*FIRED!*" Cornfield shouted, when we asked him how his day had gone. "I knew I never should have started work at one," he muttered to himself.

"Five card stud," he told us." Then he reached for his tape machine and pushed the button in.

"EPILOGUE. *What Kind of Job Are You Applying For?*" Cornfield's taped voice asked.

And Cornfield's real voice told him, "Baker. Well bake, bake, bake! It's *BURNED!*" he screamed. "You're *FIRED!* Next."

And Cornfield told him plumber. "Well fix it, fix it, *fix* it! Can't you even stop a *leak*?" he yelled. "You're *FIRED!*"

And on and on and on. Every kind of job you ever could imagine.

"Wanna be a shoveler? Well shovel, shovel, *shovel*. Can't you shovel *faster*? You're *FIRED!*" Cornfield screamed.

Then he really started losing it.

We were sitting at the table and his real voice started saying things like, "Solstice. Summer Solstice."

And then he'd bet a lot of money. "I'm right there at the peak," he told us. Then he'd look down at his chart and start to get real crazy.

"Wanna play no limit?" Cornfield asked. And I told him that was fine with me. "Well I'll bump you five," he said. Then I didn't pull the queen and Cornfield won the game.

"*FIRED!*" Cornfield screamed. "Can't you even teach a *class*? FIRED! FIRED! *FIRED!*" And the tape went on and on.

Cornfield kept on winning for a while, then we went into the Equinox. That's what Cornfield called it.

Round and round, and round - and the money that I had stayed just about the same. I never really lost, but then I never really won.

"Flush," I said. And I might have won two dollars.

It must have been a little after three by then. Then all at once, I started getting decent cards. Full house, straight, aces over.

"Lowball. Nothing wild," I said.

But Cornfield wouldn't play. "Going into Winter Solstice," Cornfield said. "I've gotta take a break. I'll play again in eighteen minutes."

Kingpen got his sleeping bag and put it on the floor. "I'm gonna try to get some sleep," he said. And then he got down with the dust balls, underneath the table, and put his hand across his mouth.

"So you wanna be a trucker, but don't know how to *drive?*" Cornfield asked. "Can't even pass the *test*? Well you're fuckin' *FIRED!*" Cornfield's voice roared. "*FIRED!*"

"How about we play some cards?" I asked.

We looked at the alarm clock and Cornfield checked his chart. "I've got another minute," Cornfield told me.

So I tried to wake Kingpen, but I couldn't get him up. "We'll just play one-on-one," I said. Cornfield started dealing.

Sometimes, you can tell, right there from the start, how it's gonna go. But still you keep on going. That's what it was like.

"Bullets," Cornfield said. "I guess they've got your jacks." He pulled in the whole pile, maybe ten or fifteen bucks.

And all that I kept thinking then was how we'd walked down to the bank that morning, me and Kingpen. Walked down to the bank and put in all those checks.

Son of a bitch, I thought. *If I'd only kept the money.*

And by then I must have been down forty and I only had a hundred left. "Five card stud," I said. "Deuces wild."

I had to give him credit after that. I started with a two and then I got a queen. All that Cornfield had, that I could see, was a six. Six of diamonds. So I started betting like a wild man.

"Well, I'll match your ten and bump you five," Cornfield said. And I knew he had at least a hundred twenty bucks from the money we had paid him, to sleep in his room.

"Here's your five and I'll bump you ten," I said.

And *up* and *up* and *up* we went, until everything I had was sitting in the pile. But I never got another card that I could use.

"You're late again?" Cornfield's voice asked. "Well you're *FIRED*!" Cornfield shouted. And then I handed him another six.

BUSTED! I thought. And it turned out I was right. "*THREE* of 'em," Cornfield shouted. And he flipped the first one over.

I borrowed all of Kingpen's money after that. Woke him up enough to get forty-seven bucks, then I worked it up to eighty, but I lost it all in the end.

You don't know how to play, I thought. *You fuckin' idiot. You're FIRED!*

"How about an I-O-U?" I asked.

But Cornfield wouldn't do it. "I'm going into Winter Solstice," Cornfield said.

He picked up Kingpen's money, then he stood there for a minute, shaking like a leaf. "I've never won this much before," he said.

"Well you can lose it back to me tomorrow night," I told him. Then I went to get my sleeping bag, but Cornfield kept on talking.

"I'm asking you to leave," he said.

"Leave?"

"Suppose you try to kill me."

"What?"

"Kill me. You and Arthur."

304

I couldn't talk to Cornfield after that. He started pacing back and forth and all he ever said was "Solstice. Winter Solstice." Then he'd look down at his charts, while his other voice asked, "Really? You think that you can type?"

I crawled down between the dust balls and started shaking Kingpen.

"Come on," I said. "We've gotta go."

And it might have been because he thought the clock went off, I never really asked him, but he never asked me why.

We just got it all together, then we started to the stairs, and I told him what had happened.

"Well the *heck* with that guy," Kingpen said. "We don't need *his* room." And it turned out that we didn't.

We got down to the bottom of the stairs and Kingpen pointed to a door. "How about the *closet?*" Kingpen asked. So that was where we slept. And it was just like you would picture. We crunched up all our legs and sat there in the dark and never got to sleep. But in some ways it was better than you'd think.

"Listen," Kingpen said. And I heard a little snap, the sounds of something being unscrewed and then, *GULP, GULP, GULP.*

"You know it could be worse," he said. "Just be thankful that we're warm. Happy Thanksgiving," Kingpen told me.

And then he handed me the bottle and we toasted in the dark.

It all looked pretty neat, with little paper cutouts of turkeys and the Pilgrims and lots of hanging ribbons all around the room.

"Like it?" Kingpen asked. I told him it was great. "Did it all myself," he said.

I told him I could tell. "Looks great," I said again.

We worked up in the Student Center that day until nearly four o'clock, and then we closed it down. Mr. Milt had said to put a little CLOSED sign up, so that was what we'd done.

Then we'd gone down to the Commons. And even on Thanksgiving, with the paper plates, we weren't that busy.

"What about tonight?" I asked.

Kingpen asked me, "What about it?

"Where we gonna sleep?" But Kingpen didn't know.

"What if I go find a place? I'll go on up to Stevens. There oughta be another place to sleep up there," he told me. And it turned out he was right.

It started coming in right after Kingpen left. Mashed potatoes, turkey parts and lots and lots of stuffing. In the past, I would have squeezed it through my fingers, wiped it off my hands, and brought the dishes down inside the cans – *BOO BOOM!*

But with the paper and the plastic and Styrofoam cups, it was like I told you. All I had to do was slide everything off, stack the trays, and then send 'em through the steam.

"*Here,*" somebody said. And almost without thinking, I knew that I could do it. A one-man dish room. That's exactly what I was.

I pushed the button in, and I heard it down the line…

Psschtt. Psschtt. Psschtt.

And that's when I remember thinking, *Fitch. You are fucking good.*

Kingpen came back and I could tell he was excited. "Wait until you see it. *Mattresses,*" he said.

"Mattresses?"

"Wait until you see it."

We got off from work at ten, then we started up to Stevens. I followed Kingpen through the door that someone had left unlocked. Then we kept on going up the steps.

"Third floor," Kingpen said. So we kept on going higher, until he stopped and there we were.

"Turn it," Kingpen said, pointing to the handle. I turned the silver-colored handle and gave a little push and it was just like Kingpen said. *Mattresses.* At least a dozen of them, piled there in the room.

"I guess they store 'em in here," Kingpen said. "Just think of all the times we couldn't find a mattress and now we've got too many."

And that's what it was like a lot of times back then. *Feast or famine.*

It was sometime late that night when Kingpen said he heard her. "Mrs. Grabass," Kingpen whispered. And we thought for sure that she was gonna turn the handle, open up the door and find us. But she never did.

We went down to the Commons later on that morning, and at quarter after ten, Kingpen went to call the Union. It must have been ten-twenty when Kingpen came back and told me. "There's gonna be a C list call," he said. "They're going to the C list."

It was like the Gettysburg Address, when people stood in awe. That's the way I felt. I never said a word.

"I *knew* it," Kingpen said.

And then he told me all about how the people on the Line would work right through Thanksgiving. "*Triple* time," Kingpen said. "But then a lot of them would quit and the jobs would open up. I just *knew* it," Kingpen said again. "I bet we're *there* tonight." And where he meant, but never said, was Prudhoe Bay.

We couldn't keep our mind on dishes after that. "All we've gotta do is *be* there," Kingpen said. And even if we had to *walk* the six or seven miles in thirty-five below that day to get to the Hall, we knew that we would make it.

"We'll work another hour," Kingpen said. "And then I guess we'd better go."

We snuck out by the front a little after that. Out into the twilight, and then across the snow and down the steps.

"Come *on*," Kingpen said. We made it to the bank, went across the road and stood there on the side, sticking out our thumbs.

"Two hours twenty minutes," Kingpen said, which was how much time we had to make it to the Hall. I could see it on the bank's clock, except it only took us fifteen minutes.

"Going down to 2nd Avenue," our driver said. So we told him that was great, he took us down to 2nd, then we walked another block and went to the Union.

We were a couple hours early, but even then, a couple guys were there.

"Wouldn't let us in this morning," one guy said. "You had to show ID to get into the A and B list call."

"Something's going on," I heard somebody say. And even as we talked, the Hall kept filling up. By twenty after one, it was packed so tight, with hundreds of us there, that you could hardly breathe.

"Like a bunch of cold sardines," Kingpen said. That's what it was like.

But even then, you really didn't care, because like every person that was packed into the room, you were holding to the dream.

A thousand bucks a week, I thought. And then the screen went up.

Everybody got real quiet after that. Before the moans and groans. "One minority call for Atigun Pass," the dispatcher called out.

That was it. But even then, I didn't know exactly what he meant.

"Anyone who isn't *white*," the guy behind me said.

"But didn't we *all* have the *exact same chance* to sign up on the list?" somebody else asked. And all the guys around me started nodding their heads.

"Anyone below three thousand?" the guy announced. But he never got an answer. "*Four* thousand? *Five* thousand?"

"Do you believe this shit?" another guy called out. "I'm thirty-eight fourteen!" But he was white, so it really didn't matter.

"*SIX* thousand?"

"Look," Kingpen said. There was someone coming up from back there in the crowd.

"*Indian*," I heard somebody say.

And then I saw him. Strutting to the window. This real tall guy with lots of sinew on his arms and long pink rubber gloves, and the glasses that he always wore.

"It's Keep on Truckin' Tom," Kingpen said.

And then we watched him step up to the counter, sign a piece of paper, take his dispatch slip, and hold it in the air.

And I wish you could have seen him. He never let his hand down. *Never*. He got this crazy smile and he started strutting out, but halfway through the room, he turned and called out to the crowd.

"Werg onna POP LON!" he shouted. And then he went out past the coke machine and headed out the door.

It was just like Kingpen said. *We only had to be there*. But still it was depressing.

"Where you want to sleep tonight?" I asked. "The Mattress Room?"

And Kingpen told me, "Yeah." That was fine with him.

Except it turned out that we couldn't, because some other guys were there. People just like us. Holding to the dream.

And I know it might sound crazy, but that's what it was like back then.

"Just living to survive." That's what Kingpen used to say. People crawling into every nook and cranny. Just living to survive until they got out from the list.

We went back to the closet that night. But right before we got there, I saw a little paper sign, taped up on a bulletin board.

Antonelli's Pizza. They were looking for a person to close it up at night. *Antonelli's Pizza*. I read it on the paper.

308

And the thing that I kept thinking was, if I could only get the job, we'd have a place to sleep.

"Need a quarter?" Kingpen asked.

I told him that I did, and then I went to make a phone call.

The alarm went off at six.

Then we went down to the gym and Kingpen took my clothes. "You go ahead and take your time," he said. "Take a long, hot shower. I'll take these up to Stevens and put 'em in the washer. You want to look your best to get the job. Remember all those tapes."

The night before, I had talked to Mr. Rick, the guy at Antonelli's, and he had asked if I could meet him at the pizza place sometime after nine. So I told him nine-fifteen.

"See you then," he said. And then he told me how to get there. "It's right next to McDonalds." And I told him that I knew exactly where it was.

Kingpen came back. He handed me my clothes and told me that the dryer hadn't gotten all that hot. "So they're still a little damp," he said.

And it didn't seem to matter at the time, but it turned out that it did. As soon as we went out, I told him, "Look at this." I slapped my hands down on my pants, and you could hear it.

"Sounds like cardboard." Kingpen said. "Frozen cardboard."

We ran up to the Commons, got some breakfast, then I started to the dish room, but that's when Kingpen told me. "You don't wanna smell like that," he said. "Not like in the dish room, for your interview."

So I went out by the tables and wiped 'em down awhile. Then at quarter after eight, I took a load of trash out back to the dumpster, went around the front, ran across the snow and started down the wooden steps, breathing in my nose and blinking. Always blinking in the dark.

And at twenty after eight, I saw it on the Bank clock. Thirty-eight below. But I know that it was colder with the pants that I had on. God, I was cold. Shaking like a leaf and my toes were going numb. That's what I remember. My toes were going numb in these tennis shoes that I was always wearing.

You're a fuckin' DUMB-ASS, Fitch, I thought.

309

And then I started jumping back and forth, waiting for a ride. But I don't think they saw me. The ice fog was too thick.

"It settles to the ground." That's what Kingpen told me later. "When it's really getting cold, the car exhaust will settle on the ground and you can hardly see a thing."

And that's what it was like. Giant clouds of grey, holding to the ground and floating in the dark. And there I was. Hopping in my frozen pants, in the middle of it all.

Come on, I thought, *come on.*

And then one finally stopped. "Going down to Safeway," the driver said. The corner of the page, if you remember what I told you.

"Fine," I said. And then I got inside the car and could hardly bend my legs. I finally did it though. *Crunch, crunch, CRACK!.* And I know the driver heard it, but he never said a word.

We drove past the campground, but of course we didn't see it. *Like the Chippewa*, I thought. *Or Tangle Falls.*

"This is it," my driver said. And there we were, at Safeway.

"Well, I appreciate the ride," I said. Then I got out of the car and closed the door and started walking. Fast, then faster, then fastest. *Chinese style*, I thought. And I kept on moving just as fast as I could go, until I got to Antonelli's.

"It's not that big a place, but we sell a lot of pizzas," Rick said. "I need someone to straighten up. Vacuum, sweep, and mop. You think that you can do it?"

"You mean I'd be here by myself, after everybody leaves at night?" I asked. "No one else would be here?"

"That's it," he said. "Two a.m. and everybody's out. You can have the key, but I've gotta have the place all cleaned by eleven in the morning. That's the time we open," Rick said. So I told him I would do it.

"Shouldn't take you but a couple hours every night," Rick said. "How's thirty bucks a night, seven days a week?"

"Sounds good," I said. "And I can come down here *tonight?*" I asked. When he told me that I could, I told him I would take the job.

"And if you ever feel like eating pizza," Rick said, "come in and help yourself." He handed me the key and I put it in my pocket.

I went back to the dish room at the Commons after that. "Wait until you see it," I told Kingpen.

"A real place we can sleep?"

I told him that was right. "A real place we can sleep. And it has a fireplace," I said. "Just wait until you see it. It's even got a dining room and kitchen."

The lunch crowd came in, but again, there weren't that many people. A relaxing hour and a half, and we were through.

"How about you two start unloading boxes?" Mr. Milt asked. Because the dishes had come in. Dishes, cups and small ceramic saucers like the ones we'd had before.

"Had 'em flown up from Seattle. Careful now," Mr. Milt said, when we started going through them. And I thought that he was kidding, but it turned out that he wasn't. "Money's drying up," he muttered. And he looked a little nervous.

"Things are looking up for you two, though," Mr. Milt said. "I got each of you a schedule. No more crazy hours." He gave us each a little piece of paper, and the one that he gave me had an eleven and a seven.

"You'll be mopping up the floor," Mr. Milt said. "Up there at the Center."

"From eleven at night until seven in the morning?"

"Well it would really help me out," Mr. Milt said.

So I told him I would do it. And according to the schedule, Kingpen started after me. Seven in the morning until three.

"You can work up in the Center fixing all the food," Mr. Milt said. "You're good at stuff like that." And Kingpen nodded his head.

They say you go along awhile and then it hits the fan. Good things, bad things - and always there are patterns…

Good-Bad-Good, or Bad and Good, then Better.

But I don't know that's true. Like Pinto told me later, take a guy who's had too much to drink and send him down an alley. From one side to the next, he'll bounce off of some cars, then run into a pole, and finally end up on a fence. And then when you look back, you think you saw a pattern, but you didn't.

"Patterns," Pinto told me. "It all depends on who you are and how you plan on seeing where you were."

But I don't think that Mr. Milt thought like that.

"Well now we've got that settled," Mr. Milt said, "I've saved the best for last. I got you guys a room. A place where you can sleep. I heard you didn't have a home, so I got you one. And all it's gonna cost the two of you is fifteen bucks a week, because you work here at the school. It's *subsidized*," he said.

311

"Your room is in a dorm, on the back part of the campus, up there on the top of the hill. Here's the room number," he said. And he handed Kingpen another slip of paper and a key.

"Well, you think the two of you could work up in the Student Center for a while tonight? It would really help me out," he said.

So we told him that we would and Kingpen told me later, "Work, work, work. That's all we ever do."

And that was when I told him, "At least you've only got one job," I said. "Look at me. I've got two."

And now I'll have to do 'em both at once. That's what I remember thinking.

"Well, I can help you," Kingpen said.

But I told him, "No, *I'll* get it. Go on and get some sleep."

Later on that night, after I had finished mopping up the Center, I went down past the candy counter, out the arctic entrance, and down the wooden steps to the road. Quarter after three that morning, I was standing on the corner in my tennis shoes. Thirty-two below, I could see it on the sign, and there I was. Standing on the corner, shaking like a fuckin' leaf.

And I know you think I finally got a ride. But I didn't. I never even saw a car, so I started walking. *WALKING, WALKING, WALKING.* Until I got down to the bridge and stood there for a minute looking at the Chena River, frozen like a rock. Then I went past the Campground, turned left, and walked along some more, on this long, deserted, frozen stretch of Airport Road.

Everything was dark, and you never would imagine that it wouldn't stay that way. *Think the strangest thing.*

And then the lights came out. All across the sky. Brilliant shades of white, that arched across the black and exploded into rolling streams of red and green, and rivers full of purple neon waves.

Maybe it was all that *walking, walking, walking.* I was starting to warm up. Or maybe I was numb. But anyway, I didn't feel that cold, so I watched 'em for a while. Until the colors faded out, and I told myself I thought I saw 'em, but I didn't. *Over there*, I thought, and by that time they were gone, but I stayed another minute just in case.

I started movin' on again. Walkin'. Always *walking.* Until I got down to the pizza place, stuck the key inside the lock, and turned it. Then I pulled back on the door. And even in the arctic entrance I could feel it. *Heat.*

And like the times you stick your hands underneath warm water when they're really, really cold, my arms and legs began to throb and crack and ache, until I thought my whole entire body was gonna break apart. But of course it never did.

And in another couple minutes, it was like Kingpen always said. "When the rain is pouring down you can never picture sunshine, and when the sun is out, you have trouble picturing the rain."

I got the vacuum cleaner out. I found it in a closet, put the chairs up on the tables, plugged the vacuum in and started pushing it across the carpet, sucking up whatever stuff was there. Popcorn mostly. But other things were there. Pepperonis, olives, and these little bits of crust that had fallen on the floor. And even as I pushed that vacuum, even as I walked and thought, and thought and walked, I think I thought it then. *Best damn place a guy could ever work.*

There was a film projector for the customers. After I was finished cleaning up, I went and got a salad from the cooler, added on some croutons and some dressing, and then sat there all alone and watched a couple movies. Silent ones where the people never talk out loud. So the only thing I ever heard was the crackling of this giant pizza stove that was starting to cool down from the night before, and the *CRUNCH, CRUNCH, CRUNCH* of the salad in my mouth. *Fifty times as loud*, I thought.

I walked up to a window in the front, and looked out at the ice fog on Airport Road. And all the time I stood there, I remember I was staying warm. Staying warm and smelling in the pizza smell, because that's what it was like. *Best damn place a guy could ever work.* Always warm and toasty, with this pepperoni pizza smell that never went away. So even after you had left, you could smell it on your clothes. And all the food a guy could eat. That's what Rick had said.

But the best part was in back. When you finished all the work and you headed past the kitchen on your right. A window was there, where kids could stand and watch 'em tossing up the dough.

But you'd keep on going. Keep on going, through a narrow, stretched-out hallway, that goes into the back room that has a thick, crimson colored carpet. Finally you're there. *At the best part.* Standing in a room that's kind of like a cave, because it doesn't have a single window. I think you would have liked it.

A fireplace was over in the corner. And the fire never stopped, because the whole thing ran on gas. That's what Rick had said.

"Just go ahead and let it burn," he told me. So I did.

Every night, the shadows of the flames would dance across the room, over six or seven tables, to a jukebox that was standing up against the paneled wall.

And when I looked on the back of the jukebox, I saw a button, like a lot of jukeboxes have, I guess.

Just push the button in, I thought.

Then I pushed the button in, and pushed some numbers and some letters. I never even had to pay a cent. The music started playing. This slow relaxing music that would help me fall asleep.

Then I climbed up on a table, reached for Kingpen's clock, pulled the button out, and watched the shadows of the flames for a while.

I guess you still can see 'em. Dancin' in the night. Just go to Antonelli's and walk into the back, past the kitchen and the little windowed room where you watch 'em toss the dough. Then keep on going through this narrow, stretched out hallway, till it starts to get real dark and you think you're in a cave.

The flames will start to flicker and they'll dance around the room. And then if no one else is there, go ahead. Reach behind the jukebox, push the button in, hit some letters and some numbers, and then you'll *almost* get to know just what the place was like.

Toasty, warm and cozy, with smells of pizza bread.

And see that table there? The one right by the fireplace?

That was where I used to sleep. *That* one was my bed.

Chapter 28

I guess I knew the campus like I thought I knew this dartboard that had hung up in my parents' basement years and years before. Ever since I could remember. All it had were circles, lines and numbers. And depending on exactly where you threw the dart, you got a different score. But that's not all it was.

"How about a little *baseball?*" this other kid had asked me years ago. And when he turned the dartboard over, a baseball game was there. Depending on exactly where you threw the dart, you got a single, double, triple or an out. Or you might have hit a homer.

Suddenly it all changed. Everything *I thought I knew* about the dartboard changed. That's what it was like.

"*Here,*" Kingpen said. He handed me a key and started talking all about another bunch of buildings on the campus farther up the hill. "Just wait until you see 'em," Kingpen said. "They're almost like hotels. They're really something."

So I followed his directions and started out the back, behind the Student Center, right on up the outside steps to a road I'd never been on. *Walking, walking, walking* - up and up this hill.

And then I heard it all again - *"How about a little baseball?"*

And everything I thought I knew had changed.

There were six or seven buildings, mainly research labs and dorms. And the building we were going to live in was the middle one. That's what Kingpen said.

Bartlett Hall. I read it on the sign. The place was seven stories high and made of solid rock like the other buildings. But anyway, I went in through the arctic entrance and it was just like he had said, only better in a way. Because no one else was there.

I took the elevator, nearly to the top. Sixth floor. Then I walked on down the hall, made a left, and turned a corner. I stopped and there it was. Room 613. I put the key in the lock, gave it a turn, pushed on the door, and walked in.

I looked out through the window, and could see the campus in the dusk. All of it. Rasmussen and the Commons. Stevens Hall. And then over to the left, maybe six or seven miles away, was Fairbanks, glowing in the ice fog.

315

But the thing that made it special was the mountains off there in the distance. Way off to the south. Rutherford and Hayes. Mt. Claire. Deborah and McKinley. Dozens of these huge, silver shapes that caught the final rays of sun. They glistened and they shone, until whatever light was left faded from the ragged, jagged peaks and disappeared, with all the darkness rolling in.

But even then it didn't stop. I stood there looking out, and everywhere below, the ground began to sizzle with the patterns of the lights that ran across the town. Up and down the roads, and into people's homes. You'd see them shimmer in the thirty-five below, patterns of lights.

And of all the rooms you ever could have had, I know you never could have found a better one than that. Not another one that had a better view.

Like Kingpen told me later, it was a million dollar view for fifteen bucks a week.

They say the longest journey starts with just one step. One step. First step. I don't know. But that's what it was like. Every single time when I went to Antonelli's. Every single night.

I would bust ass mopping at the Center, then I'd start off over drifts of snow, then down the wooden steps. By quarter after two, two-thirty at the latest, I'd be down there standing at the bank, looking for a ride, but of course one never came.

So I'd always end up walking. One step, two steps. *Walking, walking, walking.* And of every place I've ever walked, I think of that the most. Walking down this black and empty road in the middle of the night. Thirty-five below. Sometimes even colder.

And nothing ever changed, except the thoughts inside my head. Thinking. *Always thinking.* Sometimes thinking *this.* Sometimes thinking *that.*

I'd get down to the bridge and stand there for a while, looking at the ice. Then I'd go around the corner, over by the campground, and start down Airport Road, the right side of the page.

And it always seemed like that was where the wind would start to howl. Even breathing in your nose, you could feel it in your lungs. These sharp, cutting pains. Then your hands would start to ache and your feet would get real numb, and you'd think that there was no way you could keep on going - but you did. Then all at once it would start...

You could see it in the sky. In between the blinks, as you were walking down to Antonelli's. It would start off in the corner and reach across the night. Reds and whites and neon greens. I'd stand there all alone and watch it run and wash across the sky. On and on, until the lights began to fade and it turned back into night.

And then I'd start off walking down the road again, but by then I didn't ache. Everything was numb. Frozen solid, so I couldn't feel my body or my feet. I could barely breathe a breath, and my eyes were frozen shut.

And then just about that time, when I never had a doubt that I was gonna die, I'd see it up ahead. *Antonelli's* - with the little pizza sign.

I'd start walking faster until I made it to the door. *Faster, faster, faster.*

But even then, after I had made it, I couldn't get right in, because I couldn't feel the key. My fingers were all numb. So I'd blow on them awhile and after six or seven minutes, I could hold the key enough to get it in the hole, and then I'd turn it once around, pull the door, and get myself inside.

And then every single night I would mumble to myself, "*Well, you finally fuckin' made it, Fitch.*" That's what I remember saying. Every single night, I would say that to myself.

And then I'd fix a bowl of salad with some Thousand Island dressing and some croutons, and watch a couple movies. I'd put up all the chairs and vacuum up the floor. Popcorn mostly. But like I said before, some other stuff was there.

So that's what it was like for three or four more weeks. Every single night I'd go into the back, reach behind the juke box, push the button in, and crawl up on the table. I'd listen to the music and watch the shadows of the flames as they danced across the room.

I'd pull the button out on Kingpen's clock and try to catch some sleep. Then a little after nine... *BRNGGG!* I'd push the button in and go down to the Union Hall.

And they hardly ever had a job. That's what I remember. Even on the A list, the jobs were pretty tight. So I'd go off to the Far North Bakery and get a couple bear claws. Then I'd start off walking. But the other way around. Up to the Chapel of the Chimes, and then I'd stand there by the funeral home, sticking out my thumb. And within ten or fifteen minutes I always got a ride. Every single time. Back across the Chena, but by the bottom corner of the page this time. Then on up College Road.

Sometime close to noon, I'd go into our room at Bartlett, look down from the hill, and see it all again. Fairbanks in the distance. Rutherford and Hayes. Mt. Claire. Deborah and McKinley.

Seven minutes less, I thought. And then the darkness would roll in, filling up the dusk. And maybe it was that, or maybe Christmas coming on, or maybe just the cold a quarter inch away.

But the thing that I remember was this feeling that I had. Like everyone was gone and I was left behind. Not connected. That's what I remember feeling.

I guess I saw them first when I went down to the Union Hall, after waking up at Antonelli's. I walked down Airport Way, made a left on Cushman and saw them hanging on the lamp poles. All these reindeer, with lots of colored lights and decorations.

"Christmas," Kingpen said. And like the flowers at the University, it happened all at once.

"Maybe we should go back east," Kingpen said. "When we go up on the Line, we'll be there for a while. We might not get another chance." So we figured we would go back east for Christmas and then fly back in the spring.

"*Early* spring," I said. And Kingpen nodded.

Kingpen flew out first. I stayed another couple days to help at Antonelli's. But on December 21st, we went down to the Hall together, paid more dues, and then we hitchhiked to the Airport.

"Now remember," Kingpen said, after we got down there. "You'll get another seven minutes after this. After winter solstice it'll keep on getting better."

He gave a little wave and then he went through the walkway and got into the plane. After that, I left and started up to Bartlett Hall.

I got a couple hours sleep, and later on that night I went up to the snack room in the Student Center and started mopping up. I'd dip it in the bucket and squeeze it out just right, and then I'd push and pull the mop head across the floor, until I saw 'em all again.

Patterns. That's what I remember always seeing. Shiny, steaming patterns. I'd watch 'em for a while. They'd run and blend together. Then suddenly they'd evaporate and disappear.

I put the chairs back on the floor at seven after two that morning. I put everything away and then I started walking after that.

Walking, walking, walking, until I got to the door, down at Antonelli's, and I told myself I'd made it. I'd put the key in the hole, turn it, pull the door, and push myself inside.

And I guess it was the dressing, now that I look back...

I fixed myself a salad, but I couldn't find the Thousand Island dressing in the cooler. So I looked and looked, until I found it on the counter. And then I poured it on the lettuce and the croutons. I sat there and ate it while I started watching movies.

And then a half an hour later – *BOO-BOOM*! Right there in my stomach.

Like a giant concrete block that hit me in the gut. Like the can of berry filler I had eaten down by Haines. *A couple cans*, I thought. And then I went into the bathroom and started throwing up.

I didn't get much work done after that. I couldn't lift the chairs, so I vacuumed all around the legs. I crawled along the floor and picked up all the popcorn and some pieces of pizzas that I couldn't reach before.

And of all the jobs I've ever done, that one was the hardest. I started getting chills and I couldn't stand up straight. And every time I thought of Thousand Island dressing, I started getting sick.

But when I finished working, *that* part was the worst. When I had to put the key inside the hole, turn it once around, and start off walking up the left side of the page.

SCREW the Hall, I thought.

I started blinking faster, breathing through my nose. I was all bent up, shaking like a leaf. *Shaking, shaking, shaking*.

It must have been near five o'clock that morning, so I never saw a car. At least not for a while. I kept on walking, then I got sick for a while, and I was *sure* that I was gonna die. Just like back in Berkley. *Right there in the gutter*. That's what I remember thinking. *Fitch, you'll just die here in the gutter at thirty-five below*.

And that was when I heard it. *Honk, honk, honk*.

"How about a ride?" a lady said. And when I turned to look around, a taxicab was there, pulled off to the side. The lady who had asked me was sitting in the back. "C'mon," she said. "My treat."

She was fifty-five, maybe sixty years old, in this long fur coat. And just about the only thing she said was, "You shouldn't be out walking in this cold." That, and then she asked me where I was going.

We drove up to the dorm and I tried to thank her, but I was really getting sick.

"Merry Christmas," she called out, and I gave a little backwards wave as they drove off down the hill.

I walked into the building and I *really* started shaking. By the time I made it to the room, I couldn't stop.

Another seven minutes. Another seven minutes. "It'll keep on getting better." That's what Kingpen had said. But it didn't. I was freezing up.

Just make it to the shower down the hall. Go and turn the shower on, I thought.

And the whole time I was crawlin' there, I never saw a soul, because no one else was there. Not in the whole building. Just me. *Crawlin', crawlin', crawlin'* down the hall.

I made it to the shower room, slipped out of my clothes, got into a shower stall and turned the water on. *PSSCCHHTT!* About as hot as it could get.

And the thing about a shower in a dorm or in a gym or any place like that, is the pressure never stops. It just keeps on coming out. And even then, the temperature won't change. Not as long as you don't change it.

Just totally connected. That's what I remember thinking. Then things started looking fuzzy. I started feeling weak. And all at once, I thought I was a snowman, because I went down on one knee and I just *knew* that I was melting.

Just hold on Fitch. Or in another seven minutes you'll be going down the fuckin' drain. That's what I remember thinking. And I didn't even have a carrot or a corncob pipe.

They'll never even know, I thought. *There'll be nothin' left behind.*

And then I slumped down on the tile and I remember drifting off.

Drifting to another time. Remembering another place.

Chapter 29

When you go into McKinley Park, you drive in from the north. You can take the train or come up from the south, but the second time you go, the time you always will remember, you go in all alone in a silver Buick Special and you drive down from the north, and you think of something Kingpen told you long ago. "We can never know beforehand the adventures that we'll have." And when you turn into the Park, you know that he was right.

You feel it all around you. *Possibilities.* That's what I remember feeling.

Forests, lakes and mountains. Like Pinto told me later, "It's nothing like a mirror."

And the thing that I remember thinking was, *I'm gonna do it all. See* it. *Feel* it. *Gonna do it all*, I thought.

And then I drove in from the north.

I made a right and the first thing that I came to, besides the trees and stuff, was a little grocery store, kind of like the one in Tok, except a gas pump was there. *Only gas inside the park*, a little sign said.

And then a little farther up the road, I saw the railroad cars. Alaskan gold and blue. The ones I'd seen before, sitting on the piece of track, except of course there wasn't any snow like there had been back in April. And now the tourists were there.

"*Look* at that," I heard a lady say. "I think I see a moose." Except it turned out that it wasn't. "Just a log," her husband told her.

But there *were* a couple moose down at Horseshoe Lake. I saw a little handmade sign pointing to a trail, so I took the path for about a mile. And there it was, Horseshoe Lake. Except it didn't look exactly like I would have pictured.

It was pretty, though. Like a picture in a magazine, except some parts were moving. Black shapes on the water. Giant fluffy clouds would roll across the bluest sky and you'd see 'em on the water. Giant black reflections would glide across the lake, and then they'd go into the woods and blend in with the trees, and you'd lose 'em by the time they made it to the hills.

If only Beamish could see this, I thought. And that was when I heard a little splash and saw 'em not a hundred yards away. Moose. A couple of them browsing in the shallows. And they never even knew that I was there.

I watched the moose for about an hour, then I went back up the trail to the hotel, near where Beamish took a leak. The McKinley Park Hotel. And the thing I found so funny was how all I had to do this time, to get inside, was push the door.

Well, you finally made it Fitch, I thought.

Then I stood there in the middle of the lobby and I watched it all go by. People coming in and people going out. Back and forth, and back and forth. Then I wandered and I wondered for a while, and looked at some displays and artwork that were hanging on the wall.

But the thing that caught my interest most was a basket full of schedules for the buses that went back into the Park. Bluebird yellow buses, like the kind they used for schools.

According to the schedules, the buses went into the Park on a narrow gravel road where cars weren't allowed to go. The buses went to different places, some farther than others. Savage River, Igloo Creek, or Sable Pass.

But it all looked pretty good. And even as I stood there, I *knew* what I was gonna do. Go out into the Park and see it all. Just ride and ride and ride, until I knew that I had seen and done it all. Unnamed mountains. *Grizzlies, caribou and wolves*.

Ride and ride and ride until I couldn't go one foot farther. And when I looked up at a map they had, I saw just where that was. *Wonder Lake*. Almost ninety miles away. Ninety miles from where I was, but still inside the Park. Wonder Lake. Thirty miles from Mount McKinley.

I got a schedule from the basket and put it in my pocket. Then I walked down to the little store and started loading up. "I'll take a couple cans of *this*," I said, "and a couple cans of *that*. And lots of ravioli." Then I got an apple pie from the freezer. I gave the guy a fifty and he handed me my change.

"Going out into the Park," I told him. And the guy just shook his head.

It must have been near eight at night by then. I walked down to the campground near a place called Riley Creek and hardly anyone was there. I took out Kingpen's tent and set it up, and then I built myself a fire. A raging, blazing fire that started off real small at first, with twigs, but then I kept on adding sticks. Lots and lots of sticks. And then I piled some branches on and built it up with logs. Giant two-foot logs. Then I sat there for a while. Sat and sat and watched it all burn down.

I lifted up a rock and set it on the coals. I got the ravioli, peeled off the lid, set the can down on the rock. And it couldn't have turned out better, if I'd cooked it on a stove. It sat there getting warm at the bottom of the can, then some flames began to flicker and the paper on the can caught fire and it heated all together. And when I saw a couple bubbles near the edges of the sauce, I gave a little stir with my spoon from Jimmy Franklin's, ate a ravioli and it was just like I had thought. Absolutely perfect to the bottom of the can.

I got the pie out after that. I found a Y-shaped stick and set the straight end in between a rock and log. Then I set the pie on top of the other end, so it hung above the fire. And the way I had it figured, in just another couple minutes, I'd be eating apple pie, except I never had a bite. It all began to run and drip and melt into the fire. Little bits of icing first, but then the whole entire pie began to go. It all changed shape and reminded me of lumpy, gooey taffy drooping down. Then it plopped into the coals and I could hear it for a while. *PPSSCCHHTTT. Sonuva bitch*, I thought.

By then, it must have been near midnight. I folded back the flap on Kingpen's tent so I could see outside, and then I crawled inside my bag. I watched the burning coals and started drifting off, except I never got to sleep. The ground squirrels were out and all through the night they kept on racing back and forth across the tent. Running on the roof and jumping on the sides. *Pitter, patter. Pitter, patter. THUMP! THUMP! THUMP!*

And of all the nights I've slept in tents, that one was the best. Down at Riley Creek. About a half a mile away from the hotel up the hill. A half a mile away from everyone who was asleep. And even now, I can hear 'em when I try. *Pitter, patter. Pitter, patter. THUMP! THUMP! THUMP!* All through the night.

———————

It reminded me of elementary school as I stood there on the gravel road, waiting for the bus. Not the road so much, but waiting. *Waiting, waiting, waiting.* And then it finally came. The metal doors swung open, just the way they always do. Half in and half out. And just for a minute, I pictured Mr. Menken sitting there behind the steering wheel. The guy who used to drive us kids to school, until he'd had his heart attack.

"Welcome to the McKinley Special," the driver said. My name's Holden Morrisey, but you can call me Morris.

I got on with my pack of raviolis and some other cans, Kingpen's tent, my spoon from Jimmy Franklin's, my sleeping bag, and some of *this* and some of *that*.

Instead of little kids with nicknames like Goob and Shorty, Speedy and Chopper, there were Earl and Margaret, Tom and Lillian, Fred and Gail and a guy who didn't introduce himself.

"Welcome to the tour," Margaret said, and her husband shook my hand.

According to the schedule, they had gotten on the bus at the hotel at five-fifteen that morning and picked me up as they rattled past the campground. At five-twenty-one, we were all on our way. Headin' into wilderness. Me and Morris, three couples and another guy. *Gonna see it all*, I thought.

As I settled in the back, you could tell we were excited. "Ever seen a bear?" somebody asked.

"Think we'll see McKinley?"

"I can't believe I'm here," someone else said.

And on and on and on.

It was still kind of dark, but starting to get lighter. And even though we'd only gone a couple miles, Margaret thought she saw a black bear's silhouette. "First check," Margaret said. And she checked a little box next to a picture of a bear on a list that she had.

"Only thirty-seven more animals to go," Earl joked.

The guy who hadn't said his name told us we would see all kinds of wildlife on our way to Wonder Lake. Bears and wolves and caribou. And when I told him I was gonna camp out there, at Wonder Lake, he said, "You'll see 'em by the dozens. Critters all around you."

"Maybe millions," Lillian laughed. And she thought she was joking, but it turned out she was right.

According to our driver, Morris, the road was mostly gravel. Some dirt, but mostly gravel all the way. "Eighty-nine miles. It was built in 1938, and it's pretty much the same now, as it was back then. Nothin' fancy." He'd been driving it for thirteen years. "Love it!"

Morris said. "See something different every time." And Lillian told him that was wonderful.

We passed a sign for Morino Backpacker's Campground. Then we started up a steep hill, made it to the top, and looked out on the taiga forest. "Land of Little Sticks." That's what Morris called it. He showed us all the white and black spruce, and then he pointed down to patches of quaking aspens, poplar and tamarack trees.

"God's country," No Name said. And it really *was* pretty. The light was kind of dappled and you'd see the dew dripping off of thousands of these spindly, sketchy trees. And the birds were waking up.

"Thrushes, jays, and chickadees," Gail said. Then we saw a fox take off across the road with something in its mouth.

"Vole," somebody else said. And then I heard a raven call out from the dawn. *CAW! CAW! CAW!*

We were going up and up. Nothing really steep like Sunwapta Pass, but maybe thirty-five degrees, and everything was thinning out.

"We're heading into tundra," Gail said.

And that was when our driver, Morris, told us, "Look for wildlife. Bears and moose and caribou."

There were blotches of color as far as we could see. Reds and golds and bluish-greens. The foothills we were passing through had snow, like icing, running from the tops on down their sides.

"God's Beauty," No Name said. And we kept on creeping up and up.

There were prairie dogs. You'd see 'em standing in their holes. And Dall sheep. Little dots of white up in the mountaintops. And then I thought of *Ovis aries*. And eating ice cream with the guy in Tok. And then my mind went to the next thing, and I wondered who was there, standing in the line.

"*Look!*" Lillian yelled. The bus pulled to a stop, we all got out and Lillian pointed to a small brown shape lumbering across a riverbed about a quarter mile away.

"Grizzly." Fred said. "You can tell 'em by the *hump*." And then they all looked through their cameras and binoculars, and I guess that they could see it.

Earl began to set his tripod up and take some pictures. Fred said the bear slowed down and that was when No Name told us, "Grayling. He's hunting for some grayling." But the riverbed was dry. That's what Fred said. So he didn't think the bear was doing *that*.

Anyway, we stayed for fifteen, twenty minutes, following the small brown shape, and I remember thinking that it all was pretty neat.

But the thing that really was the best was the way we'd stop and go. *Stop and go. Stop and go.* We didn't really have a schedule. I mean, I guess we did according to the brochure, but Morris didn't seem to give a shit.

"Just tell me if you ever wanna stop," he'd say. So that's what they would do. Lillian, mostly. She was fifty-five or sixty, like everybody else, but she acted like a kid and would get all wound up and bounce in her seat. They came from Cincinnati, she and Tom. They had saved for the last five years to take this trip. Fred and Gail were from Or-eh-Gun, and Earl and Margaret let us know that they'd been here to Alaska once before. Seven years ago. No Name came from Pennsylvania.

"Where *you* from? Been up here long?" somebody asked.

And I told 'em, "Off and on about a year."

"Are you a Sourdough?" Earl asked. "Stay up through the winter?"

"Off and on." I said again.

We were driving into tundra, up and through the land above the trees. That's what Morris called it. *Tundra.* He told us all about the little shrubs and how they clung close to the ground to keep safe from the wind.

"Lots of moss," Earl said. And he was right, but there were blueberries, bearberries, horsetails and forget-me-nots, too. That's what Lillian's booklet said. And that was just the plants. There were ptarmigan and snowshoe hares and wolverines and lynx. All kind of animals. Some that we *had* seen. Some that we *hadn't*. But we knew they all were there. Somewhere in the bushes.

We crossed the Savage River and saw dozens of sea gulls flying by the bridge. "*Mew* gulls," Lillian read. And with our windows open, we could hear them squawking in the wind.

"Singing to the Lord," No Name said.

It was kind of like the Buick. Just clunkin' along. Except I was awake. And instead of Beamish driving, it was Morris. *Driving, driving, driving.*

"Primrose Ridge," Lillian said. She pointed up ahead, and I thought of Kingpen and Sunwapta Pass, and all the stuff he used to tell us. *Kind of like the Buick.* That's what I remember thinking.

God, it was relaxing. Driving in this Park as big as Massachusetts. And I knew that it would only keep on getting better, because I looked out of my window and knew that everything was out there.

Grizzlies, caribou and wolves.

Wonder Lake, I thought. And Morris kept on driving toward it.

There were a couple times that we should have seen Mt. McKinley. Mile 9.2, somewhere near Mile 10, and anywhere from Miles 14 through 19. That's what Lillian's booklet said. But the clouds were out, so we never got a view. "We'll have another chance at Mile 37.3," she told us.

We crossed the Sanctuary River Bridge, started up another short hill, and when we looked down, everywhere we looked, we saw spruce trees leaning every which way. "Drunken Forest," Morris said. And he told us how the permafrost had made the land unstable. "Now just *imagine* if you built your house on that," he said. And we looked out and imagined.

We came to a rest stop. Right there near the bridge, there were a couple porta-potties and a picnic bench. "Go ahead and stretch your legs," Morris said. So we walked around awhile and took a break, and then we walked around some more.

"Five years," Tom said. "Five *years* we saved to see Alaska. And it's been worth every penny. Every single one. Ever seen this place called Haines?" he asked me. And I told him that I hadn't, because I hadn't at the time.

We drove along the Teklanika River after that, but it wasn't like you'd picture. It wasn't really *one* river. It was called the Teklanika *River*, but really there were *dozens* of these branches to it. Rivers in a river, all intertwined, crisscrossing each other.

"An example of a braided river," Morris told us. And while the group all took their pictures, he explained how the glaciers ground the mountains into dust, which was why the river was so silty. "Then you have your ice jams, detours, permafrost . . . The whole thing is *connected*," Morris told us. "Which is why you get *this*."

We looked back to the rivers in the river, and the thing that I remember thinking was, you'd put your boat in one branch and then you'd flow into another. *One that you had never meant to go into.* That's what I remember thinking. You'd head downstream some more, branch off another couple times, and then – *think the strangest thing,* I thought. *You'd flow into the first branch. The one where you had started.*

"Symbolic of our lives, I guess," Gail said. "Look at us. Nine strangers. Together for a while. Some of us will separate, but maybe meet again."

"God's plan," No Name said. "Thy will be done."

The road narrowed as we entered Igloo Forest, and we saw a couple of moose about three hundred yards away. "Ever see a grizzly take one down?" Fred asked. And Morris told him, no, but he'd seen a cow moose kick the crap out of a wolf one time.

We saw some more Dall sheep after that. Up in the Cathedral Mountains. Twelve or fifteen small ones, you couldn't really tell for sure, jumping on the rocks. "The only wild white sheep in the world," Morris told us. And we were there to see 'em.

We were *driving, driving, driving.* At least Morris was. We were looking out the windows, taking it all in, and maybe they were taking us in, too - wolves and moose and caribou.

"It's something. Isn't it?" Gail asked. And it really was.

We were climbing up to Sable Pass. I knew it 'cause I saw it on the little, wooden sign. *Sable Pass.* Except the neat thing was, the sign was chewed apart. All around the edges. "From grizzlies gnawing on it." That's what Morris said. And everybody that was there, except for me, took a picture.

We were coming down the other side. It all began to open up and you could really see a lot. And not the little stuff you'd see back east in park-like settings, but the big stuff. Mountains, lakes and rivers, as far as you could see. And even then, you knew it kept on going.

"There's a land where the mountains are nameless, and the rivers all run God knows where." Lillian recited.

"Robert Service," Earl said. But he didn't have to tell *me.*

There are lives that are erring and aimless, I thought. And then my mind went to the next thing. *Shoes, boots, pieces of rope.*

We had been lumbering along for a couple of hours, at least. Thirty-three miles. And then Morris started telling us about the guy who had lobbied Congress to create the park. Charles Sheldon. He'd been a big game hunter back in 1907.

"Can you imagine being here back *then?*" one of the men asked. But I remember thinking it was the kind of thing you would have heard somebody ask on a bus tour back east. Like in Manhattan, when you saw all the buildings and freeways.

"Can you imagine being here when there wasn't all this shit?" you'd hear somebody say. "Imagine being here in Manhattan when the Indians sold it for eighteen dollars' worth of beads, or whatever they had sold the island for. And then I kept on looking out the bus, and remember thinking that it *is* like it was back in 1907.

"In case any of you get the idea that you want to start walking out there," Morris said, and he pointed out the window toward the tundra, "I can't let you do it. Grizzly country for the next five miles. You have to stay on the road. Anybody want to get out?" Morris asked. And they all shook their heads and started to laugh.

We passed Mile 37.3, where we had another chance to see McKinley off in the distance, but the clouds were still around it, so we couldn't. We did see Polychrome Pass though. We were driving on the gravel road that wrapped around a mountain, and when we looked off to our left, there was a valley with boulders spread around for miles. Foothill mountains in the distance with snow on top. And everywhere we looked, there were shades of red and green and tan and even shades of yellow. Bright purple. Light purple.

"It changes all the time," Morris told us. And you would have thought there would have been a million people sitting on the gravel road taking photographs or sitting at their easels, painting. But none of them were there. Just us.

"Tell me when you're ready to go," Morris said. We sat another 15 minutes and Lillian said we could leave.

"Imagine having this in your back yard." Fred said. "Living up in Fairbanks, you could come here all the time."

"Jess, ever been here in the Park before?" Tom asked.

And I told him, "Yeah. But only once. And not this far back."

It was light out now, and in the next twenty miles Margaret checked off thirteen boxes. Ptarmigan, red squirrel, a mother moose and her calf. Lots of different kinds of birds. We even saw a porcupine waddling across the road. But mostly we saw sheep, up there on the mountains.

We had about fifteen miles to go to the Visitor Center, which reminded me of the time I had climbed the mountain and found the little building at the top. The little building where I had left one of my hamburgers. *Just when you knew things were getting more and more remote, then think the strangest thing,* I thought . . .

"Surprise! We're here," Morris announced. "Eielson Visitor Center. According to Morris, it was named after a Bush pilot, Carl Ben Eielson, whose portrait I had seen one day in the Rasmussen Library, when I was going there to sleep.

"Pit Stop!" Morris called out.

There were a lot of "Yeahs and yays." Then we got off the bus and headed toward the Visitor Center, which was really a lot nicer than anything I would have pictured. More modern, with a lot of glass, so you could stand on the inside and see everything on the outside. There were even toilets that flushed, a gift shop and a bookstore. It was a little like the Visitor Center out at Mount Rushmore, if you've ever seen pictures of that one.

"Twenty minutes good?" Morris asked. We told him it was and then I started walking around, looking at all the stuff.

There was a lot of Alaskana, like little statues of Mt. McKinley, stuffed toy animals like polar bears and whales, and lots of jade jewelry. Most of it was made in China. Then there was a slide show that never ever stopped, and I wondered if it ran throughout the night. Photos of the Park, grizzly bears and pictures of the mountains. A lot of nature things, which I guess you would have figured. And the more I stood and watched, the more and more I wanted to get going. *Gonna see it all*, I thought. And then we got back on the bus.

It was another twenty miles to Wonder Lake and along the way we saw a moose down in some muskeg. We even saw some beavers. "How long you plan on staying out here?" Gail asked. "A couple weeks?"

In my head, I started counting all the cans of ravioli and spaghetti that I had in my backpack. "Yeah. A couple weeks," I said. But then I started thinking. *Maybe I would stay out here a couple months. Maybe I would catch some fish and eat some berries. Maybe even trap some rabbits and some squirrels. Yeah. Maybe I would stay out here a couple months*, I thought.

We were coming to a fork in the road, and if we went off to the left, we would go to some kind of private campground. The only buses that could go that way were the big tourist buses.

"Double-deckers," Morris told us. But there were only two of them allowed back in the Park. "We go to the *right*," Morris said. So that's the way that *we* went. The way to Wonder Lake.

We pulled to a stop about fifteen minutes later and there wasn't really all that much around. There weren't any trees for one thing. "Too close to the mountains," Lillian said. And I figured she meant like an Alpine area. There *was* a lot of scrubby stuff, though.

"Now, remember what I said about the buses," Morris told me. "They won't all be coming back here. Some only go to Eielson and turn back. Or Igloo Creek. "You need a schedule?" he asked me. And I told him I had one.

I lifted up my backpack and the group said their goodbyes. "Have a special time," Lillian told me. I told her I would.

"You might want to read this while you're out here by yourself," No Name said. He handed me a pamphlet and I stuck it in my pocket.

"You all have a good trip back," I said.

Morris pulled on the crank, the door opened, and I went down the steps, onto the ground. The door shut behind me and off they went, driving away. "Thanks again", I yelled. And then most of them pulled down their windows and we all waved.

There was nobody there. *Nobody.* Maybe ten or fifteen little pull-off spaces for tents, and the gravel road, which went on a little farther and then circled back around. But that was it. I never got to see the lake.

There were a couple of giant mosquitoes that were circling my head. I thought they were flies at first. I smacked one on my forehead and then one got in my mouth. It couldn't have been two minutes later, there were hundreds of 'em, swarming all around me. And now that I look back, that was when it started. This constant little *bzzz* that started just outside my ears and worked its way into my head. *Bzzzzzz* . . . It was really getting bad.

I had my hand across my mouth and was breathing through my fingers, but even then, they would get up in my nose and down my throat. And that's when I think I started getting kind of frantic. I had my jacket on 'cause it was kind of chilly, so I pulled it up around my head and zipped the zipper tight. But then I couldn't see, and I was stumbling around. And I knew that I was gonna throw up from mosquitoes in my throat. Throw up vomit and half drowned mosquitoes, inside my jacket, all over myself.

So I pulled it down off of my head, and no bullshit, there were millions of these giant, black mosquitoes, buzzing all around me. Dozens of 'em on my face and getting in my nose and ears. And the worst part was, when I wiped my hand across my head, I could feel 'em in my hair. Hundreds of these little lumps. And they'd pop and they'd squish, and our blood would mix together, and then it all began to start streaming down my face and neck after that.

I threw my backpack on the ground and ripped the zipper. Some cans fell out, and I grabbed Kingpen's tent from inside the pack. And of all the tents I ever set up, I set that one up the fastest. At least most of it. The poles were never exactly right. Somehow the back was higher than the front.

But anyway, I opened up the front flap, dove inside, and zipped it shut. And the thing that I remember is that six or seven hundred of 'em came in with me. Flying all around the inside of the tent. *Bzzz bzzz bzzz . . .*

It was six or seven minutes before they started landing, and that was how I finally got 'em. They'd set down on me or the floor of the tent, and my hands would come down. Chinese Style. As fast as they could. And then faster – Boo-*BOOM!*

The other ones, sitting on the walls and ceiling of the tent, I'd flick with my finger. They'd start to lift off, then I'd wrap my hand around them as they started to fly, bring 'em to the floor, and maybe just an inch above the nylon, I'd open up my hands and keep 'em coming down. They never had a chance. *SPUH-LAT!*

There were little pools and smears of blood everywhere I looked. Hundreds of 'em. Pieces of mosquitoes, little black clumps all throughout the tent. My eyes were closing up from the welts on my face. But all in all, things were getting better.

There might have been five or six mosquitoes still alive, and I picked 'em off until only one was left. And then I thought of the Romans and how they'd let the last guy go, at the end of the battle. After they had killed everybody else.

"Wanna go and tell your buddies not to fuck with *me*?" I asked him. But he didn't give a damn. He landed on my forearm, and then I tensed my muscle up and brought my arm to my face so I could see him up close. It was pretty interesting really. He had his feet set apart to stabilize himself and he was drilling me with this needle that he had. *Drilling. Drilling. Drilling.*

And I guess he had a tough time because my arm was all tensed up. It took six or seven seconds, but he finally got it in. And the thing that made it interesting was his face. All screwed up, he was sucking really hard, but he wasn't getting much. I felt sorry for him in a way.

332

"You want some blood? I asked. And then I untensed my muscle, the straw opened up, and then - think the strangest thing - *Ka-BOOM!* I swear to God. He exploded right there on my arm.

Sweat was running down my face along with the blood. And it wasn't just that I'd been working hard. It was really heating up. *Greenhouse effect*, I thought. And somehow I figured the rays of the sun were coming *into* the tent, but they weren't getting *out*. Except it wasn't all that sunny, but it turned out that it was.

I was lying on my back, on the floor of the tent, and when I looked straight up, I could see it was dark. I thought it was a cloud at first. But when I looked out the front screen, I could see that it was sunny. And then I tapped on the ceiling with my foot and the cloud went away. But then it came back. Came and went. Came and went. And when I sat up to look more closely, to see what was going on, I could see millions of these little needles sticking through the nylon.

The *bzzz, bzzz, bzzz* kept on getting louder. *BZZZ, BZZZ, BZZZ.* And I could almost hear 'em saying, "Gonna get you Fitch. Gonna suck your skinny ass completely dry. *BZZZ, BZZZ, BZZZ.*"

And the way I had it figured, if one of them could make it through the nylon, they all would. That's what I had figured.

I was tired, hot, and bloody, and I remember, I was really hungry. Sitting in the tent and looking out the front screen at cans of ravioli and spaghetti lying on the ground. Ten or fifteen feet away. I was gonna go and get 'em, but then I thought the strangest thing - and figured somehow it would end up *more*. So, I didn't.

Another problem was the schedule. It was outside, in the pack. And as I sat there in the tent, between the *BZZZ,BZZZ,BZZZ!* in my head, I could hear Morris saying, "You know about these buses, right? They don't all come back, way out here to Wonder Lake."

So then I started thinking maybe I would starve or die of dehydration in the tent.

But then maybe I could make it to the cans. But I didn't know if I could make it back. *Thinking.* Always *thinking.* And then I sat there for a long time, until I think I fell asleep.

I remember I would wake up, tap the ceiling with my foot, or look out through the front screen to see if it was light, or dark. Or dark, or light. And then it started getting cold. Not like numb cold. Just cold. And my teeth began to chatter and my legs began to shake, and I figured it was night.

Just make it through the dark, I thought. I sat there, and I sat there, shivering and shaking. And a couple hours later, somewhere in the distance, I knew I saw a light. I saw it through the nylon.

I waited half a minute, till I knew it was a bus, and then I pulled my jacket up above my face, unzipped the front flap of the tent, and dove out into the dusk. I could hear it getting closer. This big double-decker that Morris had told us about.

I spun around, and with my arms stretched out as wide as I could get them, I scooped up the tent. Just dove into it and started grabbing the nylon and poles. *Just scoop it up,* I thought. By that time the bus was there, and I started running toward it.

There was the faintest sound of an air hose, the door opened, and I jumped inside the bus. "What's up? the driver asked. He was maybe forty years old, wearing a shiny blue uniform with a little matching hat.

"Mosquitoes," I said. "I can't thank you enough. If you could hold on for just a second, I've got a pack and some cans."

I took a big gulp of air, held it in, jumped off the bus and ran toward my stuff that was lying on the ground.

Just get 'em back in the pack, I thought. But the zipper was broken and I couldn't get 'em in. I tried to pick them up, but couldn't keep 'em in my hands. *So just stuff 'em in your pockets, Fitch*, I remember thinking. But of course *that* didn't work.

So after two or three minutes of screwing around, I started toward the bus, dragging my pack and kicking eight or nine cans of ravioli and spaghetti. *Just kick 'em down the road*, I thought. *Kick 'em to the bus*.

The door was still open and the driver was standing on the steps. "I wish I could help you son", he said. "but I'm not supposed to be here. Took the wrong fork."

He tossed my tent and poles to the ground, said, "Good luck to you." He got back in his seat, closed the door, and then he and maybe some passengers he had with him drove away. *Him? Them?* I wasn't sure. The way they had the windows tinted, I couldn't really see.

It was funny in a way. I could hear the *bzzz, bzzz, bzzz* down in my ears, but there weren't that many mosquitoes out. Maybe just a dozen of 'em flying around. I guess that was because it hadn't warmed up yet.

I got out some matches that I had in my backpack. Maybe a dozen of the heavy-duty kind you'd use in the kitchen. I collected some scrub that was lying around, and tried starting a fire. But the scrub was too thick, so I couldn't. There was only one match left, and then I remembered and reached in my pocket.

It was thirty-five pages, maybe four-by-six inches, and was called "Bring Jesus Into Your Life and Let Him Work Miracles." It was just what I needed. I crumpled it up one page at a time, took some of the brush on the ground, and set it on top of the papers. One last match. And you probably think that I screwed it up. But I didn't. And as I stood there getting warm, I could see the sun coming up. Just like it had the day before and a zillion days before that, I guess. But this time it was different.

For six or seven minutes, there were shades of pink and orange and then it all turned to dawn and morning began. It was still pretty cold. I could see my breath. And then as I turned and looked off to my right, I saw it. A range of foothills, but then right there in the middle was a mountain, bigger than I ever would have pictured. Covered in snow, with a half a dozen ridges. I knew it was McKinley. And the thing that I kept thinking was that eighty-four percent of all of the people coming to the Park would never, ever see it. Eighty-four percent. That's what I remember thinking.

And even though I knew I'd only see it for a minute, at least I'd know I saw it. *Just soak it in*, I thought. *Just keep on looking.* Because this super giant cloud was coming from the right.

I stood there and I watched and I waited, and the way it all turned out, the funny thing was, I didn't really see McKinley till the cloud began to move and cover what I thought had been the mountain. And of all the mountains that I've ever seen, that one was the best. Not because it was the biggest, even though it was. But because of *how* I saw it.

This super giant cloud began moving to the left and then I thought I saw this other super giant cloud behind it. But that wasn't what it was. It was McKinley. *The Great One*. Better than you ever could imagine. The greatest mountain that I thought I saw, but almost didn't, because I didn't know that it was there.

I stood there six or seven minutes after that. The mosquitoes were all coming back and buzzing up around my head. But I didn't give a damn.

I stood there with my tent all busted up and my cans of ravioli and spaghetti lying on the ground. And when the clouds kept moving right to left across the sky, I saw them cover up the summit, but I knew they'd never float across the picture that I'd put up in my head.

The *bzz, bzz, bzz* turned to *bzzz, bzzz, honk. Bzzz, bzzz, honk.* I could hear it in the distance. A Bluebird Yellow School bus was coming down the road.

I put my fire out, grabbed my backpack, collected all the cans, put 'em in the tent, and put it all up on my shoulder. By then the bus was there. I turned and looked back one last time. Then I started to the bus, the doors swung open, and I stepped inside.

"Holy *shit*" somebody said. "What happened to you?"

And I remember walking down the aisle and asking them if they'd seen it.

"Too many clouds," a lady said. "Are you all right?"

And then I counted two men, four women and me and figured that was right. *Eighty-four percent*, I thought.

They kept on asking questions. *Bzzz, bzzz, bzzz* . . . "How long were you out there? Did you see any grizzlies? Any big horn sheep?"

And then the last one I remember, before I fell asleep. "Where you from?" somebody asked.

And I don't think that I answered, but I know I heard it for the first time in my head.

Alaska. Grizzlies, caribou and wolves.

I slept the whole way back, almost. From Wonder Lake to Eielson to the Toklat River rest stop and then it wasn't that much later I heard "*Bzzz, bzzz,* many colors," so I figured we were at Polychrome Pass. And then I fell asleep again.

I missed the drop-off at the campground, which was better in a way. I got off at the hotel with everybody else, walked down to the train and went inside.

God, it was nice. There were a couple people there, but not in the last car. Six or seven tiny rooms, and every one was empty. And the thing that I remember best was the smell.

This musty, clock-stopped smell, like you were going back in time, to a summer home after winter, before you opened up the windows.

Always going back. And as I sat there on the bed I could still hear 'em in my head. *Bzzz, bzzz, bzzz.* And even when I took my clothes off, they were there. Six or seven of 'em, flying out from up inside my shirt and down inside my underwear. *Fuck you, Fitch.*

And I was gonna grab 'em as they tried to fly away. Bring 'em to the floor and SPAH-*LATT.* Except it turned out that I didn't. I let 'em fly away.

I went into the shower, turned the handle on and saw the bloody water going down. Down, down, down the drain. I watched it for a while, then I got the soap and started soaping. *Just lather up and keep on washing till you wash it all away*, I thought. But I don't think I ever did.

I must have been there for an hour, until I finally sat down on the shower floor. I put more soap on the top of my head, and then the *BZZZ, BZZZ, BZZZ turned to bzzz, bzzz, bzzz.*

And finally it all began to stop, because I think I fell asleep.

Chapter 30

I felt the water coming down.

I turned the shower off and grabbed a towel, but instead of crawling this time, I *walked* down the hall to our room in Bartlett. I remember feeling better. Better than I *had* felt. *Oughta head on down to work,* I thought. But when I looked at Kingpen's clock I saw I had a lot of time. It was only quarter after two.

So I figured I would go down to the airport and get myself a ticket before I went up to the snack room. *Maybe you could even call the airport, Fitch.* That's what I remember thinking. But of course I never did.

Instead I started walking. *Walking, walking, walking* to the bottom corner of the page, up the right hand side. And then instead of turning left, I made a right on Airport Way and started toward the planes. But I never saw a car. That's how I finally knew. I walked down to the airport in the middle of the day, but I never saw a car and then I realized it was *night*. But by that time I was there. Right there at the airport at 4 a.m., and of course everything was closed.

You are such a DUMB-ASS, Fitch, I thought.

And then I stood there for a minute deciding what to do, until I saw 'em in the dark.

The lights were pretty far away at first and then they started getting closer, till they pulled up right beside me. "Need a ride?" the cabbie asked. And I told him that I did.

I didn't work up at the snack room that night. I asked if he would take me down to Antonelli's, so after I had gotten in the cab, we started going back the way I had come. Up to a point. But then we stayed on Airport Road.

He was a pretty interesting guy, who had come up from the states a couple months before and he was gonna be a Guide. "Hunt big game and take people from the Lower 48 fishing, he said. "Run a trap line in the winter. But you ever see the *paperwork?*" he asked. "Oh *shit*. Nothin' but red tape. You gotta fill out all these forms and then you apprentice for a while and then they put you on a list because they're runnin' outta land.

"A state this big and they say they're running outta land! I'm like a liquor store, they told me. They only want a certain number or it starts to get too crowded. A fucking liquor store. The hell with that," he said. "I'm only gonna drive another couple weeks and then I'm heading back to Indiana. Fuggit."

We got to Antonelli's and he pulled up to the door. "Well, I appreciate the ride," I said. And then I handed him a twenty and I thought that he was gonna tell me that the pizza place was closed or ask me why I walked down to the airport, but he didn't. Instead he reached into the back and handed me this piece of fur.

"Trapper's hat," he said. And of all the hat's I'd seen till then, *that* one was the best. Made of martin, with a trim of wolverine. "The only fur that won't ice up," he said. And then he told me how he couldn't wait to wear it back in Indiana.

"You're gonna look just great," I said. And then I thanked him for the ride again.

I watched him drive away, and then I turned the key around and pulled the door open. And as usual, the first thing that I thought was, *you finally fuckin' made it Fitch.*

Only this time I had made it from the dorm down to the airport, then out to Antonelli's, but I'd made it just the same. Then I went into the back and pushed the button in, and all at once it hit me. This is really it.

You're flying out tomorrow, Fitch. No more Antonelli's. No more watching the reflections dance across the room. No more salads. No more smelling all those hot bread smells. No more jukebox. *The best place you could ever work*, I thought. And this is it.

I really started working after that. Cleaned and cleaned and cleaned. Better than I ever had before. Better than a hundred people could have cleaned the place that night. I vacuumed up the crumbs, and then I washed down all the walls, and scrubbed the red brick tile that went around the oven.

And then, just when it looked great, when I should have walked away, I found this glass and mirror spray. *Now we're going to REALLY shine it up*, I thought.

I started on the glass on the inside of the door and went around the sides. *Windows, windows, windows.* All these picture windows - and I'd cover them with spray. After I had done that, I would wipe 'em down and *REALLY* make 'em sparkle. That's what I remember saying to myself. And then after I had sprayed them all, I went and got a towel to wipe the windows off, but by then the glass and mirror spray was frozen on the glass. Frozen, sticky foam. That's what it was like. Because a quarter inch away, maybe less, it was thirty-eight below. *Thirty-eight below zero.*

I must have spent three hours after that, at least, scraping it all off with this little metal spatula I found back in the kitchen. And even now, I bet you still can see 'em. Go ahead and look. Thousands of these tiny, little scratches that'll show up when the light comes in just right. Thousands of 'em.

I went off to the back and sat there for a while, looking at the flames. I thought for a minute, then I got up and put a quarter in the slot. I pushed in J-14 and started walking.

And even then - even when I walked out through the front - I heard it coming from the back. The voice of Elvis Presley singing in the dark.

"North to Alaska - the Gold Rush is on."

Chapter 31

I had a lot to do that morning. I went down to the Hall from Antonelli's, to check things out, then I walked on down to Far North Travel and bought myself a ticket.

"Ball-tuh-more," I said. The lady that was working said the flights were booking up. She said it wouldn't be as easy as I thought, but she found one in the end.

"Fairbanks down to Anchorage, then you'll fly down to Seattle, Chicago, and finally Baltimore. You leave at one a.m.," she told me.

I handed her some money from the roll that I had gotten from the bank a couple days before. Then she handed me the ticket and I put it in my pocket. And that's when I remembered. *The key.*

"Well you have a Merry Christmas," she said, "You, too," I told her. And then I went out the door and started walking through the ice fog, back to where I'd come from. Back to Antonelli's.

It's funny in a way how certain things will change, but still remain the same. At least up in your head. I put the key inside the hole and began to give a turn, but then a couple people started out the door and I remembered it was already open.

There was a party going on. Over to the right, there was a group of kids with party hats and streamers. And the thing I thought was funny was that all the stuff that I was used to cleaning off the floor was sitting on the tables. Pizza crust and popcorn. Little pepperonis.

"Help you, sir?" somebody asked. And when I looked up to the counter, a girl was standing there, maybe 17 years old. "Wanna buy a pizza?"

But I told her that I didn't. "I *work* in here,' I said. Or at least, I *did*. But she didn't understand.

"You want an *application*?"

"No," I said. "I worked in here at night. *Late* at night." But still she didn't get it.

"Well anyway," I told her, "I want to give the key…" And just then, when I said it, Rick came out from the back.

"Hey Fitch!" he shouted. "Still flying out tomorrow?" And when I told him that I was, he started telling me about this other guy he'd gotten. The one to take my place.

"Probably won't be half as good as you," he said. And then he asked me if I had a minute.

"Come on back," he said. We went into the kitchen and a birthday cake was there. HAPPY BIRTHDAY, MARGARET. That was what the icing said, with little polar bears and mountains on the side.

"Think that you could help me out?" Rick asked. "I'm really low on people. All you've gotta do is sing. Just take this cake and give it to the kid and sing her 'Happy Birthday.' It would really help me out."

And the thing he promised me was that *all* the kids would sing. "They *always* do," he said. "It's not like you might think. Even other people, not there at the table. *Everybody* joins in."

But they didn't join in *that* day. And halfway through my solo, my voice kept getting weaker, weaker, *weaker*, till I really wasn't sure the girl could even hear me. I got down to the end, and by then, all that I could do was *whisper*. "Happy birthday, dear Margaret," I whispered. "Happy birthday to you."

I thought that it would get a little better after that, but it didn't.

"C'mon," Rick said. "I've got something you can sign. It's a Merry Christmas card that's going in the paper." He handed me a pen and then opened up a drawer. "Half a page," he said. "Fairbanks Daily News Miner, but I've gotta take it down there now, so go ahead and sign it."

He took it from the drawer and when I looked, it reminded me of the Declaration of Independence because that's what it was like. There was a written letter at the top wishing everyone in Fairbanks a Merry Christmas. And then down there in the middle, printed right across the page, you could read it . . . "From all of us at Antonelli's." And then the workers had written their names. Edna Conners, Harry Dee. On and on and on. People who had cooked and served up all the food that I had picked up off the floor.

"Well maybe since I'm not exactly working now, I shouldn't really sign it. Maybe I should *skip* it, Rick," I said.

But that's not what Rick thought. "You worked just as hard as anybody here," he told me. "Besides, I need the names. So go ahead and sign it. I've gotta take it to the paper."

So I signed it in a way. Right beneath Rebecca Slade and to the left of Lester Stone. Jerry Pitch, I wrote. Just to distract Rick, I asked him how he thought the new guy would work out as I handed him the pen.

342

"OK, I guess," he said. Then he kept on talking. And even though *I* never got to see it, I think *you* can if you want. Just call the Miner up, and tell 'em that you want to order a back issue from the archives.

The one with the Antonelli Christmas card.

The one from "all of us."

Almost.

I left Antonelli's, pulled on my facemask that I'd found, and walked into the ice fog. And I remember that it must have been near lunchtime then, because for maybe twenty minutes, it got a little light.

I bought a donut at the Far North Bakery, then I did a little shopping for the folks back east. Handicrafts and souvenirs. I even bought myself a pair of canvas mukluks for my frozen feet.

"Perfect for the kind of cold dry snow we have," the salesman told me. "Not so good for the *wet* stuff."

So I put 'em on and kept on walking. And I found out later he was right. But the thing I *really* wanted, that I couldn't seem to find, was a trapper's hat. Like the one the guy from Indiana had, back in the cab.

But anyway, I kept on walking. *Walking, walking, walking.* Then I got up to the Chapel of the Chimes and I never will forget. This dog was standing there. Right next to the fire hydrant. At forty-five below, I saw him take a leak. And the thing that I remember was that it froze and formed this giant urine icicle, right there on the valve, and all that I kept thinking was, it wouldn't thaw till spring.

People all around would pass it every day, but no one else would know. Not unless they broke it off and ate it. Someone just like me. Someone who'd been standing there waiting for a ride. Then a car pulled to the side and took me to the University.

I went up to my room in Bartlett and got some sleep. Then six or seven hours later, I pushed the button in and started thinking. *Anchorage.*

I remembered all the stores and gift shops, and somehow I just knew that one of them would have it. *You could hitchhike down*, I thought. Start down there tonight, because I figured I could get the hat with the money from the flight I didn't take. A hundred sixteen

343

bucks. That's what it would cost to fly from Fairbanks down to Anchorage. They had told me on the phone.

So at quarter of eleven that night, I thought I had it figured out. I'll put on everything I own, pack up all my gear, take a long, last look out the picture window, then I'll head down to the snack room.

And when I made it there, I wish you could have seen me. I put up all the chairs and started busting ass. *Hit the third button twice*, I thought. And the fastest I had ever mopped was slow compared to *that* night. Just *mop and mop and mop. CHINESE* style, I thought. And then I mopped *faster*.

I put the chairs back down on the floor and took a look around. Then I went out through the arctic entrance and started walking off across the snow in my mukluks. Rolling drifts of snow. I walked and walked and walked with my presents and my spoon, Kingpen's tent and clock, my sleeping bag, and some other stuff.

And by quarter after twelve, *quarter after twelve* - I could see it on the clock - there I was. Standing on the corner at the bottom of the page. I was on the left hand bottom corner, but instead of going right, I was trying to get off.

And I almost thought I wouldn't for a while. But like the kid who figures he can sell some lemonade for twenty bucks a cup, that's what I kept thinking. *All it takes is one*, I thought.

And then I stood there on the corner like the cup of lemonade, waiting for a ride. Colder, colder, *colder.* And then the lemonade was frozen.

Get as cold as you can get, I thought, *and then it keeps on getting colder.*

And then at seventeen till three, it got down to the coldest. *Forty-six below.* I saw it on the bank sign. And from seventeen till three until quarter after four, that's the way it stayed. So damn cold I didn't think that I could stand it, but I did. *Forty-six below.* And then at sixteen after four, it moved on up to forty-*five* below. *Getting toasty now,* I thought.

I tried to laugh a little, but I couldn't. I was shaking like a fucking leaf. *Shaking, shaking, shaking.* And I kept on blinking faster and breathing through my nose. But even as I stood there shaking, I kept thinking to myself. *All it takes is one.*

And then at twenty-five till five, the street light blew, and a couple minutes later, this repair truck pulled up. A couple guys got out and started working on the light, about thirty feet away.

"Pretty motherfucking cold," the one guy said. And then the other guy said, "Yeah. You know it's getting cold when resisters freeze up. Then they got inside the truck and warmed up for a while. Got back out. Went back in. Out and in. In and out. Until finally, they got it.

"*FIXED!*" the one guy said. And then the streetlight came back on. They got back in the truck and you'd think they would have asked me, "Aren't you fuckin' *cold*?" Or told me, "Get inside the truck and warm up for a while." Something. But they didn't.

"Let's go and get a cup of coffee," the one guy said. He gave a little wave, shut his door, they started off down College Road, and *BOOM!* The light went out. *Resister froze back up again*, I thought. But I don't think *they* saw it. The ice fog was too thick.

I kept on waiting after that. Waiting, blinking, breathing through my nose. And shaking. Always shaking. *Forty-five below,* I thought.

Then my mind began to wander and I thought back to Prince Rupert, Armpit of the World, and the fire that we'd built and the time that I had stood there, looking at the map until I realized I *was* there. *This* is *it*, I thought. Forty-five below. *This* is what it feels like.

And then I pictured what I'd say when they asked me stuff back east. Like, "How cold does it get?" Or, "Tell us what it's like." And that was when I knew what I would tell 'em…

Picture standing naked on a giant, solid piece of ice. Standing bare-ass naked. And the wind begins to blow and then it starts down deep inside of you at first. This sharp cutting pain that reminds you of the times you've gulped down ice cold water on a hot and steamy day. (Because I knew that they would understand that.) *Except it doesn't go away. The pain down, deep inside. It doesn't go away. And then your lungs begin to burn and so you breathe in through your nose and start to breathe out through your mouth. Tiny, little breaths. In and out. In and out.*

And the whole time that you're breathing, your mind is thinking, SHIT. Because it's starting to get blurry. Not up in your mind, but everywhere you look, because you're shaking like a leaf and your eyes are freezing shut. Forty-five below, you think. THIS is what it's like. And then you smash 'em with your fingers. Little balls of ice you pull off of your lashes. And then your toes start going numb. And you keep on shaking, shaking, and you breathe in through your nose and breathe out through your mouth and you keep on smashing ice balls until your fingers are too numb. And then just about that time… Just about that time when you know you're gonna die, you feel it wrap itself around you like a giant sheet of cellophane that someone's soaked in water. Forty-five below, you think. THIS is what it's like.

And then the cellophane begins to freeze, the cold you felt is gone, and numbness takes its place. A welcome numbness, like you thought you never could imagine.

And then for every reason that there ever was to turn and walk away, you keep on standing there instead. Like a frozen cup of lemonade. All it takes is one, you think. And then your mind begins to wander and somewhere in the night you think you hear a sound. Like an *echo, echo, echo* in your brain, brain, brain. Th ump. Th *ump.* Th*ump. Thump, thump, thump. Frozen tires warming up,* I thought.

Then at nineteen after six, forty-three below - I saw it on the bank sign - this guy pulled his eighteen wheeler to the side, rolled his window down and shouted to me. "How about a ride? Aren't you fuckin' *cold*?"

We started off toward Ester. He ran it through the gears and then he turned and asked me. "How long were you there? Fifteen, twenty minutes?"

And I told him damn close to an hour, because I felt a little stupid.

Then he shook his head and told me, "*I* never could have done it."

And it's funny in a way. My mind went back to the people down in Tok, and I wondered who was there. *Everybody's someplace.* That's what I remember thinking.

Then the water started rolling down my face, from the ice balls in my eyes, and my feet began to ache, and my fingers and my bones, till I thought that I was gonna just explode from all the pain, except I didn't.

"Gotta weigh it in up here a couple miles ahead," my driver said. But I knew we never would. And when we got where we could see it, it was just like I had thought.

"Closed," he said.

So we kept on heading south, with Ester on our right. A tiny, little town we never really saw, but even in the dark we both could see the road that went on up the hill. And like a dozen times before, I passed the frozen veldt out there in the night. Forests, fields and streams. All you could imagine.

Shoes, boots, pieces of rope.

And then somewhere south of there, somewhere south of Ester, I think I shook myself to sleep.

It was just like Beamish used to say. "Bullet holes. You can tell we're getting close." And that was how I knew we were. We drove into the city, somehow got to 4th Street, and pulled up to a light.

I told him, "This'll be just fine. I appreciate the ride. I really do." And I think he knew I meant it.

"Well, at least I saved you from that cold," he said. He helped me with my gear, I opened up my door, and I stepped down into a pothole that was filled with water that must have been eleven inches deep.

"Damn it to *hell*," I said. And that was when he told me.

"Yeah, those mukluks that you have aren't that good in water." Then he pulled his rig away.

He was right. For all the good they were in dry, cold snow, that's how bad they were in water.

I made it to the sidewalk and must have spent an hour looking in the windows of the shops, but I never found the hat. I never found the hat, and the whole entire time I thought my feet were going to freeze.

Just keep on walking, Fitch. That's what I remember thinking. *Keep on walking till you make it to the a*irport.

And when I finally did, I went into the bathroom, wrung out the mukluks, put 'em both back on, and then went up to the ticket counter. And the crazy thing was, the lady who was there told me that I couldn't get a refund.

"Now, if you had an *unused* ticket, just from Fairbanks down to Anchorage, that's one thing. But any flight back east, it's all the same. It really doesn't matter. Anchorage or Fairbanks. Same price," she said. And then she threw her hands up in the air.

I left the ticket counter, after I had checked my baggage. Kingpen's tent, my sleeping bag and all the other stuff I had. Then I went and sat with all the other people. Sat and waited till a guy came out and told us, "Your flight has been delayed. Should leave within the hour." But it didn't.

We sat around some more and then the same guy came out again and told us to relax. "Could be a little while," he said. So we relaxed and we waited and we waited.

And at seventeen to eight, he told us, "Engine part went up. We're waiting for Seattle to send us a replacement, but the weather's got 'em socked in. Your flight won't go out until the morning. That's the bottom line. But we *will* give you hotel vouchers, if you're here from out of town."

You could tell from the crowd that a lot of them were angry, but I didn't give a damn, because all that I kept thinking was I'd finally get a shower. A nice hot shower. I'd stand there just as long as I could take it. *Just turn it up*, I thought. *Turn it up Chinese style. As hot as it would get, then HOTTER. A hundred ninety-eight degrees above*, I thought.

And then I'd lie down on the bed, call down to the desk and tell 'em, "Call me in the morning, because I don't want to push the button in." And then I'd go and eat a giant breakfast. *Just put it on the bill*, I'd say, because I knew they'd pay for supper, so I figured they would pay for breakfast, too. But they didn't. Not for me.

"See your ticket? The flight from Fairbanks down to Anchorage wasn't used," she said, "so you're originating *here*. Now if you had flown from Fairbanks…

So I sat and waited thirteen hours after that. I curled up on a plastic orange chair and every time I thought I fell asleep, the vacuum cleaners came.

"Excuse me sir," I heard 'em say. "Could you please move your feet?" And then I'd pull 'em up and put 'em down and pull 'em up again, all throughout the night.

I finally got some breakfast. Not inside the restaurant. I got some on the plane. I walked across the skyway, got onto the plane, took my seat, and a couple minutes later the engines started up.

"Well I guess the part got here," somebody said.

And then we all began to cheer. That's what I remember. Everybody cheering as we started down the runway, and lifted up.

And I wish you could have seen it…

"Holy cow," the guy beside me said. And even though there wasn't that much light, it still looked pretty neat. Mountains to our left, the Cook Inlet to our right, and up ahead, as far as you could see, miles and miles of forests.

Wilderness, I thought.

And then we flew into the clouds.

We made it to Seattle by twelve o'clock, but the pilot didn't take it down.

"Heavy fog," he said, so we kept on going around and around, until I guess he figured we were almost out of fuel. Then he told us, "Fasten your seatbelts. I'm gonna take her in."

We must have started to the ground right after that, but you never would have known it. Looking out the window, all that I kept thinking was *Sunwapta Pass, Sunwapta Pass*, because that's what it was like. You couldn't see a thing. And then just when you were thinking, *how the hell...?,* you felt it, then you heard it.

Eee EEE *EEEK*! The wheels touched down and everybody started cheering.

"Merry Christmas," I heard somebody say.

The intercom came on and they told us, "Please stay in your seat. Puh-Leez stay seated until we come to a full stop."

But of course nobody did. We all lined up, and then a couple minutes later, the stewardess opened up the door, and off we went. Right across the sky bridge and down the steps.

And a minute later you could hear it. "HOLD ON TO THE RAIL! PUH-LEEZ. HOLD ON TO THE RAIL!"

"This is great," I heard somebody say. We went around the airport on the subway and when we made it to the terminal, you should have seen it.

Thousands of people. I mean *thousands,* standing all around, because they only had three flight going out. Two flights south, and one flight east.

"And that's only if the fog lets up," the lady said. She pointed down a ways and told me, "Check down *there*. Flight 116. They're boarding for D.C."

If you've ever seen those movies of the lines in the Depression, that's what it was like. A long and strung out bread line of at least six hundred fifty people. And according to a guy standing near me, they only had a hundred sixty tickets.

"They're letting people on who have *connections* first," he said, "so you never really know. We *might* get on."

Way off in the distance, I saw the line begin to move, and I thought of something Kingpen used to tell me all the time. "All we have to do is *be* there."

Then I pulled out the alarm clock, and saw that the time was seventeen till four. I left the line, walked up to the front, and memorized the ticket giver's name. *Mr. Murdock.* I could see it on his badge.

Then I walked around the airport for a while. At six minutes *after* four, I went back to the front. It was just like I had pictured. *Shift change.*

"Well I'm back," I said. Then I gave a frown and asked where Mr. Murdock was.

"Just missed him," the new man told me. "He went home."

"Home?" I said. "He was gonna change my ticket." And then I told the new guy how the old guy was gonna change my ticket, but I got paged and had to leave.

"But I told him I'd be back," I said. "And here I am. Didn't you hear the page on the intercom? JESSE FITCH, you're wanted on the phone. JESSE FITCH." And he told me that he had.

"So Mr. Murdock won't be coming back?" I asked.

The new guy told me, "No." But *he* could change it. He took the ticket, changed it, and told me, "You'll have to make your own connections out of D.C." I told him that I would.

I started to the subway and a part of me felt bad, but I kept on going. I heard "HOLD ON TO THE RAIL," and so I did, and went around to gate fourteen.

Destination Washington, D.C. I read it on the sign. And then I sat and sat and sat, until finally I heard it. "Flight 116 is now ready for boarding."

Going east, I thought.

I walked across the skyway, made it to my seat, and sat around some more, while they figured out exactly who should and shouldn't be on board.

"We have a half a dozen people who shouldn't be in here," a stewardess announced. And I thought one might be me, but it wasn't. Anyway, they figured all that out, but even then we didn't leave. We sat around some more, waiting for the fog to lift.

"I bet we're *never* gonna leave," I heard somebody say.

But in another hour and a half, the engines started up, and I pictured everybody on the plane would let out a big cheer. But no one said a word.

Too tense. That's what I remember thinking.

I started smelling this real strong musty, putrid body odor after that. Only worse than you can picture. Like something almost dead, but just not quite. *I'm gonna die if I keep smelling this*, I thought.

Then my mind went to the next thing and I realized it was *me*. *Fitch, you really smell like shit,* I thought. And even with the mukluks that were soaked and the sweaty clothes I had, it wouldn't have been so bad if I'd been sitting all alone. But these business guys were there. One on either side.

We lifted up and had been flying for a while. "How about a drink?" I heard one of them say.

And the other guy said, "Yeah." As though I wasn't even there, except I knew that they could smell me.

Fitch, you really smell like shit, I thought again.

Then just when I was thinking how to tell them that I *knew* they knew, I think the one guy was embarrassed, because he asked me, "Where you coming from?"

Coming from? It was funny in a way, because I'd always pictured people asking, "Where you going *to?*"

But the answer was the same. I turned real slow.

"Alaska... *Grizzlies, caribou and wolves*," I said.

And then I started with the stories of Beamish and the Buick, Kingpen's tent, and the mountains that we'd seen. "Ever stood in forty-six below?" I asked. And for a couple thousand miles, maybe more, I bought them drinks out of the pile, kept up with the stories, and they both sat there amazed.

"I hope to get up there one day myself," the one guy said. But I knew he never would.

And the only thing the other guy ever said was, "You've gotta write it down. Write a book," he told me. "*I'd* buy it."

And then I looked him in the eye and nodded, and I told him that I knew he would.

We kept on flying east, and in a way, it reminded me of driving west. Siting in the car. Moving in a way, but in another way you weren't. Just sitting, but you knew that in another couple hours, there you'd be. Someplace else.

We made it to D.C. I caught a connecting flight to Baltimore a little after that. We landed close to midnight, and then I caught a cab, and took it to my parents' house.

"Where you coming from?" the driver asked, as I handed him the money. "Alaska?"

He looked down at my mukluks and I know he thought that I looked kind of goofy, but my mother didn't care.

"Well, look who's home," she said. "Merry Christmas."

My father came into the room and my dog ambled by.

"Been a little skittish since he got back from the trip," my mother said. "Won't go near a car."

"But except for that, he's doing fine," my father said. He gave my dog a little pat.

Welcome home, welcome home. Some of *this,* and after *that*, we sat there. Sat and sat and sat, and I told them of my plans.

"A couple thousand bucks a week," I said.

"And all you have to do is *be* there."

Chapter 32

It's funny in a way. They say you can't go home again, but I don't think that's true. Sometimes it's a *different* you, that's all.

You see it from the little things that didn't change at home. Like this little grocery store where I used to go to buy donuts every day. Before I took the trip, I'd go into the store, and tell the server, "I'll take two of those." And I'd point to apple crullers, but I didn't know that they were apple crullers at the time.

Then the lady, she would always tell me, "Sixty-seven cents. They'll be sixty-seven cents." After I was gone all those months, not a single thing had changed. "Sixty-seven cents. They'll be sixty-seven cents."

And I wondered if she ever wondered where the hell I'd been.

Grizzlies caribou and wolves, I thought.

I pictured sleeping in the weeds, standing by the lake at Haines, and watching all the salmon in the middle of the night.

"Sixty-seven cents?" I asked.

And I thought back to the trip and sleeping in the car and standing on the corner at forty-six below.

"Sixty seven cents? Here's five bucks," I said. "Keep it for yourself."

I walked out of the store and started walking down the gutter. Walking down the gutter, eating apple crullers. And even though this time it was forty-three *above,* I could feel myself still breathing through my *nose* and breathing out of my *mouth*. And every single second, *blinking, blinking, blinking. Push the button in*, I thought.

I started goin' all around in circles, like the time I couldn't get a ride until I went out to the truck stop. *Sixty-seven cents*, I thought. After all that I had been through. Sixty-seven cents?

And that was when I figured that you really *can* go home again, except it really isn't *you*. Not exactly.

And then my mind went to the next thing. *Home of Maryland Crab Cakes*. That's what I remember thinking.

I hiked a couple blocks and went downtown to the market. But it wasn't like you'd picture. There were a couple giant buildings, with hundreds of different stalls inside. They had anything you'd ever want to eat. Vegetables and really good corned beef. Different kinds of fruit, pastries, soup and candies. And everything was fresh. Anything and everything you'd ever want to eat. Right down there at Lexington's. That's what it was called. *Lexington Market.*

I walked along the aisles, smelling all the food. Then I ended up in back, where I always used to go, with the mullet and the flounder and the crappies. Every kind of fish you ever could imagine, laid out on the ice. But not just fish. Lots of things were there. Smoke dried eels, different kinds of shrimp, lobster, crabs and clams. And when you closed your eyes and smelled, it was just like you were there. Right there on the dock, when the boats had just come in.

"I'll just start with half a dozen." That's what I remember saying. "Chincoteagues." Then I sat up on a stool, watched him take his oyster knife and pry the first one open.

I must have sat there for an hour after that, knocking down some beers, squeezing lemons, glopping on this cocktail sauce and slurping down oysters. "I'll take a half a dozen more," I said. And then I got another half a dozen and another, and I know I had *two* dozen by the time I finally left.

"That's sixteen thirty-five," he said, when I asked him what I owed. I gave him twenty-five bucks and told him thanks for all the shucking. "Didn't get a single piece of shell," I said, even though I'd had a few.

I climbed off of the stool, went out of the building, and saw a little sign for Bailey's Seafood. *We ship anywhere,* it said. And right there on the door was an article from a Maryland Magazine that told about the store and how they'd even shipped some crabs to Vietnam, years ago. "Sent our troops the best!" it said, and below it was a picture of a pile of hot steamed crabs.

"We ship *anywhere*," I read again. But it turned out they didn't.

I guess they really specialized, because the only thing they seemed to sell was crabs. Live crabs, steamed crabs, and then I saw 'em sitting in the counter showcase. "Soft crabs," I said. "I wanna mail 'em to Alaska."

I thought I'd send 'em to the Kraxins, because I knew she liked to cook. I'd send her some directions, too, that told about the crabs and how they grew out of their shells and stayed soft for a while.

"And the only thing you have to do is cover 'em with batter. Then you throw 'em in a pan and fry 'em up," I'd tell her. "Fry 'em up until they're golden brown."

"A dozen softies? " the man asked. "You wanna send 'em *where*?"

"Ketchikan," I said. And then he started laughing, until I thought that he was gonna split his side.

"Never sent none there," he squealed. "Catch a *can*? Where the hell's a city with a name like that? Holy mother Moses. Get a load of this," he yelled.

He went into the back where they were steaming all the crabs, and I heard him telling all his buddies, "Catch a fuckin' can. Do you believe it?"

He came back to the counter. Tears were running down his cheeks, but he lifted up a book that was underneath the counter, rifled through some pages and he told me, "Well, I guess that we could do it, but it's gonna be expensive. Two hundred fifty bucks. There's a minimum," he said. "Forty-seven pounds. You could send a dozen if you want to. Two-fifty either way, but I'm not so sure that we can even ship 'em *there* if you wanna know the truth."

"Just forget it. Never mind," I said. "I'll just take some up the next time that I go."

There are things that you remember, but you've gotta be reminded.

"What do you want to do?" my mother asked.

And I thought of being little, when I used to sit around with all my friends in the middle of the summer. It seemed like the only thing we ever asked each other was, "Whaddya wanna do?" And then we always told each other, "I dunno." "I dunno."

So that was what I told her. "I dunno. Wait until the spring and then go on up to work, I guess. Doesn't make much sense to go looking for a job here, if I'm only gonna quit."

"Well, have you thought of going back to school?" she asked.

I told her it was all the same. "I'd only have to quit." And then I started up again about the gravy train. "Things will loosen up this spring," I said. "And all I have to do is be there."

I didn't do much after that. At least not for a week. Visited some people, went around town, but all in all, I didn't do a whole lot.

And then one day I thought that I would go and visit Beamish. Go and see him, talk about the trip, and tell him all about the Union.

"Gonna work up on the slope," I'd say, except it turned out that I never got to see him, because Beamish wasn't home.

"Bob took off for school," his mother said. "I know he'll wish he'd seen you. He's gone off to New York. But wait a minute. Take a look at *this*."

She went off to the clubroom and came back with a book. A photo album. "Pictures from your trip," Mrs. Beamish said. And there weren't that many photographs, but the whole display was pretty good.

There were dozens of these pictures out of travel magazines. Places where we'd been and different things we'd seen. There was a picture of Chicago, with some maps. An ad from Eddie Bauer's. And animals. One was of a beaver.

Like I said, the pictures that he had from magazines were pretty good, but the photographs he'd taken on our trip weren't all that great. One was of the Buick, but most of them were scenery. Lots of snow. And even then, a lot of them were blurry, because he took them from the inside of the car, through the toothpaste and the frost.

"*Here's* a good one," Mrs. Beamish said. She turned to the back cover and a couple photographs were there. The one she meant was of a tall Alaskan spruce, and Beamish had drawn a circle up near the top.

"Remember seeing this?" she asked. And I'm not so sure that any of us *saw* it, but I *read* it. Right next to the circle. "Bald eagle," he had written.

"Now isn't this a perfect way to look back on your trip?" Mrs. Beamish asked. I told her that it was. "All Bob wanted to do was talk about it," Mrs. Beamish said. "Just *talk and talk and talk*. You ever think of going back?"

I told her that I was. "Going back this spring," I said.

I left a little after that. I asked her to say hello to Beamish for me and she told me, "Say hello yourself. Here's his number," and she handed me a piece of paper.

I guess you look back at your life and there are times you see these pivotal points. Times and places where you could have gone and done one thing, but instead you did the next. Roads less taken.

Anchorage was like that. I think of that a lot. Sleeping in the car and waking up that morning and seeing all the snow. And then we did the next thing. *Fairbanks*, I remembered. And that had made the difference.

356

But anyway, I think I hit another pivotal point later on that night, after seeing Mrs. Beamish. I hit a pivotal point and then I think I hit another. Times and places when I could have chosen one way, but instead I went to something else. And it started after dinner. That's what I remember.

We finished with dessert and then my father started asking, "Now tell me, Jess. Exactly what is it you're planning?"

"Planning?"

"Are you going back to finish college? Are you going to get a job? I only want to know your plans," he said.

And so again I told him all about the lists. "It starts out with a dispatch slip," I said.

"But the number that they gave you is four thousand, nine hundred and seventeen?" my mother asked. "And that's the number on the *third* list?"

"*Eighteen*. Forty-nine *eighteen*," I said. "But it's really not that bad. The job calls went past us once, but we were *here*. We've gotta be up *there*." I said.

I told them how they'd fly us in to camps right after that. "Coldfoot, Five Mile, Dietrich. Or I'll fly up to the Bay," I said. Prudhoe Bay. On the far side of the Slope. *Grizzlies, caribou and wolves*, I thought. "And I'll make a couple thousand bucks a week."

"Doing *what*?" my father asked. And I think you could have heard a pin drop when I told him washing walls.

"Well maybe *I* could go up there and get a job," my mother said. And I thought they'd get to laughing, but they didn't.

"Well take a long hard look at THIS," my father said. And then he went out to the other room and came back with the evening paper. "*Look* at THIS," he said. He folded back a page and an article was there. All about the Trans-Alaska Pipeline. One whole page, that told all about the project and the workers and the people just like me, trying to get on. They even had some pictures.

"Now look at THIS," my father said again. And I told him I had seen 'em all in person. Hundreds of these goofy looking people standing in a room. *Holding to the dream. Waiting for the gravy train*, I thought.

I started reading after that. *Reading, reading, reading*. Unions getting rich, I read. Very few get on. Even those with skills are turned away. And then it told of these Outsiders who had been up there awhile, and they'd all run out of money.

"And now they're living in a Rescue House," my mother read. And you could see it in the picture. The place I'd seen on Airport Road, when I'd been looking for her friend's son.

It didn't get much better after that. The article went on to say how they'd be wrapping up the project in another couple years, but even now, things were slowing down because of winter.

"In a lot of ways, it's like the Gold Rush of the past. Everybody going north, but hardly anybody getting rich." That's what it said. But the thing that really got me, the icing on the cake, was this *residency* thing.

"Now read *this* part," my father said, but instead he read it to me. "Due to an influx of workers from outside the state, officials are considering a residency test. Future workers on the Trans-Alaska Pipeline Project will be required to prove that they have lived here in Alaska for one full year prior to employment."

And the thing that I remember thinking was *this is it. After washing all those dishes and sleeping in the weeds and being stuck there in the closet - BUSTED.* That's what I remember thinking.

And I guess my folks could see it, because we really started talking after that. *TALKING, TALKING, TALKING.*

"Now take a look at Bob," my mother said. "Bob Beamish. He's out there setting goals."

"*Long*-term goals," my father said.

But Beamish was the kind of guy who knew exactly what he wanted. That's what I remember saying.

"Well maybe you should go and get some help," my mother said. "How about that center at the college where you went? Career Counseling? Isn't that what it was called?"

And for the first time in my life, I thought it made some sense.

"You need to get yourself a plan," my father said. And I told him that I would.

Chapter 33

If you ever go to Baltimore, you can see it if you want. Towson State, where the only thing they used to do was teach you how to teach, until they started branching out. Then they started teaching people how to run a business, be an insurance adjuster. How to do a thousand things you'd ever want to do.

Except I never *knew* exactly what *I* wanted to do, so I left and went off to Alaska. And now, here I was. Going back. Going back again to where I'd been.

Like the time that I was out there on the highway, heading down to Haines. *Just turn yourself around.* That's what I remember thinking, driving back to Towson.

I made a right on York Road, turned again on Towsontown Boulevard, went about a quarter mile and started up a side road. The neighborhood was still there. The one I always used to go to, to find a place to park, because there never was an empty spot on the campus.

And like a hundred times before, I drove around and drove around, until I saw an empty space. Then I parked my father's car and started walking toward the campus. Walking, walking, walking.

Push the button in, I thought.

The tape began to play and I could hear it in my head. *Do you wanna be an astronaut? A carpenter? A laboratory worker? How about a running coach?* I wondered, because then I started going past this old dirt track. But then I didn't think I'd like that, so my mind went to the next thing. *Open up a shoe store. Be a teacher. Drive a taxi. Yeah. That was it. Just drive and drive and drive.* And I think I would have done it, except I knew that I'd get lost or fall asleep.

I started up a little grassy knoll and a little after that, if you ever want to go there, it's the house up on the hill. A big white house. And they never even asked if I went to school there, so I guess that you could go. But anyway, you see it on the sign at first. This little wooden sign that's stuck there in the grass. *Counseling Center.* That's exactly what it says. And so you walk up to the door.

A lady met me there. She handed me a card and said I had to fill it out. "Part of the routine," she said. "You know regulations."

But the thing I thought was funny was it didn't have a thing to do with *me*. That's what I remember thinking. "I," and then there was a little blank where I guess you put your name, "have voluntarily entered the Mental Health Clinic at TSC." That was what it said. And then another little blank was there for you to sign.

"Need a pen?" the lady asked.

She handed me a pen, but I told her I was looking for a job. Just trying to decide exactly what I want to be, I said. A Ca-Reer.

"Well, to get some help with that you'll have to go *upstairs,*" she said. "But even then you're going to have to sign that card. According to the law, you can't come in the building unless you volunteer to do so - and I've got to have that card to prove it."

"But I'm going *up* the stairs," I said. "I'm not here for mental health."

She said it didn't matter. "I know *we're* on the first floor," she said. "But it really doesn't matter. Same building. You know regulations."

"Well, I guess if it's routine."

And I wasn't sure exactly how to spell it, but I wrote it down. Allen Whizakoris. A guy I knew up at the Union Hall. I gave her back her pen, handed her the card and started up the steps. Up and up and up.

Gonna find out what I'm gonna be, I thought. But of course I never did. I found out what I wasn't, though…

At first, he asked me, "How about a nurse? You want to be a nurse? There aren't that many guys . . ." But I said I didn't think so. "A scientist? Interested in biology? Of course you'd have to finish school. Are you a people person?"

On and on and on. And then he finally asked me, "Art? You ever think of that? There's lots of different kinds. There's advertising, cartoon, commercial. Ever think about it?"

And I asked him for a pencil and a piece of paper.

"Look at this," I said. I drew a couple circles and added on some lines. "See this?" I asked. "This to me's a person. Now you think that I could be an artist?"

"Well how about a salesman?"

But the point that I was making was that there oughta be a test. Some way that you can tell, I told him, what a person's really good at.

"You mean their *aptitude*?" he asked. He was getting all excited. He reached down in his desk and pulled some papers out. I must have sat there for at least an hour after that, playing mix and match, and answering his questions.

"Looking for a job," he said. "Now what's that make you think of?"

But the only thing I thought of, the only thing I pictured, was breathing giant dust balls and drawing to an inside straight.

"Ever thought of using tapes?" I asked. "I know where you can get some. Everything you'd ever wanna know about looking for a job and more. How to pick the job you want. How to interview."

And don't forget to check your fly, I thought.

And then I started looking down and all at once he told me, "Maybe you should join the army. Join the army, or at least go back to college. I think you need a base. Some kind of foundation. You need some time to think."

And I told him that I thought a lot.

He gave me piles of papers after that. Colorful brochures mostly. I thanked him for it all, started down the stairs, and wondered if *he* had to fill the card out for the lady every morning.

Regulations. That's what I remember thinking.

And that was when she told me, "Mr. Whizakoris - I hope I'm pronouncing it right. I *know* you'll get a job."

Later on that night, I spread 'em out on the kitchen table. Every pamphlet that I'd gotten. Every catalog and little piece of paper. Then we read them all. Every single one.

My mother told me, "Maybe you *should* go on back to college."

And the way it all turned out, that's what I did. But not like you would think.

The phone began to ring and it was Kingpen.

"Here," my mother said.

She handed me the phone and I could tell that he was shaking. I could hear it in his voice.

"You're never gonna guess, he said. "We got it. The lady called tonight. The post office box. Up at College. She told me that we got it."

361

We talked for a couple minutes about the residency test and how so much was changing. And it was just like Kingpen told me.

"One more thing to use for evidence. A post office box," Kingpen said. "A permanent address."

And then he told me he had made a call to Mr. Milt, who told him we could have our jobs back, just as soon as we got up there.

"So I think we oughta go," Kingpen said.

And right away I felt it. *Grizzlies, caribou and wolves.*

But then I started feeling guilty. Thinking maybe I should stay and visit for a while. So I told him, "Go ahead and I'll follow you on up in a couple days. Meet me at the Fairbanks airport this Thursday, 11:25 at night," I said.

"I'll see you back in Dodge," he said. And then we both hung up.

I turned and saw it in their faces first. This disbelieving look. Like *tell us it's a joke.* Tell us you're not flying six thousand, seven hundred miles to rent a post office box. *Tell us.*

But I couldn't. "I guess I'd better go," I said. "If it turns out that the paper's right, and there's gonna be a test . . . Well, anyway, I guess I'd better go."

And they both just shook their heads.

I went across the skywalk at eight-fifteen on Thursday morning, then I settled in my seat and thought of something I had thought of months ago…

All these people, only now I *knew* I knew.

And when we started coming down almost twenty hours later, including changing planes, I looked around and saw that I was right.

Only one to make it, Fitch, I thought. Only one to make it to Alaska.

The plane kept descending and the pilot told us, "Current temperature is thirty-five below," which was warmer than the last time I had been there. "Estimated time of arrival eleven twenty-five p.m.," he said.

We kept on going down, but I couldn't see a thing. At least not for a while. Just miles and miles of black. But then we started seeing tiny lights. Isolated lights that I knew were cabins scattered in the hills.

"I bet a guy would have to be a little nuts to live down there alone," I heard somebody say.

And then the fasten seatbelt sign came on and the intercom went *bong, bong, bong.*

I could see it waiting in the distance. Fairbanks. Crazy, hazy Fairbanks, glowing in the ice fog.

And if you've ever wondered what it would be like to land on frozen ground, it's not like you might think. We never slipped or slid or flipped around, or anything like that. Just kept on going down and down, and when the tires hit the runway, I never even heard a sound.

"Smooth as silk," I heard somebody say.

That's what it was like.

"Hey Fitch. Where ya been?" And when I turned around, I saw him. Kingpen. Standing there in these faded corduroy pants he always wore, with a new down jacket and a new pair of boots.

"Sorrels," he said. "I bought some stuff back east. I thought I'd come up here prepared this time." He gave a nervous laugh. "But I didn't. Not exactly. I think we're really in a jam *this* time."

We started walking toward the luggage, looking for the tent and backpack.

The way that he explained it, the company we had worked for at the University had lost its contract.

"Mr. Milt's working down in San Francisco now," Kingpen said. "And the new guy said he doesn't need the help. Said they've got as many people now as they're gonna need."

"And how about the room?" I asked. "The one for fifteen bucks a week?"

"Gone."

"And all the food that we could eat?"

"Gone."

I pointed to the backpack that was going around the circle. Kingpen picked it up and then I grabbed the tent.

"Well what about a place to stay?" I asked. "Where have you been staying?"

"Well, I met this guy," Kingpen said. "I met him up at the University. We've been staying out in Ester in a cabin that he's watching for another guy who lives in Massachusetts. But the problem is that some other guys were there and they're leaving for the states. But they can't afford the plane fare, so we're taking them to Haines to catch the ferry."

"When?"

363

"*Now*," Kingpen said. "We're driving there tonight."

"Tonight?"

"Yeah. But the thing I want to talk to you about is beer cans," Kingpen said.

"*Beer cans?*"

"Yeah. Beer cans." And then he started looking kind of nervous.

Like a lot of things back then, I guess it sounded kind of crazy when I heard it for the first time.

"But listen," Kingpen said.

And the more and more I listened, the more it all made sense.

"According to this guy I'm staying with," Kingpen said, "there's no place in the whole entire state that makes beer except a place in Haines. There's a small operation down there and the cans are selling for a little over twenty bucks apiece back east. And that's *empty*. Beer can collectors are paying twenty bucks apiece. And you know what our cost is? A dollar twenty-three a can. We'll make millions."

So that's another reason that we're going down there.

"But we haven't said a thing to the guys we're taking to the ferry. So mum's the word," Kingpen said, and he put his finger to his mouth.

We went another couple steps and then he stopped. "Listen, I feel a little stupid, but how you fixed for money?"

And before I even looked, I knew. "Thirteen hundred and twenty-seven bucks," I said.

"Well, we're kind of in a jam, Kingpen went on. "Buying stuff for Christmas and paying for my plane ticket, I only had eleven bucks the night I got up here. But I didn't think it mattered because I only needed seven for the room and I could eat down at the dish room.

"But the way it all worked out... The guy that I've been staying with is a trapper, so he doesn't have much money either. His name is Pinto. But, anyway, if we can get those cans . . ."

"Well, we're *gonna* get those cans," I said. I slapped him on the shoulder, we started from the building, and I felt it in my lungs.

Thirty-five below, I thought. And then I started blinkin' like I had a couple weeks before, and I started breathing in through my nose and out through my mouth.

"The guys are in the back," Kingpen said. "The guys we're taking to the ferry." A pickup pulled up to the curb.

"Go ahead and ride up front and stay warm for a while. I'll go in the back." He took my gear, and I opened up the hatch and helped him climb inside, underneath the cap. Then I went around and opened up the door.

It's funny in a way. The times that you look back and remember how you looked at things you never really knew. People mostly. I mean you only get a first impression once, and then a lot of times it starts to fade and change, until you wonder if it ever really was exactly what you thought.

But Pinto wasn't like that. Right there from the start, I knew him. *Knew* I knew him.

"I'm Pinto," Pinto said. He reminded me of Daniel Boone with his buckskin pants and trapper's hat and mukluks. "I appreciate your help. I'm a little low on money, but if we can get these cans, we oughta make a couple bucks at least. Eighteen seventy-seven apiece, minus postage. It should help us through the winter. We'll mail 'em to the states. We'll *advertise*."

And I said it sounded great.

We drove through downtown Fairbanks and a couple minutes later we had left it all behind and were heading toward the black. Moving. Always moving. To places in the distance. Delta Junction, Beaver Creek. Haines. And the thing that I remember thinking was, it never seemed to be like that back east. I mean, the plane would take you down and then fifteen minutes after landing, you were always where you thought you would be.

But Alaska wasn't like that.

"Look!" Pinto said. We started slowing down and he pointed to the side. "Moose." And when I looked real closely, I could see it down in the brush.

We were someplace east of Dot Lake, driving in the night, and it reminded me of when we'd come up in the Buick. Star-filled skies and frozen forests. Gravel crunchin' underneath the tires.

"Buy a one-way ticket?" Pinto asked.

"What?"

"One-way ticket, or are you planning to go back?"

"Well, I'm going back one day, but I'm trying to get out on the Pipeline now," I said.

"Yeah. You and everybody else. Things are changing fast, so you oughta see it while you can. There's a lotta stuff out there," Pinto said, and he pointed out the windshield.

We kept on driving, past places I had been. Bear Creek. Moon Lake. Tanacross. And then we saw it up ahead. Tok. *Where the*

365

people stand in line waiting for a ride, I thought. But we only saw one guy.

"Going down to Haines?" he asked.

"Yeah," Pinto told him. "Get inside the back." So he went around and climbed inside, and it really made you wonder.

Four a.m., in the middle of the winter. It was just like I told Pinto. You can be anywhere, at any time, doing anything, and there's one thing you can always know. Someone's standing there in Tok. Waiting for a ride.

We hit the border later on that night. Early morning, really. Drove on in, where I'd ridden on the toilet months before.

"Gotta check inside," the Customs agent said. And then everyone got out and he rifled through the truck. "Heading down to Haines?" he asked. Pinto told him that we were.

"But we're coming back tonight," Kingpen said.

I let someone else up front and climbed into the back after we'd left Customs. It wasn't all that bad. Wasn't warm and toasty, but we weren't completely frozen either.

"We've both been through a lot worse," Kingpen said. And I told him that I knew. "And it's only gonna keep on getting better," Kingpen said.

We started off, but then we started slowin' down and I could feel it underneath. The old plank bridge. Snag Creek. And then even though I never saw them, I knew that we'd be passing the Alaskan Border Lodge, Beaver Creek and the Pine Valley Motel, where we'd stopped and gotten cookies.

"Kind of brings it back, doesn't it?" I asked.

Kingpen told me, "Yeah. But somehow this is different. Like we're *living* here this time."

And even though we didn't have a car, or place where we were staying, I knew just what he meant. Then a little further down the road, we hit 'em. Frost heaves. And then I think I fell asleep.

Like I told you once before, unless you've really been there, you should get yourself a map to see just what it's like. You drive out of Alaska, into Canada, then you go back into Alaska again. Near Jarvis Glacier.

And by then, it was really early in the morning. "Only forty miles to Haines. Wait until you see it. Like pictures of fiords in Norway." That's what I told Kingpen. "Lots of mountains, trees and lakes."

And even in the winter, I wish *you* could have seen it.

"Unbelievable," Kingpen said, when we finally got to Haines. And in a way, it was.

"Not too many things you can find that *always* look good," I told him.

But *Haines* did. God, it looked good.

We went down Front Street, right along the cove. I thought the water would be frozen, but it wasn't.

"Ferry couldn't get out if it was," one of the guys said.

We kept on going out to Lutak Road, with Pinto driving. And for all that he had driven, you'd think that we'd have been really early, or a couple hours late, or something. But we weren't.

"Right on time," somebody said.

We took out all their gear and the guys walked onto the ferry. And it must have been about fifteen minutes later, at the most, they sailed away.

"Well that's five more outta here," Pinto said.

I didn't get it at the time, but Kingpen told me later, "He doesn't like Outsiders. He wants them all to leave." And when you looked at the back of his truck, there was a bumper sticker there. *Happiness is 10,000 Oakies headin' south, with a Texan under each arm.*

"Pipeline workers," Kingpen said. "But I think he thinks we're different."

We didn't know exactly where to go for the beer cans, but we started driving into town. "We can go inside a store and ask somebody where they brew it," Kingpen said.

But Pinto told him, "No. We'll find out for ourselves."

But we didn't. Not exactly. Like Beamish, Pinto drove and drove and drove. And it's not that big a place, so we kept on going all around. Seeing everything six or seven times. Then we finally pulled up to a store and went inside. *The Totem Liquor Cache.*

"We're here to buy some beer," Pinto said. "The kind they make in Haines, but we'd like to buy it from the brewer if we could."

"We want to make a deal." Kingpen said. "We need to buy a *lot*."

But the guy just shook his head. "Mountain Brew. You want to buy some Mountain Brew. Don't make it any more," he said. "It tasted just like shit. There was a little canning operation around here, but there wasn't nothing to it. The guy that ran it went up on the Slope. I got a couple cases here, if you really wanna buy 'em."

So we did. Then we went off to the next place. *Far North Liquors.* And then the next place, and the next place. And by the

367

time that we were finished, we had every can you could have bought in Haines. Fifty-seven cases.

"Wiped 'em out," Kingpen said. And I thought he meant the stores, but he didn't. "We wiped 'em out," he said again. "The whole entire town."

We filled the gas tank, grabbed some food, and were gonna start on up the highway. Except the truck could barely move.

"The beer is making us drag ass," Pinto said. And it was the kind of thing you didn't really think about until it happened. But he was right.

So we scrounged around and found some old, rusty fencing on the side of the road. I pictured somebody saying, "Someone will take it," just like Beamish used to say. But this time, I knew it would be *us*.

"*Here*," Pinto said. He'd found a few small logs underneath the snow, and put the fencing on top. "Hand me down those beers. *Hand* 'em to me," Pinto said. So I reached in for a case and we stood there by the road.

"Pop 'em from the bottom," Pinto told me. And then he showed me how to do it with his hunting knife. "Don't mark it on the top. Collectors want 'em perfect."

And at ten o'clock that night, if you'd been coming down the road, you would have heard it. *Psshtt! Psshtt! Psshtt!*

We set the beer cans on the wire fencing that was lying on the logs, and the beer poured out into the snow. Then Kingpen put the empties in the truck.

And from ten o'clock that night, until five o'clock that morning, that's what it was like. Take 'em out, *Psshtt! Psshtt! Psshtt!*, set 'em on the rusty fencing, then put 'em in the truck.

"Twenty-seven cases. That oughta lighten up the load enough," Pinto told us.

We got back in the truck and I don't know *how* he did it, but he did. Kept on driving until we got up to the checkpoint - and they never even checked.

"Go on through," one of the Customs agents said.

So we kept on driving into Canada, and then we kept on going north, past Rainy Hollow and the North Elias Mountains. "Could have gone and seen the eagles, back there at the river," Pinto said. "If we didn't have this beer. Chilkat River Flats. Ever seen the eagles?"

When I asked him what he meant, he told me they would gather in the fall, and fly out around the middle of the winter.

"They should be leaving pretty soon. If you hike back down to the shore, you can see 'em by the thousands," Pinto said. "More than in all the states combined. Bald eagles. Everywhere you look."

It started getting windy and we almost didn't make it, but we did. Up and up and up. "Chilkat Pass," Pinto said. And I thought that we were gonna blow away, except we didn't. "The cans we left full will hold us to the ground," one of us said.

We kept on climbing to the top, over drifts of snow, and then we started going down. Driving over streams that came from Crestline Glacier. That's what Kingpen said. On and on and on. Moving in the night. Lake Kluane. Burwash Landing. Sakiw Creek. And then it started getting crazy after that.

I guess I fell asleep, but a couple hours later, I could feel him tugging on my arm.

"Come on," Kingpen said. "I think you'd better wake up." And when I opened my eyes, we were sitting there at Customs. U.S. Customs. And according to the sign, it wasn't even open, but it was.

"Going up to work?" one of the agents asked. And we told him we were coming back from Haines.

"Went and bought some beer," Kingpen said.

"All the way to Haines? Well maybe we should have a look. How much did you buy?" the agent asked. "A case or two?" And then he looked back in the cab, and the thing that I remember was his eyes. They started getting wide and then he asked again, "*How* much did you buy?"

"Fifty-seven cases," Kingpen said.

"Well I hope you've got a permit," the agent said. But of course we didn't, so we went into the little building, and he told us that according to the law, we could only move twelve cases at a time.

"That's *bootleg* beer you've got," he said. "We're gonna have to charge you. Now take it from the truck and put it all over there." And he pointed to a spot on the ground.

So we took out all the cans and we put 'em where he wanted, and the thing that I remember was I thought that I was gonna die, I was so damn cold. Geez, it was cold. People blinking *faster, faster, faster* and breathing through their noses, and I know if I had stayed out one more minute I'd have frozen to death. Right there at the border.

Just lock me up, I thought. *And get me into the warm.*

But it turned out that they didn't. Lock me up, that is. "Now what about *these* cans?" another agent asked. "You drink 'em from the *bottom*?"

"No. We didn't drink the beer at all," Kingpen said. But then I guess he thought that we'd be charged with some kind of pollution law, so he didn't do too much talking after that.

"Well now, I've really seen it all," the other agent said. "Come on into the building. I'll tell you what we're gonna do. We're gonna let you all go, but we've gotta confiscate the beer. You seem like normal guys. Everybody working?" And I told him that we were.

"Far North Music Machines," I said.

We went outside and Pinto asked him, "How about the empty cans? Can we at least have *them*?"

But the agents told us, "No, we have to confiscate them *all*." They walked into the building and the three of us just stood there in the freezing cold, staring at our cases of cans.

Then Kingpen told us, "*Listen.*"

And we listened and it started with a tiny sound at first. A tiny, little *czzz* from a can down near the bottom case. And then another, and another. *CZZZ, CZZZ, . . . POP! POP! POP!* All along the seams. Every can we hadn't opened, froze, and started to explode.

"Over $27,000 bucks!" Kingpen said. And I remember that we stood there for a minute. *Blinkin', blinkin', blinkin'.* Breathing *in* through our noses and *out* through our mouths. Then we got inside the truck and Pinto started driving.

We got to Fairbanks sometime the next morning. We would have gotten there sooner, but I think we followed a small snowstorm on the way. The road would ice up, and then it would be clear, and then we'd run into some ice again. It seemed like forever we'd be putting on these snow chains Pinto had. Put 'em on, take 'em off, put 'em on. And then we'd take 'em off. and each time we did, we'd tell ourselves, "That's it." But of course, it never was. So we'd get 'em out and put 'em on again, and our hands and fingers would be bleeding from the metal and the ice, but we never really felt it. All you *really* felt was *numb*.

"I bet it's fifty-five *below*," Kingpen said.

We kept on going north, past Northway, Tanacross and Sawmill Creek. Then a couple hours later, I knew that we were starting to get close. *Fewer bullet holes*, I thought. Then we started seeing lights and restaurants and cars.

We're back, I thought. *After driving down to Haines and buying all their beer and leaving it behind. We're back, with freezing, bloody hands. Yeah, we're back.*

But like the lady in the bakery, the people who were living there in Fairbanks never even knew that we'd been gone.

We turned left off of Cushman, got on College Road, and went out past the corner where I'd stood a couple weeks before. *Shaking, shaking, shaking.* Eleven forty-two. That's exactly when we passed it. I saw it on the clock. *Resistors haven't frozen up yet,* I thought.

We kept going west, past the University and Chena River, out past Sheep Creek Road, six or seven miles till we saw it on the left.

"CLOSED!" Kingpen told me. And I knew it would be. And then a little past the place where they never weighed the trucks, Pinto made a right, and we started toward the town I thought was up there on the hill.

"Ester," Kingpen told me. "Just wait until you see it."

Chapter 34

If you ever want to go, I think you'd really like it. It reminds you of a Christmas garden in a way, except it doesn't have a train. The houses are a lot like you would picture though. Ten or fifteen houses all snuggled in the snow.

But anyway, you drive in on the turnoff and then you go about a half a mile and make a right. You make a right, and then you take another little road and you drive in on the snow for a couple hundred yards to a little intersection. And depending how you turn, you go on into town, or you can go and get a drink and see a show.

"Malamute Saloon," Pinto said. And he pointed to his left. "Ever been in there? It's a tourist trap. Round-trip tickets. No one else goes in there."

He stepped down on the gas and pulled down on the wheel. The back end of the truck swung around and we started to the ten or fifteen houses that were Ester. But of course we didn't stop there.

Think the strangest thing, I thought.

We kept on going up. Up and up and up this long, narrow, winding road with banks on either side. It reminded me of bobsled runs you see. That's what it was like. Smooth and icy. You could see it glaring in the dark.

"ICE!" Pinto said. And he punched down on the gearshift and dropped it into four-wheel drive.

"That should do it," Kingpen said. We went another half a mile. Up onto the hill. Up and up and up, until we pulled off on a little gravel pad and Pinto shut his truck off.

"I'll leave the keys right here," he said, and put them on the dashboard. "Take it in tomorrow, if you want to go to town. Use it if you need it," Pinto told me.

We got out of the truck and it might have been mid-morning. I don't know. But I remember it was black. Pitch black. But even in the dark, you could see 'em. Millions of birch trees, with the bark peeling off. That's what I remember.

"Wait until you see it," Kingpen said.

We walked along a beaten down, snowy path for a hundred yards or so. And sitting in the night, with the birch trees all around, there it was.

"Our new home," Kingpen said.

It wasn't like you'd picture a cabin in the woods. It was better. Better than you ever could imagine. Giant hand-cut logs with a huge picture window. No one else around.

"Only have it for another couple weeks," Pinto said. "A guy I know from Massachusetts owns it, and he's coming back. But we'll get another place. I'll go out into the woods and build one if I have to." And even then, just the way he said it, I never had a doubt that that's what he would do.

When you wake up in the woods in the middle of the winter, in the middle of Alaska, it stays with you forever. We slept that night in a loft that looked down on a Springfield airtight woodstove. The traps that Pinto had for martin, mink and wolverine were hanging on the walls. There were snowshoes and a lantern and some jugs that we would use to haul our water. A Ruger 44 and a thirty-ought-six. Alaskan kind of stuff. The stuff that you might picture.

But the things that made it better were the things you never saw. The things you *felt*. The things that stay with you forever. Like little crackling sounds. Hissing, steaming, cracking sounds you heard, coming from the stove. *Tsst, tsst, pttt. Tsst, tsst, pttt.*

And then the shadows of the embers would dance and flicker all around the room, and you'd lie there in your bag, and everything would seem as good as it was ever gonna get. Absolutely perfect. *Tsst, tsst, psst. Tsst, tsst, psst.* Like you're lying there all bundled in a womb, except the whole thing smelled like wood. That's what I remember.

Giant log walls, wooden chips spread down on the floor, and the woodstove smell, all mixing up together. Absolutely perfect. As good as you could picture it was ever gonna get.

But even then, it still kept gettin' better, because sometime, somewhere in the night, you'd hear one all alone. First one, and then another and another, till they echoed in your head. *AH ooo. Ah ooo. Ah ooo.*

Timber wolves.

I crawled out of my bag, pulled on my mukluks, got my jacket, threw another log inside the stove, then started out the door.

Grizzlies, caribou and wolves.

I stood there in the birch trees, on the snowy, frozen ground, and listened for a while until the only thing I heard was, "I'll leave the keys in here, in case you wanna take it out tomorrow morning." That's what he had said. "Go out and see the sights. I'll leave the keys in here." And when I pulled back on the handle and opened up the door, that's exactly where they were.

I climbed up on the bench seat, and it reminded me of concrete. Only harder. "Frozen fuckin' solid." That's what Pinto used to call it. And everywhere you looked, little frozen cola chips were lying on the seat, and on the floor, and even on the dashboard. *From a plastic soda bottle that Kingpen must have left there from the night before.* That's what I remember thinking. Cold, then colder, then it must have exploded. BOOM! Little frozen cola chips everywhere you felt.

I put a chip into my mouth, turned the key, and pumped down on the pedal. *Grer er, Grer er.* And then absolutely nothing. *Busted*, I thought. But then I waited a few minutes and tried it again. *Grer er, Grer er, Er er.* Then it started sputtering and I finally got it going.

I started down the long and winding chute that I was telling you about. Kind of like a bobsled run, banked up on either side. *Going for the gold*, I thought. *Thump, thump, thump, thump.* And then I guess the air inside the tires started warming up, because I didn't feel the thumping quite so much. Just little, tiny, faster thumps. And then my toes began to thaw, and I looked off to my right, and just like I had figured, *CLOSED.* Then I started eating all these cola chips for breakfast.

Thinking, thinking, thinking. Driving down the road, eating cola chips and always thinking. That's what I remember thinking. *Where you gonna go? No place you can go, but it really doesn't matter, 'cause you're always with yourself. Everybody's someplace. Even if it isn't where you wanna be.* On and on and on.

And then I went up to the gym and went inside, got undressed and went into the shower. And it made me think of Abraham. The guy up on the mountain who was gonna kill his son. The guy the Bible tells you about, who stood the test of faith. But I don't think he did.

Because he thought he knew he heard from God and did what he was told.

Faith, I thought, *is when you're standing bare-ass naked underneath the shower, and you turn the water on, and even though it's cold, you stand there anyway. Come on. Come on. Have faith*, I thought.

And just like I had figured, it started heating up, until I thought that I was gonna melt. *Just turn that shower dial around*, I thought up in my head. *Hot, then hotter, then as hot as you can take it. Even hotter. Soak it up, and hold onto the heat like you used to do last spring.* Then my mind went to the next thing. "The building will be closing . . ."

I turned the shower off and all the steam began to rise up from my arms and legs and feet. Like dry ice in a way, except that I was wet and hot. But anyway, I got some paper towels and started drying off, and then I pushed the dryer button in and stood there for a while and let the hot air do the rest. *Psschtt*. And in another twenty minutes, I was dressed and back in the truck.

I went down to the Union first. And even on a Sunday, even with it closed, a couple guys were there, standing on the sidewalk, making all these plans. Standing in the dark, in the middle of the winter, thirty-five below, maybe even colder, and the passengers were waiting. *All aboard*, I thought. And then one guy told the other, "We should be up on the Slope next week.

I walked down to the bakery and got a couple bear claws. Then I started walking all around town some more. *Walkin', walkin', walkin'.*

It was kind of like before, with the reindeer and the other decorations, except somehow it was different. We'd made it through the solstice. The light was coming back for one thing. Another seven minutes, but of course you couldn't really tell it all that much.

I started thinking of the time we'd come up in the Buick and how you couldn't picture being hot when you were cold, and how you couldn't picture anything but snow when it was snowing. So, a couple hours later I walked up Wendell, made a left on Lathrop and decided I would see it all again. Every bit of green I never could imagine out there in the dark.

There was a path someone shoveled up the walk, that went onto the porch that I was telling you about. *Window to the world*, I thought. I kicked the snow off of my mukluks, pushed in on the door, and everything was just the way it had been months before. Rows and rows of books, and wooden tables. Magazines. And standing there behind the counter, running everything, was Mrs. Ogatok. I read it on her name card. Mrs. Ogatok, in her little business suit.

I guess the first thing that you think when you go into a library is what book you're gonna read. What you're gonna read, where you're gonna sit, but it wasn't like that then.

Just breathe it in and soak it up, I thought. Breathe it in and soak it up, until your toes begin to tingle and the ice begins to melt and run down on your face.

Everywhere you went back then, that's what it was like. The first thing that you thought of. No matter where you went. In the bakery, in the Hall, when you went to check the mail. *Just breathe it in and soak it up*. And when the ice began to melt and your toes began to tingle, then you took a look around and figured out which doughnut you would buy. Or you turned the key and checked for mail inside the box, or started looking for a book, or did some other thing.

I knew right where to go. There was a section over to the side, where I'd been once before. Alaskana. With books and magazines and even record albums of Alaskan kind of stuff. *Grizzlies, caribou and wolves.*

And right there in the middle, on display, was *The Wildness of Alaska*, by Richard Lorris. Thirty-seven ninety-five. That's how much it cost. And it must have weighed nearly six or seven pounds with all the pictures of the icebergs and the rivers and the mountains and the bears. *Pictures, pictures, pictures*. All the green I never could imagine.

And then just like Kingpen said, it kept on getting better. *Seven minutes more,* I thought, because I glanced up to my right and saw a record album. *Sounds of the Far North.* And when I read the small print, I knew it was *exactly* what I wanted. *Authentic sounds recorded in Alaska.* That's the way they described it on the album cover. And when I went into the little room and put the needle down, that's *exactly* what they were.

It was a goofy little room. Smaller than a bathroom. And it used to be a closet. That's what I remember thinking. But anyway, it had a little wooden table and chair, and a plastic, orange-colored record player you could use, to listen to the records that were there. Records like you'd play at home, I guess, of famous people singing. Except my record wasn't like that. Not exactly.

It started with a moose at first. *Mwaa. Mwaa.* Way off in the distance. And then you heard some rustling in the grasses and then another gruffer sound, only closer in this time, and really loud, like *URUGH! URUGH!.* "Its mate." That's what the narrator said.

Around and round the record went, on the little plastic turntable. *Mwah, URUGH! Mwah, URUGH!* On and on, until I guess they wandered off, because it started getting quiet for a while.

But then you started hearing birds. Alaskan arctic terns, the narrator called them. And they sounded just like seagulls. *Agh. Agh.* Dozens of 'em flying all around. And that's the way it went. Moose, birds, and then you heard an owl. Kind of like a zoo, except it wasn't all together. Every animal and little sound was recorded by itself, so you knew it was authentic. Just the way somebody taped it. Baying wolves at night, geese honking at each other. But the one I really liked, the one that was my favorite, was called "The Calving of a Glacier."

It started out real quiet, and I said to Kingpen later, it reminded me of Horseshoe Lake. You heard a couple birds and could almost feel the gentle breezes. Then you heard a real soft *swish, swish,* the dipping of the oars I guess, because the one guy whispered, "Well, we're pushing off." Then you heard a clunk and a click and he whispered, "Ladies and gentlemen, this is Earl Rollins for KFAC. Today Bill Quigley and I are broadcasting live from a rowboat, directly in front of the Matanuska Glacier, just outside of Juneau. It is our hope to capture and broadcast live to you, our audience, the authentic sounds of a glacier calving."

And I figured what that meant was some pieces of the glacier breaking off. But anyway, he whispered, "Now picture if you can, miles and miles of ice, either way you look. A wall," he whispered. "At least four hundred feet, maybe taller. Just *picture* it."

And so I pictured it and listened, and I really felt like I was there. From the whispering, I guess. But anyway, I couldn't hear a thing until he said, "We'll be sitting here all throughout the day. *Listening,*" he whispered. But for now, let's return you to our regularly scheduled program."

I heard a click, and then the record went around, and then I heard another click. "Well, we're back," Earl whispered, "and I really have to tell you, this is *very* disappointing. See any signs of calving yet?" And I guess Bill shook his head, because you couldn't hear Bill answer. "Well, like I said before," Earl broadcast, "we'll be sitting here all day, if we have to." *Listening*, I thought. And then I heard another click.

He came back when the record turned around, but it wasn't quite that fast in real time. "We've been sitting out here for eleven hours now," Earl said, "so I think we're finally going to have to pack it in. So for KFAC . . ."

"Hey, Earl!," Bob shouted.

"This is Earl Rollins signing . . ."

"Hey, Earl! I think the glacier's movin!"

You could have heard a pin drop after that. A total, eerie silence. Then it turned into a rhythmic, disbelieving chant.

"Oh my God," Earl whispered. "Oh my God! Oh my God!"

And then you heard a crack that sounded like it should have split the sky, and you knew it split the ice. "HOLY FUCKIN *SHIT!!!*" Earl screamed. Right there on the record.

And then it all came tumblin' down, louder than you ever could imagine. *KA KA KA RASH! SMASH! THWUMP! THWUMP! THWUMP!*

"Hold on to the fuckin' *boat*!" one of them yelled. Then I heard a clunk, and figured right away that Earl had dropped the microphone. But you still could hear the roar. *Chinese style*. Like you're lying on the beach and the waves are crashing down right there on your head. *Sa-MASH! MASH! MASH!*

But the way it all worked out, I guess they made it in the end. I mean the sounds are on the record. And if you don't believe me, look it up. I think you'd really like it. The album's called *Sounds of the Far North*, and it's "The Calving of a Glacier," with Bob and Earl.

Chapter 35

Pinto swore that we were wrong, but I didn't know it at the time. "Best darn place a guy could ever live," Kingpen said. And I thought that he was right. Everything seemed perfect. Just about. The only thing we never really liked was walking to the road, me and Kingpen. Walking, walking, walking down this frozen bobsled run, because the truck had frozen up. But then we didn't really have the money for the gas, so it didn't matter.

But anyway, we'd walk and walk, and then we'd get down to the main road and stand there on the side. And soon enough, "How about a ride?" somebody'd call out from their window, and then we'd head off to the Union.

And every single time, it always was the same. "No C list calls today," they'd tell us. "No C list calls today."

I remember feeling down and disappointed, but then Kingpen always used to say, "One day we'll get out. All we've gotta do is *be* there." So every day we were. Every single day. We'd go up to the door, see the sign - and then we'd turn around, walk up to the Chapel of the Chimes, catch a ride up College Road, check the mail, go up to the school, hang around awhile, and then catch another ride on back to Ester.

Geez, that town was pretty. I wish you could have seen it. With the snow, the little houses with the chimneys, and the Christmas lights. Us walking in the dark with the wolves howling in the night.

And then right there at the turn, where you started up the hill, there was a well that people used. A springhouse really. And every time we got there, one of us would ask, "How about we stop and get a drink?" And then we'd lean inside the springhouse, dunk the bucket, ladle out some water and talk for a while. Talk and talk and talk, look up at the lights when they rolled across the sky, and listen to the wolves. Then after all of that, we'd start off walking, walking, walking, up and up and up.

"Would make a perfect bobsled run," we always used to say. And then we'd hike up in the dark, up between the birch trees. Our toes would lose their feeling, and our faces would get numb. And right about the time we thought that we were gonna die, we'd pull back on the cabin door and there it was. Best darn place a guy could ever live. *Almost perfect.*

We didn't see a lot of Pinto after living there a couple days. He was always coming in or going out. Then one day he left with his snowshoes and a rifle and some other gear. "Going out to check my traps," was all he ever said. So at twenty-eight below, Pinto started walking out into the birch trees, toward the hills behind our cabin.

"Pinto should have been a mountain man," Kingpen told me. And that was when I said I thought he was one.

At first I thought it might have been the way the snow had drifted from the wind. A little pile that sat out in the field. But that's not what it was.

"There's something *under* all of that," Kingpen said. And we stood there on the road right outside of Ester. Looking. Always looking. Looking through the winter night, out into the field, staring at this lumpy little pile, until we both began to know there wasn't any doubt. "It's *something*," Kingpen said. And I told him that I knew.

We started walking after that. Walking through the snow, down into the gully, just like at McKinley. "It's *something*," Kingpen said again. And then we started jumping from one tussock to another. That's what Kingpen called them. The things that grew out of the muskeg. Squatty tufts of grass that stood above the snow. We'd leap and we'd jump, but we hardly ever made it. Not because we missed. They weren't that far apart.

But the nature of the tussocks was they were a little bit like giant mushrooms. You had to hit the center or they wouldn't hold you up. You'd wiggle and you'd wobble and then you'd fall off in the snow.

But it didn't really matter at the time. Because *SOMETHING* kept us going. "See it?" Kingpen asked me. "*Something's* underneath that snow." And when we got a little closer, we knew that we were right.

It wasn't what you're thinking, if you're thinking it was Pinto. It was about as long as Pinto, though. "Now grab hold and help me pull it out," Kingpen said. He handed me this piece of rope that he had dug out of the snow. "One, two, PULLLL. One, two, PULLLL," Kingpen shouted.

And of all the things I've ever found, that one was the best. Even *how* we found it, underneath the snow. *Like treasure.* That's what Kingpen told me later. Everything about it was like treasure. Especially the name.

"One two, PULLLL," Kingpen yelled again. And then we leaned back on the rope and I remember we could feel it breaking loose that time. "PULLLL, PULLLL, *PULLLL,*" Kingpen shouted. And it took another minute, but we got it. *The Flying Golden Eagle.* You could read it on the wood.

"Hot darn!" Kingpen said. And he didn't have to say another word, because I knew what he was thinking. It just keeps on getting better. Seven minutes every day. *No more walking down the hill,* I thought.

We started toward the road, went up through the town, and told ourselves that we would wait until morning, but of course we didn't. We never even stopped to get a drink. We kept on walking to the top, dragging it along. Up and up and up. And then we turned the sled around, I sat up in the front, Kingpen got in back, and we started down.

Six o'clock at night and we couldn't see a thing, but we started. "Think I should *push* us?" Kingpen asked.

"Yeah. Give a little shove," I said. But it turned out that he couldn't, because we started going faster all at once. Faster, faster, *faster.*

"HOLD *ON!*" Kingpen yelled.

And I wish you could have seen us. The Flying Golden Eagle. *Zoo Zoo ZOOM!* As fast as we could go, and then a little faster.

The Flying Golden Eagle.

The road began to curve and I guess I lost control, because we started up the bank and hit a pile of snow.

"Damn," I said.

And then we laid there on the ice and laughed and laughed, until I thought that we were gonna fuckin' die.

I read a story once about this guy who liked to fly. Or it might have been a bird. I don't know. But anyway, it kept on flying better and better until it got to be the best. Ultimate perfection. And I never understood how anyone would want it that much, until we got the sled. But then I did.

Later on that night, as we sat there by the fire with a pencil and a little piece of paper, Kingpen drew out how the road went down into the town. "Here's the first curve," Kingpen said. "The one we didn't make." He drew a little turn that went off to the right. "And then it comes back to the *left*," he said. "Remember? You go a couple hundred feet and then it goes back to the left? And then . . ."

"And then you go a ways, into this sweeping right hand curve," I said. "And then another little ways and then a gentle right hand turn."

"And then the *straight* part," Kingpen said. "On down to the springhouse for about a half a mile. And then you make a sharp right and go into the town."

We looked at the map and we knew it wasn't perfect. But just like Kingpen said, "At least we both can *see* it. We'll go down in the morning. Take it really slow and then we'll hitchhike to the Hall. And tomorrow afternoon, when we've got a little light . . . "

"We'll run her down into the town," I said. "Run her down to Ester."

And we really had a hard time sleeping after that. *Turn left. Turn right.* Then all that I could picture was the Flying Golden Eagle on the straight part at a hundred miles an hour. Maybe even faster.

"Night," I said.

And that's when Kingpen told me, "That Flying Golden Eagle, it's kinda like a treasure. Isn't it? " he asked. "The way we found it in the snow?"

And I remember telling him it was.

Kingpen had the map. "How about we *walk* it down the first time?" Kingpen asked.

So we pulled the sled behind us and walked on down, and it wasn't all that different than the way that we had pictured it the night before. The only thing we noticed was this root that ran across the straight part, halfway to the springhouse. And I guess we could have cut it, but we didn't.

"Let's go to the Hall," Kingpen said. "We'll see what's with the A list and then come back when it's light." So that's what we decided.

We hid the Flying Golden Eagle right behind the weigh station, walked back to the road, and waited awhile. And like it always seems to happen when you've got the time to wait, someone comes along and hollers out, "Need a ride?" And then you tell 'em you'd appreciate the ride, they ask you where you're headed, and you start off where you're going.

"Anyplace downtown," I said. Because it really didn't matter. "Going to the Hall?" he asked.

And when we told him, "Yeah," he shook his head.

We started getting into ice fog after that. Fifteen minutes out of Ester, we hit these clumps of clouds. And then the closer we got, the more they drifted together, until you could just barely see.

"Well, I guess this should do," our driver said. Then we felt a little bump and knew we'd pulled up to the curb. "Hope you get a job," he said.

The Union Hall had changed the rules back, so you could go in for the morning call, even if you weren't on the A or B list. We walked through the door and it looked funny in a way, without the yellow sign. But it was just like Kingpen said. "One day we'll *belong* here, if we wait for long enough. We'll be *with* 'em on the A list."

When I looked around the room, it was just like I remembered. Tough and grizzled faces staring into space. Zombies who had ridden on the train. Cold Foot, Five Mile, Happy Valley, Prudhoe Bay. And maybe for a second, maybe for an instant, I thought of what I'd read of residency cards and people from Outside.

But then it all began to drift and fade away, and my mind went to the next thing. *Grizzlies, caribou and wolves.* And I stood there in the Hall and listened to the stories.

There was one guy there who had just flown down from Prudhoe. "Fifty-eight below," he said. But kind of like the time we'd been at Ice Worm Gulch, it kept on getting colder.

"Went down to sixty-six below when I was there," another person said. Then they all began to talk and of course it kept on getting better. Sixty-eight below, then seventy.

Then the first guy said that he was going to Hawaii. "*Fuck* it all. I'll come back in the spring," he said.

And then they started saying things like, "Hours oughta pick up early March."

"No more seven nines."

"That's *BULLSHIT*," one guy said. "A lousy *thousand* bucks a week? Fuggit."

And then they all began to say the one thing that my father's newspaper article never mentioned. Another couple months and things were gonna break. "All the work a guy could ever want," I heard somebody say.

Just hold on to the dream, I thought. All we've gotta do is *be* here.

Across the room the screen went up. The guy tapped on the mike and told us, "Mornin'."

But it wasn't like the summer. "Not a lot of jobs this time of year," the guy announced. He rattled off a few. "Two for Prudhoe, one for Five Mile and one for Chandalar." But even then, we didn't walk away.

"Let's stay and see how far they go down the list," Kingpen said. So we waited and we waited, maybe six or seven minutes.

"A hundred eighty-nine. Anybody lower than a hundred eighty-nine?" the dispatcher asked. And it turned out no one was, so the last job went to him. Number one eighty-nine.

And I guess when I look back, we could have seen it differently. At least another million jobs before they got to us. But of course we never did. "That's four more off the list," Kingpen said.

And then my mind went to the next thing and I guess Kingpen's did the same. The Flying Golden Eagle. Racing down that hill as fast as we could go and then we'd keep on going faster. Faster, faster, faster. *Ride it down Chinese style.* That's what I remember thinking.

Then we started out the door and Kingpen asked me, "Wanna head on back and try and make it down the hill?"

And I breathed in through my nose, and I breathed out through my mouth, and I started blinking faster.

And I told him that I did.

I guess you do it the most when you're little. But I don't think the feeling ever really goes away. The times you stand there and you picture that you're gonna do it all. Save the game. Break the record. Be the hero.

That's what it was like. We stood there for a minute and we looked on down the hill, and even though we never said a word, we knew what each of us was thinking. *This is it. Just like the Olympics. Fitch and Kingpen going down the chute.*

"Think we oughta *sit* the first time?" Kingpen asked. "Maybe we should try it sitting first." So that was how we started. Kingpen sat up front and I got in the back, then Kingpen told me how he thought that he could steer. "Like this," he said. And then he pulled up both his legs and pushed down with his left foot.

We must have sat there on the sled for five minutes after that, looking at the map on the paper that we had. "Watch this curve." "Lean hard left here." "Hold on tight at this point," and on and on and on.

"Well I guess we're just about as ready as we're gonna be," I said. Then Kingpen turned around and told me to push off.

And I heard it in my head. *Three, two, one...*

It wasn't like back east. I never felt the runners hold and then break free. "Cold's too dry for them to freeze into the ice," Kingpen told me later. But anyway, I gave a little push and all I ever felt was gliding. Going down the ice like a paperclip on a slanted piece of mirror. Gliding, gliding, gliding. Gliding kind of slow at first, but then we started going along, and let me tell you - we were really movin'.

"Hold *ON!*" Kingpen shouted. And it was kind of like the last time when we were heading toward the bank. Except this time we could see it in the dusk. "Hold *ON!*" Kingpen yelled again, and then, just about the time when I thought that we would crash, he pushed down to his left and we started to the right.

Push the button in, I thought. And then we started going faster. Faster, faster, faster. *And then it comes back to the left,* I thought. Remember? It goes a couple hundred feet, and by that time we were moving. *Faster, faster, FASTER!*

Only this time, Kingpen couldn't make the turn. "HOLD *ON!*" Kingpen screamed. And it was funny in a way, because neither of us did. We fell off of the sled and we watched it slide into the bank. Then we sat there for a while. Sat there on the icy road and planned it out some more. Then we did it all again.

We must have gone on down that hill at least a dozen times that day, before we finally made the turn. And the way we finally did it, was we built it up. Banked it even higher, like the bobsled runs you see. We took a lot of snow and then we got a bucket and some water from the springhouse. And by the time that we were finished, it was really looking good. All built-up and really icy.

"Like a pro's course," Kingpen said.

And even though it was pretty dark and we could hardly see a thing, we told ourselves that we would try it one more time.

"Just once more," Kingpen said.

So we walked on up the hill, got back on the sled, and Kingpen asked, "You sure you want to go?" But he knew what I was gonna say. "Well hold on," Kingpen told me. Then I gave a little push and we started gliding down into the dark.

It always seemed a little slower in the dark. That's what I remember. I mean, you never really saw the trees go flying by for one thing. Not like we would later. But you still went pretty fast.

"Hold *ON!*" Kingpen yelled. And all at once we started to the right. Right there in the groove. Faster, *faster*. Holding tight and always going faster, till we started up the bank. Up and up and up, and then just where we'd gone over all the other times, we started coming down, like we'd been shot out of a sling. Ka ZOOM! *Heading toward the next curve.* That's what I remember thinking.

We were heading toward this sweeping right hand curve, except we never made it in the dark.

"Didn't see it," Kingpen told me later.

So we crashed into the bank. But just like Kingpen said, we were getting there.

"We'll make it down to Ester one day," Kingpen told me. And the way it all turned out, one day we almost did.

I think I told you that I could have lived in Ester for a while. I mean we only stayed about another week, but I think I would have liked it. With the birch trees all around, and the Springfield stove, and the springhouse and the wolves howling in the night. "Best darn place a guy could ever live," Kingpen used to say.

And I thought it at the time. Mostly in the mornings, when we'd climb out of the bags and start it all again.

"Can you think of any better way a guy could go to work?" Kingpen asked.

We'd sit there near the cabin on the Flying Golden Eagle, and even though we weren't exactly heading off to work, I'd tell him, "No. I couldn't think of any better way." People taking cars and buses. People down in subways. And there *we* were, gliding from the start, and flying up around the banks. You'd shoot out of the slingshot and then you'd hear it in your ears. *Whooo-oosh.*

"Ready?" Kingpen asked. Except this time it was different. We were lying down this time to cut down on the wind. "Ready?" When I told him that I was, he started pushing off, laid on top my back, and we started gliding down. Faster than we'd ever glided down before. "Hold *ON!*" Kingpen yelled.

I started thinking I was gonna bust up all my teeth, because my face was right up front. Then all at once, Kingpen grabbed my arm and told me, "*PUSH* it. Push it *DOWN.*" So I pushed down to the left and I wish you could have seen it. "Perfect," Kingpen told me later. "Couldn't have done it any better myself."

We went off to the right and started toward the ice bank we had built up earlier that week. Faster, faster, faster. Always going *faster*.

"Hold *ON!*" Kingpen yelled again. I pushed down on the right, but even then we kept on going up, because we couldn't steer that well on ice. So we shifted all our weight. Shifted to the left.

And just like all the times that Kingpen steered us through, we kept on going up. Up and up and *up*. But faster than before cause we were lying down I guess. But anyway, I wish you could have been there. Up and up, then right there at the top – "HOLD *ON!*" Kingpen yelled.

We both let out a scream, and – *ZOO OOM!* We were fucking flying!

Down the frozen bank, blasting through this straight part for a couple hundred feet, and all these trees just flying by. Fucking flying! *ZOOM! ZOOM! ZOOOM!*

"Shift right!" Kingpen yelled again, and almost right away I pushed down on the left, and we shifted to the right. We started whipping 'round this longer, lower bank that swerved off to the right. "Fishtail One." That's what Kingpen called it later.

We went another eighty-ninety yards and entered Fishtail Two. And the thing with Fishtail Two was, it really started dropping down right after that. "Thirty-six degrees." That's what Kingpen figured later. Thirty-six degrees.

And then from Fishtail Two, you started down the chute. *Short Chute One.* And you couldn't really talk by then, because you couldn't even breathe. All that you could do was blink. Faster, faster, *faster.* Blinking in the dusk.

The sled began to rattle and I thought back to the Buick and the frost heaves and the shocks. *Ejong, Ejong, Ejong.*

Then we banked up to our left and must have started down the long chute a hundred miles an hour. Maybe even faster. Just like the Olympics.

Gonna do it all, I thought.

Then we saw it up ahead.

Kingpen saw it first. I felt his feet go down and he tried to shift his weight, but of course it didn't help. By then it was too late. The runner slammed into the root and we went flying down the hill. Flying down the hill with the Flying Golden Eagle stuck back on this root.

And I bet you think that one of us got hurt, but we didn't. We just tumbled for a while. Then we got a sharp rock, cut the root out of the ice, and covered up the hole with snow.

We stood there for a minute. "Wanna get back on and ride it down to Ester?" Kingpen asked.

But I told him, "No. We're gonna take it from the top. Tomorrow afternoon."

We walked down to the road, hid the Flying Golden Eagle, and caught a ride down to the Union Hall.

And even though it was the A list call, it was kind of like the C list. Not one single job. But even then, they didn't put a notice on the door. "No Pipeline jobs today," the guy announced.

The screen went down and Kingpen told me, "Bottomed out. Things have bottomed out. Only way from here is up. Can't get worse than zero." And it was funny in a way. I mean that's what you would think. But now that I look back, it didn't get a whole lot better for a while.

We hitchhiked back to Ester after that. Hitchhiked back, and then we spent all that afternoon walking up and down the hill, until we knew we had it right. Every little detail.

"Note this bump," I said. And then we'd draw it on the map. Every little bump and every little bend.

"Better check the last part of the ride," Kingpen said. "End of Long Chute One. Check it really well."

And I thought he meant because we'd never sledded down that far before, but that wasn't what he meant. "We'll be flying so darn fast we'll have to memorize it," Kingpen told me. "*Memorize* the map." So that's just what we did.

Checked and re-checked Long Chute One. Mostly near the bottom. And it was just like Kingpen said. All we had to do was make that right hand turn and we would go into the town. "Think that you can do it?" Kingpen asked. And I told him that I could.

We got the sled and walked up to the cabin after that. "Sandwich or noodles?" Kingpen asked me. And I told him noodles would be fine, because that was all we ever had. Sandwiches or noodles. Every single day. Sandwiches or noodles, sandwiches or noodles, because we didn't have much money.

"Want to tell it to me one more time?" Kingpen asked. And I sat there eating noodles and told him one more time.

"I'll start off lying down," I said. "I'll start off lying down and then you rock it back and forth. Back and forth. Just like the Olympics. And when you rock it back the third time, really give a push. Give it all you've got."

"And then I'll dive on top," he told me. "That should really get us moving." And the way we had it figured, we had six or seven seconds until we made it to the first turn. "Six or seven seconds, then we'll go off to the right and head down to the Slingshot."

"Like a rocket," I told Kingpen. "We'll shoot out like a rocket."

"But you've gotta keep it low enough to stay inside the bank," he told me, "or we'll go into the trees." FASTER, FASTER, *FASTER*! "Then a couple hundred feet and we start down Fishtail One. Then Fishtail Two. Then we go into the short chute. Short Chute One."

And the thing that we both knew was, we couldn't do much breathing after that. "Take a big breath *here*," Kingpen said. And he pointed to the map and told me, "Don't forget it starts to angle down. Thirty-six degrees. And then the little bend that goes off to the right."

"Yeah," I told him. "And then we hit it. Long Chute One."

Long Chute One must have been about a half a mile long, with banks on either side, and solid ice that slanted down thirty-six degrees. A perfect bobsled run that went down past the springhouse, curved off to the right, and went into the town. "We could even make it down onto the highway," Kingpen said, and he gave a little laugh.

I guess it happens with a lot of things. You think you get to know them and then they change. But I don't think *they* do.

"*We've* changed," Kingpen always used to tell me.

And maybe he was right.

Except for Slingshot One, which we had built up some, nothing else was different. Just us, and the *confidence* we had.

"Now we *know* that we can make it," Kingpen said.

We stood there on the hill and it was eerie in a way. Every single foot was up there in my head. Even parts I couldn't see. Every lump and bump and curve. Every patch of snow.

"Ready?" Kingpen asked.

"Yeah," I said.

Then we started rocking back and forth. "One, two . . . Hold *ON!*" Kingpen yelled. He gave a hard push and we started off faster than we'd ever started off before. Faster than we'd ever go again.

Glidin', glidin', glidin'.

Gonna bust up all your teeth, I thought, and then I pulled it to the right and it was perfect. Just like the last time. Only *faster*. Then we kept on going for a couple hundred feet, and Kingpen told me, "Keep the Eagle down. Keep it in the bank." But by then, I knew that we were gonna make it. Even flying down as fast as we could go, I *knew* it.

"HOLD *ON!*" Kingpen yelled. But the problem wasn't going in as much as coming out. Up and up and up, and then right there at the top – VA- ZOOOM! Right out of the slingshot! I mean we were really moving. Shot out of the slingshot and heading down to Fishtail One.

Seven seconds, six seconds, "Shift *RIGHT!*" Kingpen yelled. I pushed left on the handle and we shifted to our right. Like the bucket full of water that never spills a drop when you swing it round your head, that's what it was like. *Just stay inside the bucket*. That's what I remember thinking. *Stay inside the bucket*. Then the sled began to rattle and we started on down Fishtail Two.

Gonna do it all, I thought.

Then Kingpen yelled, "Shift *LEFT!*" I felt him take a breath and we started down the chute. Short Chute One. Only this time we were going faster than the last time, because we went up in the air. Right there where it dropped down thirty-six degrees.

And I know you think I knocked my teeth out, but I didn't. We went up in the air, slammed down on the ice, and kept on gaining speed. Faster, *faster*. Heading into Long Chute One and I couldn't even breathe.

But even though we couldn't talk, we knew what we were thinking...

Gonna do it all. Just like the Olympics.

And I know we would have done it, but we didn't. Because of all the things we wrote down, out of all that we had noticed, *that* one wasn't there.

"*Awe shi...* " I thought.

I pulled down on the left and tried to turn the sled around. Kingpen started rolling underneath the pickup, and the last thing I remember was a thud.

"Like a mud ball hitting bricks." That's what Kingpen told me later.

Right into the springhouse. Spa-latt!

I guess I went unconscious after that. Empty pages in a book. *Nothing, nothing, nothing.*

"Got a pulse?" I finally heard somebody ask.

"C'mon Fitch."

Come on where? I thought. And then the pages started filling up with thinking I was dead. But then I thought that I was thinking, so I thought I was alive.

Thinking, thinking, thinking. Always thinking.

Fucking teeth are broken all apart, I thought. And then I stuck my tongue between my lips to check, and that's when Kingpen said, "I *knew* he was alive. I *knew* it," Kingpen yelled. "I *knew* he wasn't dead."

I started coming 'round right after that. I opened my eyes, and there were Kingpen and the driver of the pickup that had been coming up the hill.

"We thought that you were dead," he said. And everywhere around me was the Flying Golden Eagle. Smashed as much as it could smash and then smashed more. Little pieces of the treasure, everywhere I looked.

"Think that you can walk?" the driver asked. And I told him that I could, except it turned out that I couldn't.

So they put me in the pickup. I think we would have gone on into Fairbanks, except that Pinto happened by. Came back from the woods and I wish you could have seen him. All these little furs of mink and martin. One small wolverine. And ermine. Lots of ermine.

"We'll take him to the cabin," Pinto said. They put me in the back of the pickup, and we started driving up the hill.

And it was funny in a way. Because of all the roads I've ever known, I knew that one best. "Watch out for the bank," I thought. "Pull down real hard left. Faster, *faster*." Then we started on up Fishtail One and I think I fell asleep.

———

We only stayed in Ester for six or seven days after that. "Kenny's coming and he wants his cabin back," Pinto said.

So we had to find a new place and eventually they did. Kingpen and Pinto. Because I couldn't do a thing. Couldn't even walk.

So I sat inside the cabin, with some ice that Pinto packed around my legs. I'd watch 'em both go out each day and get into the truck and start off looking. *Looking, looking, looking.*

Then just like Pinto'd said we'd get another place in another couple days, we did. Just outside of Fox. They came home late one night, and Kingpen told me, "Wait until you see it. Kind of like an old Wild West saloon with a pair of swingin' doors and a candle chandelier."

"You'll like it," Pinto said.

"And the guy that owns it told us we could clean it for the first month's rent," Kingpen said. "And only pay a hundred fifty after that. But we've really gotta clean it."

"Because of all the *cat shit*." That's what Pinto told me later. From a couple dozen cats who had lived there with the lady who had rented it before us. But I never got to see it. Not the cat shit.

I stayed back in the cabin, while they both went off to clean. We moved a couple days after that. Packed up all our sleeping bags and blankets and my spoon from Jimmy Franklin's.

Then we got into the truck and started down the hill. Right there at the bottom, Kingpen asked if I could see these little cracks and indentations in the springhouse wall. "Like a mud ball hitting bricks," he told me. And they're probably still there.

We got out to the road, made a left and started down the page - if you're still looking at the book. Straight on down the right hand side.

"CLOSED," Kingpen told me.

A couple minutes later, we started past the University and Pinto asked us, "Wanna take a shower?" But we didn't. So we kept on going. Down College Road, heading into the ice fog.

"Forty-two below, you start to get inversion," Pinto said. He swung the truck down Lacey, made a left on Steese, and we started past the pipe yard, to a place I'd never been.

"Just wait until you see it," Kingpen said. And that was all that I could do.

We kept on driving. Went out on the Steese Highway, but it wasn't like you'd think. It was a wide road really. That was all it was. And the more we drove, the more we started getting into the country. Suburbs, Pinto called them. But there weren't that many homes. A couple cabins and some trailers.

We went another couple miles and came to a bar. Kingpen read the sign. *Fox Roadhouse.*

That was really all there was of downtown Fox. We never saw a house, or a person, or a car. Just this little roadhouse bar. And everywhere we looked, there were giant hills of snow. But none of 'em had trees.

"Overburden," Pinto said. He told us how they had run it through the crushers years before. "Tons and tons of rock and dirt," he said. "They'd take out all the gold and leave these giant mounds."

And you'd think that they'd be worthless, but they weren't. "Not to fuckin' tourists." That's what Pinto said. "Just wait until the summer. They'll be swarming here like ants, looking for some color. Dozens of 'em. Sleazy-ass Outsiders."

We made a left and started up the Haul Road after that. North to Prudhoe Bay, but of course we never drove that far. "Nine miles," Kingpen said. And we kept on driving, through hills that were covered with little, scrawny trees. Driving, driving, driving in the dusk, until we started going up, and somewhere close to mile six, we saw it on our left.

The Hilltop Cafe. "Where the guy who owns our new place works," Kingpen told me.

We started going down after that. Down and down. Then the asphalt turned to gravel, and the only thing we ever saw were trees, from then on out. Hilltops and valleys, full of scrawny little trees. *Wilderness,* I thought.

Another couple miles, we saw it sitting on our right. *Nine Mile.* The name we came to call the place we lived in through the spring.

It was just like Kingpen said, only somehow it was better. A western-style saloon, but there wasn't any town. No town, no electric, no running water. Nothing really. Just the Haul Road out in front, that was heading up to Prudhoe, and the Fox bar, nine miles back. "Just keeps on getting better," Kingpen said. Then we pulled off to our right and drove onto a gravel pad that was covered up with snow.

"Like it?" Kingpen asked. We were standing there in Olnes. That's what Pinto told us. Just outside of Fox.

"This used to be a town of twenty thousand people," Pinto said. "For the Gold Rush. But then they all packed up and left. Only things they left behind were cabins. And most of them are gone."

But *Nine Mile* was still standing. And I wish you could have seen it.

There was a hitching post out front. A couple logs were stuck into the ground with another one across the top. And right in back of that, it was just like in the movies. "Façade," Kingpen told us. And that was kind of what it was, with a big square front. But the part that was attached, the building right behind it, was a triangle.

And everything was red. That's what I remember. Weathered wood, painted like a barn. And even in the snow, it looked like something you would see out West. A little platform porch, with a rocking chair sitting on the snow, and little panes of glass in back of that.

Then right there, in the middle of it all, were these swinging wooden doors. But that wasn't how we got inside. No. We went around the left side, to the back, around a giant mound of snow. We went in that way. Through a door we couldn't lock.

As soon as we got in, Kingpen asked me, "Smell it?"

"Cat shit," Pinto said. "Smell it?"

But I couldn't, so I told them, "Only smells like pine to me."

Then Kingpen told me one last time, "Scrubbed and scrubbed and scrubbed." He told me how a guy had come out from the *News Miner*. "Took a couple pictures of me fixing up the place. They're gonna do a spread on people living in the bush," he said, and Pinto rolled his eyes.

As we walked in, I saw a bunk bed to our right. A homemade wooden bunk bed. That was in the back room, along with a double-barrel wood stove, a table and some chairs, and a cabinet full of plates down at the other end. That's what I remember.

All these plates and none of 'em quite matched. Some were white, or blue, or blue *and* white. Most were different sizes. There were spoons inside a drawer, with a couple forks and knives.

But anyway, if you went on past the woodstove, you could walk on through a narrow doorless doorway, that opened to the next room. The front room. With windowpanes, so you could look out to the hitching post.

And of all the things you'd guess that were sitting in that *front room*, you'd never guess it right. So I'll give you a big clue...

"Rack 'em." That's what Pinto told us later.

That's it. And every ball was there. Every single one. Just waiting to be shot with these cue sticks that were leaning up against the wall.

And right above the table, there was an antique chandelier. But of course it didn't work. At least not how you'd think. No electricity. Instead, there were candles. Six or seven candles taped up there with duct tape; with little metal dishes underneath to catch the melting wax.

And hanging on the plywood wall, the only other thing you saw, the only other thing there, was a giant faded map of Alaska. *Grizzlies, caribou and wolves.*

We started to get ready for the night. I couldn't do much, but Pinto went and cut some wood. Then we got into his truck and drove down to the spring at Fox.

It was a pull-off really, where a pipe came from a hill, and all the water you could drink came pouring out. Forty-two below and you'd think it would have been frozen. But it wasn't.

"Ever try it?" Pinto asked, and he pointed to the water. "Supposed to keep you coming back," he said. "To Alaska. If you're fool enough to ever leave."

"A folktale," Kingpen said. Then we put a five-gallon jug underneath the pipe and waited. Stood there in the cold and waited, with the water splashing all around. Then we pounded on the top of the container, put the jug back in the truck, and started off again.

We started past the overburden, driving through the hills of scraggly trees, going up and *up*. Then right there at the hilltop, Pinto stopped the truck. "Look," he told us. "A storm is coming in."

Over to our right, you could see it coming through the valley. A foggy kind of haze, all windy, white and swirling.

"I love it," Pinto said, more to himself than to us. And then we started down the other side, on asphalt, then on gravel.

We drove onto the pad and parked by the hitching post. Kingpen got the jug of water, while Pinto got some tools and took the battery from the truck, so it wouldn't freeze.

And then right about that time, it started snowing. But not like you would think. Not those giant flakes you're used to, but the really, really small ones, because it was so cold. "Like sugar," Kingpen said.

I guess the times when you look back, your mind sees different pictures. Like slides, I guess, but Nine Mile wasn't like that. It was more like a movie, that started when you went around the cabin to the back and through the door we couldn't lock. A story in a story. Slides that kept on moving. That's what I remember.

"Spaghetti?" Kingpen asked. And we told him that was fine, so he cooked it on the little metal tray that Pinto rigged on top the woodstove. Spaghetti, Italian bread, and a salad that was brown, because that's what it was like in Fairbanks in the winter. Brown wilted lettuce, black bananas, and oranges you barely could eat.

"Like it?" Kingpen asked. We told him it was great. And if you wanna know the truth, it couldn't have been better. We sat there at the table, slurping down the noodles on the different colored plates, and mopping up the sauce with lots of bread. Eating, eating, eating.

Then we went into the front room, lit the candles on the chandelier, and started shooting pool.

"Rack 'em," Pinto said. And then for hours and hours, we stood there thinking we were good, but always getting better.

I dusted off the eight ball, dropped it in the corner pocket, and that was it for the night.

"Gonna get some shut eye," Pinto told us. "I'll sleep back on the floor."

Then for maybe five more minutes, we stood there. Kingpen and me.

"Hear it?" Kingpen asked. And I told him that I did. Just one more echo of a sound that we'd been hearing through the night.

"Headin' up to Prudhoe," Kingpen told me, which was something that I already knew.

And then we looked out through the little panes of glass, into the tiny flakes of snow, and we kept on watching. Watching, watching, *watching*. Until the tail lights of the semi that was hauling pipe to Prudhoe were completely out of sight.

I guess that next day must have been a Sunday, because we didn't go to the Union call. Pinto took his snowshoes and went off someplace. I put more wood inside the stove, and all we did was sit around that day. Kingpen and me. Sat around and shot the shit and a little pool. Then I think it hit us all at once.

We had to get some money. Get some kind of job. But the thing about a job was that we really couldn't take one. At least not a *day* one, because then we'd miss the Union call. So we had to start our own jobs. That's what Pinto told us later.

"Making money isn't all that hard," he said. But I don't think he cared. About the money. Because the thing I found with Pinto was that he liked the challenge. Like the guy who'd dug a tunnel with a spoon, when he could have used a shovel.

"So then just how *do* we make it?" Kingpen asked. And once we started talking, it really didn't seem that hard.

I remember lots of people making lots of money back then. Not us. But a lot of *other* people were. And they weren't just working out of the unions, either.

Like this lady who had put an ad in the *News Miner* to sell a five-acre lot out at Chena Ridge, just outside of town. Except she didn't even own it. That came out later. There was to be a showing on Sunday and with $5,000 down, you could buy the lot and settle on Monday. Except by then she was gone, with the $75,000 that different people had given her. That's what the paper said.

There were people clearing out their homes and replacing all their furniture with bunk beds. Dozens of 'em. And from what people said, they were making up to twenty, thirty thousand bucks a week, renting beds to people who were looking for work.

And a mailman, out at Ft. Wainwright, had signed up everyone on his route for book and record clubs, except they didn't know it. He bought the first ones for a penny, cancelled the subscriptions, and was selling thousands and thousands of records and books on a street corner, for a couple bucks apiece.

"And how about that *robot*?" Kingpen asked.

"That robot" was this guy who had shown up in Fairbanks six or seven weeks earlier. He had covered himself in aluminum foil and some kind of silver paint, and then wouldn't move until you put at least a dollar in his bucket. He started outside at an intersection, but then I think the paint froze to his face, so he moved into the mall.

"Here, give him a quarter," I heard a mother tell her kid once. And the little girl dropped a quarter in, but he wouldn't move. Not even for the little girl, until she put a dollar in the bucket.

"I bet that guy makes three hundred dollars a day," Kingpen said.

"Five hours," I said. "I bet he makes that in *five* hours." And then we figured three.

"You know how everyone Outside is always saying they want to come up here, except they never do?" Kingpen asked. And I told him I knew. "Well suppose we sold them some land?"

"Yeah, $5,000 down," I said.

"No, listen," he told me. "Suppose we were to buy an acre? Some place really cheap - and sold it in *inches*? With a certificate to people Outside. You know how many square inches would be in that acre?" But neither of us knew.

So Kingpen figured it out and according to him, there were over six million square inches, and we could sell 'em for a dollar apiece.

"So even if we bought a place for a couple thousand bucks and had to pay for the certificates and marketing... Can you imagine?" Kingpen asked.

But that was just it. It was all we could do. *Imagine*.

We had no money. It had all gone for beer cans.

It was the spring of '76 and there would be a lot ahead of us, but of course we didn't know it at the time. My dog would die for one thing, and Kingpen would go blind for another.

But for the time being we focused on the residency cards. The state had passed a law that required anyone working on the Pipeline to have proof of residency for one continuous year. It didn't look good; but still, there were the good times.

My birthday was the next day, and I remember that we started out at this place in town called The Arctic Bar. Kingpen and I had a couple of drinks, then we went off to another place and another place. We finally ended up in Ester at the Howling Dog Saloon, where they gave you six free shots on your birthday. Maybe they still do. I don't know. But anyway, it got to be a lot like that time in

Anchorage when I was trying to read Beamish's lips in the mirror, except Beamish wasn't there.

"Did you hear that he's getting married?" I asked Kingpen.

"Yeah, you told me," he answered. I nodded my head and thought of the guy in Prince Rupert. "You think he's still there, bobbing his head?

"Beamish?" Kingpen asked.

"No. But I'll give you a clue. The Armpit of the World." And I held my nose. I really wasn't doing too well.

The Dog closed at five that morning, but for some reason Kingpen got all upset when he found out we were still there at three.

"Oh no," he said. "We're late." But he wouldn't tell me what we were late for.

We left The Dog, managed to get outside and into Pinto's truck, and started driving back to Olnes. "Shoot, Kingpen said. "Shoot. Shoot. Shoot." And then I think I drifted off to sleep.

We hit the gravel on the Haul Road and that woke me up. "Almost there," Kingpen said.

And geez, it was pretty. Even in the dark. Silhouettes of all these scrawny spruce trees everywhere you looked. The moon was up above us and it was just starting to snow. That's what I remember. Clear patches of sky, along with snow clouds. All mixing together in a pattern and a way that I had never seen. And except for the gravel underneath the tires, everything was quiet. Absolutely quiet and still. That's what I remember, too.

We drove another couple miles and could see a glow up ahead, where our cabin was.

"Looks like Pinto's home," I said, but Kingpen didn't answer.

The closer we got, I could see there were at least a dozen cars and trucks parked around the place. And then I started hearing all this music. Banjos, fiddles, and guitars. Even people singing. And the way it all turned out, the whole thing was for me.

"Sorry that we're late, but happy birthday, Jess," Kingpen told me.

And then we went into the cabin, Pinto handed me a box, and I laid down on the floor and went to sleep.

It was a cardboard shoebox he had found somewhere, and when I opened it the next morning, a pair of moccasins was inside. Pinto had made 'em. Handmade leather moccasins of moose hide with rawhide laces. And they fit just right.

"They'll last you for years," he told me. And if you've ever seen Walter Dyer moccasins, they were a lot like those, except I think that these are better.

"You can even wear 'em in the winter," Pinto told me. And I do.

Another gift was there. Down in the box, it had been underneath the moccasins. "I think you'll like this too," Pinto told me. And I did.

I unwrapped the tissue and I wish you could have seen 'em. Dozens of rent receipts, paychecks, and official looking papers for the entire past year. And all of them in order. That's what I remember. All of 'em in order and the older ones were smudged and wrinkled. All crinkled up.

"That oughta do it," Pinto said. And it turned out that it did.

We spent the next few weeks working on Kingpen's receipts, and going up to the library to look in the *News Miner* for the article about Kingpen living in the cabin. Kingpen and I did. Pinto had gone out into the woods.

But as hard as we tried, we could never get the receipts to look as good as the ones that Pinto had made for me. And the newspaper never had the article. At least not for a while.

"I guess we oughta head on down to the Government Building at some point, to apply for the cards," Kingpen told me. "Doesn't make much sense to go down to the Hall, if we don't have the residency cards."

So eventually we did. And the way that it worked was, you went in person for an interview. To the Government building. You showed them your receipts and answered some questions. Then exactly five days later, you went back. If they handed you a small envelope, well, that was great, because there was supposed to be a residency card inside.

But if they handed you a large envelope, well, you were screwed.

Because according to what we had heard, there was a letter inside explaining that you would be prosecuted for fraud. And it didn't sound like they were playing around either.

"Have you heard that 27 percent of people applying are getting the large envelopes?" Kingpen asked me. And I told him I had. "Well what will we do if *we* get one of them?" he asked me. I told him we wouldn't.

It must have been the following week when we decided to go in. We got our papers together and practiced what we'd say. "Talk about frost heaves and mukluks, so he knows we were here in the winter. And don't forget you pronounce it *Val-DEEZ*," Kingpen told me. And I told him I wouldn't.

We took Pinto's truck out to the Steese Highway, made a right, and went into town, like we had so many times before.

"Maybe they'll see these Alaskan license plates and that'll help, too," Kingpen said. But I told him that it wouldn't matter.

"We've got all kind of things," I said. A driver's license. A library card. And even though they weren't a year old, I figured they would count for something. "And what about that post office box?" I said.

But Kingpen wasn't smiling. He was really nervous. I could see it on his face.

We parked the truck next to the building, went inside, and found the office. There must have been a dozen people there in the waiting room. One guy was from the Hall.

"They look good," Kingpen said. "They look real Alaskan," he told me, pointing at my moccasins. "Maybe they'll help you get the card."

It didn't take that long. About twenty-five minutes and they called me in.

"How are you today?" the man asked. Mr. Brockman. He was sitting behind a grey metal desk with a nameplate, and he motioned me to the empty chair.

"Great," I said, sitting down. "Can't believe this weather though. I mean compared to last year. Remember that?" But he'd only been in Alaska for a month, he told me.

"Still a Cheechako," he said and started to laugh. "But anyway, here's how it works. You show me your receipts, and then I'll ask you a few questions and take it from there. You OK with that?" And I told him I was. "So what do you have?"

I had all the receipts in a blue and gold folder I had bought at the bookstore up at the school. "Ever been up there?" I asked. I pointed to the folder's cover. U of A? And when he told me he hadn't, like I knew he would, I told him I thought that he should go. "Pretty interesting place, with the ski trails, the museum, and the stairway that goes to the ceiling."

"You like bush pilots?" I asked him. "You know. They fly into the *bush*? The paintings of them in Rasmussen - they're really something to see."

The more I talked, asked questions, and saw him shaking his head, the more I knew he didn't know shit. Which was fine by me. So I really laid it on with the Fairbanks flood of 1967, and what it was like before all these Outsiders came into the state. "No offense, of course," I said. And he told me none taken. Then he gave a little nervous laugh and asked if he could see the papers.

"Now I only brought the ones from last year," I said. "Is that OK?" When he told me it was, I took 'em from the folder, at least a couple inches' worth.

"Now the oldest one I have is from... " But before I said another word, he said that was fine. "But you've gotta see the rent receipts," I told him. "And the car insurance papers, and what about the... ?" But he said it was all settled. Then he wrote himself a note.

"So where you living now?" he asked. And when I told him Olnes, just outside of Fox, he got this real strange look. He told me that he'd heard of it, and even when I was sure that he hadn't, it turned out that he had.

I went back to the waiting room. Kingpen went to talk with Mr. Brockman and when he came out, he wasn't sure exactly how it had gone.

"I don't know," Kingpen said.

And after that he didn't want to talk about it, so we just kept walking. *Walking, walking, walking.* And that was when we finally saw it on the front page of the *Miner* in a newspaper sales case. Fifty cents to get it out, but of course we didn't have it. So we went to the truck and found some quarters on the floor.

I wish you could have seen it, when we finally got it in our hands. It was a front page spread, showing Kingpen and our cabin. "Living in the Bush," the title said. It told all about the candles on the chandelier, hauling water from the spring, and cooking on the woodstove.

"Look," Kingpen said. There were photographs of Kingpen playing pool and pointing to the outhouse. "This is really something, isn't it?" he asked.

But like a lot of things back then, it turned out it was more.

Think the strangest thing, I thought.

And then five days later, when he was shaking like a leaf, he asked, "Suppose I get the *larger* envelope? Will it be perjury or fraud?"

On and on, until we got up to the waiting room and the secretary handed me my little card. "Now Mr. Kingpen, Mr. Brockman wants to see you in his office."

And I thought that Mr. Kingpen was gonna puke right there, except it turned out that he didn't. Instead he got this nervous look, started shuffling off, and was gone for fifteen minutes. And the thing that I kept thinking was that maybe it was *BOTH* - perjury *AND* fraud.

But it turned out that it wasn't. Kingpen got his card. Mr. Brockman said that he had seen the article in the *Miner*, Kingpen told me.

And that with all the liars he had met, Mr. Brockman said that it would really mean a lot, just to shake the hand of a real Alaskan.

Man to man.

Chapter 36

It was the end of March, and somewhere along the way I had met this guy up at the University who knew a lot about chemistry. Marty Goldman. One day I had gone into his dorm room and I heard this little explosion down by my foot. "Pretty wild, huh'?" he said, and then he explained how he mixed up this ammonia with some other stuff. When it dries into a powder and you put pressure on it . . ."

"It *explodes*," I said.

But Marty said, "No, it *implodes*." But anyway, he told me how to mix it up and handed me some of the stuff. Then I took it to the cabin. And I wish you could have seen it...

Kingpen came into the cabin with the duffel bag of laundry that he'd done in town. He threw it on the upper bed of the bunk bed - and *BOOM!*

"Geez. Did you hear *that*?" Kingpen asked me. But I told him I hadn't. "You didn't hear *THAT*?" And I told him no again.

And then it only kept on getting better.

He walked across the room and almost everywhere he walked... *boom, BOOM,* or *Ka-BOOM,* depending on how much of the stuff I'd mixed together. And then think the strangest thing, there was a knock on the back door. "Anybody home?"

"Mr. Jackovitch," Kingpen told me. "The guy who owns the cabin." Then Mr. Jackovitch asked if he could talk with us for a minute.

"Didn't want to do it guys, but I've gotta raise the rent. At least a couple hundred, with things booming like they are. Lottsa people looking for a place to rent." Then he sat down on this chair and it sounded like he farted. Only *louder*. "What the *FUCK*?" he yelled.

It was funny in a way, because I knew exactly where I'd put the powder. I could walk anywhere I wanted, and you'd never hear a sound. And then I started giving Kingpen hints, until he finally started catching on. But Jackovitch never did.

"Now how long's *this* been going on?" he asked. We told him just about a month.

"Funny thing is, it doesn't happen in the front room," I said. And it really started getting crazy after that.

There was a pickaxe on the wall. Mr. Jackovitch took it down and started pushing on the floor. And every time he hit a little pile, you'd hear it. *BOOM. BOO BOOM!*

"Holy *shit!*" he yelled. And from the look on his face, you could see that he was getting scared. "Maybe I should *insulate* myself," he said.

I found a pair of gloves. Big pink latex gloves I had brought home from the dish room. "Try these," I said. Then we found a pair of fishing waders Pinto had, that Mr. Jackovitch thought were great. So he put them on, too.

"Now maybe if I get a picture," Kingpen said, "we can tell just what they are. The explosions, I mean."

So Kingpen got his camera and kneeled down to take the picture. And the funny thing was, every time Kingpen asked him, "Ready?" Mr. Jackovitch told him, "Aim the camera down. Why do you keep aiming up at me?" And I swear to God, I kept trying not to laugh, until I thought that I was gonna throw up.

Mr. Jackovitch left after an hour and told us he'd come back, except he never did. Not for a while. I think he was afraid.

"Think he'll still increase the rent?" Kingpen asked.

"Just think the strangest thing," I said. And then of course the way it all turned out, it turned out to be *more*.

We didn't get out of the Hall, but in a way, it didn't really matter. We knew we would that spring.

"Let's just focus on our lives," Kingpen used to say.

So that was what we did. Focused on our lives, did odd jobs to get by, and kept on meeting people as we went along.

There was this guy who lived about a quarter mile away. We met him on his snowmobile and even though I think he was from Rhode Island, he thought he was an Indian. He called himself Coldwater. He had a long ponytail and was always looking at the sky, saying things like, "Good Day to Die," or talking about spiritual circles. And I remember him telling me that I should *always* look for signs. He was a pretty interesting guy, really.

He lived about a quarter mile away, and his place was pretty neat. It was a small log cabin, like a lot of 'em I guess, but the stuff inside was kind of different. I saw it when I went inside to see him once. And then it turned out that I went in there another time, too.

He had a red, black and white wool blanket hanging on the wall, a dream catcher hanging from the ceiling, and some eagle feathers tied together with a strip of rawhide. There were moccasins and different furs. Strips of salmon and moose meat. He even had these sewing needles that he had made from different animal bones.

"Look at these," he said. He showed me some traps that he had made for mink and ermine and snowshoe rabbits. And sitting near the wall, on a homemade wooden table, were some little dried-up buttons. Tan and greenish buttons, about the size of a quarter. And when I asked him what they were, he told me peyote.

"Ever tried it?" he asked. And when I told him I hadn't, he told me I should.

"It'll tell you *who* and *what* you oughta be," he said.

———————

That's what it was like that spring. We hardly had a dollar; but overall, things were pretty good. We were focusing on our lives and meeting interesting people.

Pinto finally came back, after being in the woods. We sat around for days and nights after that, listening to his stories, shooting pool, and trying to get out of the Hall.

Then it all turned to shit.

I had seen Mr. Jackovitch one night up at the Hilltop Café. He told me he was coming out to the cabin the next night with a friend of his, to check it out.

"You should have seen it," we told Pinto. "Jackovitch pushing the pickaxe, wearing your waders and the pink rubber gloves." And we showed him the photographs.

"But now what are we gonna do?" Kingpen asked. "He'll be here in two hours."

Then Pinto asked, "Could you do it all again?"

"What?"

"The powder," he said. "You still have the stuff?"

I told him I did, then we spent the next hour or so mixing it together and spreading it around in little clumps. Only this time they were *bigger* clumps and we put 'em in *both* rooms. By the time Jackovitch showed up, everything was ready.

He had this little guy with him who never gave his name, but he looked just like an Albert. And the thing that I remember is, they came in the door, and Jackovitch lifted his hands up toward the ceiling and asked him, "Feel it? Can you *feel* it?"

And the other guy said, "Yeah. I can feel it."

So I guess because they *felt* it, they decided not to walk around the room. Instead, Jackovitch picked up a boot that was lying on the ground and told him, "Watch *this*."

And I swear to God - out of all the places that he could have thrown that boot, he never could have hit a pile of powder bigger than the one he hit. You could feel it shake the window. *BA-OOM!*

"See?" Jackovitch asked him. "What did I tell you?"

And his buddy nodded and told him, *"Shit!"*

"It's *everywhere*," I said.

And Kingpen told him, "Everywhere. Except it's not out in the outhouse."

"Not yet," I said. And then we started walking all around, where we knew that we had put it. Boom, boom, *BOOM!*.

"Watch this," I said. And then just for effect, I rolled a couple balls across the pool table, where I knew there wasn't any powder. Then when both guys looked relieved, I sent the eight ball rolling toward the bottom left hand corner pocket, where I knew there *was* some, and – *Ka-BOOM!* The ball flew right off the table.

"My God!" the guy who looked like Albert told him.

And Jackovitch said, "Yeah, I know. I told you, didn't I?"

They didn't stay long after that, but they said they'd be back. "Electrical," I heard the small guy tell him as they tiptoed past. "I think that it's *electrical*." But Jackovitch just shook his head.

We put some music on after they left. We had a cassette player hooked up to Pinto's truck battery, that we kept high up on a shelf inside the cabin, to keep it warm.

"How about Christopher Robin?" Pinto asked, which was our favorite, by Kenny Loggins. So Kingpen stood on his toes, reached way up, connected the wires, and you know how it starts - *KA-RIST-AH-FER-RAH-BIN.*

God, it was perfect. Little ice flakes were pinging on the windows. Pinto threw another log in the stove, we got in our bags, the part *"CHASE ALL THE CLOUDS GOING BY"* was playing, and like I said, it was absolutely perfect.

And then Kingpen told me, "Night. I'll see you in the morning."

But I don't think he ever did.

Like most mornings back then, I was crawling down deep in the bag. *I can do it,* I thought, except I knew that I couldn't. I was too damn cold.

Then Kingpen said he'd take care of the thing I knew I couldn't do. "I'll get it going," he said. And what he meant was the fire in the stove. "I'll get it."

I heard him climb down from above me, and a few seconds later I heard Kenny Loggins start singing.

Then I heard a loud thud, and Kingpen screamed. I mean *really* screamed. By the time I got out of my bag, Pinto was there.

"Battery tipped over," he yelled. A cap had come off and all of this acid was dripping down Kingpen's face. "Get the Igloo!" Pinto screamed. And what he meant was the 5-gallon Igloo water jug that was over by the door.

It turned out that the water was frozen, but I got it anyway. Pinto tore Kingpen's shirt off. Then he made a fist, lifted it over his head and brought it down inside the Igloo. *Ca-rack!* And then he pounded it again with his bloody hand.

"*Hold* him!" Pinto yelled. We managed to get Kingpen's hands down from his face, and I got him into a bear hug from the back. "Now *hold* him," Pinto said again. "Hold him *tight*." So I did.

Pinto lifted the Igloo and brought the water down. Three or four gallons washed across Kingpen's face.

"Oh my God!" Kingpen screamed.

We hooked the battery up to the truck, but as hard as we tried, we couldn't get it going.

"Battery's all fucked," Pinto said.

That was when we heard it. An 18-wheeler coming from the north. I ran into the road and started waving like crazy - and the driver brought it to a halt. *Pssshhtt.*

"Gotta help!" I yelled. And then the three of us got Kingpen up into the cab, and the guy took him into town.

It wasn't going well. Kingpen had been in the hospital for a week and would be losing his sight. Not all at once, the doctors had told him, but he would over time.

"I guess I should be going home," he told me. "My mother sent me some money." But the way it turned out, he didn't go like you would think.

"I want to see it one more time," he told me. "The mountains, the rivers, the lakes."

"All one million of 'em?" I asked, and we both tried to laugh.

"I'm gonna hitchhike out," he said. "Go down to Haines, get on a ferry, and see Southeast. Maybe I'll fly out of Seattle. I don't know exactly what I'm gonna do." But I think he did. Because when I went back the next day to see him, they told me he was gone.

We only stayed in the cabin for another week after that. Pinto went off into the woods and I might have been there in Olnes for another couple days. Until they started on the cabin, tearing it up.

I was driving back to Nine Mile one day in Pinto's truck, when I saw them standing there in front. Mr. Jackovitch and his buddy and a couple other guys. Each of them had a pickaxe or a shovel. That's what I remember. I parked and then I heard him.

"Tear it up. Just tear it *UP*," Jackovitch told his buddies. And they started on the floor. I wish you could have seen them ripping up the boards and looking all around the windows. Every now and then, you'd hear *Boo-Boom*, from a clump of powder we had missed.

"Hear it? *Hear* it?" And on and on it went. But not for me. I got my stuff out of the cabin, climbed back behind the wheel, and drove away.

I went up to the school after that and starting living out of Pinto's truck. It was late April, and I was buying pieces of toast with all kinds of jelly up at the Student Center, just to stay alive. Five cents a slice. I guess it was supposed to be like a little side dish or something, but it was the main meal for me. I'd cook the bread up in a little toaster and then I'd pile the jelly on. Grape or peach, or sometimes marmalade. I'd slap the toast together and have the greatest jelly sandwich anybody could have made. A couple inches thick for just a couple nickels. Then I'd go on down to Stevens and watch television for a while. I'd head off to the Union in the afternoon, then maybe go up to Rasmussen.

I had a gallon can of corned beef hash I'd gotten someplace. I kept it in the truck. Every night, I'd eat some from the can, except I had to chip away at it first, because it was so damn cold. In fact, it was frozen. So I'd get my spoon from Jimmy Franklin's and bring it down inside the can - *chip, chip, chip* - and then I'd put the little pieces in my mouth to melt.

Just heat it up, I thought.

And then I'd crawl down in the bag and I'd shiver and I'd shake and then I'd crawl on down some more.

God, it was cold.

I started watching Westerns a lot that spring. Every afternoon. They'd have these marathons on the TV up in the dorm, with Roy Rogers and Trigger, and Daniel Boone. The Big Valley and Bat Masterson. All the Westerns you ever could imagine. Even ones I'd never heard of like *Range Rider*, *Sheriff of Cochise* and *Trackdown*.

But the one I liked the best, with Lil' Joe and Hoss, was *Bonanza*, with the Ponderosa and Hop Sing. And the very best part of the very best show was always the beginning. *Just start it up,* I thought, when I knew that it was coming on. But the last time I thought that I was gonna see it, it turned out that I didn't.

The guitar began to twang, the map of Nevada started to burn, and then I started smelling smoke. *Wow,* I thought. I started smelling smoke and then the fire starting come out. All around the screen. But even then, they kept on coming. *Dent, deh deh, dent, deh deh, dent, deh deh, dent, dent dent dent.* All four of 'em. They rode up on their horses and then suddenly, they were gone. Just like that.

They replaced the TV about a week after that. Tube burned out, I'd heard. But I had lost interest by then and figured I would focus on getting a job. Anything, as long as it gave me time to check in at the Hall. And then finally I saw it. An ad that guaranteed you could work your own hours.

It didn't say exactly what it was, but the place was uptown at 12th Street and Cushman. When I got there I knew I had $3.27, so I figured I would have to take the job, no matter what it was. I walked up a set of stairs that was connected to the building, but still outside. When I got up to the top, I knocked on the door and went in. Everywhere I looked, I saw different colored streamers and lots of balloons. And all these teenage girls were talking into phones. All around the room.

A bell went off. "We have another three sales," a man announced. A girl stood up and waved, and then she went and moved a marker on the wall. "Three hundred eighty *seven!*" the man yelled out, and the girls all clapped.

They were selling coupon books. Over $5,000 worth of coupons for 15 bucks. The way it all worked, Mr. Barry said, was you called the number on the list and then you read this speech.

"We pay you five bucks an hour, plus 50 cents a book," he said. "You'll be surprised how fast it all adds up." And as if to make his point, the bell went off.

He handed me one paper with the speech and another with a list of phone numbers.

"Just pick a number," he said. "And give it a try. Don't worry if they don't buy one - it's just your first call."

So I gave it a try. I really did. I dialed the numbers and hoped no one was home. And when they answered, I pretended they hadn't.

"Not home," I said, and hung up.

"Well try *this* one," he said. And he pointed to another number.

But I needed to practice. That's what I told him.

"Hold on for a minute," I said. I started reading the speech. "*Hello. How are you today?*" And then it said "PAUSE." Until they *told you*, I guess. "*My name is _____,*" I read. And I guess that was where you told them your name. I thought of the mental health clinic back east and the paper that I'd signed, and the guy upstairs. *Maybe he'd buy one,* I thought.

"Are you ready, Mr. Fitch?"

I told him that I would be. "In a minute," I said.

The bell went off and the clapping began. And I knew that I could sell 'em by the hundreds, if he'd only let me read my own speech. But that wasn't gonna happen. He wanted to, he said, but it was policy that everybody's had to be the same.

"We need to be consistent. I'm sorry, Mr. Fitch."

I told him I was too, but I really didn't think that I could do it. And the thing that I remember as I walked away, was that they suddenly hit four hundred. The bell went off, and a couple of the girls got up and waved. I heard it as I was going out.

"Four hundred!" Mr. Barry yelled. "*Four hundred* coupon booklets sold! Give yourselves a hand."

I spent the weekend feeling pretty down and thought that I was getting sick. The food that I'd been eating wasn't all that good for one thing. I'd been eating corn beef hash in the dark one night, like I always had, except it wasn't quite as frozen and it tasted kind of furry. And when I saw it in the morning I wished that I hadn't. All this whitish-green mold was on top, so I threw the can away. I was gonna get a toasted jelly sandwich, but I was kind of sick of them, too, so I got a Bit-O-Honey.

And I've gotta tell you. If you're ever really hungry, but don't have a lot of money, you really oughta try it. It comes in seven pieces and you can spread 'em out throughout the day. *Chewin', chewin', chewin'*. Every couple hours. *Just chew 'em up*, I thought. And even then, they stick up in your teeth, so when you think that you're all finished, it turns out that you're not. *Kind of like the burp-up foods*. That's what I remember thinking.

I had a little over three bucks left. Nine Bit-O-Honeys, if I bought 'em up at school where they were 10 cents less than they were at the stores. I think my mind was getting kind of fuzzy, 'cause it all began to mix together - Bit-O-Honeys, living in the weeds, A list, B list and all the balloons. *Just keep on doing what you're doing Fitch*, I thought. And then I kept on walking to the Union Hall for the C list call.

I thought the sign would be on the door, but it wasn't. So I went on in and sat down by the Coke machine with another couple guys.

"Fucking *bullshit*," one of 'em mumbled. I nodded my head and asked him if he had ever been to The Armpit of the World. "Fucking *BULLSHIT*," he said again.

My head began to wobble and bobble and bobble and wobble. I remember I started *hearing* it first. This *Blup, Blup, Blup* down deep inside. And then I started *tasting* it. And even though I never saw exactly what it was, I pictured it was greenish black and figured it was bile. Even though I didn't know exactly what *that* was. *Blup, Blup, Blup*. This bitter stuff would come up in my throat and then I'd send it down again. Up and down and up and down.

There must have been a hundred people there. I couldn't really tell 'cause I was sitting on the floor. But the thing that I was thinking was that every one of 'em, every single one, had a story. Pipeline stories, stories of Alaska, but then there were the other stories. More personal.

The screen went up and I pictured he would call out, "Who's not wearing any underwear?" And a giant magnet in the ceiling would pull up their hands. "Who got laid last night? This morning? In just the past few hours? Which ones of you were on a telephone today in a room full of girls, surrounded by balloons?"

I raised my hand and the crowd let out a cheer. "All *right*," somebody yelled. And then I felt it coming up. *Blup, Blup, Blup.* I could taste it in my mouth.

The place went crazy after that. There were people slappin' each other and giving high fives. A couple people started crying, and this lady started thanking Jesus.

I asked the guy beside me what was going on, but he didn't know. So I got up on my feet and asked this other guy who was clapping.

"Forty-seven fucking calls!" he shouted. "Forty-seven!"

Then the screen went down and stayed down for a couple minutes.

When it went back up, the dispatch guy blew into the microphone and told the crowd to settle down. "Now this is how it's gonna work," he told us. "I've got twenty jobs for Prudhoe Bay. Seven twelves. Seventeen for Atigun. Seven tens. Six jobs up at Cold Foot. Seven tens. And five at Five Mile. Seven tens. All general laborers. We'll start at thirty-five hundred. Anybody lower? Come up front."

You could have heard a pin drop as we looked around, but nobody moved. "Thirty-seven hundred. Anybody have a *lower* number?" the dispatcher called out. One guy went up to the window.

You could hear the murmur start at the front window and build, until it got back to the Coke machine where I was.

"Thirty-six fourteen," someone said. "He's number thirty-six fourteen. Signed for Prudhoe Bay." And you figured that he would, with seven twelves.

"Anybody else below thirty-seven hundred? Thirty-seven fifty?" Two guys went up. And that's the way it went. Up and up, and up.

And even though I never heard a person ask, I knew exactly what a lot of them were thinking. "What about the people with the numbers in between the people going to the window? Where the hell are they?"

But it really didn't matter. "Forty-nine fifty. Anybody lower?"

I walked up to the window and remembered what we'd said so many times...

"All we've gotta do is *be* there."

And there I was.

There were three jobs left. Two at Atigun and one at Five Mile. I took that one. The one at Five Mile. Don't ask me why. I didn't even know where it was at the time. And I think, looking back, maybe it reminded me of walking. *Walking, walking, walking.* I don't know.

The guy handed me a dispatch slip and then a bigger piece of paper with instructions. "Now follow these directions," he said. And I told him that I would.

I walked over to the map right after that. The one on the wall with the Pipeline camps. Happy Valley. Coldfoot. And there it was. Five miles north of the Yukon River. Five miles farther north than I'd ever been before.

It was the first week in June. I spent the rest of the day hanging out up at the University. I took a shower and then I washed some clothes. I wrote a letter to my folks. And I put a note to Pinto, with the key to his truck, into our post office box.

That night, I tried to get some sleep down in the weeds. Except it turned out that I couldn't. I was afraid I'd be late. *All you've gotta do is be there*, I kept thinking. But then I thought that I wouldn't.

So at quarter after four the next morning, I started walking, until I made it to the bus stop down on 2nd Avenue. And at seven-thirty sharp, a little white Alyeska shuttle bus picked up about a dozen of us, and drove us to Fort Wainwright for our physicals.

We went in past the guardhouse, but it was kind of like the weigh stations we had seen. No guards. Then we kept on driving past some guys in army uniforms, poking sticks at some trash on the ground.

"Bet those fuckers aren't making $20 a day," somebody said.

We drove a little farther, to the other side of the Fort, the side that Alyeska was leasing. And the people who were there, in regular clothes, were doing the exact same thing. Except they were making hundreds. A couple hundred bucks a day to pick up trash.

"And all the lobster they can eat," somebody said.

The bus pulled up to a small, two-story building, where we had our physicals that day. And for all the people going through, you would have thought it would have been more like those Army physicals you hear about. "You're fine. You're fine." All up and down the line. But it really wasn't like that. Not at all.

They put me in a box at first, with some earplugs on my head. "Now *listen*, and when you hear the *BEEP, BEEP, BEEP*, push the button in." And I told them I was good at that. But it was harder than you'd think. Sometimes they were loud, but then other times they weren't.

And I know a couples times I pushed the button and I heard *PSSCHttt, PSSCHttt, PSSCHttt*, up inside my head. So then I'd push it in again. And there never was a pattern. That's what I remember thinking.

They checked my vision to see if I was colorblind. And then they told me, "Here, read across the chart." They examined both my eyes for farsightedness, nearsightedness, and maybe in-between. I don't know. E F P. Next line – d m r a z l. And then they stuck me with a needle and drew out some blood. A doctor told me to *cough, cough, cough*. And then he stuck his finger up my butt. And that was just the start.

They took an x-ray of my lungs and checked my heart. They tapped me on my knee and my leg went up. On and on and on. And then just when I knew they couldn't check me anymore, they handed me a checklist.

Psychological Profile.

And that was seven pages long with questions like, "Do you show anger quickly? Do you like to travel? If you could live with seven million people or just seven, which would you prefer? Favorite vegetable? Potatoes or carrots? And how about . . . ?" *Blah. Blah. Blah.* On and on and on.

And I guess with everything that day, I bet it cost a thousand bucks, at least. And that was just for me.

A doctor came in at the end and the only thing he asked was, "Think you're predisposed to being by yourself?"

And I told him that I thought about a lot of stuff, but I'd never thought of that.

"But I am an only child," I said. "So maybe."

"Now how about the test results?" I asked.

I thought he'd say, "We'll mail 'em," but he didn't. "Well, all in all, you passed with flying colors." That was what he said.

And then he looked down at my chart and told me, "The only thing that you have wrong with you is flat feet."

Chapter 37

My plane was flying out at seven-thirty-five that night. So by six o'clock, I was there. At the airport. I finished up some Bit-O-Honeys and walked around looking at the animals.

Then I went to talk with the lady at the counter next to Northwest, where they sold tickets for the flights that went up into the ghost towns. "Still here?" I asked.

She smiled and I could tell that she remembered me. "We'll be here until next March," she said. "And then we're shutting down for sure. Going up to work?"

I nodded my head and gave her a big smile.

Then at quarter after seven it all started up. "Five Mile, Happy Valley, Atigun, and Prudhoe Bay," they announced.

And even though I'd heard it all before, this time it was different...

This time, they were calling out to me. *Jesse Fitch.*

I walked to the lady at the Alyeska counter and handed her my ticket. Then with thirteen other guys and one woman, I walked across the tarmac - and up the porta-steps into the plane.

We can never know beforehand the adventures that we'll have, I thought.

And then the engines started up. We headed down the runway, and in another couple seconds, we lifted off. Lifted off, and as we circled to the right, I saw the University and some houses down below.

But after that, it all turned into trees. Millions of these scrubby, half-ass trees. *Wilderness*, I thought. And then I saw about a half a dozen lakes, of the million that Kingpen had told me were there.

Just push the button in, I thought.

In another couple minutes, we flew above these giant boulders that looked like giant breasts. Dozens of 'em, pushing up out of the ground. And then we heard it on the intercom. *Bong. Bong. Bong.*

"Going down," the pilot said. And I wish you could have seen it. The mighty Yukon. Eight o'clock at night and it was gleaming in the sun. And then we landed.

We were sitting on a makeshift gravel pad in the middle of the woods. About a half a dozen of us got off and walked over to a van that said *Alyeska*.

"I'll take you to the camp," the driver said. We went about a quarter mile, to maybe fifty-five or sixty trailers that were all hooked together. ATCO trailers. All connected.

And once you were inside, you never would have known that was what they were. *Kind of like a labyrinth.* That's what I remember thinking. Long straight hallways with rooms off to the sides, where people stayed. Then there was a rec room with Ping-Pong tables and a TV, plus a weight room and a movie room.

I checked in with the guy in charge of the rooms, and he told me, "Your roommate works at night, so there shouldn't be a problem. Room 14D," he said. And what that meant was the hallway and the letter for the room. Then he handed me my key.

The thing that I remember was that I was gonna eat. Before I'd see my room, I'd go down to the chow hall and eat and eat and eat. Just fill me up. That's what I remember thinking. *Fill me up Chinese style.*

And I wish you could have seen it. I found a set of double doors and I thought back to the pool at the University and the pulp mill in Ketchikan, because that's what it was like. You smelled it first. Turkey, ham and roast beef sandwiches and homemade apple pies. Buckets full of ice cream. All kinds of fruit - and none of it was black. Six or seven soups. Ravioli and lasagna.

I must have sat there for an hour after that. Thinking of the rain and the sun and the snow and the flowers. *Just one more piece of chocolate cake*, I thought. And then I ate one more.

After I'd finished, I went to my room and my roommate was there. Gary Carune. We shook hands and he said that he was heading off to work.

"And how about that Dining Hall?" That's what I remember asking. "Have you ever seen so much good food?" But it turned out I was wrong.

Because after I described it, Gary told me, "Jesse, You weren't even *in* the Dining Hall. You were in the fuckin' *snack* room."

———————

The way it worked was, there were maybe fifteen or twenty of these Bluebird school buses that were yellow. They were parked by the camp, along with a couple dozen pickups that were mostly Chevy 1500s or Ford 150s. You had a number that they gave you for the bus, and that's the one you had to be on by six o'clock each morning.

Before I started to the bus, I went down to the Dining Hall. I guess you think I had a lot to eat but I didn't. *Still full from the food I'd eaten in the snack room.* That's what I remember thinking. But I could have had an awful lot to eat, if I had wanted to.

The way they had put it together, they must have cut the sides out of the trailers and then connected them together. Because the space was open like a cafeteria, but kind of like a restaurant. The Dining Hall was nothing fancy, but not as plain as you would think. There were posters of Jamaica and Bermuda, I guess so you could picture you were there, when you weren't.

But anyway, you'd go and get in line, and anything and everything you'd ever think that you could eat for breakfast was there. Even *more.*

A couple chefs were standing back behind the counter and you'd hear the guys in line call out to 'em, "Gimme a steak well done and a three-minute omelet." "How about some tortillas?" "Where's that egg benedict?" On and on. And then one guy asked for a dill feta scramble and the chef handed him a plate full of something, so I guess that was it.

There were biscuits and gravy, different kinds of grits, sausage links, sausage patties, hot cakes, waffles, and every kind of juice you could imagine. Everything was there.

Then after you were finished, you went into the snack room and packed yourself a lunch. *Just put it in the bag,* I thought.

I got a roast beef sandwich, a can of lemonade, an apple, a couple candy bars, and a piece of lemon pie. And I really thought I had myself a lunch. That's what I remember thinking.

I passed a clock on the wall at ten of six, went outside, found my bus, and got on board. A few minutes later, it must have been six sharp, we started rolling out. *Rolling, rolling, rolling.*

Heading south on the Haul Road. Every once in a while, we would cross on over to the Pipeline pad and drop some workers off. Then back to the Haul Road and drive some more.

It must have been five miles, we made it down to the Yukon and another worker asked me, "First time up here?" And I told him that it wasn't. Not to the Yukon, but it was to work.

He told me how they'd used a giant pump and ice machine the year before to make an ice bridge, when they hadn't had the real bridge. "Shoulda seen it," he said. And I told him I wished I had.

We passed a guardhouse on the south side of the bridge, to keep the regular people from driving farther north. It wasn't that much farther, when we passed a tipi that was set up in the muskeg over on our right.

"Molly's," the same guy told me. And I nodded my head.

Guys were getting dropped off all along the way, at places where they worked. And then finally there was me.

"Know where you're working?" the Teamster asked. And I had to tell him no. So then I sat there on the bus by myself with the driver, and the thing that I kept thinking was that now I would get fired.

Don't know where your job is? I screamed inside my head. *Couldn't figure out your bus stop? You're FIRED!*

But the Teamster told me that it happened all the time. "Look. Here's a magazine," he said. And he handed me some porn from a box that was there. "Just relax," he said. "They'll come and get you."

"But what about some gloves?" *I didn't have the money...*

"There. In the bag," he said. He pointed to a large plastic bag filled with new leather gloves.

"How about a doughnut?" he asked me. "You like crullers? How about an apple crumb? You like Boston Crème?"

"What I'd really like is to work," I said. "I've been living in the weeds and chipping frozen corned beef hash."

But he didn't give a damn. All he said was, "Fuggit." Then he pulled his baseball cap down across his face and went to sleep.

A guy came in a pickup after that. "General foreman," he said. "Name's Mike Garrett." He told me where to stand outside the bus, and to look for a red pickup that might be around. "A Belly Dump will be here and some pickup trucks are coming by. Now if you see a *blue* pickup, that's trouble. So wave your hands." But I never saw it, so I never did.

Looking back, I think it was a beer run. Pickups would drive up from Fairbanks, loaded full of beer. Then they'd put it into the Belly Dump to take to the camp. Hundreds of cases.

Like us heading back from Haines, I thought, without the *Psshtt! Psshtt! Psshtt!*

Then Mike came back and told me, "You see those three guys? You can work with them and be the foreman." He drove away.

By the time that I joined them, it was time for lunch. Not that they'd been working, because the Union said they needed *four* guys for that. That's what they told me later. But anyway, I got my roast beef sandwich out and one guy asked me, "Zat all ya got?"

Zat all I got? I thought. And I remember thinking that I really did have something, until I saw the steak and lamb chops that he had.

"Want a lobster tail?" another guy asked. "I've got too many."

"Just getting out of the Hall?" the first guy asked. And I nodded my head. "Snack room's for *shit*," he said. "Take a bag with you to supper." He began to start a fire on a grill made of rebar that had been welded together.

We really hit it after that. All up and down the pad, giant drilling rigs were drilling into the tundra. Schramms and Texomas. We were on a Taurus, and the guy up in the cab, the operator, wound it up - *Ba-ROOM!*

This long, foot-wide bit would start to go around, and then head down into the permafrost. The reason we were drilling was to put long metal pipes into the ground. Maybe forty-five or fifty feet deep, set about a dozen feet apart. Vertical support members – VSMs for short. You can see 'em if you ever see a picture of the Line.

After they were in the ground, a slurry truck would pour cement-like stuff down and all around the VSMs. It would all freeze down there in the permafrost. Eventually, this metal crossbeam would connect the VSMs and the 48-inch Pipeline would sit on that. Eventually. But for now, we were working on the VSMs, and almost every person had a different job.

There was the guy who gave directions with his fingers and hands to the operator of our rig. Up or down. Left or right. A little of *this*. A lot of *that*.

Then the operator revved it up, just like I said. *Ba-ROOM!* And then he'd send the drill bit down into the ground.

The slurry guy was there, and a Teamster, to drive the slurry truck. There was an archeologist we named The Squeeze, who felt the mud and permafrost for artifacts. Then another guy would put a level on the VSM, just as it was getting frozen in the ground, to make sure it was straight.

But the thing that I remember is it all came down to me. Couldn't start without a *fourth* guy on a shovel, somebody said. So even though they'd gotten there at six o'clock that morning, it wasn't until two o'clock that we started.

Ba-ROOM! Ba-ROOM! The giant bit started toward the ground. The way that it worked was that after it had come up, the operator spun it and the mud flew off. Except when it didn't. Then one of us would tap it with his shovel till the mud came off. *BA-ROOM!* Up, down. Up, down. And then every dozen times or so, one of us would tap it.

"You can be the foreman." That's what Mike had said. But I knew I didn't want to be a prick, so every ten or fifteen minutes, when a guy would tap the drill bit with his shovel, I would say, "Nice job," or "That was great."

But then I started thinking, *Come on, Fitch.*

I thought of Churchill and Patton. Rosa Parks. *Lead from the front. Just set an example.*

So every couple times, even when it didn't need it, I would tap it. Down, up. Tap. Clink. Clink. Clink. *Just hit it with my shovel.* That's what I remember thinking.

I must have done that at least a dozen times when one guy asked, "What the fuck?" And the way it all turned out, there was a misunderstanding.

He pointed to the one guy in the circle. "He's ONE. We go in order. This guy's TWO. I'm THREE, and you're *FOUR*. Got it? You're the *FOUR*man."

Things went pretty well after that. We put down thirteen holes that day. Even though the four of us with shovels weren't that busy. The mud turned into permafrost after six or seven feet, and it would spin right off the bit. *Zeeee.* And even though the guy we called The Squeeze had been there all day squeezing, he never found a thing.

We shut down at six and got back on the bus. I grabbed a couple of bear claws to take to my seat and we started to the camp. Driving back to where we'd come from, picking up workers all along the way.

And then just before the bridge I saw her, standing on the tundra.

"Hey Molly!" somebody on the bus yelled.

And you could have seen her too if you had been there. Standing next to her tipi, with the full-sized, naked picture of herself.

"Hey Molly, we'll see you tonight!" another couple guys yelled. And Molly smiled and waved.

———————

There was a raffle in the Dining Hall that night. Ten bucks for a chance to spend all night with Manuela, who was a culinary worker. There were card games and people selling whiskey and jewelry. One guy was cutting hair for twenty bucks a head, in a closet by the rec room.

I walked to the Dining Hall and got some lobsters, prawns, and giant king crab legs. I put 'em in a couple brown paper lunch bags, and then I headed down to watch TV.

Just settle down and get into the groove. That's what I remember thinking. *Just get into the groove.*

I watched a tape of a newscast from a couple days before, but a dog kept barking. Every time the lady talked, *bark, bark, bark.* Anybody watching it could tell it was an audio over-ride. Except it turned out that they couldn't.

"Oh, shit," I said. And I started laughing, until I reminded me of Beamish.

"What's so fucking funny?" one guy asked. I really tried to tell him, but I don't think he got it. I don't think any of the guys listening to the lady bark did. So I got up and left.

In a way, it was relaxing. Every day was the same. *Brngg. Brngg. Brngg.*

Push the button in.

Then I'd go down to the Dining Hall with my bags of prawns and lobster tails, or maybe prime rib, and tell the guy, "Ham and cheddar cheese." And he knew I meant an omelet, because I got it every day. I'd get some sausage on the side. Big links. And a giant glass of orange juice.

I'd head out to the bus, maybe eat a cruller or a bear claw while we drove out to the site, and then we'd hit it. The Taurus would start up, *Ba-ROOM! ROOM. ROOM. ROOM!* The bit would go down, and every fourth time the mud was still there when it came back up. *Clink, Clink.* I'd tap it with my shovel.

You are really something, Fitch, I thought.

And the best part was that I could think all day. That's what I remember thinking.

"Want a double-stuffed?" one guy asked at lunch. And what he meant was a pork chop, but I told him I was full of steak.

Then we'd drill, drill, drill for the rest of the day. *Clink, Clink, Clink.*

I'd head back to the camp, eat more prawns and lobster, and then take in a movie or watch TV. After all of that, I'd head back to my room, and just about that time, I'd meet Gary heading off to work.

"See ya, Fitch", he'd say.

Then I'd lay down on my bed. And the thing about the bed was that it was absolutely perfect every single night. Because a culinary worker had made it. Folded down the sheet, pulled the blanket back, and then they always fluffed the pillow. That's what I remember. Always fluffed the pillow. *Absolutely perfect.*

I'd lie there on the bed thinking for a while, till I thought to pull the alarm clock button out. I'd get underneath the blanket, and start drifting off to sleep. *Drifting, drifting, drifting.*

Then sometime later on, I'd hear it in my sleep. *Brnggg, Brnggg, Brnggg.*

And it all would start again.

It was the first of July and depending on the hours, I was making thirteen, fourteen hundred bucks a week.

But the big news was the Fourth. *Triple time.*

And according to the rumors, we wouldn't even have to work.

There was gonna be a picnic and a raft race down the mighty Yukon. "All kinda shit," somebody said. And the way it all turned out, it was *sort* of like that. Except it started on the *third*.

They laid off a bunch of 798ers that day, ones who were counting on the triple time. Welders from Texas, Oklahoma and Louisiana. And the thing about those guys was you didn't mess with them.

They tore up the camp that night, for one thing. I stayed in my room, but could hear the bottles crashing outside. There were all kinds of fights and then the smoke detectors started up... *Wee, wee, weeeeeeeeee!*

All night long.

But as bad as that was, the worst part was the next day. We went out to work and all of the equipment had been welded together. Backhoes and loaders, dozers and graders. Like this giant pileup of equipment, except you couldn't really move one piece anywhere without moving the other.

And the way it all turned out, whoever had said it had been right. We didn't work on the Fourth, even though I think we were supposed to. We spent the day on the bus. "How about another jelly-filled?" somebody asked and the Teamster passed one back.

There was a cookout for us that night. Right on the Yukon. Hot dogs and hamburgers, barbecued ribs. All cooking on grills that were really barrels cut in half and welded onto metal legs. All the salads you could eat. Potato and Jell-O, marshmallow and fruit. Then they had this coleslaw that was really good. Chopped real fine and not too thick.

And in the middle of the whole celebration, there was a giant bonfire going, with a group of guys nearby, playing their guitars and singing country music.

But the thing that was the best was the raft race. There were thirteen entries, and almost all of 'em looked like you would think. Pieces of plywood nailed onto four-by-fours, with barrels underneath.

But then just before the start, a flatbed truck came across the bridge, and I wish you could have seen it.

"Holy *shit*," somebody said. It was carrying a huge raft, kind of like a houseboat. The driver backed it down the bank and the guys who'd built it took it off, with a forklift that was by the bridge.

It must have taken them at least a month to put it all together. And I could tell that they had used at least twenty-five or thirty thousand dollars' worth of wood and stuff to build it.

But anyway, the rafts were in the water. The idea was to race 'em down the river for a mile, and then a guy in a powerboat would go along to bring the rafters back, because there wasn't any road. *Just float 'em down and powerboat 'em back up.* That's what I remember thinking.

Then all at once, this guy pulled out a .357 and *Ka-BOOM!* I mean that thing *blasted* off.

"GO!" he yelled. But the way it all worked out, not one raft made it. They all started breaking up, almost right away.

Then not too far off, you heard, *BLUB, BLUB, BLUB.* It was coming from the houseboat. "Forklift put a hole in it," one guy standing near the shore said. You could see it going down. *BLUB, BLUB, BLUB.*

But the funniest thing was when one guy grabbed a box of cellophane. He got some giant trash bags and started wrapping up his

424

arms and legs and feet. And then he got an empty barrel, made sure it was plugged, and started wading out. And I think he would have won, if they'd given him a chance.

"Over *here*," somebody yelled. "We're going down."

"No. *Here*," another group would scream. And the powerboat would race around.

It wasn't till he'd saved them all that he noticed the one man. The plastic-covered guy, floating farther down the river on his barrel.

"Let him go. He'll *win!*" we all began to scream. But the guy in the powerboat went down and got him anyway.

The days pretty much turned into weeks. I'd gained fifteen or twenty pounds, so I started working out in the gym and cut back on the pies. I was making all kinds of money and had this great looking tan from being out in the sun. It was almost too good.

Then I thought of something Pinto used to say. "When you're eating that prime rib, this is what you'll miss," he used to tell me. And then he'd point to a pile of spaghetti that Kingpen had made, when we lived back in Olnes. "This is what you'll remember."

And he was right in a way, but I wasn't sure why. Maybe you missed what you had, or had what you missed up in your head, or . . .

"Your turn," one of the guys said, and I tapped the drill bit with my shovel.

A plane was flying out. Fifteen or twenty guys, heading to Fairbanks. We all stopped to watch until it was too far away.

"Fuggit," somebody said. "Four more days." And what he meant was until he'd put in his full nine weeks. Nine weeks on, and then you could take two weeks off, if you wanted. But I never did. You didn't have to, unless they thought that you were cracking up.

The thing that I kept thinking, like I said, was *keep it in the groove...*

Get up in the morning, after *Brnggg, Brngg, Brngg*. Then push the button in. Get my ham and cheddar cheese omelet, head on out to work, *CLINK, CLINK, CLINK*. Head back to the camp, eat some prawns and lobsters, then go back to my room. Pull the button out, lay down on my bed and put my head down on the fluffy pillow.

425

Then just when I had figured I really had a plan, a truck pulled up and a guy that I had never met gave each of us a pink slip. "Sorry guys," he said. And then he drove away.

We were drilling someplace north of Five Mile and all that we could figure was that the crews from Cold Foot, the next camp up, would be coming down to finish up the holes. So they wouldn't need us anymore. But anyway, I remember one guy was *really* upset.

"Now what? Now what?" he kept asking. The problem that he had was that he'd only been out of the Hall for forty-seven hours. "I can't move up to the B list," he said. "I'd need two hundred hours. Do I get my number back or do I go down to the bottom of the C list with over 18,000 names? Now what? Now what? I got really screwed."

And even though I never said it to his face, I thought it to myself. *Yeah, Chinese style.*

We took the bus back to the camp a little later on. I went to the office and picked up my last check. Then I went down to the Dining Hall and ate all that I could eat. *Just eat it up,* I thought. And I pictured toast and jelly and chipping corned beef. And just when I was thinking that I couldn't eat another thing, I got a piece of pie. Lemon meringue. With this homemade topping that they put on top.

I went into the snack room, got a couple of the lunch bags, then I went back to the Dining Hall and started toward the prawns.

Just fill 'em up, I thought. So I did.

I was flying out at seven forty-five that morning. I got my gear together, wrote a note to Gary, and turned my key in at the office. Then I went to find the van to take me to the plane. But the way it all turned out, they used a bus instead.

"Lotta people getting RIFFED," the driver told me. "Winter's coming. Gonna be a lotta layoffs." And I wondered who would drive *him* to the airport.

We heard, *BONG, BONG, BONG,* and then, "This is the Captain. Please fasten your seatbelts." But nobody did. And maybe a half an hour later, *BONG, BONG, BONG.* We started coming down.

We landed and I walked down the steps from the plane. And as I crossed the tarmac, I remember thinking back to Anchorage and Tok.

Now where you gonna go? I thought. Even when I knew that I was going to the terminal.

I caught a ride up to the University, climbed the wooden steps and went into the Student Center. Not that much had changed. People playing Ping-Pong and watching TV. Maybe not as many people, but the stuff was the same. Then I walked into the snack room and asked the guy how much it would cost for a half-dozen ketchup packets. But he waved me on. Then, with all of my other stuff, I took 'em to the ceiling. As usual, no one was there.

I sat on my chair, at the table at the top. Then I opened up a packet, put some ketchup on one of my prawns and ate it. But I was feeling kinda full from all the lobster tails and prime rib, so I quit right after that.

I got out all my checks and added them up. I remember thinking, *Over $16,000, Fitch. Who wouldda thought?* But the thing that was so funny was that I couldn't really spend it, because the banks were all closed.

And right about then, *"Attention puh-leez. Attention puh-leez. The Student Center will be closing in five minutes."*

So where you gonna go? But that was me thinking.

I was gonna go spend the night in a laundromat, but I never did. I walked on down to set up my tent in the Chena River weeds, except they weren't there. I guess the cold had killed them. And when I looked around it was kind of like the campground in Prince Rupert. There weren't even any campers.

Just pick a camping spot, I thought. So I did. Then I set up Kingpen's tent, crawled down deep in the bag with my ketchup and my prawns - and all I can remember is, I shook myself to sleep.

I packed up my stuff the next morning and started walking to the Union Hall. Kind of like a hobo, but with sixteen thousand bucks.

It was the middle of September and a lot of guys were there who had been laid off from up and down the Line. They were flying to Hawaii, or the British Virgin Islands. Flying *here*, flying *there*. Anywhere...

"Fuck this shit." You heard it all around.

"Got a pocket fulla money. I'm heading out."

"Unemployment, here I come."

427

The line was moving up. The way that it worked was, you gave the window guy your layoff slip and he figured out your hours. Over two hundred hours, you were placed on the bottom of the B list. If you'd worked over eight hundred, you made it to the A list.

"Twenty-one fourteen," he told me. "That's your number on the A list." And the way I had it figured, maybe they were right. Maybe I *should* go and see the world. *Go out and see it all.* That's what I remember thinking.

But then they started with the calls.

Two general laborers for Prudhoe Bay. Seven fourteens. One specialized job. Fiberglass man at Coldfoot. Seven twelves. And the more that I listened, the worse and worse it sounded.

"Haven't had a guy get off the B list for the last three weeks."

"Yeah. This is *it* for this year," somebody said. "Fuggit. I'm heading south. I'll come back in the spring when the jobs are picking up."

And on and on and on.

I stood there with my ketchup and my prawns, and all that I kept thinking was, *Where you gonna go? Where you gonna go?* And I thought about the lady in the bakery and the people standing there at Tok.

Maybe I could buy some land with my sixteen thousand bucks and sell a zillion square inches. Or fly on down to Vegas and just put it all on red. Yeah, that was it. *Put it all on red.* That's what I remember thinking. But then I heard it coming from the microphone...

"Anyone lower than *ten*?"

I went up to the window to get a closer look, and a guy was there with fourteen.

"Anyone lower than twenty?" the dispatcher called out. And the guy with fourteen took one of the jobs at Prudhoe Bay. The other Prudhoe Bay job went to twenty-seven.

One job left. And the thing about *that* job, the one at Coldfoot, was that it was *specialized*. Like a powder man or high rigger. They would go out of our Union, but they were different, in a way. More specialized.

"Fiberglass man," the guy called out. "You need to know your shit. Anyone lower than five hundred?"

But no one went up. "Six hundred? A thousand?" And this guy said he was nine eighty-three.

But the dispatch man started asking questions. "Now what about the mix?" he asked. "The catalyst and resin? You know how to do that? And the roving and the mat? How to layer 'em together?"

I guess it was too much, because the guy finally told him no. He really wasn't sure. So then it went to anybody lower than fourteen hundred, and I started walking to the door. Walking to the door with everybody else. And that was when I realized, stopped, and turned around.

"Eighteen hundred? Anyone?" That was when I started back to where I'd been. Walking to the window.

"Twenty-one hundred. Anyone lower? Twenty-two?"

And the way it all turned out, I told him I had worked at Bay State, a fiberglass repair yard just outside of Ball-tuh-more. "Mostly worked on boats," I said. "But some other stuff, too."

I told him I had been in charge of mixing all the catalysts and resins, and then we'd had to layer all the mats and rovings and make sure they were tight.

"Can't be too careful with that stuff," I told him. And he told me I was right.

He handed me the dispatch slip and I signed it. Then I walked out the door, and figured I would head up to Rasmussen.

"Fiberglass?" the librarian asked.

And I told her, "Yeah. Repair mostly."

And she knew right away. "Boat building," she said. That's where we found it. *Everything You've Ever Wanted to Know about Building a Fiberglass Boat,* by William Hendle.

I went to the bank after that. Cashed the last check I had gotten and then went down to Samson's Hardware. I bought a RefrigiWear suit and a pair of bunny boots. I threw away my backpack that was falling apart, bought a duffel bag, and started walking. And even with all the screwed up, goofy people living there that year, somehow I just knew...

Fitch, you've gotta be the only person walking here in Fairbanks, eating prawns out of a bag.

My plane flew out at seven forty-five that night. *BONG. BONG. BONG.*

We lifted into the air, and I turned another page in William Hendle's book. *Just mix the resin up,* I thought. It really didn't seem that hard. Just mix the resin up with catalyst and pour it on the mat. Then layer on the roving. Mat, roving, mat, roving, mat. And the guy who wrote it did a great job of having pictures in his book. Pictures, pictures, pictures. Pictures of the tools, and of people doing the work. And photographs of every kind of boat you ever could imagine.

But the thing about the book was that it started getting harder two-thirds through. More specialized. *BONG. BONG. BONG.*

We started heading down and that's when I realized, *First time north of the Arctic Circle, Fitch. First time.*

I made myself a peanut butter and jelly sandwich in the snack room, then I went back up the hall until I found it. C13. The guy who was there told me he was leaving the next morning.

"Only been here a month," he said.

I threw my gear in the closet, told him I was sorry, and then kept on reading. "Chapter 12: How to Build a Mold." And it really started getting kind of complicated after that.

The idea was, to fix or repair the damage that was there, you had to spray this silicone everywhere the damage was. Then you had to form some kind of mold over that, with the resin that you'd pour on the roving and the mat. After it had dried, you could lift it right off. Because of the silicone. That was Chapter 12. Chapter 13 told you how to finish the repair, except I never got to that part.

"Any chance you could turn that light off sometime soon?" my roommate asked. "It's one-thirty."

So I told him I was sorry and turned off the light.

"Really like to read, don't you?" he asked.

And I told him that I did.

Chapter 38

The thing about Coldfoot was that it used to be a town. Slate Creek. And from what I had read, thousands of miners had passed through in 1898, and then eventually most of them had moved on. But some of them were still there - in a cemetery down by the entrance to the camp. There were a couple dozen small stone crosses and headstones that had fallen over. I wanted to straighten them up but never did. Not for a long time.

There were maybe a hundred and fifty of us, living in eighteen or twenty trailers that had been welded together. *Cozy*. That's the word I would use to describe it. I loved living there. And it all started the next morning.

I was looking for Bus Fourteen, but it turned out to be a van, and then it only took me about a quarter mile. We went past the cemetery and down to the Haul Road. I thought that we were going to go left or right, but we went straight, on a smaller gravel road, until we drove into a clearing about the size of a football field, in the middle of the trees.

"Here you go," the Teamster said. "You get out here."

So I got out there - and I could hear it all around. This *SQUISH, SQUISH, SQUISH*. Because that's what it would do. Every time I walked. *SQUISH, SQUISH, SQUISH.* Listen if you ever get one. A RefrigiWear suit. And it really doesn't matter if they're new or not. Every time you walk... *SQUISH. SQUISH. SQUISH.*

"Hey Fitch!" A pickup truck was coming toward me and the guy was calling from his window. "Hey Fitch! Are you Fitch?"

And I told him I was.

"Worked with fiberglass before?"

And I told him I had.

"Jimmy Willers," he said. "General Foreman."

There were at least a couple dozen tents throughout the clearing. Big canvas tents with diesel heaters.

"This is where you'll work," Jimmy told me. I followed him inside the closest one, and saw six or seven guys sitting there.

"Break's over!" Jimmy yelled.

"Ever work on *transitions*?" he asked me.

"No, just boats."

"Well, the transitions are where the Pipeline goes into the ground. For caribou crossings," he said. "Sometimes the fiberglass shells get damaged. If they're not too bad, we repair 'em. Otherwise, they need to be replaced. And then there are the bumpers that get beat to shit. They go between the Pipeline and the VSMs."

"Vertical support members," I said.

And he told me, "Yeah."

But as nice as he was, I think the guy was tricky.

"Well how about you get started?" Jimmy said. And then of all the things he could have asked me, he said, "Fitch, what about a mold?" And then he pointed to this dented piece of crap and asked, "How about you fix it?"

And of all the things I've ever looked for in my life, I looked for that the most. *Can't find the damn silicone? Get outta here!* I heard up in my head. *You're fired!*

I looked and I looked and then finally I asked one of the guys, "Where you keep *it*?"

"Keep *what*?"

"The *silicone* spray," I said. "For the molds." And the way it all worked out, I thought that I was fired.

Jimmy told me, "Get into the truck." And I was sure that we were heading to the camp.

But then once we got inside, he shook my hand and told me, "Christ, Fitch, you really *do* know what you're doing."

The way that he explained it, I would go around and check everybody's work. Like quality control. 'Make sure they're doing it right."

And I told him that I would.

I loved that place. I really did. I had a room to myself and every morning I would tell the guy with the chef's hat, "Ham and cheddar cheese."

Then I'd walk on down the entrance road, past the cemetery. And the whole time I'd be thinking that even if I'd had a job up in a lighthouse, it never would have been as good as this. *Thinking, thinking, thinking.* That's what I remember thinking. And then I'd go into the clearing, and depending how I felt, I'd pick out a tent, start walking, and then think, *fuggit.* And I'd go the other way.

Just keep on walking, Fitch, I thought. And then I'd point to something when I got there. "Got enough of *this*? How about the

432

resin?" "Got enough of *that*? Catalyst?" And then I'd tell 'em, "Don't forget to smooth out the air holes in the mat." That was what I'd tell 'em.

But then I always ended on a good note. Like, "Thanks for all you're doing. Sure appreciate your work." But even then, for fifteen, sixteen hundred bucks a week, I knew it didn't matter what I told 'em. They didn't give a shit.

Now how about some soup? And every day I told myself that sounded great. And I'd walk up to the camp and have myself some hot soup, maybe steak or lasagna, and a couple pieces of cake or pie. And then I'd head down to the tents again.

Walking and thinking all these crazy things. And then I wondered why I thought of *them*. Like this guy I'd met in town who had worked in a book store. He'd told me every single night, this old man would come in and go to Section 180. Philosophy.

"And I wish you could have seen him, Fitch." That was what he'd said. "Real unkempt. Hair down to here. Totally disheveled. But even then, the thing that I kept thinking was why would he go *there*?"

"Where?"

"Section 180. Philosophy. So anyway, one night I finally met him. Introduced myself while he was reading Plato. But he wouldn't say a word. And do you know what, Fitch? I swear to God. As I was standing there, this piece of feces came right out of his pants. Right down by his shoe."

And I guess from how I looked, he could tell I was confused.

"Feces?" I asked.

"Shit, Fitch. *SHIT!*"

And that's when I remember that I finally got it, but in some ways I still didn't.

It was late September, and the snow that was coming down would stay until the spring. The snow was coming down and staying, the creeks were freezing up, and the lights were really getting good. I thought of the moon breaking into pieces and the time we sat up on the cache. I figured I would go outside the camp that night to watch 'em sway across the sky. But I never got the chance.

"Hey Fitch." It was Jimmy. The way he explained it, the operation that we had was going mobile. "We need to get out into the field," he told me. "We'll keep the tents, but I want you and another guy to make repairs out on the Line. He's been out there working for the last two weeks, but needs some help. I've never met him. His name is Mr. Pasquale. He works out of Dietrich, one camp up. He'll be the foreman."

And all that I could think of was *Clink, clink, clink, CLINK. Tap, tap, tap, TAP*.

"How many guys?" I asked.

"What?

"How many?"

"Just you and him," he told me. "That's *TWO*," he said. "I'll watch the guys in the tents."

And then I told him, "Just make sure you check the mats for bubbles."

I stayed up late that night, reading the book and looking at the pictures. The next morning, I met Jimmy with my gear, and together we starting driving north to look for Mr. Pasquale. *Driving, driving, driving*.

Along the way, I thought I heard him ask me, "Fitch, are you asleep or awake?" And I remember I told him I wasn't.

We were somewhere north of Coldfoot and somewhere south of Dietrich.

"Do the two of you have radios?" I asked, but Jimmy just ignored me.

"He should be working on the Line," he said. Which explained why we were driving on the Pipeline pad until we came up to a creek or gully, and then we'd go back to the Haul Road to get around it. And then we'd go back to the pad. Looking. Always *looking*.

We saw a lot of workers but none of them were Mr. Pasquale. "He should be working by *himself*," Jimmy said. "I think he's near here."

But it reminded me of the Chippewa Campground, because then we started south, then north, then south again. The only person that we ever saw *alone* was this kid sitting in a pickup over by the pipe.

"Maybe we should ask *him*," I said. And of course when we did, *that* was him. *Mr. Pasquale*.

"Well here's the plan," Jimmy told us. "You'll be working out of Dietrich. I'll send you the list of the stuff to fix. Bumpers mostly. But I'll send you the coordinates."

What he meant were the numbers, like mileposts, so we could find the problems out on the Line. "Now how about resin?" he asked Pasquale. "You got enough of that?"

"One full drum," Pasquale told him.

"And what about catalyst?"

"Good with that, too," Pasquale said. "And I've got mat and roving. Everything we'll need. We're good to go."

With that, Jimmy told him once more, "I'll send you the list. Check at the office tomorrow morning at Dietrich." Then he drove away.

Pasquale's truck reminded me of the Buick, except the smell was somehow different. More sharp and tangy, from the catalyst. And less sweet, without the dog food and beer.

It was a total fucking mess though. Like someone had mashed together the inside of their bedroom closet with the place where they worked, and then put it in their truck. Hammers and chisels and saws. A canteen and some little metal rollers to roll out the bubbles, and two or three sweaters and hats. Hairdryers. And everywhere you looked, cantaloupes and bananas, apples and pears.

"Like fruit?" I asked. And all of these oranges and most of them were black.

It must have been ten thirty or eleven, neither of us knew. Then I remembered.

"Hold on," I said. I got out and went to the bed of the truck where my duffel bag was. "Hold on," I said. But then when I checked it had frozen at nine forty-five.

"You bring any lunch?" he asked. And of course I'd forgotten from working near the camp, so we went up to Chandalar.

"We'll hit the repairs tomorrow," he said. "When we get the list." Then we started driving.

There weren't that many rules, but if you wanted to get paid, you had to be out of camp by six, and you couldn't come back until the end of your shift. Which is why we went to Chandalar, the next camp up from Dietrich.

"Ever been up there?" he asked. When I told him no, he said, "Try the bouillabaisse. It's pretty good."

And the way it all turned out, it was. We had bouillabaisse and lemon pie. Then I filled a paper bag with prawns, and got a little cup of cocktail sauce, and by that time we were ready to go home.

Just dip 'em in and head on home and get it all fluffed up, I thought, except it turned out we were early, or at least we *thought* we were. So we went back to the place where we'd met earlier that morning and went to sleep. And every now and then one of us would wake up.

"What time you think it is?" one of us would ask.

"Ugh?"

"What time?"

And then we'd wonder and we'd guess, until we saw some other pickups heading to the camp. Then we went on in.

I moved in with Pasquale that night. Room D14. And the thing about Pasquale was he was a pig. Not that I was all that neat, but he was pretty bad.

"Wanna listen to a tape?" he asked. And as hard as we looked through all his stuff, we never found the cassette. Or even the player.

"Might be in the truck," he said. And then he sat there on the bed, and almost every night, I swear to God, you could watch him fall asleep. We'd be sitting there talking, or even eating food, and then just like that, his eyes would start to close, and "Zzzzzzzz..."

I was sitting in the truck at five of six, when Pasquale came out. He told me the same thing that he'd said the day before. "Nothing. No list." Then he got in the truck and starting driving. Because like I said, you needed to get out.

"Where you wanna go?" he asked. "Someplace to sleep, or maybe for a ride? How about Atigun? Ever seen the Pass?" I shook my head, so we headed north.

There were sections of the Pipeline assigned to different contractors. I think there were five altogether, but I know that there were three from Fairbanks to Prudhoe Bay. We were with Associated Green.

There was another contractor from Chandalar up to someplace farther north, and then another one up near Prudhoe Bay. But anyway, the problem was, it could really hit the fan if you went into another contractor's section, where you weren't supposed to be.

"So we've gotta *watch* it," Pasquale said. And he kept on driving. Further up, into the Arctic.

Unless you've been there, it's different than you think. Up above the Arctic Circle, the trees don't all stop. They do get smaller, though. Really small and scrawny and all spread out. God, it was pretty, with maybe half a foot of snow and these mountains all around us. Kind of like Denali, in a way.

"How about you take some pictures? There's a camera there, somewhere," Pasquale said. *Somewhere.* So I looked and I looked, until I finally found it back behind the seat. Then I started taking pictures of the mountains and the trees. But I got some other good ones, too - of cantaloupes and bananas and even my alarm clock, sitting on the dash.

"How about we get some sleep?" Pasquale asked. So we crossed on over to the Pipeline pad and rested for a while before heading up to Chandalar for some bouillabaisse. Man, that stuff was good. Lobster, shrimp, mussels and clams.

Then we started driving and it wasn't that much farther to the mountains, so we kept on going. Up and up and up, through Atigun Pass.

"Brooks Range," Pasquale said. And I remember thinking that I wished Kingpen could have seen it. Mountains all around, and then we started down the other side. The North Slope. And I thought that we would keep on heading down, but instead we stopped about a half mile from the bottom.

Pasquale turned the truck around and told me, "Better head on back." So we started heading south.

Coming out of Chandalar after lunch, we had passed a crew that was putting on some insulation. Wrapping it around the pipe. And the neat thing was the machine that they had. A manipulator. That was what Pasquale called it. And of all the machines I've ever seen, *that* one was the best. For one thing, it was *huge*. The manipulating part. Maybe thirty-five feet long, it would take the insulated foam wrapped in shiny metal, and then bend it all around the pipe and fasten it.

"So, let's stop there," Pasquale said, "and take some pictures."

"Yeah, they'll be great," I said. "But, I've only got a couple shots left."

So we drove and we drove, Pasquale did, and then we saw 'em on the Pipeline pad. All these workers and a lot more equipment than when we'd seen them the first time. Cranes and cherry pickers and a couple more buses. We parked and got out of the truck - and the whole thing was amazing.

Just wrap it up, I thought. Because that's what it was like. Giant extenders on the machine would bend the metal together and then wrap it all around the pipe just right. We even got some pictures. But the guy who was in charge of the jobsite never did.

"Hey, who the hell are *you*?" he asked. "Put that camera down."

"Me?" Pasquale asked. And it reminded me of the cartoon where the guy is asking, *"Me? You mean me?"* and the other guys says, *"Yeah. You."*

"And who the hell are *you*?" he asked, looking at me.

"Allen Whizakoris," I said.

"You guys with Arctic Construction?" he asked. And I swear to God, I almost blurted out Aurora. *Music Machines*, I thought. And then my mind went to the next thing and I pictured lying on the table listening to songs from the jukebox. Stevie Nicks, Rod Stuart, Al Green. And then my mind went to the next thing.

"Associated Green," I mumbled.

"What the *fuck*? I'll get you fired," he started.

"Associated Green," Pasquale said again. "We just came up from Associated Green. We're working for the *News Miner*, going up and down the Line, taking photographs, and writing interesting stories about the men who make our country great. Now what's *this* called?" Pasquale asked him, pointing to the machine

"This?"

"Yeah. *This*," Pasquale said. "Are you the guy in charge?"

And when it turned out that he was, we started taking pictures - or at least he *thought* we did. A couple of the crew and then lots of him and the machine.

"Now that's B-R-U-M-B-L-E-M-A-N-N," he told me, as we drove away. "With two N's."

Then I remember we waved, and I pretended to write it down with this frozen pen I had found in the back of our truck.

It had been two weeks. At least. Fourteen times. Nothing. *No list.* Nothing. And it started getting boring. That's what I remember.

"Whaddya wanna do?" "Ugh?" "Whaddya wanna do?" "Ugh?" Every single day. "Ugh?" "Ugh?" "Ugh?"

But then we finally got it. Eighteen repairs on seven different bumpers up near Chandalar.

It was getting pretty cold. Close to zero. But we didn't care. We had our mat and our roving. "And how about the resin and the catalyst? Got enough of that?" one of us asked. And we both started laughing.

The best part was that we had my clock. Up there on the dashboard, so we didn't have to guess the time. "Three till six," I said. "We'd better go." And then we pulled out of the camp.

We might have gone an hour, then we found it. It wasn't very hard with the numbers from the list. Kind of like the Milepost.

"Bumper's dented in on the back," Pasquale said, looking at the list. And when we got out of the truck, we could see it. "Probably from forks," Pasquale said.

"Now how about the silicone?" I asked.

"The *what*?" he asked.

"The silicone," I said. "For the mold."

"What mold? This isn't moldy."

"No. For the . . ."

"Have you done a lot of this?" he asked.

And at first I told him yeah, but then I started feeling guilty and I told him no. "Not exactly. But I've checked a lot of other people's work," I said. And for all the work I'd checked, none was quite like his. That's what I remember.

We started with an orange. "Now stuff it in real tight. They're the best for forks," Mr. Pasquale said. And what he meant were the holes the forklifts left behind.

"Get it all down in there." He showed me with a chisel how to get it right. "Now maybe a banana, 'cause there was still a little space. Yeah. That's it," he said. "Shove it in."

We measured and cut the mat right after that, and then we used it as a template to cut out the rest. Mat, roving, mat, roving, mat. But to do it right, we put the resin on one layer at a time.

"Gimmee a cup," Pasquale said. And then I handed him one from down at my feet. He went around back to the big barrel of resin that was sitting in the bed of the truck.

439

Just open up the valve, I thought. And then he opened up the valve and it started coming out real slow, like molasses, except that it was gray.

"Here," he said. And then I poured a little catalyst in.

"Now stir it with this." He handed me a Popsicle stick and I whipped it all around in the cup. Then we went to the dent and laid the first patch down.

Just cover up the fruit. That's what I thought. And then we poured it on the mat and rolled it out real smooth. *Just get the bubbles out.* That's what we said.

And then we put on the roving, which was more heavy-duty than the mat. Pour the resin on, roll it out and on and on. Except then we had a problem.

"Generator's frozen," Pasquale said. And the thing was, we needed it to run the hair dryers that we used to heat the patches.

"Fuggit," Pasquale said. And the way it all worked out, we finished putting on the patches, but they never really dried until we heated 'em the next day. But all in all, I'd say they turned out pretty good.

It must have been November. Late November, getting really cold, and a lot of guys were getting laid off.

"Heard they closed down the tents," Pasquale said. But *we* kept working.

Every once in a while, they would send somebody out for us to train, but then we'd always ask 'em, "You really wanna work with this shit?"

And we'd point to the barrels and make up names like acetone and carbolic acid.

"Are you good at *math*?" Pasquale would ask. And of course they never were.

"You can blow yourself sky high, if you can't do the equations for the catalyst and resin. Remember Kyle?" he would ask. And I'd nod my head.

"This job is *specialized*," Pasquale always told 'em. And then they'd always say how they were gonna go back to the Hall and see if they could take another kind of job instead.

Things were going great. *Patch. Patch. Patch.* Then we'd go back to Dietrich, and even though it wasn't Coldfoot, it was a pretty decent place. And as I walked into the Dining Hall, I wondered how they ever put it all together, out there on the tundra. All the wires and resisters and the showers and the cafeteria.

"I'll take one steak, *rare*," I said. That was for Pasquale. I got one *well done* for me. The next day, we would heat 'em up for lunch with these hairdryers that we had in the truck. Heat 'em *up* and eat 'em *down*. Things were going great.

"Ever think of what you're gonna do after this?" Pasquale asked one day, when we were sitting in the truck.

I told him no. "How about you? Gonna start a fruit business?" And he started to laugh. "Think you'll stay here in Alaska?"

"I don't know," he said. He told me how he had hitchhiked up from Virginia a couple years ago, when he was just seventeen.

"Just had to see it," he said. He reached into his pocket and pulled out a photograph, all crinkled and bent. "Here."

And the thing that I remember was that he was crying. Pasquale was. Right there in the photograph. Tears coming down his cheeks. He was standing by the side of the road with his backpack on and his thumb stuck out. You could see it in the photograph.

"Started in Manassas," he said.

And when I asked him who had taken his picture, he looked off to a nearby mountain and told me his old girlfriend had.

We'd found a heated shed and kept the generator there at night. We'd start it in the morning and keep it running on the back of the truck near the barrel of resin. *Weh eGH eGH eGH.* But every now and then *eGh, egh, eh.* It would start running slower. Then it would stop.

"Is there *gas* in there?" one of us would ask.

"Yeah."

"What?"

"Yeah."

And the thing was, you had to get it running in about two minutes tops or it would freeze. "Pull it *harder!*"

Wee ee ee.

And then when you pulled the rope, maybe after six or seven times, you'd see a little smoke coming out from someplace. Maybe from the carburetor. I don't know.

It always started slow at first. *Wuh, wuh, weh.* But then it started getting faster and you knew that it was gonna make it. *Weh, Weh, eGH, eGH.*

"Got it!" one of us would yell. But by then, most of the hair dryers wouldn't work. I mean you heard the fan inside, but the air coming out was cold. Kind of like the Buick.

"Try *this* one. Or how about *this* one?" And sooner or later we could usually get one to work.

It was Thanksgiving. The only way I knew was because of all the decorations in the Mess Hall. Lots of cardboard turkeys with their wings spread out. And centerpieces on the tables with I think you call them horns, with little gourds and pumpkins coming out. Different shades of corn everywhere. Then there was the food. All the normal stuff. The lobsters and prime rib, but they also had some oyster stuffing that looked really good. Sweet potato pie and of course the turkey with the homemade cranberry sauce.

Eating, eating, eating. Everybody *eating*.

Then just as I sat down, all at once this guy a couple feet away started choking. *UGh, ugh, uh.* And the thing that I remember thinking was, *pound him on the back. Get the guy going.*

So I got up from my mashed potatoes and my gravy, which made me think back to the dish room, and *BOOM. BOO BOOM!*

He finally barfed it out, whatever it was. Right there on his food, in the middle of his plate.

And the thing that I remember is, he didn't miss a beat. He picked up his fork, stuck it in this stuff that he had just barfed out, and put it all back in. I thought that I was gonna puke and so I left.

And the way it all turned out that Thanksgiving night, *think the strangest thing*, I never even ate.

Chapter 39

Her name was Laura and she'd given him a cassette of herself singing, before he'd left Virginia. And he wanted me to hear it.

"She's really good," Pasquale said. But I didn't think she was. At least not for a while. "Listen," he told me, and I really tried. But the words were all garbled and she sounded kind of slow.

"She made it just for me," he said.

We listened for a minute, but by then even he knew it didn't sound quite right. *Pa hut yaur hade on mah pilloah.*

"Tape recorder's fucked," he said. "Maybe it's the batteries." Then he opened up the back of the recorder to check. "It'll just take a couple minutes," he said.

I went down to the bathroom and by the time that I got back, I swear to God, "*Zzzzzzz...* "

"Got news," Pasquale said. It was five of six and we were leaving the camp. "Jimmy just called. We're going up to Prudhoe and working down from there."

"You and Jimmy?"

"No. *Us,*" he said. "Jimmy's working on another project. We'll be living up at Pump One." That was the Pump Station at the top of the Line.

"Supposed to go to *sixteens,*" he said. "Now we're *really* gonna make some money."

So that was the plan. The very next morning we left the camp, just as it started to snow.

Anchorage or Fairbanks? I thought.

Then I started telling Pasquale about our trip from back east.

"The Embers?" he asked. I nodded. "Yeah. I've been there," he said.

We were up near Chandalar, heading north, and we had these special papers. "Think we'll see that prick Brumblemann again?" Pasquale asked.

And I told him if we did, it wouldn't matter. "Not with *these* papers." Because the thing about the papers was that we were free to go anywhere we wanted up and down the Line. Top clearance, Pasquale said. We kept on driving up into the Pass, then down the other side. We were heading to the Bay. And all the time, the snow was swirling all around and I bet that it was fifty-five below.

"Want another prawn?" I asked him.

And he told me, "Yeah. And how about some cocktail sauce?"

We had the Brooks Range to our back, and everything in front of us was flat. Like a desert, except that it was white. We would drive and drive and sometimes we could see the Pipeline on our left. This silver tube that would rise or dip into the ground, where they placed the crossings for the caribou.

"Ever seen a caribou?" he asked me and I told him that I had, down at McKinley.

"Ever been to Wonder Lake?" I asked him. And before he could answer, I told him he should go. "But you'll hear it in your head for weeks," I said. "Bzzzzzzzzz."

There was a long winding river on our right, except you couldn't see the water because of all the ice and snow. "Sagavanirktok," Pasquale said. And he reminded me of Kingpen, pointing out the rivers and the mountains on our trip.

"Want to stop at Pump Three?" one of us asked. "Get some lunch?" But the other person didn't answer. I think I might have been asleep. I don't know. But anyway, we kept on driving. Pasquale did.

"A hundred fifty-three miles to go," he said. And the way that he knew was from these markers on the pipe. Driving, driving. But it wasn't quite as fast as you would think.

We finally got there though, at nine o'clock that night. We came in near the airport at Deadhorse, made a left, and in another ten or fifteen minutes we were there.

Pump One. Prudhoe Bay.

We were the only people there who worked for Associated Green. Me and Pasquale.

"You sure that you're supposed to be here?" the guy at the window asked.

We showed him our clearance papers and he told us, "OK, but according to this you'll be working *outside* the camp. Everyone else living here is working either in or on the camp. Have you *seen* that back gate?"

We told him we hadn't.

"Well anyway, here are your room keys. B23."

We got some roast beef sandwiches in the snack room. Then I watched some TV in the rec room, while Pasquale went down to B23 with our stuff. And of all the shows that could have been on - you guessed it. *Dent, deh deh, dent, deh deh, dent, deh deh, dent, dent dent dent. Bonanza.*

And I thought for sure the TV was gonna catch fire and explode. But it didn't.

We'd forgotten to store the generator, so of course by the time we came out the next morning, it was frozen and covered in snow. But it really didn't matter.

"*Look*," Pasquale said. We had driven around to the back of Pump One, where the Pipeline came out of the ground. A gate was there. A big chain link gate that was connected to the metal fence that ran around the pump station. And on the other side, where there should have been a gravel pad that ran along the pipe, there was a field of snow, about seven feet high. Kind of like the road into Denali, when we tried to drive back there. Me and Kingpen and Beamish.

"Well at least the gate opens *toward* us," I said. But it really didn't matter.

"I'm gonna see if I can find an operator with a front-end loader to clear this out," Pasquale said. He opened the truck's door and went out into the cold. "I'll be back," he said. And then I think I went to sleep.

It must have been an hour later, I heard *Vroom, Vroom, Vroom.* When I looked out from in the truck, Pasquale was there.

"Help me pull this back!" he yelled. So I got out and we pulled the giant gate back, then the front-end loader went to work. *Vroom. Vroom. VROOM!*

"Told me he can only clear out a space big enough for the truck," Pasquale said. "He's not even supposed to work on the other side of the fence."

But for ten or fifteen minutes, he did. We watched him. He cleared out a little spot and then turned around and came back through the gate. *Vroom. Vroom. VROOM!*

"Thanks!" Pasquale yelled.

We got back in the truck. Pasquale drove us ten or fifteen feet and then he had to stop because of all the snow.

"Now whaddya wanna do?" I asked. But Pasquale didn't know, so we sat there for a while. *Sat and sat and sat.* It must have been around eleven or eleven-thirty.

"How about I turn the truck around?" he asked. "We'll have a better view."

And it couldn't have been worse. That's what I remember thinking.

"Imagine you woke up and this is what you saw," I said. "White on white on white. You'd think that you were blind."

"Yeah," Pasquale said. Then he turned the truck around.

"Well look at *that*. Just think. This is where it starts," Pasquale said. "Pump One."

In a way, he was right. But in another way, he wasn't. There were hundreds of these smaller lines that ran into the camp. Gathering lines, Pasquale called them. The way he explained it, they carried oil from the wells into the Pumping Station. From there it was pumped into the main line, that was buried underground until it came up right behind us.

Pump One. Maybe two football fields wide and of course there was the Pumping Station. But a lot of other stuff was there, too. ATCO trailers, warehouses, and maybe ten or fifteen Quonset huts where people worked inside. Front-end loaders going by. *Vroom. Vroom. VROOM!*

"I'm gonna go and get a hot lunch," Pasquale said. "You want anything? You want some prawns?"

"Yeah, and a couple of pork chops," I said. "Unless they're double-stuffed. Then just one."

"Gottchya," he said. I watched him walk through the cold, into the camp, and then I think I fell asleep again.

Pasquale called Jimmy that night. "They're sending somebody up from Associated Green," he said. "He's coming up the pad in a front-end loader."

"From where?" I asked. But Pasquale didn't know.

446

"I guess he's not *that* far away, or they would have sent him up the haul road. He could have started south on the pad from here. But anyway, he'll be working with us."

"Who?"

"The operator with the loader. Jimmy said there are lots of high spots on the pipe up here. Caribou crossings. He'll have to lift us up in the bucket."

"Who?"

"The operator with the loader. We're supposed to call him on the radio every couple hours."

And before I could ask, "Who?" again, he told me Charles Ivey. "His name is Charles Ivey."

———

God, it was cold. There was a little chart at the camp, and every morning I would pass it on my way to get my omelet. Fifty-eight below. Minus eighty-three with the wind chill.

But it wasn't all that bad. Like everything that was up there, our truck was running all the time so it wouldn't freeze. And we only had to walk maybe twenty-five feet to get to it every morning. Then, with the heater and our bunny boots and RefrigiWear suits, we were pretty warm.

"How long you think this truck's been running?" I asked.

"What?"

"The truck," I said. "How long has it been running? A year?"

"Nah. Only a couple of months," Pasquale said. And what I had forgotten was that it had been turned off in the summer.

But anyway, every single day was the same. Every day. We'd pull up to the gate and Pasquale would always say, "You wanna get the gate?"

Then I'd get out in the cold and the dark, and I'd lift the little hatch and pull back on the gate.

Just open up the gate. That's what I remember thinking. Sometimes I would stand there looking south and think, *Fitch, you are really something.* Just me, standing there alone, looking down the Line. And then I'd go and get inside the truck.

We'd been doing it for weeks. Every day Pasquale parked the truck inside the cleared out space, I set my alarm clock, and then we went to sleep. Three, two, one, *BRNGGG!*.

447

"Well, I guess I'll try again," Pasquale always said. And then he pushed the button in on the microphone and asked the same thing he had asked a hundred times before...

"Charles Ivey? Can you hear me? Over."

And like a hundred times before, dead air. *Nothing.*

So we'd sit there some more and some more. Then we started playing tic-tac-toe on the ceiling with some resin that we had in the truck.

Just fiberglass it up. That's what I remember thinking. Then Pasquale started painting a picture on the dashboard with some paint he had found.

"Watch *this*," I said.

There was a fire extinguisher right behind my seat. "Watch *THIS*."

I rolled my window down an inch, pushed the hose out, pulled the pin, and squeezed the trigger. *PSCCHHTTT...*

And I wish you could have seen it. The sun was coming up and I had it aimed right into the light.

"*Christ!*" Pasquale yelled.

And it really was amazing. The foam blasted out, and then it turned to rain. But only for a second - and then the whole thing turned to billions of these tiny frozen crystals that reflected all the light.

"That's *amazing*," Pasquale said.

We got out of the truck, and for ten or fifteen minutes it was kind of like the dish room. *PSCCHTTT, PSCCHTT, PSCHTTT.*

But God it was pretty. And then we heard it in the truck. *Ba-RINGGG!*

"Maybe we should turn the truck around," Pasquale said. "For better reception."

So we got back in the truck, parked *this* way and then *that* way.

And the thing that I kept thinking was what we must have looked like to anybody watching. Every day, we'd go out the back gate and drive up to the snow pile. Then we'd turn around and turn around. Blasting foam up into space.

"Just whaddya think they think we do?" I asked. "For a job, I mean."

"Who?"

"The workers," I said. "Inside the fence," Because I knew they must have seen us.

"Fuck if I know," Pasquale told me.

And then he pushed the button in. "Charles Ivey? Can you hear me? Over."

I figured that he didn't, because he never answered. *Kind of like praying.* That's what I remember thinking.

And then my mind went to the next thing, and I thought of that play. *Waiting for Godot.* These two guys, waiting, waiting, waiting. And I don't think Godot ever even got there.

"You think that he exists?" I asked.

"Yeah. I guess he does. Jimmy said to just keep trying."

But that wasn't what I meant.

"No. Not Ivey. *God*," I said. "We've never *seen* him. We never *hear* from him. Doesn't he have a responsibility to let us know he's *there*?"

"What?"

"Any of 'em. Jesus, Buddha… How are we supposed to *know*?"

And then I swear to God, *that very second*, we heard it on the radio…

"This is Charles Ivey. Over."

You could have heard a pin drop after that.

We looked at each other, then Pasquale pushed the button in. "Charles Ivey, this is Pasquale from Associated Green. What is your location? Over."

"I'm thirteen miles south of Pump One, coming up the pad on a front-end loader. Should be there later on tonight. Over."

"Sounds good," Pasquale said. "We'll meet you at the back gate at six o'clock tomorrow morning. Over and out."

We really got it all together after that. We got the generator going, and made sure the tools and the mat and roving were in the truck.

"We can get a bag of fruit in the morning," I said. "We can't forget *that*."

After putting in our sixteen hours, we went into the camp, had some lobster and prawns, and watched a movie. Then later on that night, we laid there in our beds, talking catalyst and resin, until we drifted off to sleep.

The pad that went along the Pipeline was ploughed out, but Ivey wasn't there.

"Look," Pasquale said. And when you looked down the Line, where the snow had been, you could see what Jimmy meant about the caribou crossings.

"Probably nine feet off the ground, Pasquale said. "I guess we'll just start working our way down, checking all the fiberglass. That bucket will come in handy."

"Where do you think he is?" I asked, but Pasquale didn't know. So that was when we started driving all around. Looking everywhere.

"How about you try him on the radio?" I asked. So Pasquale tried it, but that didn't work.

Anyway, we finally found him. He was over by one of the Quonset huts with his front-end loader. Except it wasn't running.

"Frozen," Ivey said. "I accidentally turned it off last night. Wasn't thinking."

So we told him it was no big deal and the three of us built a Visqueen tent around the oil pan and the engine. Pasquale found some two-by-fours, and it took a while because it was so cold. But we finally got it. We found a diesel space heater, just inside the Quonset hut. That was all we needed. We connected it to an extension cord, put it in the Visqueen tent, and flipped the button on. At first you heard it, then you saw it in the dark. *WHOOOOSH* - and then the fire started blasting out.

"Shouldn't take but an hour," Pasquale said. The two of us got back in the truck and I thought that Ivey would get up in his cab. But instead he just stood there. Then he went into the Visqueen tent. Then out again. In and out. In and out. Just trying to stay warm. That's what Pasquale said. But then all at once he got too hot.

"FIRE!" Ivey screamed.

He came running out of the tent and you could see the fire in the background. All around the bottom of the front part of the loader. "Fuel line came off!"

"Fire! Help!" he screamed. He was running toward the truck. "Gimmee the extinguisher!" he yelled.

I knew it wouldn't work, but I gave it to him anyway.

"Come on," Pasquale said.

Then we got out of the truck and stood there for a minute. And the thing that I remember is that Ivey that was so sure. He ran up to the fire, with the Visqueen melting all around. He leaned into the flames, aimed the hose, pulled the pin, and squeezed. *Pth* . . . Just a little bit of air. That's all that was left.

But Ivey didn't think so. "Fucker's frozen up," he yelled. And then he threw it on the ground.

"Come on," Pasquale said.

A lot of frozen blocks of snow were there, where a grader had passed by.

"Start *throwing* them!" Pasquale shouted.

I thought I couldn't lift them at first, but I did. Three-by-three-foot chunks. I lifted one over my head and it hardly weighed a thing. Not compressed like regular snow, because it was so cold. That's what Pasquale told me later.

But anyway, we got 'em to the loader, threw them toward the fire, and I wish you could have heard 'em. *Ca-Link. Ca-link.* Like giant champagne glasses toasting in the dark.

Except they didn't shatter, they bounced right off. And then a crowd began to gather.

"Who the hell built *THAT?*" one guy asked, pointing to the melted Visqueen and the burning two-by-fours. "You use *CARPENTERS?*

"What?"

"Who *built* that? he yelled. "And how about that *diesel heater?* That belongs to *US!*" he screamed.

And that's when I figured that the Quonset hut was theirs. The *carpenters'.*

"We're gonna card you for your time!" What that meant was filing a grievance. However long it had taken us to build the tent, *they* would get the time.

Yelling! Screaming!

All this going on, and then we started hearing *GONG, GONG, GONG!*

It came out of another Quonset hut, not too far away. The siren started up and right before it hit the peak, the fire truck was there.

"Fire truck," somebody said.

They sprayed a bunch of foam all over everything, but it really didn't matter.

"That's one fucked-up, toasty loader," one guy said.

But it was worse than that. From the bottom of the oil pan to the roof of the cab, it was totally burned up.

I thought we'd all get fired, but instead, they brought us up another loader on a flatbed the next morning. And man, that thing was nice.

There was a bucket on the front, and then on the back there was a giant platform that lowered and raised up. That was where we were gonna keep our generator and our hair dryers. Our mat and roving, and our fruit. But the best part was, it would lift us up to work.

Just lift me up and up. That's what I remember thinking.

And it all worked pretty well for a while, until the dryers started freezing, or burning up.

It was easily sixty-five below. You'd measure out the crack on the bumper, but you couldn't write it down. It was too damn cold. So you'd yell it to the window of the truck that was rolled down a half an inch.

"FOUR BY EIGHT INCHES!" And you could only hope he heard you.

And then the guy inside, me or Mr. P, would mix a little catalyst and resin in a plastic cup and pour it on the mat that we had cut. Just pour it on and on.

We had a little wooden board to work on. We'd add the roving and more mat, and then roving and more mat. Then just when you thought you had it right, you'd yell out through the half inch, "READY!"

And you really had to time it right, because the patch would start to set up from the heater in the truck.

But the worst of it was Ivey. He was almost always sound asleep.

So the guy up on the platform would yell or throw some snow at the window of the loader.

"Hey Ivey!" Splat. "Bring it down."

And then Pasquale or I would go and get the patch from the one of us who was in the truck, and then he'd step back on the platform.

Just lift me up. That's what I would think when it was me. *Lift me up and up.*

I'd get up by the pipe and lay the patch just right. I'd start to roll it out and turn the dryer on. Hot air, warm air, then freezing cold. Then *RATTLE, RATTLE, RATTLE.*

We must have started with at least a dozen of them. But by the end of the day, all of 'em were broken. Every single dryer. We tried taking them apart, and mixing different pieces together, but nothing ever worked. Just *RATTLE, RATTLE, RATTLE.*

It did seem kind of silly. Standing on the platform, heating the outdoors that was sixty-five below with little hair dryers. Especially when they didn't work.

"Fucking things are *useless!*" Pasquale said. "I'm gonna call Jimmy." So later on that night he did.

And the way it all worked out, we got more dryers. Small industrial ones that worked a lot better. At least for a while.

And then we got a bus and three more people.

Chapter 40

It was the middle of December, when Jimmy had come up to tell us they were putting on the push.

"They wanna get it *done*," he said. And "they" meant Alyeska. "They want to get it done and get the oil flowing."

So he was sending up a bus. Jimmy was. With a teamster to drive it, and a couple more workers.

"And dryers," Pasquale said. "We need *better* ones."

"And how about the catalyst and resin?" Jimmy asked. I told him we were good. "Got another crew working up from Atigun," Jimmy told us. Pasquale and I nodded our heads.

It was all going pretty well. The camp was filling up with welders and operators from Associated Green, and together we all started working down the Line.

Just open up the gate.

So every morning, right a six o'clock, I would pull the two sides back and wave everybody through. Just wave and wave and wave, until Pasquale yelled, "C'mon Fitch," and then I'd get inside the truck.

And then the morning came when we finally got our bus.

"Ever seen one this nice?" Pasquale asked.

I told him I hadn't. "At least not up here."

It really was nice. More of a shuttle really. And it only had nineteen thousand miles. No cracks on the glass. It was really something.

"Ever drive one?" Pasquale asked. Our Teamster, Darlene, told him no, but it didn't look that hard. And I bet you think I'm gonna tell you later that she smashed it all apart. But she didn't.

We started driving down the Line in the truck that morning, with Ivey right behind us in the loader and the other three in the bus. Darlene, Tony and a girl named Violet Gully. I swear to God.

"Ever heard a name like that?" Pasquale asked. And I told him that I hadn't.

Except for the cold, it was really pretty nice. We all met inside the bus and Pasquale told us, "I'm gonna *delegate*. We'll set up an assembly line. Fitch and I will work outside measuring the cracks.

Violet, you cut the mat and roving and the mat and roving and the mat. Tony, you mix the catalyst and resin and pour it on the patch. Violet, you bring it out, and then me and Fitch will roll it on. *Got it?*"

And then he told Tony how much of the catalyst to put in.

"And Ivey?" he added. "We really need you to stay awake. *Got it?*"

When you looked up and down the Line, everything was clicking. At least as far as you could see, with all the snow that was falling down and blowing all around.

The welders were there. Some cutting. Some welding. They were all working in heated tents that had been placed around the pipe.

"Look at that," Pasquale said. An x-ray truck was there. Quality control, taking x-rays of the welds. And if an x-ray didn't pass, a welder had to cut out the weld and then weld it back again. That's what Pasquale said.

But anyway, everything was moving. Moving along. And the main reason was that they had these fuel trucks that kept it all going. Or at least they were supposed to.

They would fill up at the camp. The tankers would. At Pump One. And then for two twelve-hour shifts, twenty-four hours, the drivers would go up and down the Line filling everything that moved, except for people.

"Fill it up with diesel?" the fuel truck driver asked.

And Darlene told him, "Yeah. Fill it up."

Except it turned out that the bus used *gas*.

And when it stopped and wouldn't start, I heard Pasquale ask her, "*Diesel?* Didn't you *KNOW* the fucking thing took *GAS?*"

And then I heard him, screaming in my head, *You're FIRED!* But instead they kept us. I remember that we waited three days for the mechanics to put another engine in.

We were winding down for Christmas and a lot of guys were heading out for R and R.

"Going anywhere?" Pasquale asked.

I told him, No, I was staying right there. "Gotta open up the gate," I said.

"Well just how long have you been here?"

"What?"

"Working here?" he asked.

I told him that I didn't know. "I'll just cut out all the mat and roving and the mat and roving and the mat, mix the catalyst and resin, pour it on, and I'll keep on rolling. *Just roll it on*," I said.

"But Jimmy thinks you oughta go," Pasquale said.

"What?"

"He thinks you need a break."

"What?"

"Take a break. Just for Christmas. Go and see your folks. I don't know."

And then I thought about it and figured maybe he was right. At least it couldn't hurt.

"You going out?" I asked.

"Yeah, I'm heading out tomorrow."

"What?"

"Going back to Virginia. Listen. I've thought about a lot of things," he said. "I'm giving this up. I'm gonna head back east and see if I can make it work with Laura. You'll be in charge the next couple days until you leave. Then Jimmy's gonna have the other three go on R and R, and come back after Christmas."

"Well what about the catalyst and resin?"

"What?"

"Do you think we have enough?"

And that was when he told me, "Fitch - you really need a break."

My plane flew out of Deadhorse at nine o'clock that morning. And all the way to Fairbanks, all we did was party.

"I wanna buy everybody on the plane three rounds," one guy yelled. "Except that asshole *there*." And he pointed to this man who you *knew* he couldn't stand.

The thing about the people on the plane was, a *lot* of us were there. Not like when they'd fly us up to Five Mile on these *small* planes. Oh no. There were at least a hundred of us now. *At least.*

And all of us got three rounds, except for *THAT* guy. We bought our own drinks after that. And all around you heard, "I'm finally gonna get some ass."

"Gonna get that *Poo* Tang," one guy yelled.

And I felt kind of bad for the stewardess, but I don't think she cared. *Probably heard it all before.* That's what I remember

456

thinking. And the way these guys were talking, they weren't waiting till they got back to their wives in Texas and Louisiana. They were figuring on getting it on 2nd street. "Rosie's!" one guy roared. And another couple guys let out a cheer.

We touched down at ten-o-five and by quarter after, I was walking around with my duffel bag. And everywhere I looked, there were people standing around. Hundreds of people - and of course the animals were there behind their glass. People, people, people, going nowhere - but hoping that before too long, they'd be up *there*, flying in the air.

But unless you had a ticket, you weren't going *ANY* where. That's what I remember. Because I was *there*. December 22nd.

Standing in line. And when I got up to the counter, that was what she told me. "You're not going *ANY* where, Mr. Fitch. At least not on Northwest. Not until Dec. 26th."

So I got a round-trip ticket leaving then, and coming back on the 29th. All these checks inside my pocket, and then I finally found some money left from the check I had cashed to buy my winter gear.

"Four hundred eighty dollars and twenty-one cents," she said. So I handed her five hundreds and then I stuck it all back in. The round-trip ticket and all the checks and extra money that I had. The spoon from Jimmy Franklin's.

Just stuff it all back in, I thought.

Then I started walking. *SWISH. SWISH. SWISH.* Gonna hitchhike up to school and buy myself a jelly sandwich. Maybe grape or marmalade. And then a Bit-O-Honey. And after that I'll climb up all the stairs, and I'll sit there at the top and watch it all go by. People playing Ping-Pong or walking all along. *I'll chew it up a seventh at a time.* That's what I remember thinking. Just chew and chew and chew, and when I thought that I was finished, it would be there in my teeth, so I'd take my tongue. . .

"HEY *FITCH*!"

And then, I'd eat some burp-up food. Like an orange or a tangerine. That would *really* keep me going. Burp it up and chew it up and work it with my tongue. *You are really something ....*

"FITCH! HEY *FITCH*!" And when I finally turned around and looked, there he was. *Pinto.* I swear to God.

"Hey Fitch! Where ya going?" And like a lotta times back then, I told him that I didn't know, but I thought that I might go and get a jelly sandwich.

457

"Jesus. *LOOK* at you," he said. "Where's your tennis shoes?" And then we started laughing.

He was taking flying lessons, Pinto was, from a guy named Charlie.

"We met him up at the University. Remember?" Pinto asked me. "Maybe twenty-five years old, kinda short, with a wispy little beard?"

"Did he have a dog?"

"What?"

"A dog? Did Charlie have a dog?"

"I don't think so," Pinto told me. So I told him that I thought I didn't know the guy.

"Well anyway, we go out every Wednesday in his Cessna. Been up a half a dozen times. Just went out this morning. I hope to get my license," Pinto said.

And the thing about Pinto was, nothing that he ever did surprised me. *Nothing.* Because he always had *something* going on.

"You flying out?" he asked.

I told him that I'd finally gotten out from the Union Hall and was flying back for Christmas. Back east. Except I couldn't get a ticket. "Not until the 26th," I said. "So I'm flying back then, and coming back here the 29th."

And one hour later, we were ice fishing. Me and Pinto. Because that's what it was like.

We bought a couple dozen eggs and drove out to a small frozen lake just past Ester.

"Here, you start choppin'," Pinto told me, "while I get the stuff together."

So I started with this axe, *CHOP, CHOP, CHOP.* Went six or seven inches down and in another foot I hit the water.

"Here," Pinto said. "Peel these." And he handed me the eggs he had boiled in a metal bucket, on a fire he had going. "Now throw the eggshells in the hole," he said.

The way that he explained it, they reflected the light and the fish would go *there*, to the bottom of the hole. And I wish you could have seen it.

We had three or four lines with weights and lures that he had made. They were all tied to sticks that we laid across the hole. And we hadn't been there ten minutes. "One's on yours, or check on that one there," one of us would say. And then we'd give a pull.

But it was harder than you'd think. The arctic char weren't so hard to catch, but the rainbow trout were. They could really fight. And God, they were pretty. Different shades of blues and greens and pinks. Kind of like the Northern Lights squirming on the ice.

"We'll keep a dozen of 'em," Pinto said. He cut off their heads and fileted them right there, then threw 'em in the bucket that was sitting on the ice.

We got the fire going, even better than before. *Roaring*. So at forty-five below or whatever it was, we started feeling warmer. "Here," Pinto said. And he handed me this flint fire starter. "You keep it, you might need it. I've got another one in the truck."

We set the fish in between some woven braches Pinto had put together. We held 'em up above the fire just right. And of all the fish I've ever eaten, they sure were the best. Man, they were good. And we ate 'em right there, where we were standing on the ice.

I stayed with Pinto after that, until the 26th, when I flew out. He was living in a trapper's cabin, which wasn't very big, but at least it was warm. Kind of like a log shack that had been thrown together, with a wood-burning stove and a couple of windows. Pinto had his thirty-ought-six, his snow shoes, and some other stuff.

"Ever read this?" he asked.

He handed me a book about a guy named Albert Johnson. *The Mad Trapper of Rat River*. And it really was amazing.

"Can you *imagine*, being chased on foot by all these Mounties, for hundreds of miles, in the middle of winter? The guy made it through blizzards and went over a mountain that was 7,000 feet high. During a *whiteout*," Pinto said. "And he killed his food by hand. So the sound of a gunshot wouldn't give him away. You oughta read it," he said.

I read about Albert Johnson, chopped wood, and hauled water from a nearby spring. Then sometimes, I'd help Pinto skin the mink and marten he brought in from his trap line. Just being around trees again was a little overwhelming. But all in all, it was a pretty good transition.

And anything could happen. Like I said, there was always something going on.

"Shhhh… " one of us said one night. And it wasn't like the trip with Kingpen and Beamish when you'd *think* something was there. This time you *knew* it.

459

I was sure it was a bear, but Pinto didn't think so. "Not unless his den was flooded out," he told me. "They should be hibernating now. Grab the .44," Pinto whispered. The Ruger Magnum was right there, holstered and hanging on the wall.

Pinto lifted up the thirty-ought-six. "I've got the windows covered," he told me. "You take the door."

And I know if whatever it had been had tried to get inside, it never would have gotten very far. *Just pull the hammer back,* I thought. Then I heard a click, and *Ka-BOOM!* I swear to God, I blew off half the fucking door.

"HOLY *SHIT*!" Pinto yelled.

And the funny thing was, when we went outside, nothing was there. That's what I remember seeing. *Nothing.*

It was Christmas morning and the best part was, you didn't have the feelings you get when you're all rushed. *Hurry here* - and then we're going *there. Hurry, hurry, hurry. And don't forget Aunt Sarah's present.*

"I love this," I said. And then I went and got some water from the spring and put more wood on the fire.

"I've gotta go out on the trap line," Pinto said, "so you can come with me on the snow machine, stay here, or I can drive you into town. Whatever you want."

The way I had it figured, I would stay with the transition. See the buildings and the cars and all the decorations. *Heading back to normal.* That's what I remember thinking.

So a couple hours later, there I was. Standing at the corner of Cushman and 2nd Avenue. I dropped a quarter in the slot and dialed the number.

Beep. Beep. Beep. Like a front-end loader, only going backwards. *Beep, beep, beep.* "We're sorry, but all circuits are busy. Puh-Leez try your call again later." For two and a half hours.

And then finally when I got through, I thought they wouldn't be there, but they were.

"Well, Merry, Merry. Will you accept the charges?"

"Of course we will," my mother said. And then I told her I'd be back there Monday morning.

"But what about *today*?" she asked. "Are you building that Pipeline?"

"No, I'm staying with a friend who's here in Fairbanks. We're living in a little house, except a little smaller."

"Sounds nice," she said. And I told her that it had been, until I blew off half the door.

"Well, we'll see you soon. I love you," she said.

"Love you, too."

"...*You, too,*" my echo said.

Then for all the crazy things that were drifting through my head, I knew what I was gonna do.

Shoes, boots, pieces of rope.

Chestnuts, I thought. Pass out chestnuts roasting on an open fire.

There was a little place like Lindey's Grocery store, except more oriental, with exotic kinds of foods. And maybe the owners were Buddhists or Hindus, because the place wasn't closed on Christmas. But anyway, they had everything that you never even heard of. Fried crickets and rooster balls. A million kinds of noodles. Quail eggs and mocha ice cream. And there above it all, on the highest shelf, was a five-pound bag of Ariano Farm chestnuts.

I got three large cans of Sterno and some matches and a pan. And then I found a bag of plastic cups and headed to the front.

"Find everything you need?" the cashier asked. I told her I had, and then I paid her and headed back to Cushman, singing all the way.

"CHES-nuts roasting on an O-pen fire..." *SWOOSH. SWOOSH. SWOOSH.*

There was a trash container at the corner. I set the cans of Sterno down and found a little metal stand inside the bin. It didn't take that long, maybe two minutes.

I had everything set up. Everything was perfect. And you probably think something screwed up, but it didn't. I wasn't even cold. I'd just pour 'em in the pan and then I'd put 'em right above the burning can of Sterno and stir 'em with my Jimmy Franklin's spoon.

Stir 'em up, I thought. The steam would seep out and the shells would start to crack. Then that's when I would put about a dozen of 'em in a cup and shout, "CHES NUTS! Get your hot roasted CHES NUTS!"

And there weren't that many people, but the ones who walked by and got 'em, really seemed to like them. And I never charged a cent.

I spent a couple hours doing that. Giving away these plastic cups of hot roasted chestnuts. And then Pinto came to get me, helped me clean everything up, and we started home.

"Any luck?" I asked. And he said he'd gotten a marten.

"But except for that, sixteen traps of nothing."

And I remember riding home wondering and thinking how it all fit together. *One little marten, just hopping along on a popular trail or the one less travelled. 'Oh, there's a little something good to eat.' SLAM! Then what?*

And then these people walking, walking, walking all along, chewing on these chestnuts that they never would have had if *I* hadn't been there. And what about the lady at the bakery? And the people standing there at Tok? Everybody's *someplace*. Doing *something*.

But why was it *THIS*? Or why was it *THAT*? And then I started thinking I was I was getting too focused on *THIS and THAT*. *THIS* and *THAT*. *Just think of something different.* That's what I remember thinking. Except I couldn't.

"Holy cow! Look!" Pinto said. He pointed up ahead through the windshield and the Northern Lights were there. Christmas night - and they were swaying in the black.

"Come *on*," he said. He turned the truck off, we went into the dark, and we must have stood there for an hour.

And I know if you're like me, you can look or hear almost anything, but after a while you start to say, or at least you think, I've had enough of *this* or like I told you, *that*. Almost anything. At some point you know you wanna walk away.

But the lights were never like that. I'd stand there and I'd shiver and I'd shake, but I never walked away. *Ever*.

"Look," one of us said. And the different shades of red and purple, neon green and white would shimmer right above us. Then it all would start to roll across the sky until we thought it had completely rolled away. But then it started coming back.

"Ever heard of the Light Riders?" Pinto asked.

When I told him I hadn't, he told me how some Athabaskans believed that when you died, your spirit rode out on the Lights. And I guess he meant to heaven. I never asked.

"But what about the *black*?" I asked.

"What?"

"Maybe you come *in* that way," I said. "Riding on the Lights." Because I thought it made more sense. "You kind of break into the universe," I said. "This giant, living bubble. You sneak in from the back, through this infinitesimal hole. You come in from the black, through the back, and the next thing that you know, you're riding on these colors you could never have imagined. Then all at once it's coming in."

"What?" Pinto asked.

"Consciousness," I said. "But then you'd have to figure how to deal with *that*. Hearing *THIS* and feeling *THAT*. Seeing and smelling and touching all this stuff. It probably would be easier staying in the *BLACK*."

"Except I guess you wouldn't really know that you were there." That's what Pinto said. "So what would be the point?"

But the thing that I kept thinking was, you wouldn't really need one, because it wouldn't really matter, unless you came in from the *BLACK*. You wouldn't need a point.

"*NOW* is when you need one," I said. "Or at least it would help. Do *you* know what it is?"

"What?"

"The *point*. You ever wonder what it is?" I asked.

The lights were dying out, and we leaned against the engine trying to stay warm.

"What time you leavin' in the morning?" Pinto asked.

"Eleven o'clock," I said. "Can you drive me down?"

"Wouldn't miss it," he said. Then we stood there for another minute.

"You OK?" Pinto asked me.

I told him I was, but that sometimes I thought that I thought too much. "You know. Why are we *here*? What does it mean? Stuff like that."

"You wanna live a life that has meaning?" Pinto asked me. "I'm not sure it's the point, but one that has meaning?"

And when I told him I did, he nodded his head, walked around to the side of the truck, pointed to the side view mirror and told me, "Come here."

We got to the airport around ten the next morning, and then we sat around and talked for a while.

"Now Fitch, you bought yourself a round-trip ticket, right?" Pinto asked. I nodded my head. "And how about that book that I gave you to read about the mad trapper of Rat River? Albert Johnson."

463

"Read it," I said. "And if you wanna know the truth, he reminded me of you."

I thought that he'd let out a laugh, or joke, or something. But he looked at the ground and asked, "You ever wanna do something like that? Not tell anybody ahead of time? Just go out somewhere and let 'em think that you're dead? Just go out and never come back, except maybe once in a while, but you'd have a disguise? See if you could make it?"

I told him I knew what he meant, but I couldn't see it for me. "I know *you* could do it though," I told him.

"If I ever do, I'll leave you a clue," he said with a smile.

And then they called for boarding. Fairbanks to Anchorage, to Seattle, to Baltimore.

And as I started across the ramp, I remember looking back and calling out, "Hey Pinto. Did I ever tell you about the time I hitchhiked down to Anchorage?" But then I stopped talking because I knew I wouldn't have the time.

So instead I told him, "Hey, listen. I'll look you up in the spring." But the way it turned out, I never saw him again.

Chapter 41

Going back was a blur. I remember I was gonna buy some stuff at the SeaTac Airport for my parents, but I hardly had any money. Thousands and thousands of dollars in papers, but none of it was green.

I knew what my mother would say. "Oh, Jesse. You're the only gift we need."

Which is exactly what she told me when I let her know I hadn't brought them anything. "Just this duffel bag," I said, as it was coming around on the conveyor belt. And I wondered who had been there with Beamish to see the mold on his stuff.

"I'll get it," my father said. We walked to the car, I got in the back, and all at once it hit me. *Everything was so intense.*

"Lotta buildings going up," I said. "And look at all these trees. *WATCH OUT!"* I yelled. *"ARCTIC FOX!"*

And after we drove over it, my father asked, "You mean that piece of trash?

"What?"

"Why don't you relax?" my mother said. So I closed my eyes and tried to sleep, except I couldn't.

"Shoes, boots, pieces of trash."

"What?" my mother asked.

"Hey Dad. You like roasted chestnuts?" I asked.

"What?"

"I got 'em up in Dodge in a five-pound bag and then I roasted 'em," I said. "I stirred 'em with my spoon in a pan I held above the Sterno, and then I gave them out in plastic cups. Kind of like the catalyst and resin. Just stirred it up and stirred it up." That's what I remember saying.

We got back to the house a little after that. God, I was beat. "Well, again, I'm sorry about the presents," I said, "but how about the three of us going out to dinner? Tomorrow night. My treat."

And then it started back and forth, "Oh, you don't have to do that."

"Oh, I know, but I *want* to," I said.

"But really, you don't *have* to . . ." *Blah, Blah, Blah.*

And the more they said no, the more I kept thinking this could really be nice. Kind of like Jimmy's.

"You ever been there?" I asked.

"Where?"

"Jimmy Franklin's," I said, and I showed them my spoon. "It's out in Chicago."

I started up the stairs to my bedroom and told them we could go wherever they wanted, as long as it was fancy.

"I don't want 'em plain. I want hamburgers with everything," I said. "*EVERYTHING!*"

I tried calling Kingpen, but nobody was home. And Mrs. Beamish told me that Bob was in Florida with his wife.

"Are you doing OK?" she asked. And I told her just fine. "Well Bob still talks about his trip," Mrs. Beamish said. And I told her I figured he would. "I'll have him call you, if I hear from him," she said. And I told her that would be great.

"Just ask him to call me at my parents' house," I told her. And she told me she would.

I really didn't want to go outside. I'd been looking out the windows at all these things I hadn't seen for the longest time, like houses and grass and trees. All these cars going by.

And girls and women. Oh my God. It was like the Miss Universe Pageant. And all I could do was *stare*. I started to think about this girl who had liked me back in school, Chrissy something. And I figured I would try and find her number and give her a call, except I never did. I thought about her a lot, though.

I went down to the bank and tried to cash a $1,400 check, so I could pay for dinner. But I didn't have an account, so I had to open one. Even then, they'd only give me $400.

"This is an *advance*," the manager told me. "You can withdraw the other $1,000 in a couple days. We're really doing you a favor. Suppose it doesn't clear?" he asked.

Later that night, there was a knock on my bedroom door.

"Just about ready, Jess?" my mother asked. "Your Dad and I found a Chinese restaurant that we can go to, if that's all right with you." And of course I told her that it was, but it kind of turned out that it wasn't.

I could tell when I looked on the window, before we even walked in the door. Too many choices. That's what I remember seeing. And after we sat down, it turned out it was worse, because of all the combinations. You know. Choose one from list A and two from C, or two from B and you get a soup, but no dessert.

And the thing I could never figure out was how you got more choices on one plan, and the meal was less expensive than if you got fewer choices on the other.

"Now how can *that* be?" I asked.

"Because it's *proportioned*." That's what my father told me.

"Now Jess, are you still sure this is OK?" my mother asked.

And I told her, sure. It was just different than where I'd come from.

"We eat differently up there. We don't have menus," I said. "It's more of a buffet."

But anyway, it was all kind of confusing. Chow mein, lo mein, Cantonese and mu shu. They had these pictures of little chili peppers, up to five, telling you how hot and spicy all their stuff was.

And of all the things I could have gotten, I told the waitress, "I'll take *that*," and pointed to the picture. "Number one-o-five. Wanton soup and sweet and sour giant prawns." And even though the giant prawns were little shrimp, the sauce was pretty good. In fact, everything was great.

At the end of the meal, they gave each of us a little complimentary bowl of sherbet, with a fortune cookie. And a small warm towel, like the one the stewardess had given me the day before, at the end of my flight.

"Well this was really nice," my parents said. As they headed to the door, I took a couple hundreds from the pile and left them there, underneath my unopened cookie.

After we got home I thought that I would go to sleep, but instead we got to talking. *Talking, talking, talking.*

"So how are things at work?" my father asked.

"What?"

"Up there where you're working? You're working. Right?"

"Well, no. Not now, I'm not," I said. "They said I oughta take a break."

"What?"

"Jimmy told Pasquale that he thought that I should take a break," I said.

"What? Now let me get this straight," my father said. "As long as it took you to get *on* this project, now they want you *off*?"

"They do?"

"What?"

"Jesse, what is it exactly that you do up there?" my mother asked. And I told her that I opened up the gate, for one thing.

"I'm the guy who opens up the gate at the back of Pump One, there at Prudhoe Bay. Without me, the work can't get started."

"So you're the *gatekeeper*?" my father asked.

And I told him in a way, but we also spent a lot of time calling out to Charles Ivey. "Over." And then I pictured turning the truck, this way and that. "And when you aim the hose just right and pull the trigger - *PSCHTTT*!"

"Mom, you should have seen it," I said. "Millions of these foamy sparkles blasting at the light. *PSCHTTT*! But anyway, I think it took two weeks but we finally got him."

"Who?"

"Ivey. With his front-end loader. He came up that next night."

"Well, that's good," my mother said.

"Yeah, but it all burned up."

"What?! What burned up?" my father asked.

"The front-end loader," I said.

"The front-end loader?"

"What?"

"Jesus Christ! Jess! Are you all right?"

"What?"

"Look. I know we've talked about this before. Just what would you say your chances are of moving up the ladder with your job?"

"No chance," I told him. "We don't have one. They brought up a platform instead."

And then I was going to tell them about the diesel in the bus, and the catalyst and resin, and the mat and the roving and the mat and roving and the mat. But I was too damn tired, and started heading off to bed.

"I'll see you tomorrow," I said.

468

But then think the strangest thing, *Ba-Ring, Ba-Ring.* "Just push the button in," I said.

Then my mother told me, "The only time it rings is when you're home."

And how he got the number, I'll never know, but it was Jimmy.

"You gotta get yourself back up here," he said. "They want this finished by the spring."

So I told him I could be up there on the 30th.

"Well, I'll put you on the plane's manifest for nine that night. Fairbanks to Prudhoe."

"Sounds good," I said.

And then I hung up the phone and my Dad said, "Let me guess. They want you back *on.*"

And that was when my mother put her arm around me, looked at my father, and I swear to God, she said, "They need our son to open up the gate."

It was Tuesday morning, December 28th.

"Here," my mother said, and she handed me the phone. It's Bob," she whispered. "Calling from Florida."

"Hey, FITCH!"

"HEY, BEAMISH!" On and on. But about halfway through, he started asking what I was gonna do in September.

"Have you thought any more about Law School? You know, Fitch, it's not a bad idea." He told me how he knew this guy in Admissions at the University of Baltimore School of Law. "It's nothing fancy. But I think this guy can get you in. I got you an appointment for 3:15 today, if you want to meet with him."

It all sounded so crazy, I figured I would do it.

So that was what I did. Went to meet with Mr. Baker. At three-o-five I was there. Sitting in the waiting room, with my little coat and tie, listening to his secretary talk about a massage chair that she had. I told her that I'd never had one, but I'd heard that they were pretty good. And then she said that she was gonna join the gym, but I said I didn't know a good one. Then she said more of *this* and I said more of *that*. Talking, talking, *talking*. Then she told somebody goodbye, and took off this little headset she'd had on.

"Now are you here for your meeting with Mr. Baker?" she asked. And when I told her I was, she walked me to his office door, gave it a knock, and he invited me in.

He was younger than I would have pictured, maybe twenty-four years old. "So you're the ringleader, I heard?"

"What?"

"Robert told me it was your idea to go to the Far North," he said. "You and Robert and that other man. I've seen the pictures. Quite an adventure, you guys had. Now are those Alaskan shoes?" he asked, pointing down at my moccasins that Pinto had made.

"Yeah. That's them," I said.

"And you're building that Pipeline?" he asked.

"Well, I open the gate each morning at Prudhoe Bay, and then we head on down from there," I said. "We find all the cracks and roll on the patches with mat, roving, mat, roving and mat. And then for the bigger holes, we use bananas and grapefruits and lemons. And sometimes a cantaloupe.

"Now about this Law School…" I said.

"How *cold* does it get?"

"The Law School?"

"No, the Pipeline," he said. "Where you work."

"Well today, it's probably seventy-below, at least," I said. "Are they introductory courses? The first year? How does that work?"

"Well assuming you get in, and that's a big assumption, that's how it would work the first year. Just what kind of law would you want to focus on?" he asked.

I told him Corporate. Criminal. Maybe Environmental. It really didn't matter. "I've always had a passion for justice," I said. But I don't think he really cared.

"So from what I understand, you work in these camps?" he asked.

"Yeah," I said. "That's right." And like the lady at the airport, I announced the names …"Five Mile, Cold Foot, Dietrich, Happy Valley, Atigun."

"And what about when it's cold?" he asked. "How do you get there then?"

And I remember I told him, they fly us in.

"But when it's *really* cold?" he asked. "Do you take a train?"

"What?"

"Do they send you on a train?"

I thought of sitting in the shower with the blood all running down. "No, they stay there in the Park," I said.

"At Prudhoe Bay?"

"What?"

"Look, I understand that when it's not that cold, you take a plane to go up to the camps. And then I know that you could drive. But when it's really, *really* cold, like it is up there now, do you go up on a train? To the Pipeline camps?"

And it took me a while, but I finally figured what it was that he wanted to hear. *TRAIN. TRAIN. TRAIN.*

"Oh, I got it," I said. "You mean when it's *really, REALLY* cold? Yeah, we do take a train. It's called The Gravy Train," I said. Tell me *THIS* and tell me *THAT*. On and on.

And then I waited and I waited, until he finally asked, "How cold does it get?" And after I had told him, I knew that it would come. *Just ask me. ASK me.* That's what I remember thinking. And then finally he asked me, like I always knew he would. "Tell me what it's like," he said.

"Well, picture standing naked on a giant solid block of ice and the wind begins to blow. Breathing in through your nose and breathing out through your mouth." *And don't forget the ice balls, Fitch*, so I added them all in and then I wrapped it all in cellophane. *Just wrap it up*, I thought, and I went on and on and on.

And when I saw that he was numb, and couldn't take it anymore, I asked him, "Ever seen an outhouse?" And when he told me that he had, I told him how we had these vacuum trucks go up and down the Line.

"Well Billy Bob went on R and R," I said. "Rest and Relaxation. So, another guy came up to camp to do the job, and the first day at work, he's right there at the end. Last outhouse. So he unrolled the hose and he pushed the lever *down* to suck the outhouse out. The only thing was, he was supposed to pull it *up*."

"What?"

"Yeah. The shit came pouring out the hose, covered up the man and he flopped around for ten or fifteen seconds after that. Then he just froze up solid, all covered in crap. Sixty-eight below."

"Oh my God."

"Yeah," I said. "He *died*." Because I'd heard he really had.

"Now can you imagine calling that guy's wife?" Mr. Baker asked. "To explain what had happened?" I told Mr. Baker that I couldn't.

471

"Well I appreciate your time," I said. Because I'd been in there at least an hour. "I'll get my transcripts to you," I said. And Mr. Baker told me I should hear one way or the other by mid-March.

"Stay warm," he said. I told him I'd try, and closed the door.

My mother drove me home. I was gonna try and drive that day, but with everything around me, I knew I couldn't do it.

"So how'd it go?" she asked. And I told her it went fine, but the talk with the lady in the waiting room had been a little strange.

"And now I've gotta get my transcripts figured out," which my mother said *she'd* do.

"Now is there anything else?"

"Nope. All packed and ready to go," I said.

"Well, it's just another option," my mother told me. "I can see you as a lawyer. You're good with people and you like solving problems. And you've always been willing to take a chance. You've got a lot ahead of you."

And when she said that, it reminded me of a board up at camp for the Super Bowl. A thousand bucks to buy a square. You got a number from the side and one from the top, and put 'em together. If the number in your box turned out to be the final score, you won a hundred thousand bucks. But the thing you had to agree to, when you bought in, was that if you won, you'd drag up. Quit. *Adios.*

"So when do you think you'll be home next?" my mother asked.

"It could be in the fall, if I get into Law School, or it could be the tenth. January tenth. But that's just if I win the Super Bowl pool. It's a thousand bucks a square, but I haven't bought in yet." And I think she thought I meant that I could win a thousand dollars.

"Well I know that's a lot of money, but you just stay away from that stuff," she said. And I told her that I'd try.

I went down to the bank, cashed a check, took out the other money, and flew out of Baltimore on the 29th. I bought a square as soon as I got up to the camp the next night.

In a way it was almost like I'd never been away. *Just eat 'em up,* I thought, as I sat there in the Dining Hall, eating all these prawns with cocktail sauce. I thought that I would mail some to the Chinese restaurant, to show 'em what a giant prawn *really* looked like, but I didn't.

Instead I decided I would make the phone call. *Call her up*, I thought. So I went down the hall to the seven phone booths that were there, and I started waiting. *Just hurry up and wait.* That's what I remember thinking. Because I knew that it would take at least a half an hour. Just wait and wait and *wait*. Kind of like the airport, down in Juneau.

And when it all was said and done, I wasn't even sure that she'd remember who I was.

So instead of calling her, I said it in my head. *Hello Chrissy? Chrissy? This is Jesse. Yeah. Jesse Fitch.* But then that was where I got stuck. Thinking what to say. *Come on Fitch. Come on Fitch.*

And then I heard her voice, that I didn't really hear, up there in my head. "What's that echo?" ... *echo, echo...*

"That's the satellite, I'd say. I'm in Alaska. Pump One."

And then I'd tell her how I opened up the gate and mixed the catalyst and the resin. "Just stir and stir and stir it in the cup, and then I pour it on. The mat and the roving and the mat and the roving and the *mat*." But after hearing myself say or think all *that*, I figured, screw it. *Screw it.*

So instead, I got a piece of paper and wrote a note to a philosophy professor that I'd had instead...

> *Dear Dr. Madden,*
>
> *I doubt that you remember me. I cut more of your classes than I attended. My loss. Not yours. Ha, Ha!*
>
> *Anyway, I remember you asking us once in your philosophy class, "Just what will a degree in philosophy get you? Why it won't even buy you a ham sandwich." Remember asking us that?*
>
> *Well anyway, I'm here to tell you that I've seen a number of people who wouldn't even get off the planes, but I'm here at Pump One eating king crab, lobster, and roast beef sandwiches.*
>
> *At least I think, so I am, or maybe I am, so I'm thinking. Get it? Anyway, I'm up here thinking, thinking, thinking.*
>
> *Keep up the good work.*
> > *Your former student,*
> > *Jesse Fitch*

The little post office they had at the camp closed at eight. I bought a stamped envelope, put the note inside, and addressed it to Professor Madden at Towson State College, Towson, Maryland. I handed it to the man behind the counter, just in time. Then I went down to see about a room.

I thought I'd get the same room that I'd had. B23. But instead, the room assigner handed me the key to D14. I could hear myself walking to the room. *SWISH, SWISH, SWISH.*

And even though I knew he wouldn't be there, I pictured Pasquale sitting on his bed.

"Hey, FITCH!" he'd say. And then we'd talk a little bit and he would fall asleep, like he always did. But of course that didn't happen.

Nobody was in the room, but the guy who was living there had a lot of stuff. A popcorn popper, a coffee pot, a mixer, and a bunch of other odds and ends to keep him busy. *Just make it all your home. Make it all real comfy.*

And then my mind thought of the next thing - and when I looked at my bed, there it was. The blankets all turned down and the pillow all fluffy. And I thought of my mother, asking me, the last night we were standing in my room at home. "Now do you make your bed up at the camp? Before you go to work?" And when I told her I didn't, she told me I should. "Don't get into bad habits," she said.

I set my alarm clock, turned off the light, settled in, and lay there thinking. *Two of column three? One of A or B? Moo Shu pork or Cantonese?* But instead I knew he'd just look at me and ask, "Same?" And I'd tell him "Yeah," and he'd give me a three-egg omelet of ham and cheddar cheese, with a couple of big sausages.

The alarm went off at five-thirty. I sat up and heard, "Who the hell are you?"

"Me? You mean *me?*"

"Yeah. *You,*" he said. Like he thought I was a dream.

"I'm *Fitch,*" I said. "Got up here last night." I stuck out my hand. "Nice to meet you. And your name is ...?

"Last night? Well where was I?"

"What?"

It reminded me of two guys you would visit in a nursing home. Talking, talking, *talking,* but neither of 'em made any sense.

"Well, I've gotta go to work," I said. "I'll see you when I get home."

I went and got my omelet, and Jimmy was there eating pancakes with blueberry syrup.

"Hey, Fitch! You have a good Christmas?" But you could tell he didn't care. "Listen, we really gotta get this moving. I'm bringing in more people and another couple buses."

"And what about the catalyst and resin?"

"What?"

"We have enough of *that*?" I asked. "And what about the dryers? Most of them are fucked."

"Yeah, yeah. I'll take care of *that*," he said. "But, listen. This is turning out to be big. We've got the contract for the fiberglass repair on the bumpers from Pump One down to Atigun. A hundred seventy-one miles. And then we've got the valve work to the Yukon."

Whatever that meant. That's what I remember thinking.

"I'll be supervising *that*," he said. He told me how he wanted me to supervise the work being done on the bumpers. "You'll have your own truck," he said. "Just make sure everybody's working and putting all the patches on right. Now here's a list of all the cracks and holes." I was gonna ask him how he got it, but I didn't.

"Now you think that you can do it, Fitch?" I told him that I could. "Well get your truck out of the yard for now," he said. "Two crews will be up here tomorrow, and a couple more will be down there in Dietrich the day after that. You can meet with them on Saturday. You've got a red 150 out by the entrance to the camp. I'll get back to you in about a week."

"And what about the catalyst and resin?" And then he told me everything I'd needed would be in the warehouse.

"Warehouse FBG, here at Pump One. Same thing down at Dietrich. You'll have your own warehouses. Now you'd better get going. It's almost six o'clock."

I thought the truck would be a wreck, but it was really pretty nice. A few cracks in the windshield, but it only had about 67, 000 miles, and the heater worked. But the big thing I noticed was it didn't smell like rotten bananas and hot grapefruits and resin and catalyst and stuff. *Moving on up.*

I started toward the back of the camp and saw that someone else had opened the gate, so I kept on driving.

And the thing that I kept thinking was, *This is it, Fitch. You're the man in charge. Patch this, patch that. And what about the catalyst and resin? Did you mix it all just right? Well, DID YOU?*

All in all, it was great. Kept on driving, and because it was just one road, I didn't get lost. And the way it all turned out, I didn't even fall asleep. Just kept on driving in the dark. And then, for a couple minutes, it turned a little light and I drove on some more. *Driving, driving, driving.*

The thing that I kept thinking was, *Who could have a job like this?* Driving on the northern slope, checking all these patches, eating giant prawns with cocktail saucc, and making who knew how much money every week. And I never even had to spend a cent.

And I swear to God, if I'd had a phone, I would have called that guy who worked upstairs back east. "Yeah, it's me," I'd say. "The guy who couldn't draw. Now can you hold on for just a minute? I seem to have a piece of lobster stuck between my teeth."

It was freezing cold on the outside, but I was staying warm inside my truck, in my RefrigiWear suit and my bunny boots. Then every once in a while, I'd turn up the heat and get real hot, just because I could. And all the time, I'd just keep on driving.

Except for some pickups and some buses, and the people that I'd see standing around, everything was flat. Just like a desert, like I told you, except that it was white. I started heading higher after that. Going farther south, on up the slope. Up and up and up, through Atigun, then down the other side.

A couple trees, then more trees - and then I saw it on my right…
Chandalar.

And of all the things Pasquale told me, he was absolutely right about *that*. Crabs and mussels, clams, and shrimp. It was nothing but the best.

The bouillabaisse at Chandalar - it was absolutely great.

I didn't see my roommate that night. I saw him the next morning. Somebody told me later that people would give him stuff to get him to leave their rooms.

That morning he had a new board game and a toaster.

But anyway, I met my crews out by the warehouse. We had two buses and the first thing I said was, "Gasoline. You got it? Not diesel but *GASOLINE*." And Darlene and the other driver nodded their heads.

The way I had it figured, I was going to have one group work from Pump One to Pump Two, and then the other crew could work from Pump Two down to Pump Three. But then I figured the first crew would be working longer, so I said, "Now the next day we'll turn it around." But that seemed kind of stupid. "We'll start working down together," I said. "From Pump One down."

"Now who's done this before?" I asked. Violet Gully raised her hand. "All right," I said. "It's almost six. Let's get out of the gate. Move those buses about a quarter mile down the pad."

I took Violet with me to Warehouse FBG. We loaded up the bed of the truck with a barrel of resin, three quarts of catalyst, and some rolls of roving and mat. Then we got the rollers and heaters, and some scissors and little plastic cups.

"Don't forget the *stirrers*," I said. "And get a couple of those plywood pieces from the ground." Then we got inside the truck, Violet turned the heater up as high as it would go, and we headed out the gate toward the buses.

I spent the morning teaching them about the patches. How to measure the cracks and the dents on the bumpers - and then cut all the mat and the roving and the mat and roving and the mat.

"And then you pour it in the cup. The *resin*," I said. "You get it from the back, in the bed of the truck. You turn the little valve on the barrel to let the resin out, then you add the catalyst." And like I said, we only had quarts for that, because we only used a little bit.

"You can measure it with the cap," I said, "except when it gets really cold."

"Like now?" somebody asked. Which was really pretty funny, because when you read the directions, none of it was supposed to work at less than fifty-five degrees *above* zero.

"That's over a hundred degrees *hotter* than it is now," somebody said.

Which is why I told 'em we had *THESE*. "See these dryers?" I said.

And I had 'em practice after that.

"Now pretend you had a crack maybe five inches long and a half-inch wide." I had 'em cut their mat. "That's it, but not so *exact*. Maybe an inch bigger all around. You lay it out on the crack," which was really on their practice piece of plywood. "Then you fill your cup with resin and maybe add an inch and a half of catalyst and stir. That's it. *Stir and stir and stir.* Now pour it on the patch. That's it.

Not too much. Now roll it with the roller, until it's nice and flat. You got it."

"And now you cut the roving, do the same thing, then the mat, same thing, roving, same thing and then the mat. Then you take your dryer that is plugged into the generator and you heat it all up. *Heat and heat and heat.* And don't forget to roll out any bubbles with your roller. Any questions?"

"And don't forget to keep the generator filled, or else we'll all be screwed," I said. "Any of you working up here in the cold for the first time?" I asked.

When one guy raised his hand, I told him to have someone check his face every ten or fifteen minutes. "For *frostbite*," I said. "You won't begin to feel it until your nose falls off."

The way I had it figured, I'd assign 'em different jobs. Like, *you* can be the measurer and the cutter. *You* can mix the catalyst and resin. *You* can be *THIS.* And *you* can be *THAT. Blah, Blah, Blah.* On and on and *on.* But then I figured, *Screw it.*

And it all worked out great. "How about I cut some patches out ahead of time?" one guy said. So that was what he did. Some people liked working outside, but then they'd get cold and switch off with some people in the bus. Then even the crews started switching back and forth. Everyone except the loader operators were moving all around. At one point, I remember, there were eight people on one crew and two on the other.

"Is this gonna be OK?" one guy asked. And I remember I told him I couldn't give a shit.

"Just keep it *moving, moving, moving*," I said. "You guys are doing great."

I left at lunch time. They all ate on one bus and I didn't want to intrude, so I took the truck and parked it just outside the gate. Then I walked up to the camp for some soup.

"Anybody want anything?" I asked before I left, but nobody did. Almost all of them had steaks and pork chops that they were gonna heat with their hair dryers.

And by the time we went home that night, we'd finished almost a mile.

"Couldn't have asked for more," I told them. And I really couldn't have.

Chapter 42

It wasn't that it was lonely at the top, it just was kind of different. *No direction*. That's what I remember thinking.

My roommate was this guy named Pooch, a welder, who was really kind of nice. Except I hardly got to see him until he'd come into the room with a bunch of crap. Then he'd wake me up and ask me if I wanted coffee, or some popcorn.

We'd get to *talking, talking, talking*, and it was never very long before one of us would fall asleep. And I swear to God, you'd wake up an hour later and you'd hear, " ...was working down in Oklahoma and the pipe split wide open, and the water they were using for the hydro test leveled out a field of beans."

"No shit," I said. And then I'd tell him all about this, "*POP, POP, POP...*" And the whole time I was talking, I could tell that he was snoring, and then he'd wake up and tell me, " ...killed one of the guys on the hydro test crew." And then I'd say it turned out they were turtles.

But anyway, one night I told him, "Hey Pooch. How about we go to this show that's coming?"

There were some flyers in the camp that told about some girls who were coming up from Fairbanks to sing. March the 18th at eight o'clock. He said that sounded great.

So there was that and the football pool, and then a lot of other stuff started.

It was cold for one thing. I mean *really* cold. You'd hear on the TV how the nation's low was minus thirty-seven in Minot, North Dakota, even though the little chart near the snack room said that it was eighty-five below at Deadhorse.

The wind would start to blow and sometimes there would be a whiteout. Then every time the warehouse workers left the camp and headed to a warehouse, they'd have some other guys on radios. One in the housing trailer the guy was leaving, and the other one in the place where he was going.

"He's leaving the trailer. Heading to the Millwork shop," someone would announce. Even though the Millwork shop might have been only fifty feet away. "ETA seven minutes."

If the guy didn't get there, they'd send out a search party, because all you had to do was miss the building by a couple feet in the whiteout, and you'd be dead, because you'd freeze. I think one guy did, so then they hooked up a couple ropes as guides between the buildings.

Anyway, it was getting pretty crazy. A lot of the machinery was freezing up and I know some other people died.

Then on the morning of January 4th, they told us, "Anybody working for Associated Green, get on the buses." They were there, just outside the entrance to the camp. Eleven of 'em, with a D9 dozer out in front.

"Get on. Get on," a guy announced, and then he took our names. We started out the entrance to the camp and I thought that they were taking us over to the Deadhorse airport, but we went the other way. They said it was too dangerous to work *outside*, so they were sending us to a camp called Service City to work *inside* instead.

I was in the second bus, first seat, so I could hear the Teamsters talking on their radios. From what I heard, Service City was about fifteen miles away.

Depending on our trades, we would work inside, like I said, building stuff, or welding, or washing walls, like Rockett had. *Just wash it up, then wash it down.* That's what I remember thinking.

I started adding thirty wipes up plus thirty wipes down a minute, times sixty, times sixteen. I thought that I could figure out how much money I would make a wipe, except I couldn't. So I started counting snowflakes landing on the windshield. *One, two, three, four* - but by the time I got to *fifteen*, they were smashed into a pile of frozen slush.

On and on we pushed. Kind of like driving in the Buick to Chicago, except that this was worse. Way worse. We hadn't gone three miles and if it hadn't been for the radios, we would have lost some of the buses. In fact, we finally did.

About three miles in, it got so bad we could barely move, so we left the last three buses there and everybody crowded onto the eight in front. We chained 'em all together after that, and hooked the front one to the D9.

Then a guy came around and asked for volunteers to go up front. "We need one man on the dozer's windshield," he said, because the windshield wipers' motor had frozen up. All you'll have to do is wipe. So one guy raised his hand and that's exactly what he did.

Climbed up on the roof of the dozer, hung down over the windshield, and wiped and wiped and wiped.

Another two guys and I went up in front, ahead of the D9. We each waved a flag to try and keep it on the road. And I wish you could have seen us.

"More *this* way, or more *that way*!" we'd yell.

But there was no way the operator driving the D9 could hear us. So we'd wave our flags and then this other guy, the one hanging over the windshield, would wipe and wipe and wipe.

Then he'd point, the chains on the buses would catch, and we'd probably go another twenty feet. We did that for an hour, then some other laborers came out and took our places.

I think, now that I look back, we would have turned around - except by then we were over halfway there.

We finally got to Service City at four o'clock in the morning. What a dump.

This little camp, with no TV or Ping-Pong. Nothing like Pump One. We didn't even get a bed. Not that *I* cared that much, but a lot of guys did. They gave us mattresses instead.

We put them in the hallways. I laid down on mine, pulled the button out, and figured in a couple hours I would push it back in.

But the way it all worked out, we never did a thing during the four days we were there. They were gonna have us wash some walls, but I found out later they had figured we'd be groggy and get hurt, so they never did.

And of all the paychecks I ever got, that one was the largest for a week… three thousand, seventeen dollars and seventeen cents. *Take home*. Because they didn't give us beds.

"They have to give us each a *bed* to sleep in," one guy told me, "or they have to pay us twenty-fours. Union rules."

I had Oakland 24 and Minnesota17, which wasn't that bad, but it wasn't that great. One hundred thousand bucks, but then I'd have to get another job.

But maybe then I wouldn't. I could live on that. Plus all of my checks. *It takes money to make money,* that's what I remember thinking. And I would have it. Money, money, money.

I could buy a bunch of suits and walk around the courtroom in my moccasins, all the time objecting, "But your honor, what about *this* or what about *that*?"

Or I could buy a fancy restaurant, work back in the dish room, and push the button in. *Pschttt, pschttt, pschttt.*

And then there was the lighthouse. I could look out at the water, eat my burp-up food and every time I burped it up, I could think. *Chinese* style.

Think as much as you can think, Fitch. Look out at the water, burp up some orange and then think more. Burp. Burp, burp, burp.

We didn't have live news. Everything was taped. But think the strangest thing…

On January 5th, the camp put in a Reuters teletype machine. Every morning and every night, they'd post the latest news on the bulletin board, right outside the Dining Hall. "The quick brown fox jumps over the lazy dog." And then the news would be there. Right below it.

There were articles about computers, bombings in Russia, and one about a guy named Gary Gilmore, convicted of killing two people. And instead of appealing his sentence, he wanted to be shot. *Just fuggit.* That's what I remember thinking he was thinking.

It really made you wonder about coming into the black and going out on the light. I mean, *where would it all go?*

The feelings that you had… The stuff in your head…

Pschttt, pschttt, pschttt.

Would it keep on going?

A couple of days later, the Raiders took the game 32 to 14. I wasn't even close. It turned out that one of the chefs was, though. He won the pool and he didn't even quit. That's what I remember. You'd see him cooking food in his whites and fancy hat, and you'd wonder if he had it in his pocket. A hundred thousand bucks. Money, money, money.

Things were going great at work. Too great, really. There wasn't all that much to do. I'd check in on my workers and give 'em their supplies. And every other day, I'd hand them all a list of the cracks they should be fixing.

"Dryers working OK?" And they all would nod their heads.

"Cantaloupes and lemons?" *Check.*

"And how about Ivey?" I'd ask. "Is he staying awake?"

"Fuck you," he'd answer. And then we all would laugh.

After that, I'd go driving. Head on down to Atigun, pull the truck off in a pull-off on the way, pull the button out, go to sleep, and in a little while—*Brngg.* And then I'd push the button in and start driving again.

Jimmy was right. They must have wanted it finished, because things were really picking up. I could see it every day, driving up and down the Line. Even in January.

There were welding tents around the pieces of forty-eight inch pipe being welded together. There were dozens of buses, hydro test crews, backhoes, cherry pickers, and manipulators. Fuel trucks to keep it all going.

And up and down the Line, there were dozens of break shacks to keep everybody warm. They were trailers, really. ATCO trailers, except they weren't hooked together like the ones at the camp. They sure were nice, though. They had tables and chairs and like all of the buses, all the lewd magazines you would ever want to look at. All kinds of food and microwave ovens. Cups and utensils. And doughnuts. Holy shit. You shoulda seen the doughnuts.

There was one break shack a little down past Pump Two near the Sagavanirktok River, where they said the river ran north. But you couldn't really tell, because like I think I told you, it was frozen.

But anyway, a lot of 798ers were there. Welders. And that break shack was *really* something, let me tell you. They had a laborer who worked there, and his whole job was to take care of the break shack and keep those welders happy. He had all kinds of doughnuts in rows with little labels, telling what they were. There were tablecloths on the tables, steak sauces, napkins and silverware, and hot fresh coffee every hour. That break shack was the *best.* And the more that I stopped there, the more they thought it was me who made it that way.

"Just what the fuck do you *do*?" one guy asked one day, when I was sitting in there.

And before I could think of an answer, another one asked, "Check the break shacks?"

So I told him, "Yeah. That's it. I drive up and down the pad and check the break shacks." Which is what I told a lot of people after that. "Check the break shacks and make sure they're up to standards."

"Everything here in good order?" I asked. And when the one guy told me they could use another microwave, I looked at the laborer and he told me he would get one.

Chapter 43

You think and wonder and ponder in your head - and then something hits you and it doesn't fit in. Gary Gilmore. Life is a range, but some people aren't in there. Not in the range. You only think they define it. But they don't.

I got back to my room late one night and a package was sitting on my bed. Inside the cardboard box was a tape, a player, and a note from Pasquale.

"Try *this*," he had written. "I think it was the batteries."

I put the package aside and walked down to the Dining Hall, but I wasn't hungry. There was the sentence about the fox jumping over the dog, and then the headline below it. Gary Gilmore to be executed by firing squad tomorrow morning. And I wondered how he got there.

Shoes, boots, pieces of rope.

Anchorage or Fairbanks?

I went back to my room and sat on my bed for a long time, looking at a popcorn popper, board games, and a toaster.

What was his last meal? Steak and potatoes? Prawns? Did he even want one?

Pooch came in sometime after one o'clock, with a bunch of stuff somebody had given him.

"Fugga job," he said. "I'm gone home." He didn't say a word after that. He crawled into bed and I didn't bother to ask him about what he'd said.

Going home, I thought, and I wondered where that was. Not for him so much, but for me. Ester? Olnes? Down in the weeds?

I couldn't get to sleep that night and around five o'clock that next morning, I went down to the board. It was already there. Gary Gilmore executed by firing squad. The last words he was quoted as saying was "Let's do it."

They did.

Chapter 44

I needed a plan. I was making lots of money, and the food was great. But it was all gonna end. Just like Careers. *Drive your little car around the board,* I thought.

I started driving down to this break shack by Franklin Bluffs. The break shack itself wasn't all that great, but the people sure were nice. They were a mix of operators, laborers, and a couple 798ers - but they all got along.

"How the break shacks looking?" somebody asked when I stepped inside. And I told him pretty good, for the most part.

"Couple little problems here and there," I said. "Nothing major."

"Well, that's good," he told me.

It was lunchtime, and like a lot of guys, they were grilling steaks and ribs, pork chops and shrimp and even salmon, on these grills that the 798ers had made by welding rebar together. They would grill the food outside, with the snow coming down, and then bring it inside. Everything was there. Salads and rolls, baked potatoes. Just about anything you'd ever want to eat.

"Watch *this*!" one guy said. He took a hardboiled egg, peeled the shell, and threw it outside. Go on and get it he yelled. And almost right away, a seagull flew down, scooped it up, and started flying off.

"Ya see that?" somebody asked. "Try another one."

So the first guy did. Peeled another egg and threw it out the door. And in the middle of the winter there at Prudhoe Bay, you never would have thought you'd see a seagull. But let me tell you. They were there. Dozens of 'em, flying all around the break shack.

"I'll bet a hundred bucks he can't eat *two*," another guy said. And he pointed to a seagull over on the side, all by himself.

"You're on," the first guy said. The money started flying on the table after that. At least a thousand bucks. And the way it all turned out, the seagull scooped 'em up and ate 'em, but then he couldn't fly. I guess he was too heavy. He could only waddle on the ground.

"Still ate 'em," the first guy said. And then he and the guys who had bet with him collected their money.

It all started getting better, or maybe *worse* after that.

"Here," an operator said. He took an egg, peeled the shell, and cut the egg in half. "Watch *this*." he said. He scooped the yolk out of both halves with a spoon, filled the holes with some Louisiana Hot Sauce and smushed the halves of the egg back together.

"Now watch *this*." He threw it out the door, and it couldn't have been more than six or seven seconds, a bird came flying down, scooped up the egg, and I wish I hadn't seen it in a way.

He scooped up the egg, then he started flying up. Up and up and up. And right around a hundred feet, you would have thought that he was shot out of the sky. Just a total nosedive. He slammed into the ground. Ka-Boom!

"See *that*?" the operator asked. And then he grabbed the hot sauce and another egg.

Some time ago, there had been a rumor, but I think it was the truth. When it was almost impossible to get out on the Line, people would call into the Hall and request their own names... "James Jefferson, seven twelves for Arctic Construction at Prudhoe Bay."

And then the Hall would give him the dispatch slip, he'd fly up north, and wing it from there.

"Well here's my dispatch slip," the guy would say. And from what I understood, the company would usually take him in. But finally they all caught on and the requestor would have to give a code word.

But anyway... *Maybe I could do that*. That's what I was thinking. Not request my name, but keep on driving, finding cracks and checking break shacks. *Just keep on keeping on.* Hydrochloric acetate and break shack generators.

"Do you *understand*?" I'd ask. "Do you know what you're dealing with? Lay me off and it's *your* responsibility," I'd say. "It's on *your* head now." That's what I was thinking. But that was just another option.

But when all was said and done, I had it pretty good. And the thing that I was looking forward to was just relaxing that night. *Take a long hot shower.* And that was how it all started...

I poured shampoo from a bottle that somebody had left in the shower stall, and rubbed it in my hair. But it didn't lather up. So I poured on *more. Just pour it on and lather up,* I thought. But it still didn't lather, so I thought it must have been conditioner. But I didn't really care. At the time, I didn't give a shit.

Just gimmee that hot water. And then I got the soap and washed myself all over. God, it felt good. Then I stepped out of the shower and a stack of towels was there. Big white fluffy towels, that made me think of the little brown paper ones I had used on the Ferry. *Fitch, you have come a long way,* I thought.

I put my clothes on, walked to the Dining Hall, and had a couple lobsters. *Rest and relaxation. Just bring it on,* I thought. And then I started walking.

I went back to my room, and Pooch's brush was there, sitting on the table. *Well here's to new things,* I thought, because I never brushed or even combed my hair.

First, I pulled out all the hair that was in the brush, and threw the hair in the plastic bag in the trashcan. Then I started brushing it all back. Every hair that was up on my head. *Brushed and brushed and brushed.* Then I pulled my own hair from the brush, and dropped that into the plastic bag in the trashcan, too.

Then I looked in the mirror on the back of the door and I didn't even say a word. I just nodded to my head.

Nodded to my head, took off my clothes down to my underwear, and got into my bed. I put my head on the pillow, and then I pulled one button out, and pushed another one in. And I wish you could have heard her.

Pasquale had been right. It *was* the batteries. She had this gravelly voice that was absolutely perfect, when she was singing at the right speed. God, she sounded good. There were fast songs and slow songs and songs in between, where she'd start off real low and then lift up her voice, until you thought the fuckin' windows would break.

And then there was this lullaby. It almost put me to sleep. This really, sexy, gravelly voice singing, "Go to sleep my baby. Baby go to sleep." And I was right there with her. Singing in my head. Right there with her. Right there…

"What the *FUCK,* Fitch?! Come on. Wake up. We're gonna *party.*"

It was Pooch. He was pretty well screwed up, and he wouldn't take no for an answer. I put my clothes back on, and we headed down a couple doors to a room full of 798ers.

"Now who the fuck's *this*?" one of 'em asked. And Pooch told him I was his roommate. "An OK guy, even if he is a Laborer." There were laughs all around.

There was a guy strummin' a banjo and another one had a fiddle. There were bottles everywhere.

"Here," somebody said. He handed me some whiskey in a plastic cup. "Here's to us 798ers," he said. They all toasted with their cups and we drank 'em down. Then he poured me another one.

It was kind of like my party in Olnes, but more like the Embers in a way. You didn't mess with these guys. *They would kill for each other*. That's what I remember thinking. You'd look at 'em the wrong way and... *that was that*.

"Ever play cards?" this one guy asked. And I told him that I didn't think I did. "Well, stop on down if you do. Friday nights. No limit."

We weren't running out of drinks, but we were running out of ice.

"Well, you're the *laborer*," one of 'em said. "So how about you go on down to the Dining Hall and get some?" And that was when I asked how much.

"Well, unless you wanna keep on running down there, you oughta get a fuckin' *nuff*. Don't you think?"

And I told him, "Yeah, I think a lot."

Pooch had already gotten some ice and put it in our room. That's what he said. So I went down there and found the ice, in the plastic bag in the trash can. I got a couple handfuls and put it all in a popcorn popper that was there, so I could carry it. *Pop, pop, pop.* Then I took it back to the party.

I remember Pinto told me once, "You can pretend to pick yourself up, turn yourself around, and back yourself into someone else's body. Of course it will all be in your head, but it's good if you get bored," he'd said. "You can forget about being yourself and become somebody else."

So that's what I was doing. Becoming Harley Cooter, the guy across from me...

I *pretended* to stand up, turn myself around, back on over, and sit in Harley's lap, because he was sitting down. And the thing about Harley was, he was so damn *fat*. That's what I remember. So I started puffing out my stomach and leaning back in my chair. And he had these real short arms, so I started pulling up my hands. And then there was his face. Dozens of these wrinkles, all sagging down.

489

Totally relaxed. You could tell that he was drunk, or maybe it was just he didn't give a shit. I don't know.

But I started with my forehead, and then I let my eyes droop down. And by the time I let my mouth drop, I could feel the spit sliding off my chin.

"What the *fuck*! Are you all right?" somebody asked. "Here. Have another drink."

So I did. And then I stopped being Harley and started looking at this other guy named Beau. And the thing about him was this buckle he had on.

They were all dressed the same. The guys that were there. Paisley welder hats, all turned around, cowboy boots and jeans. And fancy buckles for their belts. But this one was *huge*.

It reminded me of a riddle that was written on a stall down in the bathroom. *What's the difference between a 798er and a piece of shit? They both should be flushed down the toilet, but the welder can't. His belt buckle would get stuck.* It went something like that. But anyway, I got to laughing and kept looking at the middle of his belt.

"Whaddyou, a *faggot*?" Beau asked. He had his face screwed up real tight, just the opposite of Harley's. And just for a minute I thought about sitting in his lap.

"Are you a *faggot*?" he asked again.

And the thing that I remember was I was gonna ask him, "What?" But a piece of hair was hanging down my throat and I couldn't talk, until I finally pulled it out.

"What?" I finally asked.

"Holy shit," somebody said. "Remember Bubba, down in Texas? Was up here working two years…"

"Yeah," somebody said. "What about him? Wasn't he working to buy a Prize Bull?"

"Yeah. That's him. Well anyway, it turned out he was queer."

"No shit! *Bubba*?"

"No. The fucking *bull*."

"What?"

"*Queer steer*," somebody said. "Bubba lost his fucking money. All of it."

"No shit." And I thought that they were kidding, but they weren't.

490

"Well, the thing I've always wondered," Harley asked. "If a guy was bent that way, would he get himself excited looking in the mirror, if he didn't have his clothes on?"

"What?"

"I mean if you looked at a naked lady you would get a hard-on, right? So what if you liked guys, and stood there looking at yourself naked, wouldn't it be the same thing?"

I looked over at Beau, who was looking at me.

"Fuck if *I* know," I said. "Maybe you could put a mirror in front of the bull, and see what happens."

The banjo player started to say something, but then he put his fingers down in his mouth.

"Who wants another one?" somebody asked, and I held out my cup. I was really getting messed up. And I think it started with the shower.

They started talking all about the Givers and the Takers. And they wanted you to know *they* were the Givers.

"*Fuck* the Company. They oughta send us on a paid vacation every couple weeks. Send us to Hawaii. All that *we* do," one guy said. And he meant the 798ers. The rest of us weren't *shit*.

And then there was the Government. "With their bullshit taxes. Just *take* and *take*." And I think that he was gonna say another "take," but then he started choking, until he pulled something from his throat.

"*Fuggit*," one guy said. He started telling all the rest of us how he'd bought a bottle of shampoo. "Took it with me to the shower. When I left and went back to my room, I realized I'd forgotten it, went back and it was gone. All the money people making here, and they have to steal a man's shampoo? Fuck 'em," he said. "Just another taker. But I fixed *somebody's* ass," he said. "I bought another bottle, poured most of it out, peed in the sucker, and put it back in the shower."

And that was when I knew, it hadn't been *conditioner*.

The guy with the banjo started playing, and then the guy with the fiddle. But they couldn't keep in step, because one or the other would have to stop to stick his fingers down his throat.

I pulled a hair out of my mouth and I remember thinking, *Just who the Hell are you, Fitch, to judge these guys? You've got pee in your hair, you can't draw for shit, and you couldn't even find your way out of a tent. Just let it go.*

491

And that's when I decided I would just try and be one of the guys.

I started slapping my knees to the part time music, let out a few *ya-hoos,* and looked all around to see what else I should do. One guy tapped his foot and I thought that looked pretty good, so I was just about to start tapping.

But then I noticed that nearly everybody there had his hand down his throat, or was at least trying really hard to cough something up. Everybody there, except this one guy who was sitting in the corner.

They called him "The Bishop." And that might have been his name, but he seemed really religious, so I think it was because of that. He didn't drink, play cards, or smoke. And he always had his Bible. I had seen him once before, in the little welding shop he ran, about a mile down the pad. It had a sign that he had carved above the door that said, *Jesus is my friend. Don't use his name in vain.* And from what I could tell, most of the guys didn't. They were pretty respectful, except for Beau sometimes.

"Where's the *goddamned* ice?" Beau roared. So I told him I would get some, but it turned out that I didn't.

I went down to my room and turned on the light. And the thing that I remember was I had this real weird sensation like something was wrapped, or maybe just stuck, around that thing that hung down my throat between my tonsils. Epiglottis? Toovula? *Uvula.* Yeah, that was it. *Uvula.* But anyway, I stuck my tongue way back and started moving it around, but I couldn't get whatever it was, until I stuck my fingers back there. And of course it was a hair. *Just pull out one more hair*, I thought.

I reached in the trashcan to drop it in, and more of it was there. More hair. All the hair from Pooch's brush, mixed in with the ice he had put there, in the plastic trash bag. Probably some pee hair, too. That's the last thing I remember thinking before I started throwing up.

And of all the times that I've thrown up, that time was the worst. It went on and on and on - and even then I knew that it would never be enough.

Like the oil down at Earthquake Park, you could wait a hundred years. *Drip. Drip. Drip.*

Some of the hairs would never come up and something told me they would never go down. They would just stick behind my tonsils or slide around in my esophagus. And what about my sinus cavities? Could they even get in *there*?

And what about my future? I could be about to kiss some girl or give an argument in court.

Then what would I say?... "Please excuse me while I extricate a pee hair from my mouth?"

I really didn't try to plan much after that. If a nice quiet evening could turn into a night of puking, *screw it*.

Think the strangest thing. But it always turned out *more*. That seemed to cover it. And you couldn't even think it, because it was *more*. That's what I remember thinking. *Fuggit*.

I was earning quite a bit of money and was thinking of investing, but then I decided I should keep it for law school. But lots of guys *were* investing. Or doing something with their money. They were buying penny stocks, playing the market, buying real estate or racehorses. Sending their money home, but then you would hear stories of their wives running off. Other guys would gamble it away, and you'd hear that their wives were writing to them, asking for some money for the kids. A lot of stuff was going on. Just like down in Fairbanks.

There was one guy named Tom, a Teamster who drove a bus. Every penny that he made, he put into pornography. Not pornography itself, but some kinds of stocks that were connected to it. According to him, he was even a part-owner of some X-rated movie theatres and a couple of sex shops. They were the big thing, he thought.

And the reason he thought *that* was because everywhere you looked, there must have been a thousand porn magazines. In the break shacks, buses and camps. Thousands of 'em. And since his only job was to drive the workers to the break shack in the morning, then wait fourteen hours until he drove them back to camp, I think he had probably seen every picture in the magazines. Probably twice. And I guess like someone living in an apple orchard, he figured everybody in the world would want them.

"And don't forget the sex toys," he would tell anyone who would listen. "That market is gonna *explode*. It's poised for a take-off," he said. "Mark my words."

But for all of the pictures in all the magazines, the picture that *I* really liked was this one of a peach, on a can of sliced peaches in a break shack down by Atigun. God she was pretty. She was the one in the middle with two others on each side. She had beautiful blue eyes, kind of coy and inviting. And right where the stem came up at the top, there were these leaves that hung down. And her color was perfect. Kind of yellow in some parts, but mostly orange in others. But the best part was her lips. Just like I like 'em. All juicy red and pouty. *Really, really* pouty. God, she was a knockout. The only parts that weren't that good were her legs that were spindly, and these little red tennis shoes she had on.

I could feel myself slipping away. Not that it was bad. Just different.

I think Violet had something to do with it. And now that I look back, I really should have thanked her more than I did. She was the one who held it together. I would meet her each morning, and we would talk about roving and mat and vegetables and fruit and generators and heaters - *and where were the cracks?*

"You have enough catalyst and resin?" I'd ask.

And then I would start driving. I loved that. Driving down to Atigun, stopping every once in a while. Checking the break shacks. And then I'd usually find a pull-off and go to sleep.

It was dark almost all the time. I started taking so many naps during the day that I couldn't sleep at night. I'd have my times mixed up, plus the days were always the same. I didn't know if it was Tuesday or Saturday, except I knew that we got paid on Fridays. At least I thought that we did.

But anyway, even with the snow and the dark and the flatness all around, you'd still see things, or else you wouldn't, that would make you *think*. Like the forest, for example.

There was a silhouette of a Christmas tree that someone had made out of three-quarter-inch plywood. It was about eight feet tall and they had painted it green. I guess they had pounded a pole into the ground somehow and then nailed the plywood tree to that. We called it *The Prudhoe Bay National Forest*. It was about a quarter of a mile south of Pump Two, on the side of the Haul Road.

But anyway, the thing had fallen down. So of course I started asking myself, "Fitch, do you think it made a *sound*?" And I can tell you, *that* one didn't because of all the snow.

But what if it was summer and no one was around?
What if this? What if that?

And then I started thinking, *there weren't even any trees. But did it really matter?*

And that was when I knew it didn't, because no one would be there to give it all any meaning. It was a meaningless question, that deserved a meaningless answer.

Yellow, hop, tangerine, gravy.

So at least that was one less question I had to answer from myself. Or anyone else, for that matter.

I could see it on the Bar Exam... "If a tree falls in a forest and no one is there to hear it, does it make a sound?"

"Yellow, hop, tangerine, gravy," I'd say.

And when they asked me, "Mr. Fitch. What did you say?"

That's when I'd tell 'em... "You heard me."

More people were flying in to work, some guys were going out on R and R, and the rest of us, the ones who just kept staying, were slowly going crazy. Not me so much, but a few were. *Like Tom the Teamster.* The guy who'd put all his money into pornography.

It was the first week of February when the box came. And apparently it wasn't all plain brown like I think they advertise. It was shipped from Desiree's Gift shop down in California. According to the rumors, Tom had ordered this full-sized, realistic blow-up doll he named Martha. I guess at first, the guys who worked around him thought that it was funny, but then his roommate moved out and Tom couldn't get another one. But he didn't give a damn. Because he'd rather room with Martha. At least that was what he said.

But anyway, it all came to a head one night, when I went down to the Dining Hall and everything was red and pink. There were hearts and arrows everywhere.

"Valentine's," somebody said.

And you should have seen the food. Flaming *this* and flaming *that.* And hundreds of these really fancy pastries, like you'd see in bakeries in France. But for all of the tuna and the oysters and the tarts, and the steaks that were grilled to perfection, I knew Pinto had been right about the food. *The spaghetti in the cabin had been the best.*

I thought of that and about walking in my mukluks down the snowy steps. And hiking down to Antonelli's in the middle of the night. *Walking, walking, walking.* And then maybe I would stop along the way and watch the lights. But finally I'd get there. I'd take the key, and if my hands weren't frozen solid, I'd stick the key into the hole, and turn it once around. *I pulled back on the door, and started feeling warm...*

And then I heard the whistling. All this crazy whistling.

The place was going crazy.

"Is she your fucking *DATE?*" somebody yelled.

Guys were whistling, screaming out "YaHoo!" and shouting out anything and everything you could imagine.

And the cause of it all was Teamster Tom, who was walking through the Dining Hall entrance with his blow-up girlfriend, Martha. She was wearing this little purple negligée or nightgown. I didn't know the difference, but it didn't cover much.

You could tell that he was crazy, or maybe he thought he was in love. You could see it in his eyes. I think he thought that he was gonna take her out for a dinner of steak or lobster. Maybe both. But then he changed his mind.

There was a column in the middle of the Dining Hall and when they started toward that, he and Martha, you could tell that things were gonna happen. *And they wouldn't be good.* That's what I remember thinking.

You didn't wanna look, but you knew you kinda had to.

Just think the strangest thing, I thought. But of course it turned out *more*.

The Bishop started toward him, but he wasn't fast enough. Tom had Martha's nightgown up, or whatever it was called, and then he pulled his pants down.

I got up, left my lobsters, crème brûlée, and sorbets sitting on my plate, and started walking. *Walking, walking, walking.*

But even then, I took a look. And the way it all turned out, I really wished I hadn't.

"Just put it *in*," Tom said. And then I guess he did, because he started banging Martha up against the column.

Just keep on walking, Fitch. That's what I remember thinking.

And then one guy started, another and another, and before long everybody there was chanting... "GO! GO! GO! GO!"

I made a left, started down the hall, and like a chorus I could hear 'em, all behind me, "GO! GO! GO! GO!"

And then it finally happened. Like every time it does. *More.*

Because as loud as they were chanting you could hear him scream above 'em. From the Dining Hall, to the rec room, to the living quarters, to the far ends of the camp. "I'm COMING!" Teamster Tom roared. "I'm fucking *COMING*."

I heard they flew him out that night, and his stuff the next morning. I don't know *what* they did with Martha. One guy said they popped her and threw her away, which really got me thinking...

Here you are Fitch, with a picture of a peach that you keep in your pocket. And even if she did look good, she wasn't what I needed. *You need a real girl, Fitch.*

And then I thought of Chrissy and pictured how maybe I would call her again, even though I never had. And what about that female teamster? The one who drove the trash truck. She looked pretty good. Not from the front so much, but the back of her head wasn't all that bad, with the swinging pony tail.

And even Violet Gully. She was kind of squatty, but we got along real well. And then there was that girl in Rasmussen, who worked in the library.

Hell. There were all kinds of options. So I thought and thought and thought about them for a while, until I figured I would go and take a shower.

We were getting into March and really being pushed. That's what Jimmy said.

"Doing a great job, Fitch, but we've gotta get this finished."

They were bringing in the hydro test crews and the PIGS, which stood for Pipeline Intervention Gadgets. They were really cylinders, that were used to clean the inside of the pipe.

Just clean the pipe, I thought, and then I pictured leaving Prudhoe Bay riding through the pipe, heading down to Valdez on a PIG. *Souie! Souie!*

I was staying up at night. Kind of *Chinese* style. Late. Then later. Then finally all night.

I couldn't get to sleep. There was a little library in the camp, and so I started reading. I remember getting interested in survival stuff. There were books about edible plants and making different kinds of traps. And then there was one about this guy in New Jersey. He had lived near the woods when he was little, and he liked it so much that his parents let him live there. In the woods. But anyway, he had written all about it and then, after that, he had started a survival school.

So at least that part was different. I'd started reading books. But pretty much everything else was still the same.

Brngg. Brngg. I'd push the button in, even though I was awake.

"Ham and cheddar cheese?"

"Yeah. Ham and cheddar cheese," I'd say.

Then I'd take my bag of prawns and cocktail sauce, and I'd get into my truck that was always out there running in the dark. Then I'd go and meet with Violet and the gang. Mat and roving? Mat and roving? Mat? *Blah. Blah. Blah.*

And then I'd start off driving, stop and get some sleep, and visit in the break shacks. I'd watch these birds who couldn't fly, but would wobble very happily across the frozen ground.

Kind of like the Buick. That's what I remember thinking. *KaJong. KaJong. KaJong.*

And later on that night, I'd head back to the camp, and eat a couple lobsters or a steak, and some pieces of pie. And then maybe some peach ice cream, because that was pretty good. And then I'd go and read, until one night it hit me...

Walking heads.

There were dozens of them. All around me in the rec room - and every one was different. Hundreds of them all throughout the camp. They all were pretty much the same size and shape; but the thing that was amazing, even incomprehensible to me, was that each of these spheres was filled with all kinds of bullshit. They were all sitting on shoulders, that were resting on waists, on top of these legs, on feet that were walking them around.

Walking, talking heads that could choose what they said. And they *knew* they were there. That was the *BIG* thing.

They knew they were there, and unlike the chairs, they took it all in. Through their eyes and their noses and their ears and their mouths.

And then I started thinking about all the stuff up *in* there. Human drama stuff. High points and low points. All rolling around. Up in these heads. Everything they ever could imagine.

And then they had their *subconsciouses*, so you knew there was *more*. Little drifting thoughts and giant explosions. All wrapped up there, in walking, talking heads.

How did it start? Where would it end?

Relationship issues. Human drama. Everything you ever had experienced or thought you'd want to know. If a tree fell in the forest? What about your head? A tree would never hear it. Much less even know.

And that's when I began thinking about all this meaning that wouldn't even be there without these people's heads.

Yellow, hop, tangerine gravy.

Clocks and street signs and all kinds of things, except they wouldn't mean a thing.

And what about the thinking, up there in a head?

I wondered how it all began. Not *what* so much, but *when*. Your senses took stuff in, you turned it into words, and there you were. But suppose you couldn't talk, or you didn't know words? You were six months old. Then what?

So I started picturing an apple, except every time I saw it, I heard it in my head. *Apple. Apple.* And that's the way it was with everything I pictured. *Lamps and lemonade. Mat and roving. Mat and roving. Mat.*

Just try putting them together in a paragraph of pictures… You can't *begin* to do it.

Fuggit, I thought. And the funny thing was, *then* I saw a picture.

Just make it really simple, Fitch. That's what I remember thinking.

So I started saying words, just to hear 'em in my head. Just send 'em out of your mouth and bring 'em in your ears. But then, just like that time I was looking in the mirror, it all began to change.

Take *wobble* for example. It doesn't sound that bad. But try saying it again, and again, and again. *Wobble. Wobble. Wobble.* It sounded really stupid. And every word was like that. It didn't make sense. Like t*hat'll.* Yeah, that's a good one… *That'll. That'll. That'll.*

Then I started thinking of the times I'd called back east and the words would bounce off of the satellite. *Satellite. Satellite. Satellite.* They all sounded stupid and didn't make sense. Nonsense.

Now *there* was another one. *Nonsense. Nonsense.*

Every one was like that. Long words, compound words.

So I thought I'd try a really little, simple one, but I think that made it worse…

IT.

Now there's one for you, Fitch. It. That's what I remember thinking. But it sounded even worse. *It. It. It.*

So then I started talking faster. *Just turn it up Chinese style.* That's what I remember thinking. Then *IT* went up through my ears and I heard *IT* in my head. *It. It. It. It... Tit. Tit. Tit.*

And then my mind went to the next thing... I reached into my pocket and took out the picture of my peach that I had cut off of the can. I took one last look at her *really* pouty lips, and threw her in the trashcan.

Just Fuggit. That's what I remember thinking.

Just. Just. Just... Fuggit. Fuggit. Fuggit.

Chapter 45

I think it was the middle of March when we started having storms. Really bad ones. You could barely work or even drive, because of the winds and the whiteouts.

"Probably won't send us to Service City again," Violet said, and we all started laughing.

They did make sure we left the camp though. Associated Green. They'd open up the back gate and send these dozers down the pad for a quarter mile or so, and then the buses followed. I don't think anybody ever got out, unless they had to pee or take a crap.

But anyway, dozens of buses were there, all gathered around, people in them sleeping, reading books, or looking at the pictures in the magazines.

"Anybody wanna play tic-tac-toe?" one of the guys on my crew asked. When Violet said that she would, he got out a brush and some resin, and started to paint lines on the ceiling of the bus.

"My father always said I was a lazy son of a bitch," one guy said. "I remember him asking me once if I thought there was an employer out there who would be crazy enough to pay me to sleep."

"Well you should call him and tell him you found one," somebody said. "You can tell him you just didn't know they would pay you this much."

"Yeah."

And we were really making money then because of all the overtime. Taking home a little under or over a couple of thousand bucks a week. All of these paychecks, in all of my pockets.

Then I started wondering how much it would cost. *A lighthouse in Maine.* I would probably have enough. I could sit up there and think - and then every once in a while, turn the light this way or that. *Just keep it all lit up.* That's what I remember thinking.

The storms lasted through the week. The planes weren't getting in and neither were the trucks. And you really had to wonder. What about the food? Maybe we would starve. But of course we never did. I never understood exactly how it worked, but the food was always there. *Ham and cheddar?* Ham and cheddar. And lobsters and doughnuts and twenty kinds of pies. *Roast beef well? Or do you like it rare?* Everything. Every single thing was there. Except for the tapes. And that was the problem.

I was sleeping through the days and was staying up at night, watching the tapes that were preset on the TV in the rec room. Of course it wasn't live, but it really didn't matter. There were tapes of all different shows. But when the planes stopped coming in, or it might have been the trucks, the tapes stopped, too. So they only had one. Family Feud. The New Year's Eve episode.

But anyway, one night, all night, all I did was watch *that* tape. Over and over and over, because that's how it was set. The Family Feud tape would start and then run to the end, then rewind to the beginning. Start and then run to the end. Then back to the beginning. Over and over and over.

And by five o'clock that next morning, I knew my life had changed. I became totally convinced that anything and everything I had ever thought of in my head, the one that was up there on my shoulders, really didn't matter.

Yellow, hop, tangerine gravy. I was sure of it.

The episode that I was watching, the only one I *could* watch, the New Year's Eve one, started with some hokey music and a sign that said *Family Feud*, with little light bulbs all around it. Then they introduced two families, the Tullises and the Vaughns. And each of them had five or six people, including the children.

But anyway, I watched the show the first time and Mrs. Tullis had a kerchief on, that right away reminded me of a corncob. Even though it didn't look like one, except that it was yellow. A couple minutes later, the show's host started kissing all the ladies and I could hear it in my head – *SMACK that man! SMACK that man!*

Then after that, the questions started. Name the strongest man. So Mr. Vaughn hit the buzzer first and told him Samson. And right away I saw the movie in my head, even though I'd never really seen it, with this really strong guy with no shirt on, chained to marble pillars. He'd give a pull and they'd all come crashing down. All but one. And on and on it went.

The first time I watched it, there were six or seven times I would see or hear something on the show that triggered something in my head. Like this kid, for example.

One of the boys on the show sounded just like Elmer Fudd. He didn't talk that much, but every time he did, I'd hear up in my head -

I tawt I taw a puddy tat. Even though I knew that it was really Tweetie Bird who said that.

But anyway, that was the first time that I watched it, and I really didn't think that much about it at the time. But then the show went off, there was a couple minute pause, and it started up again. The hokey music and the little light bulbs and the sign. And then six or seven seconds later, I saw the lady's kerchief, and right away I pictured seeing the exact same corncob I had seen up in my head before.

Yeah, you kiss that lady. Smack that man! Smack that man! And every single time I watched that show, the columns would come down exactly the same way. Exactly. And the same one was always left there standing, up in my head.

Name a little animal a child has for a pet. *A Wabbit? I tawt I taw a puddy tat.* Over and over and over and over. The same six or seven things - and then my stupid connections.

And that's what got me thinking. *Why would that happen? They're not even connected.* That's what I started thinking. Then my mind went to the next thing, but maybe it wasn't. Maybe it *wasn't* really my mind.

Maybe they both worked *together.* You were predestined to have free will - but not *all* of the time. Maybe there were some things you could choose, but others you couldn't. Could some things set off certain other things? But how would you know, unless each of your days was exactly the same? Like the tape?

And what about God? Where was He in all of *this* or *that*? Was He really *there*, or something predestined to be in your head?

And that was another word that didn't make sense. *God. God. God.* Wasn't that *dog* spelled backwards? Man's best friend. That had to mean *something.*

But hadn't He drowned millions of children? What if I finally met Him, but didn't like Him? *Then what?*

I really started worrying after that. But then I thought that maybe I was *supposed* to, so I didn't get that upset. And then I finally figured I would play it *backwards* sometime. Sit up in the lighthouse with my TV and video machine - and do *that* if I could.

Just start with the people un-clapping at the end of the show. And then when it got back to the place where the kid said, "tibbaW," right before the host asked the question - well, I'd just see what would happen *then*, up there in my head.

Fuggit, I thought. I stopped watching the tape.

Then I walked to the Dining Hall for breakfast, and I told the guy I thought I wanted ham and cheddar cheese...

At least I *thought* that I was *thinking* that I *thought* that it was me.

———————————

There were all these *News Miners*, in the break shacks and camps, and out on the buses in boxes. Nobody ever threw 'em away. New ones and old ones, they just piled up.

That was how I found out. Looking through one in a break shack near Pump Two. Pinto was dead. But now I think maybe he isn't. I don't really know for sure.

There was a small column on page eight, in a paper from late January. A plane had gone down, and according to the flight records, the only one who had been aboard was an inexperienced pilot named David Pinto, age 21. The plane had gone down in a small stand of trees about 12 miles northwest of Fairbanks. It had apparently become engulfed in flames and exploded. Very little was left. No signs of life. Nearly everything had been incinerated. There weren't even any bones. It was assumed that animals had dragged off whatever, if anything, was left.

I spent the next three days making phone calls to the State Police, the Aviation Center they had referred me to, and some people Pinto had known at the University. No one could tell me any more than what I had already read, from what had been written two months ago. And that was kind of weird. For two months he was up there in my head alive - when really he was dead.

I wrote him a note a couple of days later and mailed it to our post office box in Fairbanks. I included my address at Prudhoe and my parents' address and phone number back in Maryland, but I never heard back.

So many times after that, for a *long* time, I would think of what he had said at the airport. I still do. "I'll leave you a clue," he had told me.

But now that I look back, I think he *took* one instead.

Chapter 46

The winds had been whipping up. It was still pretty cold, but not like it had been. And the sun was staying out a little longer. *Seven more minutes a day.*

I drove back to the camp that night, grabbed a couple of pork chops and a piece of lemon pie, and put it all on a paper plate from the snack room. Then figured I'd go for a ride, out to the dock where the Sea-Lift came in during the summer. It was about thirteen miles from the camp.

I went out the front way, past the guard shack, made a left, and followed the signs. Except for the natural gas flaring off high in the night, it was pretty dark. The further I drove, the blacker it got, except for the part of the road where my headlights were shining. After a half an hour, I pulled up to the dock.

It wasn't the kind of dock *you* would probably picture. Like all of the things we drove on up there, it was made of gravel. It was about fifty feet wide and went for maybe an eighth of a mile, out into the Beaufort Sea. There were a few places where it would branch off along the way.

I thought some people might be there, but nobody was. Kind of like Prince Rupert, at the campground in April. I pictured how different the dock would be in the summer, for maybe two months, with the all the barges coming in and the giant cranes offloading.

I had seen it all in an Alyeska building on Ft. Wainwright. Pictures on the walls, of giant crawlers, that would carry the modules and buildings maybe an eighth of a mile an hour, until they got them to where they were going. But none of that was at the dock that night.

I drove to the end of the dock. I couldn't go any further or I would have been out on the sea, which was all frozen over with giant chunks of ice. Then I sat there a minute. Eating my lemon pie. I sat and I sat, and then I flashed on the brights. I couldn't see it clearly, but I *know* a polar bear was there. Way out on the ice pack, where the lights turned dim. I could see this little white speck that was moving real slowly and then it was gone. Into the black.

And that's when I began to hear 'em. Cocktail glasses, all clinking together, up in my head. Then this attorney, in his little bow tie, would start telling his stories. "Now can you *imagine* that?" the guests would ask. And all of his stories would be so lame, I would already have forgotten them, if they had been mine. *Talking, talking, talking*, until I knew I couldn't stand it anymore.

He'd go on and tell us, "I was driving one time in Australia and got to the end of the road. You should have seen it," he'd say. "Got to a river and I couldn't even cross. It was the end of the road." And that was when I *knew*.

You've gotta tell him, Fitch. You've gotta tell 'em all.

And it wasn't just for me. I thought of Artemus Tischman and Pinto, and Kingpen and even Violet Gully. And what about Meatman and Kolis and that girl with my Buick? Where was she now? *On the side of a road, looking for a cotter pin?*

So that's when I told him - "End of the road? *BULLSHIT!*"

I flashed on the brights. "End of the road? See those giant chunks of ice?" I asked him. "That's the Beaufort Sea. It's sixty-five or seventy below, I'm sitting here eating pork chops and a lemon pie, and looking for a polar bear. So you know what, Asshole? Don't tell *me* about the end of the road... Because I'm *here*."

Yeah. That's what I'd say. *Fuggit.*

I drove back to the camp and had a Teamster fuel up the truck. I went inside and there were little flyers posted, telling about the women from Fairbanks who were coming to sing. It was tonight.

The show started at eight in a large conference room and it must have been eight-thirty or nine o'clock, so I went down to my room to look for Pooch. Nothing was there.

I mean *my* stuff was. Pretty much one duffel bag, but that was it. No toasters, coffee makers or popcorn poppers. *Well think the strangest thing*, I thought. *Maybe he did go home.*

But just to be sure, I went down to the Dining Hall, checked the rec center, looked in the phone booths, and then went to the conference room. But everyone was gone. And that's when I thought he could be with those friends of his, a couple doors down from my room. So I started walking.

I could hear 'em inside, laughing and cussing and carrying on, but there wasn't any music playing. I knocked a few times, but I didn't think they heard me, so I turned the handle and pushed the door in a little way.

I nodded, said, "Hey guys," and then asked if they had seen Pooch.

"Went home to his wife," somebody said. "Left about an hour ago."

"*Gone home.*" I could hear him in my head.

"Aren't you that little twerp that was here a month or so ago?" Beau asked. And I was gonna *say*, but instead I think I *thought*, "Aren't you like that piece of crap, except you won't go down the toilet?"

There were seven guys in the room. Four were playing poker, two were watching, and the Bishop was sitting on the corner of the bed marking his Bible. There were chips in the pot. Dozens of 'em.

And it took me a while, but finally I caught on to the colors and how much each was worth. They had green, orange, black and purple. Twenty-five, fifty, a hundred, and five hundred bucks. There was a couple thousand dollars in the pot - and this guy named Watson won it with a straight.

The way it all worked was, you traded in your paychecks for the chips, and then when you dropped out, you traded back whatever chips you had for paychecks. And then they had a couple thousand in cash to make it all work out. Paychecks for chips, to trade back for paychecks and maybe some money. Give or take. It was pretty simple, really.

They'd been playing five-card draw, five-card stud and seven-card stud. Nothing wild and nothing fancy. No in-between or games like that.

"Your deal," Beau said. He handed the stack to the guy on his left, who shuffled the cards and then handed them back to Beau. Beau cut 'em and handed 'em back and then the guy dealt them around.

"Seven-card stud," he said. And after four and a half, or maybe five minutes, Beau was at least six thousand dollars richer. *Full house. Queens over.* Which was a pretty good hand, when you figured it was stud and nothing was wild.

"Any chance I could get a drink?" I asked. "No ice?"

507

The cards kept going around and Beau was the big winner, until he lost a sixteen thousand dollar pot. "God *DAMN* it," Beau said. The Bishop looked up, but he didn't say anything.

"Now you're back to what you started with," Watson said. Beau gave a fake little laugh.

It must have been ten-thirty, maybe eleven o'clock, and the two guys who had been watching were heading out.

"Sec you tomorrow," one of 'em said. A couple of the players nodded and mumbled something, and the Bishop told the two guys good night.

"See you tomorrow," he said.

The cards were going around and so was the money. No big winners and no big losers. At least not for a while.

But then there was one game of five-card stud, first one down. Beau had played two cards and dropped out, then Watson started upping the pot. *Big time.* "I'll bet you four thousand," Watson said. BJ saw him, and then a guy named Bobby saw BJ and bumped them both eight thousand.

"*Eight* thousand to you," Beau said. And I really thought that would make Watson stop and think. But it didn't seem to.

"Here's eight and I'll raise you another five grand," Watson said, which made BJ drop out.

"Too much for me," he said.

There was one card left to be dealt, and like everybody does, Bobby looked at his card that was down. I've seen everybody do it. Like you really think it's gonna change. Bobby threw in ten purple chips, Beau announced, "Last card," and they started coming around, first to Watson and then to Bobby.

"Your bet," Watson said, because Bobby was high, with a queen.

"Five thousand," Bobby said. And for all of the raising, it stopped there.

"I'll call you," Watson said. And with the five thousand he put in, there must have been twenty-five or thirty thousand dollars in the pot.

Both hands were unbelievable. Watson had a straight, a six to a ten, but then Bobby laid down a flush. All spades. And I really felt bad for Watson, when I pictured what he'd lost.

Because the way it all turned out, he left the table and didn't even get a full paycheck back. Eight hundred and seventy-five dollars...

that's what he left with. And I know he must have come to the game with a lot more than that.

I thought it would all end, with only three guys left. But that was where I came in. That's what BJ said.

"Come on. Give us some of that Laborers' money." Beau handed me another drink. I knew I had six or seven hundred dollars in my pocket. And the thing I remember thinking to myself was I had never spent a cent on recreation. Nothing. *So maybe now it's time to just kick back and play a game or two*, I thought.

I got out my money and handed in two checks for a total of $3,850. The way I had it figured, that was *that*. If I lost it all, it was over. *Finished*. That's what I remember thinking.

But then I started winning. After ten or fifteen minutes, I was up a couple thousand bucks. But then I missed an inside straight and dropped a grand.

"Here, have another drink," Beau said. "I know, no ice."

So I took it and I drank it, thinking it would help me focus. But I don't think it did. I started getting all distracted, with the dust balls that I'd see up in my head. And then I'd wonder if the picture of my peach was still there in the trashcan.

"Two bills to you," BJ said, and I remember tossing two black chips in the middle of the pile. And even though I wasn't sure exactly what I'd had when I called him, I won.

I was doing great, but then I started losing. I had to cash another check for chips, but I knew that I would get it back. Just as soon as the pressure started up, that was when I'd play my best. Just rack 'em up, or better yet, we'll start eighteen to one. Even if I got down to a dollar…

"*Your* deal," somebody said. I told 'em we were playing stud. Five-card. And I didn't get the flush that I was hoping for, but I won a couple thousand with an ace-high bluff. I was getting hot. Things were getting better. Round and round it went. The cards and all the money.

"Now what about the time?" somebody asked. "You wanna stop at eleven-thirty?"

"Yeah," everybody said. No matter who was up, or who was down, that's what we decided. *Eleven-thirty*.

I missed a few good pots, but then I won a couple. One for sixteen thousand. So with that, I knew I must have been up six or seven grand.

"It's eleven twenty-five," the Bishop said. "So if you wanna stop, you have five minutes."

Then BJ said we'd play one more hand, but Beau said two. "All right, two," we all agreed.

Then Bobby started dealing. "Five stud. First one down."

My down card was an ace. And then I got another one. Two bullets. But I didn't get a damn thing after that. The way it all worked out, I lost the six or seven thousand I was up, to BJ's straight.

"Believe that shit?" he said. And I had to give him credit for a five-card straight. No draw.

"All right. Last hand," BJ said. "Seven-card stud. First two and last one down. Nothing wild." And then he started dealing.

I got a four of hearts and then I got an eight. Another heart. Both down. And when the next ones came around, the first ones up, I got a bullet, with a red heart in the middle. And I knew I had it made.

"First ace bets," BJ said. So to keep 'em all playing, I only bet a thousand. I tossed two purple chips in the pot, but Beau decided that he'd raise it up another grand, even though he only had a ten of hearts showing.

"Two to you, Bob," BJ said.

Bobby also had an ace, which is why BJ looked at me and told me first ace bets. Anyway, Bobby tossed ten black ones and a couple purples in the pot, BJ stayed in with a three of diamonds on top, and I met Beau's raise with another grand. Eight thousand bucks sitting in the middle - and we'd hardly even started.

"Next one coming at ya," BJ said, and then he started dealing. A five of diamonds came to me. "No help," BJ said. He tossed a two of spades to Beau, dealt another ace to Bob, gave himself a king of diamonds, said "Awe, *shit*," but I think that he was bluffing.

"Pair of bullets will go four thousand," Bob said, putting his chips in the pot. BJ sat there for a minute, but he finally put his money in.

Just bluffing, bluffing, bluffing. That's what I remember thinking.

"Well are you in, or are you out?" somebody asked.

"What?" And that's when I remembered. I'd forgotten what my cards in the hole were. "Just thinking," I said.

And then I looked at my hole cards and knew I could remember from the Buick. Sixty-four. Close to my heart. Sixty-four. Sixty-four. And I wondered where it was.

"I'm in," I said. And then I thought maybe New York. Or maybe Ohio. I didn't really know. And then my mind went to the next thing, and I started wondering all about the dog food and the toothpaste on the windows.

"I'm in," Beau said. And I noticed that he didn't hesitate, even though he didn't seem to have a thing, except a ten of hearts and a two of spades.

"Coming round," BJ said. I got an eight of clubs and then I think it hit me that maybe, just maybe, I didn't have it made. But then I thought the strangest thing and figured maybe I could get a straight. *And then there's always more.*

"Two of clubs," BJ said, and Beau was sitting with a pair of 'em.

"Were deuces wild?" I asked.

But I don't think he got it. Instead he started looking all intense, his eyes squinched up, and he just sat there and stared.

Bobby got a ten of diamonds and then BJ gave himself an eight, same suit.

"Aces bet," Beau said.

"A thousand," Bobby told him, and tossed some chips in the pot. Then BJ folded, which kind of surprised me.

"I don't have *shit*," he said. He tossed in his cards.

"A thousand to you," somebody said. And this time I knew what I had in the hole without looking. With a four and a five and a six and an eight, it wasn't very likely, but there was always *more*.

Just think the strangest thing, I thought.

I was gonna put in the money, but first I needed to sign on of my checks over for some chips. So that's what I did. Checks for chips, for checks. It, it, it, it, ti... But then I stopped before I started thinking of the next thing, because I knew I'd lose my focus.

"Here's your thousand, and I'll bump you *three* thousand," Beau said. And that's when Bob dropped out.

"Three thousand to *you*," BJ said. "If you still wanna play."

He had a couple of deuces showing and maybe one in the hole. But the thing that I knew was, if I could just get a seven, or even two hearts, I could beat him.

"Here are three more checks," I said. And I pulled 'em out of my pocket and signed them.

"All in," BJ said. "Last card that'll be face up."

I couldn't believe it. I saw the red and then saw the heart. Or maybe I saw them together. I don't know. But the thing I remember thinking was, *just keep it all together. Don't get all excited. One more to go*, I thought. *You know you can do it.*

And then it kept on getting better.

"Jack," BJ said. And he put it with the rest of Beau's cards.

"Bet's to you," BJ said. And he pointed to Beau, who didn't have *squat*. Not that I did. But I did have potential. Beau didn't have *shit*. At least not that I could see.

"The bet's ten thousand," he said, but he didn't have that many chips, and neither did I. So we got out more of our checks, and that was when Beau started getting angry. *Really* angry.

"*Fuck* this bull*shit*," he said. I'm not playing for goddamned paper." What he meant was the checks that you'd get with your chips. At least if you won. "And what about *taxes*?" he roared. "*Fuggit*. I wanna win *real* money."

Which is where Henry Osbourne came in.

I think it was BJ who brought up Henry's name. He was a guy they all knew who worked in the office, in the payroll department. According to the law, any remote place in Alaska where you worked had to guarantee you money for your check if you needed it. "You're entitled to your funds by law," Beau said.

So we were going to go down there. Room A17. We were going to get Henry, go the Payroll Department, and make the trade. But first we would trade in our chips. Chips for checks - and then we'd go down to get Henry, go the Payroll Department and get the money. *REAL* money for our checks.

At least that was the plan. But what about the cards? We couldn't just leave 'em on the table.

So the Bishop would stay and watch 'em. That's what BJ said. But *I* wasn't really sure, until Beau told me, "Look at the man. He's sitting there on the bed, reading a goddamned Bible. Whaddya *think* he's gonna do?"

So that's when I figured, *Fuggit. Just let him stay and watch 'em.*

The four of us left the room, went down to the main hall, turned right, and then right again at another side hall. *Walking, walking, walking.*

"Here," Beau said. Then he knocked on the door, turned the handle, and pushed the door open. "Hey, Henry. HENRY!" he called.

You could hear some rustling, and in another couple minutes an older man came out with Beau. You'd think he would have been a little more upset, but he wasn't. Then I figured maybe Henry did this all the time. Got woken up in the middle of the night, went down to the Payroll Room, and got people money. Maybe *THIS*. Maybe *THAT*. It made me think back to the time when Kingpen had traded all that crispy, burned up money from the light bulb.

"Hey, Henry. You ever get crispy, burned up bills?" I asked him. But I don't think he heard me.

We all went another two halls down, made a left this time, and came to the offices.

"This way," Henry said. He took us to a door that was locked. Henry chose a key from his big metal ring, unlocked the door, and the five of us went in.

There were two rooms inside, except instead of a wall, there was wire mesh in between them. "Now you all stay here in this room," Henry said.

He took all the checks that Beau and I had given him, unlocked a little wire door, and shut it behind him. And even though he didn't want us in there, we could still see what he was doing.

There was a huge walk-in safe, maybe three-feet-by-three and six feet high. And when Henry unlocked it, I wish you could have seen all the money. It was all stacked up in fist-sized bundles, and I think that most of the bills were hundreds. There must have been millions in there. *At least*. All behind this little wire door.

"Now how you wanna do this?" Henry asked. "It's just you two, right?"

Beau told him, "Right."

But it wasn't just us two, because of all of the chips in the pot. BJ figured that out. He and Bobby signed some checks and got it squared away.

Then Henry sat down at a desk, got his adding machine and told us, "OK. I'll add up all the checks from Mr. Fitch and give him his money. And then I'll do the same for you, Beau. Then I'll add up the checks from these other two guys. Sound good?"

"Sounds good," Beau said.

We must have stood there a good fifteen or twenty minutes after that. *CLICK CLICK CLICK CLICK CLICK*. Kinda like the time down at the train with all that buzzing in my head. *Bzzzzzzzzzzzzzzzzzz*.

Henry finally finished. BJ figured the out the pot and Henry handed each of us our money. Hundreds of hundreds. Thousands and thousands. And when I wondered how I would count it, then came *MORE*.

"Here Mr. Fitch," he said. "You might want this." And when I looked at the bottom of the slip of paper from the adding machine, there it was... $47,890.21.

I thanked Henry for his trouble and gave him a hundred dollar tip. Then we went back to the room. Everything was the same.

"Three guys broke in," the Bishop said. "But I fought 'em off." And then he gave a little laugh.

There was over thirty thousand dollars in the pot. No chips. No checks. Real money. Hundreds, mostly.

"Twos bet," BJ said. And Beau told me again, ten thousand. And just for a minute I thought I'd tell him, "Fold." After all that we had been through with Henry. I'll fold. And the adding machine. I'll fold. *CLICKCLICKCLICKCLICKCLICK. Bzzzzzzzzzzzzzz.*

"Jesus Christ. Are you IN or are you OUT?" Beau yelled. "God *damnit*! What the hell!"

"I'm IN," I said. And then it took me five minutes, but I counted out a hundred hundreds and put 'em in the pot.

I needed a seven for a straight. But the way I had it figured, it would even work out better if I could get a heart. One pair, two pair, three of a kind, straight, flush, full house. And then it went to four of a kind, Royal straight. The kinds of hands that no one ever really got.

A seven. Or a heart. And I thought of the movies, *The Hustler* and *The Cincinnati Kid*.

But mostly I thought of something Pinto had said when we were looking through some change. "I think that I've got 'em all," I had told him. And I meant all the quarters. But I remember him telling me, "There's always one more. Look," he'd said, as he took the last one from the pile.

So, anyway. That's what I was thinking. A seven or a heart. *There's always one more.*

"Last one down," BJ said. He dealt us each one card.

I was gonna play it cool and not even look at the card. But then I started thinking it wouldn't really matter. It was his bet, so if I *did* look, but maybe if I *didn't* . . .

He was over there counting all his money. And then at one point, he told me he was putting it all in, so if I planned on sticking around, I could start counting, too.

"Thirty-four thousand, eight hundred," he said. He pushed it all in. That's when I looked at my card.

It was the five of hearts. And of all the cards I've ever seen, I thought *that* one was the best. *Just picture all those hearts*, I thought, and as soon as I thought it, I saw 'em bouncing in my head. It took six or seven minutes, but I counted up my money, and pushed thirty-four thousand, eight hundred dollars in. And I still I had a couple thousand left.

"Call," I said. And then he flipped over his cards and that was when I knew that I was gonna puke. Just push up some more hairs.

He had two jacks in the hole and with the one on top, he had three. And then he had the deuces. Full house.

"Jacks over," he sneered. And the thing that I remember is that for the first time in a long time, I couldn't even think. I tried to think of pictures, to get 'em in my head, to turn 'em into words, but everything was blank. Which was all that I could think of. *BLANK. BLANK. BLANK. And what does that look like? WELL?! What? WELL?! What?*

"WHADDYA HAVE?" he screamed. But my hands didn't work. I couldn't flip the cards. So BJ turned 'em over.

I was gonna say Flush, but my mouth didn't work, so all I kept saying was fuh-fuh-fuh …

But when I looked at my cards, the ones that had been red, my six and my four, had both turned to black.

"Holy SHIT," BJ said. "Four fives." And there they were. Three had been down, but now four were up. And that's when I think I started thinking again.

"Why you goddamned motherfucker."

"We're gonna keep playing," Beau said. "We can take a ten minute break, I'm gonna get some more money, but we're gonna keep playing."

"How about we play to one o'clock," Bobby said. "But that's it. No matter what."

"Well I'm going to bed," the Bishop told us. "You all have a good night."

Beau went storming out the door, I got the plastic bag from the trashcan and dumped the money in. "I'll be back in a minute," I said. "I've gotta take a leak."

Then I left with the money and went down to my room.

There were a half a dozen legal pads with a pencil that I used for recording the smashes and cracks on the fiberglass we fixed. I put it all in my duffel bag, along with the money and my alarm clock. I grabbed my RefrigiWear suit and my bunny boots, left the room, and started walking toward the door that went outside.

God, it was cold. Especially without wearing my boots and my suit. And I thought of the transistors. Had they blown out yet? Was someone standing on the corner? *And what about Tok?* Someone *HAS* to be there, I figured. But I really didn't know. *Yellow, hop, tangerine, gravy.*

The truck was running. Just like it had been the last five months or so. And just like Antonelli's, it was freezing cold on one side and warm on the other. Or in this case, maybe not warm, but warmer. *Just pull back on the door*, I thought. And then I got behind the wheel, flipped the heater switch to high, and started driving.

I went out the front way, like I had before. I passed by the guard shack and we both waved to each other again. I went out to the main road and turned right this time. I drove a couple hundred feet, pulled a little over to the side, and stopped the truck. I put on my RefrigiWear suit, bunny boots, and mittens. Then I started driving again.

There were a lot more lights this way than there had been on the way to the dock. I passed the natural gas towers that were flaring off into the night. I was one hundred, maybe two hundred feet from them, and you could hear 'em in the sky… *Whooooooooooooosh.*

And, just like the truck, they were never turned off. Just this constant *WHOOOOOSH* - and then they sounded more dim as you got further away.

There were huge oil tanks. Giant cylinders all lit up. And pressure stations. All kinds of stuff. You'd see these gathering lines, maybe twelve or eighteen inches around, that would bring the crude in to the main line, like I told you before, from places farther north.

Driving. Driving.

I started passing signs. There was one for Deadhorse Airport. It said two miles, but I never made it there. I turned right about a half a mile before that and started down the Haul Road. Going south.

I started feeling better after that. More relaxed. My brain was back to thinking, or it might have been my mind. But whatever it was, it felt pretty good.

And as for Fitch, I was toasty warm. *Just toast 'em up,* I thought.

I pictured the eggs Kingpen would cook in the pan and the bread and the jelly for only a dime. And then I started to wonder how many slices I could buy with the money that I had. "Just toast 'em all up. *Chinese style*," I said.

And I kept on driving.

I hadn't given it much thought, but there might have been a minute when I thought about flying out. I mean from Deadhorse. But I knew they'd have a schedule. A plane probably wouldn't be flying out until the morning.

And even if one had been flying out sooner, what was I supposed to do? Stand there and reach down in my duffel bag, pull out a handful of thousands… and go through all of that at the counter?

But the thing that really made me wanna drive was what Kingpen had said. "I wanna see it all just one last time."

Except it turned out I couldn't. Everything was black, including the gravel the headlights lit up.

It was a pretty decent road, though. There was the pad that ran along the Pipeline, and then there was the Haul Road, which was really the main road that the supply trucks would use. The ones we'd hear at night, heading up north, when we lived down at Olnes.

But anyway, the Pipeline was off to my right. Every once in a while, I could see it, when the Haul Road went near it. Giant lights were set up all along the pad, and I could see the night shift people, welding, driving loaders, and working on the manipulators. The roads were pretty much parallel, but like I said, the Haul Road was more stable than the pad. It was built of gravel, right there on the tundra. Maybe six feet high, twenty-five feet wide. I was up high enough that I could have seen all the way down to the Brooks Range, if it had been light out that night.

I had been driving for a little over an hour. I had passed Franklin Bluffs some time back, and now I was passing Pump Two, all lit up, on my left. It was smaller than One.

Not as many heads. That's what I remember thinking.

In a couple of minutes I started slowing down, hoping I would see it stuck on the pole. But I didn't. *Couldn't see the tree for the forest, or the forest for the tree?* How did it go? But then I figured that it really didn't matter. It wasn't there. But if it had been, I guess I would have seen them both. That's what I remember thinking.

Things were going great. And even though I didn't have Kingpen or Beamish or my dog in the car, it reminded me of that. Driving to

Kluane Lake, or on the best parts of the logging road. Everything was black, and you knew where you were headed, but not where you were going.

God, I loved it. Just being by myself.

Jesse Fitch.

And I thought of the time that Pinto had told me how eternally thankful he was to be who he was. "I mean it," he'd said. "I think about it a lot. I could have been somebody else." And I hadn't understood him at the time. But now I did.

Just push the button in, I thought. And I kept on driving.

I think I might have only seen a dozen trucks that night. All heading north with supplies. I'd always pull to the side to give 'em enough room. But a couple times, when the gravel flew, it put another crack or chip in my windshield. But I didn't give a damn.

I passed Happy Valley and started to head up into the Range. Foothills for a while. I remember it was sometime, somewhere, before Pump Three, I stopped the truck, and went outside to take a leak.

And I wish you could have seen it. Not me taking a leak, of course, but the caribou that were there. Down in this valley. It was really a herd, I guess. Probably the Porcupine, from what Kingpen had said.

But anyway, there were *thousands* of 'em. *Tens* of thousands. I stood there for a long time after that. Stood there and watched and listened.

CLIP CLOP, CLIP CLOP, CLIP CLOP. That's the way they sounded, moving in the group. And I thought it might have been their antlers at first, but the more that I watched, I think it was their feet.

The truck kept climbing up. Kind of like Sunwapta Pass. Heading up and up through Atigun, then down the other side. And after that it, started getting different.

For one thing, trees were there. Little scrawny ones at first. I could see 'em, even in the dark. Small, misshapen, little wisps of shadows, standing in the snow. Always alone. Never in a group.

Now suppose you fall? I thought. And I remember laughing.

God, I was happy. The happiest I'd been in all my life. Heading the right way on the only road there. Passing by a herd of caribou.

And then just to make it perfect, the lights started up. God, they were wild. Brilliant pinks and reds and orange.

Maybe we do ride out that way, I thought. *Maybe*.

And then I knew what I would do.

I kept on driving for a long time, until I made it to the Camp. There were twenty-three in all. Little markers, some with crosses - and most of them were down. I spent an hour, standing them back up. And you can see 'em if you ever get there. Right in front of Coldfoot.

I drove throughout the night. Around one-thirty the next afternoon, I was almost home, wherever that was. At least it was familiar. Just a couple miles north of Olnes.

I thought that maybe somebody would be there, but nobody was. I pulled the truck up to the hitching post, shut it off, got out, and walked around to the back.

The door had been kicked in. The stove was gone and I thought that maybe someone would have replaced the floor, but it was still dug up. The mismatched plates were there. All smashed to pieces. The cupboards were bare.

I went into the front room and it was more of the same. Someone had taken the pool balls and broken all the windows. The chandelier was gone. A few of the candles we had duct-taped to it were lying on the ground.

And the map was gone. That was the worst part.

I left after that. I was gonna drive away, but I wanted to walk, so I started toward Coldwater's cabin, trudging through the snow. And when I got there, he was gone, too. The cabin was fine, just vacant. I could tell that he wasn't coming back.

The cabin was one large room, with a stove in the back. There was a small table and a chair. There was a bed he had made out of some scrap wood. There was even a sort-of kitchen. Of course there was no running water, but the idea was there, with a countertop, sink, and some homemade drawers that I pulled open.

Nothing and *nothing* and *nothing*. But in the fourth drawer, there was *something*, but I couldn't tell what, at first.

And then I realized they were the buttons. Little dried-up tan and green buttons, about the size of a quarter. There were at least a dozen

519

in a small plastic bag, the only thing Coldwater had left behind. I put the bag in my pocket and left.

There was a small roadhouse at Fox, where I stopped to get gas. The truck had what they called side-saddle tanks, one on each side, so I filled them both. A hundred and forty-three dollars. I took out two hundreds, told the guy to keep the change, and then started driving to Fairbanks. But once I got there, I kept on going to College instead. To the post office.

I took my duffel bag in, and walked over to the box. Just for a minute, I was sure I had lost it. I hadn't though. It was down deep in my pocket. I found the key, pushed it in the hole, turned it around, and opened the door. There were three envelopes inside. Two were pretty much the same. Regular size and shape, and both of them looked like they had been addressed by kids. The other one was a large manila packet from the University of Baltimore Law School.

On the way out, I was gonna say hello to the lady who worked there. The one who had helped us so much. But I was told she had left. So then I did, too. I threw my duffel bag over my shoulder and for the last time, I walked out of the post office with my mail. Three envelopes.

I realized much later, there should have been four.

Chapter 47

I was going to drive, but thought for old times' sake I would walk. So I crossed the street and started up. Up and up and up the snowy steps - and then I walked a little ways to the Student Center and started up again. And just like old times, no one was there. I went up to the chair and the table by the ceiling, looked down below, and it was all the same. People buying snacks, playing pool, and watching TV.

I sat in the chair and thought for a minute. Then I opened one of the envelopes. It was kind of hard to read. The letters ran together and there were places where the sentences overlapped.

> *Dear Jesse*, it started...
>
> *I hope you don't get this letter for a while, because it will mean you finally made it to the Slope. Was it everything we hoped it would be? You will never believe this, but as I was going through Haines, I ran into that girl I liked. Her name is Marie. We are working together to start a restaurant here. My eyes are not doing so well, but she seems to like me anyway. I think this might really turn into something. But anyway, good luck with everything you are doing.*
> *Your friend, Arthur Kingpen*

I put his letter back in the envelope, put it in my duffel bag, and then opened the second one. It was from New Hampshire.

> *Dear Mr. Fitch,*
>
> *I hope that you remember me. My name is Isabella Rose and you met me and my family on a beach in Oregon. The reason I am writing is because the kids in my class are studying the United States. Each of us was supposed to pick a state and then try and get someone who lives there, or the Chamber of Commerce, to send us a postcard. I picked Alaska. If*

*you get my letter and it's not too much trouble, could
you send a postcard to me at my school?* ...and then
the address was there.
Thank you.
Your friend,
  Isabella Rose
P.S. Stay away from those bears!!!!!! Ha! Ha!

I did the same thing with her letter that I had done with
Kingpen's. I put it in the envelope and then I put it in the duffel bag.
And then I took the manila envelope and put it in there, too.

I took one last look from the top, started down, went out across
the campus, down the snowy steps, crossed the street, and got in the
truck. Then I drove around to the back of the post office where the
dumpster was, and took the money from the duffel bag. I put two
thousand in my pocket and then I started counting the rest, putting it
all into two piles. I took out a legal pad and pencil and started
keeping score. One thousand. One thousand. On and on. And by the
time I was finished, nearly an hour later, I had two piles. Over
$63,000 each.

That's when I opened the last letter. The one in the manila
envelope.

It was more a collection of pamphlets than a letter, even though a
letter was on top. The bottom line was, I was accepted. Apparently it
was a geographical diversity issue.

It began, *Dear Mr. Fitch,* like you figured it would. And then it
went on to say how pleased they were to offer me a position in the
upcoming class, starting in September. *Although your grades do not
reflect our current standards, we believe that you, as an Alaskan,
will have much to offer our University.* And then there were all kinds
of pamphlets and brochures about the place.

I drove back around to the front of the post office, got out, locked
the truck and went inside. There was a display of all kinds of boxes
and envelopes you could buy. I picked a medium-sized box, gave the
lady a hundred from my pocket and waited for my change. After
that, I went back outside to the truck. It took a couple of minutes, but
I got it all into the box. The sixty-three thousand.

Then I tore a piece of paper from the legal pad, took my pencil
and wrote Kingpen a note...

Hey Kingpen,

Thank you for your letter. It really meant a lot. And as
for your question, (and this was the best part), I wrote,
It was MORE. Because he'd know exactly what I
meant. *Way MORE. But anyway, here's a little*
something for your restaurant, or whatever you want.
All the best, Fitch

I closed the top of the box, found some duct tape on the floor mat, and used it to cover the edges and flaps. Then I found Kingpen's return address on his envelope, and I took it and the box full of money inside. I borrowed a magic marker and addressed the box. And the lady told me they'd send it. Overnight. Except she said he'd get it on Monday, the 21st. "Spring solstice," she said. And my mind started thinking of Cornfield... and somehow it all seemed so right.

I got back in the truck and started downtown to a place called Arctic Gifts, because I'd been in there before, and I knew they had it all. Everything Alaskan you ever could imagine. Jade necklaces and watches made with gold nuggets, ivory carvings from Athabaskan villages. They even had dried salmon, so I got some of that. Dried salmon, little snow globes with dog sleds inside - and the globes would snow when you shook 'em. I bought twenty-nine post cards and every one was different. Pictures of these huge mosquitos, Mt. McKinley, the Pipeline and Prudhoe Bay. "Just give one to each kid." That's what I remember saying.

I got a piece of whale baleen and little boxes full of gravel with tiny flakes of gold included. "Guaranteed." There was a slide show you could put in a projector, so I got that and some grizzly teeth. A totem pole and a book of Robert Service poems. *There's a Land Where the Mountains Are Nameless.* And I thought about the one that I had climbed with the hamburgers. *CAW. CAW. CAW.*

I started buying *Chinese style* after that. Buying, buying, *buying.* A little bit of *THIS* and then a lot more of *THAT.* And when I was finished, she added it up. Seven hundred fifty-nine dollars and eighty-four cents. Except I *wasn't* finished, because then I saw the *best* thing.

There was a display box, on the counter, back behind the cash register. I asked if I could see it, so the clerk put it on the counter. There were little vials of water, with a label on each one.

"They're from Fox," the lady said. Then she started to tell me where that was and how a spring was there, but I told her that I knew.

"Dumped an igloo full of it on a good friend's head," I said. "But he's still going blind."

"Oh my," she said.

But anyway, the label told all about how if you drank the water, you would stay there in Alaska, or at least come back. So I told the clerk to put a vial in there. In the gift box she was filling up.

"Well that will be a conversation piece," she said. "It's a nice added souvenir."

But that wasn't why I was sending it. I knew that little girl.

"She'll *drink* it," I said. "Just as soon as she reads the label."

I left Isabella's name and the address to her school, and the lady promised to gift-wrap the stuff and mail it. I thanked her, walked out of the store, and started heading back. Back to the post office where I'd just been.

Always going back, I thought.

And then I was reminded of something Pinto always said…

"We do it for the memories. That's all you'll ever have left. Fuck this *North to the Future* bullshit," he'd say. "It's north for the past."

I knew there was a plane leaving at five. The problem was, I didn't know what to do with the money.

Think the strangest thing, I thought.

And then it wasn't all that hard. Something would go wrong. Mechanical failure, the wheels won't come up. The flaps won't go down. And then just like that time with the dog, we'll land in the Yukon, or maybe Vancouver. Quebec? Then what about Customs? "What's all this money?" Something would screw up.

So I decided to mail it. To my parents at first. But that wouldn't go well. "You wanna be a lawyer, but you're sending all this money in the mail? Cash money?" "What's this all about? Why would you send all of your money here like that?" And that's when I thought I would tell 'em I didn't. "I sent another box down to Haines," I'd say. But then I thought that wouldn't help.

So the way it all worked out, I sent it to Beamish. At his mother's house, because I knew the address. I bought another box, stuffed the money in with a note asking him to keep it in a safe place, but not in a bank. And then I wrapped it all up with duct tape. Wrapped and wrapped and wrapped. Then I went back in and addressed it on the front.

"Same way?" the lady asked, and what she meant was overnight.

"Same way," I said.

And then I thanked her, walked out, and never went in again.

I thought I was gonna be late, but in fact, I was a little early. I parked the truck in the lot, left the key in the ignition, lifted up my duffel bag and went inside.

It was all still there... the animals in glass boxes, people flying here, people flying there. I gave a wave to the lady selling tickets for the flights to the ghost towns up north. And then I kept on walking to the next counter over.

There were about thirty or maybe thirty-five people at the Northwest station, the one that I was going to. Fairbanks to Anchorage, to Seattle, to Baltimore. At least if they didn't land in Ontario.

But by then I figured that it really didn't matter. *Just fly me to Caracas. I won't give a shit.* Because all at once it hit me. I was so damn tired.

Just get up under the bridge, I thought. *Whoosh, Whoosh, Thump. Whoosh, Whoosh, Thump.*

At first I thought that I'd get in the line, but then I figured it would take a while, so I went to get something to eat. God, I was hungry. And the first thing that I saw, when I went inside the little restaurant in the airport, was a pie case. Four feet high, maybe two feet across, it was a plastic cylinder, with lots of different kinds of pies in it. Not like up at Prudhoe. But there must have been a dozen.

And the one that I wanted was strawberry shortcake, even though I knew that it looked better than it tasted, because I'd had it before. It had this yellow cake and then a layer of strawberries, except they were glazed and didn't look quite real. *Even better*. That's what I remember thinking. And then there was another layer of the cake, six or seven more strawberries on that, more glaze, and then all this whipped cream on top. And even though, like I told you, I knew from before that it wouldn't taste as great as it looked, I still got it.

I went to a table in the back and sat there a minute, because I'd forgotten to get a fork. I was gonna hunt inside my duffel bag for my spoon from Jimmy Franklin's, or maybe I could just go get a plastic one...

THIS or *THAT*? Anchorage or Fairbanks?

And then I started thinking of the Chinese restaurant. Two from A or three from C? Now how many little peppers do you want it to taste like?

What did it all mean?

Then my mind went to something Pinto had told me the night we had watched the lights. I thought a couple more minutes, and then I pushed the strawberry shortcake away, got up and left.

There was no line at the counter this time. "Round trip?" she asked and she gave a little smile.

"Yeah. Round trip," I said. Even though I figured that I'd never use it.

I had just enough money for the tickets, maybe three hundred dollars more. That was it. She took my duffel bag and put it on the conveyer belt. I watched it go around, then out through the flap, and I thought of Beamish.

"We're boarding now," she said. I thanked her and I walked out the door, out onto the tarmac, and climbed up the stairs.

We can never know beforehand the adventures that we'll have, I thought.

And then I found my seat and we slowly began to roll. We made it to the front of the runway, the engine revved, we started moving, picked up speed, and lifted into the air.

"You see this, Fitch?" Pinto had asked me. And he'd pointed to the side-view mirror of his truck. "Whaddya see?"

And I remember telling him hills full of trees.

"And you think you can go there?" he'd asked.

"Where?"

"Can you go *there*, Fitch? Into the mirror?"

And I remember telling him *Yeah*, because I was pretty screwed up at the time and thought that was what he wanted to hear.

But it wasn't.

"Then try it," he said. And he made me punch the mirror really hard until it started to break.

And then I'll never forget...

He pointed every other way and told me, "There's your gift," he'd said. "Mountains and rivers and valleys. Forests and lights in the midnight sky. It isn't a mirror," he told me.

"Go see it. Go see and experience it all. And you want to know what it all means? Just wait until you're hungry. Then start off walking till you find what you need. The moment you kill it and eat it, or pull something from the ground and you know that it kept you alive... that's meaning," he told me. *"Nothing can mean more than that."*

The plane veered off to the right and I could see the lights of the University down below. It was another ten or fifteen minutes, and then the pilot called back to me. I was the only one there.

"Now you understand tomorrow's our last flight up here? You'll have to meet us there at the runway, so we can fly you out."

"Got it," I called back. And even though it was dark, I knew we were near 'em. The giant breasts. And then just about that time, I could feel the plane bearing to the left.

"Not much up here," the pilot called back.

And maybe there would be, or maybe there wouldn't. But I knew there would be something. There always was.

Shoes, boots, pieces of rope.

Except, for now, none of it meant a thing.

Yellow, hop, tangerine, gravy.

But soon it would.

And just how do you know that? I asked myself.

And, I swear to God. As clearly as I've ever heard a voice up above my shoulders, I heard it that day...

Because Fitch, I told myself. *My head is on the way.*

Made in the USA
Middletown, DE
31 January 2015